D1317162

Houghton Mifflin

HOUGHTON MIFFLIN BOSTON

Education Place® is a federally registered trademark of Houghton Mifflin Company.

Weekly Reader® is a federally registered trademark of Weekly Reader Corp.



Printed in the U.S.A.

ISBN-13: 978-0-618-59034-6

ISBN-10: 0-618-59034-X

23456789-DW-16 15 14 13 12 11 10 09 08 07

# Program Authors & Consultants

## Authors

**Dr. Carole Greenes**

Professor of Mathematics Education

Boston University
Boston, MA

**Dr. Matt Larson**

Curriculum Specialist for Mathematics

Lincoln Public Schools
Lincoln, NE

**Dr. Miriam A. Leiva**

Distinguished Professor of Mathematics Emerita

University of North Carolina
Charlotte, NC

**Dr. Jean M. Shaw**

Professor Emerita of Curriculum and Instruction

University of Mississippi
Oxford, MS

**Dr. Lee Stiff**

Professor of Mathematics Education

North Carolina State University
Raleigh, NC

**Dr. Bruce R. Vogeli**

Clifford Brewster Upton Professor of Mathematics

Teachers College, Columbia University
New York, NY

**Dr. Karol Yeatts**

Associate Professor

Barry University
Miami, FL

## Consultants

**Strategic Consultant**

**Dr. Liping Ma**

Senior Scholar

Carnegie Foundation for the Advancement of Teaching
Palo Alto, CA

**Language and Vocabulary Consultant**

**Dr. David Chard**

Professor of Reading

University of Oregon
Eugene, OR

**Houghton Mifflin Math and Math Expressions Blended Usage Advisor**

**Dr. Matt Larson**

Curriculum Specialist for Mathematics

Lincoln Public Schools
Lincoln, NE

# Reviewers

## Grade K

**Stephanie Bagley**
M. Agnes Jones Elementary School
Fulton County
Atlanta, GA

**Charisse Byers**
Emma Hutchinson Elementary School
Fulton County
Atlanta, GA

**Irene Perez**
Morningside Elementary School
Fulton County
Atlanta, GA

**Marquel Pollard**
Seaborn Lee Elementary School
Fulton County
College Park, GA

## Grade 1

**Camille Lawrence**
Capitol View Elementary School
Fulton County
Atlanta, GA

**Paula Rowland**
Bixby North Elementary School
Bixby, OK

**Stephanie McDaniel**
B. Everett Jordan Elementary School
Graham, NC

**Juan Melgar**
Lowrie Elementary School
Elgin, IL

**Sharon O'Brien**
Echo Mountain School
Phoenix, AZ

## Grade 2

**Eileen Misluk**
Mary Lin Elementary School
Fulton County
Atlanta, GA

**Erin Price**
Mount Zion Elementary School
Clayton County
Jonesboro, GA

**Mark Martin**
Carter G. Woodson Elementary School
Fulton County
Atlanta, GA

**Kiesha Doster**
Berry Elementary School
Detroit, MI

**Marci Galazkiewicz**
North Elementary School
Waukegan, IL

**Ana Gaspar**
Lowrie Elementary School
Elgin, IL

**Elana Heinoren**
Beechfield Elementary School
Baltimore, MD

**Kim Terry**
Woodland Elementary School West
Gages Lake, IL

**Megan Burton**
Valley Elementary School
Pelham, AL

**Kristy Ford**
Eisenhower Elementary School
Norman, OK

## Grade 3

**Julie Jasnic**
Kedron Elementary School
Fayette County
Peachtree City, GA

**Melanie Laycock**
R. N. Fickett Elementary School
Fulton County
Atlanta, GA

**Randy Iddins**
McGarrah Elementary School
Clayton County
Morrow, GA

**Allison White**
Kingsley Elementary School
Naperville, IL

**Amy Simpson**
Broadmoore Elementary School
Moore, OK

4000017993

# Reviewers

## Grade 4

**Aja Davis**
A. D. Williams Elementary School
Fulton County
Atlanta, GA

**Travis Thornton**
B. E. Usher Elementary
Fulton County
Atlanta, GA

**Claudia Weiss**
Vaughan Elementary School
Cobb County
Powder Springs, GA

**Tracy Smith**
Blanche Kelso Bruce Academy
Detroit, MI

**Brenda Hancock**
Clay Elementary School
Clay, AL

**Karen Scroggins**
Rock Quarry Elementary School
Tuscaloosa, AL

**Lynn Fox**
Kendall-Whittier Elementary School
Tulsa, OK

## Grade 5

**Pam Thompson**
J. Milton Lewis Elementary School
Cobb County
Kennesaw, GA

**Jessica Carley**
Morris Brandon Elementary School
Fulton County
Atlanta, GA

**Patrick Logan**
Chase Street Elementary School
Clarke County
Athens, GA

**Jennifer LaBelle**
Washington Elementary School
Waukegan, IL

**Anne McDonald**
St. Luke The Evangelist School
Glenside, PA

**Ellen O'Rourke**
Bower Elementary School
Warrenville, IL

**Gary Smith**
Thomas H. Ford Elementary School
Reading, PA

**Linda Carlson**
Van Buren Elementary School
Oklahoma City, OK

## Across Grades

**Jacqueline Lampley**
Hewitt Elementary School
Trussville, AL

**Rose Smith**
Five Points Elementary School
Orrville, AL

**Winnie Tepper**
Morgan County Schools
Decatur, AL

# Place Value and Money



## 1 Place Value



Georgia

Performance Standards in Chapter 1
M4N1

**Algebra** Indicates lessons that include algebra instruction.

# 2 Compare, Order, and Round Whole Numbers and Money

Georgia

**Performance Standards in Chapter 2**
M4N1
M4N2.a
M4N2.b
M4D1.b



## FINISHING THE UNIT



Unit 1 Literature Connection *Beyond Pluto* pages 644–645

**Process Standards covered in Unit 1:** M4P1, M4P2, M4P3, M4P4

(WR) Indicates WEEKLY WR READER eduplace.com/map

# Operations and Algebraic Reasoning



Georgia

**Performance Standards in Chapter 3**
M4N2
M4N7

## 4 Multiplication and Division Basic Facts



Georgia

**Performance Standards in Chapter 4**
M4N3
M4N4
M4N7

**Algebra** Indicates lessons that include algebra instruction.

# 5 Algebraic Reasoning



Georgia

**Performance Standards in Chapter 5**
M4N7
M4A1

## FINISHING THE UNIT



Unit 2
Literature Connection
*Kid Camp*
page 646

**Process Standards covered in Unit 2:** M4P1, M4P2, M4P3

WR Indicates WEEKLY WR READER eduplace.com/map

# Multiplication of Whole Numbers



## 6 Multiply by One-Digit Numbers

Georgia

**Performance Standards in Chapter 6**
M4N2.b
M4N3
M4N7.d

**Algebra** Indicates lessons that include algebra instruction.

# 7 Multiply by Two-Digit Numbers



Georgia

**Performance Standards in Chapter 7**
M4N2.b
M4N3
M4N7.c
M4N7.d

## FINISHING THE UNIT



Unit 3 Literature Connection *Gone Prawning* page 647

**Process Standards covered in Unit 3:** M4P1, M4P2, M4P3, M4P4, M4P5

WR Indicates WEEKLY WR READER eduplace.com/map

# Division of Whole Numbers



**Algebra** Indicates lessons that include algebra instruction.

# 10 Number Theory and Mean



Georgia

**Performance Standards in Chapter 10**
M4A1.a
M4D1

# 11 Divide by Two-Digit Divisors



Georgia

**Performance Standards in Chapter 11**
M4N4
M4N7.a
M4N7.d

## FINISHING THE UNIT



Unit 4 Literature Connection *But I'm Not Tired* pages 648–649

**Process Standards covered in Unit 4:** M4P1, M4P2, M4P3, M4P4, M4P5

WR Indicates 

eduplace.com/map

# Measurement and Graphing



## 12 Customary and Metric Measurement



Georgia

**Performance Standards in Chapter 12**
M4M1

## 13 Time and Temperature



Georgia

**Performance Standards in Chapter 13**
M4N7.a
M4N7.d
M4M1.c

**Algebra** Indicates lessons that include algebra instruction.

## 14 Collect and Analyze Data



Georgia

**Performance Standards in Chapter 14**
M4D1.b

## 15 Graph Data



Georgia

**Performance Standards in Chapter 15**
M4D1

## FINISHING THE UNIT



Unit 5
**Literature Connection**
*Lengths of Time*
page 650

**Process Standards covered in Unit 5:** M4P1, M4P2, M4P3, M4P4, M4P5

WR Indicates WEEKLY WR READER eduplace.com/map

# Geometry and Measurement



## 16 Plane Figures



Georgia

**Performance Standards in Chapter 16**
M4M2
M4G1
M4A1.a

## 17 Congruence, Symmetry, and Transformations



Georgia

**Performance Standards in Chapter 17**
M4M2.b
M4G1





**Algebra** Indicates lessons that include algebra instruction.

# 18 Perimeter, Area, and Volume



Georgia

**Performance Standards in Chapter 18**
M4G2

## FINISHING THE UNIT



Unit 6 **Literature Connection** *Dividing the Cheese* page 651

**Process Standards covered in Unit 6:** M4P1, M4P2, M4P3, M4P4, M4P5

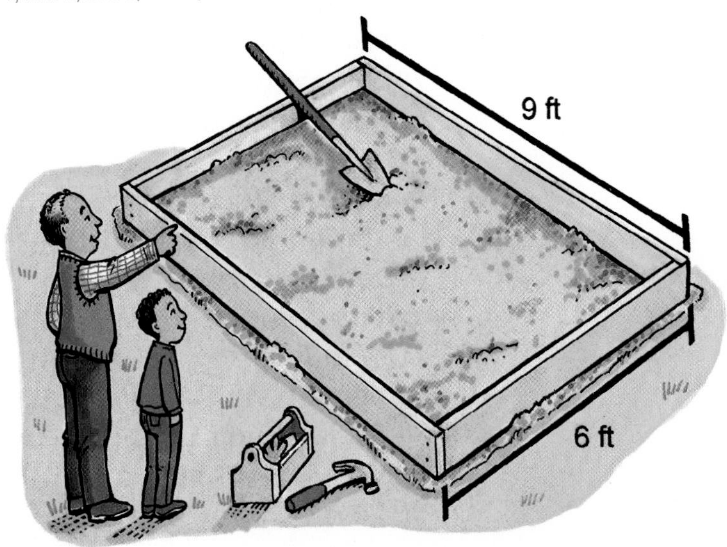


WR Indicates WEEKLY WR READER eduplace.com/map

# Fractions and Decimals



**Algebra** Indicates lessons that include algebra instruction.

# 21 Understand Decimals



Georgia

**Performance Standards in Chapter 21**
M4N1.a
M4N5.a
M4N5.b
M4A1.a

# 22 Add and Subtract Decimals



Georgia

**Performance Standards in Chapter 22**
M4N2.c
M4N2.d
M4N5.a
M4N5.c
M4N7.d

## FINISHING THE UNIT



Unit 7 Literature Connection *Hold the Meat!* pages 652–653

**Process Standards covered in Unit 7:** M4P1, M4P2, M4P3, M4P4, M4P5

(WR) Indicates 

# Multiply and Divide Decimals/Graphing



## 23 Multiplication and Division of Decimals



Georgia

**Performance Standards in Chapter 23**
M4N5.d
M4N5.e

**Algebra** Indicates lessons that include algebra instruction.

UNIT 8 Multiply and Divide Decimals/Graphing

# 24 Algebra and Graphing



Georgia

**Performance Standards in Chapter 24**
M4G3
M4A1.a

## FINISHING THE UNIT



**Process Standards covered in Unit 8:** M4P1, M4P3, M4P4, M4P5

## STUDENT RESOURCES



Unit 8 Literature Connection *The Perfect Present* pages 654–655

WR Indicates WEEKLY WR READER eduplace.com/map

# Back to School

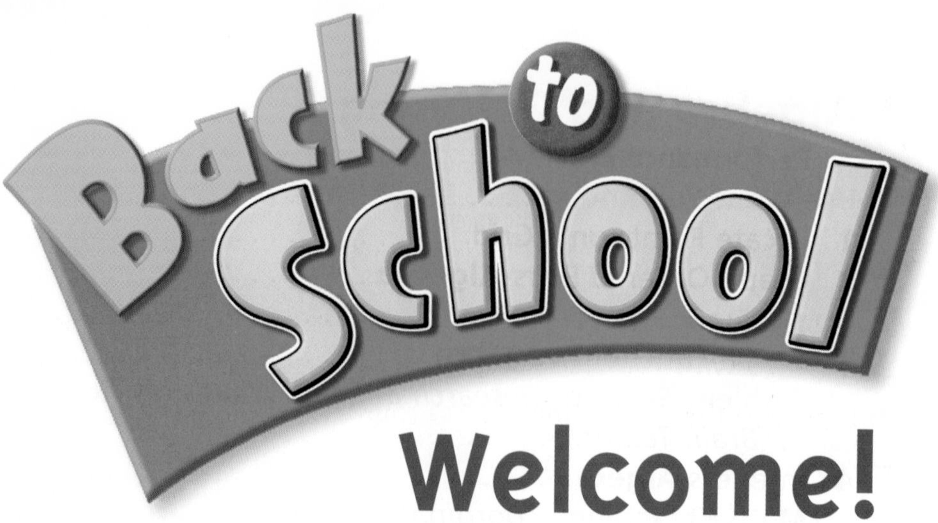

# Welcome!

Scientists, athletes, artists, and health-care workers all use math every day—and you will too. This year in math you'll learn about numbers, patterns, shapes, and different ways to measure. You'll use the mathematics you know to solve problems and describe objects and patterns you see. You can get started by finding out about yourself as a mathematician and about the other students in your class.

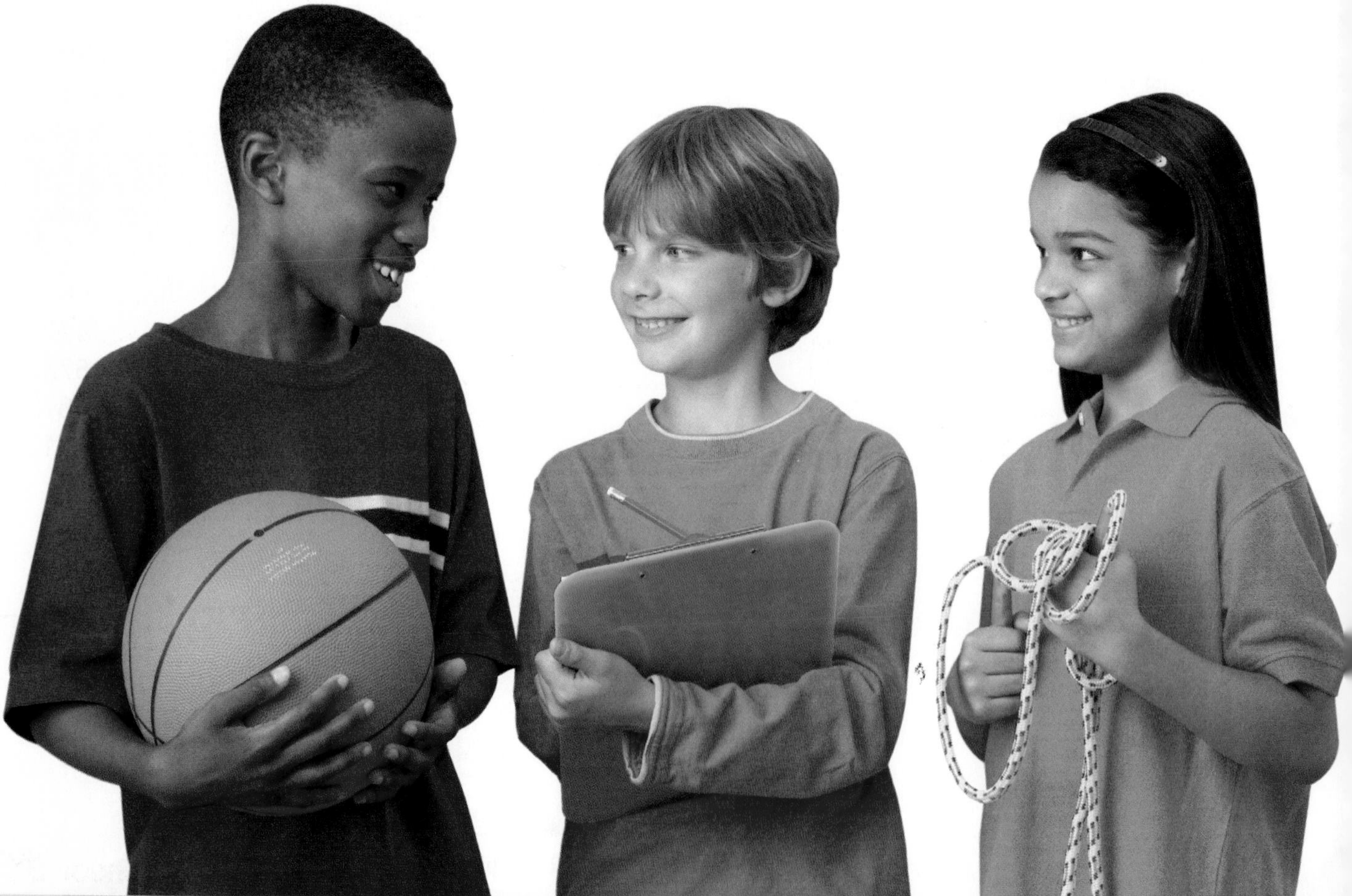

Activity

**Real World Connection**

# Collecting Data

## About Me

Write your math autobiography by answering these questions. You can draw a picture to go with your autobiography, if you want.

- Tell about a time you first remember doing math, even if you were very young.
- What are you good at in math?
- What would you like to improve or know more about?
- How do you (or someone in your family) use math outside of math class?

## About My Class

Your classmates may be just like you in some ways and different in other ways. You can collect data to find out something about the whole class.

- Think of one topic you'd like to know about all your classmates.
- Write a survey question for your topic.
- Take a survey among your classmates. Use tally marks to collect the data.
- Make a bar graph or picture graph to show your results.
- Use your graph and data to write what you learned about your class.

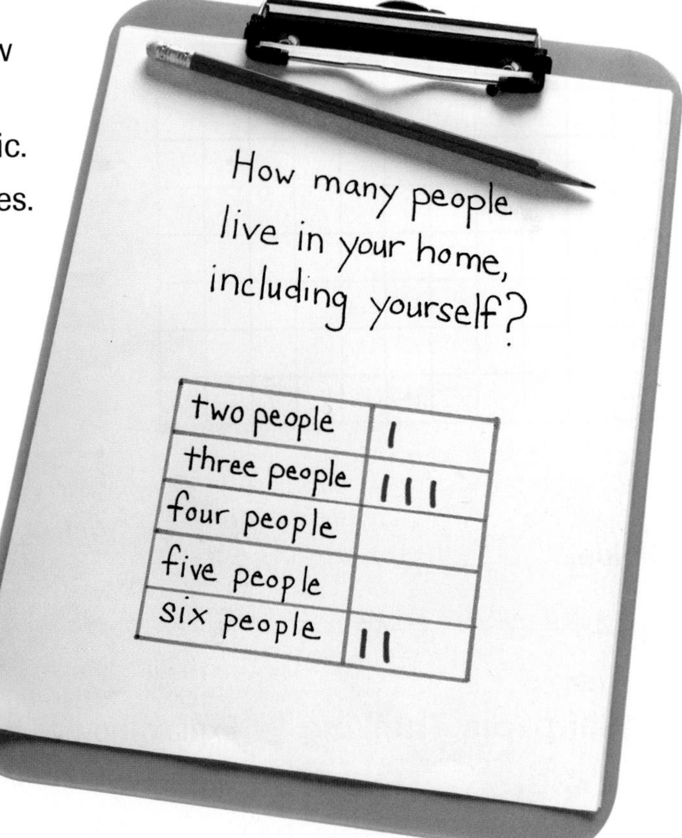

Back to School
**Lesson**

# Problem Solving and Numbers

**Objective** Maintain basic number and problem-solving skills

 **STANDARDS** Maintains M3N4 and M3P1.d

## Learn About It

In this lesson, you will review the basic multiplication and division facts. You will also use basic facts to solve problems.

## Guided Practice

1. Copy and complete a multiplication table like this one.
2. Highlight any facts that gave you trouble. These are facts to practice and learn.

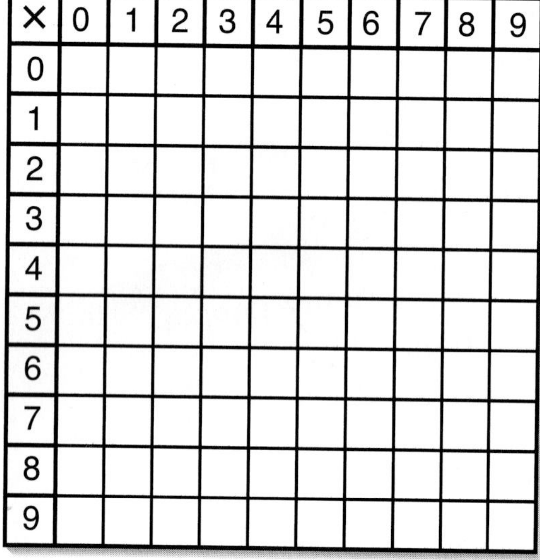

| × | 0 | 1 | 2 | 3 | 4 | 5 | 6 | 7 | 8 | 9 |
|---|---|---|---|---|---|---|---|---|---|---|
| 0 | | | | | | | | | | |
| 1 | | | | | | | | | | |
| 2 | | | | | | | | | | |
| 3 | | | | | | | | | | |
| 4 | | | | | | | | | | |
| 5 | | | | | | | | | | |
| 6 | | | | | | | | | | |
| 7 | | | | | | | | | | |
| 8 | | | | | | | | | | |
| 9 | | | | | | | | | | |

**Ask Yourself**

- What strategies and patterns can I use to complete the table?

**Divide.**

3. $45 \div 5$
4. $42 \div 7$
5. $2 \div 2$
6. $56 \div 8$
7. $36 \div 6$

**Explain Your Thinking** ▶ Explain how to use your completed multiplication table to find answers to division facts.

## Practice and Problem Solving

**Multiply or divide.**

**8.** 6 × 4 **9.** 54 ÷ 9 **10.** 7 × 7 **11.** 35 ÷ 5 **12.** 6 × 8

**Solve each problem. Choose the strategy and computation method that works best for the problem.**

**13.** How many students and teachers are in your classroom right now?

**14.** How many human elbows and knees are in your classroom right now? Explain how you found your answer.

**15.** An after-school group found that there were 28 elbows and knees. How many people were in that group?

**16.** **Multistep** Suppose that 15 students in your class are 10 years old and the rest are 9 years old. How many years have all the students in your class been living?

**17.** In one class, students built a pyramid. They put 9 cans on the bottom row, 8 cans on the next row up, and 7 cans on the third row. They continued building until they put 1 can on the top row. How many cans did they use in the entire pyramid?

**You Choose**

**Strategy**
- Find a Pattern
- Use Models
- Make a Table
- Write a Number Sentence

**Computation Method**
- Mental Math
- Estimation
- Paper and Pencil
- Calculator

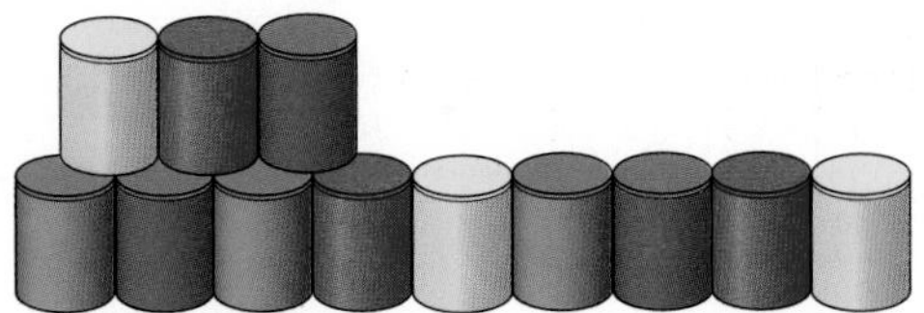

## Sharpening Skills for CRCT

**Open Response**

**Write each number in word form.** (Grade 3)

**18.** 7 hundreds, 6 tens, 5 ones

**19.** 120

**20.** 300 + 90 + 2

**Multiple Choice**

**21.** Paula bought 8 beads for 7¢ each and 2 bracelets for $3 each. How much did she spend? (Grade 3)

A. 56¢ B. 62¢
C. $3.62 D. $6.56

# Measurement

**Objective** Maintain basic measurement skills needed to start fourth grade.

 **STANDARDS** Maintains M3M2.c

## Work Together

You can use math to describe objects in your classroom. First, review how to measure length with a ruler.

Work with a partner. Estimate the length of the pencil below to the nearest inch. Record your estimate; then measure.

**Vocabulary**

- **centimeter (cm)**
- **foot (ft)**
- **inch (in.)**
- **meter (m)**
- **yard (yd)**

**STEP 1** Line up the left end of the pencil with the zero mark of the inch ruler. If there is no zero mark, line up the pencil with the end of the ruler.

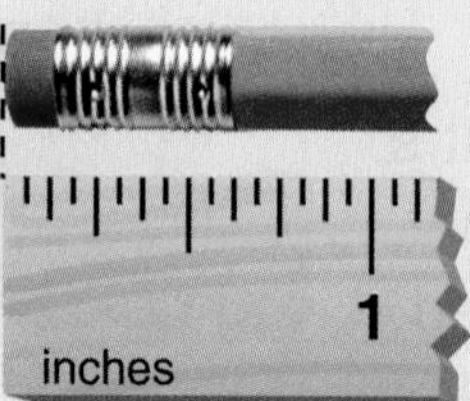


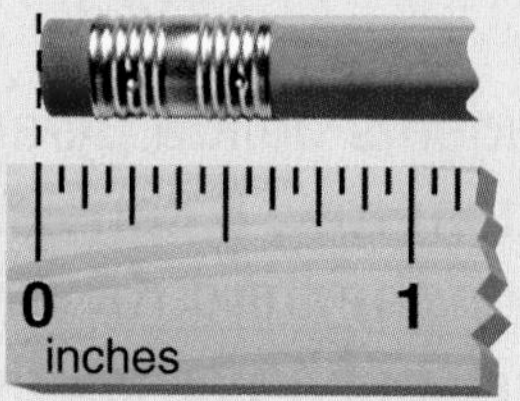


**STEP 2** Find the inch mark closest to the right end of the pencil.

- What is the length of the pencil to the nearest inch?
- How close is your measurement to your estimate?

Repeat the steps above to estimate and measure the length of the pencil to the nearest centimeter.

## On Your Own

**Find 3 classroom objects to measure. Copy each table. Then follow the directions.**

- Estimate the length of each object to the nearest inch. Record your estimate.
- Measure the object. Record your measurement.

| | Object | My Estimate | Length to the Nearest Inch |
|---|---|---|---|
| 1. | | | |
| 2. | | | |
| 3. | | | |

- Estimate the length of each object to the nearest centimeter. Record your estimate.
- Measure the object. Record your measurement.

| | Object | My Estimate | Length to the Nearest Centimeter |
|---|---|---|---|
| 4. | | | |
| 5. | | | |
| 6. | | | |

**Use an inch ruler, a centimeter ruler, a yardstick, or a meterstick to solve each problem.**

12 inches = 1 foot
3 feet = 1 yard
100 centimeters = 1 meter

7. Find three objects that you estimate are each about 1 foot long. Measure each object to check your estimate.

8. Find 3 objects that you estimate are about 20 centimeters long. Measure each object to check your estimate.

9. Find an object about 1 yard long or wide. Measure to check your estimate.

10. Find an object about 1 meter long or wide. Measure to check your estimate.

## Talk About It • Write About It

11. Describe how to find the length of the pencil.

# Math Connections

## Geometric Pieces

**STANDARDS** Maintains M3M3, M3M4, and M3P5

**Vocabulary**
**area**
**perimeter**

**Materials**
grid paper

The figure below was made by tracing around two rectangles on grid paper.

Can you find each rectangle?

Compare your answer with a classmate.

The distance around any figure is called the **perimeter**.

Find the perimeter of this figure.

Can you find the perimeter in more than one way?

How do you label your answer?

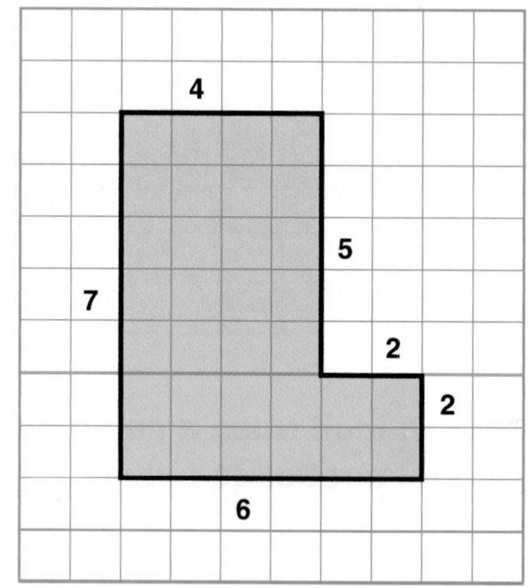


The **area** of a figure is the number of square units needed to cover the figure without overlapping.

Find the area of the figure at the right.

Can you find the area in more than one way?

How do you label your answer?

**Use grid paper. Follow the directions.**

1. Draw a rectangle. Find its perimeter and area.
2. Draw a figure that combines two rectangles or squares. Find the perimeter and area of the entire figure.
3. Draw the front of a rectangular apartment building. Put in doors and windows. Use other geometric shapes to finish your picture.
4. Find the area of the building you drew in Exercise 3. The area of the building should NOT include the area of the windows or doors.

# UNIT 1

# Place Value and Money

## Place Value

page 2

CHAPTER 2

## Compare, Order, and Round Whole Numbers and Money

page 22

# Reading Mathematics

## Reviewing Vocabulary

**Here are some math vocabulary words that you should know.**

| | |
|---|---|
| **digit** | any one of the ten number symbols 0, 1, 2, 3, 4, 5, 6, 7, 8, or 9 |
| **place value** | the value of a digit determined by its place in a number |
| **standard form** | the usual, or common, way of writing a number, using digits |
| **expanded form** | a way of writing a number as the sum of the values of the digits |
| **word form** | a way of writing a number using words |

## Reading Words and Symbols

Look at the base-ten blocks below. You can read and write the number they represent in these ways.

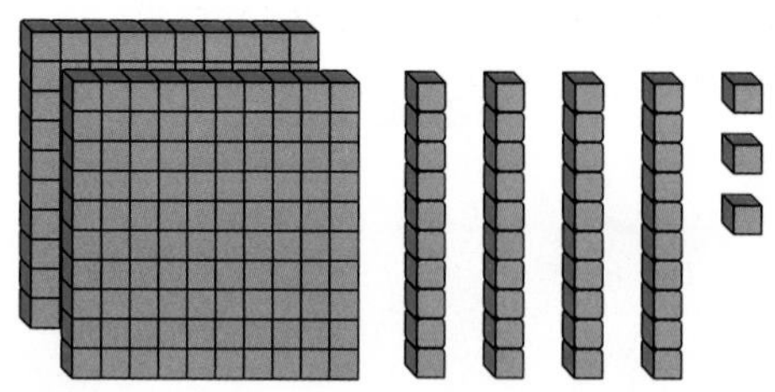

**Read:** There are 2 hundreds blocks
4 tens rods
3 ones cubes.

**Write in standard form:** 243

**Write in expanded form:** 200 + 40 + 3

**Write in word form:** two hundred forty-three

**Use words or symbols to answer the questions.**

1. What is the expanded form of 562?
2. What is the word form of 300 + 70 + 5?

# Reading Questions on CRCT

**Choose the correct answer for each.**

**3.** Select the answer that represents the blocks at the right.

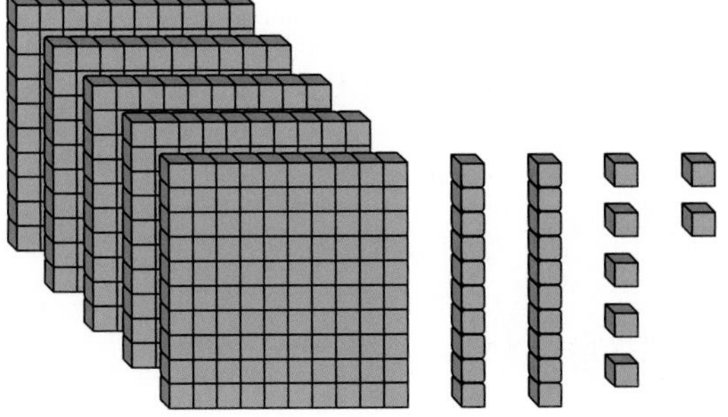

A. 725

B. 572

C. 527

D. 275

**Select** means "choose" or "pick."

**4.** What answer is equivalent to 318?

A. 8 + 100 + 30

B. 300 + 80 + 1

C. 800 + 10 + 3

D. 300 + 10 + 8

**Equivalent** means "equal."

**5.** Which of the following is NOT an alternate way to show the value of the number 89?

A. 80 + 9

B. eighty-nine

C. 8 tens 9 ones

D. 80 tens 9 ones

**Alternate** means "different."

# Learning Vocabulary

**Watch for these words in this unit. Write their definitions in your journal.**

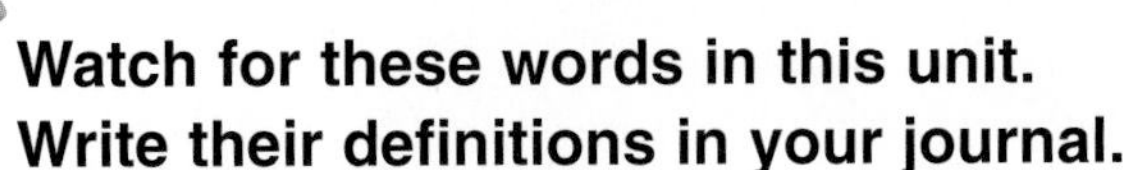

**ordinal number**
**short word form**
**period**
**million**
**hundred million**

## Education Place

At **eduplace.com/map,** see eGlossary and eGames—Math Lingo

## Literature Connection

Read "Beyond Pluto" on Page 644. Then work with a partner to answer the questions about the story.

CHAPTER 1

# Place Value

## Georgia PERFORMANCE PREVIEW

### Using Data

The tallest building in Georgia is located in Atlanta. Look at the facts about the building. Which number is used to count? Which numbers are used to measure?

Use numbers to write 3 facts about another building that you know.

**Georgia's Tallest Building**

- The building is **1,023** feet high.
- The building has **55** floors.
- The building took **14** months to build.

# Use What You Know

**Use this page to review and remember what you need to know for this chapter.**

## VOCABULARY

**Choose the best term to complete each sentence.**

1. 1, 2, 3, 4, 5, 6, 7, 8, 9, and 0 are ____.
2. In the number 1,045, the 4 is in the ____ place.
3. 1st, 3rd, and 7th are examples of ____.
4. The number 400 + 30 + 5 is written in ____.

**Vocabulary**

- tens
- digits
- standard form
- expanded form
- ordinal numbers

## CONCEPTS AND SKILLS

**Copy the place-value chart and write each number in it. Then write the value of the digit 7 for each number.**

5. 37
6. 785
7. 478
8. 1,075
9. 7,564

| thousands | hundreds | tens | ones |
|---|---|---|---|
| | | | |
| | | | |
| | | | |
| | | | |
| | | | |

**Write each number in standard form.**

10. 9 tens 3 ones
11. 6 hundreds 8 tens 5 ones
12. 800 + 20 + 4
13. 4,000 + 600 + 20
14. six hundred eighty-four
15. nine thousand, sixteen

**Write the value of the underlined digit.**

16. 6<u>3</u>4
17. <u>4</u>72
18. 7,<u>5</u>82
19. <u>4</u>,339

20. How many tens are there in 1,000? How many hundreds are there? Explain your answers.

Facts Practice, See page 664.

Lesson 1

Audio Tutor 1/1 Listen and Understand

# Uses of Numbers

**Objective** Use numbers in different ways.

**STANDARDS** Extends M4N, M4P4

**Vocabulary**
ordinal number

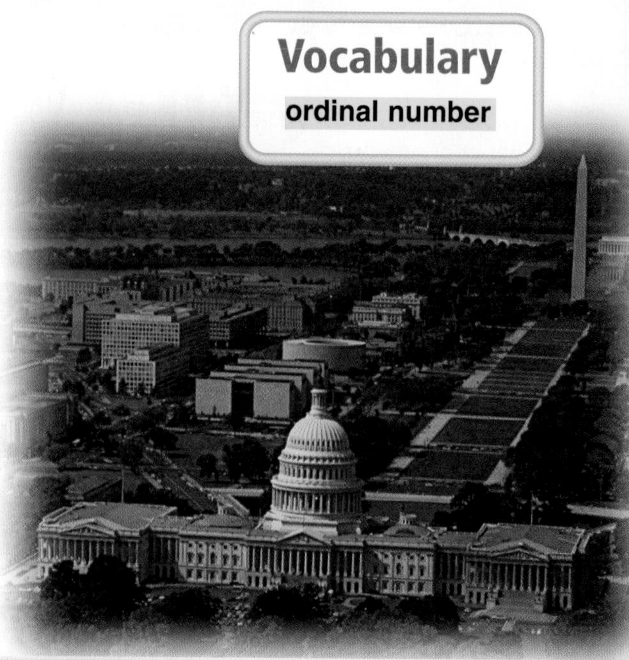

## Learn About It

Washington, D.C. became the capital of the United States in 1791. It has 3 famous monuments. It is the 21st largest city in the country.

Numbers are used in many different ways. How are the numbers **1791**, **3**, and **21st** being used?

**Ordinal numbers are used to show position.**

- 2nd President
- 1st President

*John Adams was the 2nd President but the 1st President to live in the White House.*

**Numbers are used to count.**

- 540 rooms
- 658 windows

*The U.S. Capitol building has 540 rooms and 658 windows!*

**Numbers are used to measure.**

- 30 feet
- 40 tons

*The famous Bartholdi Fountain is about 30 feet high and weighs almost 40 tons.*

**Numbers are used to label.**

- X-15
- Apollo 11

*At the Air and Space Museum, there is the X-15 airplane, and the Apollo 11 command module.*

In the paragraph above, **1791** is used to measure, **3** is used to count, and **21st** is an ordinal number used to show position.

## Guided Practice

**Tell how each number is being used. Write *position, count, measure,* or *label*.**

**1.** 

**2.** 

**3.** 2,399 visitors

**4.** 25th person in line

### Ask Yourself

- Is the number an ordinal number?
- What does the number tell me?

**Explain Your Thinking** ▶ For each number on Page 4, tell if it is an estimate or an exact amount. Explain your reasoning.

## Practice and Problem Solving

**Tell how each number is being used. Write *position, count, measure,* or *label*.**

**5.** 

**6.** 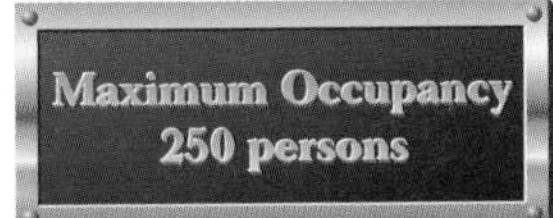


**7.** 

**8.** Carmel, IN 46033

**9.** 16th president of the U.S.

**10.** 750 pounds

**11.** 29 miles

**12.** 5 boxes of 12 pens each

**13.** Apartment 4B

**14.** 50 states

**15.** 3rd place

**16.** Row 65F

**17.** **Reasoning** Tanya went souvenir shopping. At the 3rd shop, she bought 4 souvenirs. The souvenirs weighed a total of 8 pounds. Which number in this problem is being used to count? Which number is used to measure? Explain how you decided.

## GPS Sharpening Skills for CRCT

**Open Response**

**Write each number in word form.** (Grade 3)

**18.** 4,285

**19.** 2,049

**20.** 753

**21.** 14

**22.** 620

**23.** 359

**24.** 5,005

**25.** 290

**26.** During John's 5th trip to Washington, he traveled about 100 miles and bought 3 gifts. How is each number in the problem being used?
(Ch. 1, Lesson 1)

Extra Practice See page 21, Set A.

Lesson 2

 **Audio Tutor 1**/2 Listen and Understand

# Place Value Through Hundred Thousands

**Objective** Read and write numbers through 999,999.

**STANDARDS** M4N1.a, M4N1.b

## Vocabulary

**period**
**standard form**
**expanded form**
**short word form**
**word form**
**base-ten**

## Learn About It

Anaya lives in Tallahassee, the capital of Florida. In the year 2000, the population of Tallahassee was 150,624.

What does the number 150,624 mean?

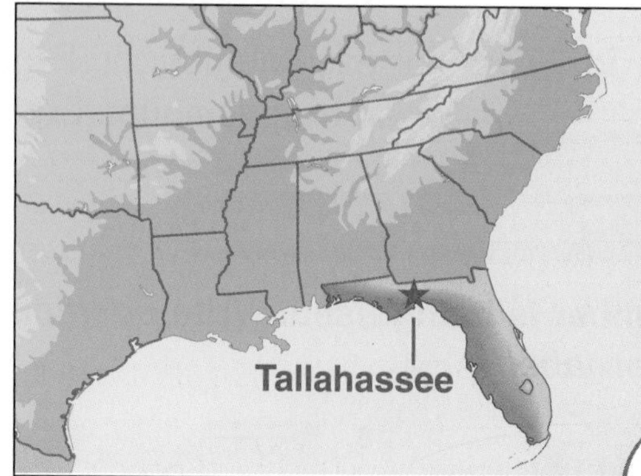


Each group of 3 digits separated by a comma in a number is called a **period**.

▶ **A place-value chart can help explain what this number means.**

| Thousands | | | | Ones | | |
|---|---|---|---|---|---|---|
| hundreds | tens | ones | | hundreds | tens | ones |
| 1 | 5 | 0 | , | 6 | 2 | 4 |

- The value of the 1 is 100,000.
- The value of the 5 is 50,000.
- The value of the 6 is 600.
- The value of the 2 is 20.
- The value of the 4 is 4.

▶ **There are different ways to write 150,624.**

| | |
|---|---|
| You can use **standard form**. | 150,624 |
| You can use **expanded form**. | 100,000 + 50,000 + 600 + 20 + 4 |
| You can use **short word form**. | 150 thousand, 624 |
| You can use **word form**. | one hundred fifty thousand, six hundred twenty-four |

▶ We use a base-ten place-value system. Each place is ten times greater than the place to the right of it.

| Thousands | | | Ones | | |
|---|---|---|---|---|---|
| hundreds | tens | ones | hundreds | tens | ones |

× 10 × 10 × 10 × 10 × 10

## Guided Practice

For Exercises 1–3, write each number in three other ways. You can use a place-value chart to help you.

**1.** 104,002 **2.** 104,020 **3.** 104 thousand, 200

**4.** What is the value of the 7 in 702,209?

**Ask Yourself**

- What is the value of each digit?
- Do I need a comma?

**Explain Your Thinking** ▶ Do you think the population of a city is an estimated or exact amount? Why?

## Practice and Problem Solving

Write the value of the underlined digit.

**5.** 7$\underline{0}$1 **6.** 5,$\underline{2}$60 **7.** 63$\underline{9}$,572 **8.** 5$\underline{6}$,112

**9.** $\underline{1}$2,048 **10.** 3$\underline{5}$0,237 **11.** $\underline{7}$63,299 **12.** 89$\underline{0}$,973

Write each number in both short word form and word form.

**13.** 1,201 **14.** 300,200 **15.** 99,909 **16.** 332,332

**17.** 70,000 + 4,000 + 100 + 3 **18.** 500,000 + 20,000 + 1,000 + 600 + 3

Write each number in three other ways.

**19.** 80,000 + 4,000 + 200 + 2 **20.** 200,000 + 60,000 + 7,000 + 100 + 80 + 1

**21.** 405 thousand, 603 **22.** twenty thousand, eight hundred

**23.** 170 thousand, 815 **24.** six hundred four thousand, ninety-nine

Go On

## Algebra • Equations Find each missing number.

25. 6,000 + 400 + 30 + ■ = 6,439

26. 2,000 + 900 + ■ = 2,950

27. ■ + 600 + 50 + 1 = 1,651

28. 8,000 + ■ + 4 = 8,204

29. ■ + 5,000 + 60 = 905,060

30. 70,000 + 8,000 + ■ + 7 = 78,067

**Rewrite the number to show each change.**

31. 2,146
   a. Increase by 10,000.
   b. Increase by 100,000.

32. 279,153
   a. Decrease by 1,000.
   b. Decrease by 10,000.

33. 509,986
   a. Decrease by 10,000.
   b. Decrease by 100,000.

34. 90,884
   a. Increase by 1,000.
   b. Increase by 10,000.

35. 192,906
   a. Increase by 10,000.
   b. Decrease by 1,000.

36. 99,090
   a. Decrease by 1,000.
   b. Increase by 1,000.

## Data Use the table for Problems 37–40.

37. What is the population of Austin, Texas? Write this number in three other ways.

38. Which cities have at least 200,000 people?

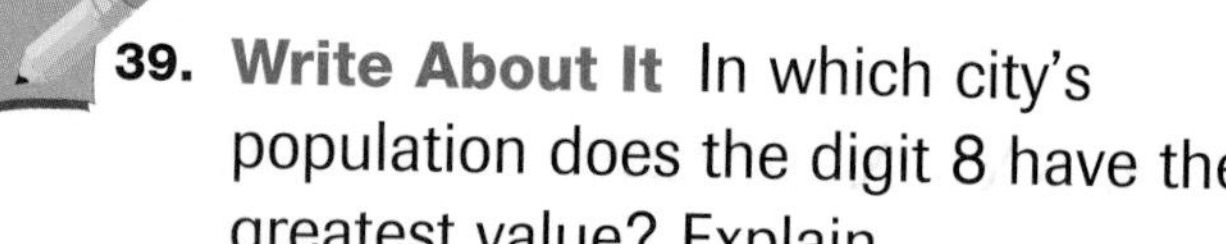

39. **Write About It** In which city's population does the digit 8 have the greatest value? Explain.

40. **Create and Solve** Use the table to write a problem. Give it to a friend to solve.

**State Capital Populations in the Year 2000**

| Capital | Population |
|---|---|
| Indianapolis, IN | 781,870 |
| Austin, TX | 656,562 |
| Raleigh, NC | 276,093 |
| Frankfort, KY | 27,741 |
| Montpelier, VT | 8,035 |



Extra Practice See page 21, Set B.

**Problem Solving** GPS

# Visual Thinking
## Benchmark Numbers

STANDARDS M4N7.d

Benchmark numbers like 50, 100, and 200 can help you estimate an unknown amount.

If you know Jar A holds 250 marbles, you can use it as a benchmark to estimate how many marbles are in Jar B.

Jar A

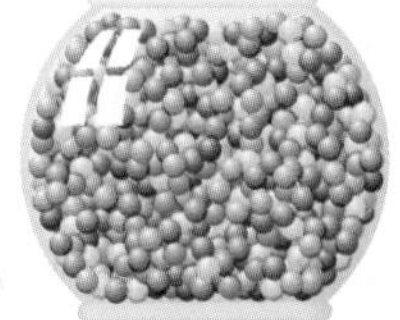
Jar B

**Think** There are about twice as many marbles in Jar B as Jar A.

So, there are about 500 marbles in Jar B.

**Use each benchmark to choose the best estimate.**

**1.** 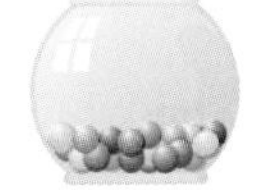

Benchmark 25 marbles

**a.** 50 marbles
**b.** 100 marbles

**2.** 

Benchmark 500 gallons

**a.** 10,000 gallons
**b.** 1,000 gallons

**Quick Check**

**Check your understanding of Lessons 1–2.**

**Tell how each number is being used. Write *position, count, measure,* or *label*.** (Lesson 1)

**1.** 2,305 books on a shelf **2.** 350 inches long **3.** Room 5C

**Write each number in three other ways.** (Lesson 2)

**4.** 45,207 **5.** 50 thousand, 203 **6.** 900,000 + 6,000 + 700 + 80 + 4

**Write the place of the underlined digit. Then write its value.** (Lesson 2)

**7.** 4<u>5</u>7,239 **8.** 12<u>7</u>,488 **9.** <u>5</u>64,220

**Solve.** (Lesson 1)

**10.** Sophia went to the mall to find a pair of X-20 sneakers. She bought the sneakers she wanted at the 3rd store she went into. How is each of the numbers in this problem being used?

Extra Practice at **eduplace.com/map**

Lesson 3

Audio Tutor 1/3 Listen and Understand

# Problem-Solving Strategy
## Use Logical Reasoning

**Objective** Use logical reasoning to solve problems.

**STANDARDS** Extends M4D, M4P1.b

**Problem** Al, Ron, Jo, and Di are each holding one of the state flowers shown. Di's flower is white. Al's flower is not red. Ron's flower is not purple. Jo's flower is not blue or red. Which color flower is each person holding?

**This is what you know.**

- Di's flower is white.
- Al's flower is not red.
- Ron's flower is not purple.
- Jo's flower is not blue or red.

**How can you use logical reasoning to solve?**
You can make a chart to show what you know and then use logical reasoning to complete it.

SOLVE

**Use logical reasoning to fill in the chart.**
Write *yes* or *no* for the facts you know.

- Di's flower is white, so it is not red, purple, or blue.
- Jo's flower is purple because it is not white, blue, or red.
- Al's flower is blue, because it is not white, red, or purple.
- Ron's flower must be red.

When you write *yes* in the chart, you can write *no* in the rest of that row and column.

| | White | Red | Blue | Purple |
|---|---|---|---|---|
| Di | **yes** | no | no | no |
| Jo | no | no | no | **yes** |
| Al | no | no | **yes** | no |
| Ron | no | **yes** | no | no |

**Solution:** The flower Al is holding is blue. Ron's is red. Jo's is purple. Di's is white.

LOOK BACK

**Look back at the problem.**
Does the solution match the facts in the problem?



Extra Help at **eduplace.com/map**

## Guided Practice

**Use the Ask Yourself questions to help you solve each problem.**

1. Rita, Gail, Rae, and Barb each have a state flag that is either red, blue, green, or black. Barb's flag is not red or green. Rita's is not red. Rae's is black. What color is each person's flag?

2. Dana, Nell, Bob, and Raj each take either Exit 1, 2, 3, or 4 off the state highway. Dana does not take Exit 1. Bob takes Exit 2. Raj does not take Exit 4. Nell does not take Exit 1 or Exit 4. Which exit does each take?

   **Hint** What are the heads of the columns and rows in my chart?

### Ask Yourself

**UNDERSTAND** What facts do I know?

**PLAN** Can I use logical reasoning?

**SOLVE**
- Did I fill in a chart with what I know?
- Did I use logical reasoning to complete the chart?

**LOOK BACK** Does my solution match the facts in the problem?

## Independent Practice

**Use logical reasoning to solve each problem.**

3. Mai, Lu, and Jo are playing a game about U.S. states. Their scores are 20, 25, and 30. Mai does not have the most points. Jo does not have the fewest points. Lu has 30 points. How many points does each girl have?

4. Vicki, Mary, and Tyra each own either a motorcycle, a car, or a van. Vicki does not own a vehicle with 4 wheels. Tyra owns a van. What vehicle does each person own?

5. Joe, Tom, Hal, and Bob are standing in line. Tom is first, Hal is not second or fourth. Joe is directly behind Hal. Bob is in front of Hal. In what order are the boys in line?

Go On

# Mixed Problem Solving

**Solve. Show your work. Tell what strategy you used.**

6. **Multistep** Choi and Ana are playing a game. Choi scored 50, 40, and 80 points. If Ana has scored 60 and 70 points, how many more points does she need to tie Choi's score?

7. Tony and Aaron collect state patches. Tony has 4 more patches than Aaron. Together they have 14 patches. How many patches does each boy have?

8. Jeff bought a shirt for $12.00 and a pair of pants for $15.00. He paid with a $10 bill and a $20 bill. How much change did he receive?

**You Choose**

**Strategy**
- Guess and Check
- Solve a Simpler Problem
- Work Backward
- Write an Equation

**Computation Method**
- Mental Math
- Estimation
- Paper and Pencil
- Calculator

**Data** **The line plot shows the number of books read by students in a class. Use the line plot for Problems 9–11.**

9. How many students are in the class?

10. Students who read 4 or more books get certificates. How many students will get certificates?

11. Before the survey, Juan guessed that most people in his class had read more than 4 books. Was his guess correct? Explain.

12. **Reasoning** Erin, Hal, KC, and Juan each read either 3, 4, 5, or 6 books. Juan did not read 6 books. KC read 4 books. Hal did not read 5 or 6 books. How many books did each student read?

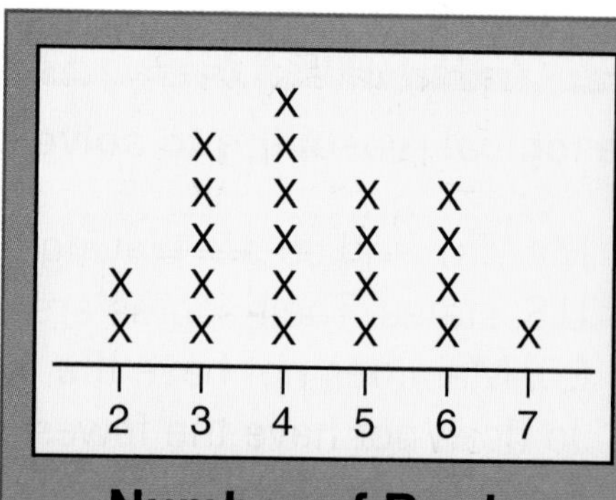


Number of Books Read by Students

# Problem Solving on CRCT

**Multiple Choice**

**Choose the letter of the correct answer.**

1. Leon has 7 pencils. His sister has 2 fewer pencils than he does. They want to share all the pencils equally among 3 people. How many pencils will each person get?

   A. 4
   B. 6
   C. 12
   D. 24

(Grade 3)

2. The number below is being used to _____.

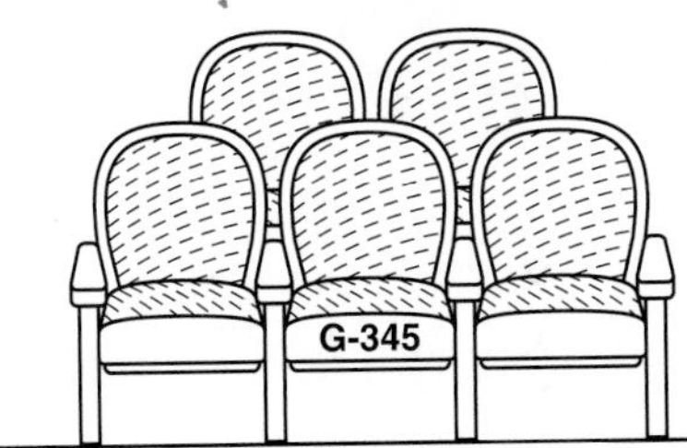


   A. count
   B. show position
   C. label
   D. measure

(Chapter 1, Lesson 1)

**Open Response**

**Solve each problem.**

3. Rita's piano lesson starts at 11:35 A.M. and lasts for an hour. What time does it end?

   **Explain** how you know.

(Grade 3)

4. The instruments below belong to Ned, Tom, and Belle. Ned's instrument does not have strings. Tom does not play the guitar.

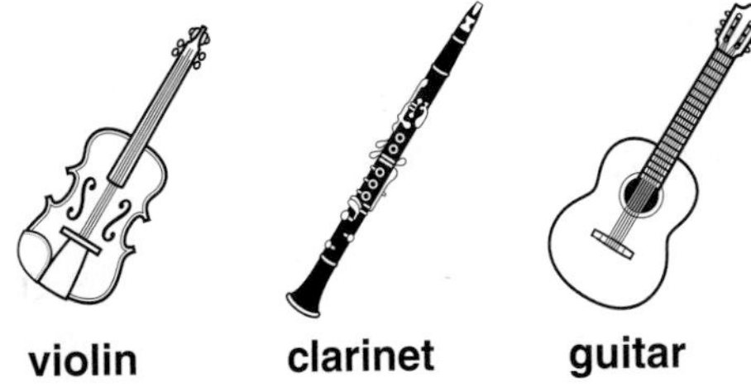


   Tell which instrument each person plays. Explain how you know.

(Chapter 1, Lesson 3)

5. The table below shows the number of people who took raft trips with the All Water Rafting Company.

| Raft Trips | |
|---|---|
| **Year** | **Number of People** |
| 2003 | 70,065 |
| 2004 | 104,300 |
| 2005 | 132,586 |

   a. How many people took rafting trips in 2003? Write the number in word form and in expanded form.

   b. Which year did one hundred four thousand, three hundred people take rafting trips? Explain how you know.

   c. Look at the number of people who took raft trips in 2005. What is the value of each digit in the number?

(Chapter 1, Lesson 2)

**Education Place**

See **eduplace.com/map** for more Test-Taking Tips.

# How Big Is One Million?

**Materials**
Newspapers

**Objective** Relate one million to hundreds and thousands.

**STANDARDS** M4N1.a, M4N1.b, M4P3

## Work Together

Randy claims that he reads more than one million words each day. How many words is that?

A place-value chart can help explain what this number means.

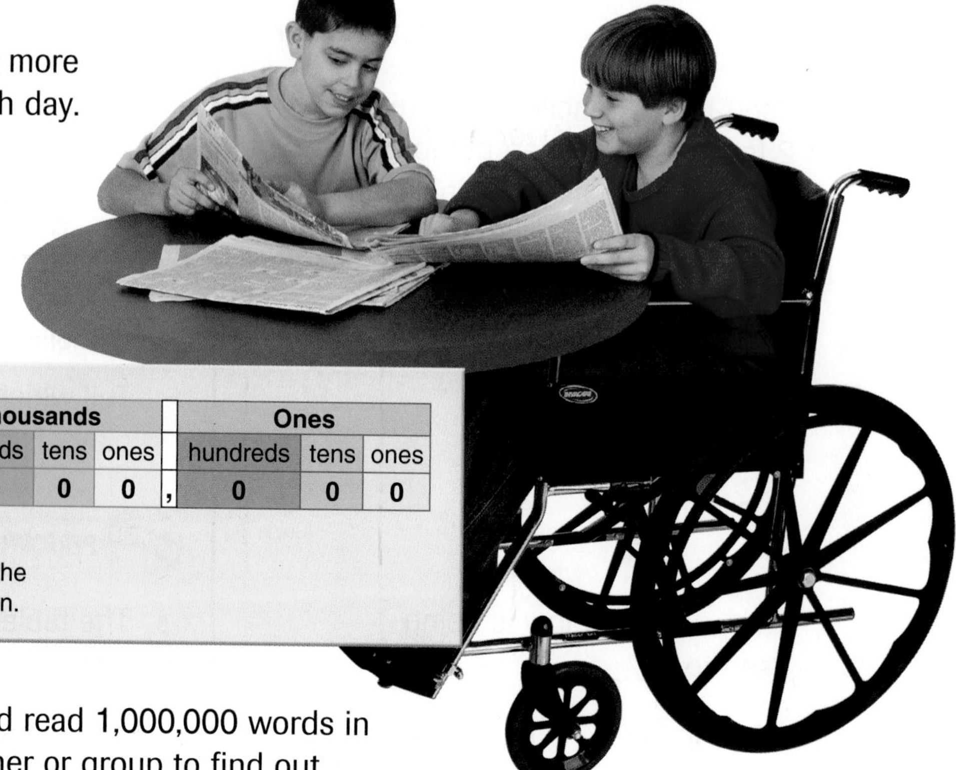

| Millions | | | | Thousands | | | | Ones | | |
|---|---|---|---|---|---|---|---|---|---|---|
| hundreds | tens | ones | | hundreds | tens | ones | | hundreds | tens | ones |
| | | 1 | , | 0 | 0 | 0 | , | 0 | 0 | 0 |

The value of the 1 is one million.

Do you think a person could read 1,000,000 words in one day? Work with a partner or group to find out.

**STEP 1** Take a page from a newspaper. Count and circle 100 words in an article. Write "100 words" on the circle.

**STEP 2** Make a chart like the one shown. Estimate how many groups of 100 are on the first page. Write your estimate on the chart.

| | |
|---|---|
| How many groups of 100 words are on the page? | |
| How many pages to read 1,000 words? | |
| How many pages to read 10,000 words? | |
| How many pages to read 100,000 words? | |
| How many pages to read 1,000,000 words? | |

Estimate how many pages you will need to read 1,000 words. Write your estimate on the chart.

Use a calculator to complete the chart.

## On Your Own

**Use this chart to answer each question.**

| MILLIONS | | THOUSANDS | | | ONES | | |
|---|---|---|---|---|---|---|---|
| | millions | hundred thousands | ten thousands | thousands | hundreds | tens | ones |
| | 1 | 0 | 0 | 0 | 0 | 0 | 0 |
| | | | | | | | |

1. How many thousands are there in 10,000?
2. How many thousands are there in 100,000?
3. How many thousands are there in 1,000,000?
4. How many hundreds are there in 1,000,000?
5. Describe the patterns you see in your charts.
6. Do you think Randy could read 1 million words in one day? How many newspaper pages would he have to read?

## Talk About It • Write About It

**You learned how 100 and 1,000 are related to one million.**

7. How many thousands are in half of a million? Explain.
8. Would you use hundreds, thousands, or millions to count the following things? Explain your reasoning for each.
   **a.** the people in your state
   **b.** the students in your school
   **c.** number of miles from New York to California

Lesson 5

# Place Value Through Hundred Millions

**Objective** Read and write numbers through 999,999,999.

 **STANDARDS** M4N1.a, M4N1.b, M4P3

## Learn About It

Derek is collecting state quarters. The first state quarter the U.S. Mint made was the Delaware quarter in 1999.

The Denver mint made 401,424,000 Delaware quarters that year. A place-value chart can help you understand the value of the digits in the number 401,424,000.

**A place-value chart can help explain what this number means.**

| Millions | | | | Thousands | | | | Ones | | |
|---|---|---|---|---|---|---|---|---|---|---|
| hundreds | tens | ones | | hundreds | tens | ones | | hundreds | tens | ones |
| 4 | 0 | 1 | , | 4 | 2 | 4 | , | 0 | 0 | 0 |

The value of the 4 is 400,000,000.

The value of the 1 is 1,000,000.

**Remember**
Each group of 3 digits separated by a comma in a number is called a **period**.

**There are different ways to write 401,424,000.**

| | |
|---|---|
| You can use **standard form**. | 401,424,000 |
| You can use **expanded form**. | 400,000,000 + 1,000,000 + 400,000 + 20,000 + 4,000 |
| You can use **short word form**. | 401 million, 424 thousand |
| You can use **word form**. | four hundred one million, four hundred twenty-four thousand |

## Guided Practice

**For Exercises 1–5, write each number in three other ways.**

1. 560,790,341
2. 56,298,743
3. 506,709,341
4. 500,000 + 200
5. 914 million, 887 thousand
6. Write 2$\underline{3}$0,207,090 in expanded form. Then write the value of the underlined digit.

**Ask Yourself**

- What is the value of each digit?
- Do I need a comma?

**Explain Your Thinking** ▶ What pattern do you see in the place-value chart on Page 16?

## Practice and Problem Solving

**Write each number in word form and short word form.**

7. 6,007,002
8. 606,707,202
9. 45,213,450
10. 911,394,116
11. 4,000,000 + 200,000 + 30,000 + 6,000 + 400 + 20 + 5
12. 900,000,000 + 60,000,000 + 6,000,000 + 40,000 + 600 + 5

**Write each number in standard form and expanded form.**

13. 16 million, 201 thousand, 856
14. 439 million, 898 thousand, 312
15. sixty-three million, seven hundred ninety-six thousand, nine hundred three
16. five hundred twenty-seven million, nine hundred thousand, six hundred forty

**Solve.**

17. In one year, the U.S. Mint made a total of 939,932,000 Georgia quarters. Write this number in short word form.

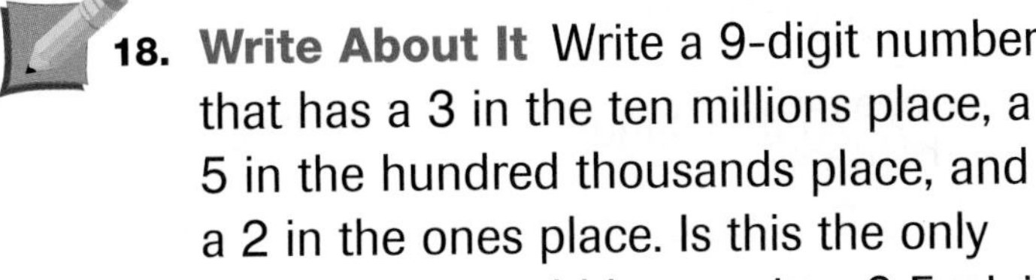

18. **Write About It** Write a 9-digit number that has a 3 in the ten millions place, a 5 in the hundred thousands place, and a 2 in the ones place. Is this the only number you could have written? Explain.

*The Georgia quarter was the 4th state quarter to be minted.*

Go On

**Write the place of the 7 in each number. Then write its value.**

**19.** 708,993,040 **20.** 37,990,841 **21.** 16,007,845 **22.** 122,799

**23.** 20,895,227 **24.** 78,901 **25.** 107,912 **26.** 19,870,001

**Match each standard-form number to its expanded or short word form.**

**27.** 567,890,000 **a.** 243 million, 500 thousand

**28.** 56,789,000 **b.** 243 thousand, 500

**29.** 243,500,000 **c.** 567 million, 890 thousand

**30.** 243,500 **d.** 50,000,000 + 6,000,000 + 700,000 + 80,000 + 9,000

**Data** **The table shows the corn produced by four states. Use the table for Problems 31–34.**

**31.** How many bushels of corn did Kansas produce? Write this number in two ways.

**32.** Which number has a 7 in the hundred thousands place?

**33.** Which states produced at least 100 million bushels of corn?

**34.** **Explain** How many bushels of corn did Oklahoma produce? In this number, does the digit 7 or the digit 8 have a greater value? Explain.

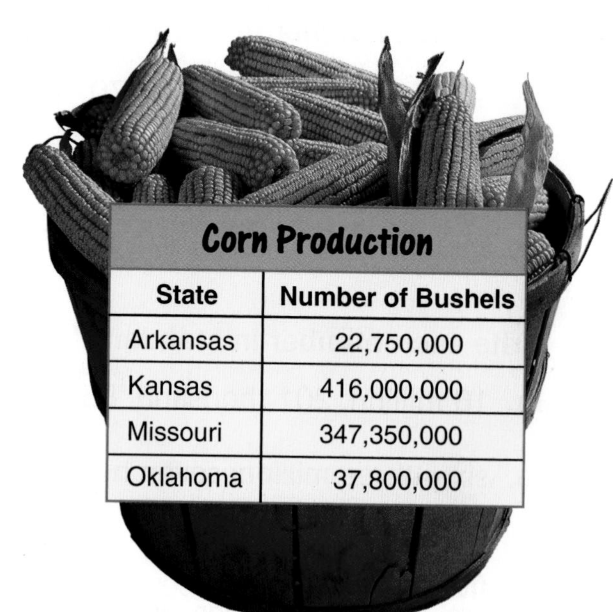

**Corn Production**

| State | Number of Bushels |
|---|---|
| Arkansas | 22,750,000 |
| Kansas | 416,000,000 |
| Missouri | 347,350,000 |
| Oklahoma | 37,800,000 |

## Sharpening Skills for CRCT

**Open Response**

**For each pair of measurements, tell which is greater.** (Grade 3)

**35.** 4 ounces or 4 pounds

**36.** 2 yards or 2 feet

**37.** 1 meter or 10 centimeters

**Multiple Choice**

**38.** What is NOT another way to write the value of the underlined digit in <u>7</u>8,206? (Ch. 1, Lesson 2)

A. 70 thousands C. 70,000

B. 7 ten thousands D. 70 hundreds



Extra Practice See page 21, Set C.

# Math Reasoning

## Different Bases

STANDARDS Extends M4N1

Our place-value system is based on tens. Other systems use different bases.

### Base Ten

Each place value in base ten is 10 times greater than the one to the right of it.

To read the number, add the values.

× 10 × 10 × 10

| thousands | hundreds | tens | ones |
|---|---|---|---|
| 1,000 | 100 | 10 | 1 |
| 2 | 1 | 0 | 4 |

Base 10 uses the digits 0 – 9.

2 × 1,000 + 1 × 100 + 0 × 10 + 4 × 1

2,000 + 100 + 0 + 4 = 2,104

### Base Two

Each place value in base two is 2 times greater than the one to the right of it.

To read 1101 in base ten, add the values.

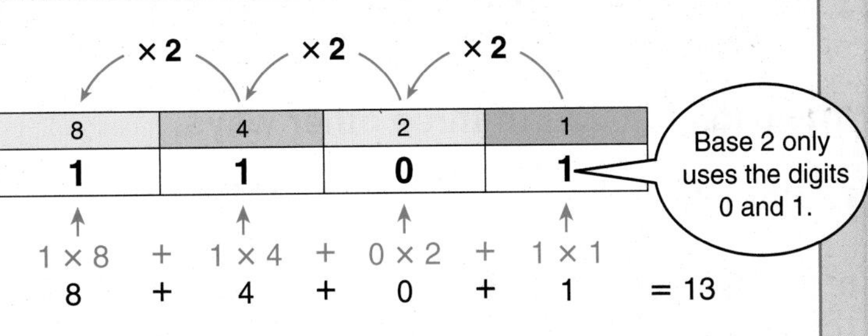


### Base Five

Each place value in base five is 5 times greater than the one to the right of it.

To read 1403 in base ten, add the values.

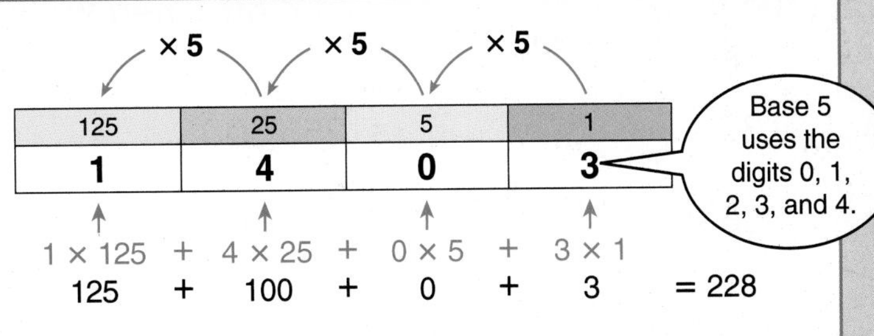


**Write each base-two number in base ten.**

**1.** 100 **2.** 101 **3.** 11 **4.** 110

**Write each base-five number in base ten.**

**5.** 201 **6.** 332 **7.** 41 **8.** 224

**9. Challenge** Look at the charts above. What are the next 2 place values in base two and base five? Explain your answers.

# Chapter Review/Test

Study Guide page SG5

## VOCABULARY

**Vocabulary**
**base-ten**
**standard form**
**ordinal number**
**expanded form**

**Choose the best term to complete each sentence.**

1. A number that is used to show position is an ____.
2. Our place-value system is a ____ system.
3. 10,000,000 + 5,000 + 20 + 9 is the ____ for 10,005,029.

## CONCEPTS AND SKILLS

**Tell how each number is being used. Write *position, count, measure,* or *label.*** (Lesson 1, pp. 4–5)

4. 4th in line
5. 16 ounces
6. 25 marbles

**Write each number in three other ways.** (Lesson 2, pp. 6–9, Lesson 4–5, pp. 14–19)

7. 395,123
8. 1 million, 619
9. 56 million, 432 thousand
10. 500,000,000 + 8,000 + 600 + 9
11. 20,000,000 + 300,000 + 4,000 + 1
12. seven hundred fifty-six million, six
13. three hundred nine thousand, fifty-one

**Write the place of the underlined digit. Then write its value.**
(Lesson 2, pp. 6–9, Lesson 5, pp. 16–19)

14. <u>1</u>09,377
15. 2<u>5</u>6,300
16. <u>3</u>,589,605
17. 48,<u>5</u>56,215
18. 2<u>0</u>6,000,015
19. <u>3</u>46,157,021

## PROBLEM SOLVING

**Solve.** (Lesson 3, pp. 10–13)

20. Four children stand in line to see a movie. Elise is second in line. Brian is not last. John is directly in front of Elise. Chris is not second or third in line. List the children in order from first to fourth.

**Show You Understand**

Why do we call our system of numbers a base-ten system? Explain your thinking.

# Extra Practice

## Set A (Lesson 1, pp. 4–5)

**Tell how each number is being used. Write *position*, *count*, *measure*, or *label*.**

1. 52 miles
2. Charlotte, NC 08088
3. 50th anniversary
4. 76 people
5. Apartment 9C
6. 325 pounds

## Set B (Lesson 2, pp. 6–9)

**Write each number in three other ways.**

1. 59 thousand, 505
2. 200,000 + 6,000 + 60
3. 300,991
4. 230,000
5. five hundred six thousand
6. 49,300
7. 800,000 + 50,000 + 400 + 70
8. 400,000 + 20,000 + 900 + 70 + 7
9. thirty thousand, nine hundred
10. five hundred fifty thousand, three

**Write the place of the underlined digit. Then write its value.**

11. $5\underline{0}{,}862$
12. $\underline{5}05{,}432$
13. $99{,}9\underline{9}0$
14. $4\underline{9}{,}887$
15. $110{,}02\underline{2}$
16. $8{,}\underline{8}92$
17. $\underline{7}28{,}683$
18. $1\underline{4}6{,}170$

## Set C (Lesson 5, pp. 16–19)

**Write each number in three other ways.**

1. 4,005,000
2. 909,990,099
3. 15 million, 304 thousand, 794
4. 700,000,000 + 5,000,000 + 40,000 + 600 + 7
5. seventy-six million, two hundred fifty-seven thousand, four hundred forty-two

**Write the place of the 9 in each number. Then write its value.**

6. 780,090,001
7. 97,341,203
8. 109,866
9. 923,011,233
10. 65,901,235
11. 573,280,908
12. 59,605,511
13. 600,390,885

Extra Practice at **eduplace.com/map**

CHAPTER 2

# Compare, Order, and Round Whole Numbers and Money

## INVESTIGATION

### Using Data

A student claims that, according to the graph on the right, there are more species of fish than mammals in the Grand Canyon. Is she correct? Why, or why not?

What other comparisons could you make, using the information in the graph?

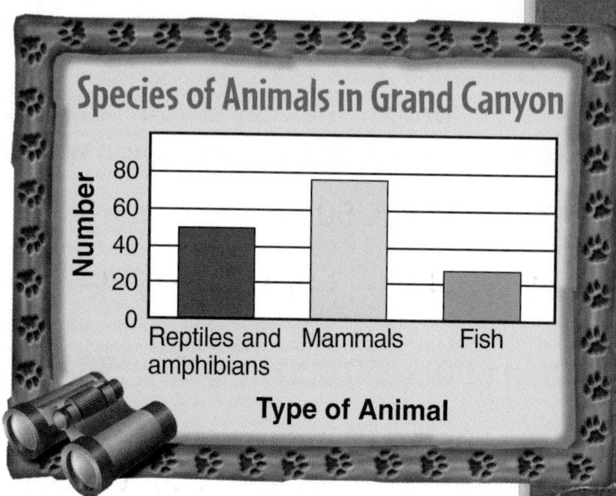

**Use this page to review and remember what you need to know for this chapter.**

## VOCABULARY

**Choose the best term to complete each sentence.**

1. The symbol < means _____.
2. A symbol used to write numbers is called a _____.
3. A number that is close to an exact amount is an _____.

**Vocabulary**

- digit
- estimate
- less than
- greater than

## CONCEPTS AND SKILLS

**Compare. Write >, <, or = for each ○.**

4. 86 ○ 85　　5. 75 ○ 57　　6. 260 ○ 260　　7. 400 ○ 500　　8. 362 ○ 326

**Tell whether the digit 6 is in the hundreds, thousands, or ten thousands place.**

9. 6,723　　10. 1,645　　11. 63,908　　12. 86,709　　13. 2,603

**Write the numbers in order from least to greatest.**

14. 65　73　45　　15. 175　204　192　　16. 1,973　1,745　1,945

**Write *true* or *false* for each.**
**If false, write a statement that is true.**

17. You can write forty-five cents as $0.45 or 45¢.
18. You can use two coins to give someone 31¢.
19. The value of two quarters and one nickel is less than the value of five dimes.

**Write About It**

20. What two bills are equal to the value of 4 five-dollar bills? Are there other combinations of bills that would equal that same amount? Explain your answer.

Facts Practice, See page 665.

## Lesson 1

**Audio Tutor 1/4** Listen and Understand

# Compare Numbers

**Objective** Compare numbers up to nine digits.

**STANDARDS** M4N1.a

**Vocabulary**
compare

20,766 acres

20,454 acres

## Learn About It

Our country has many beautiful national parks. **Compare** the number of acres each park occupies. Which park has the greater number of acres?

## Different Ways to Compare Numbers

**Way 1** You can use a number line.

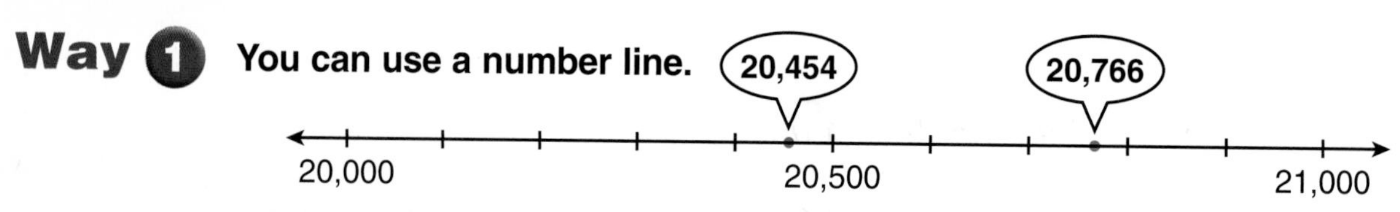


20,766 is to the right of 20,454 on the number line. So 20,766 > 20,454.

**Way 2** You can use place value.

**STEP 1** Begin at the greatest place. Find where the digits are different.

20,766
20,454

Same   Different

**STEP 2** Compare the digits that are different. Write > or <.

20,766
20,454

7 hundreds > 4 hundreds

So, 20,766 > 20,454.

**Solution:** The park that occupies 20,766 acres has the greater number of acres.

## Guided Practice

**Compare. Write >, <, or = for each ⬬.**

1. 1,001 ⬬ 979
2. 968,305 ⬬ 968,305
3. 19,009 ⬬ 19,090
4. 2,300,062 ⬬ 2,030,062

**Ask Yourself**

- Which digits do I compare first?
- What should I do when digits in the same place are the same?

**Explain Your Thinking** ▶ In Exercise 1, did you need to compare the digits in the hundreds, tens, or ones places? Explain.



Extra Help at **eduplace.com/map**

## Practice and Problem Solving

**Compare. Write >, <, or = for each ⬬.**

5. 808 ⬬ 880
6. 1,207 ⬬ 1,207
7. 2,347 ⬬ 2,487
8. 5,648 ⬬ 6,548
9. 1,035 ⬬ 1,340
10. 72,066 ⬬ 72,600
11. 11,001 ⬬ 92,876
12. 135,734 ⬬ 55,724
13. 869,621 ⬬ 879,566
14. 112,311 ⬬ 99,902
15. 190,098 ⬬ 19,098
16. 495,339 ⬬ 494,340
17. 98,760,032 ⬬ 98,790,032
18. 444,440,004 ⬬ 404,004,004
19. 40,000 ⬬ 400 thousands
20. 7 ten thousands ⬬ 7,000
21. 5,000 ⬬ 500 thousands
22. 9 thousands ⬬ 9,000

## Data **Use the table for Problems 23–25.**

The table shows the number of people who took part in activities at Colorado National Monument during one fall month.

23. Which activity was the most popular? Which was the least popular?
24. Did more people choose to go bicycle riding or mountain climbing?
25. **You Decide** Do you think the data would be similar or different for a month in summer? Explain.

**Activities at Colorado National Monument**

| Activity | Number of People |
|---|---|
| Auto Tour | 11,908 |
| Bicycle Riding | 834 |
| Horseback Riding | 11,025 |
| Mountain Climbing | 943 |
| Wildlife Tour | 10,169 |

## Sharpening Skills for CRCT

**Open Response**

**Write the value of the underlined digit.**
(Ch. 1, Lesson 5)

26. $\underline{2}$,090
27. $\underline{9}$2,001
28. $\underline{1}$20,900
29. $\underline{2}$0,090,029
30. $\underline{3}$79,536,221
31. 63$\underline{9}$,726,503

32. A museum has two thousand sixteen gems and one thousand ninety-eight minerals on display. Are there more gems or minerals on display? (Ch. 2, Lesson 1)

Extra Practice See page 45, Set A.

Lesson 2

Audio Tutor 1/5 Listen and Understand

# Order Numbers

**Objective** Order numbers up to nine digits.

**Vocabulary**

order

## Learn About It

**STANDARDS** M4A1.b, M4N1

The Wright Brothers National Memorial in North Carolina is a fun place to visit! One summer, there were 72,566 visitors in June, 77,465 visitors in July, and 71,324 visitors in August. Which month had the most visitors? Which month had the least number of visitors?

*This monument honors the first successful airplane flight achieved on December 17, 1903.*

## Different Ways to Order Numbers

Ordering numbers is like comparing numbers.

### Way 1 You can use a number line.

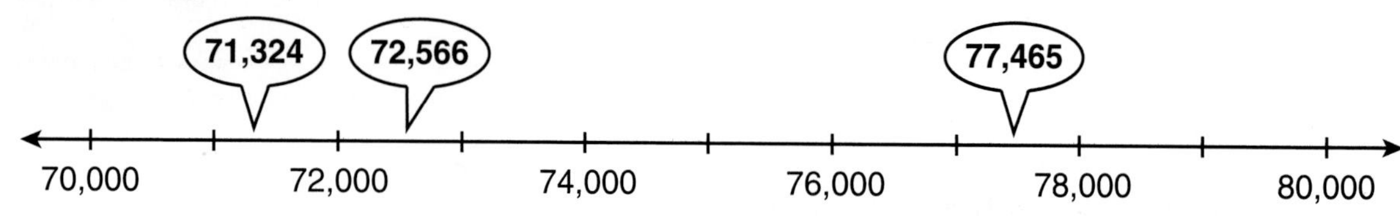


71,324 is farthest to the left. 72,566 is between 71,324 and 77,465.
77,465 is farthest to the right.

So, $71,324 < 72,566$ and $72,566 < 77,465$.

### Way 2 You can use place value.

**STEP 1** Line up the digits by place value. Begin at the greatest place value. Find the place where the digits are different.

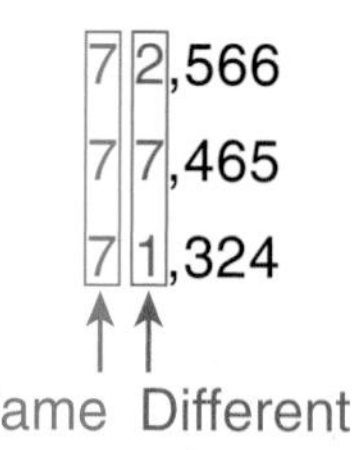


**STEP 2** Compare the digits that are different. Write $<$ or $>$.

72,566
77,465
71,324

$7 > 2$. So, $77,465 > 72,566$.
$2 > 1$. So, $72,566 > 71,324$.

Ordered from least to greatest, the numbers are: 71,324 72,566 77,465

**Solution:** July had the most visitors. August had the fewest visitors.

## Other Examples

### A. Order 4- and 5-digit Numbers

Order these numbers from greatest to least.
12,345  12,700  7,890

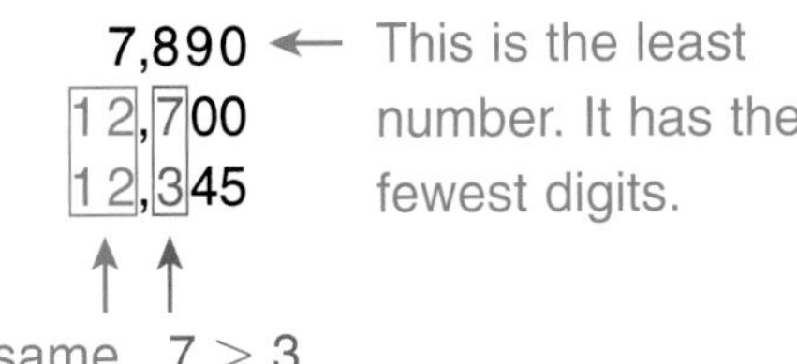


7 > 3. So 12,700 > 12,345.

So, the order from greatest to least is
12,700  12,345  7,890

### B. Order Greater Numbers

Order these numbers from least to greatest.
719,264,198  708,345,562  719,263,001

719,264,198
708,345,562
719,263,001

0 < 1  3 < 4

0 < 1. So, 708,345,562 is the least number.

3 < 4. So, 719,263,001 < 719,264,198.

So, the order from least to greatest is
708,345,562  719,263,001  719,264,198

## Guided Practice

**Ask Yourself**

- Am I ordering from least to greatest or from greatest to least?
- Which digits do I compare first?

**Write the numbers in order from least to greatest.**

1. 1,209  12,909  9,102
2. 69,541  689,541  68,541
3. 1,202,334  1,220,334  1,022,030
4. 993,457,601  994,574,601  993,574,601

**Explain Your Thinking** ▶ How does looking at the number of digits in some numbers help you order the numbers? Explain.

## Practice and Problem Solving

**Write the numbers in order from greatest to least.**

5. 4,040  4,404  4,044  4,004
6. 102,000  12,000  100,200  10,200
7. 85,407,363  8,407,363  85,073,630
8. 225,522,145  25,522,145  252,522,145

*The glider shown here was one of several used by the Wright brothers.*

**Write the numbers in order from least to greatest.**

**9.** 3,199  2,233  8,872

**10.** 2,110  1,911  2,345  2,350

**11.** 19,588  10,002  9,855

**12.** 57,601  574,601  576,601  506,960

**13.** 365,844  365,448  356,882

**14.** 642,951,316  645,746,892  604,682,637

**Find each missing digit.**

**15.** 6,106 > 6,■19

**16.** 2,117 = ■,117

**17.** 4,382 < 4,3■2

**18.** 91,472 > 9■,472

**19.** 114,899 < 114,■99

**20.** 703,9■1 = 703,981

**21.** 11,234 > 1■,785

**22.** 67,813 > 67,8■3

**23.** 82,■88 = 82,588

**24.** 179,00■ < 179,001

**25.** 856,■34 < 856,134

**26.** 683,129 < 6■3,129

**Solve.**

**27.** Use the information in the picture. Thomasville's population is 30 more than Lincolnton's. Write the populations in order from greatest to least.

**28.** Mr. Marcel drove 1,038 miles, Ms. Lok drove 752 miles, and Mrs. Alba drove 1,093 miles. Order the distances they drove from least to greatest.

**29.** A seven-digit number has a 7 in the millions place and a 3 in the ten thousands place. All other places have ones. Write the number in words.

## Sharpening Skills for CRCT

### Open Response

**Write the missing number.** (Grade 3)

**30.** 5 + ■ = 11

**31.** 9 × ■ = 27

**32.** 14 − 7 = ■

**33.** 42 ÷ 6 = ■

**34.** 8 × 7 = ■

**35.** 13 − ■ = 6

**36.** ■ ÷ 4 = 9

**37.** 9 − 7 = ■

### Multiple Choice

**38.** Look at the numbers below. Which number is greatest? (Ch. 2, Lesson 2)

A. 62,102  
B. 61,902  
C. 62,109  
D. 61,002



Extra Practice See page 45, Set B.

Problem Solving

GPS

STANDARDS M4N1.a

## Social Studies Connection

### Thai Numerals

Students in Thailand use both Arabic and Thai numerals. The Thai number system is very similar to the base ten number system.

**Here are the Thai symbols for 0–9.**

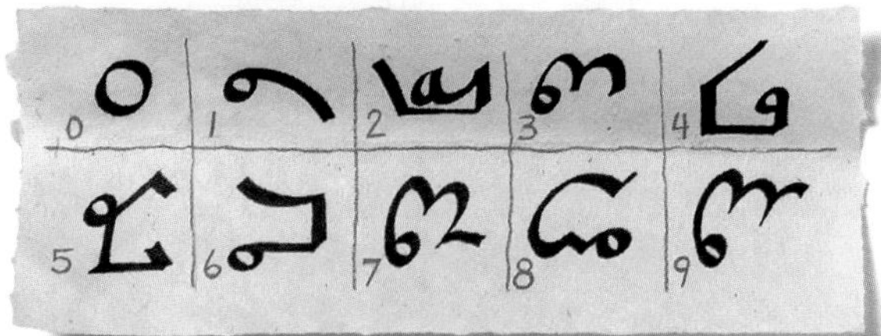


- Think about how we put our symbols for 0–9 together to make the numbers from 10 to 20.
- Then look at the Thai symbols for 11, 17, and 19 in the chart. Now write the missing Thai symbols to complete the chart.

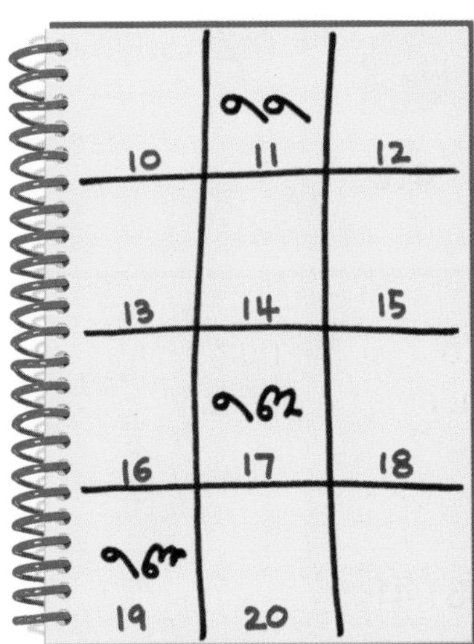


## Math Reasoning

### How Big is 100,000?

- 100,000 is big if you are carrying that many pounds of rocks.
- 100,000 is small if you are filling a bucket with that many grains of sand.

**Choose the best number.**

1. The number of people that would fit in an elevator

   **a.** 100 people **b.** 10 people

2. The time it takes to brush your teeth

   **a.** 2,000 minutes **b.** 2 minutes

3. When might 2,000 minutes seem like not enough time?

## Brain Teaser

**Use the clues to find the mystery number.**

- It is a four-digit number.
- Its tens digit is 2.
- Its thousands digit is 4.
- Its hundreds digit is the sum of its ones digit and its tens digit.
- Its ones digit is two times its tens digit.

What is the number?

**Education Place**

Visit *Education Place* at **eduplace.com/map** to try more Brain Teasers.

Lesson 3

# Compare and Order Money

**Objective** Count and compare amounts of money.

 **STANDARDS** Extends M4N1, M4P2

## Learn About It

Sean and Maria are visiting the Kennedy Space Center. They are buying a gift for $32.00. They have 1 twenty-dollar bill, 2 five-dollar bills, 1 one-dollar bill, 1 quarter, 1 dime, 1 nickel, and 1 penny. Do they have enough money?

**Follow these steps to find out.**

**STEP 1** Find the total value of the bills.

Start with the bill with the greatest value. Count on.

**$20.00** → **$25.00** → **$30.00** → **$31.00**

**STEP 2** Find the total value of the coins.

Start with the coin with the greatest value. Count on.

**25¢** → **35¢** → **40¢** → **41¢**

**STEP 3** Write the total amount as $31.41.

Then **compare** $31.41 to $32.00.

$\$31.41 < \$32.00$

**Solution:** No, they do not have enough money, since $31.41 is less than $32.00.

**Follow these steps to order $25.30, $21.00, and $25.20 from least to greatest.**

**STEP 1** Find the greatest place value with different digits.

$2[1].00 ← least

$2[5].30

$2[5].20

↑

1 < 5

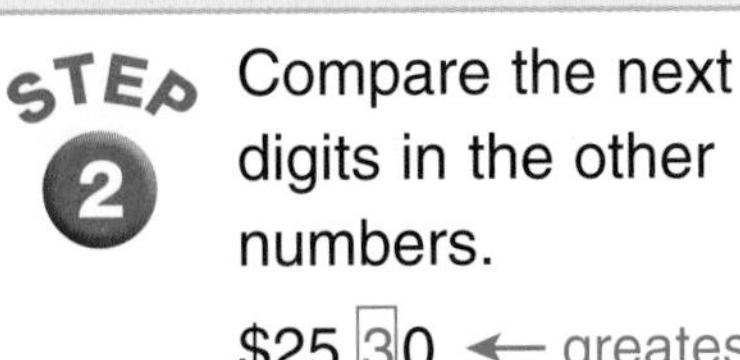

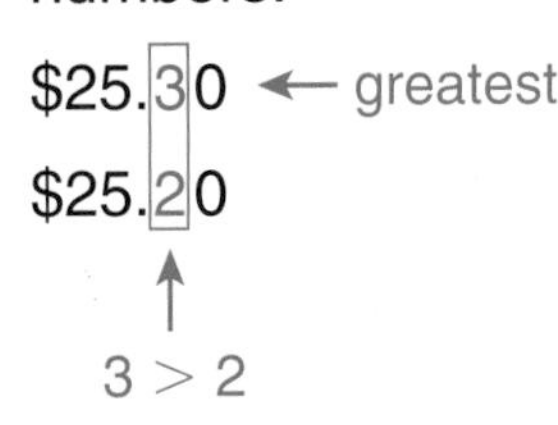

**STEP 2** Compare the next digits in the other numbers.

$25.[3]0 ← greatest

$25.[2]0

↑

3 > 2

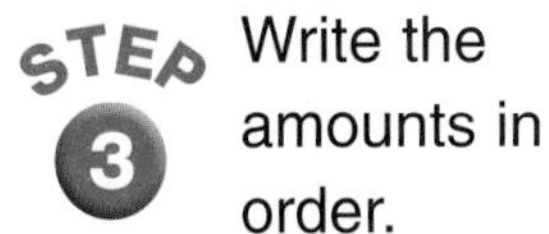

**STEP 3** Write the amounts in order.

$21.00 < $25.30 and $25.30 > $25.20

So, from least to greatest, $21.00 < $25.20 < $25.30

**Solution:** From least to greatest, the amounts are $21.00 $25.20 $25.30

## Guided Practice

**Ask Yourself**

- In what order will I count the bills?
- In what order will I count the coins?

**Write each amount. Then write the greatest amount and the least amount.**

1.   

2. 

3. 

4.  

**Explain Your Thinking ▶** Is it usually easier to count the bills or coins with the greatest value first? Why or why not?

Go On

## Practice and Problem Solving

**Write each amount. Then write the greater amount.**

**5.**   or 

**6.**    or   

**7.** 6 dimes, 2 quarters, 4 nickels
**or**
7 nickels, 2 half-dollars

**8.** 4 one-dollar bills, 6 quarters,
**or**
1 five-dollar bill, 4 dimes

**9.** 3 five-dollar bills, 8 quarters
**or**
1 twenty-dollar bill, 5 dimes

**10.** 7 ten-dollar bills, 6 quarters
**or**
1 fifty-dollar bill, 3 five-dollar bills

**11.** 2 fifty-dollar bills, 5 quarters
**or**
5 twenty-dollar bills, 6 dimes

**12.** 13 one-dollar bills, 9 dimes
**or**
1 ten-dollar bill, 6 quarters, 8 dimes

## Data Use the pictures for Problems 13–16.

**13.** Which souvenir is most expensive? Which is least expensive?

**14.** Adela has 1 twenty-dollar bill, 3 quarters, and 1 five-dollar bill. Does she have enough money for a Space Blanket and two NASA Travel Mugs?

**15.** **Estimate** About how much would it cost to buy one calendar and two T-shirts?

**16.** Using the least number of bills and coins, how would you pay the exact amount for a NASA Travel Mug?

**17.** **Write About It** Explain how you compare $53 and the sum of 4 ten-dollar bills, 3 five-dollar bills, and 2 one-dollar bills.

Extra Practice See page 45, Set C.

## Real World Connection

### Braille Numbers

STANDARDS M4N1.b

Braille is a code made with raised dots. A blind person can read letters, words, numbers, and symbols by touching the raised dots. Here are the Braille symbols for the numbers 0–9:

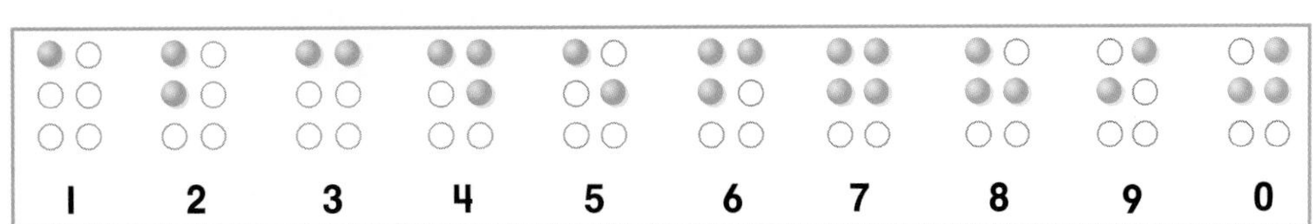


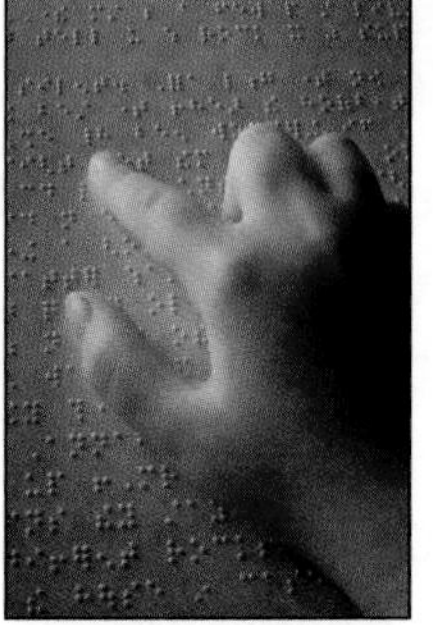

▶ This symbol appears before a number.

▶ So this is the number 12.

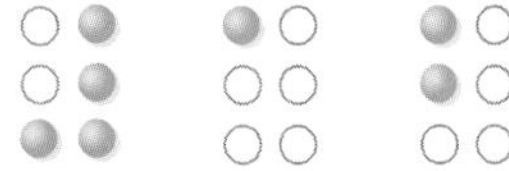

**Write each of these Braille numbers in three ways.**

**1.**

**2.**

WEEKLY WR READER eduplace.com/map

## Quick Check

Check your understanding of Lessons 1–3.

**Compare. Write >, <, or = for each ⬬.** (Lesson 1)

1. 6,057 ⬬ 12,032
2. 5,564 ⬬ 5,654
3. 204,568 ⬬ 204,567
4. 567,034,789 ⬬ 593,694,129

**Write the numbers in order from least to greatest.** (Lesson 2)

5. 212 2,002 1,212
6. 4,004 4,440 4,044
7. 43,120 39,021 26,707
8. 512,678 34,762 710,094

**Write each amount.** (Lesson 3)

9. 6 ten-dollar bills, 4 quarters, 2 dimes, 4 pennies
10. 3 twenty-dollar bills, 2 five-dollar bills, 3 nickels, 2 pennies

Lesson 4

# Make Change

**Objective** Count on to make change.

 **STANDARDS** Maintains M2N1.c

## Learn About It

The Bailey family is vacationing at Mammoth Cave in Kentucky. They are buying a poster of the stalactites and stalagmites in the Great Onyx Cave. The poster costs $23.89. They give the clerk $30.00. What amount will the Baileys get as change?

You can count on from the cost of the poster to make change.

*Stalactites form downward from the roof of a cavern. Stalagmites form upward from the floor. Both are caused by the dripping of mineral-rich water.*

**Follow the steps below to find the change that the Bailey family will receive.**

**STEP 1** Start with the cost of the poster.

Count the coins and bills until you reach the amount they paid.

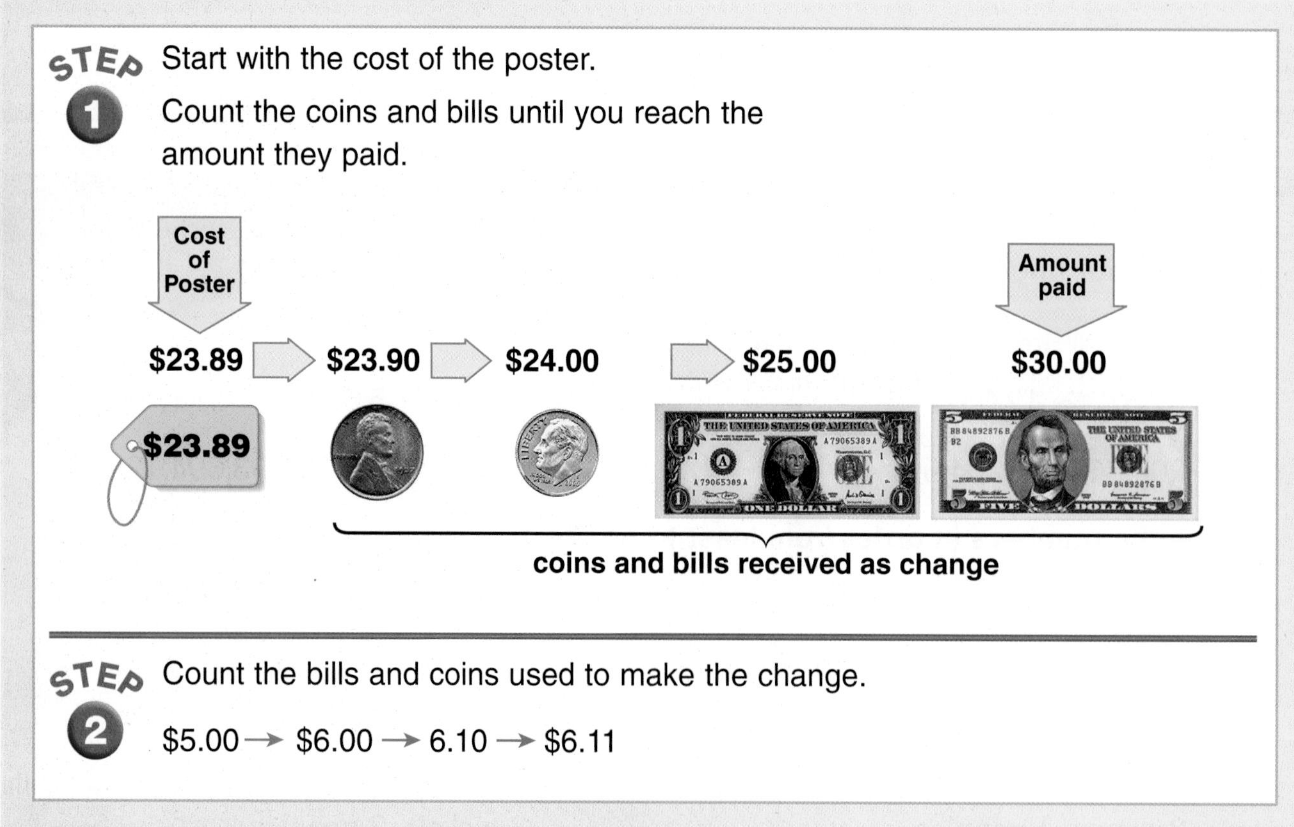


**STEP 2** Count the bills and coins used to make the change.

$5.00 → $6.00 → 6.10 → $6.11

**Solution:** The Baileys will get $6.11 as change.

## Guided Practice

**Ask Yourself**

- What amount do I start with?
- What coins and bills do I need to count up to the price?

**A $10 bill was used to buy each item below. List the coins and bills you would use to make change.**

**1.** $3.28

**2.** $8.77

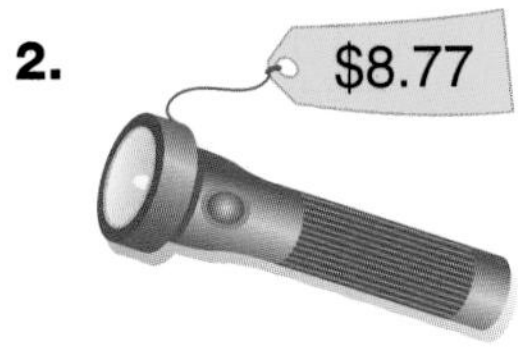

**3.** $5.99

**Explain Your Thinking** ▶ Look at Problems 1–3. Why do you start with coins when making change?

## Practice and Problem Solving

**A $20 bill was used to buy each item below. List the coins and bills you would use to make change.**

**4.** $12.75

**5.** $8.29

**6.** $6.55

**7.** $4.35

**8.** $5.98

**9.** $18.19

**Write the amount of change you would receive for each.**

**10.** You bought popcorn for 79¢. You paid with 4 quarters.

**11.** You bought a pen for $0.86. You paid with 1 five-dollar bill.

**12.** You bought a CD for $7.74. You paid with 2 five-dollar bills.

**13.** You bought a sandwich for $3.17. You paid with 1 ten-dollar bill.

Go On

 **Data** **The table on the right gives information about tours of Mammoth Cave. Use the table for Problems 14–18.**

14. Mr. Orestes and his 12-year-old son are going on the Great Onyx tour. How much will they pay for one adult and one youth tour?

15. Mrs. Tyler goes with her two children on the Travertine tour. She pays with 1 twenty-dollar bill and 1 ten-dollar bill. How much change does she receive?

16. The Trog tour is planned only for 8- to 12-year-olds. If Pam and Tom's parents pay for their tickets with 1 twenty-dollar bill and 1 ten-dollar bill, how much change will they get?

17. You buy 1 adult ticket and 1 youth ticket to the Discovery tour. If you pay with 4 one-dollar bills and 1 five-dollar bill, how much change should you receive?

18. **Create and Solve** Use the data in the table to write a new problem. Exchange your problem with a friend and solve.

**Mammoth Cave Tours**

| Tour | Adult | Youth |
|---|---|---|
| Discovery | $5.00 | $3.50 |
| Frozen Niagara | $11.00 | $8.00 |
| Grand Avenue | $21.00 | $15.00 |
| Great Onyx | $15.00 | $11.00 |
| Historic | $11.00 | $8.00 |
| Travertine | $10.00 | $8.00 |
| Trog | — | $14.00 |
| Violet City | $15.00 | $11.00 |

## Sharpening Skills for CRCT

**Open Response**

**Tell what time it will be.** (Grade 3)

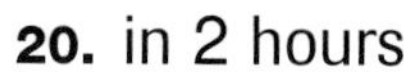

19. in 20 minutes

20. in 2 hours

21. in 15 minutes

22. in 35 minutes

23. Jason bought the game below. What are the fewest coins and bills he could have used to pay for it if he received no change? (Ch. 2, Lesson 4)

$14.87

Extra Practice See page 45, Set D.

Game Activity

GPS

# Dollar Dunk

**2–4 Players**

STANDARDS Extends M4N

What You'll Need • 40 index cards or Learning Tool 4

**Practice using money by playing this game.**

Dollar Dunk is like the game Go Fish. Try to be the first to use all your cards.

10 cards

10 cards

10¢

8 cards

25¢

8 cards

50¢

4 cards

## How to Play

1. Make 40 cards like the ones shown or use Learning Tool 4.
2. Shuffle and deal 5 cards to each player. Stack the rest facedown.
3. Players look at their cards. The object is to get rid of the cards by making $1.00 with some or all of the cards. Whenever players can make $1.00, they place those cards faceup in front of them.
4. If a player cannot make $1.00, he or she asks another player for a card. For example, the player might ask, "Do you have 25¢?" If that player has the card, it must be given to the first player. If not, the first player "dunks" into the deck by taking the top card.
5. Players take turns repeating Steps 3 and 4. The first player with no cards is the winner.

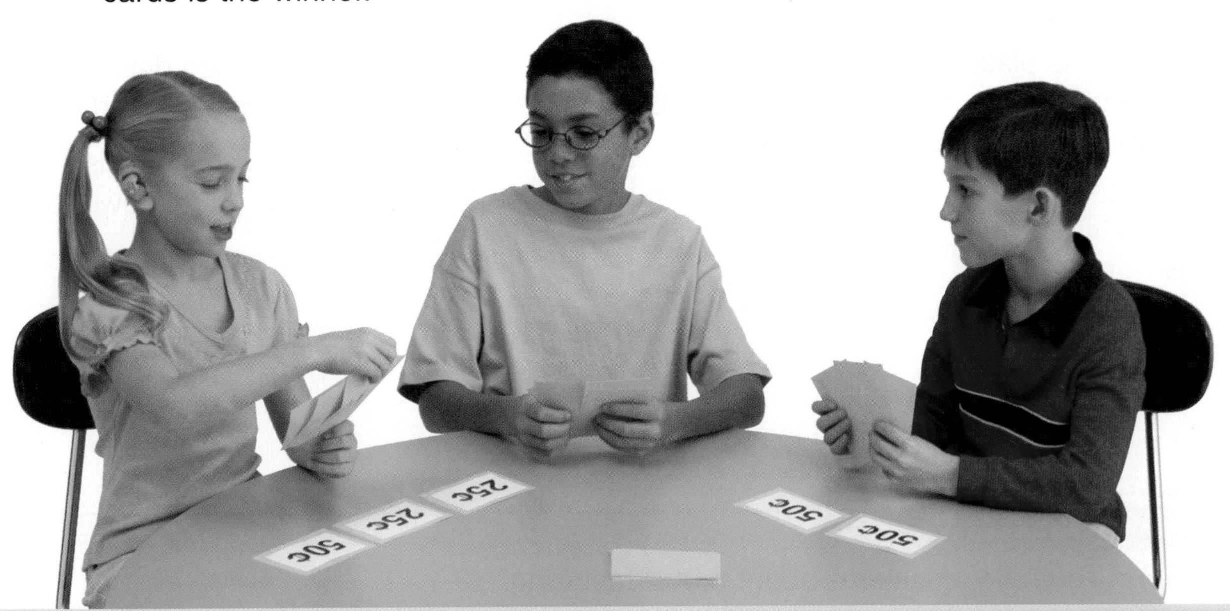

Lesson 5

Audio Tutor 1/6 Listen and Understand

# Round Numbers

**Objective** Round numbers and money amounts.

**Vocabulary**
estimate
rounding

STANDARDS M4N2.a, M4N2.b

Jeff visited an amusement park on his vacation. He rode a roller coaster that is 5,843 feet long. About how long is the roller coaster?

Since you do not need an exact number, you can **estimate** by **rounding** the number.

## Different Ways to Round 5,843

### Way 1 You can use a number line.

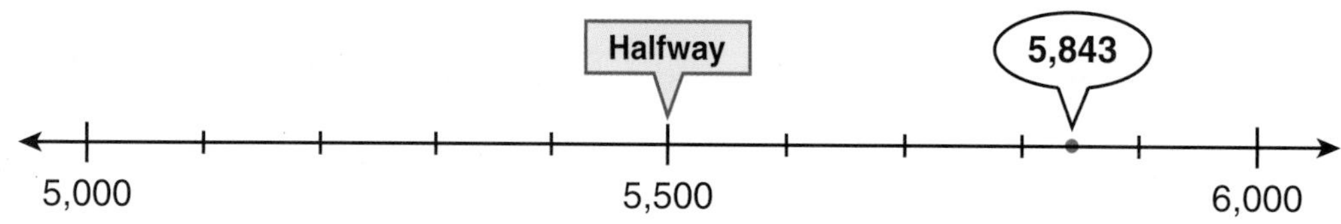


5,843 is closer to 6,000 than to 5,000.
So, round 5,843 to 6,000.

### Way 2 You can use place value.

**STEP 1**

Find the place you want to round to. Underline the digit in that place.

5,843
↑
thousands place

**STEP 2**

Look at the digit to its right. Circle that digit.

5,(8)43
↑
digit to the right

**STEP 3**

- If the circled digit is 5 or greater, round up.
- If the circled digit is less than 5, round down.
- 8 is greater than 5, so

5,843 **rounds to** 6,000

**Solution:** The roller coaster is about 6,000 feet long.

## Guided Practice

**Round each number to the place of the underlined digit.**

1. $\underline{3}$,812
2. 1$\underline{4}$,731,200
3. \$4$\underline{4}$.92
4. 12$\underline{5}$,601
5. \$$\underline{1}$57.72
6. 792,3$\underline{6}$9

> **Ask Yourself**
> - What is the digit to the right of the rounding place?
> - Is this digit 5 or greater, or is it less than 5?

**Explain Your Thinking** ▶ Can a three-digit number round to 1,000? Use an example to explain why or why not.

## Practice and Problem Solving

**Use the number line to round each number to the nearest thousand.**

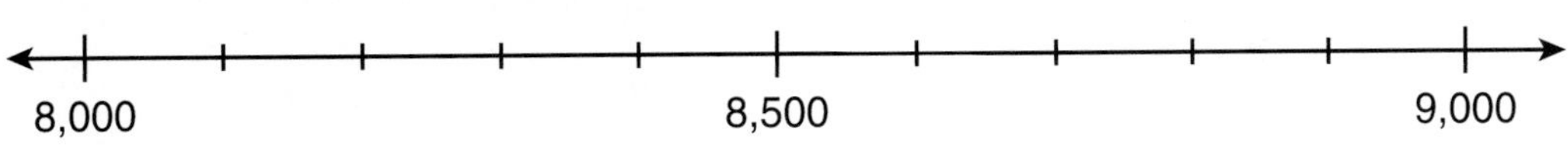


7. 8,900
8. 8,210
9. 8,350
10. 8,732
11. 8,499

**Round each number to the place of the underlined digit.**

12. 2$\underline{6}$,754
13. 19,8$\underline{8}$7
14. 3$\underline{3}$,501
15. 1$\underline{1}$3,772
16. 42$\underline{8}$,001,674
17. 209,$\underline{1}$21,456
18. 7$\underline{8}$,901,223
19. 7,$\underline{4}$25,333

**Round to the nearest ten cents. Then round to the nearest dollar.**

20. \$4.57
21. \$9.45
22. \$13.84
23. \$578.34
24. \$827.16
25. \$391.72
26. \$4,398.79
27. \$3,287.95

**Solve.**

28. Rosemarie rode one of the longest roller coasters in the world. It is 8,133 feet long. How long is that to the nearest hundred feet?

29. There were 2,638 riders for the roller coaster. A park official rounded that number to 3,000. To which place was the number rounded?

## Sharpening Skills for CRCT

**Open Response**

**Complete each number sentence.** (Grade 3)

30. ■ + 9 = 16
31. 8 × ■ = 48
32. 18 − 5 = ■
33. 42 ÷ 7 = ■
34. 4 × ■ = 24
35. ■ + 3 = 12

36. Round 99,603 to the nearest ten thousand. Then round it to the nearest thousand. What do you notice about your answers? Explain. (Ch. 2, Lesson 5)

Extra Practice See page 45, Set E.

Lesson 6

# Problem-Solving Application

## Use a Bar Graph

**Objective** Use a bar graph to compare data.

 **STANDARDS** M4D1.b, M4P1.c

**Vocabulary**
bar graph

**You can use a bar graph to compare data.**

**Problem** A community center takes people on day trips. The bar graph shows how many people went on various trips last summer.

Which activity had twice as many people participate as the zoo?

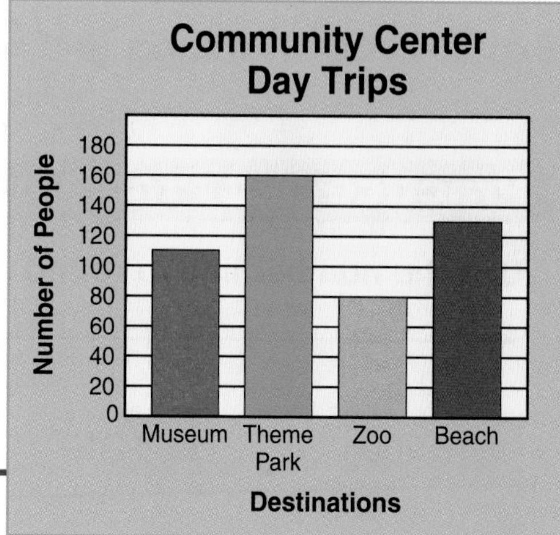


**UNDERSTAND**

**This is what you need to find.**

You can use the height of the bars on the graph to compare the number of people on each trip.

**PLAN**

**Get information from the graph.**

Find the bar that is about twice as tall as the bar for zoo. Then find the number of people for the two trips.

**SOLVE**

**Use the bar graph to compare data.**

The bar for the zoo reaches to 80. The bar for the theme park is twice as tall as the bar for the zoo. It reaches the 160 line.

160 is twice as much as 80.

**Solution:** Twice as many people went on the theme park trip as went to the zoo.

**LOOK BACK**

**Look back at the problem.**
How could you check to see if your answer is reasonable?

## Guided Practice

**Use the bar graph on Page 40 to solve Problems 1–4.**

1. How many people visited the theme park?
2. Did more people visit the museum or the zoo?
3. Did fewer people visit the beach or the theme park?
4. About how many more people visited the beach than the museum?

   **Hint** Estimate each number, then subtract.

### Ask Yourself

**UNDERSTAND** — **What does the question ask me to find?**

**PLAN** — **Can I get the information from the graph?**

**SOLVE** — **Did I read the graph correctly?**

**LOOK BACK** — **Is my answer reasonable?**

## Independent Practice

**Data** **Use the bar graph for Problems 5–10.**

The graph shows the coins that Gabriel has saved for summer trips.

5. Which coin does Gabriel have the most of?
6. Which coin does he have the least of?
7. **Mental Math** How much money does Gabriel have in pennies?
8. Does Gabriel have more quarters than nickels? How do you know?
9. **Multistep** If Gabriel gives all of the nickels and dimes to his younger brother, how much money will he give his brother?
10. **Create and Solve** Write a problem about the graph. Then exchange problems with a friend and solve.

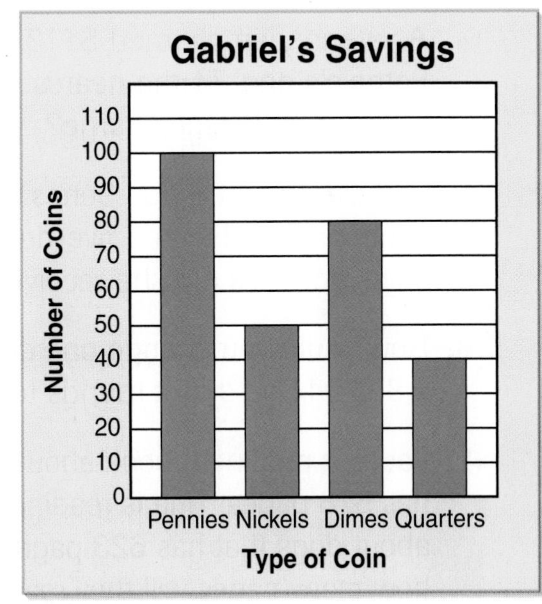

Go On

# Mixed Problem Solving

**Solve. Show your work. Tell what strategy you used.**

**11.** Ali, Jim, and Sue are members of either hockey, soccer, or swimming teams. Ali doesn't play soccer. Jim doesn't play soccer or swim. Each person plays one sport. What team is each person on?

**12.** Mark added 36 in. to his race car track. Then he removed 4 in. This made his track 94 in. long. How long was the track before he started changing it?

**13.** The prize for a competition doubles each day. The prize was $1 for the first day. What will the prize be on the seventh day?

### You Choose

**Strategy**

- Draw a Picture
- Find a Pattern
- Use Logical Reasoning
- Work Backward

**Computation Method**

- Mental Math
- Estimation
- Paper and Pencil
- Calculator

**Solve. Tell which method you chose.**

**14.** A veterinarian charged $113 for treating Patricia's dog. To the nearest ten dollars, how much did she charge?

**15.** Patricia bought 3 dog bones for $0.60 each. She paid with 1 five-dollar bill. What coins and bills did she receive as change?

**16.** How could you change one digit in 7,856,041 so that it rounds to 7,800,000?

**17.** Laura is reading a book about horses that has 578 pages. Tina is reading a book about dogs that has 623 pages. About how many pages will they read altogether?

**18.** **Multistep** Maria earned 3 ten-dollar bills, 4 quarters, and 2 nickels. Alex earned 5 five-dollar bills, 3 one-dollar bills, and 3 quarters. Who has more money?

# Math Reasoning

## Round Numbers to Estimate

STANDARDS M4N2.b

Rounding can be used to estimate numbers. You can round numbers to the tens place, hundreds place, thousands place and so on.

For example:

- Rounding 2,349 to the tens place gives 2,350
- Rounding 2,349 to the hundreds place gives 2,300
- Rounding 2,349 to the thousands place gives 2,000

The place to which you round a number depends on how large a number is and how the number will be used.

**Round numbers to estimate. Tell whether you rounded to the nearest ten, hundred, or thousand.**

1. Lin wants to collect 1,000 baseball cards. If she has 720 baseball cards, about how many more does she need?
2. A baseball bat can be no longer than 42 inches. About how long is a baseball bat?
3. The Turner Stadium in Atlanta can seat 50,096 people. 25,810 people attended a recent game at the stadium. About how many seats were empty?

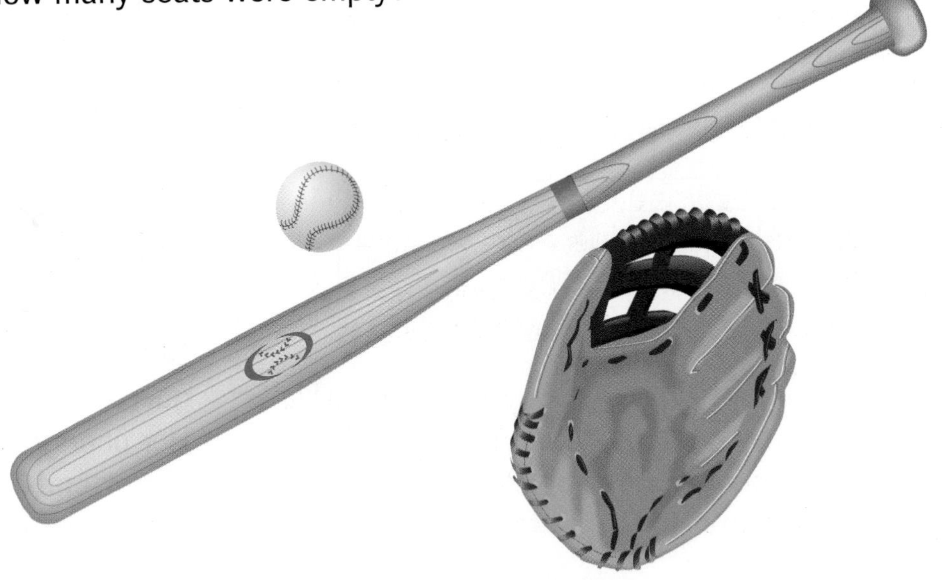

# Chapter Review/Test

Study Guide page SG7

### VOCABULARY

**Choose the best term to complete each sentence.**

1. To tell about how much is to ____.
2. To compare numbers you can use ____.
3. One way to display data is to use a ____.

**Vocabulary**
- order
- estimate
- bar graph
- place value

### CONCEPTS AND SKILLS

**Compare. Write >, <, or = for each ⬬.** (Lessons 1, 3, pp. 24–25, 30–32)

4. 8,032 ⬬ 8,132
5. 82,435 ⬬ 83,435
6. 1,111,111 ⬬ 1,111,011
7. $0.60 ⬬ 12 dimes
8. $2.35 ⬬ 9 quarters
9. 4 ten-dollar bills ⬬ $25

**Write the numbers in order from least to greatest.** (Lesson 2, pp. 26–28)

10. 1,653 1,335 1,356
11. 45,397 54,201 45,937
12. 202,765 201,777 202,762
13. 426,729 426,792 426,279

**Round each number to the place of the underlined digit.** (Lesson 5, pp. 38–39)

14. 56,<u>7</u>64
15. 2,3<u>4</u>3,890
16. 1,<u>1</u>43,251
17. $23<u>4</u>.56
18. $<u>6</u>51.22

### PROBLEM SOLVING

**Use the graph for Problems 19–20.**
(Lesson 6, pp. 40–42)

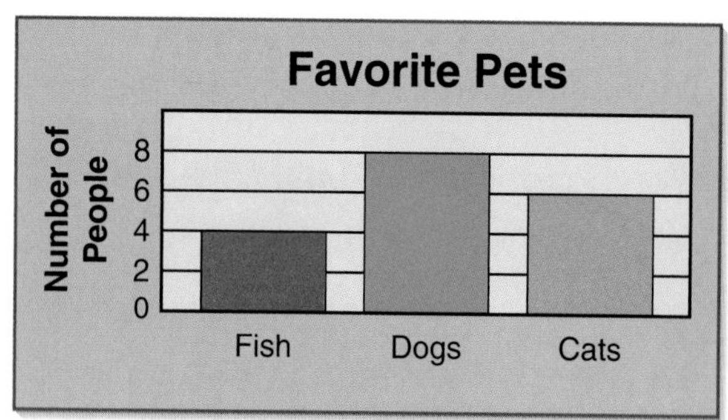


19. How many more people prefer cats than fish?
20. How many people were surveyed?

**Write About It**

**Show You Understand**

Carol bought three books. She gave the clerk 3 ten-dollar bills. Her change was 2 quarters, 1 nickel, and 2 one-dollar bills. What was the cost of the books ?

Explain how you got your answer.

# Extra Practice

## Set A (Lesson 1, pp. 24–25)

**Compare. Write >, <, or = for each ●.**

1. 125,427 ● 125,407
2. 501,100 ● 500,001
3. 60,000 ● 60 thousands
4. 3 ten thousands ● 3,000

## Set B (Lesson 2, pp. 26–28)

**Write the numbers in order from least to greatest.**

1. 33,503 31,000 23,427
2. 126,522 126,351 130,000
3. 5,416,000 15,000,000 9,333,151
4. 122,341,984 122,347,000 122,347,050

## Set C (Lesson 3, pp. 30–32)

**Write each amount. Then write the greater amount.**

1. 5 quarters, 3 dimes, 2 pennies **or** a one-dollar bill, 5 dimes, 6 pennies
2. 1 five-dollar bill, 4 quarters, 7 dimes **or** 4 one-dollar bills and 7 quarters

## Set D (Lesson 4, pp. 34–36)

**Write the names of the coins and bills you would use to make change for each of the following.**

1. You bought a pen for $0.63. You paid with a five-dollar bill.
2. You bought a book for $7.52. You paid with a twenty-dollar bill.
3. You bought a game for $14.89. You paid with a twenty-dollar bill.
4. You bought a sandwich for $3.47. You paid with a ten-dollar bill.

## Set E (Lesson 5, pp. 38–39)

**Round each number to the place of the underlined digit.**

1. 1,567
2. 6,352
3. 9,884
4. $17.42
5. 16,276
6. 787,322
7. 4,295,401
8. $5.98

Extra Practice at **eduplace.com/map**

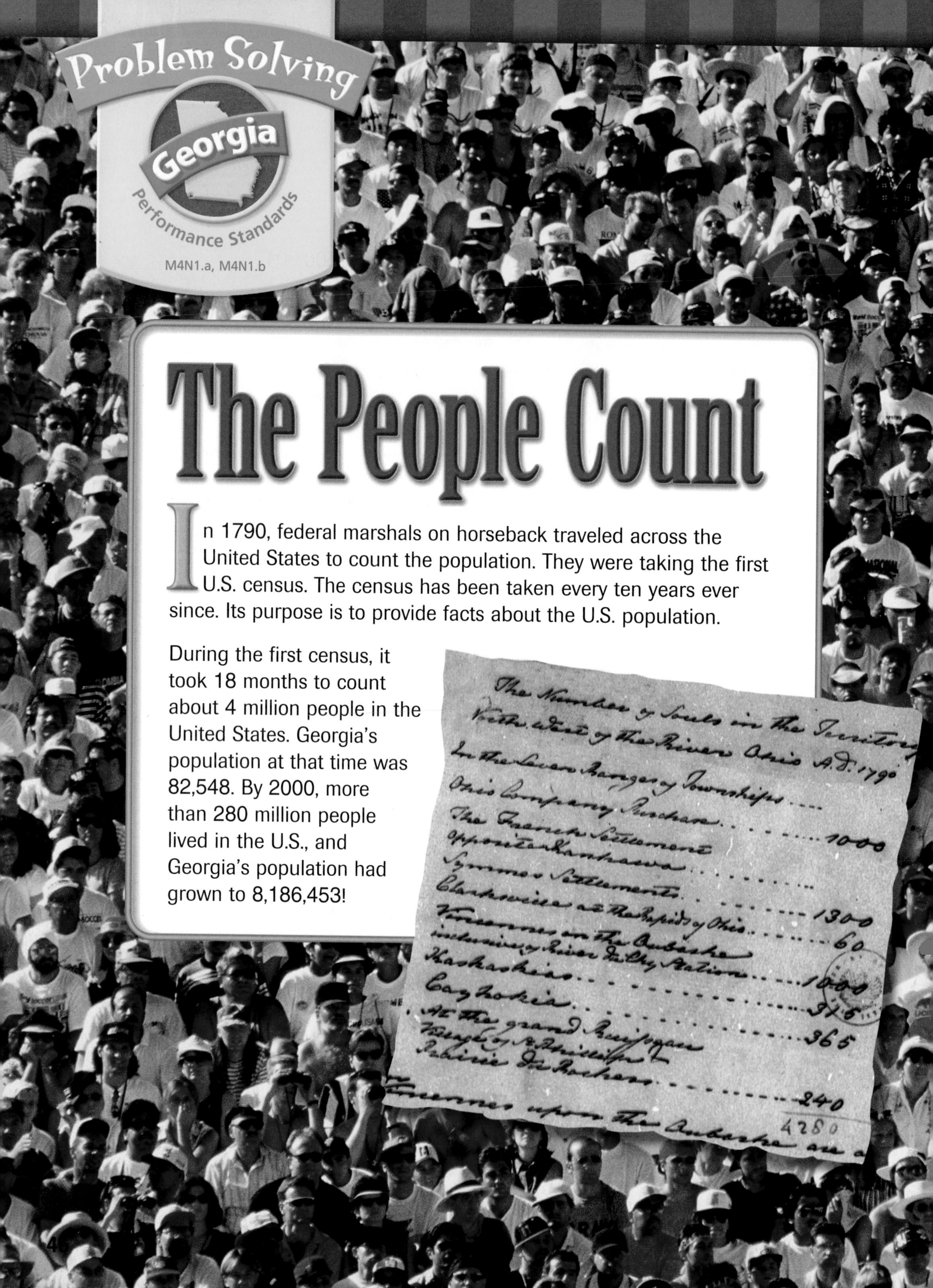



# The People Count

In 1790, federal marshals on horseback traveled across the United States to count the population. They were taking the first U.S. census. The census has been taken every ten years ever since. Its purpose is to provide facts about the U.S. population.

During the first census, it took 18 months to count about 4 million people in the United States. Georgia's population at that time was 82,548. By 2000, more than 280 million people lived in the U.S., and Georgia's population had grown to 8,186,453!

The Number of Souls in the Territory
North West of the River Ohio A.D. 1790
In the Seven Ranges of Townships ....
Ohio Company Purchase ........ 1000
The French Settlement
Opposite Kanhawa ........
Symmes Settlements ........
Clarksville at the Rapids of Ohio ........ 1300
Vincennes on the Oubashe ........ 60
inclusive of River Du Chy Station ........ 1000
Kaskaskias ........ 375
Cayhokia ........ 365
At the grand Ruisseau
Village of St. Phillips
Prairie Du Rochers ........ 240
Vincennes upon the Oubashe are a
4280

## Problem Solving

**This map shows the location of 6 major cities in Georgia. The table shows the population of the cities in 2000. Use the table to answer Problems 2–5.**

**2000 Census Data for Major Cities in Georgia**

| City | 2000 Population |
|---|---|
| Athens | 100,266 |
| Atlanta | 416,474 |
| Augusta | 195,182 |
| Columbus | 185,781 |
| Macon | 97,255 |
| Savannah | 131,510 |

1. Write Georgia's 2000 population in expanded form and in word form.

2. What number is in the tens place in Atlanta's population? What is the value of the 7 in the Columbus population? What is the value of the 7 in Macon's population?

3. Round Augusta's population in 2000 to the nearest thousand.

4. One city's population in 2000 has the same digit in the tens, thousands, and hundred thousands places. Which city is it?

5. Which city's population in 2000 was one hundred thousand, two hundred sixty-six?

## Enrichment: Math History

**STANDARDS** Extends M4N

# Roman Numerals

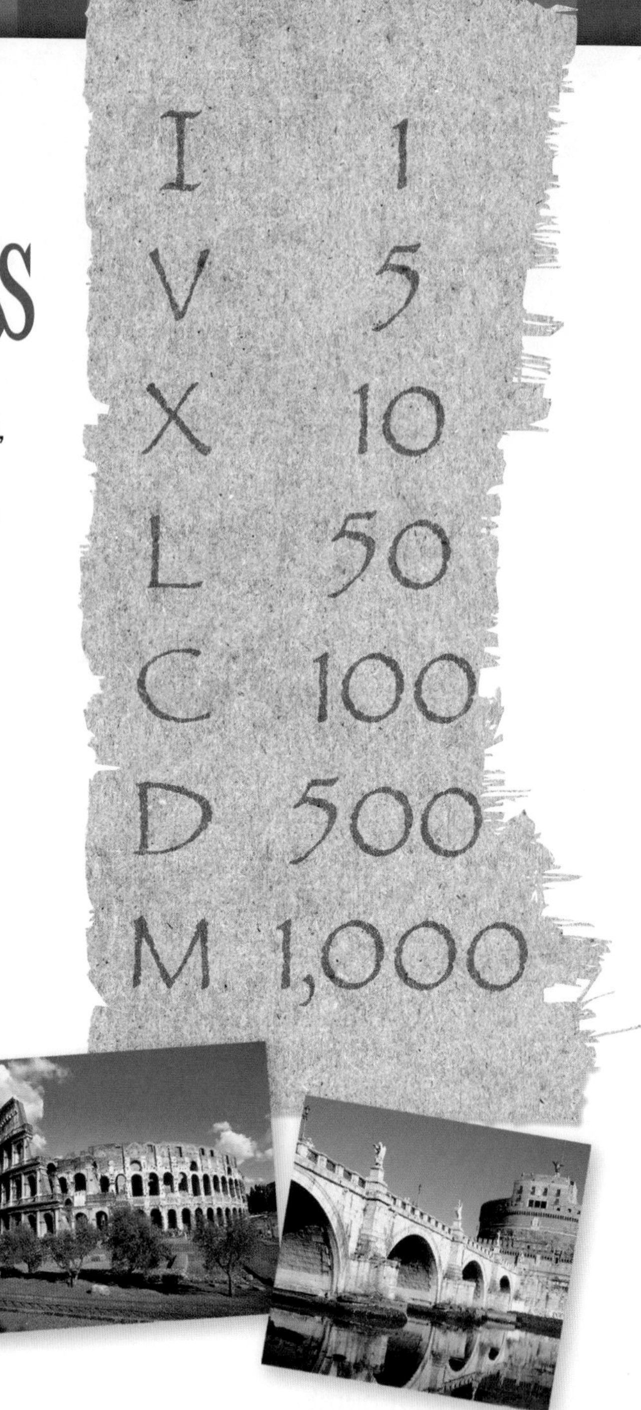


When we write the numbers 0, 1, 2, 3, 4, 5, 6, 7, 8, and 9, we are using the Arabic number system. When you look at a clock or a building, sometimes you will see letters that represent numbers. These are called Roman numerals.

The picture at the right shows Roman numerals and their equivalent Arabic numerals.

- When Roman numerals are alike or the values decrease from left to right, add to find the value.
  III = 1 + 1 + 1 = 3
  VI = 5 + 1 = 6
- When a numeral of lesser value appears to the left of a numeral of greater value, subtract the value of the lesser numeral from the value of the greater numeral.
  IV = 5 − 1 = 4
  CM = 1,000 − 100 = 900
- A numeral never repeats more than 3 times.

## Try These!

**Write these Arabic numerals as Roman numerals.**

**1.** 7 **2.** 111 **3.** 56 **4.** 341 **5.** 2000

**Write these Roman numerals as Arabic numerals.**

**6.** XVII **7.** CLXXIII **8.** CXLV **9.** XXIV **10.** CIX

**11. Analyze** Write the year that you were born in Arabic numerals. Then write it in Roman numerals. Which system is easier to use? Why?

# Change, Please

STANDARDS M4D1.d

Mr. Diego bought lunch every day for one work week. Each day he gave the clerk a ten-dollar bill.

The table shows how much his lunch cost each day.

| | Cost | Change |
|---|---|---|
| **Monday** | $6.47 | |
| **Tuesday** | $4.23 | |
| **Wednesday** | | |
| **Thursday** | $7.72 | |
| **Friday** | $5.41 | |

**Use the table to answer Questions 1–2.**

1. Use a calculator to find how much change Mr. Diego received for every day of the work week except Wednesday.

2. If the total cost of lunch for one work week was $29.02, what was the cost of lunch on Wednesday? How much change did Mr. Diego receive?

Mr. Diego wants to compare the cost of lunch for each day of the week. He can compare the costs by making a bar graph.

3. Copy the graph at right on a separate sheet of paper. Use your answers from the table above to create a bar graph. Round your answers to the nearest dollar.

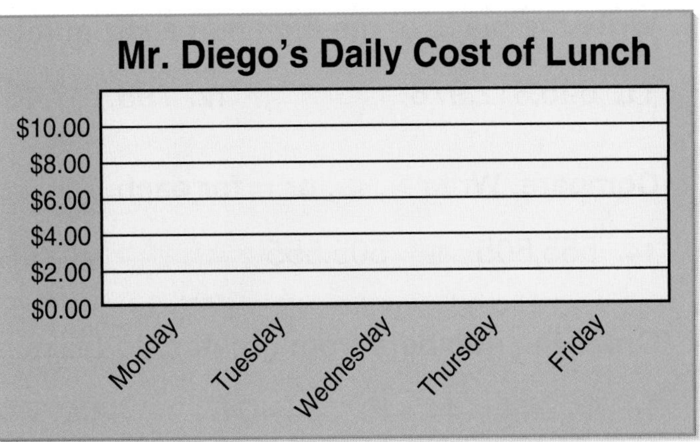


4. Look at your bar graph. Did Mr. Diego spend more money for lunch on Monday or on Wednesday?

5. Mr. Diego decides he does not want to spend more than $7.00 on lunch again. On which day did he spend more than that?

# Unit 1 Test

Study Guide pages SG5, SG7

## VOCABULARY Open Response

**Choose the best term to complete each sentence.**

**Vocabulary**
- round
- period
- estimate
- base-ten
- ordinal number

1. Each place is tens times greater than the place to the right of it in a ____ system.
2. To show the order or position of something, you would use an ____.
3. Each group of 3 digits in a number is separated by a comma and is called a ____.
4. Words such as *about* or *almost* tell you that a number is being used to show an ____.

## CONCEPTS AND SKILLS Open Response

**Tell how each number is used. Write *position, count, measure,* or *label* for each.** (Chapter 1)

5. 3rd fastest sprinter
6. 15 cats
7. Apartment 42A
8. 124 Hayward Street
9. 523 kilometers
10. 34 marbles

**Write the place of the digit 4 in each number. Then write its value.** (Chapter 1)

11. 645,312,978
12. 798,132,465
13. 321,654,987

**Compare. Write >, <, or = for each ●.** (Chapter 2)

14. 555,505 ● 505,555
15. $1,987,654 ● $1,978,654

**Order the numbers from greatest to least.** (Chapter 2)

16. 44,044  44,440  44,404
17. 716,844  617,488  761,844

**A $20 bill was used to buy each item below. List the coins and bills you would use to make change.** (Chapter 2)

18.

19.

**Round to the place of the underlined digit.** (Chapter 2)

**20.** 754,<u>8</u>42,182 **21.** 9<u>8</u>9,434,123 **22.** 672,81<u>8</u>,432

## PROBLEM SOLVING Open Response

**Use the bar graph to solve Problems 23–24.**

**23.** The zoo has the most of which reptile? the least?

**24.** About how many reptiles are at the zoo?

**25.** **Reasoning** Rae, Tai, and Gia either have a turtle, a lizard, or a snake. Rae's pet does not have legs. Gia loves the feel of her pet's shell. What reptile belongs to each girl?

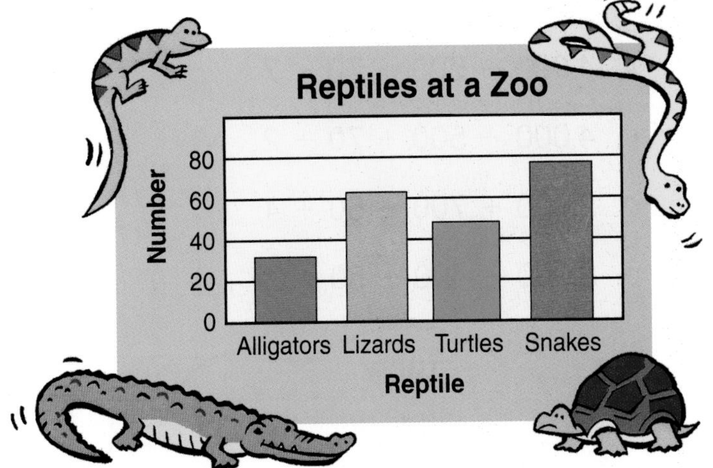

# Performance Task

| Georgia's Historic Capitals | |
|---|---|
| **Capital City** | **Population in 2000** |
| Savannah | 131,510 |
| Augusta | 195,182 |
| Louisville | 2,712 |
| Milledgeville | 18,757 |
| Atlanta | 416,474 |

**Task** Georgia has had five different state capitals. The information above shows the five capital cities and their populations in 2000.

Use the data in the table to complete the following.

a. Use place value to order the cities by population, from greatest to least.

b. Draw a number line on a strip of paper two feet long. Mark one end as zero and the other end as 450,000. Fold the number line to make smaller, equal units. Label them.

c. Plot points on the number line to show the populations of the five cities.

d. Measure five strips of paper using the number line. Each strip will represent the population of one of the five cities. Use the strips to create a bar graph on the class bulletin board.

# Getting Ready for CRCT

**Solve Problems 1–10.**

*Look at the example below.*

What is the expanded form of the number 4,572?

A. 4,000 + 500 + 70 + 7

B. 4,000 + 500 + 70 + 2

C. 2,000 + 700 + 50 + 4

D. 2,000 + 400 + 50 + 7

THINK

You know that the value of the first digit in 4,572 is 4,000.

So you can eliminate choices **C** and **D**.

## Multiple Choice

1. There were 2,678 visitors to the town fair. How many people is that to the nearest ten?

A. 2,670

B. 2,680

C. 2,700

D. 2,800

(Chapter 2, Lesson 5)

2. Which of the following shows 45,937 rounded to the nearest hundred?

A. 45,990

B. 45,900

C. 46,000

D. 50,000

(Chapter 2, Lesson 5)

3. How many thousands are in 2,000,000?

A. 2

B. 20

C. 200

D. 2,000

(Chapter 1, Lesson 4)

4. What is the place of the underlined digit in 3,4<u>8</u>7,663?

A. millions

B. hundred thousands

C. ten thousands

D. thousands

(Chapter 1, Lesson 5)



For Test-Taking Tips, See page 658.

## Open Response

5. Write 247,365 in word form.

(Chapter 1, Lesson 2)

6. Write the number eighty million, twenty-three thousand, one in standard form.

(Chapter 1, Lesson 5)

7. The bar graph shows the number of apples Bernadette's friends picked.

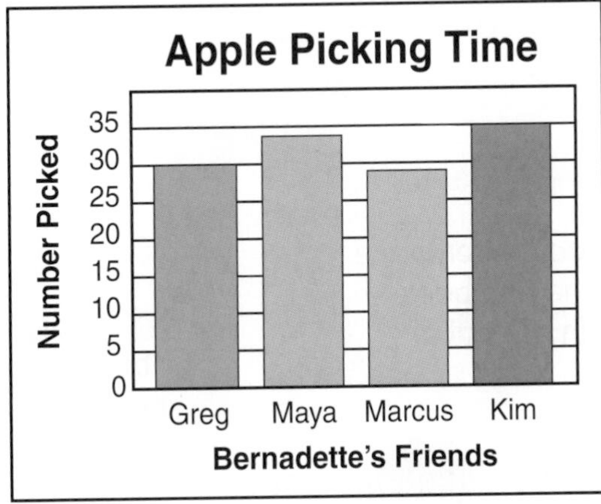


Bernadette picked 33 apples. Which of her four friends picked almost the same number as Bernadette?

(Chapter 2, Lesson 6)

8. Oscar and Yvette each have 5-digit numbers. Yvette's number has 4 sixes. Oscar's number has 3 sixes. Yvette is sure she has the greater number. Could she be wrong? Explain.

(Chapter 2, Lesson 1)

## Extended Response

9. Use each number tile below once.

| 6 | 4 | 1 | 5 |
|---|---|---|---|

a. Make the greatest number possible.

b. Make the least number possible.

c. What two numbers can you make if the six is in the tens place and the five is in the thousands place?

(Chapter 1, Lesson 2)

10. The chart shows the number of pennies the third, fourth, and fifth grades collected for the pet shelter.

| Pennies Collected | |
|---|---|
| **Grade** | **Pennies** |
| 3 | 941 |
| 4 | 1,368 |
| 5 | 1,126 |

a. Round the number of pennies each grade collected to the nearest hundred and to the nearest thousand.

b. Suppose you want to find which grade collected the MOST pennies. To which place should you round? Explain.

(Chapter 2, Lesson 5)

**Education Place**

Look for Cumulative Test Prep at **eduplace.com/map** for more practice.

# Vocabulary Wrap-Up for Unit 1

**Look back at the big ideas and vocabulary in this unit.**

## Big Ideas

You can write a number in standard form, expanded form, short word form and word form.

You can compare numbers using a number line and using place value.

### Key Vocabulary

**standard form**
**expanded form**
**word form**
**compare**

## Math Conversations

**Use your new vocabulary to discuss these big ideas.**

1. Write nine hundred nine thousand, nine hundred ninety in three ways.
2. Explain how to round 8,934 to the nearest ten, hundred, and thousand.
3. Show how to order these numbers from greatest to least.

   2,765 2,739 2,768

4. Explain how you would make change from $20.00 for an item that costs $17.38.
5. **Write About It** Brainstorm a list of five places you want to visit. Research how far they are from where you live. Order them from farthest to nearest.

I need to compare the numbers in my data.

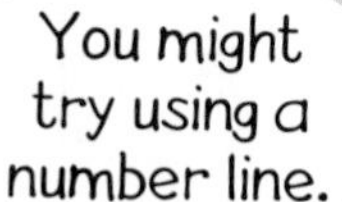

# UNIT 2

# Operations and Algebraic Reasoning

# Reading Mathematics

## Reviewing Vocabulary

**Here are some math vocabulary words that you should know.**

| | |
|---|---|
| **dividend** | the number that is divided in a division problem |
| **factors** | numbers that are multiplied together to give a product |
| **quotient** | the answer in a division problem |
| **regroup** | to use 1 ten for 10 ones, 10 tens for 1 hundred, 15 ones for 1 ten 5 ones, and so on |

## Reading Words and Symbols

You can use words and symbols to show addition, subtraction, multiplication, and division.

| Write: | Read: |
|---|---|
| $12 + 8 = 20$ | Twelve plus eight equals twenty. |
| $15 - 5 = 10$ | Fifteen minus five equals ten. |
| $2 \times 9 = 18$ | Two times nine equals eighteen. |
| $24 \div 3 = 8$ | Twenty-four divided by three equals eight. |

**Use words and symbols to answer the questions.**

1. Use the numbers 4, 6, and 10 to write an addition sentence and a subtraction sentence.

2. Use the numbers 2, 8, and 16 to write a multiplication sentence and a division sentence.

# Reading Questions on CRCT

**Choose the correct answer for each.**

**3.** Which of the following describes the model below?

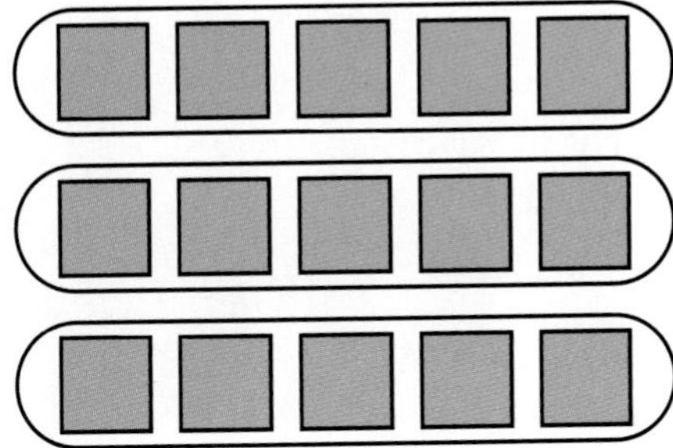

A. 12 ÷ 3

B. 15 ÷ 3

C. 15 ÷ 5

D. 18 ÷ 3

**Describes** means "represents."

**4.** The sum of 430 + 135 is between which two numbers?

A. 450 and 500

B. 500 and 550

C. 550 and 600

D. 600 and 650

**Between** two numbers means "after the first number and before the second number."

**5.** Which number is the best estimate of the difference?

324 − 155

A. 100

B. 140

C. 160

D. 200

**Best estimate** means "closest estimate."

# Learning Vocabulary

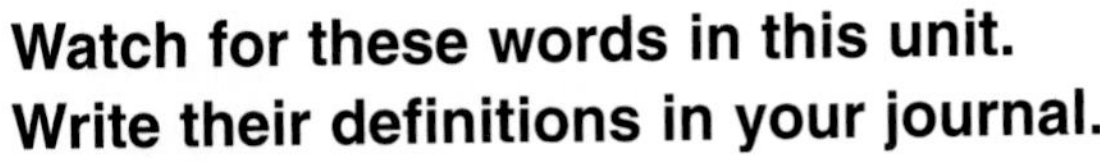


**Zero Property of Addition**

**Commutative Property of Addition**

**variable**

**inverse operations**

**expression**

**equation**

## Education Place

At **eduplace.com/map**, see eGlossary and eGames—Math Lingo

## Literature Connection

Read "Kid Camp" on Page 646. Then work with a partner to answer the questions about the story.

# CHAPTER 3 Add and Subtract Whole Numbers

## Georgia PERFORMANCE PREVIEW

### Using Data

You can eat peach cobbler hot or cold. You can even eat it with ice cream! The recipe shows how to make 1 batch of peach cobbler. How would you change the recipe if you wanted to make 2 batches of peach cobbler?

**Peach Cobbler**

8 tablespoons butter
1 cup flour
1 cup sugar
2 teaspoons baking powder
2 pinches of salt
1 cup milk
1 can peaches
1 pinch cinnamon

Preheat oven to 350°. Melt butter in baking dish. Mix next four ingredients. Stir milk into mixture and pour into dish. Place peaches on top. Sprinkle with cinnamon. Bake for 45 minutes.

# Use What You Know

**Use this page to review and remember what you need to know for this chapter.**

## VOCABULARY

**Choose the best term to complete each sentence.**

**Vocabulary**
- sum
- addend
- difference
- estimating
- regrouping
- number sentence

1. In 6 + 3 = 9, 6 is an ____.
2. In 7 + 5 = 12, 12 is the ____.
3. You can subtract two numbers to find their ____.
4. A ____ shows how numbers are related.
5. When you change 1 ten to 10 ones you are ____.

## CONCEPTS AND SKILLS

**Add or subtract. Regroup if you need to.**

6. $\begin{array}{r} 62 \\ +\ 37 \\ \hline \end{array}$
7. $\begin{array}{r} 40 \\ +\ 28 \\ \hline \end{array}$
8. $\begin{array}{r} 87 \\ +\ 54 \\ \hline \end{array}$
9. $\begin{array}{r} 56 \\ -\ 19 \\ \hline \end{array}$
10. $\begin{array}{r} 71 \\ -32 \\ \hline \end{array}$

**Round each number to the place of the underlined digit.**

11. $4\underline{2}5$
12. $3\underline{8}5$
13. $\underline{2},476$
14. $\$14\underline{4}.69$
15. $92,\underline{2}39$

**Compare. Write >, <, or = for each ⬭.**

16. 18 − 9 ⬭ 4 + 4
17. 8 − 3 ⬭ 9 − 4
18. 7 + 7 ⬭ 9 + 6
19. 9 + 6 ⬭ 10 + 5
20. 4 + 5 ⬭ 6 + 2
21. 15 − 7 ⬭ 14 − 6
22. 8 + 3 ⬭ 12 − 1
23. 12 − 4 ⬭ 11 − 5
24. 13 − 5 ⬭ 6 + 5

### Write About It

25. There are 175 more boys than girls at the hobby show. There are 256 girls there. How many boys are at the hobby show? Explain how you know.

Facts Practice, See page 666.

son
1

Algebra

# Addition Properties and Subtraction Rules

**Objective** Use properties of addition and rules of subtraction.

**STANDARDS** M4N7.c

**Vocabulary**
- Zero Property
- Commutative Property
- Associative Property

## Learn About It

Here are some properties and rules you can use when you add and subtract.

### Properties of Addition

**Zero Property of Addition**

- When you add zero to a number, the sum is that number.

$7 + 0 = 7$

**Commutative Property of Addition**

- When you change the order of the addends, the sum stays the same.

$5 + 7 = 12$
$7 + 5 = 12$

**Associative Property of Addition**

- When you change the way addends are grouped, the sum stays the same.

$(3 + 5) + 6 = 3 + (5 + 6)$
$8 + 6 = 3 + 11$
$14 = 14$

**Remember**
Do what is in the parentheses first.

### Rules of Subtraction

**Zeros in Subtraction**

- When you subtract zero from a number, the difference is that number.

$7 - 0 = 7$

- When you subtract a number from itself, the difference is zero.

$7 - 7 = 0$

## Guided Practice

**Copy and complete each number sentence. Tell which property or rule you used.**

1. 11 + 0 = _____
2. 45 + 34 = _____ + 45
3. 17 − 17 = _____
4. (4 + 6) + 8 = _____ + (6 + 8)
5. 25 − 0 = _____
6. 3 + (3 + _____) = (3 + 3) + 1

**Ask Yourself**

- Is one of the numbers zero?
- If there are parentheses, what do I do first?

**Explain Your Thinking** ▶ How could you group 50 + 387 + 950 to make it easier to add?

## Practice and Problem Solving

**Copy and complete each number sentence. Tell which property or rule you used.**

7. 34 + 99 = _____ + 34
8. 342 + 0 = _____
9. (7 + 3) + 67 = 7 + (3 + _____)
10. 24 + (7 + 8) = (24 + 7) + _____
11. (7 − 0) + 3 = _____ + 3
12. 5 + (9 + 0) = 5 + _____

**Use the Associative Property to help you find each sum mentally.**

13. 75 + 25 + 46
14. 92 + 421 + 8
15. 179 + 345 + 21
16. 490 + 84 + 10
17. 328 + 291 + 9
18. 820 + 78 + 80

**Solve.**

19. Marta needs to find the sum of 24, 105, and 66. How can she group the addends to make it easier to add?
20. Cara had 92 stamps. Leah gave her 48 more. If Mel gives her 8 more stamps, how many will Cara have?

## Sharpening Skills for CRCT

**Open Response**

**Round each number to the greatest place or to the nearest dollar.**
(Ch. 2, Lesson 5)

21. 481
22. 3,597
23. $5.25
24. $316.37
25. 32,877
26. 481,921

27. Do you think there is a Commutative Property for subtraction? (Ch. 3, Lesson 1)

    Why or why not?

Extra Practice See page 81, Set A.

Lesson 2

# Mental Math Strategies

**Objective** Use mental math to add and subtract two- and three-digit numbers.

**STANDARDS** M4N7.d

**Vocabulary**
breaking apart
compensation

## Learn About It

Mental math strategies can help you add and subtract.

**You can use breaking apart to add or subtract mentally.**

**Find 44 + 18.**

- Break apart the numbers. 44 = 40 + 4; 18 = 10 + 8
- Add the tens. 40 + 10 = 50
- Add the ones. 4 + 8 = 12
- Add the tens and ones. 50 + 12 = 62

So, 44 + 18 = 62.

**Find 58 − 25.**

- Break apart the numbers. 58 = 50 + 8; 25 = 20 + 5
- Subtract the tens. 50 − 20 = 30
- Subtract the ones. 8 − 5 = 3
- Add the tens and ones. 30 + 3 = 33

So, 58 − 25 = 33.

**You can use compensation to add or subtract mentally.**

**Find 38 + 56.**

$$\begin{array}{r} 38 \\ +56 \\ \hline \end{array}$$

Add 2 to 38 to make 40.

$$\begin{array}{r} 40 \\ +56 \\ \hline 96 \\ -\ 2 \\ \hline 94 \end{array}$$

Subtract 2 to compensate for adding 2.

So, 38 + 56 = 94.

**Find 145 − 17.**

$$\begin{array}{r} 145 \\ -\ 17 \\ \hline \end{array}$$

Add 3 to 17 to make 20.

$$\begin{array}{r} 145 \\ -\ 20 \\ \hline 125 \\ +\ 3 \\ \hline 128 \end{array}$$

Add 3 to compensate for subtracting 3 extra.

So, 145 − 17 = 128.

## Guided Practice

**Use mental math to add or subtract. Tell which strategy you used.**

**1.** 27 + 31

**2.** 34 + 29

**3.** 68 − 24

**4.** 116 − 97

> **Ask Yourself**
> - Which strategy makes the calculation easier?
> - If I use compensation, what number should I adjust?

**Explain Your Thinking** ▶ Would you use mental math or paper and pencil to find 361 − 174? Explain.

## Practice and Problem Solving

**Use mental math to add or subtract.**

**5.** 34 + 27 **6.** 33 + 49 **7.** 88 + 96 **8.** 314 + 498

**9.** 78 − 15 **10.** 59 − 22 **11.** 391 − 58 **12.** 212 + 107

**Algebra** • **Symbols** **Compare. Write <, >, or = for each ⬬.**

**13.** 48 + 26 ⬬ 46 + 28

**14.** 76 − 16 ⬬ 92 − 20

**15.** 173 − 45 ⬬ 120 + 45

**16.** 453 − 53 ⬬ 224 + 176

**17.** Carolyn collected 136 colored beads. She traded 25 of them for 13 wooden beads. How many beads does she have now?

**18.** Jim removed 16 silver beads from a necklace. The necklace now has 65 beads. How many beads did the necklace have before?

## GPS Sharpening Skills for CRCT

### Open Response

**Find the next two numbers in the pattern.**
(Grade 3)

**19.** 14, 12, 10, 8, 6, _____, _____

**20.** 125, 120, 115, 110, _____, _____

**21.** 2, 4, 8, 16, 32, _____, _____

**22.** 3, 6, 5, 10, 9, 18, _____, _____

### Multiple Choice

**23.** Lily used 294 beads for her craft project. Patty used 193 beads. How many beads were used?
(Ch. 3, Lesson 2)

A. 397 C. 487

B. 401 D. 497

Extra Practice See page 81, Set B.

Lesson 3

 **Audio Tutor 1**/7 Listen and Understand

# Estimate Sums and Differences

**Objective** Use rounded numbers to estimate sums and differences.

**STANDARDS** M4N2.b, M4N2.d

The Community Center in Riverville offers an after-school arts program. 478 grade school students and 188 middle school students sign up for the program. The Community Center has enough space for 675 students. Does the center have enough space for all of the students that signed up?

You do not need to know the exact number of students that signed up. You only need to know if the total is less than 675. So, you can estimate the sum.

**Remember**
To estimate is to find a number close to an exact amount.

**Estimate the sum of 478 and 188.**

Round each addend to the nearest hundred. Then add the rounded numbers.

| | | |
|---|---|---|
| 478 | rounds to | 500 |
| +188 | rounds to | +200 |
| | | 700 |

Since both addends were rounded up, the actual number will be less than 700. But will it be less than 675?

To get a closer estimate, round to the nearest ten. Then add.

| | | |
|---|---|---|
| 478 | rounds to | 480 |
| +188 | rounds to | +190 |
| | | 670 |

Both addends were rounded up and their sum is less than 675. So, you know the actual total is less than 675.

**Solution:** The Community Center has enough room for all the students.

## Other Examples

**A. Round to the Nearest Dollar**

| | | |
|---|---|---|
| \$4.89 | rounds to | \$5.00 |
| +\$1.59 | rounds to | +\$2.00 |
| | | \$7.00 |

**B. Round to the Nearest Thousand**

| | | |
|---|---|---|
| 6,742 | rounds to | 7,000 |
| −2,575 | rounds to | −3,000 |
| | | 4,000 |

**C. Round to the Nearest Ten Thousand**

| | | |
|---|---|---|
| 73,465 | rounds to | 70,000 |
| −19,287 | rounds to | −20,000 |
| | | 50,000 |



Extra Help at **eduplace.com/map**

## Guided Practice

**Round each number to the nearest ten. Then estimate.**

1. 45 + 32
2. 586 − 98
3. 4,567 + 1,111

**Ask Yourself**

- Which place am I rounding to?
- Am I finding a sum or a difference?

**Round each number to the nearest hundred or dollar. Then estimate.**

4. $4.52 + 3.26
5. 873 − 256
6. 6,359 + 1,703
7. 87,623 − 24,401

**Explain Your Thinking** ▶ If both addends are rounded down, will the sum of the rounded numbers be greater than or less than the actual sum?

## Practice and Problem Solving

**Round each number to the nearest ten. Then estimate.**

8. 526 + 313
9. 672 − 259
10. 427 + 777
11. 821 − 482
12. 5,426 + 479
13. 3,550 − 1,743
14. 724 + 255
15. 10,207 − 4,520

**Round each number to the nearest hundred or the nearest dollar. Then estimate.**

16. 266 + 142
17. 397 − 151
18. 701 + 884
19. 925 − 478
20. 2,436 + 553
21. 4,444 − 3,858
22. $34.99 + 96.78
23. $49.99 − 46.27
24. 25,492 + 2,321
25. 46,591 − 25,427
26. $135.61 − 93.48
27. 359,513 + 233,642

Go On

**Round each number to the greatest place. Then estimate.**

28. $\begin{array}{r} 57{,}834 \\ -53{,}619 \\ \hline \end{array}$

29. $\begin{array}{r} 23{,}509 \\ -\quad 837 \\ \hline \end{array}$

30. $\begin{array}{r} 346{,}899 \\ +271{,}585 \\ \hline \end{array}$

31. $\begin{array}{r} 3{,}277 \\ 6{,}503 \\ +5{,}499 \\ \hline \end{array}$

## Algebra • Number Sentences **Find a number at the right that makes each number sentence true. Use each number only once.**

32. $453 + ■ < 800$

33. $325 - ■ = 215$

34. $755 < 169 + ■$

35. $■ - 256 = 344$

36. $■ + 662 > 1{,}000$

37. $■ - 372 > 400$

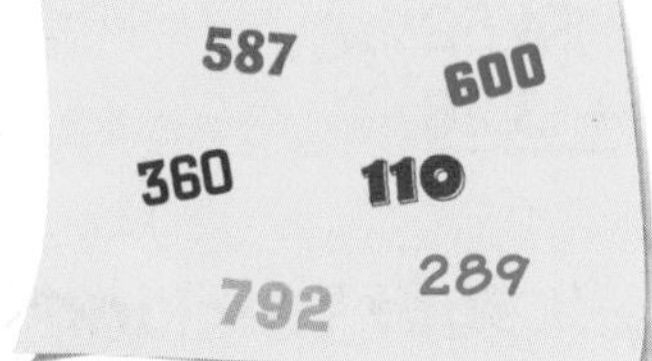


## Data **Use the poster for Problems 38–41.**

38. Doug bought 4 canvases. About how much money did he spend?

39. Karen bought a paint box and 3 tubes of paint. About how much money did she spend?

40. **Money** Ramon bought a canvas and a paint brush. About how much change should he get back if he paid with a $10 bill?

41. Emma estimated the cost of an easel and a paint brush by rounding each price to the nearest dollar. Was her estimate more or less than the actual amount? By how much?

**Painting Supplies**

| | |
|---|---|
| Canvas | $3.79 |
| Paint brush | $2.29 |
| Tube of paint | $1.95 |
| Easel | $10.38 |
| Frame | $7.49 |
| Paint box | $14.67 |

## Sharpening Skills for CRCT

**Open Response**

**Round each number to the greatest place.** (Ch. 2, Lesson 5)

42. 3,496

43. 62,549

44. 876

45. 752,385

46. 5,689

47. 24,985

48. Rob sold 350 tickets to a play on Monday and 324 tickets on Tuesday. About how many tickets did Rob sell? (Ch. 3, Lesson 3) Explain how you got your answer.



Extra Practice See page 81, Set C.

# Math Reasoning

## Front-End Estimation and Clustering

You learned that one way to estimate is by rounding. Here are two other ways to estimate.

**Vocabulary**

**front-end estimation**

**clustering**

**You can use front-end estimation to estimate.**

▶ **Estimate 573 + 228.**

- Add the front-end digits.

```
  573
+ 228
  700
```

500 + 200 is 700.

- Adjust the estimate.

```
  573
+ 228
  800
```

73 + 28 is about 100 more. 700 + 100 = 800.

The estimate is about 800.

▶ **Estimate 311 − 196.**

- Subtract the front-end digits.

```
  311
− 196
  200
```

300 − 100 is 200.

- Adjust the estimate.

```
  311
− 196
  100
```

96 is about 100. So subtract another hundred.

The estimate is about 100.

**You can use clustering to estimate sums. Clustering is used to estimate addends that have similar values.**

▶ **Estimate 117 + 105 + 91.**

117 + 105 + 91 is about 300

The addends are all close in value. I can skip count by 100s. 100, 200, 300.

The estimate is about 300.

**Use front-end estimation to estimate each sum or difference.**

**1.** 663 + 141 **2.** 441 + 248 **3.** 866 − 450 **4.** 937 − 297

**Use clustering to estimate each sum.**

**5.** 48 + 49 + 52 **6.** 214 + 206 + 187 **7.** 375 + 407 + 389

Lesson 4

# Problem-Solving Decision

## Estimate or Exact Answer

**Objective** Decide whether an estimated or an exact answer is needed to solve a problem.

 **STANDARDS** M4N2.b, M4P1.b

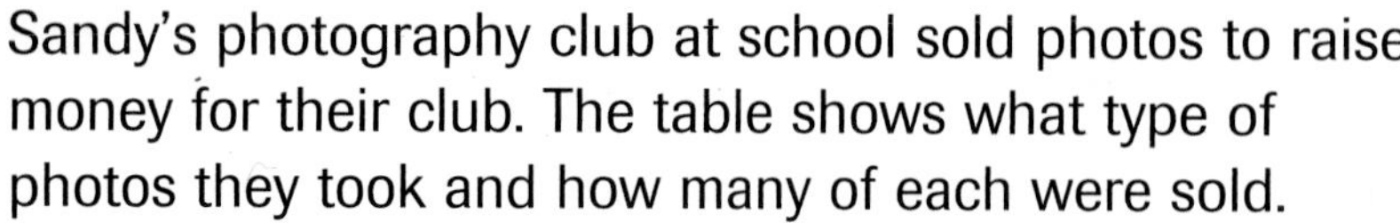

Sandy's photography club at school sold photos to raise money for their club. The table shows what type of photos they took and how many of each were sold.

**Photography Fundraiser**

| Type of photo | Number sold |
|---|---|
| Landscapes | 123 |
| People | 105 |
| Animals | 216 |
| Other | 87 |

Look at these examples. They show when to use an estimate and when to use an exact answer.

**Sometimes you can estimate to solve a problem.**

About how many photos of people and animals were sold?

Since the question asks you to find *about how many* photos were sold, you can estimate the sum.

$$\begin{array}{r} 105 \\ +\ 216 \\ \hline \end{array} \quad \text{rounds to} \quad \begin{array}{r} 100 \\ +\ 200 \\ \hline 300 \end{array}$$

About 300 photos of people and animals were sold.

**Sometimes you need an exact answer to solve the problem.**

How many more photos of landscapes than photos of people were sold?

Since the question asks you to find *how many more,* you need to find the exact difference.

$$\begin{array}{r} 123 \\ -\ 105 \\ \hline 18 \end{array}$$

123 ← number of landscape photos
105 ← number of people photos

18 more photos of landscapes than people were sold.

## Try These

**Solve. Tell whether you need an exact answer or an estimate.**

1. Were there more than 700 photos sold at the fundraiser?
2. How many photos of animals and of landscapes were sold altogether?
3. The club raised \$193 selling photos of people and \$212 selling photos of animals. About how much was raised by selling photos of people and animals?
4. The club raised a total of \$685. About how much more do they need to reach their goal of \$1,200?

# Social Studies Connection

## Magic Squares

 **STANDARDS** Extends M4N

A Chinese tale from B.C.E. 2200 tells about a turtle with a magic square on its back. Look at the rows, columns, and diagonals of numbers in the picture on the right. The numbers add to 15 each time!

**Copy the magic squares.**
**Then fill in the missing numbers.**

**1.**

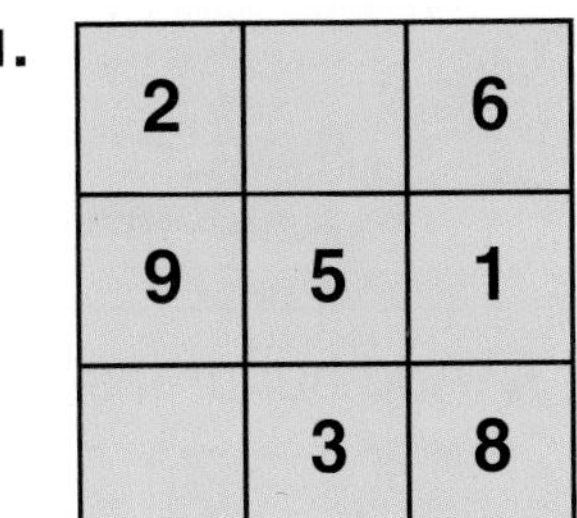

| | | |
|---|---|---|
| 2 | | 6 |
| 9 | 5 | 1 |
| | 3 | 8 |

**2.**

| | | |
|---|---|---|
| 6 | 1 | |
| | 5 | 3 |
| 2 | 9 | 4 |

**3.**

| | | |
|---|---|---|
| | 3 | 4 |
| 1 | | 9 |
| 6 | | 2 |

WEEKLY WR READER eduplace.com/map

## Quick Check

Check your understanding of Lessons 1–4.

**Copy and complete each number sentence.** (Lesson 1)

**1.** 85 − _____ = 85 **2.** (24 + 21) + 9 = 24 + (21 + ___)

**Use mental math to add or subtract.** (Lesson 2)

**3.** 128 + 139 **4.** 72 + 46 **5.** 215 − 98 **6.** 481 − 57

**Round each number to the greatest place. Then estimate.** (Lesson 3)

**7.** \$81.31 − \$23.66 **8.** 2,693 + 5,396 **9.** \$426.18 − \$162.27

**Tell whether you need an exact answer or an estimate.** (Lesson 4)

**10.** This year 1,285 people competed in a fishing contest. Last year 974 people competed in the contest. About how many people competed both years?

Extra Practice at eduplace.com/map

Lesson 5

Audio Tutor 1/18 Listen and Understand

# Add Whole Numbers and Money

**Vocabulary**
regroup

**Objective** Add numbers using regrouping.

**STANDARDS** M4N7.d, M4N, M4P2

## Learn About It

Mr. Shaw has a large collection of model trains. He has 129 pieces of track. He plans to buy 97 more pieces of track. How many pieces of track will he have altogether?

**Add.** 129 + 97 = ■

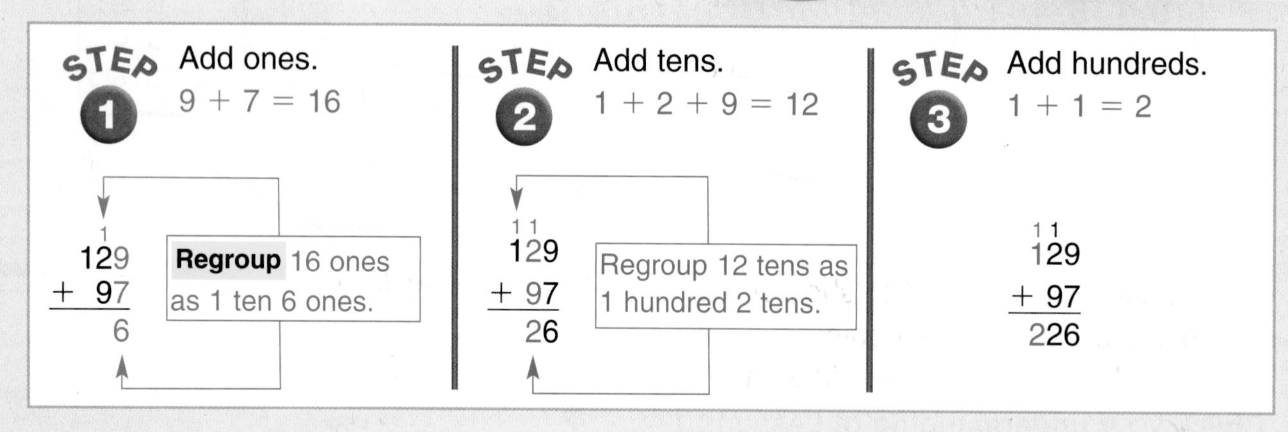


**Solution:** Mr. Shaw will have 226 pieces of track.

## Other Examples

**A. Add Thousands**

```
 1  11
 18,293
+ 2,048
 20,341
```

**B. Add Money**

```
    1 1
 $15.64
+  3.87
 $19.51
```

**Remember**
Bring down the decimal point and the dollar sign.

## Guided Practice

**Find each sum.**

**1.** 283 + 55

**2.** 6,582 + 298

**3.** $27.93 + 5.24

**4.** 4,571 + 2,714

**Ask Yourself**
- Are the digits lined up correctly?
- Do I need to regroup?

**Explain Your Thinking** ▶ How can adding numbers in a different order help you check that your answer is correct?

## Practice and Problem Solving

**Add. Check by adding in a different order or by estimating.**

| | | | | |
|---|---|---|---|---|
| **5.** 652 + 145 | **6.** 732 + 88 | **7.** 6,714 + 8,600 | **8.** \$51.95 + 32.61 | **9.** \$37.80 + 6.47 |
| **10.** 894 + 4,717 | **11.** 5,182 + 3,957 | **12.** 9,832 + 761 | **13.** 3,431 + 768 | **14.** 3,984 + 1,079 |
| **15.** 8,623 + 382 | **16.** \$143.21 + 78.99 | **17.** 54,186 + 11,983 | **18.** \$142.31 + 56.28 | **19.** \$323.05 + 184.95 |

**Data** **Use the price list for Problems 20–23.**

**20.** What is the cost of 1 railroad station and 1 colonial house?

**21.** Is \$30 enough to buy the railroad station and the hardware store?

**22.** Harold bought a barber shop and a hardware store. What coins and bills would he receive if he paid with a \$20 bill?

**23.** **Create and Solve** Use the information in the price list to write an addition word problem. Then solve it.

**Miniature Village**

| Building | Price |
|---|---|
| Barber Shop | \$5.59 |
| Railroad Station | \$26.35 |
| Colonial House | \$15.67 |
| Hardware Store | \$13.25 |
| Butcher Shop | \$11.79 |

## Sharpening Skills for CRCT

**Open Response**

**Write each amount.** (Ch. 2, Lesson 3)

**24.**    

**25.** 

**Multiple Choice**

**26.** Janai collected 381 cans to recycle. Ed collected 526 cans. How many cans were collected? (Ch. 3, Lesson 5)

A. 807 C. 907

B. 897 D. 927

Extra Practice See page 81, Set D.

Lesson 6

**Audio Tutor 1/9** Listen and Understand

# Subtract Whole Numbers

**Objective** Subtract whole numbers with up to five digits.

**STANDARDS** M4N7.a, M4N7.d

**Vocabulary**
inverse operations

## Learn About It

Can you imagine spending hours creating something only to knock it down? You might if you like building domino lines!

Suppose a domino line has 2,865 dominoes in it. If 868 dominoes are knocked down, how many dominoes are left standing?

**Subtract.** **2,865 − 868 = ■**

**STEP 1** Subtract ones.

```
     5 15
  2,8 6 5
−   8 6 8
        7
```

Regroup a ten as 10 ones.

**STEP 2** Subtract tens.

```
     15
    7 5 15
  2,8 6 5
−   8 6 8
      9 7
```

Regroup a hundred as 10 tens.

**STEP 3** Subtract hundreds.

```
    1715
  1 7 5 15
  2,8 6 5
−   8 6 8
    9 9 7
```

Regroup a thousand as 10 hundreds.

**STEP 4** Subtract thousands.

```
    1715
  1 7 5 15
  2,8 6 5
−   8 6 8
  1,9 9 7
```

**Solution:** 1,997 dominoes are left standing.

**Check Your Work.**

You can check by adding because addition undoes subtraction. Addition and subtraction are **inverse operations**.

```
  2,865       1,997
−   868     +   868
  1,997       2,865
```

The numbers are the same, so the difference is correct.

## Another Example

**Subtract Money**

```
      12
    1 2 14
  $8 2 .3 4
−   2 1 .5 9
  $6 0 .7 5
```

**Remember**
Bring down the decimal point and the dollar sign.

## Guided Practice

**Subtract. Use addition to check your answer.**

1. $\begin{array}{r} 483 \\ -\ 262 \\ \hline \end{array}$

2. $\begin{array}{r} 4,674 \\ -\ 1,833 \\ \hline \end{array}$

3. $\begin{array}{r} \$65.72 \\ -\ 49.81 \\ \hline \end{array}$

4. 839 − 45

5. $53.59 − $3.48

**Ask Yourself**

- Are the digits lined up correctly?
- Do I need to regroup before I subtract?

**Explain Your Thinking** ▶ How could you use estimation to see if your answer is reasonable?

## Practice and Problem Solving

**Subtract. Use addition or estimation to check.**

6. $\begin{array}{r} 967 \\ -\ 815 \\ \hline \end{array}$

7. $\begin{array}{r} 8,397 \\ -\ 5,067 \\ \hline \end{array}$

8. $\begin{array}{r} 7,927 \\ -\ 2,639 \\ \hline \end{array}$

9. $\begin{array}{r} \$97.48 \\ -\ 46.27 \\ \hline \end{array}$

10. $\begin{array}{r} \$28.13 \\ -\ 9.24 \\ \hline \end{array}$

11. $\begin{array}{r} 757 \\ -\ 486 \\ \hline \end{array}$

12. $\begin{array}{r} 324 \\ -\ 77 \\ \hline \end{array}$

13. $\begin{array}{r} 5,188 \\ -\ 1,434 \\ \hline \end{array}$

14. $\begin{array}{r} \$73.59 \\ -\ 26.84 \\ \hline \end{array}$

15. $\begin{array}{r} 9,634 \\ -\ 4,967 \\ \hline \end{array}$

16. 9,526 − 8,410

17. $83.61 − $61.75

18. $75.26 − $29.58

### Algebra • Equations **Find each missing number.**

19. 39 + ____ = 58

20. ____ − 178 = 113

21. ____ + 412 = 938

22. ____ − 247 = 429

23. 342 + ____ = 829

24. ____ − 276 = 634

25. A club has 1,985 dominoes. A group used 928 of these dominoes to make a domino line. How many dominoes were not used?

26. **Multistep** Josh and Meg each used 350 dominoes. If 2,658 dominoes were used altogether, how many were used by other club members?

## Sharpening Skills for CRCT

**Open Response**

**What color is the next shape in each pattern?** (Grade 3)

27.  ____

28. ● ● ● ● ● ● ● ● ● ____

29. Mr. Tyson flew 1,224 miles in May and he flew 2,145 miles in June. How many more miles did he fly in June than in May?
(Ch. 3, Lesson 6)

Extra Practice See page 81, Set E.

Lesson 7

 **Audio Tutor 1**/10 Listen and Understand

# Subtract Across Zeros

**Objective** Subtract when some digits are zero.

**STANDARDS** M4N7.a, M4N7.d

*The world's largest Ukrainian egg is in Alberta, Canada. It is over 27 feet high.*

## Learn About It

Painting eggs in colorful designs using wax and dye is an old tradition in the Ukraine.

Leah guesses there are 2,500 triangles on the Ukrainian egg shown at the right. There are actually 2,206 triangles on the egg. What is the difference between Leah's guess and the actual number of triangles?

**Subtract.** **2,500 − 2,206 = ■**

**STEP 1** Subtract ones. 6 > 0, so you need to regroup. There are no tens, so regroup 1 hundred as 10 tens.

```
   4 10
 2,5̸0̸0
− 2,206
```

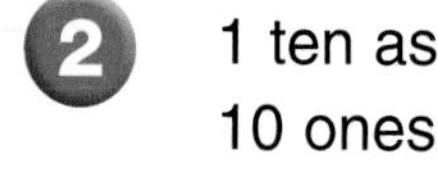

**STEP 2** Regroup 1 ten as 10 ones.

```
      9
   4 1̸0 10
 2,5̸0̸ 0̸
− 2,206
```

**STEP 3** Then subtract.

```
      9
   4 1̸0 10
 2,5̸0̸ 0̸
− 2,206
    294
```

**Solution:** There are 294 fewer triangles than Leah thought.

## Guided Practice

**Subtract. Estimate or add to check.**

1. 306 − 94
2. \$8.02 − 4.88
3. 4,055 − 1,572
4. \$70.46 − 23.15
5. 500 − 156
6. 9,070 − 2,305
7. 4,000 − 2,843
8. 6,003 − 2,346

**Ask Yourself**

- Do I need to regroup?
- Do I need to regroup more than once before I can subtract at all?

**Explain Your Thinking** ▶ Where should you start regrouping if the number you are subtracting from has no ones, no tens, and no hundreds?

## Practice and Problem Solving

**Subtract. Estimate or add to check.**

9. 404 − 159
10. 710 − 572
11. $9.00 − 7.48
12. 605 − 94
13. 7,038 − 3,251
14. 2,004 − 1,413
15. 8,080 − 637
16. $70.00 − 53.94
17. $50.50 − 32.56
18. $29.00 − 17.07
19. 9,055 − 8,215
20. $60.00 − $41.20
21. 8,009 − 5,506

**Algebra • Functions** Follow the rule to complete each table.

| | Rule: Add 2,376 | |
|---|---|---|
| | Input | Output |
| 22. | 1,542 | ■ |
| 23. | 3,721 | ■ |
| 24. | ■ | 6,922 |

| | Rule: Subtract 3,118 | |
|---|---|---|
| | Input | Output |
| 25. | 5,307 | ■ |
| 26. | 7,200 | ■ |
| 27. | ■ | 1,433 |

| | Rule: Subtract 4,628 | |
|---|---|---|
| | Input | Output |
| 28. | 5,000 | ■ |
| 29. | ■ | 1,053 |
| 30. | 6,204 | ■ |

**Solve.**

31. A Ukrainian egg artist plans to paint 400 stars on an egg. So far, he has painted 215 stars. How many stars still need to be painted?

32. A gift store ordered 6,500 Ukrainian eggs. They sold 6,221 eggs. How many Ukrainian eggs were not sold?

## Sharpening Skills for CRCT

### Open Response

**Write each amount.** (Ch. 2, Lesson 3)

33. one $10 bill, 1 quarter, 1 dime

34. four $20 bills, 3 nickels, 7 pennies

35. two $50 bills, 6 quarters, 3 dimes

36. six $5 bills, 8 dimes, 5 nickels

### Multiple Choice

37. There are 1,000 seats in a theater. So far, 762 seats have been filled. How many more seats are available? (Ch. 3, Lesson 7)

A. 362
B. 338
C. 248
D. 238

Extra Practice See page 81, Set F.

Lesson 8

# Add and Subtract Greater Numbers

**Objective** Add and subtract whole numbers with up to six digits.

## Learn About It

**STANDARDS** M4N2.b, M4N7.d, M4P1.d

*Corn and grain are used to design murals on the walls of the Corn Palace.*

Most murals are painted, but at the Corn Palace in Mitchell, South Dakota, they are made out of corn!

One mural at the Corn Palace uses 42,936 ears of corn. Another mural uses 75,658 ears of corn. How many ears of corn are used for the two murals?

**Add.** **42,936 + 75,658 = ■**

### Different Ways to Find 42,936 + 75,658

**Way 1** **Use paper and pencil.**

**STEP 1** Add ones.

```
     1
  42,936
+ 75,658
       4
```

**STEP 2** Add tens.

```
     1
  42,936
+ 75,658
      94
```

**STEP 3** Add hundreds.

```
   1  1
  42,936
+ 75,658
     594
```

**STEP 4** Add thousands and ten thousands.

```
   1  1
  42,936
+ 75,658
 118,594
```

**Way 2** **Use a calculator.**

Enter: 4 2 9 3 6

Press: +

Enter: 7 5 6 5 8

Press: =

Solution: 118594

**Check your answer.**
Estimate to be sure your answer is reasonable.

| | | |
|---|---|---|
| 42,936 | rounds to | 43,000 |
| +75,658 | rounds to | +76,000 |
| | | 119,000 |

118,594 is close to 119,000.

**Solution:** 118,594 ears of corn are used for the two murals.

**Subtract.** 275,000 − 182,500 = ■

## Different Ways to Find 275,000 − 182,500

### Way 1 Use paper and pencil.

**STEP 1**
Subtract ones and tens.

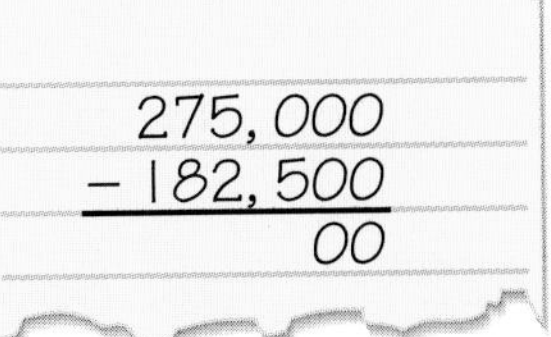

```
  275,000
- 182,500
       00
```

**STEP 2**
Subtract hundreds.

```
     4 10
  275,000
- 182,500
      500
```

**STEP 3**
Subtract thousands.

```
     4 10
  275,000
- 182,500
    2 500
```

**STEP 4**
Subtract ten thousands and hundred thousands.

```
 1 17 4 10
  275,000
- 182,500
   92,500
```

### Way 2 Use a calculator.

Enter: 2 7 5 0 0 0

Press: 

Enter: 1 8 2 5 0 0

Press: 

Solution: 92500

**Check your answer.**
Estimate to be sure your answer is reasonable.

| | | |
|---|---|---|
| 275,000 | rounds to | 280,000 |
| −182,500 | rounds to | −180,000 |
| | | 100,000 |

92,500 is close to 100,000.

**Solution:** 275,000 − 182,500 = 92,500

## Guided Practice

**Add or subtract. Estimate to check.**

**1.** 43,396 + 12,594

**2.** 78,396 − 46,239

**3.** 456,912 − 37,800

**4.** $312.75 + $357.39

**5.** 415,607 + 206,834

**Ask Yourself**

- Should I use paper and pencil or a calculator?
- How can I check that the answer is reasonable?

**Explain Your Thinking** ▶ Why should you always estimate when using a calculator?

## Practice and Problem Solving

**Add or subtract. Estimate to check.**

**6.** 14,659 − 11,584

**7.** $235.74 + 20.97

**8.** 14,508 − 13,639

**9.** 468,397 + 457,107

**10.** 125,975 − 109,300

**11.** 73,880 + 48,659

**12.** 64,340 − 8,621

**13.** 525,024 + 25,386

**14.** 413,816 + 253,109

**15.** 407,001 − 184,652

**16.** $387.91 + $413.28

**Find each missing digit.**

**17.** 53,268 + 25,■35 = 79,103

**18.** 145,397 + 94,444 = 23■,841

**19.** $36■.22 − 99.97 = $267.25

**20.** 843,■02 − 564,763 = 278,239

**Algebra** • **Symbols** **Compare. Write <, >, or = for each ●.**

**21.** 342 + 471 ● 620 + 233

**22.** 692 − 437 ● 529 − 340

**23.** 1,273 − 836 ● 236 + 201

**24.** 52,648 + 1,690 ● 83,141 − 19,302

## Choose a Computation Method

Mental Math • Estimation • Paper and Pencil • Calculator

**Solve. Tell which method you chose.**

**25.** Exactly 275,000 ears of corn will be used to make the murals this year. If 182,500 ears have been delivered so far, how many more are needed?

**26.** One mural requires 37,200 ears of corn. A different mural requires 30,100 ears. How many ears of corn are needed for both murals?

**27.** On Monday, 2,359 people visited the Corn Palace. On Tuesday, 4,697 people visited. About how many people visited altogether?

**28.** Each year over $100,000 is needed to make the murals. About how much money was spent in the last 10 years?

*Every winter, the Corn Palace becomes one of the world's largest bird feeders!*



Extra Practice See page 81, Set G.

# Use What You Know

**Use this page to review and remember what you need to know for this chapter.**

## VOCABULARY

**Choose the best word to complete each sentence.**

| Vocabulary |
|---|
| equal |
| addition |
| division |
| multiply |
| product |

1. You can ____ two factors to find the product.
2. Multiplication can be written as repeated ____.
3. In division, items are separated into ____ groups.
4. ____ can be written as repeated subtraction.

**For each fact tell if 8 is a *factor, product, dividend, divisor,* or *quotient*.**

5. $5\overline{)40}$ with quotient 8

6. $\begin{array}{r} 4 \\ \times\ 2 \\ \hline 8 \end{array}$

7. $2\overline{)8}$ with quotient 4

8. $\begin{array}{r} 9 \\ \times\ 8 \\ \hline 72 \end{array}$

9. $8 \times 4 = 32$

10. $32 \div 4 = 8$

11. $16 \div 8 = 2$

12. $2 \times 4 = 8$

## CONCEPTS AND SKILLS

**Write a multiplication sentence for each picture.**

13. 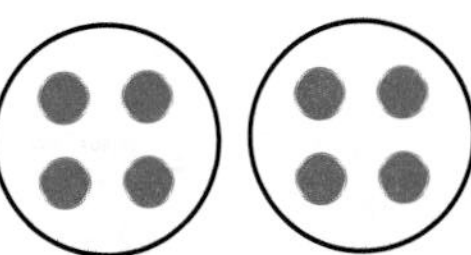

14. 

15. 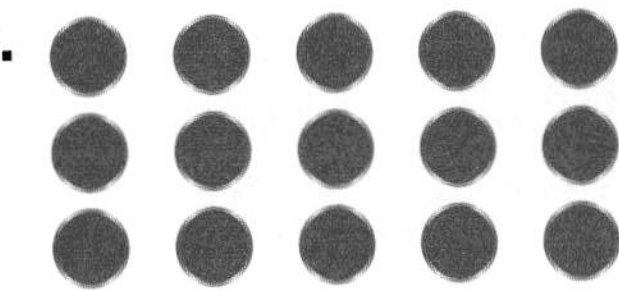

**Complete each number sentence.**

16. $4 + \blacksquare + 4 = 12$

17. $3 + 3 + 3 + 3 = \blacksquare \times 3$

18. $8 + 8 + 8 + 8 = 4 \times \blacksquare$

19. $7 + 7 + 7 + 7 + 7 = \blacksquare \times 7$

**Write About It**

20. Look at Exercise 14. How does it show $16 \div 4 = 4$? Use correct vocabulary to explain your answer.

Facts Practice, See page 667.

Lesson 1

Audio Tutor 1/11 Listen and Understand

Algebra

# Multiplication Properties and Division Rules

**Objective** Use multiplication properties and division rules.

**Vocabulary**
- Commutative Property
- Property of One
- Zero Property
- Associative Property

## Learn About It

**STANDARDS** M4N7.c, M4A1.b, M4P2

Multiplication and division have special properties and rules.

### Multiplication Properties

**Commutative Property**

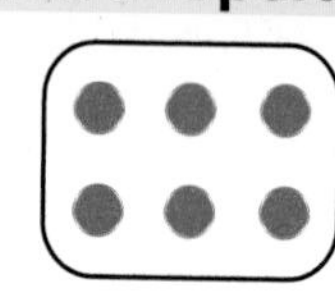

3 × 2 = 6    2 × 3 = 6

- When you change the order of the factors, the product stays the same.

**Property of One**

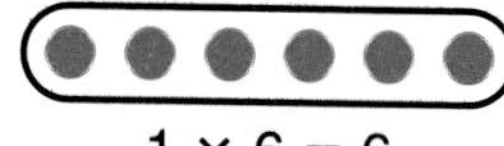

1 × 6 = 6

- When you multiply any number by 1, the product is equal to that number.

**Zero Property**

4 × 0 = 0

- When you multiply any number by 0, the product is 0.

**Associative Property**

- When you group factors in different ways, the product stays the same. The parentheses tell you which numbers to multiply first.

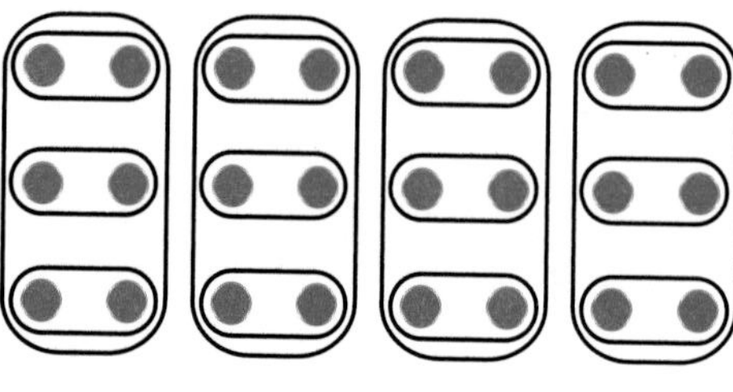

(3 × 2) × 4

6 × 4 = 24

**3 × (2 × 4)**

**3 × 8 = 24**

▶ Division rules can help you divide with 1 or 0.

## Division Rules

- When you divide a number by itself, the quotient is 1. This is true for all numbers except 0.

  $5 \div 5 = 1$ or $5\overline{)5}$ with quotient 1

- When you divide a number by 1, the quotient is the same as the dividend.

  $5 \div 1 = 5$ or $1\overline{)5}$ with quotient 5

- When you divide 0 by a number other than 0, the quotient is 0.

  $0 \div 5 = 0$ or $5\overline{)0}$ with quotient 0

- You cannot divide a number by 0.

## Guided Practice

**Use properties and rules to solve. If there is no solution, explain why.**

**1.** $1 \times 93 = \blacksquare$  **2.** $(2 \times \blacksquare) \times 4 = 16$  **3.** $9 \times (9 \times 0) = \blacksquare$

**4.** $0 \div 3 = \blacksquare$  **5.** $9 \div 9 = \blacksquare$  **6.** $4 \times \blacksquare = 0$

**7.** $8 \div 0 = \blacksquare$  **8.** $\blacksquare \times 1 = 18$  **9.** $11 \div \blacksquare = 1$

**Ask Yourself**

- Did I multiply what was in the parentheses first?
- Is 0 the dividend?

**Explain Your Thinking** ▶ Do you need to multiply $6 \times 9$ to find $(6 \times 9) \times 0$? Use multiplication properties to explain.

Go On

## Practice and Problem Solving

**Solve. Name the multiplication property you used.**

**10.** 1 × 4 = ■

**11.** 5 × 8 = ■ × 5

**12.** 0 × 72 = ■

**13.** 3 × 7 × 8 = 3 × ■ × 7

**14.** ■ × 1 = 5

**15.** 3 × 2 = ■ × 3

**16.** (3 × 2) × 4 = 3 × (■ × 4)

**17.** 8 × ■ = 0

**18.** (4 × ■) × ■ = 4

**Solve. Explain the division rule you used. If there is no solution, tell why.**

**19.** 0 ÷ 10 = ■

**20.** ■ ÷ 17 = 0

**21.** 12 ÷ ■ = 1

**22.** ■ ÷ 1 = 92

**23.** 12 ÷ 0 = ■

**24.** 10 ÷ 10 = ■

**Algebra • Properties** **Compare. Write >, <, or = in each ●.**

**25.** 6 ÷ 6 ● 6 ÷ 1

**26.** 7 ÷ 1 ● 6 ÷ 1

**27.** 0 ÷ 4 ● 4 ÷ 4

**28.** 0 ÷ 19 ● 0 ÷ 7

**29.** 8 ÷ 8 ● 0 ÷ 9

**30.** 24 ÷ 24 ● 692 ÷ 692

**31.** 15 × 1 ● 15 ÷ 1

**32.** 0 ÷ 63 ● 2 × (7 × 1)

**33.** 81 × (0 × 1) ● 0 ÷ 81

**Solve.**

**34.** When the product of two numbers is 0, what do you know about one of the numbers?

**35.** When the quotient of two numbers is 1, what do you know about the two numbers?

**36.** **Analyze** Miguel multiplied two non-zero numbers. The product was equal to one of the numbers. What was the other number? Use properties to explain your answer.

**37.** **Reasoning** Tiara is thinking of three whole numbers. The product of the three numbers is 8. Their sum is 7. What are the numbers? Explain how you got your answer.

## GPS Sharpening Skills for CRCT

**Open Response**

**Add or subtract.** (Ch. 3, Lessons 5–7)

**38.** 109 + 93

**39.** \$243 − \$66

**40.** 462 + 215

**41.** 750 − 172

**42.** \$6.08 − \$1.99

**43.** 586 + 709

**Multiple Choice**

**44.** Which is an example of the Zero Property of Multiplication?
(Ch. 4, Lesson 1)

A. 0 × 6 = 0

B. 6 × 1 = 6

C. 6 + 0 = 6

D. 6 × 6 = 36



Extra Practice See page 107, Set A.

## Game
## Mystery Number

STANDARDS M4N7.c

**Play this mystery number game with a partner.**

**Step 1:** Player 1 picks a two-digit "mystery number." Without showing Player 2, Player 1 enters that number into a calculator, presses ×, enters a one-digit number other than zero, and then presses =.

**Step 2:** Player 2 writes down the number shown on the calculator, and uses the number to try to guess the mystery number. If Player 2 guesses incorrectly, he or she must give the calculator back to Player 1. Player 1 then repeats steps 1 and 2, using the same mystery number but a different one-digit factor. Player 1 continues repeating the steps until Player 2 guesses the mystery number.

**Step 3:** Record the number of guesses made. Then switch roles. The player with the least number of guesses is the winner.

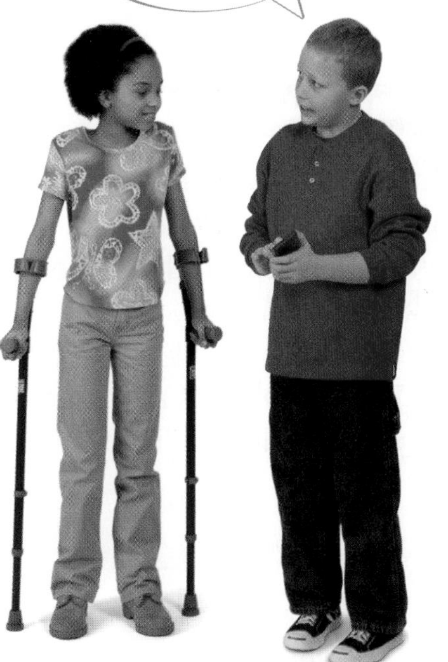


## Algebraic Thinking
## How Do They Relate?

**Complete each sentence.**

1. $3 \times 4$ is to $4 \times 3$ as $6 \times 7$ is to _____.
2. $0 \div 13$ is to 0 as _____ $\times 13$ is to 0.
3. $(4 \times 5) \times 7$ is to $4 \times (5 \times 7)$ as $(6 \times 8) \times 2$ is to _________.

## Brain Teaser

Choose digits from 0 to 9 to complete each problem.

**A.**

| | 1 | ■ | 3 |
|---|---|---|---|
| + | ■ | 2 | ■ |
| | 8 | 1 | 2 |

**B.**

| | 1, | ■ | 5 | ■ |
|---|---|---|---|---|
| + | | 4 | ■ | 6 |
| | 2, | 0 | 0 | 3 |

**C.**

| | | 4, | 5 | ■ | 3 |
|---|---|---|---|---|---|
| + | | 9, | ■ | 6 | ■ |
| | 1 | ■, | 6 | 3 | 1 |

**D.**

| | 8, | 0 | 4 | ■ |
|---|---|---|---|---|
| − | | 9 | ■ | 7 |
| | ■, | ■ | 4 | 6 |

**Education Place**

Check out **eduplace.com/map** for more Brain Teasers.

Lesson 2

 **Audio Tutor 1/12 Listen and Understand**

Algebra

# Relate Multiplication and Division

**Vocabulary**
- array
- fact family

**Objective** Use multiplication facts to help you divide.

**STANDARDS** M4N7.a

## Learn About It

A community theater stores hats on shelves. There are 15 hats arranged on 3 shelves with the same number of hats on each shelf.

A group of objects arranged in equal rows and columns like this is called an **array**.

You can write two multiplication number sentences about the array.

| 3 | × | 5 | = | 15 |
|---|---|---|---|---|
| ↑ rows | | ↑ hats in each row | | ↑ hats in all |
| 5 | × | 3 | = | 15 |
| ↑ columns | | ↑ hats in each column | | ↑ hats in all |

You can also write two division number sentences about the array.

| 15 | ÷ | 3 | = | 5 |
|---|---|---|---|---|
| ↑ hats in all | | ↑ rows | | ↑ hats in each row |
| 15 | ÷ | 5 | = | 3 |
| ↑ hats in all | | ↑ columns | | ↑ hats in each column |

Like addition and subtraction, multiplication and division are **inverse operations**. One operation undoes the other.

▶ The multiplication and division number sentences you can write using two factors and a product form a **fact family**. Fact families show how multiplication and division are related.

| Fact Family for 4, 6, and 24 | |
|---|---|
| $4 \times 6 = 24$ | $24 \div 4 = 6$ |
| $6 \times 4 = 24$ | $24 \div 6 = 4$ |



Extra Help at **eduplace.com/map**

## Guided Practice

- What are the factors?
- What is the product?

**Write the fact family for each array or set of numbers.**

1. 

2. ● ● ● ● ●
   ● ● ● ● ●

3. 4, 4, 16    4. 5, 6, 30    5. 3, 5, 15

**Explain Your Thinking ▶** Look back at Exercise 3. Why are there only 2 number sentences in the fact family?

## Practice and Problem Solving

**Write the fact family for each array or set of numbers.**

6. 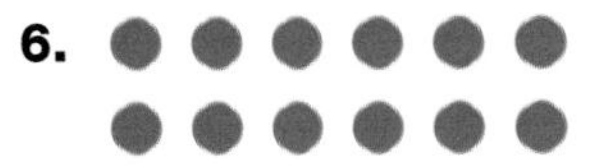

7. 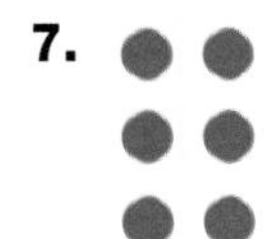

8. 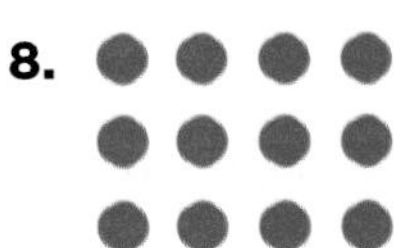

9. 3, 3, 9    10. 1, 10, 10    11. 4, 8, 32    12. 5, 8, 40

**Complete each fact family.**

13. $4 \times 6 = ■$    $■ \div 4 = 6$
    $6 \times ■ = 24$    $24 \div ■ = 4$

14. $8 \times ■ = 72$    $■ \div 8 = 9$
    $9 \times 8 = ■$    $■ \div 9 = ■$

**Algebra • Equations Use a related division sentence to find the missing number. Write the number sentence you used.**

15. $8 \times ■ = 64$    16. $■ \times 6 = 54$    17. $■ \times 9 = 81$    18. $7 \times ■ = 56$

19. $■ \times 9 = 45$    20. $7 \times ■ = 49$    21. $7 \times ■ = 63$    22. $■ \times 20 = 20$

23. Can you form a fact family using 2, 7, and 27? Explain why or why not.

24. There are 2 different fact families that contain 3 and 6. Write the 4 number sentences for each fact family.

## Sharpening Skills for CRCT

**Open Response**

**Write each number in expanded form.**
(Ch. 3, Lessons 5–8)

25. 742    26. 4,909

27. 65,015    28. 608,926

29. A theater group has 48 students. Two students drop out. Can the remaining students be arranged in 6 equal rows? (Ch. 4, Lesson 2)

Extra Practice See page 107, Set B.

Hands On Lesson 3

Algebra

# Patterns in Multiplication and Division

**Vocabulary**
square number
multiple

**Objective** Use multiplication facts to help you divide.

 **STANDARDS** M4N7.a, M4A1.a, M4P2

**Materials**
multiplication table
(Learning Tool 5)

## Work Together

You can use a multiplication table to multiply and discover patterns.

column ↓

| × | 0 | 1 | 2 | 3 | 4 | 5 | 6 | 7 | 8 | 9 |
|---|---|---|---|---|---|---|---|---|---|---|
| 0 | 0 | 0 | 0 | 0 | 0 | 0 | 0 | 0 | 0 | 0 |
| 1 | 0 | 1 | 2 | 3 | 4 | 5 | 6 | 7 | 8 | 9 |
| 2 | 0 | 2 | | | | 10 | | | | |
| 3 | 0 | 3 | | | | 15 | | | | |
| 4 | 0 | 4 | | | | 20 | | | | |
| 5 | 0 | 5 | | | | 25 | | | | |
| row → 6 | 0 | 6 | 12 | 18 | 24 | 30 | | | | |
| 7 | 0 | 7 | | | | | | | | |
| 8 | 0 | 8 | | | | | | | | |
| 9 | 0 | 9 | | | | | | | | |

↑ product

**STEP 1**

Use a table like the one shown.

Look across the row for 6 and down the column for 5 to find $6 \times 5$.

- What is the product?

Use this method to fill in the rest of the products in the table.

**STEP 2**

A **square number** is the product of two factors that are the same.

| $4 \times 4 = 16$, so 16 is a square number. |
|---|
| $7 \times 7 = 49$, so 49 is a square number. |

- Find the other square numbers in the table.
- Describe how you found them.

**STEP 3**

A **multiple** of a number is the product of that number and any whole number. The row for 6 shows the multiples of 6.

- List 5 multiples of 6 shown in the table.
- Where else can you find multiples of 6 in the table? Where can you find multiples of 8?

▶ You can also use a multiplication table to divide.

To find 40 ÷ 8, look down the column for 8 until you find 40. Follow that row to the left to find the quotient.

- What is the quotient of 40 ÷ 8?
- Use your table to find 21 ÷ 7. Describe how you found it.

| × | 0 | 1 | 2 | 3 | 4 | 5 | 6 | 7 | 8 |
|---|---|---|---|---|---|---|---|---|---|
| 0 | 0 | 0 | 0 | 0 | 0 | 0 | 0 | 0 | 0 |
| 1 | 0 | 1 | 2 | 3 | 4 | 5 | 6 | 7 | 8 |
| 2 | 0 | 2 | 4 | 6 | 8 | 10 | 12 | 14 | 16 |
| 3 | 0 | 3 | 6 | 9 | 12 | 15 | 18 | 21 | 24 |
| 4 | 0 | 4 | 8 | 12 | 16 | 20 | 24 | 28 | 32 |
| 5 | 0 | 5 | 10 | 15 | 20 | 25 | 30 | 35 | 40 |

Find the number 24 in four different places in the table. Write a division sentence for each 24 you find.

- How are your division sentences the same? How are they different?

## On Your Own

**Use your multiplication table to answer each question.**

1. Write a division sentence using a square number as the dividend. Write the fact family for the set of 3 numbers in your division sentence. Is there another division sentence that uses the same dividend and factors? Why or why not?

2. Find the product of 4 and 8 in two places in the table. Write two multiplication sentences using 4 and 8 as factors. What property do the number sentences show?

## Talk About It • Write About It

**You learned how to use patterns in a multiplication table to multiply and divide.**

3. **Analyze** Look at the multiples of 3 and 6 in the table. What do you notice? Why do you think this is true?

4. What division rule does the row for 0 show?

5. **Challenge** How could you extend the table to show multiples of 10?

Lesson 4

Audio Tutor 1/13 Listen and Understand

# Multiplication and Division Facts to Five

**Objective** Learn different ways to multiply and divide.

## Learn About It

STANDARDS M4N4.a, M4A1.b

Kerry Connolly belongs to an Irish step dance company. In one dance, there are 4 lines with 3 dancers in each line. How many dancers are there?

**Multiply.** $4 \times 3 = \blacksquare$ or $\begin{array}{r} 3 \\ \times\, 4 \\ \hline \end{array}$

### Different Ways to Find 4 × 3

**Way 1** Use skip counting.

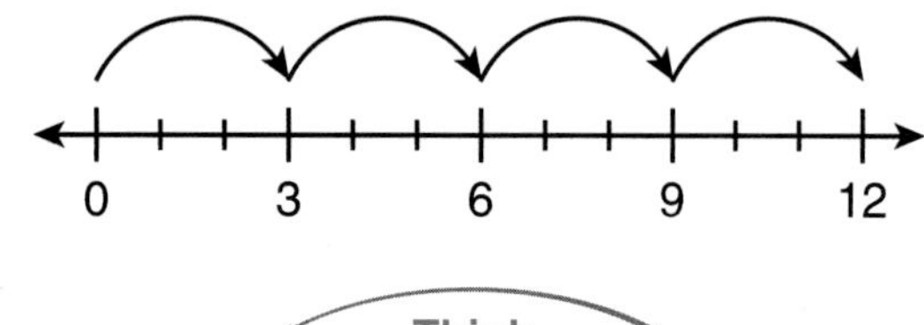


Think
3, 6, 9, 12
So $4 \times 3 = 12$.

**Way 2** Use doubles.

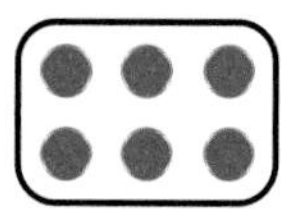
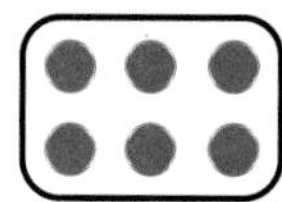

You know 4 is double 2 and $2 \times 3 = 6$.

Since $2 \times 3 = 6$

Then $4 \times 3 = 6 + 6$

$4 \times 3 = 12$

**Solution:** There are 12 dancers.

▶ You can also use different strategies to divide.

### Different Ways to Find 20 ÷ 4

**Way 1** Use repeated subtraction.

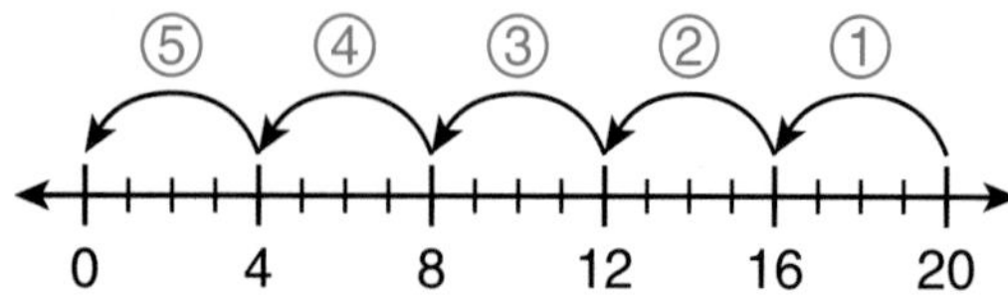


The number of 4s you subtract is the quotient.

So $20 \div 4 = 5$

**Way 2** Use a related multiplication fact.

$20 \div 4 = \blacksquare$

Think
$4 \times \blacksquare = 20$
$4 \times 5 = 20$

So $20 \div 4 = 5$.

## Guided Practice

**Multiply or divide. Use one of the methods shown.**

**1.** $6 \times 2$ **2.** $5 \times 4$ **3.** $5 \times 6$ **4.** $4 \times 4$

**5.** $2\overline{)10}$ **6.** $4\overline{)24}$ **7.** $18 \div 3$ **8.** $20 \div 5$

> **Ask Yourself**
> - Can I skip count or use doubles to multiply?
> - Can I use repeated subtraction or related facts to divide?

**Explain Your Thinking** ▶ How can knowing that $4 \times 4 = 16$ help you find $5 \times 4$?

## Practice and Problem Solving

**Multiply or divide. Show your work with a drawing.**

**9.** $3 \times 3$ **10.** $4 \times 2$ **11.** $4 \times 7$ **12.** $3 \times 8$ **13.** $4 \times 6$

**14.** $5\overline{)5}$ **15.** $5 \times 4$ **16.** $36 \div 4$ **17.** $45 \div 5$ **18.** $3 \times 7$

**Algebra • Equations** **Complete each number sentence.**

**19.** $4 \times$ ■ $= 0$ **20.** ■ $\times 3 = 18$ **21.** ■ $\times 2 = 18$ **22.** $5 \times$ ■ $= 35$

**23.** $30 \div$ ■ $= 6$ **24.** $25 \div$ ■ $= 5$ **25.** $27 \div 3 =$ ■ **26.** ■ $\div 5 = 8$

**Solve.**

**27.** **Multistep** Dancers' hair ribbons cost $5 a box. There are 8 ribbons in each box. How many ribbons can you buy for $15?

**28.** **Explain** Write and solve a multiplication number sentence for $5 + 5 + 5 + 5 =$ ■. Explain how you got your answer.

## GPS Sharpening Skills for CRCT

**Open Response**

**Order the numbers from least to greatest.** (Ch. 2, Lesson 2)

**29.** 23, 33, 32, 20 **30.** 522, 252, 325

**31.** 77, 71, 87, 18 **32.** 203, 320, 302

**Multiple Choice**

**33.** Which number sentence can help you find $32 \div 4$? (Ch. 4, Lesson 4)

A. $15 \div 3 = 5$ C. $32 - 4 = 28$

B. $8 \times 4 = 32$ D. $32 \times 1 = 32$

Lesson 5

# Multiplication and Division Facts to Ten

**Objective** Learn different methods to multiply and divide facts to ten.

 **STANDARDS** M4N4.a, M4P2

## Learn About It

An African theater company is putting on a puppet show using spider puppets. Each spider has 8 legs. How many legs do 6 spider puppets have altogether?

**Multiply.** $6 \times 8 = \blacksquare$ **or** $\begin{array}{r} 8 \\ \times\ 6 \\ \hline \end{array}$

### Different Ways to Find 6 × 8

**Way 1** **Use a known fact.**

You know $5 \times 8 = 40$ and $6 \times 8$ is one more group of 8.

Since $5 \times 8 = 40$
Then $6 \times 8 = 40 + 8$
$6 \times 8 = 48$

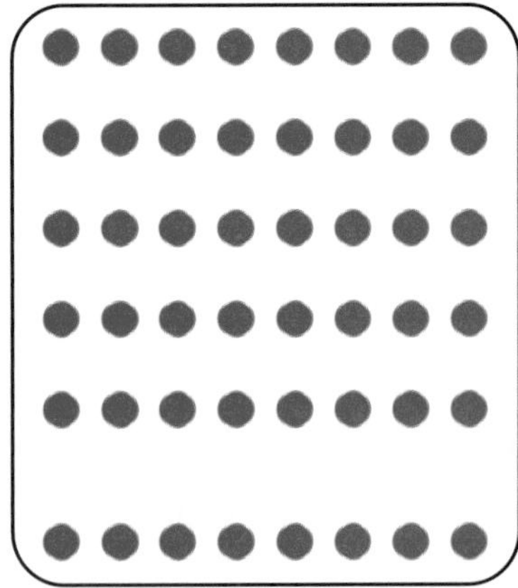

**Way 2** **Use doubles.**

You know 6 is double 3 and $3 \times 8 = 24$.

Since $3 \times 8 = 24$
Then $6 \times 8 = 24 + 24$
$6 \times 8 = 48$

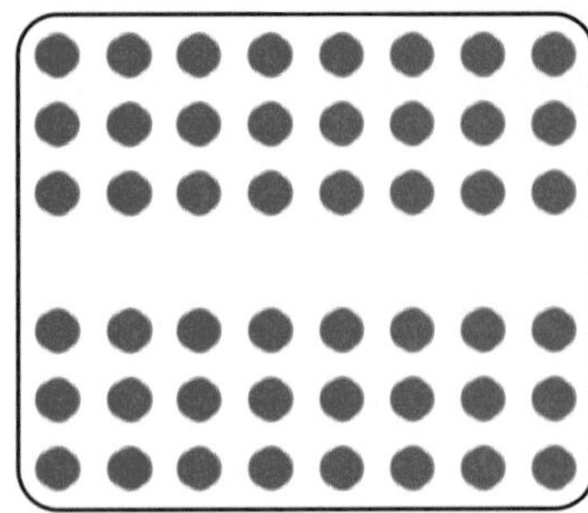

**Solution:** Six spider puppets have 48 legs.

▶ Omari is assembling spider puppets for the show. He has 24 spider legs. How many spider puppets can he make?

**Divide.** $24 \div 8 = ■$ or $8\overline{)24}$

## Different Ways to Find 24 ÷ 8

### Way 1 Use a related multiplication fact.

$24 \div 8 = ■$

Since $8 \times 3 = 24$

Then $24 \div 8 = 3$

Think
$8 \times ■ = 24$
$8 \times 3 = 24$

### Way 2 Use doubles.

8 is double 4, so 24 ÷ 8 will be half of 24 ÷ 4.

Since $24 \div 4 = 6$

Then $24 \div 8 = 6 \div 2$

$24 \div 8 = 3$

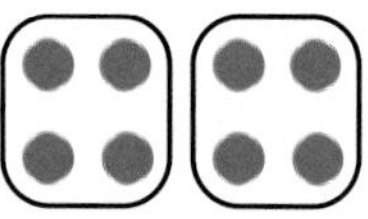
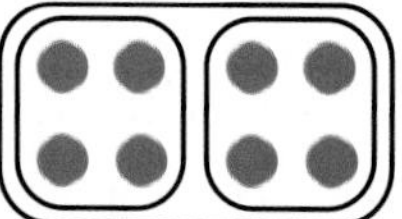
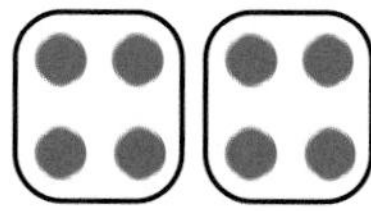

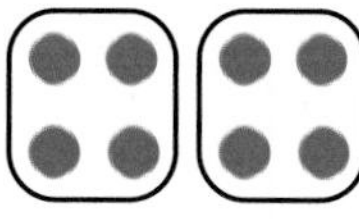
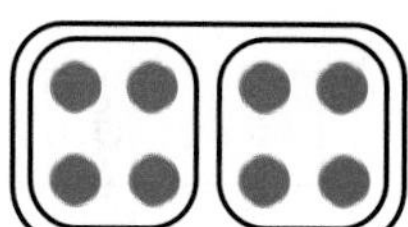

**24 ÷ 4 = 6** **24 ÷ 8 = 3**

### Way 3 Use a related division fact.

If you know $24 \div 3 = 8$

then you know $24 \div 8 = 3$.

**Solution:** Omari can assemble 3 spider puppets.

## Guided Practice

**Multiply or divide.**

1. $6 \times 6$
2. $7 \times 2$
3. $7 \times 5$
4. $6 \times 8$
5. $8\overline{)24}$
6. $6\overline{)54}$
7. $8\overline{)56}$
8. $10\overline{)70}$

**Ask Yourself**
- What strategy can I use to multiply?
- What strategy can I use to divide?

**Explain Your Thinking** ▶ How can knowing that $36 \div 6 = 6$ help you find $42 \div 6$?

Go On

## Practice and Problem Solving

**Multiply or divide.**

**9.** $8 \times 0$ **10.** $8 \times 6$ **11.** $6 \times 7$ **12.** $9 \times 7$ **13.** $7 \times 8$ **14.** $10 \times 8$

**15.** $6\overline{)6}$ **16.** $8 \times 9$ **17.** $40 \div 10$ **18.** $27 \div 9$ **19.** $40 \div 8$ **20.** $8\overline{)16}$

**21.** $6 \times 8$ **22.** $9 \times 3$ **23.** $35 \div 7$ **24.** $10 \times 8$ **25.** $63 \div 7$ **26.** $42 \div 6$

**Compare. Write >, <, or = in each ●.**

**27.** $16 \div 2$ ● $24 \div 3$ **28.** $10 \times 3$ ● $9 \times 3$ **29.** $80 \div 10$ ● $81 \div 9$

**30.** $10 \times 4$ ● $6 \times 7$ **31.** $32 \div 4$ ● $8 \times 1$ **32.** $18 \div 2$ ● $90 \div 10$

## Algebra • Functions **Complete each table.**

| | Rule: Multiply by 8 | |
|---|---|---|
| | **Input** | **Output** |
| **33.** | 4 | ■ |
| **34.** | 6 | ■ |
| **35.** | ■ | 56 |
| **36.** | ■ | 80 |

| | Rule: Divide by 7 | |
|---|---|---|
| | **Input** | **Output** |
| **37.** | ■ | 4 |
| **38.** | 14 | ■ |
| **39.** | 42 | ■ |
| **40.** | ■ | 9 |

**41.**

| Rule: ________ | |
|---|---|
| **Input** | **Output** |
| 9 | 3 |
| 24 | 8 |
| 27 | 9 |
| 12 | 4 |

## Data **Use the graph for Problems 42–46.**

**42.** How many tickets did the children in Room C sell?

**43.** How many more tickets did Room B sell than Room A?

**44.** Write 2 number sentences to show the number of tickets sold by Room B.

**45.** **Money** Tickets cost $5. What is the cost of the tickets sold by Room A?

**46.** **Analyze** Suppose Room D sold 36 tickets. How would you show this on the graph? Explain your answer.

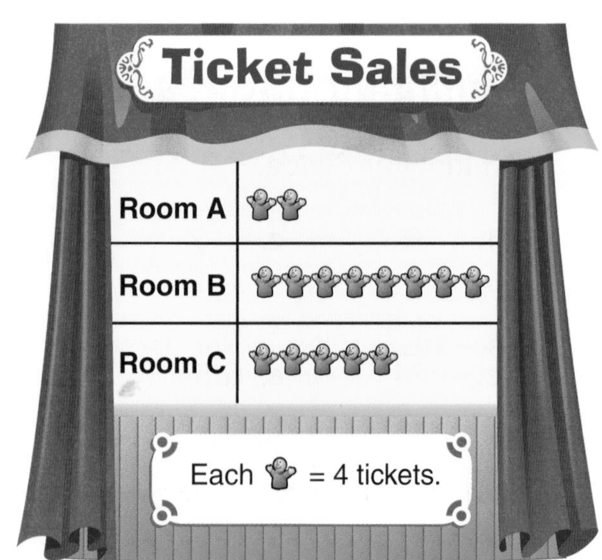




Extra Practice See page 107, Set C.

Problem Solving

GPS

# Math Reasoning
## Common Multiples

**STANDARDS** M4N4.a,
Prepares for M5N1.b

**You can use multiples to solve problems.**

What is the least number of packages of hot dogs and rolls that you can buy to have the same number of hot dogs and rolls?

- Make two tables as shown.

| Packages | 1 | 2 | 3 | 4 | 5 | 6 | 7 | 8 | 9 | 10 |
|---|---|---|---|---|---|---|---|---|---|---|
| Hot Dogs | 10 | 20 | 30 | **40** | 50 | 60 | 70 | **80** | 90 | 100 |

| Packages | 1 | 2 | 3 | 4 | 5 | 6 | 7 | 8 | 9 | 10 |
|---|---|---|---|---|---|---|---|---|---|---|
| Rolls | 8 | 16 | 24 | 32 | **40** | 48 | 56 | 64 | 72 | **80** |

- Look for common numbers in the second row of both tables. Since you want the least number and $40 < 80$, choose 40.
- To find the answer, look above the 40 in each table.

You will need to buy 4 packages of hot dogs and 5 packages of rolls.

**Find how many bags of each kind of balloon you need to buy to get the same number of each.**

**1.** Small balloons: 6 in each bag
Medium balloons: 5 in each bag

**2.** Red balloons: 12 in each bag
Blue balloons: 8 in each bag

## Quick Check

**Check your understanding of Lessons 1–5.**

**Use properties and rules to solve. If there is no solution, explain why.** (Lesson 1)

**1.** $1 \times 27 = \blacksquare$

**2.** $\blacksquare \div 0 = 2$

**3.** $(4 \times 3) \times 3 = 4 \times (\blacksquare \times 3)$

**Write the fact family for each set of numbers.** (Lesson 2)

**4.** 7, 9, 63

**5.** 4, 4, 16

**6.** 10, 6, 60

**Multiply or divide.** (Lessons 3–5)

**7.** $4\overline{)36}$

**8.** $6 \times 7$

**9.** $10 \times 7$

**10.** $56 \div 8$

**Materials**
multiplication table
(Learning Tool 6)

# Multiply and Divide With 11 and 12

**Objective** Use a multiplication table to multiply and divide with 11 and 12.

## Work Together

 **STANDARDS** M4N3, M4N4.a, M4P3

You can use a multiplication table and patterns to multiply and divide with 11 and 12.

**STEP 1** Use a multiplication table like the one shown.

- What pattern do you see in the row and column for 10?

| × | 0 | 1 | 2 | 3 | 4 | 5 | 6 | 7 | 8 | 9 | 10 | 11 | 12 |
|---|---|---|---|---|---|---|---|---|---|---|---|---|---|
| **0** | 0 | 0 | 0 | 0 | 0 | 0 | 0 | 0 | 0 | 0 | 0 | | |
| **1** | 0 | 1 | 2 | 3 | 4 | 5 | 6 | 7 | 8 | 9 | 10 | | |
| **2** | 0 | 2 | 4 | 6 | 8 | 10 | 12 | 14 | 16 | 18 | 20 | | |
| **3** | 0 | 3 | 6 | 9 | 12 | 15 | 18 | 21 | 24 | 27 | 30 | | |
| **4** | 0 | 4 | 8 | 12 | 16 | 20 | 24 | 28 | 32 | 36 | 40 | | |
| **5** | 0 | 5 | 10 | 15 | 20 | 25 | 30 | 35 | 40 | 45 | 50 | | |
| **6** | 0 | 6 | 12 | 18 | 24 | 30 | 36 | 42 | 48 | 54 | 60 | | |
| **7** | 0 | 7 | 14 | 21 | 28 | 35 | 42 | 49 | 56 | 63 | 70 | | |
| **8** | 0 | 8 | 16 | 24 | 32 | 40 | 48 | 56 | 64 | 72 | 80 | | |
| **9** | 0 | 9 | 18 | 27 | 36 | 45 | 54 | 63 | 72 | 81 | 90 | | |
| **10** | 0 | 10 | 20 | 30 | 40 | 50 | 60 | 70 | 80 | 90 | 100 | | |
| **11** | | | | | | | | | | | | | |
| **12** | | | | | | | | | | | | | |

**STEP 2** Now fill in the table for the 11 row and column.

- How can you use the 10 facts to find the 11 facts?
- How can you use patterns to find the 11 facts?

**STEP 3** Fill in the table for the 12 row and column.

- How can you use the 11 facts to find the 12 facts?
- How can you use the 6 facts to find the 12 facts?

## Practice and Problem Solving

**Divide.**

**9.** $4\overline{)6}$ **10.** $2\overline{)9}$ **11.** $5\overline{)12}$ **12.** $2\overline{)17}$ **13.** $4\overline{)23}$

**14.** 50 ÷ 7 **15.** 15 ÷ 2 **16.** 33 ÷ 9 **17.** 49 ÷ 5 **18.** 18 ÷ 6

**19.** $6\overline{)16}$ **20.** $12\overline{)100}$ **21.** $8\overline{)32}$ **22.** $3\overline{)23}$ **23.** $2\overline{)25}$

**24.** 69 ÷ 7 **25.** 44 ÷ 9 **26.** 101 ÷ 9 **27.** 39 ÷ 6 **28.** 20 ÷ 4

**Find each missing number.**

**29.** 3 ÷ ■ → 1 R 1 **30.** 9 ÷ 4 → 2 R ■ **31.** 26 ÷ 9 → 2 R ■

**32.** 15 ÷ 3 → ■ **33.** ■ ÷ 8 → 2 R 4 **34.** 125 ÷ 11 → ■ R 4

**35.** 34 ÷ ■ → 4 R 2 **36.** ■ ÷ 7 → 4 **37.** 150 ÷ ■ → 12 R 6

**38.** Suppose 9 acrobats each balance 5 sets of candles. Are 46 sets of candles enough for all the acrobats? Will there be any sets left over?

**39.** Mrs. Kim bought 2 adult tickets for $7 each and one senior ticket for $5 to an acrobat show. She paid with a $20 bill. What was her change?

**40.** **What's Wrong?** After the show, Chang packs 53 glasses into boxes. He says he can divide them evenly into 8 boxes. Use a division sentence to explain why he is wrong.

## Sharpening Skills for CRCT

**Open Response**

**Add or subtract.** (Ch. 3, Lessons 5–8)

**41.** 267 + 324 **42.** $3.52 − $1.09

**43.** $678 + $491 **44.** 701 − 645

**45.** $\begin{array}{r} \$72.79 \\ +\ \$13.21 \\ \hline \end{array}$ **46.** $\begin{array}{r} 6{,}005 \\ -\ 953 \\ \hline \end{array}$

**47.** Is this division example correct? If not, explain why not and then correct it. (Ch. 4, Lesson 8)

$$\begin{array}{r} 5\text{ R }6 \\ 6\overline{)36} \\ -\ 30 \\ \hline 6 \end{array}$$

Extra Practice See page 107, Set E.

Lesson 9

**Audio Tutor 1**/15 Listen and Understand

# Problem-Solving Decision

## Choose the Operation

**Objective** Decide what operations to use to solve problems.

**STANDARDS** M4N7.a, M4P1.c, M4P1.d

**You need to use different operations depending upon what question is asked.**

Ian the Great can juggle 6 rings in each hand at the same time! He has 4 assistants who can juggle several bowling pins at the same time. Ian has 20 juggling rings and 12 bowling pins.

| **Sometimes you add to find the total.**<br>How many pieces of juggling equipment does Ian have?<br>20 + 12 = 32 pieces | **You can multiply to find the total if you have equal groups.**<br>How many rings can Ian juggle at the same time?<br>6 × 2 = 12 rings |
|---|---|
| **You subtract to find the difference.**<br>How many more juggling rings than bowling pins does Ian the Great have?<br>20 − 12 = 8 more rings | **You divide to find equal groups.**<br>Suppose each assistant juggles the same number of bowling pins. How many pins does each assistant juggle?<br>12 ÷ 4 = 3 bowling pins |

## Try These

**Solve. Explain why you chose each operation.**

1. Ian's 4 assistants have 16 juggling balls. If they each juggle an equal number of balls, how many balls does each assistant juggle?

2. Manuela can juggle 5 rings. Carl can juggle 3 rings. Ian can juggle 12 rings. How many more rings can Ian juggle than Manuela and Carl together?

3. Ian needs to buy more juggling equipment. He buys 3 packages of juggling balls. Each package contains 5 balls. How many balls did he buy?

4. Ian's assistants can each juggle 3 rings or 5 balls at a time. Ian wants them to juggle a total of 15 balls. How many assistants does he need?

Problem Solving

GPS

# Math Challenge
## Exponents

STANDARDS Prepares for a future grade.

Becca decided to start a jogging routine last month. The first week, she ran 2 miles. Each week after that, she doubled the distance that she ran. How many miles could Becca run by the 4th week?

On the 4th week, Becca ran **2 × 2 × 2 × 2 miles**, or **16 miles**.

What is an easy way to write the product of **2 × 2 × 2 × 2**? You can write the product as an exponent. **2 × 2 × 2 × 2** written as an exponent is $2^4$. This number is read as "two to the fourth power." So, Becca ran $2^4$ miles last month.

- The **base** is the number that is being multiplied.
- The **exponent** shows the number of times that the base is used as a factor. In this case, the base 2 was multiplied by itself 4 times, so the exponent is 4.

exponent
$2^4$
base

Here are some more examples of exponents:
$3 \times 3 \times 3 = 3^3$ (Three to the third power)
$8 \times 8 \times 8 \times 8 \times 8 = 8^5$ (Eight to the fifth power)

**Look at the table below. Use what you know about exponents to fill in the missing information.**

| Expression | Exponent | Spoken form |
|---|---|---|
| 2 × 2 | $2^2$ | Two to the second power |
| | $5^3$ | |
| 6 × 6 × 6 × 6 | | |
| | | Four to the fourth power |
| | $3^8$ | |
| 7 × 7 × 7 × 7 × 7 | | |
| | | Eight to the third power |

Choose an exponent from the table above. Write an example of how that exponent might be used in a real-world situation.

# Chapter Review/Test

Study Guide pages SG12, SG22, SG25

## VOCABULARY

**Choose the best term to complete each sentence.**

1. You can find 7 × 0 = ■ using the ____.
2. 3 × 4 = 4 × 3 is an example of the ____.
3. 6 × 6 = 36 and 36 ÷ 6 = 6 are a ____.
4. The number left after you divide is called the ____.

**Vocabulary**

- fact family
- remainder
- Commutative Property
- Zero Property
- Property of One

## CONCEPTS AND SKILLS

**Use properties and rules to solve. If there is no solution, tell why.** (Lesson 1, pp. 84–86)

5. 9 ÷ ■ = 9
6. 0 × 84 = ■
7. (5 × 3) × 2 = 5 × (■ × 2)

**Write the fact family for each set of numbers.** (Lesson 2, pp. 88–89)

8. 3, 6, 18
9. 3, 4, 12
10. 2, 8, 16

**Multiply or divide.** (Lessons 3–8, pp. 90–103)

11. 5 × 3
12. $4\overline{)32}$
13. (9 × 6) × 2
14. 65 ÷ 6
15. 12 × 7
16. 2 × 4 × 6
17. $7\overline{)80}$
18. 25 ÷ 4

## PROBLEM SOLVING

**Solve.** (Lesson 9, pp. 104–105)

19. Jina has 12 stuffed bears. Her sister has half as many. How many bears does Jina's sister have?
20. Vanna reads for 10 minutes every night. Pete reads 3 times as long every night. How many more minutes does Pete read than Vanna each night?

**Write About It**

**Show You Understand**

Don has 12 coins in his coin collection. How many different rectangular arrays can he make with the coins?

Draw the arrays. Then explain how you found them.

# Extra Practice

## Set A (Lesson 1, pp. 84–87)

**Use properties and rules to solve. If there is no solution, tell why.**

**1.** $4 \times 9 = ■ \times 4$  **2.** $4 \div 4 = ■$  **3.** $0 \div 6 = ■$

**4.** $5 \times (6 \times 4) = (5 \times 6) \times ■$  **5.** $5 \div 0 = ■$  **6.** $■ \times 16 = 0$

## Set B (Lesson 2, pp. 88–89)

**Write the fact family for each set of numbers.**

**1.** 2, 3, 6  **2.** 3, 7, 21  **3.** 4, 9, 36  **4.** 5, 8, 40

**5.** 7, 4, 28  **6.** 3, 6 ,18  **7.** 4, 2, 8  **8.** 8, 8, 64

## Set C (Lessons 4–5, pp. 92–93, 94–97)

**Multiply or divide.**

**1.** $3 \times 3$  **2.** $30 \div 5$  **3.** $7 \times 4$  **4.** $4\overline{)32}$  **5.** $24 \div 6$

**6.** $7 \times 10$  **7.** $9\overline{)63}$  **8.** $8 \times 6$  **9.** $7 \times 9$  **10.** $9\overline{)90}$

**11.** $5 \times 6$  **12.** $80 \div 8$  **13.** $9 \times 4$  **14.** $8\overline{)72}$  **15.** $32 \div 4$

## Set D (Lesson 7, pp. 100–101)

**Find each product.**

**1.** $7 \times 6 \times 2$  **2.** $5 \times 6 \times 2$  **3.** $(4 \times 5) \times 2$  **4.** $(9 \times 3) \times 4$

**5.** $7 \times 3 \times 3$  **6.** $10 \times (2 \times 4)$  **7.** $5 \times (3 \times 2)$  **8.** $8 \times 7 \times 1$

## Set E (Lesson 8, pp. 102–103)

**Divide.**

**1.** $3\overline{)19}$  **2.** $6\overline{)61}$  **3.** $4\overline{)15}$  **4.** $3\overline{)37}$  **5.** $9\overline{)103}$

**6.** $7\overline{)51}$  **7.** $6\overline{)41}$  **8.** $8\overline{)94}$  **9.** $9\overline{)85}$  **10.** $5\overline{)63}$

**11.** $11\overline{)121}$  **12.** $9\overline{)98}$  **13.** $8\overline{)60}$  **14.** $6\overline{)53}$  **15.** $12\overline{)100}$

Extra Practice at **eduplace.com/map**

# Algebraic Reasoning

## INVESTIGATION

### Using Data

Some animals spend most of their day sleeping! The table shows the average number of hours some animals sleep in a 24-hour period. Myra wrote the following number sentence using the data in the table:

$n = 19 \times 3$

What fact do you think Myra's number sentence might show?

**Snoozing Animals**

| Name of Animal | Average Amount of Sleep Per Day |
|---|---|
| Gerbil | 13 hours |
| Koala | 20 hours |
| Opossum | 19 hours |
| Squirrel | 15 hours |
| Tiger | 16 hours |

# Use What You Know

**Use this page to review and remember what you need to know for this chapter.**

## VOCABULARY

**Choose the best term to complete each sentence.**

1. The number sentence $3 \times 5 = 5 \times 3$ is an example of the ____.
2. The ____ tells you the product of 0 and 218.
3. The number sentence $(2 \times 4) \times 5 = 2 \times (4 \times 5)$ is an example of the ____.

### Vocabulary

**Associative Property**
**Commutative Property**
**Zero Property**
**Property of One**

## CONCEPTS AND SKILLS

**Find the missing number.**

4. ■ + 6 = 11
5. 15 + ■ = 18
6. ■ + 22 = 45
7. 19 + ■ = 63
8. 6 × ■ = 30
9. ■ × 8 = 0
10. 7 × ■ = 63
11. ■ × 8 = 96
12. ■ − 14 = 6
13. 17 − ■ = 13
14. 45 ÷ ■ = 9
15. ■ ÷ 3 = 12

**Copy and complete each table.**

| | Rule: Add 6 | |
|---|---|---|
| | **Input** | **Output** |
| | 3 | 9 |
| 16. | 5 | ■ |
| 17. | 8 | ■ |
| 18. | ■ | 15 |

| | Rule: Subtract 8 | |
|---|---|---|
| | **Input** | **Output** |
| 19. | ■ | 11 |
| | 22 | 14 |
| 20. | 35 | ■ |
| 21. | 47 | ■ |

| | Rule: Divide by 7 | |
|---|---|---|
| | **Input** | **Output** |
| | 21 | 3 |
| 22. | 42 | ■ |
| 23. | ■ | 5 |
| 24. | 56 | ■ |

**Write About It**

25. Explain why you can multiply two factors in any order. Draw a picture to support your explanation.

Facts Practice, See page 668.

Lesson 1

 **Audio Tutor 1/16** Listen and Understand

Algebra

# Order of Operations

**Objective** Use the order of operations to simplify expressions.

**Vocabulary**
- expression
- order of operations
- parentheses

## Learn About It

STANDARDS M4N7.b

The Sea Turtle Patrol in Florida helps protect green-turtle nests. One turtle made 3 nests on the beach. Three other turtles each made 4 nests. Then 1 nest was destroyed in a storm. How many nests were left?

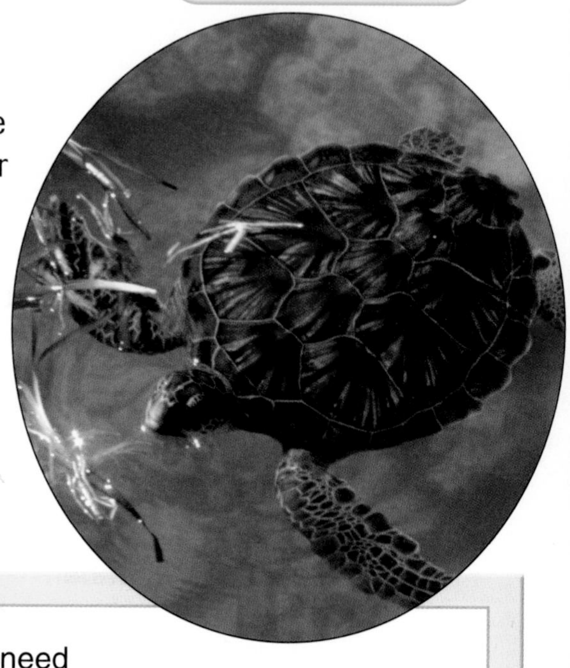

You can write an expression to solve the problem. An **expression** is a number or group of numbers with operation symbols.

$3 + (3 \times 4) - 1$ is an expression that shows the number of nests that were left.

To simplify or find the value of $3 + (3 \times 4) - 1$, you need to follow the rules for the **order of operations**.

**Order of Operations**
- First, do operations inside the **parentheses** ( ).
- Then do multiplication and division in order from left to right.
- Finally, do addition and subtraction in order from left to right.

$3 + (3 \times 4) - 1$

$3 + 12 - 1$ ← There is no more multiplication or division.

$15 - 1$

$14$

**Solution:** There were 14 nests left.

### Other Examples

**A. Simplify $12 \times (4 - 2)$.**

$12 \times (4 - 2)$ First, work inside parentheses.

$12 \times 2$ Then multiply.

$24$

**B. Simplify $14 + 10 \div 2 \times 3$.**

$14 + 10 \div 2 \times 3$ Multiply and divide left to right.

$14 + 5 \times 3$

$14 + 15$ Then add.

$29$

## Guided Practice

**Ask Yourself**

- Are there parentheses?
- Which operation should I do first?

**Simplify. Follow the order of operations.**

1. $(14 - 7) + 3$
2. $(5 + 2) \times 3$
3. $6 + 12 \div 3$
4. $27 \div 9 - 1$

**Explain Your Thinking** ▶ Does $48 - (16 - 6)$ equal $(48 - 16) - 6$? Why or why not?

## Practice and Problem Solving

**Simplify. Follow the order of operations.**

5. $42 \div 7 \div 2$
6. $8 + 12 \div 4$
7. $8 \times (5 + 2)$
8. $3 \times 9 - 3 + 1$
9. $3 \times (9 - 3) + 1$
10. $15 \div 5 \times 8 - 4$

**Copy the expression. Then insert parentheses to make the expression equal 24.**

11. $13 - 1 \times 2$
12. $4 + 2 \times 4$
13. $6 + 6 \times 2$
14. $3 \times 11 - 3$
15. $8 \times 8 - 5$
16. $2 + 2 + 2 \times 4$

**Solve.**

17. Write this expression four times.

    $8 + 12 \div 4 \times 3 - 2$

    Add one set of parentheses to each expression to get different answers.

18. **Multistep** Two pails of turtle eggs hold 8 eggs each. There are 4 more pails of eggs with 10 eggs in each pail. Find the total number of eggs in the pails.

19. **Explain** There are 20 hatchlings, or baby green turtles, in a nest. If two groups of 5 hatchlings leave the nest, how many are left? How did you get your answer?

## Sharpening Skills for CRCT

**Open Response**

**Round each number to the nearest hundred. Then estimate.** (Ch. 3, Lesson 3)

20. $943 + 512$
21. $872 - 543$
22. $5,109 + 2,286$
23. $3,679 - 1,882$

24. Jamie simplified $15 - 3 + 9$ and got 3. What mistake did he make? What is the correct answer? Explain. (Ch. 5, Lesson 1)

Extra Practice See page 131, Set A.

Lesson 2

Audio Tutor 1/17 Listen and Understand

Algebra

# Words Into Expressions

**Objective** Use variables to write expressions.

**Vocabulary**
variable
evaluate

STANDARDS M4A1.c

## Learn About It

Many people have worked to help endangered grizzly bears in the wilderness areas of Yellowstone National Park. Suppose a park ranger saw 2 cubs in each of the dens she found. How many cubs did she see?

Since you don't know how many dens she found, you can use a **variable** to stand for that number and write an expression.

**Remember**
An expression is a number or group of numbers with operation symbols.

- Let $n$ stand for the number of dens. ← You may choose any letter or symbol for the variable.
- Then express the number of cubs.
  $2 \times n$ or $2 \cdot n$ or $2n$ ← You read all these expressions as "2 times $n$."

**Solution:** The ranger saw $2n$ cubs.

▶ Now suppose the ranger found 3 dens. How many bear cubs did she find?

**Evaluate $2n$ when $n = 3$.**

| STEP 1 Write the expression. |  STEP 2 Replace $n$ with 3. |  STEP 3 Simplify the expression. |
|---|---|---|
| $2n$ | $2n$<br>$2 \times 3$ | $2n$<br>$2 \times 3$<br>6 |

**Solution:** If the ranger found 3 dens, she found 6 cubs.

▶ Which expression matches these words?

The ranger saw 2 more cubs this week than last week.

**$2y$** **$y - 2$** **$y \div 2$** **$y + 2$**

Let the variable $y$ stand for the number of cubs the ranger saw last week.

- $2y$ means twice the number seen last week.
- $y - 2$ means 2 less than the number seen last week.
- $y \div 2$ means half the number seen last week.
- $y + 2$ means 2 more than the number seen last week.

**Solution:** The expression $y + 2$ matches the words.

## Guided Practice

**Ask Yourself**

- What is the variable?
- Do I add, subtract, multiply, or divide to write the expression?

**Choose the expression that matches the words. Let *p* stand for the number of bears.**

1. 5 more than the number of bears

   **a.** $5p$ **b.** $5 - p$ **c.** $5 + p$ **d.** $p \div 5$

2. half as many bears

   **a.** $p \div 2$ **b.** $2p$ **c.** $p - 2$ **d.** $p + 2$

3. three times the number of bears

   **a.** $p + 3$ **b.** $p - 3$ **c.** $3p$ **d.** $p \div 3$

**Evaluate each expression when $n = 6$.**

**4.** $5n$ **5.** $n \div 3$ **6.** $4n$ **7.** $n + 7$ **8.** $43 - n$

**9.** $n - 4$ **10.** $15 - n$ **11.** $12 \div n$ **12.** $10n$ **13.** $n + 35$

**Explain Your Thinking** ▶ When writing an expression, how do you know when to use a variable?

Go On

## Practice and Problem Solving

**Write the expression. Let $n$ stand for the number of bear cubs seen yesterday.**

14. 5 fewer cubs than seen yesterday
15. 3 more cubs than seen yesterday
16. half as many cubs as seen yesterday
17. four times the number seen yesterday

**Evaluate each expression when $p = 7$.**

18. $11p$
19. $p - 7$
20. $2 \times p + 5$
21. $0 + p$
22. $9 - p$
23. $28 + p$
24. $2p \div 7$
25. $3p + 1$
26. $7p - 4$
27. $6 + 2p$
28. $70 - 2p$
29. $4p \div 4$

**Match each statement with the correct expression.**

30. When $n$ is 6, the value of this expression is 2.
31. When $n$ is 2, the value of this expression is 8.
32. When $n$ is 10, the value of this expression is 5.
33. When $n$ is 6, the value of this expression is 8.

a. $n - 4$
b. $n \div 2$
c. $n + 2$
d. $4n$

**Write an expression for each problem. Choose your own variables.**

34. There are 3 more bear dens this year than last year. How many bear dens are there this year?
35. Bob and Joe collect animal figures. Bob has half as many figures as Joe. How many figures does Bob have?
36. On Saturday, 572 more people visited the zoo than on Friday. How many people visited the zoo on Saturday?
37. Kendi has 5 times as many wildlife books as mysteries. She gives 3 wildlife books away. How many wildlife books does she have now?

## Sharpening Skills for CRCT

### Open Response

**Find each product.** (Ch. 4, Lesson 7)

**38.** $5 \times 9 \times 1$ **39.** $6 \times 7 \times 0$

**40.** $3 \times 2 \times 8$ **41.** $3 \times 3 \times 7$

**42.** $4 \times 3 \times 2$ **43.** $2 \times 5 \times 6$

### Multiple Choice

**44.** Which expression means "three less than ■"? (Ch. 5, Lesson 2)

A. 3 − ■ C. 3 + ■

B. ■ − 3 D. ■ ÷ 3

# Expression Match-up

Game Activity

**2 Players**

**STANDARDS** M4A1.c

What You'll Need • 16 Index Cards (Learning Tool 9)

### How to Play

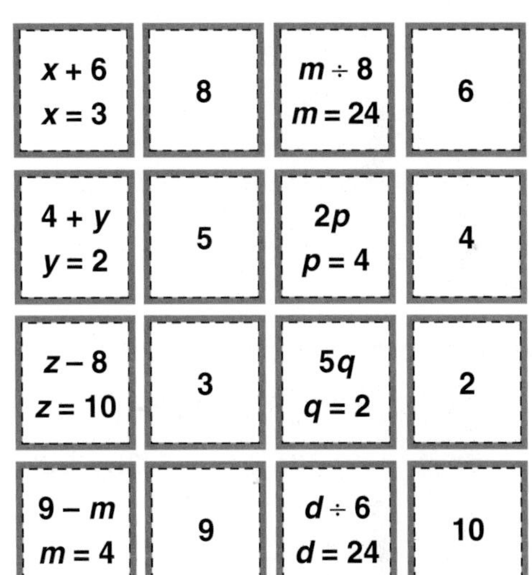


1. Make 16 cards like the ones shown.
2. Shuffle the cards. Place them face-down in any order in a 4 × 4 array.
3. A player turns over any two cards. If the cards show an expression and its value, the player keeps both cards. If not, the player turns the cards face-down in the same positions.
4. Players take turns repeating Step 3 until all 8 matches have been made. The player with the greater number of cards is the winner.

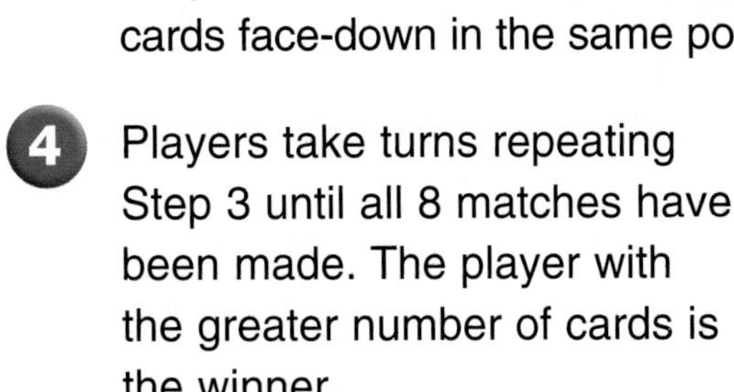
Create your own Expression Match-up game. Make 16 cards—8 with expressions, and 8 with the value of each expression. Challenge a pair of classmates.

Extra Practice See page 131, Set B.

Lesson 3

Algebra

# Compare Expressions

**Objective** Use variables to compare expressions.

 **STANDARDS** M4A1.c

**Vocabulary**

equal
equation
inequality

## Learn About It

One morning, two giant pandas ate the same amount of bamboo. In the afternoon, the male panda ate 15 pounds of bamboo. The female panda ate a total of 44 pounds of bamboo during the morning and afternoon. Which panda ate less?

Let $b$ = the amount the male panda ate in the morning.

male panda → $b + 15$ ⬬ $44$ ← female panda

You can compare these expressions if you know the value of $b$. Let's suppose the value of $b$ is 22. Let $b = 22$.

**STEP 1** Evaluate the expression, $b + 15$. Substitute 22 for $b$.

$b + 15$ ⬬ $44$

$22 + 15$ ⬬ $44$

$37$ ⬬ $44$

**STEP 2** Compare the expressions.

$37$ ⬬ $44$

$37 < 44$, so $b + 15 < 44$

**Solution:** If $b$ equals 22, the male panda ate less.

- Expressions are **equal** if they have the same value. When equal expressions are connected by an equal sign (=), they form an **equation**.
- When expressions are not equal, they form an **inequality**. The symbols $>$, $<$, and $\neq$ show an inequality.

| Remember | |
|---|---|
| $=$ | is equal to |
| $\neq$ | is not equal to |
| $>$ | is greater than |
| $<$ | is less than |

### Another Example Evaluate and Compare

Let's suppose the value of $b$ is 29.

Evaluate the expression $b + 15$. $b + 15$ ⬬ $44$

Substitute 29 for $b$. $29 + 15$ ⬬ $44$

Compare the expressions. $44$ ⬬ $44$

$44 = 44$, so $b + 15 = 44$ when $b = 29$

## Guided Practice

**Copy and compare. Let $n = 5$. Write = or ≠ for each ⬬.**

1. $25 \div n$ ⬬ $5$
2. $2n$ ⬬ $10 - n$
3. $20 + n$ ⬬ $5 \times 5$
4. $n + 6$ ⬬ $3n - 7$

**Ask Yourself**

- What is the value of the variable?
- What symbol makes the sentence true?

**Explain Your Thinking** ▶ Compare $2h + 3$ and $16 - 3$ when $h = 5$. Explain your answer.

## Practice and Problem Solving

**Copy and compare. Let $y = 3$. Write = or ≠ for each ⬬.**

5. $6 + (14 - 8)$ ⬬ $(14 - 8) + y$
6. $(14 - 7) \times y$ ⬬ $(9 \times y) - 1$
7. $(15 - 9) \div y$ ⬬ $(18 \div 6) + y$
8. $(y + 9) \times 1$ ⬬ $44 - (4 \times 8)$

**Copy and compare. Write >, <, or = for each ⬬.**

9. $8 + (16 \div 4)$ ⬬ $2 \times 9$
10. $38 + (24 + 9)$ ⬬ $38 - (24 + 9)$
11. $(23 - 10) + 7$ ⬬ $23 - (10 + 7)$
12. $6 \times (8 - 3)$ ⬬ $(4 - 1) \times 10$

**Compare the expressions. Write *equal* or *not equal* for each.**

13. $24$ and $(3 \times 9) - 4$
14. $15 + 1$ and $7 + (3 \times 3)$
15. $56 \div 8$ and $19 - (2 \times 6)$
16. $64 \div (2 \times 4)$ and $27 \div 3$

**Solve.**

17. The expression $2p + 2$ represents the weight of one panda cub. The weight of a second panda cub is $p + 10$. If $p$ is 3 pounds, which panda cub weighs more?
18. **Multistep** One panda is 3 years older than a second panda. The second panda is 2 years older than a third one. Write expressions to show the ages of the first two pandas if the third one is 5 years old.

## Sharpening Skills for CRCT

**Open Response**

**Find each product.** (Ch. 4, Lesson 7)

19. $2 \times 5 \times 9$
20. $2 \times 4 \times 3$
21. $7 \times 1 \times 8$
22. $3 \times 2 \times 3$

23. Write *true* or *false* for the expressions compared below. Explain your answer. (Ch. 5, Lesson 3)

$12 + (3 \times 2) = 6 \times 3$

Extra Practice See page 131, Set C.

Lesson 4

**Audio Tutor 1/18 Listen and Understand**

Algebra

# Variables and Equations

**Objective** Write and solve equations.

**STANDARDS** M4A1.a, M4P2, Prepares for M5A1.a

## Learn About It

Volunteers knit tiny wool sweaters to help penguins affected by oil spills. Lynn knit 4 more sweaters than Eva. Lynn knit 7 sweaters altogether. How many sweaters did Eva knit?

You can write an equation to solve this problem. Every equation has an equals sign to show that both expressions are equal.

Let the variable $s$ stand for the number of sweaters Eva knit. Then write and solve this equation: $s + 4 = 7$.

This expression shows that Lynn knit 4 more sweaters than Eva. → $s + 4 = 7$ ← This expression shows the total number of sweaters Lynn knit.

**Solve $s + 4 = 7$.**

### Different Ways to Solve $s + 4 = 7$

**Way 1 Use an addition fact.**

$s + 4 = 7$

$s = 3$

Think
$3 + 4 = 7$
So $s$ must be 3.

**Way 2 Use inverse operations.**

$s + 4 = 7$

$s + 4 - 4 = 7 - 4$ ← Subtract 4 from each side.

$s = 3$

**Check the solution.**

$s + 4 = 7$

$3 + 4 = 7$ ← Substitute 3 for $s$.

$7 = 7$

Both sides of the equals sign are the same, so the solution is correct.

**Solution:** Eva knit 3 sweaters.

Other volunteers clean oil from the penguins. Max cleaned 4 times the number of penguins that Sara did. Max cleaned 40 penguins. How many penguins did Sara clean?

Let the variable $p$ stand for the number of penguins Sara cleaned. Then write and solve this equation: $4p = 40$.

This expression shows that Max cleaned 4 times the number of penguins Sara cleaned. → $4p = 40$ ← This expression shows the total number of penguins Max cleaned.

**Solve $4p = 40$.**

## Different Ways to Solve $4p = 40$

**Way 1** **Use a related multiplication fact.**

$4p = 40$
$p = 10$

Think
$4 \times 10 = 40$
So $p$ must be 10.

**Way 2** **Use inverse operations.**

$4p = 40$
$p \times 4 \div 4 = 40 \div 4$ ← Divide each side by 4.
$p = 10$

**Solution:** Sara cleaned 10 penguins.

| Remember to Use Inverse Operations | |
|---|---|
| If the problem has addition, use subtraction to solve. | $s + 4 = 7$<br>$s + 4 - 4 = 7 - 4$<br>$s = 3$ |
| If the problem has subtraction, use addition to solve. | $t - 5 = 11$<br>$t - 5 + 5 = 11 + 5$<br>$t = 16$ |
| If the problem has multiplication, use division to solve. | $4p = 40$<br>$p \times 4 \div 4 = 40 \div 4$<br>$p = 10$ |
| If the problem has division, use multiplication to solve. | $v \div 6 = 3$<br>$v \div 6 \times 6 = 3 \times 6$<br>$v = 18$ |

Go On

## Guided Practice

**Match each equation with its solution.**

**1.** $n + 6 = 10$ **a.** $n = 12$

**2.** $9 = n - 3$ **b.** $n = 4$

**3.** $5n = 30$ **c.** $n = 6$

**Ask Yourself**

- What related fact can I use?
- Did I substitute the solution for the variable in the equation to check?

**Explain Your Thinking** ▶ If you multiply or divide equal expressions by the same number, will the expressions remain equal? Give examples to support your thinking.

## Practice and Problem Solving

**Solve each equation. Check the solution.**

**4.** $m + 10 = 35$ **5.** $7n = 42$ **6.** $r - 7 = 43$ **7.** $5 = s \div 3$

**8.** $6m = 18$ **9.** $r \div 7 = 7$ **10.** $m + 12 = 20$ **11.** $13 = k - 1$

**12.** $6 + y = 12$ **13.** $27 = 9n$ **14.** $63 \div a = 9$ **15.** $12 + 5 = d$

**Match each equation with the words that describe it. Then solve.**

**16.** $20 = 10 + m$ **a.** Three times a number is 15.

**17.** $10 - m = 6$ **b.** Twenty is 10 more than the number.

**18.** $3m = 15$ **c.** A number divided by 2 is 8.

**19.** $m \div 2 = 8$ **d.** A number subtracted from 10 is 6.

**Solve.**

**20.** **Analyze** Oliver made 7 sweaters. This is half as many as Sam made. How many sweaters did Sam make? Write and solve an equation to find the answer.

**21.** **Multistep** Tony has packed 27 sweaters and has 45 more to pack. A box holds 8 sweaters. Write an equation to find how many boxes Tony needs to pack all the sweaters. Then solve the equation.

Extra Practice See page 131, Set D.

Problem Solving

GPS

# Visual Thinking

## Balance Equations

STANDARDS M4A1.c

**Use the picture below to find the weight of one cat.**

- First, remove a bird from each side. The sides still balance because equal weights were removed from each side.
- Let $c$ stand for 1 cat. Let $d$ stand for 1 dog. Write an equation: $d = 2c$.

If the dog weighs 16 pounds, what does 1 cat weigh?

**Write an equation for each picture. Let $b$ = the weight of a ball and $c$ = the weight of a can. Solve for $c$ if $b$ = 10 lb.**

**1.**

**2.**

Quick Check

Check your understanding for Lessons 1–4.

**Simplify. Follow the order of operations.** (Lesson 1)

**1.** $6 + 7 \times 2$

**2.** $(12 - 7) \times 7$

**3.** $18 \div (12 - 9)$

**Evaluate each expression when $h$ = 3.** (Lesson 2)

**4.** $3h + 5$

**5.** $13 - h$

**6.** $21 \div h + 4$

**Copy and compare. Write >, <, or = for each ●.** (Lesson 3)

**7.** $3 \times (4 + 5)$ ● $35 - 8$

**8.** $16 \div 4 + 3$ ● $5 \times (8 - 6)$

**Solve each equation. Check the solution.** (Lesson 4)

**9.** $4x = 20$

**10.** $18 - x = 12$

Extra Practice at **eduplace.com/map**

**Lesson 5**

# Problem-Solving Strategy

## Write an Equation

**Objective** Write equations to represent and solve problems.

**STANDARDS** M4P1.b, Prepares for M5A1.a

**Problem** On Adopt-a-Pet Day, Teva adopted two cats. She paid a total of $22 for the adoption fees and rabies shots. If the rabies shots were $6 per cat, how much was each adoption fee?

**This is what you know.**

- Two cats were adopted.
- The total fees were $22.
- Rabies shots were $6 per cat.

PLAN

**Write an equation.**

You can write an equation to help you solve the problem.

SOLVE

**Choose variables and solve.**

- Let *a* stand for the adoption fee for one cat.

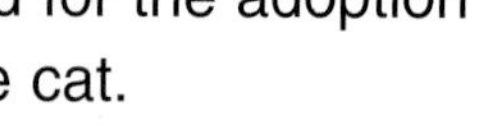

$$22 = (2 \times a) + (2 \times 6)$$

↑ total fees ↑ adoption fees for 2 cats ↑ rabies shots for 2 cats

- Solve the equation.

$$22 = 2a + 12$$
$$22 - 12 = 2a + 12 - 12$$
$$10 = 2a$$
$$10 \div 2 = 2a \div 2$$
$$5 = a$$

**Solution:** Each adoption fee was $5.

LOOK BACK

**Check if the equation is true.**

Substitute $5 for *a* in the equation. Are both expressions equal?

## Guided Practice

**Use the Ask Yourself questions to help you solve each problem.**

1. Puppies are exercised 15 minutes longer than adult dogs. Puppies are exercised 45 minutes daily. Write and solve an equation to find the number of minutes that an adult dog is exercised daily.

2. Amy bought 1 cat toy and 5 large cans of cat food. She paid $14 in all. The cat toy cost $4. Write and solve an equation to find the cost of 1 can of cat food.

**Hint** How can you show the cost of the food without the toy?

### Ask Yourself

**UNDERSTAND** — **What facts do I know?**

**PLAN** — **Can I write an equation?**

**SOLVE** — **What does the variable represent?**

**LOOK BACK** — **If I substitute my solution for the variable, are both expressions equal?**

## Independent Practice

**Write an equation to solve each problem.**

3. A student volunteer group has 38 members. Twenty-five of the members are boys. How many members are girls?

4. David has 10 pets. All his pets are either fish or hamsters. He has two more fish than hamsters. How many hamsters does David have?

5. There are twice as many cats as dogs in a kennel. The kennel has 21 animals. If there are only cats and dogs, how many cats are there?

6. A shelter has 7 poodles, 5 beagles, and 12 retrievers. The other dogs are mixed breed. There are 40 dogs. How many are mixed breed?

Go On

# Mixed Problem Solving

**Solve. Show your work. Tell what strategy you used.**

**You Choose**

**Strategy**
- Draw a Picture
- Find a Pattern
- Guess and Check
- Use Logical Reasoning
- Write an Equation

**Computation Method**
- Mental Math
- Estimation
- Paper and Pencil
- Calculator

7. A large flowerpot costs \$5 more than a medium pot. A medium pot costs \$4 more than a small pot. A small pot costs \$2. If you buy one of each size pot, what will the total cost be?

8. **Multistep** Use the digits 5, 2, 8, and 3 to make the greatest 4-digit number. Then use the same digits to make the least 4-digit number. What is the difference?

9. A scarf has 13 stripes. The first stripe is red. The second stripe is blue. The third stripe is white. Then the pattern is repeated. What color is the last stripe?

## Data Use the target to solve Problems 10–14.

10. Two of Megan's 5 darts landed in the inner circle. Her last 3 darts landed in the outer ring. What was her score?

11. Yuri scored 165 using 4 darts. Two darts landed in the outer ring. One dart landed in the inner circle. Where did his last dart land?

12. Using 4 darts, what is the greatest score possible? If all darts land on the target, what is the least score possible?

13. Where can 4 darts land to give a score of 180?

14. **Create and Solve** Write a word problem about the target. Then give it to a classmate to solve.

# Problem Solving on CRCT

Multiple Choice

**Choose the letter of the correct answer.**

1. Which numbers are NOT in order from greatest to least?

   A. 5,784 5,449 5,198 5,099
   B. 7,039 6,999 6,689 6,679
   C. 8,057 8,051 8,055 8,050
   D. 9,483 9,238 948 923

(Chapter 2, Lesson 2)

2. Mrs. Shu buys one of each state key ring. What is the total cost?

**$4.60** **$4.00** **$2.40**

   A. $6.40
   B. $8.60
   C. $10.00
   D. $11.00

(Chapter 3, Lesson 2)

Open Response

**Solve each problem.**

3. Mr. James will bake muffins for the 22 students in his class. Each muffin pan holds 6 muffins. How many pans of muffins will he bake?

   **Explain** Will Mr. James have any muffins left over? How did you decide?

(Chapter 8, Lesson 8)

4. Lee's height is represented by the expression $3h + 8$. Lee's friend Sam is 2 inches taller than Lee.

   **Represent** Write an expression to represent Sam's height. Then use $>$, $<$, or $=$ to compare Lee's height and Sam's height.

(Chapter 5, Lessons 2–3)

5. Joan is planning a block party. Use the chart to help Joan plan what to buy.

**Package Sizes**

| Item | Number in Package |
|---|---|
| Hot dogs | 8 |
| Hot dog rolls | 12 |
| Hamburgers | 10 |
| Hamburger buns | 6 |

   a. 32 people want hot dogs. How many packages of hot dogs should Joan buy?

   b. Joan has 3 packages of hot dog rolls. Should she buy more? If so, how many? Explain how you found your answer.

   c. Joan needs at least 24 hamburgers. She wants to buy the same number of hamburgers and hamburger buns. What is the fewest number of hamburgers and buns that she can buy?

(Chapter 4, Lesson 5)

**Education Place**

See **eduplace.com/map** for more Test-Taking Tips.

Lesson 6

Algebra

# Function Tables

**Objective** Relate equations to function tables.

 **STANDARDS** M4A1.a

**Vocabulary**
function table

## Learn About It

Mr. Webb works part-time for a wildlife conservation group. He earns \$8 an hour. Suppose Mr. Webb works 4 hours. How much will he earn?

Use a function table to solve the problem.

In the function table at the right, the input shows the number of hours, $h$, and the output shows how much Mr. Webb earns, $e$.

A **function table** is a table of ordered pairs that follow a rule. The rule lets you find the value of one variable if you know the value of the other.

The rule for this function table is multiply by 8, or $8h = e$. This means you multiply the number of hours ($h$) Mr. Webb works by 8 to find how much he earns ($e$).

| Rule: $8h$ = e | | |
|---|---|---|
| Input ($h$) | Output (e) | |
| 1 | 8 | ← $1 \times 8$ |
| 2 | 16 | ← $2 \times 8$ |
| 3 | 24 | ← $3 \times 8$ |
| 4 | 32 | ← $4 \times 8$ |

$8 \times h = e$

Substitute 4 for $h$. → $8 \times 4 = 32$

**Solution:** Mr. Webb will earn \$32.

### Another Example

**Use Earnings to Find Hours**

Suppose Mr. Webb earns \$72. How many hours did he work?

$8 \times h = e$

$8 \times h = 72$ ← Substitute 72 for $e$.

$h = 72 \div 8$ ← Divide to find a missing factor.

$h = 9$

Mr. Webb worked 9 hours.

*Wild turkeys were once almost extinct, but thanks to conservationists, there are now about 5,400,000 of them.*

## Guided Practice

**Write the rule for each function table.**

**1.**

| Rule: ______ | |
|---|---|
| Input ($a$) | Output ($b$) |
| 4 | 1 |
| 5 | 2 |
| 7 | 4 |

**2.**

| Rule: ______ | |
|---|---|
| Input ($m$) | Output ($n$) |
| 9 | 11 |
| 15 | 17 |
| 18 | 20 |

**Ask Yourself**

- Does my rule work for every pair of numbers in the table?

**Explain Your Thinking** ▶ If another row was added to the function table in Exercise 2, what could the input and output be? Explain how you know.

## Practice and Problem Solving

**Copy and complete each function table or rule.**

| | Rule: $b = a + 4$ | |
|---|---|---|
| | Input ($a$) | Output ($b$) |
| **3.** | 6 | ■ |
| **4.** | 3 | ■ |
| **5.** | 2 | ■ |

| | Rule: $q = p \times 6$ | |
|---|---|---|
| | Input ($p$) | Output ($q$) |
| **6.** | 4 | ■ |
| **7.** | 8 | ■ |
| **8.** | ■ | 54 |

**9.**

| Rule: ______ | |
|---|---|
| Input ($x$) | Output ($y$) |
| 21 | 3 |
| 63 | 9 |
| 77 | 11 |

**Solve.**

**10.** Dan worked 7 hours a day helping to save wild turkeys. Make a function table to show how many hours he worked in 1 day, 5 days, 8 days, and 10 days. Write an equation to show the rule.

**11. Create and Solve** Ms. Rose earns $9 an hour. Write a problem that can be answered by using this information and a function table. Ask a classmate to solve the problem.

## Sharpening Skills for CRCT

**Write >, <, or = for each ⬬.** (Ch. 2, Lesson 1)

**12.** 7 + 8 ⬬ 9 + 6

**13.** 9 − 7 ⬬ 5 − 2

**14.** 5 + 9 ⬬ 18 − 3

| **15.** | Rule: ______ | |
|---|---|---|
| | Input ($m$) | Output ($n$) |
| | 7 | 35 |
| | 9 | 45 |
| **16.** | ■ | 55 |

Extra Practice See page 131, Set E.

Lesson 7

# Problem-Solving Decision

## Explain Your Solution

**Objective** Explain your solution.

 **STANDARDS** M4N7.a, M4P2

**Problem** One Asian elephant weighs 4,875 pounds. An African elephant weighs 5,672 pounds more. About how much does the African elephant weigh? Explain your solution.

When you are asked to explain a solution, you should explain every step of your thinking.

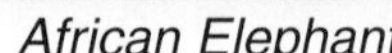

*African Elephant*

*Asian Elephant*

### ▶ Denise explained her solution with a picture.

I needed an estimate, so I rounded the numbers before adding. The long rectangle shows the total weight of the African elephant. You can see you need to add the amounts. The solution is about 5,000 + 6,000 or 11,000 pounds.

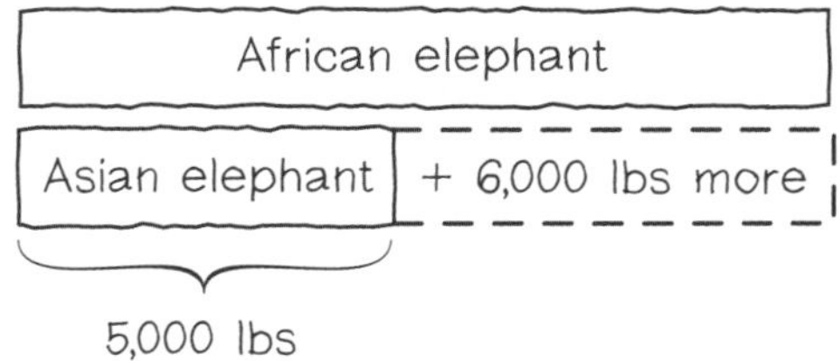


### ▶ Paul explained his solution by labeling his work.

The African elephant weighs more, so I knew I needed to add. The word "about" told me to find an estimate. First, I rounded each addend to the nearest thousand. Then I added the numbers. My answer is about 11,000 pounds.

4,875 rounds to 5,000 lbs
5,672 rounds to + 6,000 lbs
11,000 lbs

Are both explanations good? Tell why or why not.

## Try These

**Solve. Explain your solution.**

1. Elephants have 4 molars. One molar can weigh 5 pounds. In a lifetime, many elephants have 6 sets of molars. How many molars is that?
2. A sanctuary for endangered Asian elephants was founded in 1995 in Hohenwald, Tennessee. How many years ago was that?

GPS Activity

# Algebraic Thinking
## Always, Sometimes, or Never

STANDARDS M4N7.c

**Write *always, sometimes,* or *never* to answer each question.**

You can use the properties of multiplication to solve problems, even when you don't have all the information.

1. When does the value of $m + 1$ equal $m$?

2. When does the value of $3p$ equal the value of 0 times $p$?

3. When does the value of $n + 0$ equal the value of $0 + n$?

4. When does the value of $x + 1$ equal the value of $x - 1$?

5. When does the value of $r + 5$ equal the value of $5 + r$?

6. When does the value of $z$ equal the value of $2z$?

7. When does the value of $2 \times (b + 4)$ equal the value of $2 \times b + 4$?

8. When does the value of $2a$ equal the value of $3a$?

9. Write three questions about the value of variables. The answer to your questions should be *always*, *sometimes*, and *never*.

# Chapter Review/Test

Study Guide pages SG23, SG43

## VOCABULARY

**Choose the correct term to complete each sentence.**

**Vocabulary**
- variable
- equation
- inequality
- order of operations

1. A letter that stands for a number is a ____.
2. A mathematical sentence with an equals sign is an ____.
3. The rule that says to do the operations in parentheses first is the ____.

## CONCEPTS AND SKILLS

**Simplify. Follow the order of operations.** (Lesson 1, pp. 110–111)

4. $13 - (3 \times 3)$
5. $2 + (5 \times 3)$
6. $2 \times 6 \div 3 + 9$

**Evaluate each expression when $n = 8$.** (Lesson 2, pp. 112–115)

7. $9n$
8. $n \div 2$
9. $n + 24$
10. $63 - n$

**Compare. Write >, <, or = for each ●.** (Lesson 3, pp. 116–117)

11. $(64 \div 8) \times 3$ ● $100 - 67$
12. $3 \times (6 + 5)$ ● $(3 \times 6) + (3 \times 5)$
13. $25 + (36 - 9)$ ● $(25 + 36) - 9$
14. $5 \times (72 \div 8)$ ● $(6 \times 3) + 36$

**Solve each equation. Then check the solution.** (Lesson 4, pp. 118–121)

15. $p + 12 = 75$
16. $9n = 63$
17. $x - 16 = 98$
18. $6 = y \div 8$

## PROBLEM SOLVING

**Solve.** (Lessons 5, 7, pp.122–124, 128)

19. One ticket cost $10. The total cost was $60. Write an equation to show how to find the number of tickets bought.
20. On Friday, 1,976 people visited a zoo. On Monday, 786 people visited. About how many more people visited on Friday? Explain your solution.

**Write About It**

### Show You Understand

Explain how to decide if the rule is correct. Then copy and complete the function table.

| Rule: $2x + 4 = y$ | |
|---|---|
| Input ($x$) | Output ($y$) |
| 4 | 12 |
| 9 | ■ |
| ■ | 26 |

# Extra Practice

## Set A (Lesson 1, pp. 110–111)

**Simplify. Follow the order of operations.**

1. $(3 \times 9) + 8$
2. $16 \div (2 \times 4)$
3. $20 - 5 \times 2$
4. $3 \times 4 \div 2$
5. $3 + 4 \div 2$
6. $8 + 12 \div 4$
7. $(21 \div 3) \times 2$
8. $9 \times (8 \div 4)$

## Set B (Lesson 2, pp. 112–115)

**Evaluate each expression when $x = 5$.**

1. $x - 0$
2. $4x$
3. $2x + 39$
4. $52 - x$
5. $45 \div x$
6. $20 \div x$
7. $6 \times (4 + x)$
8. $x + 43$
9. $x + 9 \div 3$
10. $x + 4x$

## Set C (Lesson 3, pp. 116–117)

**Compare. Let $y = 4$. Write = or ≠ for each ⬬.**

1. $6y$ ⬬ 28
2. $63 - y$ ⬬ 51
3. $3y + 7$ ⬬ 19
4. $28 \div y$ ⬬ 7

## Set D (Lesson 4, pp. 118–120)

**Solve each equation. Then check the solution.**

1. $3x = 15$
2. $y + 5 = 19$
3. $m - 3 = 16$
4. $n \div 7 = 6$
5. $y + y = 10$

## Set E ( Lesson 6, pp. 126–127)

**Copy and complete each function table or rule.**

| | Rule: $y = x + 5$ | |
|---|---|---|
| | Input ($x$) | Output ($y$) |
| | 3 | 8 |
| 1. | ■ | 11 |
| 2. | 2 | ■ |
| 3. | 8 | ■ |

| | Rule: $y = 3x$ | |
|---|---|---|
| | Input ($x$) | Output ($y$) |
| | 5 | 15 |
| 4. | 6 | ■ |
| 5 | 7 | ■ |
| 6. | ■ | 24 |

7.

| Rule: ________ | |
|---|---|
| Input ($x$) | Output ($y$) |
| 10 | 2 |
| 15 | 3 |
| 20 | 4 |
| 25 | 5 |

Extra Practice at **eduplace.com/map**

# Super Sprinters

During the 1996 Summer Olympic Games in Atlanta, two runners broke three Olympic records and one world record on the track.

On July 29, 1996, Michael Johnson of the USA set an Olympic record in the 400-meter run. Three days later, he set an Olympic record *and* a world record when he won the men's 200-meter run. He became the first man to win both races in the same Olympics.

Defending her Olympic title from 1992, Marie-José Pérec of France set an Olympic record in the 400-meter run. On the same day that Michael Johnson set his world record, Pérec won the woman's 200-meter run. She became the second woman to win both events at a single Olympics and the first runner to win the 400-meter Olympic event twice.

## Problem Solving

**Use this table showing the runners' winning times for Problems 1 and 2.**

| **Winning Times** | | |
|---|---|---|
| **Runner** | **Distance (in meters)** | **Time (to nearest second)** |
| Michael Johnson | 200 | 19 |
| Marie-José Pérec | 200 | 22 |
| Michael Johnson | 400 | 43 |
| Marie-José Pérec | 400 | 48 |

1. Estimate how long it would take Michael Johnson to run 600 meters at his record-breaking speed. About how long would it take Marie-Jose Pérec to run the same distance?

2. Suppose Johnson ran an equal distance for each second of his races. Estimate how far he ran in 1 second.

3. Use the table on the right to estimate how long it would take an Olympic gold medalist to run 800 and 1,000 meters. Complete the table and write an expression to show the rule you used.

| **Men's Olympic Records** | |
|---|---|
| **Distance *d* (in meters)** | **Time *t* (to nearest second)** |
| 100 | 10 |
| 200 | 19 |
| 400 | 43 |
| 800 | |
| 1000 | |

# Enrichment: Finding Unknowns

**STANDARDS** M4A1.b, M4P3

# Symbols

In math, **symbols** can stand for numbers and operation signs. Symbols can be all sorts of shapes.

Look at the number sentences below. Symbols have been used to represent the unknown numbers.

| $25 \div$ ■ $=$ ■ | ■ $\times$ ▲ $= 40$ |
|---|---|
| Each symbol represents the same number, so ■ must equal 5. | Since ■ equals 5, then ▲ must equal 8. |

## Try These!

Write and solve an equation for each. Let ◆ stand for tubes of paint in the store and ● stand for paintbrushes in the store.

1. A store manager ordered 78 tubes of paint. This is 3 times the number of tubes already in the store. How many tubes of paint were already in the store?

2. The store manager checked the supplies and found that there were 15 fewer paintbrushes than tubes of paint in the store. How many total paintbrushes were in the store?

3. The store manager finished ordering supplies by solving the following problem. What did the store manager want to find out?

   ● + ★ = 78 + 26
   11 + ★ = 104
   ★ = 93

# I Need Some Order!

STANDARDS M4N7.b

You know how to follow the order of operations but your calculator may not. To see if your calculator follows the order of operations, press:

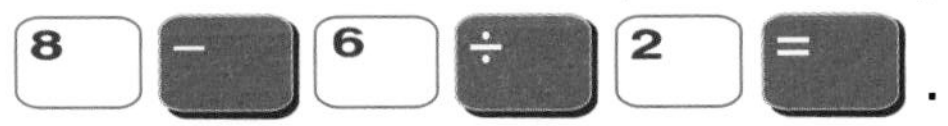

.

| Does your display look like this? | Does your display look like this? |
|---|---|
|   |   |
| That means your calculator divided and then subtracted. So, it followed the order of operations. | That means your calculator subtracted and then divided. So, it did **not** follow the order of operations. |

If your calculator does not follow the order of operations, you must enter the numbers in the correct order yourself.

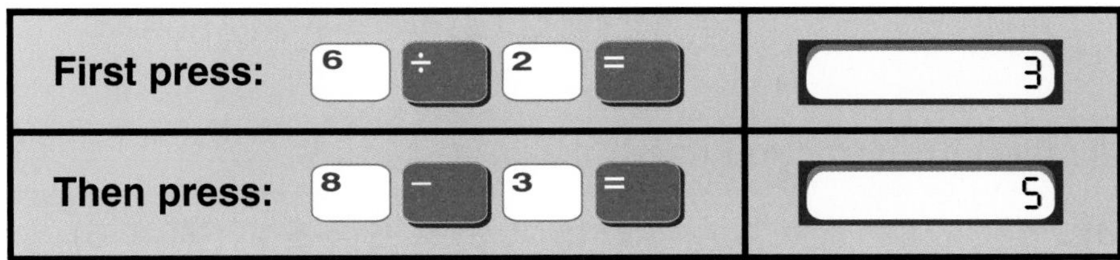

| | |
|---|---|
| **First press:** 6 ÷ 2 = | 3 |
| **Then press:** 8 − 3 = | 5 |

**Use your calculator to simplify each expression.**

**1.** 6 + (15 − 3 ) × 4 **2.** 8 − 20 ÷ (4 + 1) **3.** (7 + 9) − 12 ÷ 2

**Write operation signs in the ■ and place parentheses to make these number sentences true. Use your calculator to help you.**

**4.** 35 ■ 2 ■ 3 = 7
35 ■ 2 ■ 3 = 11

**5.** 24 ■ 8 ■ 4 = 6
24 ■ 8 ■ 4 = 2

**6.** 32 ■ 8 ■ 6 = 4
32 ■ 8 ■ 6 = 16

**7.** 27 ■ 6 ■ 3 = 9
27 ■ 6 ■ 3 = 11

**8.** 7 ■ 3 ■ 9 = 90
7 ■ 3 ■ 9 = 36

**9.** 6 ■ 3 ■ 7 = 63
6 ■ 3 ■ 7 = 21

# Unit 2 Test

Study Guide pages SG8–9, SG12, SG22–27, SG43

## VOCABULARY Open Response

**Choose the correct term to complete each sentence.**

1. A letter or symbol that stands for an unknown value in an expression is a ____.
2. The property that states that the order of factors does not change the product is the ____.
3. The property that states that when you multiply any number by 0, the product is 0, is called the ____.

**Vocabulary**

- variable
- equation
- Commutative Property
- Zero Property

## CONCEPTS AND SKILLS Open Response

**Complete each number sentence. Tell which addition property you used.** (Chapter 3)

4. $54 + 78 = ■ + 54$
5. $154 + 0 = ■$
6. $(89 + 11) + 32 = 89 + (■ + 32)$

**Find each sum or difference.** (Chapter 3)

7. 3, 400 + 201
8. 7, 906 − 804
9. 180,009 − 123,923
10. 450,189 + 312,809

**Solve. Tell which multiplication property you used.** (Chapter 4)

11. $3 \times 9 = 9 \times ■$
12. $54 \times 0 = ■$
13. $(5 \times 2) \times 6 = 5 \times (■ \times 6)$

**Solve.** (Chapter 4)

14. $11 \times ■ = 99$
15. $12 \times 7 = ■$
16. $■ \div 31 = 0$
17. $21 \div ■ = 1$

**Simplify. Use the correct order of operations.** (Chapter 5)

18. $(3 + 9) \times 3$
19. $32 - 5 \times 2 + 8$
20. $10 - (3 \times 2)$
21. $1 + (5 \times 7) - 9$
22. $4 + 15 \div 5 + 2$
23. $2 \times 8 + 9 \div 3$

**Evaluate each expression when $t = 8$.** (Chapter 5)

24. $12t$
25. $t - 5$
26. $7 \times (t - 3)$

**Solve each equation. Check the solution.** (Chapter 5)

**27.** $8k = 12 \times 4$ **28.** $45 = 4g + 5$ **29.** $5 + 25 = 6b$

## PROBLEM SOLVING Open Response

**Write an equation to solve each problem.**

**30.** Shea Stadium seats 57,775 fans. Wrigley Field seats 38,902 fans. About how many more fans fit in Shea Stadium?

**31.** The soccer team won 3 times as many games as they lost. They played 28 games in all. How many games did they lose?

**32.** Frank draws a picture using 30 shapes. He draws 8 stars, 4 circles, and 11 triangles for the picture. The remaining shapes are squares. How many shapes are squares?

**33.** There are 11 children in Uli's drawing class. If each child draws 5 pictures on Monday and 3 pictures on Tuesday, how many total pictures are drawn? Explain your solution.

# Performance Task

**Task** The picture above shows recipes for making 1 batch of pancakes and 1 batch of biscuits.

You are asked to help organize a fundraiser breakfast.

a. You need to make 3 batches of pancakes and 4 batches of biscuits. How much of each ingredient do you need? Write expressions to help you.

b. An equal number of pancakes and biscuits will be served to each of 6 tables. How many pancakes and biscuits will be served to each table? What division facts can you use to help you find your answer?

c. If the pancakes and biscuits were served to only 4 tables, how would the number served to each table change? Write your explanation using the terms *dividend, divisor,* and *quotient.*

# Getting Ready for CRCT

**Solve Problems 1–10.**

*Look at the example below.*

There are 12 rows in Mary's garden. Each row has 8 plants. How many plants does Mary have in all?

A. 4

B. 20

C. 28

D. 96

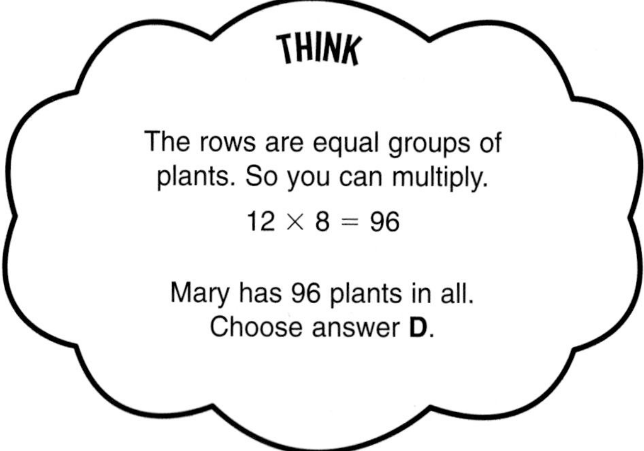


## Multiple Choice

1. A number has a 4 in the millions place and a 3 in the ten thousands place. All the other places have a zero. What is the number?

   A. three million, forty thousand

   B. four million, thirty thousand

   C. forty-three thousand

   D. four thousand, three hundred

   (Chapter 1, Lesson 5)

2. There are 5,667 people in Gia's town. In a newspaper report, the number was rounded to 5,700. To which place was the number rounded?

   A. hundreds

   B. thousands

   C. ten thousands

   D. hundred thousands

   (Chapter 2, Lesson 5)

3. Which number can go in the box to make the number sentence true?

   $$8 \times \blacksquare = 72$$

   A. 9

   B. 8

   C. 7

   D. 6

   (Chapter 4, Lesson 5)

4. A band is practicing for a concert. The flute plays for $x$ minutes. The tuba plays 3 times longer than the flute. Which expression shows how much time the tuba plays?

   A. $x - 3$

   B. $3x$

   C. $3 + x$

   D. $3 - x$

   (Chapter 5, Lesson 2)



For Test-Taking Tips, See page 658.

## Open Response

5. Look at the graph. Which team won about half as many games as the Lions?

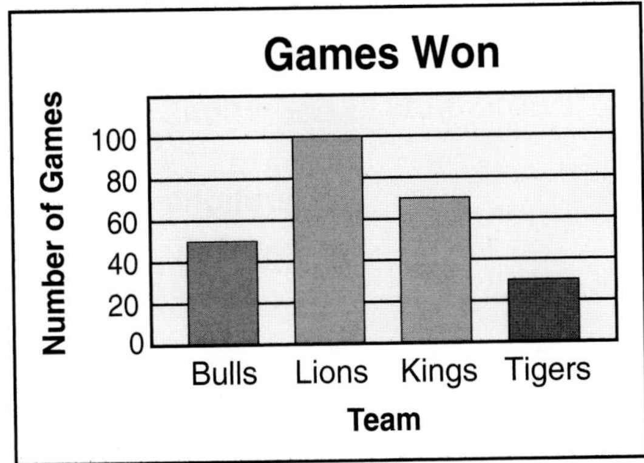


(Chapter 2, Lesson 6)

6. Simplify the expression $3 \times (4 + 1)$. Move the parentheses to write an expression with a different value.

(Chapter 5, Lesson 1)

7. Latrell collects rocks. His sister gives him 6 new rocks. Write an expression to show how many rocks he has now.

(Chapter 5, Lesson 2)

8. Kerry has 35 marbles. There are 5 marbles in each bag. How many bags of marbles does she have?

(Chapter 4, Lesson 9)

9. There are 40 students in the library. There are between 6 and 9 tables. The same number of students sits at each table. How many tables are there?

(Chapter 4, Lesson 5)

## Extended Response

10. The Ramirez family went on vacation to visit a national park. They took three days to drive to the park. The table shows how many miles they drove each day.

| Ramirez Family Vacation | |
|---|---|
| **Day** | **Miles Driven** |
| Friday | 219 |
| Saturday | 461 |
| Sunday | 113 |

a. About how many miles did the Ramirez family drive? Round to the nearest hundred.

b. About how many miles is a round trip between the Ramirez home and the national park?

c. If the Ramirez family drove only about 100 miles on Friday, about how many miles would they have to drive altogether on Saturday and Sunday to reach the park? Explain how you found your answer.

(Chapter 3, Lesson 4)

**Education Place**

Look for Cumulative Test Prep at **eduplace.com/map** for more practice.

# Vocabulary Wrap-Up for Unit 2

**Look back at the big ideas and vocabulary in this unit.**

## Big Ideas

Addition and subtraction are inverse operations.

Multiplication and division are inverse operations.

You can follow the correct order of operations to simplify an expression.

### Key Vocabulary

**inverse operations**

**order of operations**

**expression**

## Math Conversations

**Use your new vocabulary to discuss these big ideas.**

1. Explain how to use mental math to find 56 + 35.
2. Explain how you can use rounding to estimate 1,238 − 476.
3. Explain the steps needed to find 21 ÷ 6.
4. Explain how to use the correct order of operations to find $3 \times (5 - 2) - 4$.

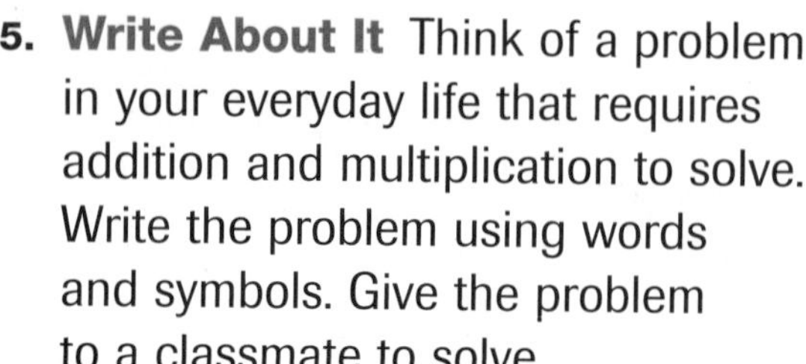

5. **Write About It** Think of a problem in your everyday life that requires addition and multiplication to solve. Write the problem using words and symbols. Give the problem to a classmate to solve.

# UNIT 3

# Multiplication of Whole Numbers

## Multiply by One-Digit Numbers

page 144

## Multiply by Two-Digit Numbers

page 170

# Reading Mathematics

## Reviewing Vocabulary

**Here are some math vocabulary words that you should know.**

| | |
|---|---|
| **estimate** | to find a number close to an exact amount |
| **factor** | a number that is multiplied in a multiplication problem |
| **product** | the answer to a multiplication problem |
| **square number** | the product of a number and itself; a number that can be shown by a square array |

## Reading Words and Symbols

When you multiply, you find the total number of objects that are in equal groups. Look at the arrays below. You can use words and symbols to describe the ladybugs.

- Four groups of three ladybugs equals 12 ladybugs.

  factors ⟶ $4 \times 3 = 12$ ⟵ product

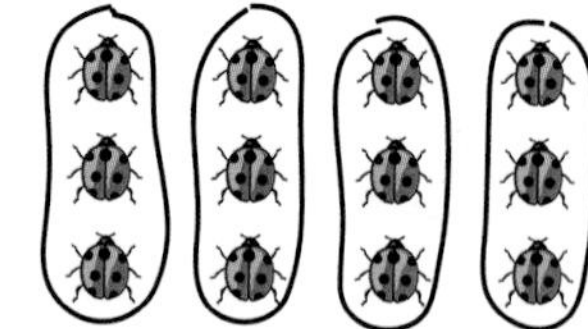

- Three groups of four ladybugs equals 12 ladybugs.

  factors ⟶ $3 \times 4 = 12$ ⟵ product

**Use words and symbols to describe each picture.**

**1.**

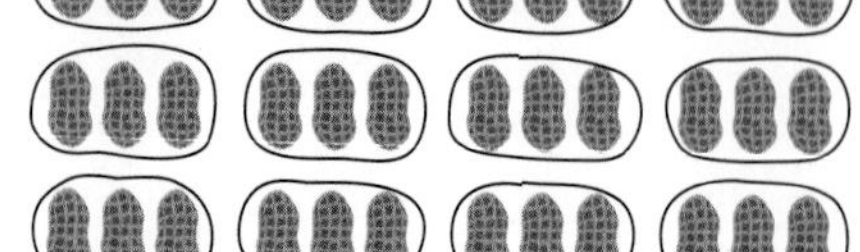

**2.**

# Reading Questions on CRCT

**Choose the correct answer for each.**

**3.** Kayla gave 12 star stickers to each of 2 friends. Which is an example of an array that shows how many stickers she gave away?

A. 

B. 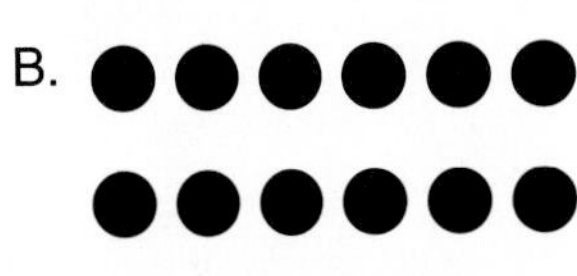

C.

D. 

An **example** is "a sample" or "something that shows a general rule."

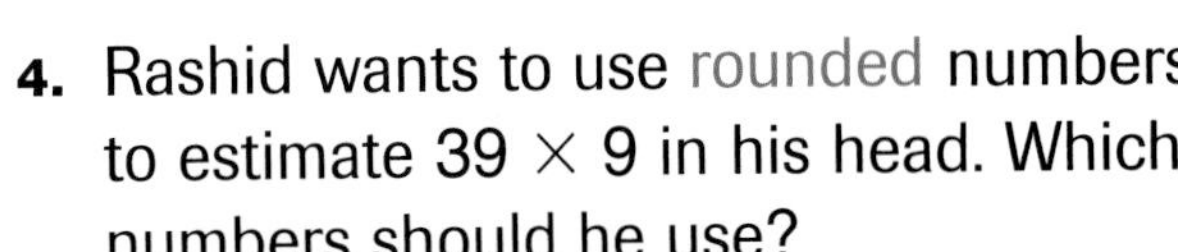

**4.** Rashid wants to use rounded numbers to estimate $39 \times 9$ in his head. Which numbers should he use?

A. $35 \times 15$

B. $35 \times 10$

C. $40 \times 5$

D. $40 \times 10$

A **rounded** number is expressed to the nearest ten, hundred, thousand, and so on.

**5.** Jung wants to find another way to calculate $18 \times 4$. Which of the following should she use?

A. $(10 + 8) \times 4$

B. $(10 - 8) \times 4$

C. $(10 \times 8) \times 4$

D. $(10 \div 8) \times 4$

**Calculate** means "solve" or "find the answer to."

# Learning Vocabulary

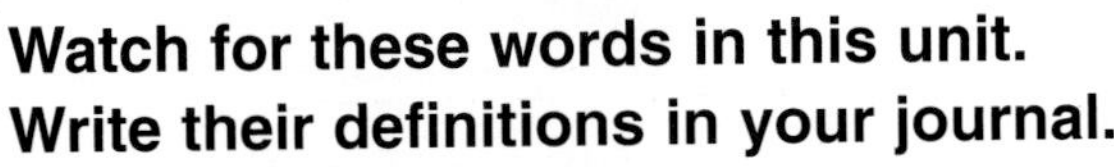

**Watch for these words in this unit. Write their definitions in your journal.**

**Associative Property**
**Distributive Property**
**product**

**Education Place**

At **eduplace.com/map** see eGlossary and eGames—Math Lingo.

## Literature Connection

Read "Gone Prawning" on Page 647. Then work with a partner to answer the questions about the story.

# Multiply by One-Digit Numbers

## PERFORMANCE PREVIEW

### Using Data

The Georgia Aquarium in Atlanta, Georgia, is one of the largest aquariums in the world. The table shows the types of places to visit at the aquarium. If you spent 17 minutes at each gallery, what would be the total number of minutes? If you spent 9 minutes at each gift shop, how much time would you need? What is the best way to solve?

**The Georgia Aquarium**

| Type of Place | Number |
|---|---|
| Gallery | 5 |
| Gift Shop | 2 |
| Café | 1 |

#  Use What You Know

**Use this page to review and remember what you need to know for this chapter.**

## VOCABULARY

**Choose the best term to complete each sentence.**

1. In $3 \times 8 = 24$, 3 is a ____.
2. The number 12 is a ____ of 3.
3. The answer to a multiplication problem is the ____.
4. You can use an ____ to represent a multiplication fact.

**Vocabulary**

- array
- factor
- quotient
- product
- multiple

## CONCEPTS AND SKILLS

**Complete the number sentence for each array.**

5. ★ ★ ★ ★ ★ ★
   ★ ★ ★ ★ ★ ★

   $2 \times 6 = ■$

6. ♥♥♥♥♥♥♥
   ♥♥♥♥♥♥♥
   ♥♥♥♥♥♥♥

   $3 \times ■ = ■$

7. ▲ ▲ ▲ ▲ ▲
   ▲ ▲ ▲ ▲ ▲

   $■ \times ■ = ■$

**Draw an array to show each multiplication fact.**

8. $3 \times 6$
9. $7 \times 4$
10. $5 \times 6$
11. $4 \times 4$

**Find each product.**

12. $7 \times 6$
13. $8 \times 8$
14. $9 \times 3$
15. $6 \times 6$
16. $8 \times 7$
17. $10 \times 3$
18. $11 \times 5$
19. $12 \times 6$

**Write About It**

20. How can you use arrays to tell that $4 \times 6$ is greater than $4 \times 5$ without multiplying? Use a picture to help explain your answer.

Facts Practice, See page 667.

Lesson 1

# Multiply Multiples of 10, 100, and 1,000

**Objective** Use basic facts and patterns to multiply using mental math.

 **STANDARDS** M4N3, M4N7.d, M4P1

## Learn About It

Stuart and his father are shopping at Music World. They are picking out some CDs to buy.

Music World displays their CDs in display racks. Each rack holds 300 CDs. How many CDs can 4 displays hold?

**Multiply.** $4 \times 300 = n$

300 is a multiple of 100. When multiplying a multiple of 10, 100, or 1,000, you can use basic facts and patterns of zeros to help you multiply.

$4 \times 3 = 12$ (4 × 3 ones)
$4 \times 30 = 120$ (4 × 3 tens)
$4 \times 300 = 1{,}200$ (4 × 3 hundreds)

**Think**
What do you notice about the number of zeros in the factors and in the product?

**Solution:** Four displays can hold 1,200 CDs.

## Guided Practice

**Use basic facts and patterns to find each product.**

1. $5 \times 7$
   $5 \times 70$
   $5 \times 700$
   $5 \times 7{,}000$

2. $9 \times 6$
   $9 \times 60$
   $9 \times 600$
   $9 \times 6{,}000$

3. $5 \times 8$
   $5 \times 80$
   $5 \times 800$
   $5 \times 8{,}000$

4. $9 \times 4$
5. $9 \times 40$
6. $9 \times 400$
7. $9 \times 4{,}000$

**Ask Yourself**
- What basic fact can I use?
- How many zeros should be in the product?

**Explain Your Thinking** ▶ Look at Exercise 3. Why are there more zeros in the product than in the factors?

## Practice and Problem Solving

**Use basic facts and patterns to find each product.**

**8.** $4 \times 4$
$4 \times 40$
$4 \times 400$
$4 \times 4{,}000$

**9.** $7 \times 3$
$7 \times 30$
$7 \times 300$
$7 \times 3{,}000$

**10.** $6 \times 7$
$6 \times 70$
$6 \times 700$
$6 \times 7{,}000$

**11.** $9 \times 8$
$9 \times 80$
$9 \times 800$
$9 \times 8{,}000$

**12.** $6 \times 5$ **13.** $6 \times 50$ **14.** $6 \times 500$ **15.** $6 \times 5{,}000$

**16.** $2 \times 80$ **17.** $9 \times 300$ **18.** $6 \times 70$ **19.** $5 \times 900$

**20.** $3 \times 200$ **21.** $7 \times 700$ **22.** $8 \times 5{,}000$ **23.** $3 \times 6{,}000$

**Algebra** • **Expressions** **Find the value of each expression when $n = 8$.**

**24.** $700 \times n$ **25.** $900 \times n$ **26.** $n \times 8{,}000$ **27.** $n \times (40 \times 10)$

**28.** $6 \times (n \times 0)$ **29.** $2{,}000 \times n$ **30.** $300 \times (n \times 5)$ **31.** $(n \times 1{,}000) \times 3$

**Solve.**

**32.** Music World displays CDs on racks. If each rack holds 200 CDs, how many CDs do 3 racks hold?

**33.** At the video store, one display shelf holds 200 videos. One display case holds 300 videos. Which holds more videos, 5 shelves or 3 cases? Explain your thinking.

**34.** **Multistep** At a computer super store, there are 40 display tables. Each table has 6 computer programs and 10 games. How many programs and games are there?

## Sharpening Skills for CRCT

**Open Response**

**Write the standard form of each number.**
(Ch. 1, Lesson 2)

**35.** four thousand, five hundred two

**36.** five hundred thousand, two hundred sixty

**Multiple Choice**

**37.** What is $400 \times 5$? (Ch. 6, Lesson 1)

A. 20 C. 2,000

B. 200 D. 20,000

Extra Practice See page 169, Set A.

Lesson 2

 Audio Tutor 1/19 Listen and Understand

# Estimate Products

**Objective** Estimate products by rounding factors.

STANDARDS M4N2.b, M4N7.d, M4P1.b

**Vocabulary**
product
factor

## Learn About It

During Kindness Week, each fourth-grader in Hunter School bought 2 small toys to donate to a children's charity. If there are 419 fourth-graders, about how many toys were donated?

You can estimate **products** by rounding **factors** to their greatest place.

**Estimate 2 × 419.**

- First, round 419 to the nearest hundred. 419 rounds to 400
- Then multiply. $2 \times 400 = 800$
  $2 \times 419$ is close to $2 \times 400$, or 800.

**Solution:** About 800 toys were donated.

### Other Examples

**A. Nearest Thousand**

Estimate $3 \times 7{,}911$.

7,911 rounds to 8,000

$3 \times 8{,}000 = 24{,}000$

So $3 \times 7{,}911$ is close to 24,000.

**B. Money**

Estimate 8 × $21.85.

$21.85 rounds to $20

8 × $20 = $160

So 8 × $21.85 is close to $160.

## Guided Practice

**Estimate each product by rounding the first factor to its greatest place value.**

1. 82 × 5
2. $4.23 × 9
3. 781 × 6
4. $8.47 × 8
5. $28 × 2
6. 180 × 4
7. $19.95 × 7

**Ask Yourself**
- What does the greater number round to?
- Do I need to write a dollar sign in the answer?

**Explain Your Thinking** ▶ How can estimating a product help you check if the answer to a multiplication problem is reasonable?

## Practice and Problem Solving

**Estimate.**

**8.** $55 \times 4$

**9.** $639 \times 2$

**10.** $\$4{,}598 \times 3$

**11.** $\$8.74 \times 6$

**12.** $637 \times 4$

**13.** $73 \times 7$

**14.** $298 \times 5$

**15.** $1{,}904 \times 2$

**16.** $\$7.35 \times 3$

**17.** $993 \times 6$

**18.** $8 \times 46$

**19.** $9 \times 663$

**20.** $5 \times 5{,}294$

**21.** $7 \times \$96.32$

**22.** This year 583 schools participated in Kindness Week. Next year this number is expected to triple. About how many schools are expected to participate next year?

**23.** A toy store donated 102 games, 3 times as many dolls as games, and 2 times as many craft kits as dolls to a children's charity. To the nearest hundred, how many of each item was donated?

**24.** **Explain** The first 5 customers to arrive at a toy store during Kindness Week will get a free toy. After that, every 5th person will get a toy. Sally is the 30th person to arrive. Will she get a toy?

**25.** **Reasoning** Mike's school collected about 900 children's books to donate. To the nearest hundred, what is the least number of books that could have been collected? What is the greatest number? Explain.

## Sharpening Skills for CRCT

**Open Response**

**Solve each equation.** (Ch. 5, Lesson 4)

**26.** $16 - n = 9$

**27.** $x \div 7 = 8$

**28.** $y + 15 = 19$

**29.** $t \times 3 = 12$

**30.** $z - 16 = 20$

**31.** $108 \div m = 9$

**32.** Jeanne has a bookcase with 3 shelves. She puts 78 books on each shelf. About how many books is this? Explain your thinking. (Ch. 6, Lesson 2)

Extra Practice See page 169, Set B.

Audio Tutor 1/20 Listen and Understand

# Model Multiplication by One-Digit Numbers

**Materials**
base-ten blocks

**Objective** Use base-ten blocks to model multiplication.

## Work Together

**STANDARDS** Maintains M3N3.c, M4P5

Yo-Yo-Mania received 3 boxes of yo-yos. Each box holds 32 yo-yos. How many yo-yos were in the 3 boxes?

**Work with a partner to find 3 × 32.**

**STEP 1** Use base-ten blocks to show 3 groups of 32.

- How many tens blocks did you use?
- How many ones blocks did you use?

**STEP 2** Record your work in a chart like this one.

| Tens | Ones |
|---|---|
| 9 | 6 |

- What is 3 × 32?
- How many yo-yos did the store receive?

**What if the store received 2 boxes of 26 yo-yos?**

**Now find 2 × 26.**

**STEP 1** Use base-ten blocks to show 2 groups of 26.

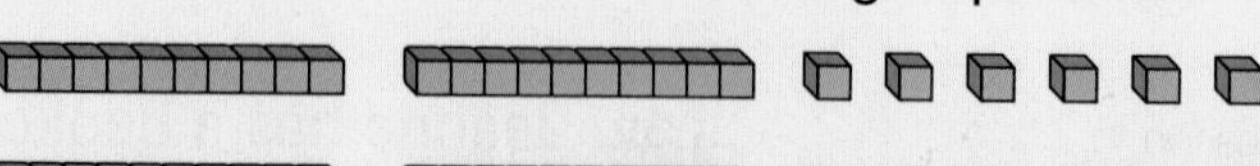

- How many tens blocks did you use?
- How many ones blocks did you use?

When the number of ones blocks is 10 or greater, you need to regroup 10 ones as 1 ten.

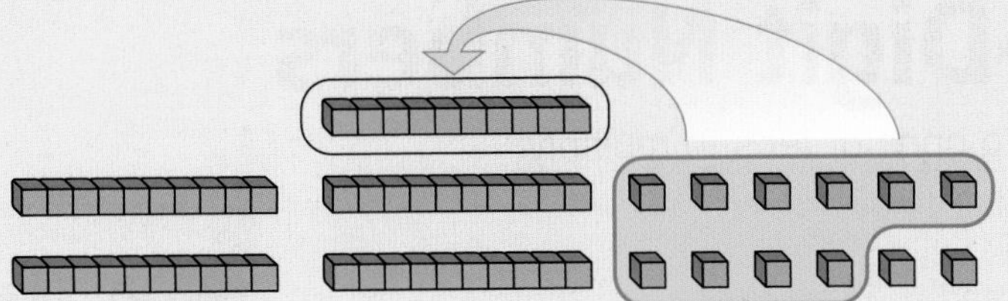

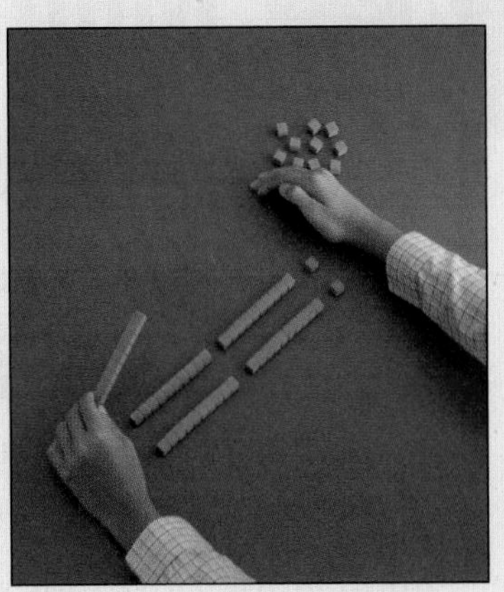

- How many tens blocks and ones blocks do you have now? Record your work in your chart.
- What is $2 \times 26$?
- How many yo-yos did the store receive?

## On Your Own

**Tell what multiplication sentence is shown by the blocks.**

1.

2.

**Use base-ten blocks to find each product.**

3. $3 \times 31$
4. $2 \times 18$
5. $4 \times 21$
6. $3 \times 22$
7. $5 \times 15$
8. $2 \times 27$
9. $7 \times 13$
10. $4 \times 16$
11. **Analyze** In which of Exercises 3–10 did you have to regroup? How can you tell if you need to regroup just by looking at the numbers in the problem?

## Talk About It • Write About It

**You have learned how to model multiplication using base-ten blocks.**

12. Which is less, $2 \times 35$ or $2 \times 36$? Explain how you can tell without multiplying.
13. **Represent** How can you use $3 \times 15$ and $6 \times 15$ to find $9 \times 15$? Use a drawing to help you explain.

Lesson 4

Audio Tutor 1/21 Listen and Understand

# Multiply Two-Digit Numbers by One-Digit Numbers

**Objective** Regroup ones or tens to multiply.

**STANDARDS** M4N3, M4N7.d, M4P2

## Learn About It

Joseph's favorite section of the Discover Science store displays dinosaurs on 3 shelves. Each shelf has 26 dinosaurs. How many dinosaurs are on the shelves?

**Multiply.** $3 \times 26 = n$

**STEP 1** Estimate.

$3 \times 26$ is close to 90.

Think
26 rounds to 30
$3 \times 30 = 90$

**STEP 2** Use base-ten blocks to show 3 groups of 26.

$$\begin{array}{r} 26 \\ \times\ 3 \\ \hline \end{array}$$

**STEP 3** Multiply the ones.
**$3 \times 6 = 18$ ones**

Regroup 18 ones as 1 ten and 8 ones.

$$\begin{array}{r} \overset{1}{2}6 \\ \times\ 3 \\ \hline 8 \end{array}$$ 18 ones

**STEP 4** Multiply the tens.
**$3 \times 2$ tens $= 6$ tens**

Add the regrouped 1 ten.
**6 tens + 1 ten = 7 tens**

$$\begin{array}{r} \overset{1}{2}6 \\ \times\ 3 \\ \hline 78 \end{array}$$ 7 tens

**Solution:** There are 78 dinosaurs on the shelves.
Since 78 is close to 90, the answer is reasonable.

### Other Examples

**A. No Regrouping**

$$\begin{array}{r} 43 \\ \times\ 2 \\ \hline 86 \end{array}$$

**B. Regrouping Tens as Hundreds**

$$\begin{array}{r} 71 \\ \times\ 4 \\ \hline 284 \end{array}$$ $4 \times 7$ tens $= 28$ tens or 2 hundreds, 8 tens



Extra Help at eduplace.com/map

## Guided Practice

**Find each product.**

1. $2 \times 14$

2. $5 \times 21$

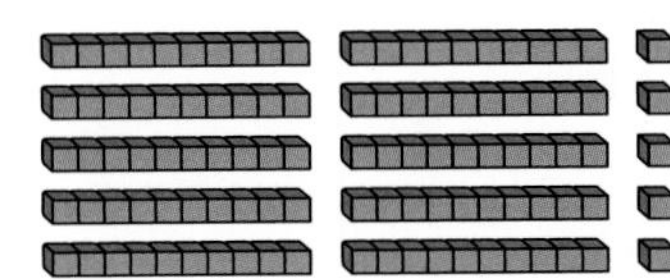



**Estimate. Then multiply.**

3. $\begin{array}{r} 14 \\ \times\ 7 \\ \hline \end{array}$

4. $\begin{array}{r} 11 \\ \times\ 8 \\ \hline \end{array}$

5. $\begin{array}{r} 19 \\ \times\ 5 \\ \hline \end{array}$

6. $\begin{array}{r} 31 \\ \times\ 4 \\ \hline \end{array}$

**Explain Your Thinking** ▶ What is the greatest number of ones you can have before you need to regroup? Why?

## Practice and Problem Solving

**Find each product.**

7. $3 \times 15$

8. $4 \times 23$

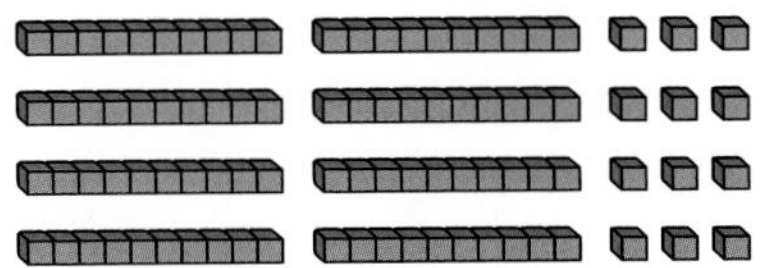

9. $3 \times 20$

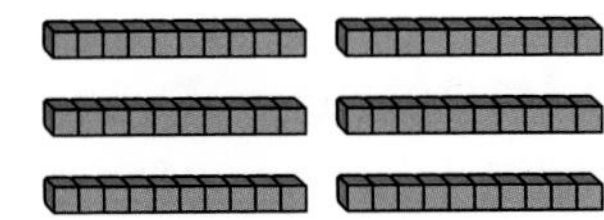

**Estimate. Then multiply.**

10. $\begin{array}{r} 73 \\ \times\ 2 \\ \hline \end{array}$

11. $\begin{array}{r} 11 \\ \times\ 6 \\ \hline \end{array}$

12. $\begin{array}{r} 90 \\ \times\ 3 \\ \hline \end{array}$

13. $\begin{array}{r} 13 \\ \times\ 5 \\ \hline \end{array}$

14. $\begin{array}{r} 46 \\ \times\ 2 \\ \hline \end{array}$

15. $\begin{array}{r} 31 \\ \times\ 9 \\ \hline \end{array}$

16. $2 \times 29$

17. $50 \times 7$

18. $29 \times 3$

19. $20 \times 3$

20. $2 \times 42$

21. $4 \times 16$

22. There are 50 pieces in one dinosaur skeleton model. How many pieces are in 7 models?

23. **Money** A toy Tyrannosaurus Rex costs \$8. A toy Stegosaurus costs \$6. Mrs. Suarez buys 12 Tyrannosaurus Rex toys and 14 Stegosaurus toys for her class. How much does she spend?

Go On

**Megan and Mark multiplied 29 × 4 in different ways. Use their work for Questions 24 and 25.**

**Megan**

I think of 29 as 20 + 9.
$29 \times 4 = (20 + 9) \times 4$
$= (20 \times 4) + (9 \times 4)$
$= 80 + 36$
$= 116$

**Mark**

I think of 29 as 30 − 1.
$29 \times 4 = (30 - 1) \times 4$
$= (30 \times 4) - (1 \times 4)$
$= 120 - 4$
$= 116$

**24. a.** How does thinking of 29 as 20 + 9 help Megan multiply?

**b.** Use Megan's way to complete this multiplication problem.

$17 \times 9 = (10 + ■) \times 9$
$= (10 \times 9) + (■ \times 9)$
$= (90) + ■$
$= ■$

**25. a.** How does thinking of 29 as 30 − 1 help Mark multiply?

**b.** Use Mark's way to complete this multiplication problem.

$38 \times 7 = (40 - ■) \times 7$
$= (40 \times ■) - (2 \times 7)$
$= 280 - ■$
$= ■$

## Algebra • Properties **Use properties to compare expressions. Write >, <, or = for each ●.**

**26.** $81 \times 3$ ● $3 \times 81$

**27.** $72 \times 5$ ● $9 \times 8 \times 4$

**28.** $8 \times 92$ ● $(8 \times 90) + (8 \times 2)$

**29.** $61 \times 3$ ● $4 \times 61$

**30.** $7 \times 2 \times 2$ ● $2 \times 7 \times 3$

**31.** $53 \times (2 + 4)$ ● $53 \times (2 + 3)$

**32.** $79 \times 9$ ● $(10 - 2) \times 79$

**33.** $65 \times 5$ ● $(60 \times 5) + (6 \times 5)$

**Solve.**

**34.** The Discover Science store displays toy bugs on shelves. The first shelf has 10 bugs. The second shelf has 20. The third shelf has 40 and the fourth has 80. How many bugs do you think are on the fifth shelf? Why?

**35. Write About It** What do you think happens to a product when you double one of its factors? Give two examples to support your answer.



Extra Practice See page 169, Set C.

# Problem Solving

GPS

## Social Studies Connection

### Mayan Numbers

**STANDARDS** Extends M4N, M4P4

In C.E. 600 the Mayan people lived in Mexico and Central America. The Maya developed a number system using just three symbols.

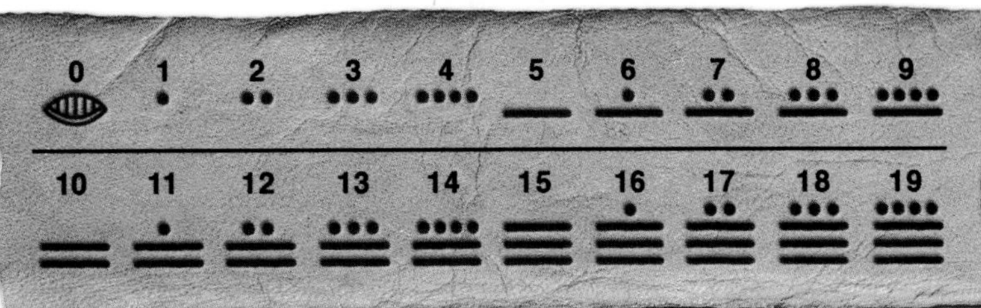


The chart shows the numbers from 0 to 19.

For greater numbers, the Maya drew the symbols in a column. Then they multiplied the top number by 20 and added that product to the bottom number.

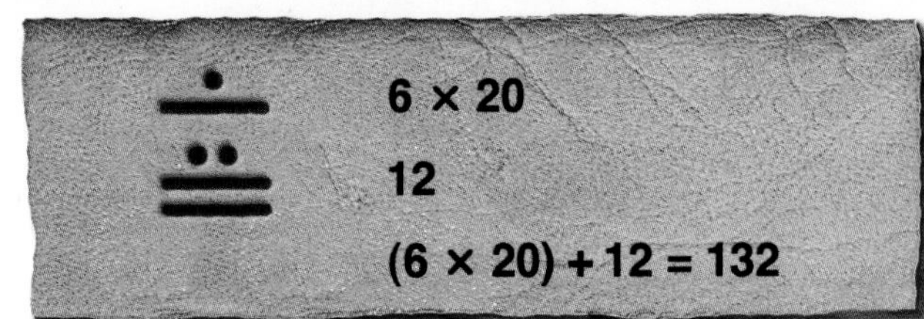


**Write the number sentence that these Mayan numbers show.**

**1.** 

**2.** 

**3.** 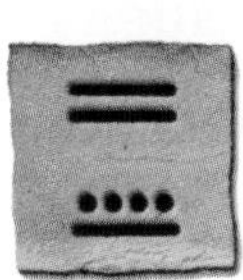

**4.** 

**5. Challenge** Write your own Mayan number problem and give it to a classmate to solve.

eduplace.com/map

# Quick Check

**Check your understanding for Lessons 1–4.**

**Use basic facts and patterns to find each product.** (Lesson 1)

**1.** $6 \times 700$ **2.** $5 \times 4{,}000$ **3.** $8 \times 9{,}000$

**Estimate each product.** (Lesson 2)

**4.** $639 \times 7$ **5.** $\$23.18 \times 5$ **6.** $9{,}812 \times 9$

**Estimate. Then multiply.** (Lessons 3–4)

**7.** $\begin{array}{r} 23 \\ \times\ 2 \\ \hline \end{array}$ **8.** $\begin{array}{r} 24 \\ \times\ 3 \\ \hline \end{array}$ **9.** $\begin{array}{r} 18 \\ \times\ 4 \\ \hline \end{array}$ **10.** $\begin{array}{r} 81 \\ \times\ 6 \\ \hline \end{array}$

Lesson 5

# Problem-Solving Strategy

## Guess and Check

**Objective** Guess and check to solve a problem.

 **STANDARDS** Extends and enriches M4N, M4P1.b

**Problem** Math Marvel is shopping at the Nifty Numbers Store. He wants to solve the puzzle and win the prize. Which numbers should he pick?

UNDERSTAND

**This is what you know.**

- The product of two numbers is 24.
- The difference between the two numbers is 5.

PLAN

**You can use Guess and Check to solve the problem.**

Guess two numbers. Check to see if they are correct.
If not, continue guessing numbers until you find the ones that work.

SOLVE

**Make a reasonable guess.**

Think of two numbers that have a product of 24.

| **1st Guess**<br>**Try 4 and 6.** | **2nd Guess**<br>**Try 2 and 12.** | **3rd Guess**<br>**Try 3 and 8.** |
|---|---|---|
| Multiply.<br>$4 \times 6 = 24$ ✔ | Multiply.<br>$2 \times 12 = 24$ ✔ | Multiply.<br>$3 \times 8 = 24$ ✔ |
| Subtract.<br>$6 - 4 = 2$ X | Subtract.<br>$12 - 2 = 10$ X | Subtract.<br>$8 - 3 = 5$ ✔ |
| 4 and 6 do not work.<br>The difference is not 5. | 2 and 12 do not work.<br>The difference is not 5. | 3 and 8 work.<br>The difference is 5. |

**Solution:** Math Marvel should pick numbers 3 and 8.

LOOK BACK

**Look back at the problem.** How can you check to be sure the answer is correct?

## Guided Practice

**Use the Ask Yourself questions to help you solve each problem.**

1. Math Marvel wants to buy two numbers with a product of 30 and a sum of 13. Which numbers should he buy?

2. Math Marvel wants to buy 2 numbers. The sum of the numbers is 26. One number is 4 more than the other. What numbers should he buy?

3. The sum of 3 numbers is 11. The product of the numbers is 36. What are the numbers?

Hint: What are the factors of 36?

### Ask Yourself

**UNDERSTAND** **What facts do I know?**

**PLAN** **Can I use Guess and Check?**

**SOLVE**
- **What numbers have the correct product?**
- **Do these numbers have the correct sum or difference?**

**LOOK BACK** **Did I find the correct numbers?**

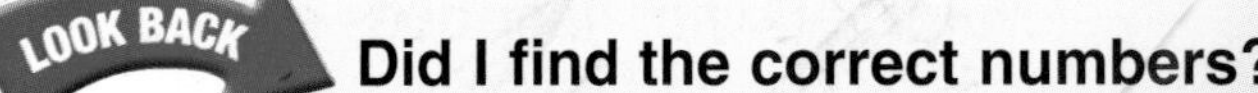

## Independent Practice

**Use Guess and Check to solve each problem.**

4. Together Otto and Zoe have 28 Math Superhero trading cards. Otto has 4 more cards than Zoe. How many cards does each have?

5. Sue has 3 times as many trading cards as Tanya. If they have 12 cards altogether, how many cards does Sue have?

6. Tara is thinking of two numbers. One number is 6 more than the other. The sum of the numbers is 30. What are the numbers?

7. Two numbers have a product of 36 and a difference of 5. What are the numbers?

# Mixed Problem Solving

**Solve. Show your work. Tell what strategy you used.**

8. **Measurement** A water park has one slide that is 538 feet long and another that is 615 feet long. How much longer is the second slide than the first?

9. Anna gets on an elevator at the fifth floor. She rides 6 floors up, then 3 floors down, then 8 floors up. Then Anna gets off the elevator. At what floor does she get off?

10. Two numbers have a product of 18 and a sum of 9. What are the numbers?

11. What is the rule for this pattern?

| 3 | 6 | 10 | 15 | 21 | 28 |
|---|---|---|---|---|---|

Use the rule to find the next number.

**You Choose**

**Strategy**
- Draw a Picture
- Find a Pattern
- Guess and Check
- Work Backward
- Write an Equation

**Computation Method**
- Mental Math
- Estimation
- Paper and Pencil
- Calculator

**Data** **Allen School collects soup can labels for computer equipment. The table shows the labels collected in 1 month. Use the table for Problems 12–15.**

12. How many more labels did the fourth grade collect than the third grade?

13. The fourth-grade students collected about twice the number of labels than what other class? Explain how you got your answer.

14. **Multistep** If Allen School needs 3,000 labels to get computer software, how many more labels are needed?

15. **Create and Solve** Write a problem using data from the table. Exchange problems with a classmate and solve.

**Soup Label Collection**

| Class | Number of Labels |
|---|---|
| Third Grade | 105 |
| Fourth Grade | 316 |
| Fifth Grade | 160 |
| Sixth Grade | 275 |

# Problem Solving on CRCT

**Multiple Choice**

**Choose the letter of the correct answer.**

1. A movie ticket costs $5. A bucket of popcorn costs $3. How much do 9 movie tickets and 10 buckets of popcorn cost?

   A. $90

   B. $75

   C. $45

   D. $30

   (Chapter 4, Lesson 5)

2. Suppose twice as many students like soccer as softball. If 499 students like softball, about how many students like soccer?

   A. about 400

   B. about 500

   C. about 800

   D. about 1,000

   (Chapter 6, Lesson 2)

**Open Response**

**Solve each problem.**

3. Patrick has 5 quarters, 4 dimes, 13 nickels, and 16 pennies in his pocket. He wants to buy the book titled *Mystery at the Falls.* How much more money does he need? Explain.

(Chapter 2, Lesson 4)

4. Fran buys 2 shirts and 1 pair of shorts. The total cost is $23. Each of the shirts costs the same amount.

Write and solve an equation to find the cost of 1 shirt.

(Chapter 5, Lesson 5)

5. The school librarian is planning a book-making project. Each book will have 9 white pages for writing and 2 blue pages for artwork.

   a. The expression 2 × ▲ shows the number of blue pages needed to make the books. In this expression, ▲ represents the number of books. Find the number of blue pages needed to make 19 books.

   b. Write an expression to show the number of white pages needed to make the books. Use ▲ to represent the number of books.

   c. Make a function table. Show how many white pages the librarian needs for the first 5 books. Use your expression as the rule.

   (Chapter 5, Lesson 2)

See **eduplace.com/map** for more Test-Taking Tips.

Lesson 6

# Multiply Three-Digit Numbers by One-Digit Numbers

**Objective** Multiply three-digit numbers by one-digit numbers.

 **STANDARDS** M4N3, M4N7.d, M4P1.b

## Learn About It

The Party Store ordered American flags to sell for the 4th of July. They ordered 2 boxes of flags. Each box had 235 flags. How many flags did they order?

**Multiply.** $2 \times 235 = n$

**STEP 1** Estimate.

Think
235 rounds to 200
$2 \times 200 = 400$

$2 \times 235$ is close to 400.

**STEP 2** Multiply the ones.
**2 × 5 = 10 ones**

$$\begin{array}{r} \scriptstyle 1 \\ 235 \\ \times \quad 2 \\ \hline 0 \end{array}$$

Regroup 10 ones as 1 ten 0 ones.

**STEP 3** Multiply the tens.
**2 × 3 tens = 6 tens**

Add the 1 ten.
**6 tens + 1 ten = 7 tens**

$$\begin{array}{r} \scriptstyle 1 \\ 235 \\ \times \quad 2 \\ \hline 70 \end{array}$$

7 tens

**STEP 4** Multiply the hundreds.
**2 × 2 hundreds = 4 hundreds**

$$\begin{array}{r} \scriptstyle 1 \\ 235 \\ \times \quad 2 \\ \hline 470 \end{array}$$

4 hundreds

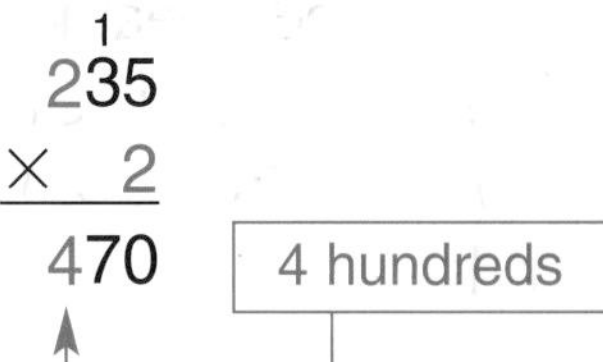

**Solution:** They ordered 470 flags. Since 470 is close to 400, the answer is reasonable.

## Other Examples

**A. Zeros**

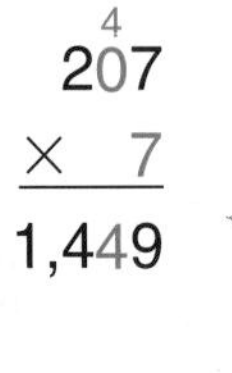

$$\begin{array}{r} \scriptstyle 4 \\ 207 \\ \times \quad 7 \\ \hline 1{,}449 \end{array}$$

Think
7 times 0 is 0.
0 plus 4 equals 4.

**B. Money**

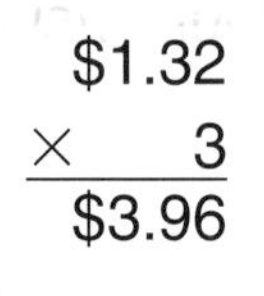

$$\begin{array}{r} \$1.32 \\ \times \quad 3 \\ \hline \$3.96 \end{array}$$

Place a dollar sign and a decimal point in the answer.

## Guided Practice

**Estimate. Then multiply.**

**1.** $\begin{array}{r} 215 \\ \times \quad 4 \\ \hline \end{array}$ **2.** $\begin{array}{r} \$1.84 \\ \times \quad 2 \\ \hline \end{array}$ **3.** $\begin{array}{r} 621 \\ \times \quad 3 \\ \hline \end{array}$ **4.** $\begin{array}{r} \$5.98 \\ \times \quad 7 \\ \hline \end{array}$

**5.** $805 \times 5$ **6.** $\$4.20 \times 6$ **7.** $909 \times 9$

**Ask Yourself**

- Do I need to regroup the ones, tens, or hundreds?
- Do I need to add any regrouped tens or hundreds?

**Explain Your Thinking** ▶ When multiplying, what must you do with the numbers that you regroup?

## Practice and Problem Solving

**Estimate. Then multiply.**

**8.** $\begin{array}{r} 321 \\ \times \quad 2 \\ \hline \end{array}$ **9.** $\begin{array}{r} \$3.08 \\ \times \quad 5 \\ \hline \end{array}$ **10.** $\begin{array}{r} 197 \\ \times \quad 4 \\ \hline \end{array}$ **11.** $\begin{array}{r} \$725 \\ \times \quad 3 \\ \hline \end{array}$ **12.** $\begin{array}{r} 790 \\ \times \quad 3 \\ \hline \end{array}$

**13.** $\begin{array}{r} 398 \\ \times \quad 2 \\ \hline \end{array}$ **14.** $\begin{array}{r} 109 \\ \times \quad 8 \\ \hline \end{array}$ **15.** $\begin{array}{r} 514 \\ \times \quad 6 \\ \hline \end{array}$ **16.** $\begin{array}{r} 136 \\ \times \quad 7 \\ \hline \end{array}$ **17.** $\begin{array}{r} \$9.21 \\ \times \quad 9 \\ \hline \end{array}$

**18.** $199 \times 7$ **19.** $508 \times 9$ **20.** $982 \times 6$ **21.** $\$4.53 \times 8$

**Solve.**

**22.** Tahni buys 2 rolls of blue streamers and 4 rolls of red streamers at the Party Store. Each roll is 972 inches long. How many inches of streamers does she buy?

**23.** **Estimate** There are 175 balloons in 1 package. How many of these packages would you have to buy to have at least 1,000 balloons?

**24.** **Money** If 3 packages of confetti cost $5.25, how much would 9 packages cost? Explain how you got your answer.

Go On

 **Algebra • Functions Copy and complete each function table.**

| | Rule: $y = 10x$ | |
|---|---|---|
| | Input (x) | Output (y) |
| 25. | 5 | ■ |
| 26. | ■ | 80 |
| 27. | 32 | ■ |
| 28. | ■ | 170 |

| | Rule: $y = x \div 4$ | |
|---|---|---|
| | Input (x) | Output (y) |
| 29. | 20 | ■ |
| 30. | ■ | 7 |
| 31. | 32 | ■ |
| 32. | ■ | 25 |

**Solve.**

33. The Party Store sells banners for $9.85 each. What is the cost of 7 banners?

34. Linh spent $51 on balloons. If red balloons cost $15 a box and blue balloons cost $7 a box, how many boxes of each type of balloon did Linh buy?

35. Ana buys 3 boxes of notes and 6 boxes of party invitations. Each box contains 20 cards. How many more invitations than notes does Ana buy?

36. **Multistep** Josh buys 8 sheets of stickers that are 5 stickers wide and 4 stickers long. He buys 2 sheets that are 10 stickers wide and 5 stickers long. How many stickers does Josh buy?

37. **Represent** Draw base-ten blocks to show $3 \times 143$. Explain how you regroup.

## Sharpening Skills for CRCT

**Open Response**

**Estimate each to the nearest dollar.**
(Ch. 3, Lesson 3)

38. $5.38 + $2.11

39. $8.49 − $3.61

40. $9.43 + $8.16

41. $7.32 − $1.76

42. If you double each factor in a multiplication problem, what happens to the product? Use examples to explain your answer.
(Ch. 6, Lesson 6)



Extra Practice See page 169, Set D.

## Guided Practice

**Multiply.**

1. $\begin{array}{r} 31 \\ \times\ 23 \\ \hline \end{array}$
2. $\begin{array}{r} 49 \\ \times\ 17 \\ \hline \end{array}$
3. $\begin{array}{r} 52 \\ \times\ 36 \\ \hline \end{array}$
4. $\begin{array}{r} \$22 \\ \times\ 45 \\ \hline \end{array}$

**Ask Yourself**

- What numbers are multiplied first?
- What numbers are multiplied next?
- What do I add to find the product?

**Use the Associative Property to multiply.**

5. $33 \times 20 = 33 \times (■ \times 10)$
   $= (■ \times 2) \times ■$
   $= ■ \times ■$
   $= ■$

6. $74 \times 20 = ■ \times (■ \times 10)$
   $= (■ \times ■) \times ■$
   $= ■ \times ■$
   $= ■$

7. $51 \times 50 = 51 \times (■ \times ■)$
   $= (■ \times ■) \times 10$
   $= ■ \times 10$
   $= ■$

8. $62 \times 30 = ■ \times (■ \times 10)$
   $= (■ \times ■) \times ■$
   $= ■ \times ■$
   $= ■$

**Explain Your Thinking** ▶ How does the Distributive Property show how each step works when you multiply?

## Practice and Problem Solving

**Multiply.**

9. $\begin{array}{r} 26 \\ \times\ 16 \\ \hline \end{array}$
10. $\begin{array}{r} 21 \\ \times\ 31 \\ \hline \end{array}$
11. $\begin{array}{r} \$34 \\ \times\ 24 \\ \hline \end{array}$
12. $\begin{array}{r} 84 \\ \times\ 42 \\ \hline \end{array}$
13. $\begin{array}{r} 71 \\ \times\ 63 \\ \hline \end{array}$
14. $\begin{array}{r} 52 \\ \times\ 25 \\ \hline \end{array}$
15. $\begin{array}{r} 63 \\ \times\ 53 \\ \hline \end{array}$
16. $\begin{array}{r} 89 \\ \times\ 92 \\ \hline \end{array}$
17. $\begin{array}{r} \$65 \\ \times\ 29 \\ \hline \end{array}$
18. $\begin{array}{r} 25 \\ \times\ 78 \\ \hline \end{array}$

**Multiply. Use the Associative Property.**

19. $18 \times 30$
20. $41 \times 50$
21. $93 \times 70$
22. $55 \times 60$
23. $98 \times 90$
24. $68 \times 20$
25. $15 \times 40$
26. $27 \times 70$
27. $54 \times 90$
28. $16 \times 30$

Go On

## Algebra • Equations Find each value of $n$.

29. $12 \times 5 = (10 \times n) + (2 \times 5)$
30. $(n + 4) \times 15 = 14 \times 15$
31. $21 \times 18 = (20 \times n) + (1 \times 18)$
32. $(n + 7) \times 12 = 17 \times 12$
33. $(10 \times n) + 9 = 349$
34. $34 \times 21 = n + 34$
35. $39 \times 20 = n - 20$
36. $25 \times (n \times 3) = 750$

**Use each of the digits 2, 3, 4, 5 once to write a multiplication sentence.**

37. What is the greatest possible product you can make?
38. What is the least possible product you can make?

## Data Use the graph for Problems 39–41.

39. The ammonites each weigh 19 grams. How much do all the ammonites weigh?

40. **Multistep** The shark teeth weigh about 64 grams each. The bugs in amber weigh about 14 grams each. Which weigh more, all the shark teeth or all the bugs in amber? How much more?

41. **Write About It** The number of fossils found by another team is 15 times the number of fossils found by Dr. Sanchez's team. Describe how you could find the number of fossils found by the other team.

42. At a science store, a leaf fossil costs \$5.95, a geode costs \$8.50, and a space pen costs \$6.75. How much less would it cost Tim to buy 6 leaf fossils than 6 pens as gifts?

43. Teva collected some rocks on Monday. On Tuesday, she collected 3 more than on Monday. On Wednesday, she collected 6 more than on Tuesday. She collected 12 on Wednesday. How many rocks did she collect on Monday?

## Sharpening Skills for CRCT

### Open Response

**Multiply.** (Ch. 6, Lesson 7)

**44.** 4 × 53

**45.** 8 × 262

**46.** 9 × 3,005

**47.** 7 × 43,715

**48.** 5 × 24,608

**49.** 6 × 5,319

**50.** 3 × 7,539

**51.** 2 × 86,425

### Multiple Choice

**52.** Each of 76 art students will decorate 15 ceramic tiles for a mural. How many tiles will be in the finished mural? (Ch. 7, Lesson 4)

A. 456

B. 760

C. 1,110

D. 1,140

Game

GPS Activity

# Multiplying Does It!

STANDARDS M4N3

**2–4 Players**

**What You'll Need** • 2 sets of number cards labeled 0 to 9 (Learning Tool 10)

## How to Play

1. Use Learning Tool 10 or make two sets of cards like the ones shown.
2. Shuffle the cards. Place them facedown in a stack.
3. Each player draws four cards from the stack to make a multiplication problem. Each player decides to make either 2 two-digit factors or 1 one-digit factor and 1 three-digit factor and then multiplies.
4. Players compare their products. The player who has the greatest product gets one point. Play until one player gets 5 points.

How fast can you multiply? As an extra challenge, award 1 extra point to the player who correctly multiplies his or her factors the fastest.

Extra Practice See page 191, Set C.

Lesson 5

# Problem-Solving Decision

## Reasonable Answers

**Objective** Decide whether the answer to a problem is reasonable.

 **STANDARDS** Extends and enriches M4N7, M4P1.b

**After you have solved a problem, remember to look back and decide whether your answer is reasonable.**

Look at these examples.

▶ **Sometimes incorrect information is used.**

Ms. Kerr is a cartoonist who draws 30 cartoon strips each month. She multiplied to find the number of strips she draws in a year.

$30 \times 52 = 1{,}560$ strips

Ms. Kerr's answer is not reasonable. She multiplied by the number of weeks in a year instead of by the number of months in a year.

The correct solution should be:

$30 \times 12 = 360$ strips

▶ **Sometimes the calculations are incorrect.**

A cartoonist drew 12 Sunday strips. For each strip, he drew 16 panels. He multiplied to find the number of panels he drew.

$$\begin{array}{r} 12 \\ \times\ 16 \\ \hline 72 \\ +\ 12 \\ \hline 84 \end{array}$$ panels

The answer is not reasonable.
An estimate of $12 \times 16$ is $10 \times 20 = 200$.
The number 84 is not close to 200.

The correct solution should be:

$$\begin{array}{r} 12 \\ \times\ 16 \\ \hline 72 \\ +\ 120 \\ \hline 192 \end{array}$$ panels

## Try These

**Solve. Explain why your answer is reasonable.**

1. Each student in art class needs 16 pastel pencils. How many pencils will 24 students need?
2. Kelly used three times as many pens as pencils in one year. She used 150 pens. How many pencils did she use?
3. Roberto buys 5 boxes of markers for $2.79 each. He pays with a $20 bill. What is his change?
4. Sonia uses about 30 sheets of paper a month to draw cartoons. About how many sheets does she use in a year?

Problem Solving

## Math Challenge

### Odd or Even?

STANDARDS M4P1.a

You may remember that **even numbers** are numbers that are multiples of 2, and **odd numbers** are numbers that are not multiples of 2.

**Explore multiplying by odd and even numbers.**

**Remember:**
Even numbers always end in an even digit.
Any whole number that does not end in 0, 2, 4, 6, or 8 is odd.

1. Multiply 2 odd numbers. Is the product even or odd? Multiply 5 more pairs of odd numbers.
2. Now multiply 2 even numbers. Is the product even or odd? Multiply 5 more pairs of even numbers.
3. Multiply an even number by an odd number. Is the product even or odd? Multiply 5 more even/odd pairs.
4. What are the multiplication rules for even and odd numbers? Write a statement to explain how you can tell whether a product will be even or odd without multiplying.

WEEKLY WR READER eduplace.com/map

## Quick Check

**Check your understanding of Lessons 1–5.**

**Use basic facts and patterns to find each product.** (Lesson 1)

1. $60 \times 90$
2. $40 \times 700$
3. $30 \times 500$

**Estimate each product by rounding each factor to its greatest place.** (Lesson 2)

4. $23 \times 36$
5. $547 \times 89$
6. $\$38.25 \times 41$

**Find each product.** (Lessons 3–4)

7. $41 \times 23$
8. $74 \times 42$
9. $24 \times 52$

**Solve.** (Lesson 5)

10. Charlotte bikes 48 miles every month. How many miles does she bike in a year? Tell why your answer is reasonable.

Extra Practice at eduplace.com/map

Lesson 6

Audio Tutor 1/26 Listen and Understand

# Multiply Three-Digit Numbers by Two-Digit Numbers

**Objective** Multiply three-digit numbers by two-digit numbers.

 **STANDARDS** M4N3, M4P2

## Learn About It

Some people get their exercise while they work! The table shows the number of miles that some people in a town walk every month on their jobs. How many miles does each person walk in a year?

Let's find out how many miles the mail carrier walks in a year.

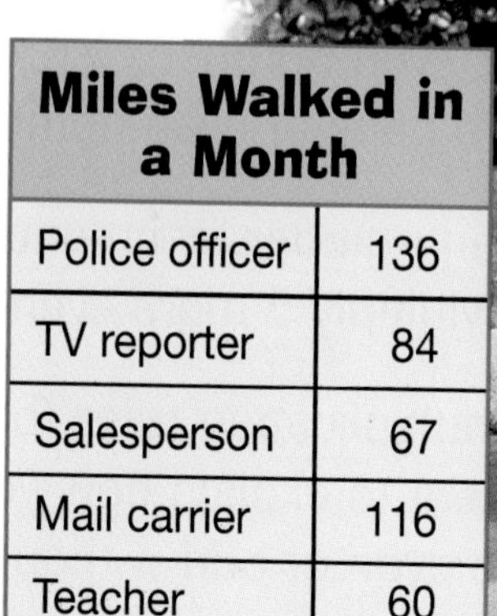

| Miles Walked in a Month | |
|---|---|
| Police officer | 136 |
| TV reporter | 84 |
| Salesperson | 67 |
| Mail carrier | 116 |
| Teacher | 60 |

**Multiply.** **116 × 12 = *n***

**STEP 1** Multiply 116 by 2 ones.

```
   1
  116
×  12
  232
```

**STEP 2** Multiply 116 by 1 ten.

```
   1
  116
×  12
  232
 1160
```

**STEP 3** Add the products.

```
    1
   116
 ×  12
   232  ← 116 × 2
+ 1160  ← 116 × 10
 1,392  ← (116 × 2) + (116 × 10)
```

**Solution:** The mail carrier walks 1,392 miles in a year!

### Other Examples

**A. Zero in the Tens Place**

```
   2
   4̸
   205
 ×  59
  1845
+ 10250
 12,095
```

**B. Zero in the Ones Place**

```
   5
   2̸
   490
 ×  63
  1470
+ 29400
 30,870
```

**C. Multiple of 10**

```
  $1.35
 ×   10
    000
+  1350
 $13.50
```

## Guided Practice

**Ask Yourself**

- What numbers are multiplied first?
- What numbers are multiplied next?
- What do I add to find the product?

**Multiply.**

1. $241 \times 14$
2. $305 \times 32$
3. $\$1.32 \times 60$
4. $574 \times 82$
5. $86 \times 427$
6. $64 \times 285$
7. $42 \times 975$

**Explain Your Thinking** ▶ What are the least and the greatest number of digits possible in the product when you multiply a three-digit number by a two-digit number?

## Practice and Problem Solving

**Multiply. Estimate to make sure your answer is reasonable.**

8. $\$1.32 \times 20$
9. $121 \times 43$
10. $208 \times 52$
11. $496 \times 71$
12. $500 \times 85$
13. $\$4.30 \times 50$
14. $734 \times 24$
15. $260 \times 65$
16. $109 \times 72$
17. $482 \times 39$
18. $30 \times \$1.49$
19. $46 \times 544$
20. $94 \times 263$
21. $81 \times 719$

**Algebra** • **Inequalities** **Compare. Write >, <, or = for each ⬬.**

22. $56 \times 24$ ⬬ $25 \times 56$
23. $(16 + 14) \times 30$ ⬬ $900$
24. $2 \times 425$ ⬬ $2 \times 400$

**Data** **Use the table on Page 184 for Problems 25–26.**

25. In 12 months, Ms. Crawford walks 1,008 miles on her job. What is Ms. Crawford's job?
26. **Multistep** How many miles more does a police officer walk in a year than a mail carrier?

## Sharpening Skills for CRCT

**Open Response**

**Multiply.** (Ch. 6, Lesson 7)

27. $9 \times 78$
28. $6 \times 325$
29. $7 \times 2{,}040$
30. $5 \times 13{,}125$
31. Hala works 20 hours and earns \$9.50 an hour. Bill works 30 hours and earns \$7.50 an hour. Who earns more? (Ch. 7, Lesson 6)

Extra Practice See page 191, Set D.

Lesson 7

# Multiply Greater Numbers

**Objective** Multiply four- and five-digit numbers by two-digit numbers.

 **STANDARDS** M4N7.c, M4N7.d, M4P1.b, M4P1.d

## Learn About It

Ms. Julian is designing a Web site for her company. The company expects about 2,250 hits a day when the site is online. How many hits does the company expect in 31 days?

**Multiply.** $31 \times 2{,}250 = n$

## Different Ways to Multiply 31 × 2,250

### Way 1 Use pencil and paper.

**STEP 1** Multiply 2,250 by 1 one.

$$\begin{array}{r} 2{,}250 \\ \times \quad 31 \\ \hline 2250 \end{array}$$

**STEP 2** Multiply 2,250 by 3 tens.

$$\begin{array}{r} \overset{1}{2{,}2}50 \\ \times \quad 31 \\ \hline 2250 \\ 67500 \end{array}$$

**STEP 3** Add the products.

$$\begin{array}{rl} \overset{1}{2{,}2}50 & \\ \times \quad 31 & \\ \hline 2250 & \leftarrow 2{,}250 \times 1 \\ +\ 67500 & \leftarrow 2{,}250 \times 30 \\ \hline 69{,}750 & \leftarrow (2{,}250 \times 1) + (2{,}250 \times 30) \end{array}$$

### Way 2 Use a calculator.

Enter:    2 2 5 0

Press:  ×

Enter:  3 1

Press:  =

Solution: 69750

**Check Your Answer**

Estimate to be sure your answer is reasonable.

31 rounds to 30

2,250 rounds to 2,000

$30 \times 2{,}000 = 60{,}000$

69,750 is close to 60,000.

**Solution:** The company expects 69,750 hits in 31 days.

## Other Examples

**A. Five-Digit Number**

$$\begin{array}{r} {\scriptstyle 1\,1\,1} \\ {\scriptstyle \not{2}\,\not{3}\,\not{2}} \\ 21685 \\ \times \quad 24 \\ \hline 86740 \\ +\ 433700 \\ \hline 520{,}440 \end{array}$$

**B. Money**

$$\begin{array}{r} {\scriptstyle 1\;\,2} \\ \$12.45 \\ \times \quad 41 \\ \hline 1245 \\ +\ 49800 \\ \hline \$510.45 \end{array}$$

**C. Multiply with Zeros**

$$\begin{array}{r} {\scriptstyle 1\quad 1} \\ 3{,}506 \\ \times \quad 20 \\ \hline 0000 \\ +\ 70120 \\ \hline 70{,}120 \end{array}$$

## Guided Practice

**Ask Yourself**

- Did I record all the zeros?
- How can I estimate to check my work?

**Multiply. Estimate to check your work.**

**1.** $31.45 × 10  **2.** 64 × 3,950

**3.** 40 × $241.28  **4.** 26 × 19,275

**Explain Your Thinking** ▶ How do you know where to place the decimal point in the answer to Exercise 3? Explain.

## Practice and Problem Solving

**Multiply. Estimate to check your work.**

**5.** 1,342 × 23  **6.** 5,121 × 43  **7.** 5,004 × 85  **8.** $26.96 × 70  **9.** 21,814 × 52

**10.** 4,832 × 50  **11.** 7,534 × 24  **12.** 4,862 × 93  **13.** 1,019 × 32  **14.** $312.65 × 60

**15.** 60 × 1,249  **16.** 46 × 6,225  **17.** 90 × $58.25  **18.** 17 × 9,644

**Use mental math, paper and pencil, or a calculator to solve.**

**19.** 190 × 51  **20.** 18 × 326  **21.** 38 × 41,624  **22.** 90 × 2,000

Go On

**Use the Distributive Property to find each missing number.**

23. $40 \times ■ = (40 \times 5{,}000) + (40 \times 20) + (40 \times 5)$

24. $50 \times 62{,}159 = (50 \times ■) + (50 \times ■) + (50 \times 100) + (50 \times 50) + (50 \times 9)$

25. $■ \times 45{,}783 = (30 \times ■) + (■ \times ■) + (■ \times ■) + (■ \times ■) + (■ \times ■)$

## Choose a Computation Method

Mental Math • Estimation • Paper and Pencil • Calculator

**Solve. Tell which method you chose.**

26. Kara's dad charges $85.50 an hour to design a Web site. He designed a Web site for 60 hours. How much did he earn?

27. An electronics superstore sells about 175 computers a day. About how many computers does it sell in 2 weeks?

28. **Money** Shelly purchased 3 gifts from an online auction store. Each gift cost $19.99. What was the total amount that she paid?

29. An online store filled 807 orders in January, 723 in February, and 1,026 in March. How many orders did it fill in these three months?

**Data** **The pictograph shows the number of hits to a music Web site. Use the pictograph for Problems 30–33.**

30. How many hits did the Web site have in November?

31. How many more hits did the site have in November than in December?

32. What was the total number of hits in October and November?

33. **Multistep** If the average sale of CDs on the site was $15 per hit, about what were the sales during September?

**Music Web Site Hits**

| Month | Number of Hits |
|---|---|
| September | 5 CD symbols |
| October | 4 CD symbols |
| November | 4½ CD symbols |
| December | 3 CD symbols |

(CD symbol) = 8,000 hits



Extra Practice See page 191, Set E.

## Sharpening Skills for CRCT

**Open Response**

**Use basic facts and patterns to find each product.** (Chapter 7, Lesson 1)

**34.** 3 × 40
**35.** 30 × 40
**36.** 300 × 40
**37.** 3,000 × 40

**Use a calculator to solve.**
(Chapter 7, Lesson 7)

**38.** Tom's Web site gets about 4,650 hits every month. About how many hits will it get in 22 months?

**STANDARDS** M4D1.d

## Math Reasoning
### Missing Products

Farmer Brown is not happy because Hungry Harry, his goat, took a few bites out of his farm bill. The partly eaten bill below shows how many of each item Farmer Brown ordered. It also shows how much 1 item cost.

**What's missing? Write a new bill for Farmer Brown that is complete.**

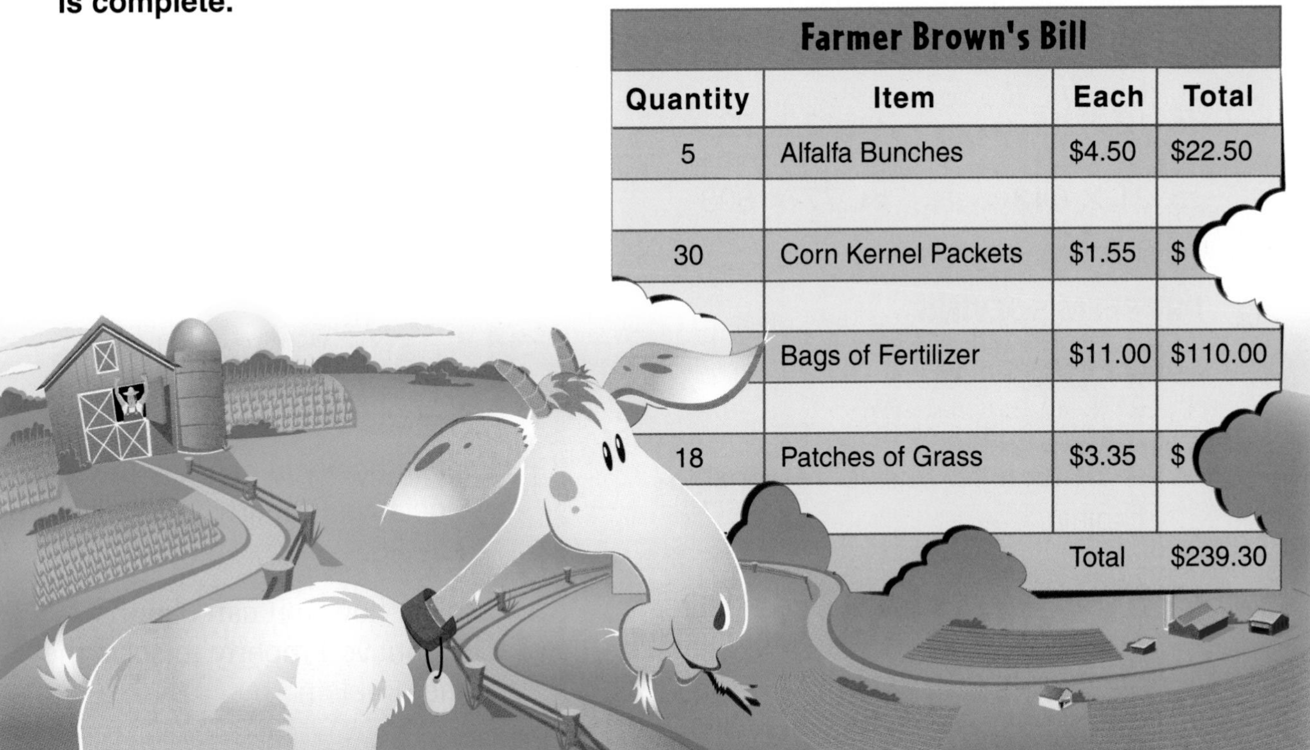

**Farmer Brown's Bill**

| Quantity | Item | Each | Total |
|---|---|---|---|
| 5 | Alfalfa Bunches | \$4.50 | \$22.50 |
| | | | |
| 30 | Corn Kernel Packets | \$1.55 | \$ |
| | | | |
| | Bags of Fertilizer | \$11.00 | \$110.00 |
| | | | |
| 18 | Patches of Grass | \$3.35 | \$ |
| | | | |
| | | Total | \$239.30 |

# Chapter Review/Test

Study Guide pages SG11, SG26, SG41

## VOCABULARY

**Choose the best term to complete each sentence.**

**Vocabulary**
- round
- estimate
- Distributive Property
- Associative Property

1. A reasonable ____ of 29 × 52 is 1,500.
2. An example of the ____ is $4 \times (5 + 6) = (4 \times 5) + (4 \times 6)$.
3. An example of the ____ is $2 \times (3 \times 8) = (2 \times 3) \times 8$.

## CONCEPTS AND SKILLS

**Use basic facts and patterns to find each product.** (Lesson 1, pp. 172–173)

4. 50 × 30
5. 60 × 400
6. 80 × 5,000
7. 20 × 7,000

**Estimate each product.** (Lesson 2, pp. 174–175)

8. 23 × 79
9. 87 × 498
10. 15 × 2,137
11. 91 × $18.75

**Multiply.** (Lessons 3, 4, 6, 7, pp. 176–181, 184–188)

12. $\begin{array}{r} 3{,}741 \\ \times \quad 14 \\ \hline \end{array}$
13. $\begin{array}{r} 3{,}847 \\ \times \quad 60 \\ \hline \end{array}$
14. $\begin{array}{r} \$18.95 \\ \times \quad 20 \\ \hline \end{array}$
15. $\begin{array}{r} 36{,}124 \\ \times \quad 26 \\ \hline \end{array}$
16. 12 × 15
17. 13 × 22
18. 24 × 39
19. 67 × 59
20. 21 × 642
21. 77 × 803
22. 40 × $6.50
23. 38 × 720

## PROBLEM SOLVING

**Solve.** (Lesson 5, p. 182)

24. Martin multiplies 62 by 99. His answer is 1,116. Is his answer reasonable? Explain.
25. Mrs. Lee bakes muffins for a muffin swap. She needs a dozen muffins for each of 25 people at the swap. Will 300 muffins be enough? Explain.

**Show You Understand**
- Explain how you can use the Associative Property to multiply 25 by 20.
- Explain how you can use the Distributive Property to solve the same problem.

# Extra Practice

## Set A (Lesson 1, pp. 172–173)

**Use basic facts and patterns to find each product.**

1. $30 \times 90$
2. $60 \times 400$
3. $80 \times 7,000$
4. $50 \times 600$
5. $70 \times 70$
6. $30 \times 80$
7. $20 \times 900$
8. $50 \times 8,000$

## Set B (Lesson 2, pp. 174–175)

**Estimate each product.**

1. $12 \times 18$
2. $16 \times 22$
3. $39 \times 416$
4. $55 \times 621$
5. $44 \times \$52.35$
6. $19 \times 5,688$
7. $61 \times 3,195$
8. $73 \times 6,796$

## Set C (Lesson 4, pp. 178–181)

**Multiply.**

1. $43 \times 22$
2. $27 \times 18$
3. $39 \times 46$
4. $58 \times 75$
5. $82 \times 61$

## Set D (Lesson 6, pp. 184–185)

**Multiply.**

1. $190 \times 14$
2. $206 \times 28$
3. $399 \times 37$
4. $\$5.07 \times 60$
5. $729 \times 15$

## Set E (Lesson 7, pp. 186–188)

**Multiply.**

1. $1,960 \times 20$
2. $5,040 \times 86$
3. $16,142 \times 29$
4. $\$263.99 \times 50$
5. $41,038 \times 18$

Extra Practice at **eduplace.com/map**

# Distances from the Sun

The huge distances between the planets and the Sun in our solar system are hard to imagine. So the North Georgia Astronomers decided to build a scale model of the solar system with its center at the edge of the square in the middle of downtown Gainesville.

In Gainesville's model of the solar system, Earth is 75 meters away from the Sun in Gainesville Square. This represents a real distance of 150 million kilometers, or one Astronomical Unit (AU). Most of the planets are many AUs from the Sun, so their models are scattered all over Gainesville!

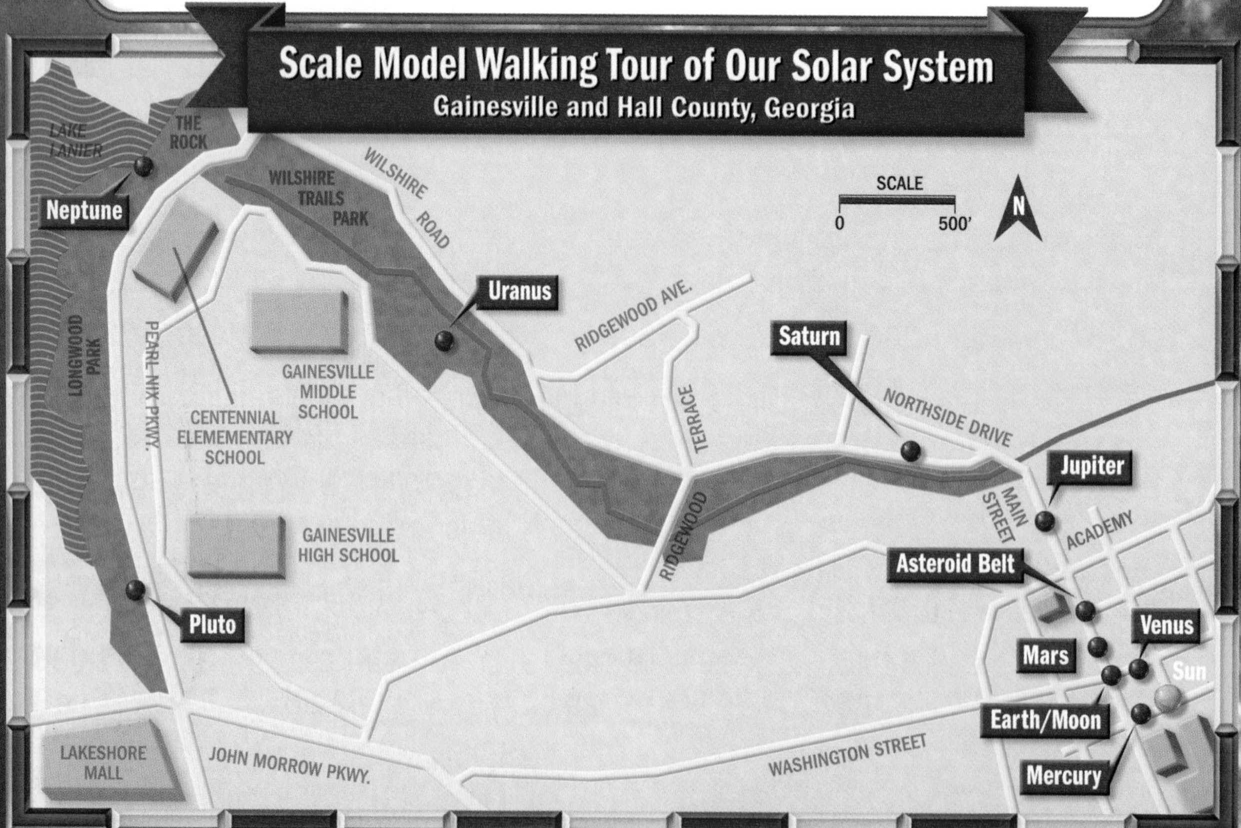

## Problem Solving

1. Copy the table below onto a piece of paper. Fill in the missing distances for the listed planets in the Gainesville solar system model.

| Planet | Average Approximate Distance from the Sun (in AUs) | Distance from the Sun in the Scale Model (in meters) |
|---|---|---|
| Earth | 1 | 75 |
| Mars | 2 | |
| Jupiter | 5 | |
| Saturn | 10 | |
| Uranus | 19 | |
| Neptune | 30 | |
| Pluto | 40 | |

2. Write an expression that shows how you found the distances in the model solar system.

3. What numbers would you use to estimate the distance from the Sun to Uranus in the model?

4. Suppose a spacecraft is 8 AUs from the Sun on its way to Saturn. If the spacecraft is being added to the model, what numbers would you use to estimate its distance from the Sun?

# Enrichment: Gelosia Multiplication

**STANDARDS** M4N3

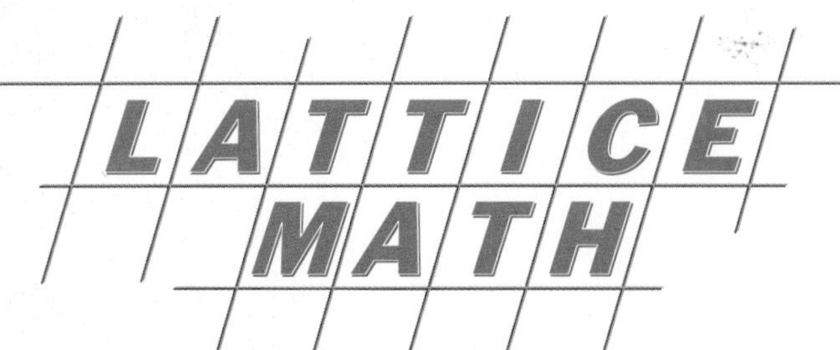

Before people had calculators and computers, they had other ways to multiply large numbers. One way became popular in Europe in the 1400s. It is known as Gelosia Multiplication.

You can use this method to find the product of 423 and 57.

**STEP 1** Make a grid like the one on the right.

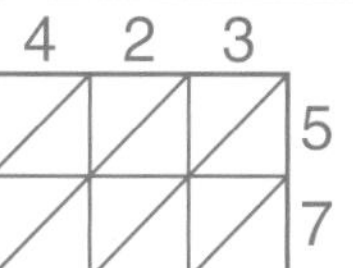

**STEP 2** Begin at the top right. Multiply $3 \times 5$. Write the product as shown, with the tens digit above the diagonal.

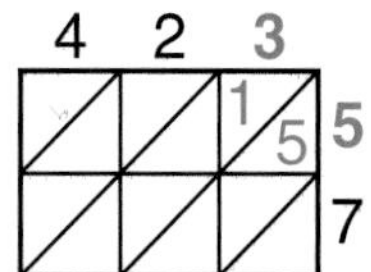

**STEP 3** Continue to fill in the grid by multiplying the numbers for each box.

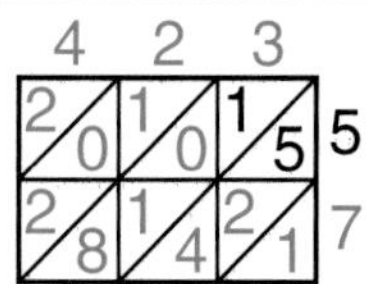

**STEP 4** Begin at the lower right. Add numbers in the diagonals. Regroup tens to the next diagonal on the left. Read the answer from top to bottom and left to right.

$423 \times 57 = 24{,}111$

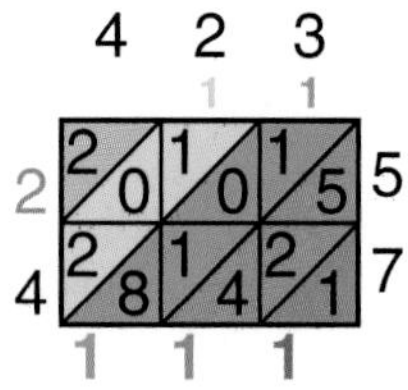

## Try These!

**Use Gelosia Multiplication to solve.**

**1.** $48 \times 35$ **2.** $26 \times 13$ **3.** $487 \times 83$ **4.** $528 \times 76$ **5.** $2{,}017 \times 21$

**6.** **Analyze** How is Gelosia Multiplication like the multiplication method you know?

# UNIT 4

# Division of Whole Numbers

# Reading Mathematics

## Reviewing Vocabulary

**Here are some math vocabulary words that you should know.**

| | |
|---|---|
| **array** | an arrangement of objects, pictures, or numbers in columns and rows |
| **dividend** | the number that is being divided |
| **divisor** | the number by which the dividend is divided |
| **quotient** | the answer in a division problem. |

## Reading Words and Symbols

When you divide, you separate a number into equal groups. All of the statements below, and the image below, can be used to represent the same division problem.

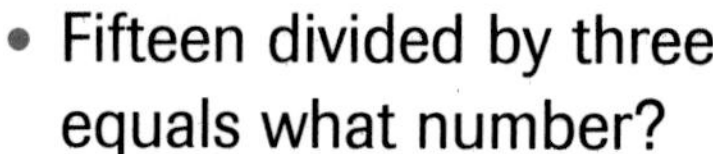

- Fifteen divided by three equals what number?
- 15 divided by 3 = ?
- $15 \div 3 = n$
- $3\overline{)15}$

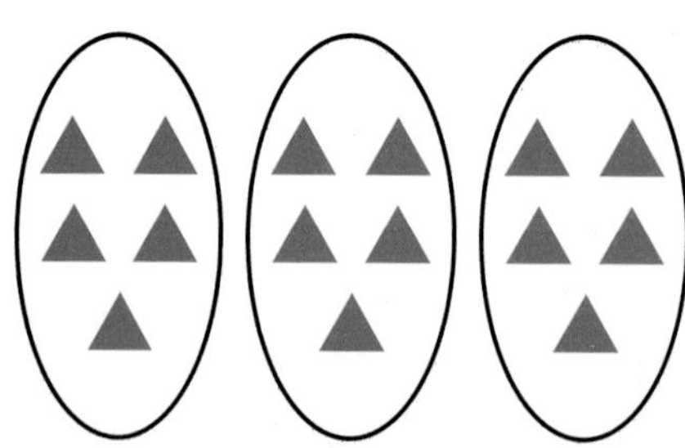

**Use words and symbols to describe each array.**

**1.** 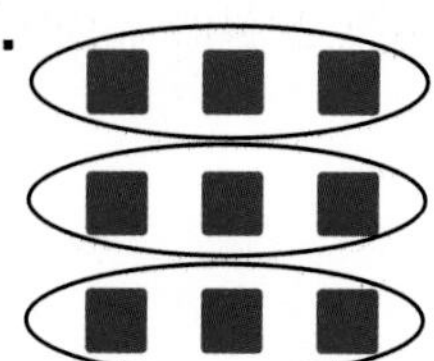

**2.** 

**3.** 

# Reading Questions on CRCT

Georgia Performance Standards

**Choose the correct answer for each.**

**4.** Which number sentence below is NOT correct?

A. $15 \div 3 = 5$

B. $14 \div 2 = 7$

C. $11 \div 3 = 4$

D. $9 \div 3 = 3$

A **number sentence** uses symbols to show how numbers are related.

**5.** Tell what the variable stands for in this problem.

$$4\overline{)n}\ \text{with quotient } 6$$

A. dividend

B. divisor

C. quotient

D. remainder

A **variable** is a letter or a symbol that stands for a number. The variable in the problem above is *n.*

**6.** Shonna divides 27 oranges into 3 equal groups. How many oranges are in each group?

A. 6

B. 7

C. 8

D. 9

**Equal groups** means "groups with the same number of objects."

# Learning Vocabulary

**Watch for these words in this unit. Write their definitions in your journal.**

**quotient**
**factor**
**multiple**
**prime number**
**composite number**

## Education Place

At **eduplace.com/map** see eGlossary and eGames–Math Lingo.

## Literature Connection

Read "But I'm Not Tired" on Pages 648–649. Then work with a partner to answer the questions about the story.

CHAPTER 8

# Understand Division

## PERFORMANCE PREVIEW

### Using Data

Ricardo and Mike bought some quartz, the Georgia state gem, for their rock collections. Look at the table. How can you find out how many pieces of quartz Ricardo will get if the two boys share the quartz equally?

**Quartz Collection**

| Type of Quartz | Pieces of Quartz |
|---|---|
| Amethyst | 25 |
| Citrine | 10 |
| Rose Quartz | 36 |
| Smoky Quartz | 3 |

# Use What You Know

**Use this page to review and remember what you need to know for this chapter.**

## VOCABULARY

**Choose the best word to complete each sentence.**

| Vocabulary |
|---|
| divisor |
| quotient |
| dividend |
| remainder |

1. In the division sentence $8 \div 2 = 4$, the _____ is 2.
2. In the division sentence $15 \div 3 = 5$, the _____ is 15.
3. When you divide 12 by 3, the _____ is 4.

## CONCEPTS AND SKILLS

**Write a division fact for each picture.**

4. 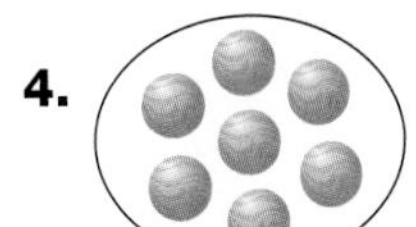 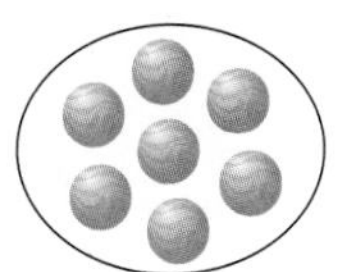

5. 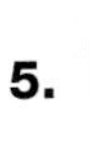  

6.  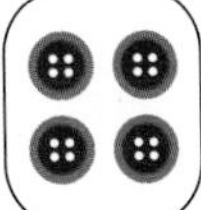 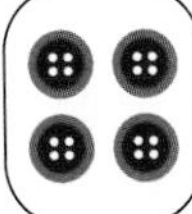

7. 

**Write two related multiplication facts for each division fact.**

8. $6 \div 3 = 2$
9. $18 \div 9 = 2$
10. $24 \div 4 = 6$
11. $35 \div 5 = 7$
12. $56 \div 8 = 7$
13. $42 \div 6 = 7$
14. $54 \div 9 = 6$
15. $72 \div 8 = 9$

**Divide.**

16. $6\overline{)6}$
17. $6\overline{)60}$
18. $9\overline{)81}$
19. $7\overline{)35}$

20. Explain how you could use multiplication to find the missing numbers.

$32 \div ■ = 8$ $\quad$ $■ \div 7 = 2$

Facts Practice, See Page 668.

Hands On
Lesson 1

Audio Tutor 1/27 Listen and Understand

# Model Division

**Objective** Use models to understand division.

**STANDARDS** Maintains M3N4.b, M4P3, M4P5

**Materials**
base-ten blocks

## Work Together

You can use base-ten blocks to model division.

Work with a partner to divide 84 by 4.

**STEP 1** Use base-ten blocks to show 84.

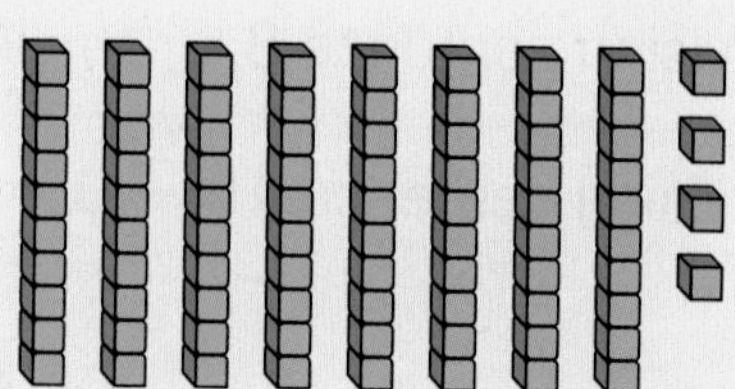

**STEP 2** Start by dividing the 8 tens into 4 equal groups.

- How many tens are in each group?

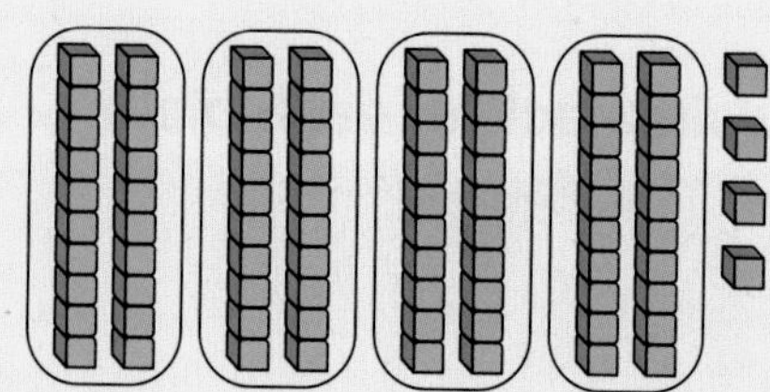

**STEP 3** Next, divide the 4 ones into the same 4 equal groups.

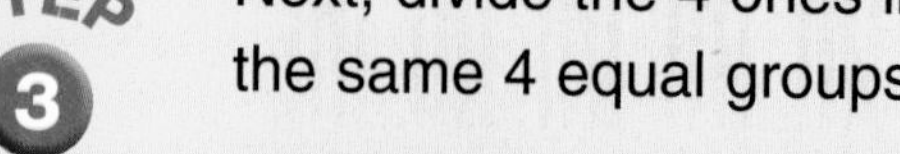

- How many ones are in each group?
- How many tens and ones are in each group?

Write a number sentence to show the division.

▶ **Remember:** A number that is left when you divide is called the **remainder**.

Work with a partner to find 65 ÷ 2.

STEP 1 Use base-ten blocks to show 65.

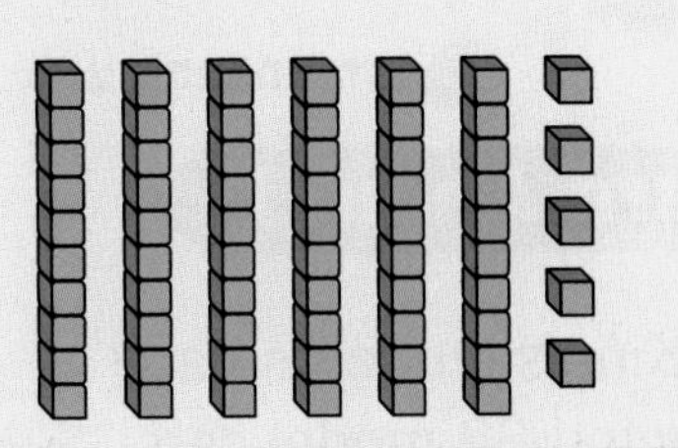

STEP 2 Divide the 6 tens into 2 equal groups.

- How many tens are in each group?

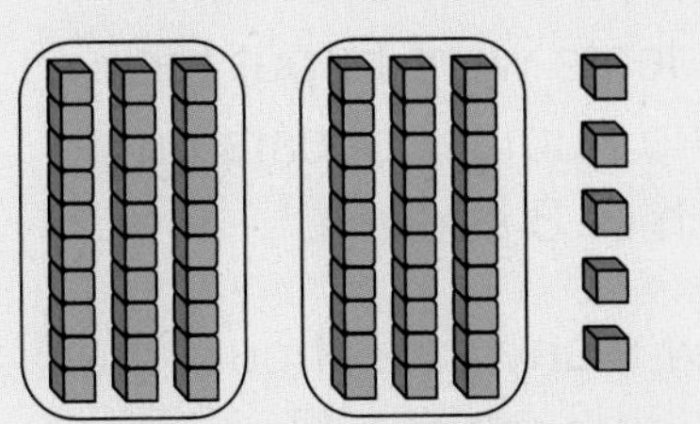

STEP 3 Try to divide the 5 ones into 2 equal groups.

- How many ones are in each group?
- How many ones are left?

Write a number sentence to show the division.

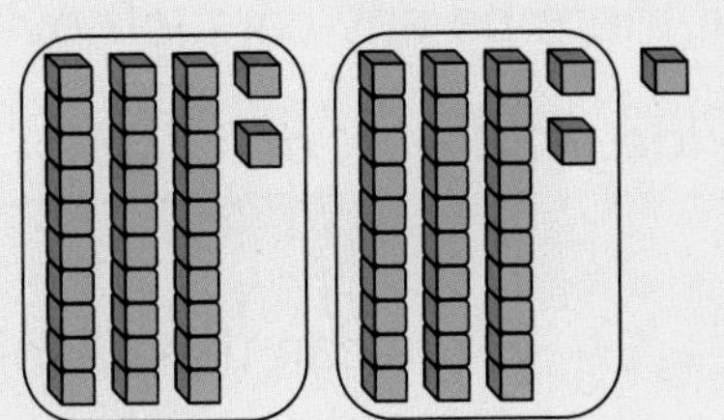

## On Your Own

**Use base-ten blocks to complete the table.**

| | Number | Number of Equal Groups | Number in Each Group | Number Left | Number Sentence |
|---|---|---|---|---|---|
| **1.** | 85 | 4 | ■ | 1 | 85 ÷ 4 → 21 R1 |
| **2.** | 63 | 3 | ■ | ■ | ■ |
| **3.** | 28 | ■ | 14 | ■ | ■ |

## Talk About It • Write About It

**You learned to use models to show division.**

4. Explain how dividing tens is like dividing ones.

5. **What's Wrong?** Ali divided 14 tennis balls into 4 groups as shown on the right. Explain what is wrong.

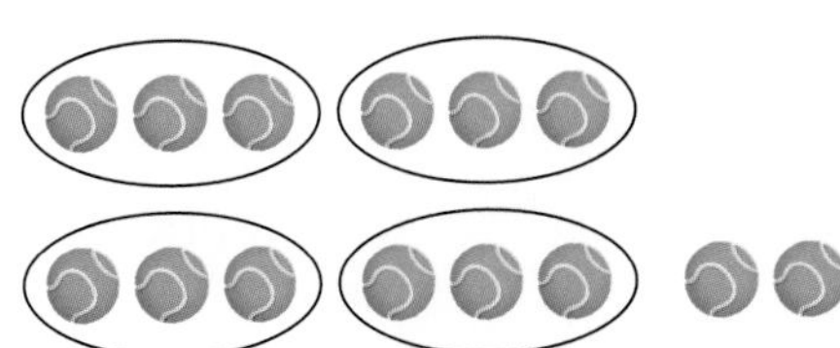

14 ÷ 4 = 3

Lesson 2

 **Audio Tutor 1**/28 Listen and Understand

# Divide With Remainders

**Objective** Find two-digit quotients with and without remainders.

**STANDARDS** M4N4.c M4P2

## Learn About It

Mr. King's students have collected 38 model cars to put on display. The students want to put the same number of cars on each of 3 shelves.

How many cars should they put on each shelf?

Will there be any cars left over?

**Remember**
The remainder is the amount that is left over when a number cannot be divided equally.

**Divide.** **38 ÷ 3** or **3)38**

**STEP 1** You can use base-ten blocks to represent the 38 cars.

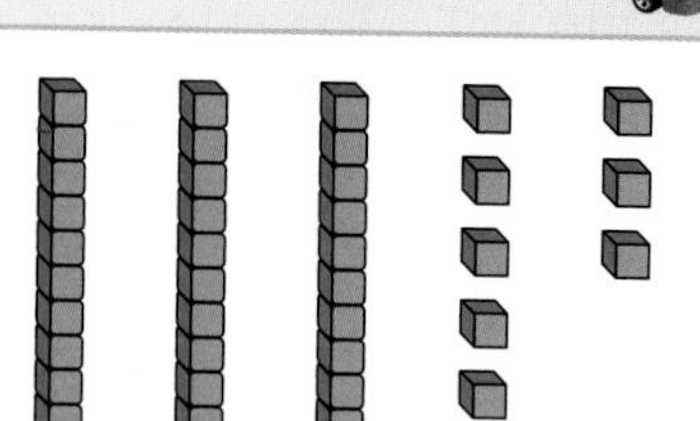

number of groups → 3)38 ← cars in all; ■ ← cars in each group

**STEP 2** Divide the 3 tens into 3 equal groups. Put 1 ten in each group.

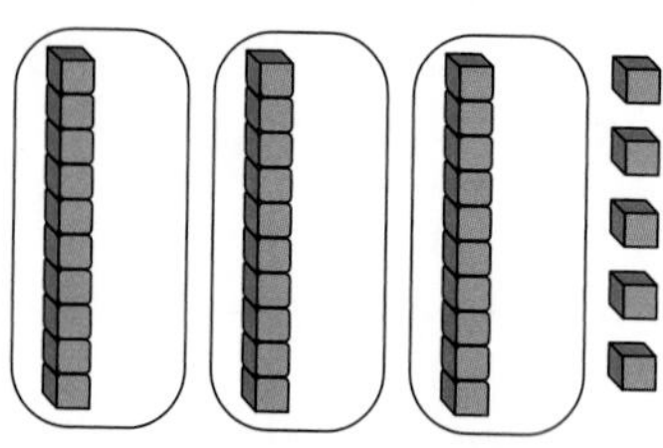

```
   1
 3)38
 - 3    ← Multiply. 1 ten × 3
            Subtract. 3 − 3
   0       Compare. 0 < 3
```

**STEP 3** Try to divide the 8 ones into 3 equal groups. Put 2 ones in each group. There are 2 ones left.

```
   12 R2
 3)38
 - 3↓
   08       Bring down 8 ones.
  - 6   ←   Multiply. 2 ones × 3
    2       Subtract. 8 − 6
            Compare. 2 < 3
```

The amount left is called the remainder. → 2
It should always be less than the divisor.

**Solution:** The students should put 12 cars on each shelf.
There will be 2 cars left over.

## Guided Practice



**Divide. Tell if there is a remainder.**

**1.** $3\overline{)39}$ **2.** $2\overline{)85}$ **3.** $2\overline{)47}$ **4.** $5\overline{)57}$

**5.** 66 ÷ 3 **6.** 85 ÷ 4 **7.** 34 ÷ 3 **8.** 94 ÷ 3

**Explain Your Thinking** ▶ How can you tell if the remainder is too large?

## Practice and Problem Solving

**Divide. Tell if there is a remainder.**

**9.** $4\overline{)87}$ **10.** $5\overline{)55}$ **11.** $2\overline{)63}$ **12.** $3\overline{)68}$ **13.** $2\overline{)69}$

**14.** 78 ÷ 7 **15.** 69 ÷ 6 **16.** 26 ÷ 2 **17.** 65 ÷ 3 **18.** 29 ÷ 2

### Algebra • Symbols **Write > or < for each ●.**

**19.** 24 ÷ 4 ● 48 ÷ 2 **20.** 36 ÷ 3 ● 60 ÷ 3 **21.** 48 ÷ 3 ● 48 ÷ 4

**22.** 66 ÷ 3 ● 60 ÷ 2 **23.** 99 ÷ 3 ● 99 ÷ 9 **24.** 39 ÷ 3 ● 48 ÷ 4

**Solve.**

**25.** José has 67 model cars in his collection. He wants to share them equally among 3 friends. How many cars will each friend get?

**26.** **Money** Jennifer has $29. She buys 2 model-car kits. Each kit costs the same amount. She has $1 left. How much does each kit cost?

**27.** How many different ways can 16 model cars be arranged in equal rows so there are at least 3 cars in each row and 1 car in a row by itself?

**28.** **Multistep** A shop sells 25 model cars for $9 each. It also sells 35 model trucks for $10 each. How much more does the shop receive for the model trucks than for the model cars?

## GPS Sharpening Skills for CRCT

**Open Response**

**Round each number to the nearest thousand.** (Ch. 2, Lesson 5)

**29.** 3,762 **30.** 112,155 **31.** 876

**32.** 16,023 **33.** 7,864 **34.** 35,561

**35.** Can 58 model cars be divided into 5 equal groups? Why or why not? (Ch. 8, Lesson 2)

Extra Practice See page 225, Set A.

Lesson 3

 **Audio Tutor 1**/29 Listen and Understand

# Problem-Solving Application

## Interpret Remainders

**Objective** Interpret a remainder to find a reasonable answer.

**STANDARDS** M4N4.c, M4P1.b, M4P1.d

When you solve a problem that has a remainder, you need to decide how to interpret the remainder.

### ▶ Sometimes you increase the quotient.

Mrs. Ross puts 4 old post cards on each page of her scrapbook. How many pages does she need for 49 post cards?

$$\begin{array}{r} 12 \text{ R1} \\ 4\overline{)49} \\ -4\phantom{9} \\ \hline 09 \\ -8 \\ \hline 1 \end{array}$$

Twelve pages will hold 48 cards. Another page is needed for the 1 extra card. So increase the quotient.

Mrs. Ross needs 13 pages.

### ▶ Sometimes you drop the remainder.

An exhibit of old post cards is on display at a museum for 79 days. How many full weeks is that?

$$\begin{array}{r} 11 \text{ R2} \\ 7\overline{)79} \\ -7\phantom{9} \\ \hline 09 \\ -7 \\ \hline 2 \end{array}$$

There are 7 days in a week. So 79 days are 11 full weeks and 2 days. Drop the remainder.

Seventy-nine days are 11 full weeks.

### ▶ Sometimes the remainder is the answer.

Mrs. Ross has 86 post cards. She divides them equally among 4 children and keeps the extras. How many post cards does she keep?

$$\begin{array}{r} 21 \text{ R2} \\ 4\overline{)86} \\ -8\phantom{6} \\ \hline 06 \\ -4 \\ \hline 2 \end{array}$$

Each child will get 21 post cards. There are 2 extra post cards. The remainder is the answer.

Mrs. Ross keeps 2 post cards.

**Look Back** How does thinking about the question help you decide what to do with the remainder?

## Guided Practice

**Use the Ask Yourself questions to help you solve each problem.**

> **Ask Yourself**
> - Do I need to increase the quotient?
> - Do I need to drop the remainder?
> - Is the remainder the answer?

1. Mrs. Webster wants to buy a post card for each of 68 fourth-graders. The post cards come in packages of 3. How many packages does Mrs. Webster need to buy?

2. Every day, Mr. Lun displays 3 post cards for his class. Mr. Lun has 38 post cards. He will not display fewer than 3 cards on any day. How many days will Mr. Lun display post cards?

## Independent Practice

**Solve. Explain why your answer makes sense.**

3. Suzanne is placing post cards in her scrapbook, beginning with page 1. She puts 3 post cards on each page. She is placing the ninety-fifth post card. Which page is it on?

4. **Money** Mr. Greene buys as many $6 post-card books as he can with $68. How much money does Mr. Greene have left after he buys the post-card books?

5. Fifty-nine fourth-graders are touring a printing plant. Only 5 students can see a printing demonstration at one time. How many times does the demonstration have to be given so that all 59 students can see it?

6. **Create and Solve** Write two word problems, one that you solve by dropping the remainder and one in which the remainder is the answer.

Go On

# Mixed Problem Solving

**Solve. Show your work. Tell what strategy you used.**

7. Vicky has twice as many shells as fossils in her collection. If she has 45 fossils and shells, how many fossils does she have?

8. Ruth and Paul sold 34 tickets to a play. Ruth sold 6 more tickets than Paul. How many tickets did each person sell?

9. Look at the sequence of numbers.

| 5 | 10 | 15 | 20 | 25 |
|---|---|---|---|---|

If the pattern continues, what will be the tenth number in the sequence?

10. Use these clues to find a mystery number.
    - It is less than 40.
    - When you divide it by 5 or 6, the remainder is 1.

### You Choose

**Strategy**
- Find a Pattern
- Guess and Check
- Make an Organized List
- Make a Table
- Write an Equation

**Computation Method**
- Mental Math
- Estimation
- Paper and Pencil
- Calculator

**Solve. Tell which method you chose.**

11. **Multistep** A band has 2 rows of 3 saxophones, 3 rows of 4 clarinets, 4 rows of 2 flutes, 2 rows of 5 trumpets, and 1 row of 3 drums. How many musicians are in the band?

12. Seats in an auditorium are arranged in 12 rows of 20 seats. Each seat is filled, and 9 people are standing. How many people are in the auditorium?

13. One collector spent $98.75 on stamps. A second collector spent $67.68 on stamps. How much more did the first collector spend than the second?

14. **Money** Is $10 enough to buy a grilled-cheese sandwich for $3.60, a salad for $2.75, and a small juice for $1.25?

Activity

GPS

# Math Challenge

## Side-by-Side Division

STANDARDS M4N4.a

**Materials:** Paper Squares (Learning Tool 12)

Make square cards like the ones shown or use Learning Tool 12.

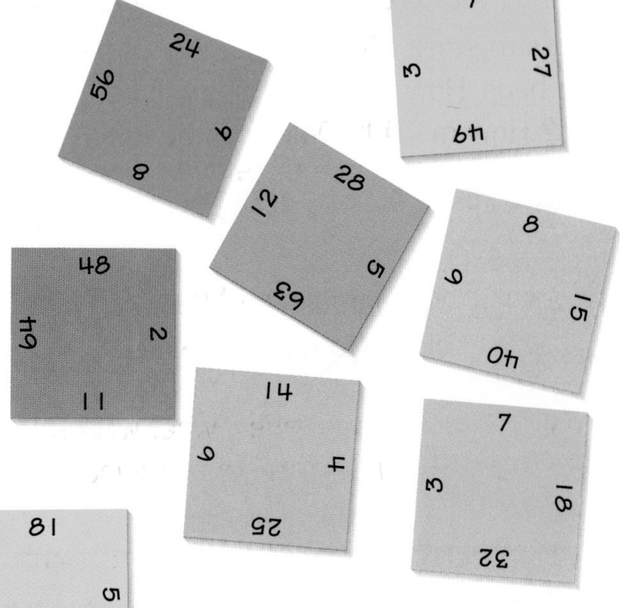

- When you find a number on one card that is the exact divisor of a number on another card, place the numbers side by side.
- Find other matches. Every time you match sides, give yourself one point. The most points you can get are 12.

The number 3 is an exact divisor of 36.

$36 \div 3 = 12$

Score 1 point.

Quick Check

**Check your understanding of Lessons 1–3.**

**Divide.** (Lessons 1–2)

1. $2\overline{)42}$
2. $3\overline{)36}$
3. $4\overline{)48}$
4. $3\overline{)96}$
5. $5\overline{)56}$
6. $2\overline{)85}$
7. $3\overline{)65}$
8. $6\overline{)68}$

**Solve.** (Lesson 3)

9. Sarah has 49 coins in her collection. If she wants to place 4 coins on each page of her coin album, how many pages will she use?

10. Mr. Torres has 23 chairs in his class. He wants to divide the chairs into 2 equal rows. How many chairs will not be in the 2 rows?

Lesson 4

# Regroup in Division

**Objective** Regroup to divide two-digit numbers.

**STANDARDS** M4N4.c, M4A1.a, M4P1.b, M4P5

**Vocabulary**
divisor
quotient
dividend
regroup

## Learn About It

Ella has 54 marbles in her collection. She wants to store the same number of marbles in four bags. How many marbles will be in each bag? How many marbles will be left?

**Divide.** 54 ÷ 4 or $4\overline{)54}$

**STEP 1** You can use base-ten blocks to represent the 54 marbles.

**divisor** (number of groups) → 4; **quotient** (marbles in each group); $4\overline{)54}$ ← **dividend** (marbles in all)

**STEP 2** Try to divide 5 tens into 4 equal groups. Put 1 ten in each group. There is 1 ten left.

$$\begin{array}{r} 1 \\ 4\overline{)54} \\ -4 \\ \hline 1 \end{array}$$

Multiply. 1 ten × 4
Subtract. 5 − 4
Compare. 1 < 4

**STEP 3** **Regroup** the 1 ten left as 10 ones.

10 ones + 4 ones = 14 ones

$$\begin{array}{r} 1 \\ 4\overline{)54} \\ -4\downarrow \\ \hline 14 \end{array}$$

Bring down 4 ones.

**STEP 4** Divide the 14 ones. Put 3 ones in each group. There are 2 ones left. 2 is less than the divisor, so it is the remainder.

$$\begin{array}{r} 13\text{ R2} \\ 4\overline{)54} \\ -4 \\ \hline 14 \\ -12 \\ \hline 2 \end{array}$$

Multiply. 3 ones × 4
Subtract. 14 − 12
Compare. 2 < 4

The remainder is less than the divisor.

**Solution:** Thirteen marbles will be in each bag. There will be 2 marbles left.

Here is a way to check that an answer is correct.

**Check 54 ÷ 4 → 13 R2.**

- Multiply the quotient by the divisor. $13 \times 4 = 52$
- Add the remainder. $52 + 2 = 54$

The sum equals the dividend, so the answer is correct.

## Other Examples

**A. Remainder of Zero**

```
   15      Check:  15
5)75               × 5
 − 5               75
   25              + 0
 − 25              75
    0
```

**B. Zero in the Dividend**

```
   12 R6   Check:  12
7)90               × 7
 − 7               84
   20              + 6
 − 14              90
    6
```

**Use place value columns to help.**

```
     1
5 )  7  4
     5
     2  4
```

## Guided Practice

**Divide. Check your answers.**

1. 5)74  2. 4)50  3. 6)79  4. 3)72

5. 40 ÷ 3  6. 84 ÷ 5  7. 78 ÷ 6  8. 63 ÷ 4

**Ask Yourself**

- When I divide the tens, are there any left?
- What should I do with any tens that are left?

**Explain Your Thinking** ▶ Look back at Example A. What would be a simpler answer check?

## Practice and Problem Solving

**Divide. Check your answers.**

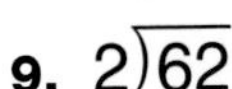

9. 2)62  10. 8)92  11. 6)74  12. 7)94  13. 8)96

14. 3)63  15. 2)76  16. 5)81  17. 4)49  18. 3)82

19. 80 ÷ 6  20. 99 ÷ 7  21. 65 ÷ 3  22. 81 ÷ 7  23. 64 ÷ 4

Go On

## Algebra • Functions Copy and complete each table.

| | Rule: $y = x \div 3$ | |
|---|---|---|
| | $x$ | $y$ |
| **24.** | 54 | ■ |
| **25.** | ■ | 15 |
| **26.** | 66 | ■ |
| **27.** | ■ | 13 |

| | Rule: $y = x \div 6$ | |
|---|---|---|
| | $x$ | $y$ |
| **28.** | 72 | ■ |
| **29.** | 66 | ■ |
| **30.** | ■ | 15 |
| **31.** | ■ | 14 |

**32.**

| Rule: ____ | |
|---|---|
| $x$ | $y$ |
| 7 | 1 |
| 14 | 2 |
| 49 | 7 |
| 91 | 13 |

## Data The graph shows the number of marbles in Ella's collection. Use the graph for Problems 33–35.

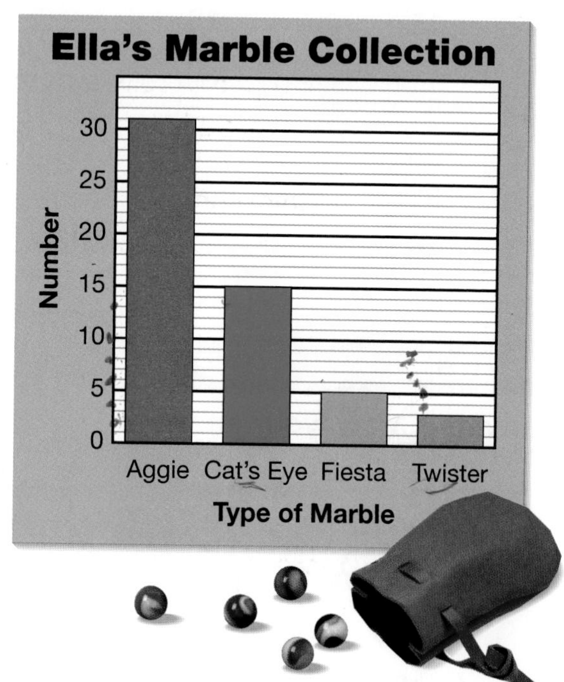


**33.** Ella wants to divide her aggies equally into two bags and give the leftover marbles to her sister. How many marbles will Ella give to her sister?

**34. Multistep** Ella and two friends are playing with all of Ella's marbles except the fiestas. If the marbles are divided equally, how many does each of the three girls have? How many marbles are left?

**35. Analyze** Ella wants to trade all her cat's eyes for twisters. She can get one twister for 3 cat's eyes. How many twisters will she have after the trade?

**36. Reasoning** Four marbles have prices of \$1, \$2, \$3, and \$5. An aggie costs less than a twister but more than a cat's eye. A fiesta is the most expensive. What is the cost of each marble?

## GPS Sharpening Skills for CRCT

### Open Response

**Solve for $n$.** (Ch. 5, Lesson 4)

**37.** $n = (2 \times 7) + 3$

**38.** $n + 15 = 3 \times 7$

**39.** $26 = (4 \times n) + 2$

**40.** $n = 4 + (5 \times 5)$

### Multiple Choice

**41.** Abdul has 67 stamps. He places an equal number of stamps on each of 4 pages. How many stamps are left? (Ch. 8, Lesson 4)

A. 1 stamp
B. 2 stamps
C. 3 stamps
D. 5 stamps



Extra Practice See page 225, Set B.

Game

Activity

GPS

# Race for the Remainder

STANDARDS M4N4.c

**2 Players**

What You'll Need
- A number cube labeled 1 to 6
- A number cube labeled 4 to 9

## How to Play

1. The first player rolls both number cubes to make a two-digit dividend.
2. Then the first player rolls a number cube labeled 4 to 9. The number rolled is the divisor.
3. The first player then divides the dividend by the divisor. The second player checks that the quotient is correct.
4. The remainder is the number of points the first player receives.

Repeat steps 1 to 4.
Have players take turns.
The first player to reach a total of 30 or more points wins.

Here is another way to play **Race for the Remainder.** Have each player roll 3 number cubes at once. The player then chooses 2 digits as a dividend and 1 digit as a divisor.

Lesson 5

# Divide Multiples of 10, 100, and 1,000

**Objective** Use basic facts and patterns to divide mentally.

STANDARDS M4N4.a, M4N7.d, M4P1.b

## Learn About It

The Delmar family collected pennies. When the jar was full, Mrs. Delmar gave the pennies to her three sons. They counted 1,500 pennies and shared them equally. How many pennies did each boy get?

**Divide.** $1{,}500 \div 3 = \blacksquare$ **or** $3\overline{)1{,}500}$

Use the basic fact $15 \div 3 = 5$.

$15 \div 3 = 5$

$150 \div 3 = 50$

$1{,}500 \div 3 = 500$

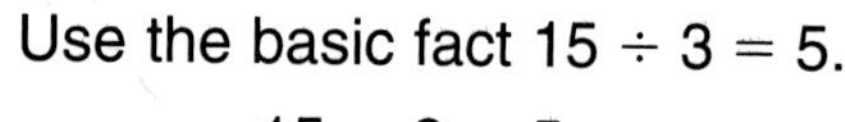

2 zeros → ← 2 zeros

What do you notice about the pattern of zeros?

**Solution:** Each boy got 500 pennies.

## Guided Practice

**Divide.**

**1.** $48 \div 8 = 6$
$480 \div 8 = 60$
$4{,}800 \div 8 = \blacksquare$

**2.** $21 \div 7 = 3$
$210 \div 7 = \blacksquare$
$2{,}100 \div 7 = \blacksquare$

**3.** $4{,}500 \div 9$

**4.** $900 \div 3$

**5.** $5{,}400 \div 9$

**6.** $4{,}000 \div 5$

**Ask Yourself**

- What basic fact can I use?
- How many zeros should be in the quotient?

**Explain Your Thinking** ▶ As the number of zeros in the dividend increases, what happens to the number of zeros in the quotient?

## Practice and Problem Solving

**Divide.**

**7.** $8 \div 4 = \blacksquare$
$80 \div 4 = \blacksquare$
$800 \div 4 = \blacksquare$

**8.** $9 \div 3 = \blacksquare$
$90 \div 3 = \blacksquare$
$900 \div 3 = \blacksquare$

**9.** $6 \div 2 = \blacksquare$
$60 \div 2 = \blacksquare$
$600 \div 2 = \blacksquare$

**10.** $270 \div 3 = \blacksquare$

**11.** $120 \div 2 = \blacksquare$

**12.** $160 \div 4 = \blacksquare$

**13.** $240 \div 8 = \blacksquare$

**14.** $120 \div 3 = \blacksquare$

**15.** $350 \div 7 = \blacksquare$

### Algebra • Equations Solve each equation.

**16.** $3{,}200 \div 4 = n$

**17.** $5{,}600 \div 8 = s$

**18.** $2{,}500 \div 5 = p$

**19.** $320 \div 8 = x$

**20.** $420 \div 6 = d$

**21.** $m \div 5 = 90$

**22.** $7{,}200 \div 8 = p$

**23.** $1{,}400 \div k = 700$

**24.** $b \div 9 = 700$

**Solve.**

**25.** Sela has 6 times as many coins now as she had 4 months ago. If Sela has 240 coins now, how many coins did she have 4 months ago?

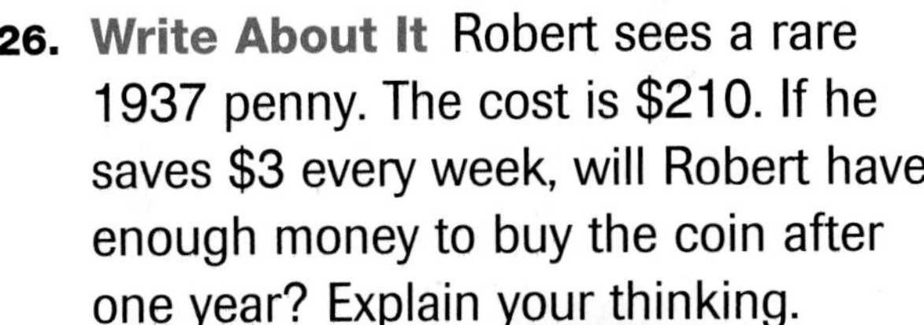

**26.** **Write About It** Robert sees a rare 1937 penny. The cost is \$210. If he saves \$3 every week, will Robert have enough money to buy the coin after one year? Explain your thinking.

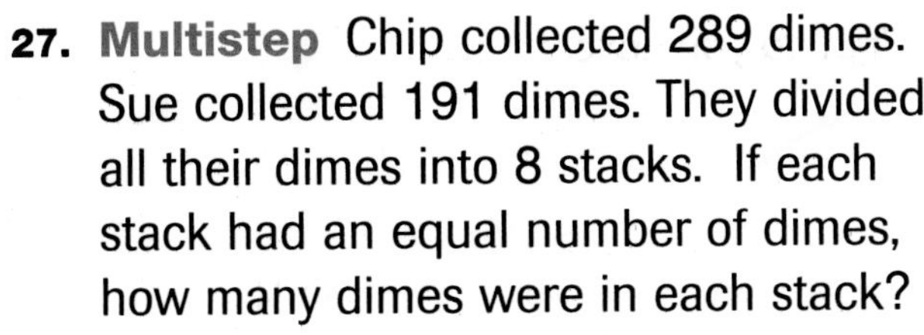

**27.** **Multistep** Chip collected 289 dimes. Sue collected 191 dimes. They divided all their dimes into 8 stacks. If each stack had an equal number of dimes, how many dimes were in each stack?

## Sharpening Skills for CRCT

GPS

### Open Response

**Multiply.** (Ch. 7, Lesson 7)

**28.** $352 \times 11$

**29.** $1{,}468 \times 32$

**30.** $12{,}914 \times 26$

**31.** $621 \times 43$

**32.** $3{,}823 \times 27$

**33.** $20{,}584 \times 30$

### Multiple Choice

**34.** Which number sentence is NOT correct? (Ch. 8, Lesson 5)

A. $150 \div 5 = 30$

B. $400 \div 8 = 5{,}000$

C. $4{,}500 \div 9 = 500$

D. $5{,}600 \div 7 = 800$

Extra Practice See page 225, Set C.

Lesson 6

 **Audio Tutor 1/30 Listen and Understand**

# Estimate Quotients

**Objective** Estimate quotients.

**STANDARDS** M4N4.a, M4N7.d, M4P1.b, M4P1.d

**Vocabulary**
estimate

## Learn About It

Maya Littlefeather collects and sells Native American crafts. One morning she sold 8 necklaces for $166. If each necklace sold for the same amount, about how much did each necklace sell for?

When you don't need an exact answer, you can estimate. An **estimate** tells about how much.

One way to estimate $166 ÷ 8 is to use basic facts and multiples of 10. Think of a new dividend close to $166 that is divisible by 8.

**Estimate.** **8)$166**

**STEP 1** Use basic facts and multiples of 10 to find a new dividend.

→

Think
8 × 2 = 16
16 × 10 = 160

**STEP 2** Divide.

$20
8)$160

Think
Is $20 a reasonable answer?

**Solution:** Each necklace sold for about $20.

## Guided Practice

**Estimate. Write the basic fact you used.**

**1.** 5)28 **2.** 3)268 **3.** 8)310

**4.** 19 ÷ 4 **5.** 177 ÷ 6 **6.** 627 ÷ 9

**Ask Yourself**
- Which basic fact can help me choose a new dividend?
- Does the answer seem reasonable?

**Explain Your Thinking** ▶ How does the divisor help you choose a basic fact?

## Practice and Problem Solving

**Estimate. Write the basic fact you used.**

**7.** $2\overline{)15}$ **8.** $3\overline{)25}$ **9.** $6\overline{)31}$ **10.** $4\overline{)35}$

**11.** $5\overline{)103}$ **12.** $7\overline{)409}$ **13.** $3\overline{)188}$ **14.** $2\overline{)157}$

**15.** $51 \div 6$ **16.** $22 \div 3$ **17.** $37 \div 6$ **18.** $338 \div 4$

**19.** $189 \div 5$ **20.** $123 \div 2$ **21.** $172 \div 8$ **22.** $263 \div 5$

**Decide whether the actual quotient is greater than or less than the estimate given. Write < or > for each ●.**

**23.** $13 \div 3$ ● 4 **24.** $15 \div 4$ ● 4 **25.** $41 \div 5$ ● 8

**26.** $48 \div 5$ ● 10 **27.** $19 \div 2$ ● 9 **28.** $52 \div 5$ ● 9

**Solve.**

**29.** Ms. Littlefeather has a collection of 128 Zuni carvings. She wants to place them in a display case. If she puts about the same number in each of 3 rows, about how many carvings will she put in each row?

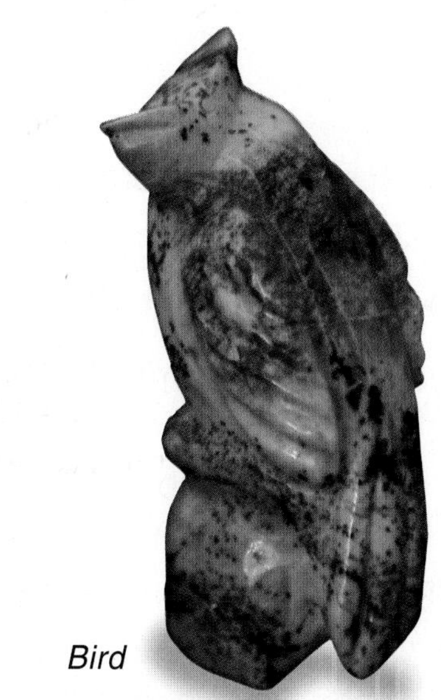
*Bird*

**30.** At a craft fair, small beaded belts cost \$8 and large beaded belts cost \$25. Write an equation in which $n$ is the cost of 3 small belts and 2 large belts. Solve for $n$.

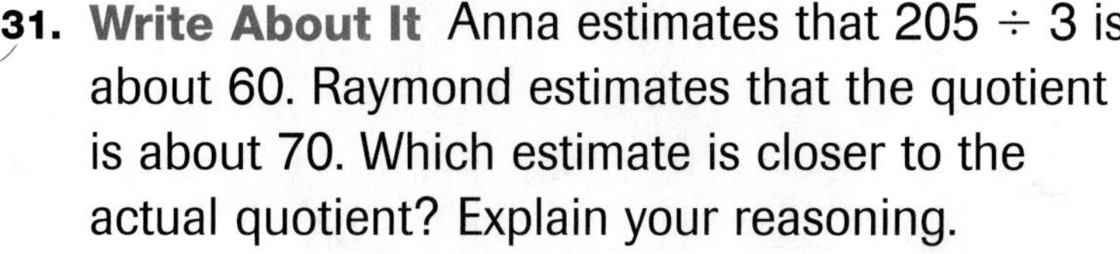

**31. Write About It** Anna estimates that $205 \div 3$ is about 60. Raymond estimates that the quotient is about 70. Which estimate is closer to the actual quotient? Explain your reasoning.

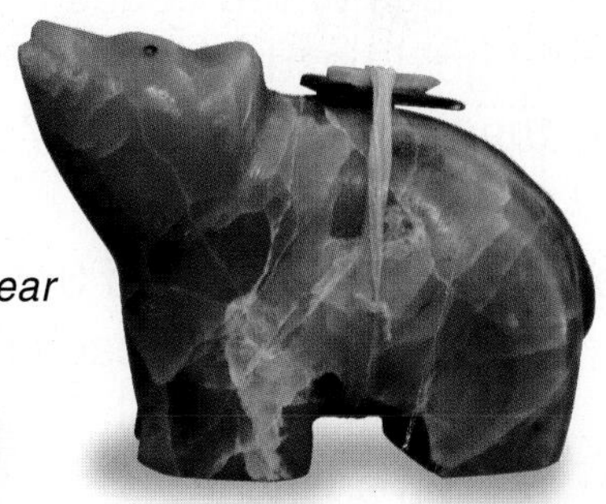
*Bear*

*Wolf*

*Rabbit*

Go On

## Data Use the pictures for Problems 32–35.

*Toy* *Drum Rattle*

*Belt*

*Necklace*

32. **Multistep** Joseph bought a necklace and one other item. He paid with four $10 bills. He received $6 as change. What other item did Joseph buy?

33. **You Decide** You have a $30 gift certificate. What two items could you buy? How much money would you receive as change?

34. **Algebra** Emily wrote this equation to find the cost of 5 items.

    $n = (2 \times 29) + (3 \times 5)$

    What were the 5 items? How much did they cost altogether?

35. **Create and Solve** Use at least three of the items pictured above to write a word problem that uses two operations. Give your problem to a classmate to solve.

## Choose a Computation Method

Mental Math • Estimation • Paper and Pencil • Calculator

**Solve. Tell which method you used.**

36. The table on the right shows the number of miles a family drove each day on a trip from Miami to Phoenix. How far did they drive?

| Mon. | Tue. | Wed. | Thu. | Fri. | Sat. |
|---|---|---|---|---|---|
| 403 | 379 | 457 | 385 | 488 | 456 |

37. **Multistep** Red beads cost $3 per bag. Gold beads cost $7 per bag. If 38 bags of red beads and 12 bags of gold beads were sold, what was the total sales amount?

38. **Analyze** Joyce and 3 friends spent $44 on jewelry. If each person spent the same amount, how much did each person spend?



Extra Practice See page 225, Set D.

## Sharpening Skills for CRCT

**Open Response**

**Divide. Check your answers.** (Ch. 8, Lesson 4)

**39.** 70 ÷ 6

**40.** 84 ÷ 3

**41.** 62 ÷ 5

**42.** 73 ÷ 3

**Solve.**

**43.** There are 8 children at a birthday party. Mrs. Mehta has 65 pieces of candy. She wants to give the same number of candies to each child. About how many pieces of candy will each child receive?
(Ch. 8, Lesson 6)

Problem Solving

# Problem Solving

## Dividing with Greater Numbers

**STANDARDS** M4N4.d, M4P4

Dividing greater numbers isn't as hard as it might look. Let's try dividing 121,000 by 11,000. How can we make this problem easier to solve?

**Step 1:** First, divide the dividend and divisor by the same amount. Let's divide each by 1,000.

| Dividend | Divisor |
|---|---|
| ↓ | ↓ |
| 121,000 | 11,000 |
| ÷ 1,000 | ÷ 1,000 |
| 121 | 11 |

**Step 2:** Now divide the new dividend by the new divisor.

121 ÷ 11 = 11

**The quotient is 11.**

**Try solving these division problems using the method shown. Tell which number you chose to divide the dividend and divisor.**

1. 32,500 ÷ 2,500
2. 144,000 ÷ 12,000
3. 250,000 ÷ 12,500
4. 1,400 ÷ 350

# Chapter Review/Test

Study Guide pages SG13–14, SG28–29

## VOCABULARY

**Choose the best word to complete each sentence.**

**Vocabulary**
- divisor
- quotient
- dividend
- remainder

1. In a division problem, the number to be divided is the _____.
2. In the division sentence $24 \div 2 = 12$, the number 12 is the _____.
3. A number that divides another number is the _____.

## CONCEPTS AND SKILLS

**Divide.** (Lessons 1, 2, 4, pp. 206–209, 214–216)

4. $2\overline{)44}$
5. $3\overline{)95}$
6. $4\overline{)86}$
7. $5\overline{)59}$
8. $2\overline{)51}$
9. $4\overline{)68}$
10. $6\overline{)72}$
11. $7\overline{)80}$

**Solve each equation.** (Lesson 5, pp. 218–219)

12. $250 \div 5 = n$
13. $3{,}600 \div a = 6$
14. $b \div 3 = 80$

**Estimate. Write the basic fact you used.** (Lesson 6, pp. 220–222)

15. $3\overline{)23}$
16. $7\overline{)346}$
17. $276 \div 9$
18. $573 \div 8$

## PROBLEM SOLVING

**Solve.** (Lesson 3, pp. 210–212)

19. Lia keeps 19 dolls on 4 shelves. If there are 5 dolls on each shelf except the top one, how many dolls are on the top shelf?
20. Daniel keeps his marble collection in boxes. Each box holds 4 marbles. If Daniel has 27 marbles, how many boxes does he use?

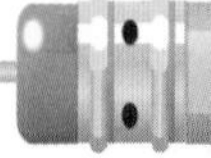

**Write About It**

**Show You Understand**

Each symbol in the division sentence below represents a different digit. Write as many different true equations as you can for the division sentence.

 ÷  = 

# Extra Practice

## Set A (Lesson 2, pp. 208–209)

**Divide. Tell if there is a remainder.**

1. $2\overline{)24}$ 2. $3\overline{)35}$ 3. $4\overline{)47}$ 4. $3\overline{)69}$ 5. $7\overline{)77}$

6. $2\overline{)67}$ 7. $5\overline{)59}$ 8. $4\overline{)85}$ 9. $8\overline{)89}$ 10. $6\overline{)68}$

11. $99 \div 9$ 12. $84 \div 2$ 13. $69 \div 6$ 14. $56 \div 5$ 15. $96 \div 3$

## Set B (Lesson 4, pp. 214–216)

**Divide. Check your answers.**

1. $5\overline{)60}$ 2. $3\overline{)41}$ 3. $2\overline{)93}$ 4. $4\overline{)55}$ 5. $3\overline{)70}$

6. $4\overline{)62}$ 7. $7\overline{)87}$ 8. $3\overline{)84}$ 9. $5\overline{)66}$ 10. $7\overline{)98}$

11. $50 \div 2$ 12. $85 \div 5$ 13. $47 \div 3$ 14. $75 \div 6$ 15. $53 \div 4$

## Set C (Lesson 5, pp. 218–219)

**Divide.**

1. $4 \div 2 = ■$<br>$40 \div 2 = ■$<br>$400 \div 2 = ■$

2. $54 \div 9 = ■$<br>$540 \div 9 = ■$<br>$5{,}400 \div 9 = ■$

3. $63 \div 7 = ■$<br>$630 \div 7 = ■$<br>$6{,}300 \div 7 = ■$

**Solve each equation.**

4. $1{,}000 \div 5 = n$ 5. $490 \div 7 = p$ 6. $640 \div 8 = d$ 7. $3{,}600 \div 4 = q$

8. $270 \div k = 3$ 9. $b \div 5 = 40$ 10. $420 \div a = 7$ 11. $s \div 9 = 50$

## Set D (Lesson 6, pp. 220–222)

**Estimate. Write the basic fact you used.**

1. $3\overline{)28}$ 2. $5\overline{)29}$ 3. $4\overline{)33}$ 4. $6\overline{)47}$ 5. $9\overline{)56}$

6. $5\overline{)395}$ 7. $4\overline{)330}$ 8. $3\overline{)251}$ 9. $6\overline{)477}$ 10. $9\overline{)550}$

11. $131 \div 4$ 12. $243 \div 5$ 13. $179 \div 3$ 14. $250 \div 6$ 15. $642 \div 9$

Extra Practice at **eduplace.com/map**

# Divide by One-Digit Divisors

## INVESTIGATION

### Using Data

A wildlife preserve provides 5,000 pounds of food for elephants each day. How many elephants could be living at the preserve? Can you find an answer in more than one way?

| The African Elephant | |
|---|---|
| Weight | 8,800–15,500 pounds |
| Height | 10–13 feet |
| Life Span | 50–60 years |
| Food | About 528 pounds per day |

# Use What You Know

**Use this page to review and remember what you need to know for this chapter.**

## VOCABULARY

**Choose the best word to complete each sentence.**

**1.** In $42 \div n = 6$, $n$ is the ____.

**2.** The answer in division is called the ____.

**3.** If equal groups cannot be made when you divide, you will have a ____.

**4.** When you divide, the ____ is divided into equal groups.

**Vocabulary**

- divisor
- dividend
- quotient
- regroup
- remainder

## CONCEPTS AND SKILLS

**Match the division example with the better estimate.**

**5.** $7\overline{)645}$  **a.** $\begin{array}{r}90\\7\overline{)630}\end{array}$  **b.** $\begin{array}{r}100\\7\overline{)700}\end{array}$

**6.** $6\overline{)200}$  **a.** $\begin{array}{r}30\\6\overline{)180}\end{array}$  **b.** $\begin{array}{r}40\\6\overline{)240}\end{array}$

**7.** $5\overline{)468}$  **a.** $\begin{array}{r}100\\5\overline{)500}\end{array}$  **b.** $\begin{array}{r}90\\5\overline{)450}\end{array}$

**Find each quotient.**

**8.** $4\overline{)12}$  **9.** $7\overline{)56}$  **10.** $9\overline{)63}$  **11.** $3\overline{)15}$

**12.** $9\overline{)39}$  **13.** $7\overline{)20}$  **14.** $5\overline{)12}$  **15.** $3\overline{)19}$

**16.** $4\overline{)48}$  **17.** $5\overline{)65}$  **18.** $3\overline{)77}$  **19.** $6\overline{)78}$

**Write About It**

**20.** A number is divided by 6. What numbers could the remainder be? Explain how you know.

Facts Practice, See Page 669

Lesson 1

Audio Tutor 1/31 Listen and Understand

# Three-Digit Quotients

**Objective** Divide a three-digit number by a one-digit number.

**STANDARDS** Maintains M3N4.e

## Learn About It

Students in the third, fourth, and fifth grades made 525 origami animals to display in the library. If each grade made the same number of animals, how many animals did each grade make?

*Origami is the Japanese art of folding paper into different shapes.*

**Divide.** 525 ÷ 3 = ■ or 3)525

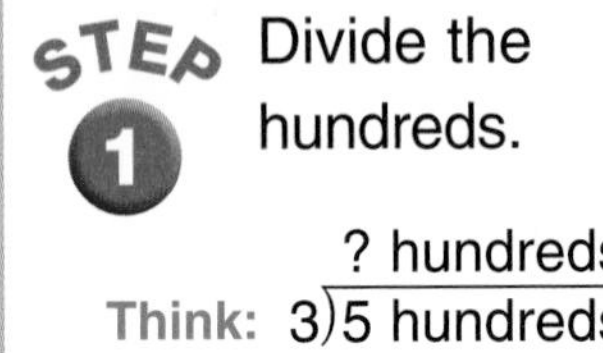

**STEP 1** Divide the hundreds.

Think: 3)5 hundreds → ? hundreds

```
   1
3)525    Multiply. 1 × 3
 - 3  ←  Subtract. 5 − 3
   2     Compare. 2 < 3
```

**STEP 2** Bring down the tens. Divide the tens.

Think: 3)22 tens → ? tens

```
   17
3)525
 - 3↓      Bring down the tens.
   22      Multiply. 7 × 3
 - 21  ←   Subtract. 22 − 21
    1      Compare. 1 < 3
```

**STEP 3** Bring down the ones. Divide the ones.

Think: 3)15 ones → ? ones

```
   175
3)525
 - 3
   22      Bring down the ones.
 - 21↓
    15     Multiply. 5 × 3
  - 15  ←  Subtract. 15 − 15
     0     Compare. 0 < 3
```

**Remember**
After you divide the hundreds, tens or ones place, the remainder should **always** be less than the divisor.

**Check.**
Multiply.
3 × 175 = 525
The product equals the dividend.

**Solution:** Each grade made 175 origami animals.

### Other Examples

**A. With a Remainder**

```
  168 R4      Check:  168     Multiply, then add
5)844                × 5      the remainder.
 - 5↓                840
   34               +  4
 - 30↓               844
    44
  - 40
     4 ← 4 is less than 5, so it is the remainder.
```

**B. Zero in the Dividend**

```
  117      Check:  117
6)702              × 6
 - 6↓              702
   10
  - 6↓
    42
  - 42
     0
```

## Guided Practice

**Divide. Check your answers.**

**1.** $2\overline{)394}$ **2.** $2\overline{)962}$ **3.** $4\overline{)450}$ **4.** $7\overline{)802}$

**5.** 685 ÷ 6 **6.** 945 ÷ 2 **7.** 775 ÷ 2 **8.** 697 ÷ 6

**Ask Yourself**

- Can I divide the hundreds?
- Can I divide the tens?
- Can I divide the ones?

**Explain Your Thinking** ▶ Think about 482 ÷ 4. Without dividing, how do you know the quotient will have 3 digits?

## Practice and Problem Solving

**Divide. Check your answers.**

**9.** $2\overline{)836}$ **10.** $4\overline{)709}$ **11.** $3\overline{)519}$ **12.** $3\overline{)404}$

**13.** $5\overline{)762}$ **14.** $6\overline{)913}$ **15.** $8\overline{)923}$ **16.** $8\overline{)889}$

**17.** $4\overline{)633}$ **18.** $6\overline{)822}$ **19.** $4\overline{)746}$ **20.** $7\overline{)934}$

**21.** 578 ÷ 3 **22.** 710 ÷ 5 **23.** 535 ÷ 2 **24.** 864 ÷ 5

**Solve.**

**25.** Each origami crane is made with either red, blue, or silver paper. The number of cranes in each color is the same. If there are 342 cranes in all, how many of them are blue?

**26.** An artist made 455 origami animals in 5 days. If she made the same number of animals each day, how many origami animals did she make each day?

## Sharpening Skills for CRCT

**Multiple Choice**

**Choose the best unit of measure.** (Grade 3)

**27.** distance from Boston to Chicago

**a.** miles **b.** yards

**28.** length of a room

**a.** inches **b.** feet

**29.** Fran read a 306-page book in 2 days. She read the same number of pages each day. How many pages did she read each day?
(Ch. 9, Lesson 1)

A. 108 C. 153

B. 135 D. 612

Extra Practice See page 249, Set A.

Lesson 2

**Audio Tutor 1**/32 Listen and Understand

# Place the First Digit of the Quotient

**Objective** Decide where to write the first digit in the quotient.

**STANDARDS** M4N4, M4N7.d, M4P1.b, M4P2

## Learn About It

Reggie has 237 photographs of insects. If he puts them into 5 groups of the same size, how many photos will be in each group?

**Divide.** **237 ÷ 5** or **5)237**

**STEP 1** Estimate to place the first digit.

237 is between 200 and 250, so use these numbers to estimate.

$$\begin{array}{r} 40 \\ 5\overline{)200} \end{array} \qquad \begin{array}{r} 50 \\ 5\overline{)250} \end{array}$$

The quotient will be between 40 and 50. The first digit will be in the tens place.

**STEP 2** Divide the tens.

Think: ? tens / 5)23 tens

$$\begin{array}{r} 4 \\ 5\overline{)237} \\ -20 \\ \hline 3 \end{array}$$

Multiply. 4 × 5
Subtract. 23 − 20
Compare. 3 < 5

**STEP 3** Bring down the ones. Divide the ones.

Think: ? ones / 5)37 ones

$$\begin{array}{r} 47 \text{ R2} \\ 5\overline{)237} \\ -20\downarrow \\ \hline 37 \\ -35 \\ \hline 2 \end{array}$$

← Bring down the ones.
Multiply. 7 × 5
Subtract. 37 − 35
Compare. 2 < 5

**Check.**
Multiply. Then add.
(5 × 47) + 2 = 237
The sum equals the dividend, so the answer is correct.

**Solution:** There will be 47 photos in each group. Two photos will be left over.

## Other Examples

**A. Multiple of 10**

$$\begin{array}{r} 83 \text{ R6} \\ 8\overline{)670} \\ -64\downarrow \\ \hline 30 \\ -24 \\ \hline 6 \end{array}$$

Check:
$$\begin{array}{r} 83 \\ \times\ 8 \\ \hline 664 \\ +\ \ 6 \\ \hline 670 \end{array}$$

**B. Multiple of 100**

$$\begin{array}{r} 85 \text{ R5} \\ 7\overline{)600} \\ -56\downarrow \\ \hline 40 \\ -35 \\ \hline 5 \end{array}$$

Check:
$$\begin{array}{r} 85 \\ \times\ 7 \\ \hline 595 \\ +\ \ 5 \\ \hline 600 \end{array}$$



Extra Help at **eduplace.com/map**

## Guided Practice

**Divide. Check your answers.**

1. $6\overline{)384}$  2. $8\overline{)672}$  3. $7\overline{)542}$  4. $4\overline{)348}$

5. $437 \div 6$  6. $235 \div 5$  7. $341 \div 9$  8. $473 \div 6$

**Ask Yourself**

- Can I divide the hundreds?
- Can I divide the tens?
- Can I divide the ones?

**Explain Your Thinking** ▶ When you divide a three-digit dividend by a one-digit divisor, what is the least number of digits that can be in the quotient?

## Practice and Problem Solving

**Divide. Check your answers.**

9. $4\overline{)396}$  10. $8\overline{)272}$  11. $5\overline{)394}$  12. $3\overline{)485}$

13. $2\overline{)162}$  14. $4\overline{)284}$  15. $6\overline{)532}$  16. $8\overline{)889}$

17. $134 \div 2$  18. $504 \div 3$  19. $317 \div 9$  20. $587 \div 6$

**Algebra • Functions Copy and complete each function table.**

| | Divide by 3 | |
|---|---|---|
| | Input | Output |
| 21. | 209 | ■ |
| 22. | 361 | ■ |
| 23. | 577 | ■ |

| | Divide by 4 | |
|---|---|---|
| | Input | Output |
| 24. | 209 | ■ |
| 25. | 361 | ■ |
| 26. | 577 | ■ |

**Solve.**

27. **Analyze** Look back at each function table. What patterns do you notice? Explain your thinking.

28. There are 452 insect photos displayed in 4 equal groups. How many photos are in each group?

29. Tim wants to sort 242 butterfly photos into 5 equal groups. How many photos will he have left over?

Go On

**Data** **The bar graph below shows how fast some animals can run. Use the graph for Problems 30–36.**

**30.** At top speed, how much faster can a cheetah run than a lion?

**31.** Which animal's top speed is twice as fast as an elephant's?

**32.** List the animals in order from the slowest to the fastest.

**33.** **Analyze** Suppose an antelope could run at its fastest speed for 15 minutes. How far would it run?

**34.** The record speed for a coyote is 43 miles an hour. Which animal runs about as fast as a coyote?

**35.** **Analyze** Suppose an elephant ran for 10 minutes at its fastest speed. How far could it run?

**36.** **Challenge** Suppose a grizzly bear can travel 9 miles in 15 minutes. What animal runs about twice as fast as the grizzly bear?

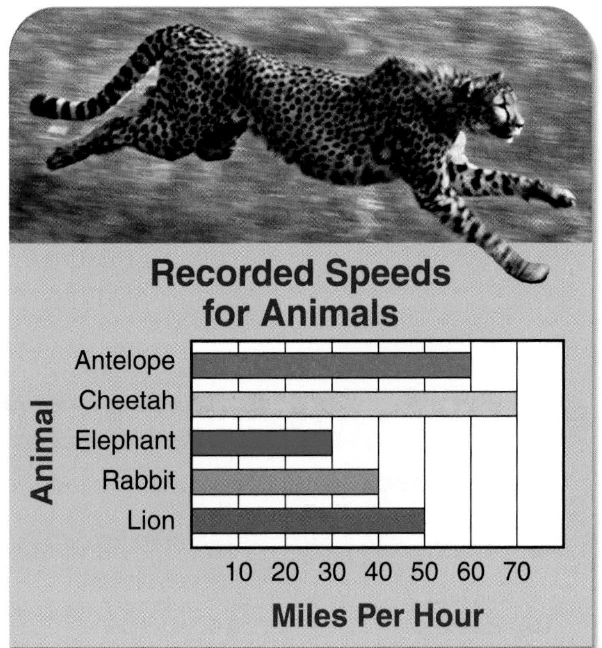

## Sharpening Skills for CRCT

**Open Response**

**Write each time to the minute before and after the hour.** (Grade 3)

**37.** 

**38.** 

**39.** 

**40.** 

**41.** Judy, Ron, and Michael have 147 baseball cards to share equally. How many baseball cards will each child receive?

**42.** Six friends shared 234 pennies equally. Explain how you would estimate the number of pennies each friend received. (Ch. 9, Lesson 2)



Extra Practice See page 249, Set B.

Problem Solving

GPS

## Logical Reasoning
### Digit Detective

STANDARDS Extends M4N4, M4P1.a

Solve these division problems by working backwards! You have the quotient, now find the divisor and the dividend.

**Use the digits in each square only once to complete each problem.**

**1.** 1 3 R1 — ■)■■

**2.** 1 6 R1 — ■)■■

**3.** 1 2 R2 — ■)■■

**4.** ■ R1 — ■)■■

1: 3, 4, 5

2: 5, 4, 6

3: 6, 7, 8

4: 1, 2, 4, 5

## Math Reasoning
### Purple Paint Prices

Pierre at the Paint Pot Store told Pat that he could sell her 9 gallons of purple paint for $216. Paco at the Perfect Paints Store said, "I have a better price! I'll sell you 8 gallons for only $208."

**Is Paco's price better than Pierre's?** Explain how you decided.

## Brain Teaser

**Education Place**

Check out **eduplace.com/map** for more brain teasers.

Lesson 3

# Divide Money

**Objective** Divide money amounts.

 **STANDARDS** M4N4, M4N7.d, M4P1.b, M4P2

## Learn About It

A mother and her three children are spending the day at the petting zoo. She paid $9.80 for their admission. Each ticket cost the same amount. How much was each ticket?

**Divide. $9.80 ÷ 4 = ■ or 4)$9.80**

**STEP 1** Estimate.

$9.80 is between $8.00 and $12.00.

```
  $2.00        $3.00
4)$8.00     4)$12.00
```

The quotient will be between $2.00 and $3.00.

**STEP 2** Divide as if you were dividing whole numbers.

```
   2 45
4)$9.80
 - 8
   18
 - 16
    20
  - 20
     0
```

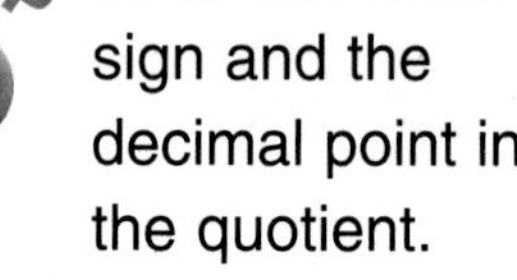

**STEP 3** Write the dollar sign and the decimal point in the quotient.

```
  $2.45
4)$9.80
 - 8
   18
 - 16
    20
  - 20
     0
```

Align the decimal point in the quotient with the decimal point in the dividend.

**Solution:** Cost of admission for each person was $2.45. Since $2.45 is between $2.00 and $3.00, the answer is reasonable.

### Another Example

**Zero in the Dividend**

**Divide.**

```
   1 68
3)$5.04
 - 3
   20
 - 18
    24
  - 24
     0
```

**Write the dollar sign and the decimal point.**

```
  $1.68
3)$5.04
 - 3
   20
 - 18
    24
  - 24
     0
```

## Guided Practice

**Estimate. Then divide.**

1. $8\overline{)\$9.20}$
2. $3\overline{)\$756}$
3. $2\overline{)\$0.42}$
4. $2\overline{)\$856}$
5. $3\overline{)\$0.81}$
6. $4\overline{)\$7.92}$
7. $1.55 ÷ 5
8. $252 ÷ 6
9. $5.39 ÷ 7

**Ask Yourself**

- Where should I place the first digit in the quotient?
- Where should I place the decimal point in the quotient?

**Explain Your Thinking** ▶ How can estimating when dividing money help you be sure the decimal point is in the correct place in the quotient? Use an example to explain.

## Practice and Problem Solving

**Divide. Check your answers.**

10. $6\overline{)\$6.72}$
11. $6\overline{)\$0.78}$
12. $3\overline{)\$0.48}$
13. $4\overline{)\$7.24}$
14. $4\overline{)\$88}$
15. $8\overline{)\$5.76}$
16. $3\overline{)\$6.36}$
17. $2\overline{)\$1.34}$
18. $45 ÷ 3
19. $0.36 ÷ 2
20. $0.88 ÷ 8
21. $0.72 ÷ 6
22. $7.56 ÷ 6
23. $5.58 ÷ 9
24. $8.19 ÷ 9
25. $464 ÷ 8

**Solve.**

26. **What's Wrong?** Look at Vera's work. What did she do wrong?

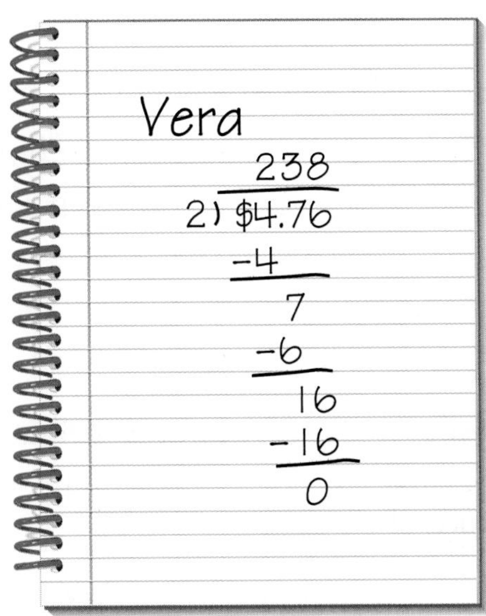


27. Tina spends $4.38 on 2 key chains at the petting zoo. Each key chain costs the same amount. How much does each key chain cost?
28. On the way to the petting zoo, Mrs. Ellis bought 6 gallons of gasoline for $8.70. How much did she spend on each gallon?
29. Paulo has $9.44 in his pocket. He wants to use the money to buy small gifts for 3 friends, and then keep the rest for himself. If Paulo wants to buy a yo-yo for each of his friends, and yo-yos cost $3.29 after tax, does he have enough money?

Go On

## Algebra • Functions Copy and complete each table.

| | Rule: $y = x \div 5$ | |
|---|---|---|
| | $x$ | $y$ |
| 30. | ■ | \$1.21 |
| 31. | \$7.50 | ■ |
| 32. | \$0.95 | ■ |
| 33. | ■ | \$0.14 |

| | Rule: $y = x \div 9$ | |
|---|---|---|
| | $x$ | $y$ |
| 34. | ■ | \$1.12 |
| 35. | \$9.99 | ■ |
| 36. | ■ | \$0.51 |
| 37. | \$4.95 | ■ |

| 38. | Rule: ____ | |
|---|---|---|
| | $x$ | $y$ |
| | \$1.50 | \$0.75 |
| | \$0.90 | \$0.45 |
| | \$6.80 | \$3.40 |
| | \$5.32 | \$2.66 |

**Compare. Write >, <, or = for each ●.**

39. \$3.99 ÷ 3 ● \$1.00

40. \$7.92 ÷ 3 ● \$2.00

41. \$6.63 ÷ 3 ● \$3.00

42. \$5.04 ÷ 4 ● \$2.00

43. \$8.46 ÷ 3 ● \$3.00

44. \$6.20 ÷ 5 ● \$1.00

## Data Use the ad for Problems 45–49.

45. What is a good estimate for the total cost of 3 T-shirts at the gift shop?

46. Mrs. Rea needs to buy 7 rolls of film. What is the least amount she might pay? What is the greatest amount she might pay?

47. **You Decide** Tony has \$20.00 to spend at the gift shop. What can he buy? Explain how you decided.

48. Kelly wants to buy mugs for her mother and her two aunts. How much money does she need?

49. **Multistep** Ann wants to send postcards to each of the 8 girls in her club. She also wants to buy one roll of film. How much money does she need?

Extra Practice See page 249, Set C.

Problem Solving

GPS

## Social Studies Connection
## Three Cheers for Division

**STANDARDS** M4N4.a, M4P4

In the 1800s, Americans could buy things with a Spanish coin worth a dollar. If an item cost less than a dollar, people broke their Spanish coin into eight small pieces, or bits. These are the "bits" in the cheer, "Two bits, four bits, six bits, a dollar..."

1. About how much was 1 bit worth?
2. If you spent 50 cents in the 1800s, how many bits would you need?
3. Suppose an item cost $2.36. You could pay with $2.00 and how many bits?
4. **You Decide** Do you think that it was practical to break off parts of the Spanish coin? What problems might this cause?

WEEKLY WR READER **eduplace.com/map**

Quick Check

**Check your understanding of Lessons 1–3.**

**Divide. Check your answers.** (Lessons 1–2)

1. $2\overline{)398}$
2. $3\overline{)736}$
3. $806 \div 5$
4. $937 \div 4$
5. $2\overline{)196}$
6. $3\overline{)260}$
7. $593 \div 5$
8. $384 \div 4$

**Solve.** (Lesson 3)

9. Juan and Roberto spend $5.70 on lunch together. Each lunch costs the same amount. What is the price of each lunch?
10. Anna and her 2 sisters each buy a key chain. They spend $4.35 altogether. If each key chain costs the same amount, what is the price of one key chain?

Extra Practice at **eduplace.com/map**

Lesson 4

Audio Tutor 1/33 Listen and Understand

# Zeros in the Quotient

**Objective** Decide when to place zeros in the quotient.

STANDARDS M4N4, M4A1.c, M4P1.b

## Learn About It

Whale Watch Company buys binoculars for visitors to use on their tours. The binoculars are shipped in boxes of 8. If the tour manager orders 824 binoculars, how many boxes should she receive?

**Divide.** **824 ÷ 8 = ■ or 8)824**

**STEP 1** Decide where to place the first digit.

Think: 8)8 hundreds → ? hundreds

```
   1
8)824   Multiply. 1 × 8
 - 8 ←  Subtract. 8 − 8
   0    Compare. 0 < 8
```

**STEP 2** Bring down the tens. Divide the tens.

Think: 8)2 tens → ? tens

```
   10
8)824
 - 8↓
   02
```

Since 2 < 8, you cannot divide the tens. Write a zero in the tens place.

**STEP 3** Bring down the ones. Divide the ones.

Think: 8)24 ones → ? ones

```
   103
8)824
 - 8 ↓
   024    Multiply. 3 × 8
  - 24 ←  Subtract. 24 − 24
     0    Compare. 0 < 8
```

**Check.**
Multiply.
8 × 103 = 824
The product equals the dividend.

**Solution:** The manager should receive 103 boxes.

## Guided Practice

**Divide. Check your answers.**

**1.** 3)924 **2.** 4)832 **3.** 5)547 **4.** 6)639

**5.** 9)972 **6.** 8)884 **7.** 7)746 **8.** 7)635

**Ask Yourself**

- Can I divide the hundreds?
- Can I divide the tens?
- Can I divide the ones?

**Explain Your Thinking** ▶ Look back at Exercise 1. Why must you remember to write the zero in the quotient?

## Practice and Problem Solving

**Divide. Check your answers.**

9. $4\overline{)804}$
10. $2\overline{)412}$
11. $7\overline{)\$7.56}$
12. $6\overline{)361}$
13. $7\overline{)\$8.40}$
14. $2\overline{)613}$
15. $9\overline{)992}$
16. $5\overline{)754}$
17. $162 \div 8$
18. $529 \div 5$
19. $420 \div 3$
20. $\$8.72 \div 8$
21. $\$6.12 \div 3$
22. $963 \div 8$
23. $947 \div 9$
24. $\$9.10 \div 7$

### Algebra • Expressions Find the value of each expression when $n = 3$.

25. $66 \div n$
26. $96 \div n$
27. $849 \div n$
28. $342 \div n$
29. $848 \div (n - 1)$
30. $(8 \times n) \div 2$
31. $742 \div (n + 4)$
32. $342 \div (n \times 3)$

**Solve.**

33. The Whale Watch Company sailed 3 times last Saturday, with the same number of tourists each time. If 324 tourists sailed on Saturday, how many people were on each tour?

34. **Write About It** Think about the problem $968 \div 8 = 121$. Without dividing, decide whether there would be a remainder if you divided by 4. Explain your reasoning.

## GPS Sharpening Skills for CRCT

**Open Response**

**Divide.** (Ch. 8, Lesson 4)

35. $8\overline{)60}$
36. $4\overline{)70}$
37. $5\overline{)60}$
38. $9\overline{)30}$
39. $6\overline{)70}$
40. $7\overline{)40}$
41. $3\overline{)50}$
42. $3\overline{)70}$
43. $7\overline{)90}$
44. $7\overline{)30}$
45. $5\overline{)70}$
46. $8\overline{)50}$

**Multiple Choice**

47. Jamie divides 321 books equally into 3 boxes. How many books are in each box? (Ch. 9, Lesson 4)

A. 17
B. 107
C. 648
D. 3,752

Extra Practice See page 249, Set D.

Lesson 5

# Problem-Solving Strategy

## Work Backward

**Objective** Work backward to solve a problem.

**STANDARDS** Extends and enriches M4N7, M4P1.a, M4P1.b

**Problem** Aurora visited an aquarium. She saw 5 more jellyfish than leafy sea dragons. There were 10 more tropical fish than starfish. Aurora saw twice as many starfish as jellyfish. She saw 120 tropical fish. How many leafy sea dragons did Aurora see?

*The leafy sea dragon is found only in Australia. It is a relative of the sea horse and is an endangered species.*

UNDERSTAND

**This is what Aurora saw.**

- 5 more jellyfish than leafy sea dragons
- 10 more tropical fish than starfish
- twice as many starfish as jellyfish
- 120 tropical fish

PLAN

**You can use what you know.**

You know the number of tropical fish.
Work backward and use inverse operations.

Remember
- Addition and subtraction are inverse operations.
- Multiplication and division are inverse operations.

SOLVE

**Use inverse operations.**

Start with the 120 tropical fish.

| tropical fish | | starfish | | jellyfish | | leafy sea dragons |
|---|---|---|---|---|---|---|
| 120 | − 10 | 110 | ÷ 2 | 55 | − 5 | 50 |
| This is 10 more than the number of starfish. | Work backward. Subtract 10. | This is twice the number of jellyfish. | Work backward. Divide by 2. | This is 5 more than the number of leafy sea dragons. | Work backward. Subtract 5. | |

**Solution:** Aurora saw 50 leafy sea dragons.

LOOK BACK

**Look back at the problem.** How can you check the answer?

## Guided Practice

**Use the Ask Yourself questions to help you solve each problem.**

1. Twice as many people went on the first aquarium tour as the second tour. Three times as many went on the third tour as the second tour. If 90 people went on the third tour, how many went on the first tour?

   **Hint** What information should you start with?

2. At a zoo, there are 2 more penguins than walruses. There are half as many seals as penguins. There are 6 seals. How many walruses are at the zoo?

### Ask Yourself

UNDERSTAND

**What facts do I know?**

**What number do I know?**

**Did I use inverse operations?**

**Did I check by starting with my answer and working forward?**

## Independent Practice

**Solve.**

3. The Dunns bought aquarium supplies. One angelfish cost 2 times as much as the fish food. The filter cost 3 times as much as the angelfish. The filter cost $12. How much did the fish food cost?

4. At an aquarium there are twice as many sharks as turtles. There are 3 fewer seals than sharks. If there are 15 seals, how many turtles are there?

5. Kelley is thinking of a number. She adds 1, divides by 5, subtracts 2, and multiplies by 5. The result is 40. What is Kelley's number?

6. **Create and Solve** Make up a number puzzle like the one in Problem 5. Give your number puzzle to a classmate to solve.

Go On

# Mixed Problem Solving

**Solve. Show your work. Tell what strategy you used.**

7. Justin is in a parade. There are 4 rows of students in front of him and 12 rows behind him. There are 5 students to his right and 4 to his left. If every row has the same number of students, how many students are there?

8. **Money** Dale buys a book and a bookmark. The bookmark costs half as much as the book. The total cost is $9.75. How much does each item cost?

9. Michael is 5 years older than Liz. Liz is 8 years younger than Carlos. Carlos is 2 years older than Meredith. If Meredith is 12 years old, how old is Michael?

**You Choose**

**Strategy**
- Draw a Picture
- Guess and Check
- Work Backward
- Write an Equation

**Computation Method**
- Mental Math
- Estimation
- Paper and Pencil
- Calculator

## Data Use the table for Problems 10–13.

10. Amy, Lisa, and Dwayne skated on different paths. Amy's path was longer than Dwayne's but shorter than Lisa's. Lisa did not skate on Windy Way. Which path did each use?

11. **Explain** Ty skated all of Speedy Street and Twisty Trail. Ed skated all of Bumpy Boulevard and Windy Way. Who skated farther? Explain how you got your answer.

12. **Mental Math** There are 3 feet in a yard. Which path at Skate Park is 960 feet long?

13. **Measurement** A mile is 1,760 yards. Edith skates Windy Way 5 times. Is that more than a mile? Explain.

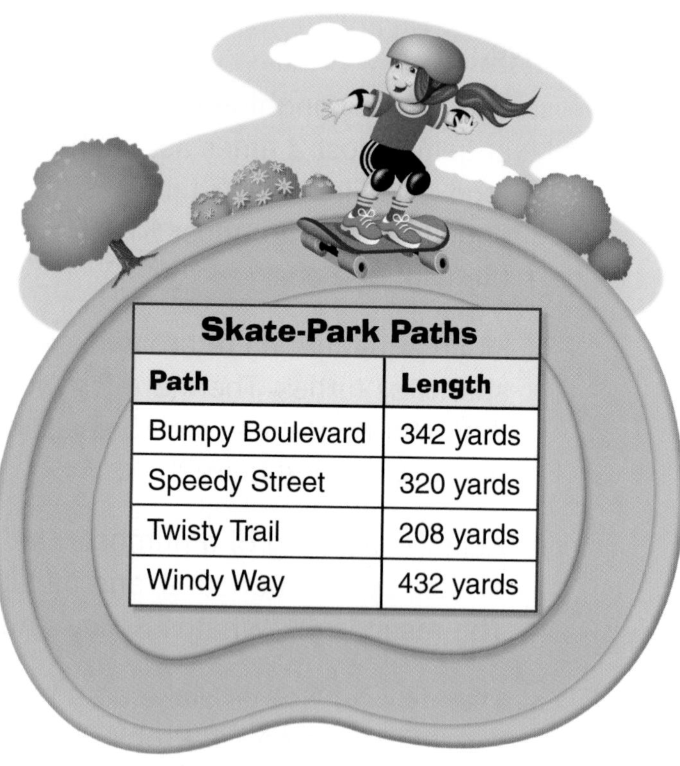

| Skate-Park Paths | |
|---|---|
| **Path** | **Length** |
| Bumpy Boulevard | 342 yards |
| Speedy Street | 320 yards |
| Twisty Trail | 208 yards |
| Windy Way | 432 yards |

## Sharpening Skills for CRCT

**Open Response**

**Divide. Check your answers**

(Chapter 9, Lesson 3)

**40.** \$4.83 ÷ 7

**41.** \$8.46 ÷ 9

**42.** \$5.60 ÷ 5

**43.** \$0.64 ÷ 4

**44.** \$12.32 ÷ 4

**45.** \$5.70 ÷ 5

**46.** \$8.10 ÷ 3

**47.** \$13.08 ÷ 4

**48.** The Panos family is planning a 7,917 mile trip for next summer. Their trip will be 7 days long. If they travel the same number of miles each day during the trip, how many miles should they travel each day?

(Chapter 9, Lesson 6)

## Problem Solving

# Math Reasoning

## Nifty Nines

STANDARDS M4A1.a

Look at the number pattern of nines.

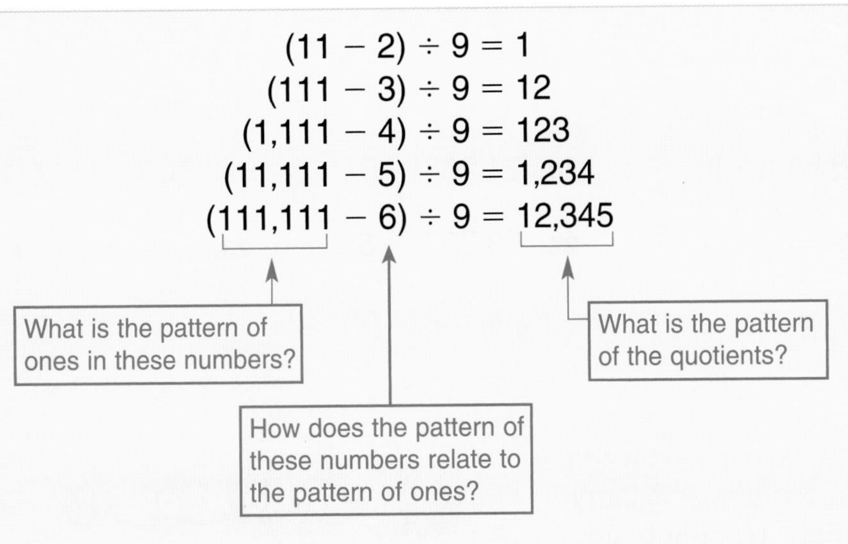

$$(11 - 2) \div 9 = 1$$
$$(111 - 3) \div 9 = 12$$
$$(1{,}111 - 4) \div 9 = 123$$
$$(11{,}111 - 5) \div 9 = 1{,}234$$
$$(111{,}111 - 6) \div 9 = 12{,}345$$

1. What is the next number sentence in the pattern?

2. What number would you subtract from 1,111,111,111? What would be the quotient?

# Chapter Review/Test

## VOCABULARY

**Choose the best word to complete each statement.**

1. The answer in a division problem is the ____.
2. If one whole number cannot be divided equally by another, there will be a ____.
3. The number that is divided in a division problem is the ____.

**Vocabulary**

**divisor**
**dividend**
**quotient**
**remainder**

## CONCEPTS AND SKILLS

**Divide. Check your answers.** (Lessons 1–4, pp. 228–239)

| | | | |
|---|---|---|---|
| **4.** 2)264 | **5.** 3)975 | **6.** 4)548 | **7.** 4)219 |
| **8.** 8)173 | **9.** 7)457 | **10.** 4)\$4.20 | **11.** 9)\$6.48 |
| **12.** 6)\$2.10 | **13.** 3)906 | **14.** 6)638 | **15.** 8)\$8.64 |

**Estimate. Then divide.** (Lesson 6, pp. 244–246)

| | | | |
|---|---|---|---|
| **16.** 9,105 ÷ 3 | **17.** 6,544 ÷ 8 | **18.** 31,268 ÷ 6 | **19.** 50,734 ÷ 7 |
| **20.** 14,533 ÷ 3 | **21.** \$768.64 ÷ 8 | **22.** 53,527 ÷ 5 | **23.** \$441.81 ÷ 9 |

## PROBLEM SOLVING

**Solve.** (Lesson 5, pp. 240–242)

24. Three people got on the bus at Asbury Street. At the next stop, 10 people got on and 5 people got off. Then there were 28 people on the bus. How many people were on the bus before it stopped at Asbury Street?

25. Ali is twice as old as Kevin. Kevin is 10 years older than Pedro. Pedro is 2 years old. How old is Ali?

**Show You Understand**

**Explain the steps you would use to solve this problem.**

5)600

Use pictures, symbols, or words to explain the steps you used.

# Extra Practice

## Set A (Lesson 1, pp. 228–229)

**Divide. Check your answers.**

1. $3\overline{)381}$
2. $2\overline{)246}$
3. $4\overline{)566}$
4. $7\overline{)859}$
5. $5\overline{)605}$
6. $675 \div 5$
7. $476 \div 3$
8. $686 \div 4$
9. $775 \div 6$
10. $937 \div 8$

## Set B (Lesson 2, pp. 230–232)

**Divide. Check your answers.**

1. $5\overline{)120}$
2. $4\overline{)396}$
3. $6\overline{)451}$
4. $8\overline{)753}$
5. $9\overline{)327}$
6. $239 \div 3$
7. $435 \div 7$
8. $126 \div 4$
9. $352 \div 8$
10. $575 \div 6$

## Set C (Lesson 3, pp. 234–236)

**Divide. Check your answers.**

1. $2\overline{)\$0.48}$
2. $3\overline{)\$3.96}$
3. $4\overline{)\$3.44}$
4. $5\overline{)\$6.10}$
5. $6\overline{)\$0.78}$
6. $\$5.12 \div 4$
7. $\$2.66 \div 7$
8. $\$1.10 \div 5$
9. $\$8.68 \div 7$
10. $\$6.48 \div 3$

## Set D (Lesson 4, pp. 238–239)

**Divide. Check your answers.**

1. $6\overline{)639}$
2. $4\overline{)880}$
3. $3\overline{)325}$
4. $5\overline{)524}$
5. $7\overline{)722}$
6. $188 \div 9$
7. $510 \div 5$
8. $612 \div 3$
9. $427 \div 4$
10. $962 \div 8$

## Set E (Lesson 6, pp. 244–246)

**Estimate. Then divide.**

1. $4\overline{)1{,}799}$
2. $2\overline{)2{,}560}$
3. $3\overline{)3{,}037}$
4. $9\overline{)4{,}554}$
5. $6\overline{)4{,}274}$
6. $6{,}413 \div 7$
7. $15{,}481 \div 3$
8. $20{,}415 \div 4$
9. $31{,}985 \div 5$
10. $65{,}738 \div 8$

Extra Practice at **eduplace.com/map**

CHAPTER 10

# Number Theory and Mean

## INVESTIGATION

### Using Data

The table shows how many children used some of the slides at a fair. About how many children would you guess used the red slide on Thursday? What information from the table did you use to make your guess?

**Children Using Slides**

| | Tuesday | Wednesday | Thursday |
|---|---|---|---|
| Red | 151 | 298 | ? |
| Blue | 160 | 321 | 638 |
| Pink | 190 | 399 | 791 |
| Green | 144 | 288 | 590 |

#  Use What You Know

**Use this page to review and remember what you need to know for this chapter.**

## VOCABULARY

**Choose the best word to complete each sentence.**

1. In the number sentence $4 \times 7 = 28$, 7 is a ____.
2. In the number sentence $32 \div 4 = 8$, 32 is the ____.
3. The number you divide by is the ____.
4. The answer in a division problem is the ____.

**Vocabulary**

- factor
- divisor
- product
- quotient
- dividend

## CONCEPTS AND SKILLS

**Skip count to find the missing numbers.**

5. 15, 20, 25, ■, ■, ■
6. 40, 50, ■, ■, 80
7. 4, 8, 12, ■, ■, ■
8. 6, 9, ■, 15, ■, ■
9. ■, 12, 18, ■, ■
10. ■, ■, 32, ■, 48, 56

**Write a division sentence and a multiplication sentence for each picture.**

11.

12. 

13.

**Solve.**

14. $6 + 134 + 23$
15. $5 + 6 + 21 + 33$
16. $100 + 98 + 178$
17. $1,976 \div 8$
18. $896 \div 7$
19. $50,670 \div 9$

20. What do the numbers 5, 10, 15, 20, 25, 30, 35, and 40 have in common?

Facts Practice, See Page 670.

Hands On Lesson 1

 **Audio Tutor 1**/34 Listen and Understand

# Factors and Multiples

**Objective** Find factors and multiples of whole numbers.

**STANDARDS** Prepares for M5N1.b, M4P3

**Vocabulary**
**factor**
**multiple**

## Work Together

**Materials**
Multiplication Table (Learning Tool 13)

You can use a multiplication table to find **factors**.

Work with a partner.

**STEP 1** Find 18 on the multiplication table.

- Look at the number at the top of the column. 6 is a factor of 18.
- Look at the number at the side of the row. 3 is a factor of 18.

$6 \times 3 = 18$

↑ factor ↑ factor

column ↓ (6)
row → (3)

| × | 1 | 2 | 3 | 4 | 5 | 6 | 7 | 8 | 9 | 10 | 11 | 12 |
|---|---|---|---|---|---|---|---|---|---|---|---|---|
| 1 | 1 | 2 | 3 | 4 | 5 | 6 | 7 | 8 | 9 | 10 | 11 | 12 |
| 2 | 2 | 4 | 6 | 8 | 10 | 12 | 14 | 16 | 18 | 20 | 22 | 24 |
| 3 | 3 | 6 | 9 | 12 | 15 | **18** | 21 | 24 | 27 | 30 | 33 | 36 |
| 4 | 4 | 8 | 12 | 16 | 20 | 24 | 28 | 32 | 36 | 40 | 44 | 48 |
| 5 | 5 | 10 | 15 | 20 | 25 | 30 | 35 | 40 | 45 | 50 | 55 | 60 |
| 6 | 6 | 12 | 18 | 24 | 30 | 36 | 42 | 48 | 54 | 60 | 66 | 72 |
| 7 | 7 | 14 | 21 | 28 | 35 | 42 | 49 | 56 | 63 | 70 | 77 | 84 |
| 8 | 8 | 16 | 24 | 32 | 40 | 48 | 56 | 64 | 72 | 80 | 88 | 96 |
| 9 | 9 | 18 | 27 | 36 | 45 | 54 | 63 | 72 | 81 | 90 | 99 | 10 |
| 10 | 10 | 20 | 30 | 40 | 50 | 60 | 70 | 80 | 90 | 100 | 110 | 12 |
| 11 | 11 | 22 | 33 | 44 | 55 | 66 | 77 | 88 | 99 | 110 | 121 | 13 |
| 12 | 12 | 24 | 36 | 48 | 60 | 72 | 84 | 96 | 108 | 120 | 132 | 14 |

**STEP 2** Find 18 in other places on the table. List other factors of 18.

**STEP 3** Repeat Steps 1 and 2 to find factors of 24.

- What factors did you find?
- Do you think these are all of the factors of 24? Explain.

You can also use a multiplication table to find multiples.

▶ A **multiple** of a number is a product of that number and any whole number.

Some multiples of 2 are 2, 4, 6, 8, and 10.



Extra Help at **eduplace.com/map**

Follow these steps to find common multiples.

Look at the column that starts with 2. All the numbers in this column are multiples of 2.

- List the multiples of 2 on the table.

Look at the column that starts with 3. All the numbers in this column are multiples of 3.

- List the multiples of 3 on the table.

These numbers that are on both lists are common multiples of 2 and 3.

- List the common multiples of 2 and 3.

| × | 1 | 2 | 3 | 4 | 5 | 6 | 7 | 8 | 9 | 10 | 11 | 12 |
|---|---|---|---|---|---|---|---|---|---|---|---|---|
| 1 | 1 | 2 | 3 | 4 | 5 | 6 | 7 | 8 | 9 | 10 | 11 | 12 |
| 2 | 2 | 4 | 6 | 8 | 10 | 12 | 14 | 16 | 18 | 20 | 22 | 24 |
| 3 | 3 | 6 | 9 | 12 | 15 | 18 | 21 | 24 | 27 | 30 | 33 | 36 |
| 4 | 4 | 8 | 12 | 16 | 20 | 24 | 28 | 32 | 36 | 40 | 44 | 48 |
| 5 | 5 | 10 | 15 | 20 | 25 | 30 | 35 | 40 | 45 | 50 | 55 | 60 |
| 6 | 6 | 12 | 18 | 24 | 30 | 36 | 42 | 48 | 54 | 60 | 66 | 72 |
| 7 | 7 | 14 | 21 | 28 | 35 | 42 | 49 | 56 | 63 | 70 | 77 | 84 |
| 8 | 8 | 16 | 24 | 32 | 40 | 48 | 56 | 64 | 72 | 80 | 88 | 96 |
| 9 | 9 | 18 | 27 | 36 | 45 | 54 | 63 | 72 | 81 | 90 | 99 | 108 |
| 10 | 10 | 20 | 30 | 40 | 50 | 60 | 70 | 80 | 90 | 100 | 110 | 120 |
| 11 | 11 | 22 | 33 | 44 | 55 | 66 | 77 | 88 | 99 | 110 | 121 | 132 |
| 12 | 12 | 24 | 36 | 48 | 60 | 72 | 84 | 96 | 108 | 120 | 132 | 144 |

Repeat Step 4. This time list the multiples of 3 and 6 on the table.

- What common multiples of 3 and 6 did you find?

## On Your Own

**List the factors on the table for each number.**

**1.** 12 **2.** 45 **3.** 100 **4.** 11 **5.** 72

**Use the table to list 10 multiples for each number in each pair. Then circle the common multiples.**

**6.** 2, 5 **7.** 6, 10 **8.** 3, 7 **9.** 9, 10 **10.** 4, 12

## Talk About It • Write About It

**You learned how to find factors and multiples of numbers.**

**11. Explain** Are all the factors of a number shown on the multiplication table? Are all the multiples shown? Give examples to explain your answers.

**12. Reasoning** Do you think a number that has 8 as a factor will also have 4 as a factor? Explain your thinking.

Audio Tutor 1/35 Listen and Understand

# Prime and Composite Numbers

**Objective** Tell if a number is prime or composite.

**Vocabulary**
prime number
composite number

**Materials**
counters

## Learn About It

STANDARDS Prepares for M5N1.a, M4P2, M4P5

You can use the factors of a number to tell if it is a prime number or a composite number.

▶ **A prime number is a whole number that has exactly two factors, 1 and itself.**

Some prime numbers are 19, 29, 31.

| Number | Factors |
|---|---|
| 19 | 1, 19 |
| 29 | 1, 29 |
| 31 | 1, 31 |

▶ **A composite number is a whole number that has more than two factors.**

Some composite numbers are 15, 18, 25.

| Number | Factors |
|---|---|
| 15 | 1, 3, 5, 15 |
| 18 | 1, 2, 3, 6, 9, 18 |
| 25 | 1, 5, 25 |

**Try this activity to tell if a number is prime or composite.**

**STEP 1** You can make arrays to find the factors of a number. Use 6 counters to make an array like the one shown.

- How many counters are in each row? in each column?
- What are two factors of 6?

**STEP 2** Continue to make arrays to find all of the factors of 6.

- What arrays did you make?
- What are the factors of 6?

Record the factors from least to greatest in a chart like the one shown.

| Number | Factors |
|---|---|
| 1 | |
| 2 | |
| 3 | |
| 4 | |
| 5 | |
| 6 | 1, 2, 3, 6 |
| 7 | |

**STEP 3** Repeat Steps 1 and 2 for the numbers 1 through 12.

- Which number has only 1 factor?
- Which numbers have exactly 2 factors?
- Which numbers have more than 2 factors?

**STEP 4** Look at your chart.

- List the prime numbers. List the composite numbers. Explain how you made your lists.
- What number is not on either of your lists? Why not?

Since the number 1 has only 1 factor it is neither prime nor composite.

## Guided Practice

**Ask Yourself**

- Can I make another array with the same number of counters?
- Does the number have more than 2 factors?

**Tell if each array represents a prime number or a composite number.**

1. ● ● ● ● ●
   ● ● ● ● ●

2. ● ● ● ● ●

3. ● ●
   ● ●
   ● ●

4. ● ● ● ●
   ● ● ● ●
   ● ● ● ●
   ● ● ● ●

5. ● ● ● ● ● ●

6. ● ● ●

**List the factors of each number. Use counters if you wish. Then tell if the number is prime or composite.**

| | | | | |
|---|---|---|---|---|
| **7.** 22 | **8.** 16 | **9.** 42 | **10.** 13 | **11.** 18 |
| **12.** 23 | **13.** 17 | **14.** 25 | **15.** 31 | **16.** 20 |

**Explain Your Thinking** ▶ How does making arrays help you tell if a number is prime or composite?

Go On

## Practice and Problem Solving

**List the factors of each number. Use counters if you wish. Then tell if the number is prime or composite.**

**17.** 21 **18.** 19 **19.** 15 **20.** 27 **21.** 100

**22.** 47 **23.** 24 **24.** 51 **25.** 26 **26.** 28

**Tell if each number is prime or composite.**

**27.** 39 **28.** 41 **29.** 37 **30.** 33 **31.** 49

**32.** 54 **33.** 53 **34.** 95 **35.** 46 **36.** 60

**37.** 52 **38.** 69 **39.** 71 **40.** 16 **41.** 30

**Solve.**

**42. Analyze** Are any even numbers prime? Are all odd numbers prime? Use examples to explain.

**43.** Are there any whole numbers that have 0 or 5 in the ones place that are prime? Explain your thinking.

**44. Explain** Do you need to list every factor of a number to tell if it is prime or composite? Why or why not?

**45. What's Wrong?** Look at Toby's work. She decided that 5 is a composite number because she can make 2 arrays with 5 counters. Explain what is wrong with Toby's reasoning.

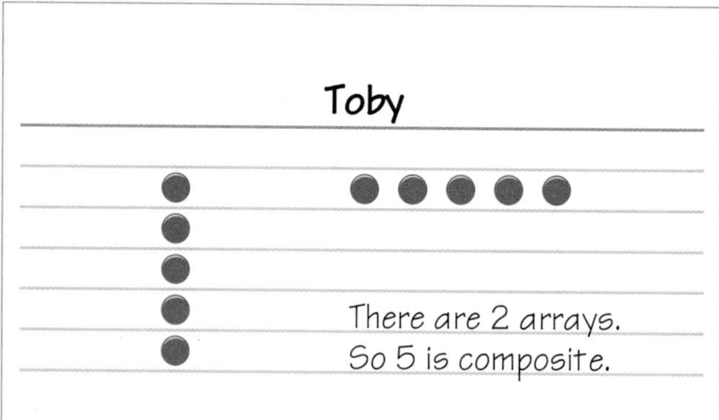

## Sharpening Skills for CRCT

**Open Response**

**Divide.** (Ch. 9, Lessons 3, 6)

**46.** \$0.36 ÷ 3 **47.** \$0.92 ÷ 4

**48.** \$7.50 ÷ 6 **49.** 1,230 ÷ 6

**Multiple Choice**

**50.** Which is a prime number? (Ch. 10, Lesson 2)

A. 1 C. 21

B. 10 D. 43



Extra Practice see page 269, Set A.

# Math Challenge

## The Sieve of Eratosthenes

Activity

GPS

STANDARDS Prepares for M5N1.a

**Materials**
Learning Tool 14

Eratosthenes was an ancient Greek mathematician who discovered a way to find prime numbers from 1 to 100.

Follow the steps below to find out how.

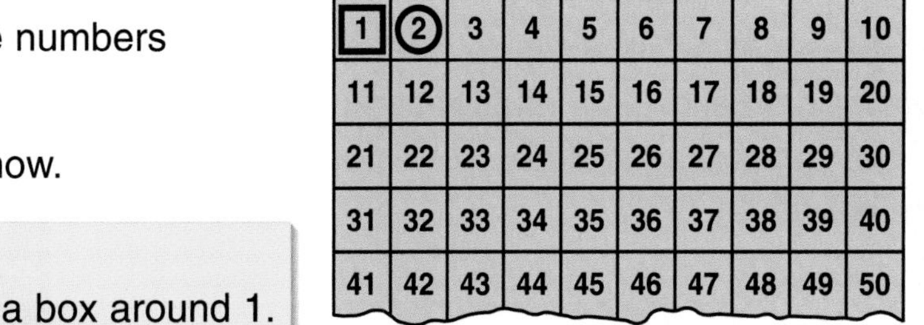

| 1 | 2 | 3 | 4 | 5 | 6 | 7 | 8 | 9 | 10 |
|---|---|---|---|---|---|---|---|---|---|
| 11 | 12 | 13 | 14 | 15 | 16 | 17 | 18 | 19 | 20 |
| 21 | 22 | 23 | 24 | 25 | 26 | 27 | 28 | 29 | 30 |
| 31 | 32 | 33 | 34 | 35 | 36 | 37 | 38 | 39 | 40 |
| 41 | 42 | 43 | 44 | 45 | 46 | 47 | 48 | 49 | 50 |

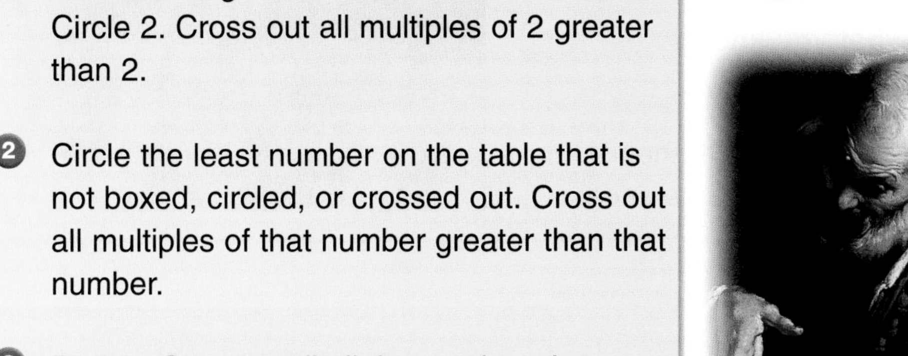

1. Use Learning Tool 14. Draw a box around 1. Circle 2. Cross out all multiples of 2 greater than 2.
2. Circle the least number on the table that is not boxed, circled, or crossed out. Cross out all multiples of that number greater than that number.
3. Repeat Step 2 until all the numbers have been crossed out or circled.
4. List the numbers you circled. What do you notice about these numbers?

Quick Check

**Check your understanding of Lessons 1–2.**

**List five multiples of each number.** (Lesson 1)

**1.** 3 **2.** 8 **3.** 6

**4.** 7 **5.** 9

**List the factors of each number. Then tell if the number is prime or composite.** (Lesson 2)

**6.** 43 **7.** 51 **8.** 24

**9.** 77 **10.** 28

Extra Practice at **eduplace.com/map**

Lesson 3

# Problem-Solving Strategy

## Solve a Simpler Problem

**Objective** Use a simpler problem to help you solve a problem.

 **STANDARDS** M4A1.a, M4P1.a, M4P1.b

**Problem** At a fair, 8 teams are in a potato-sack relay race. Each team must race against each of the other teams once. How many races are needed?

### UNDERSTAND

**This is what you know.**

- There are 8 teams.
- Each team must race against each of the other teams once.

### PLAN

**You can solve a simpler problem and look for a pattern.**

### SOLVE

**Solve the problem for fewer teams.**

**2 Teams**

*A* ⟷ *B*

**1 race**

**3 Teams**

*A*, *B*, *C*

**3 races**

**4 Teams**

*A*, *B*, *C*, *D*

**6 races**

**5 Teams**

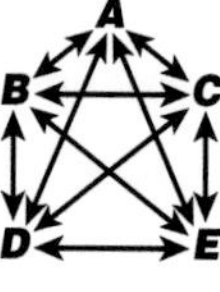


**10 races**

Look for a pattern you can use.

| Number of Teams: | 2 | 3 | 4 | 5 | 6 | 7 | 8 |
|---|---|---|---|---|---|---|---|
| Number of Races: | 1 | 3 | 6 | 10 | 15 | 21 | 28 |
| | | +2 | +3 | +4 | +5 | +6 | +7 |

- The differences increase by 1 each time.
- Continue the pattern.

**Solution:** 28 races are needed for 8 teams.

### LOOK BACK

**How does solving the problem for fewer teams help you?**

## Guided Practice

**Use the Ask Yourself questions to help you solve each problem.**

1. There are 6 judges at a race. Each judge shakes hands with every other judge once. How many handshakes is that?

2. A worker is using boards to divide a rectangular animal pen into a row of 12 smaller goat pens. How many boards does the worker need?

   **Hint** How many boards are needed to make 2 pens? 3 pens?

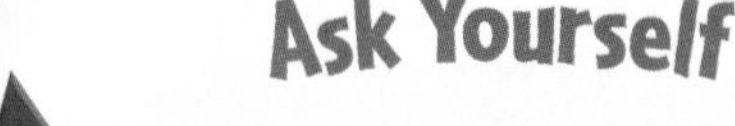


UNDERSTAND **What facts do I know?**

PLAN **Can I solve a simpler problem?**

- **What simpler problem should I start with?**
- **What is the pattern?**

LOOK BACK **Does my answer make sense?**

## Independent Practice

**Use a simpler problem to solve each problem.**

3. Cheryl works at a taco stand at a fair. A sign says: "Buy 2 Tacos, Get 3rd FREE!" How many tacos will Cheryl make if customers pay for 20 tacos?

4. Taco shells are stored in boxes. The boxes are labeled on the top and front. How many labels can be seen if the boxes are stacked in 5 rows of 4 boxes?

5. **Measurement** Six 4-foot square boards are placed end to end to make a rectangular stage at the fair. What is the distance around the rectangle they form?

6. Joshua is using straws to make a row of hexagons as shown. How many straws will Joshua need to make a row of 12 hexagons?

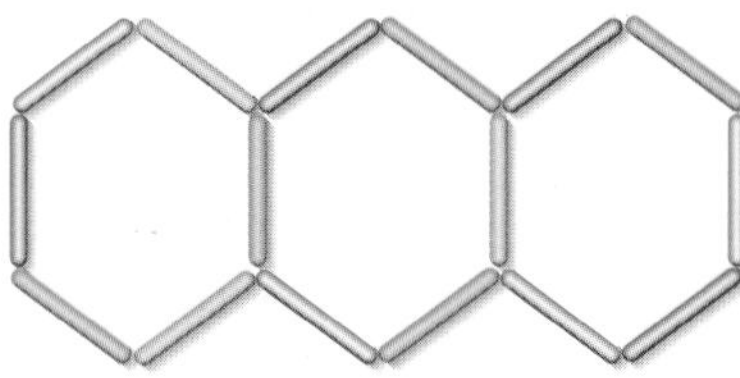

Go On

# Mixed Problem Solving

**Solve. Show your work. Tell what strategy you used.**

**You Choose**

**Strategy**
- Guess and Check
- Solve a Simpler Problem
- Work Backward
- Write an Equation

**Computation Method**
- Mental Math
- Estimation
- Paper and Pencil
- Calculator

7. Children at a picnic eat at a long table made up of 14 small tables placed end to end. Each small table seats 1 person on each side. How many people can sit at the long table?

8. There are 10 hot dogs in a package. Jameel buys 12 packages. Buns come in packages of 8. How many packages of buns should he buy so that he has a bun for every hot dog?

9. The product of two factors is 96. The difference between the factors is 4. What are the factors?

**Data** **The graph shows the number and types of pumpkins that are for sale. Use the graph for Problems 10–13.**

10. How many mini pumpkins are for sale?

11. **Money** Mini pumpkins sell for \$1 each. Sugar pumpkins sell for \$5 each. If the farmer sells all of the mini and sugar pumpkins, how much money will he make?

12. **Analyze** The Cinderella pumpkins are displayed in 5 rows of 6. Can the Giant pumpkins also be displayed in equal rows of 6? How do you know?

13. Next year, the farmer wants to sell 200 pumpkins. How many more pumpkins will she have for sale next year than this year?

# Problem Solving on CRCT

Multiple Choice

**Choose the letter of the correct answer.**

1. Mr. Lee is buying 11 baseball caps. Each cap costs $11. How much will 11 caps cost?

   A. $111

   B. $120

   C. $121

   D. $222

(Chapter 4, Lesson 6)

2. Which shirt has a prime number?

   A. 

   B. 

   C. 

   D. 

(Chapter 10, Lesson 2)

Open Response

3. A movie theater has 205 seats. A movie is shown 3 times one day and 4 times a second day. How many people can see the movie in the two days? Explain.

(Chapter 6, Lesson 6)

4. A box contains 1,215 red, white, and blue beads with the same number of each color. How many red beads are in the box?

(Chapter 7, Lesson 2)

5. Some fourth-grade students are raising money for a school trip. The table shows how much money they have raised so far.

| Money Raised for Trip | |
|---|---|
| **Activity** | **Amount** |
| Car Wash | $432 |
| Magazine Sale | $1,673 |
| Bake Sale | $387 |

   a. To the nearest hundred dollars, how much money did they raise from each activity?

   b. Did the students raise more money from the car wash and bake sale combined or from the magazine sale? Use an estimate to decide. Explain how you estimated.

   c. The students wanted to raise at least $2,000 for the trip. Have they met their goal? Explain.

(Chapter 2, Lesson 5)

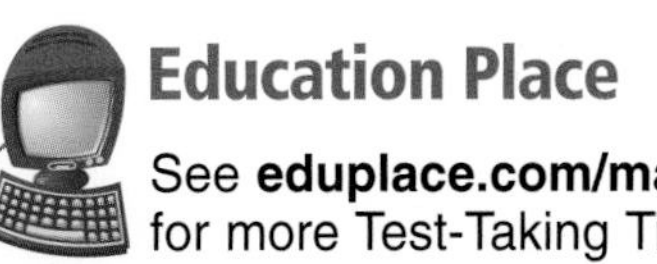

**Education Place**

See **eduplace.com/map** for more Test-Taking Tips.

Hands On Lesson 4

# Model Mean

**Objective** Use counters to model finding a mean.

 **STANDARDS** Prepares for a future grade.

**Vocabulary**

**mean**

**average**

**Materials**

counters

## Work Together

Finding a **mean** is one way to find a number that is typical of the numbers in a group. The mean of a group of numbers is sometimes called the **average**.

At a fair, Ana played Topple the Bottles. The first time she played, she hit 5 bottles, the second time 9 bottles, and the third time 7 bottles. What was the mean number of bottles Ana hit?

Work with a partner to use counters to find a mean.

STEP 1 Make a column of counters to show how many bottles Ana hit each time.

- How many columns of counters did you make?
- How many counters are in each column?

STEP 2 To find the mean, move counters from one column to another until there is the same number in each.

- How many counters are in each column?

This number is the mean.

- What is the mean number of bottles Ana hit?

**Use this page to review and remember what you need to know for this chapter.**

## VOCABULARY

**Choose the best word to complete each sentence.**

**Vocabulary**
- divisor
- multiple
- quotient
- dividend

1. In the expression 350 ÷ 5, the number 350 is the ____.
2. In the division sentence 630 ÷ 9 = 70, the number 70 is the ____.
3. The number 30 is a ____ of 6.

## CONCEPTS AND SKILLS

**Divide.**

| | | | | |
|---|---|---|---|---|
| **4.** $4\overline{)76}$ | **5.** $7\overline{)89}$ | **6.** $8\overline{)97}$ | **7.** $7\overline{)68}$ | **8.** $3\overline{)936}$ |
| **9.** $7\overline{)787}$ | **10.** $5\overline{)578}$ | **11.** $4\overline{)845}$ | **12.** $4\overline{)396}$ | **13.** $7\overline{)224}$ |
| **14.** $8\overline{)350}$ | **15.** $5\overline{)128}$ | **16.** $6\overline{)\$7.44}$ | **17.** $4\overline{)\$1.28}$ | **18.** $8\overline{)\$9.84}$ |
| **19.** \$8.75 ÷ 5 | **20.** \$7.74 ÷ 9 | **21.** \$6.57 ÷ 3 | **22.** \$9.45 ÷ 7 | **23.** \$9.08 ÷ 2 |

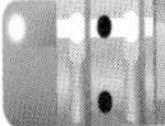

**Write About It**

**24.** What basic fact can you use to divide 4,000 by 8? How many zeros will be in the quotient?

**25.** **What's Wrong?** A van can carry 7 passengers. Danielle says that 4 vans are needed to carry 29 passengers. What is Danielle doing wrong?

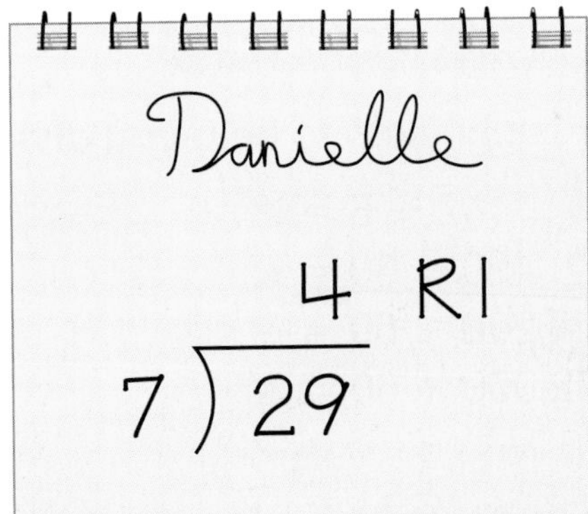


Facts Practice, See Page 671.

Lesson 1

# Divide by Multiples of 10

**Objective** Use division facts to divide by multiples of 10.

 **STANDARDS** M4N4.a, M4N4.b, M4N4.d

## Learn About It

A group of students swam a total of 80 laps at a charity swim-a-thon. If each student swam 20 laps, how many students were in the group?

**Divide.** **80 ÷ 20 = ■**

**You can use basic facts to help you divide.**

8 ÷ 2 = 4 ← basic fact

80 ÷ 20 = 4 ← Think: 8 tens ÷ 2 tens = 4

**Solution:** There were 4 students in the group.

### Other Examples

**A. Basic Fact 21 ÷ 7 = 3**

210 ÷ 70 = 3

2,100 ÷ 70 = 30

21,000 ÷ 70 = 300

**B. Basic Fact 20 ÷ 4 = 5**

200 ÷ 40 = 5

2,000 ÷ 40 = 50

20,000 ÷ 40 = 500

## Guided Practice

**Use basic facts to help you divide.**

**1.** 42 ÷ 6 = ■
420 ÷ 60 = ■
4,200 ÷ 60 = ■
42,000 ÷ 60 = ■

**2.** 40 ÷ 8 = ■
400 ÷ 80 = ■
4,000 ÷ 80 = ■
40,000 ÷ 80 = ■

**Ask Yourself**

- How many digits will the quotient have?

**Explain Your Thinking** In Exercises 1 and 2, how do the number of zeros in the quotients compare to the number of zeros in the dividends?

## Practice and Problem Solving

**Use basic facts to help you divide.**

3. $25 \div 5 = \blacksquare$
   $250 \div 50 = \blacksquare$

4. $14 \div 2 = \blacksquare$
   $140 \div 20 = \blacksquare$

5. $6 \div 2 = \blacksquare$
   $600 \div 20 = \blacksquare$

6. $81 \div 9 = \blacksquare$
   $8{,}100 \div 90 = \blacksquare$

7. $54 \div 6 = \blacksquare$
   $5{,}400 \div 60 = \blacksquare$

8. $12 \div 4 = \blacksquare$
   $12{,}000 \div 40 = \blacksquare$

9. $80\overline{)640}$

10. $10\overline{)900}$

11. $70\overline{)490}$

12. $30\overline{)1{,}500}$

13. $60\overline{)4{,}200}$

14. $30\overline{)9{,}000}$

15. $50\overline{)40{,}000}$

16. $90\overline{)63{,}000}$

### Algebra • Equations **Find each value of *n*.**

17. $2{,}800 \div n = 70$

18. $5{,}400 \div n = 90$

19. $n \div 80 = 50$

20. $n \div 60 = 600$

21. $16{,}000 \div n = 800$

22. $n \div 70 = 700$

**Solve.**

23. Twenty towns sent 180 swimmers to a charity swim. If each town sent the same number of swimmers, how many swimmers did each town send?

24. Marty swims 3,000 meters in 6 days. Each lap he swims is 50 meters. If he swims the same number of laps each day, how many laps does Marty swim each day?

25. There are 1,800 spectators seated at a regional swim meet. Each row of seats has 60 spectators. How many rows are there?

26. **Reasoning** In a race, Team D finished ahead of Team A but after Team B. Team C finished ahead of Team B. Which team won?

## GPS Sharpening Skills for CRCT

### Open Response

**Compare. Write >, <, or = for each ●.**
(Ch. 2, Lesson 1)

27. 4,386 ● 4,386

28. 725,000 ● 527,000

29. 136,200,948 ● 136,295,104

### Multiple Choice

30. What is the value of ■?
(Ch. 11, Lesson 1)

$$720 \div \blacksquare = 90$$

A. 8
B. 9
C. 80
D. 300

Extra Practice See page 291, Set A.

Lesson 2

# Estimate Quotients

**Objective** Estimate quotients.

 **STANDARDS** M4N7.d, M4P2

## Learn About It

Zoe's town held a beach cleanup. On the day of the cleanup, 19 families collected 184 bags of trash. About how many bags of trash did each family collect?

You can estimate to find 184 ÷ 19. One way to estimate 184 ÷ 19 is to use basic facts and multiples of 10.

**Estimate.** $19\overline{)184}$

**STEP 1** Use basic facts and multiples of 10 to find a new dividend and a new divisor.

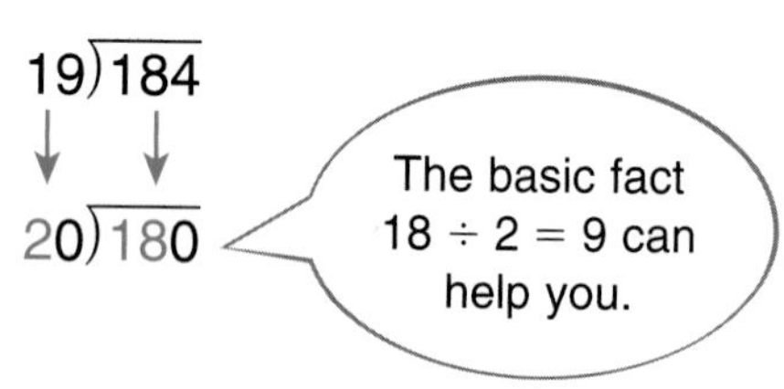


**STEP**  Divide.

$$20\overline{)180}^{\,9}$$

So $19\overline{)184}$ is about 9.

**Solution:** Each family collected about 9 bags of trash.

### Another Example

**Two-Digit Dividend**

Estimate 63 ÷ 29.

63 ÷ 29
↓ ↓
60 ÷ 30 = 2

The basic fact 6 ÷ 3 = 2 can help you.

63 ÷ 29 is about 2.

## Guided Practice

**Ask Yourself**

- What basic fact can I use?
- What is the quotient of the new dividend and divisor?

**Use a new dividend and a new divisor to estimate each quotient.**

1. 82 ÷ 18
   ↓ ↓
   80 ÷ ■ = ■

2. 488 ÷ 67
   ↓ ↓
   490 ÷ ■ = ■

3. 158 ÷ 42
   ↓ ↓
   ■ ÷ 40 = ■

4. $62\overline{)368}$
5. $43\overline{)250}$
6. $69\overline{)355}$
7. $84\overline{)491}$

**Explain Your Thinking** ▶ How can an estimate help you decide where to place the first digit in the quotient?

## Practice and Problem Solving

**Estimate each quotient.**

8. $48\overline{)99}$
9. $19\overline{)83}$
10. $63\overline{)379}$
11. $71\overline{)223}$
12. $89\overline{)448}$
13. $68\overline{)559}$
14. $78\overline{)637}$
15. $18\overline{)138}$
16. 98 ÷ 52
17. 42 ÷ 18
18. 562 ÷ 81
19. 308 ÷ 52
20. Volunteers collected 719 pounds of trash in 81 bags. About how many pounds of trash did each bag hold?
21. **Analyze** There are 96 bottles in 12 boxes in Juan's garage. Each box holds the same number of bottles. Juan says that number is 6. Is he right? Explain your thinking.
22. Some creative people make art from trash. Suppose an artist uses 312 pounds of scrap metal to make 36 sculptures. About how much does each sculpture weigh?

*This sculpture is made with discarded metal from tool chests, cabinets, and cars.*

## GPS Sharpening Skills for CRCT

**Open Response**

**Use basic facts and patterns to find each product.** (Ch. 6, Lesson 1)

23. 7 × 50
24. 7 × 500
25. 9 × 600
26. 4 × 8,000
27. What is the best estimate for 481 ÷ 79? Explain your thinking. (Ch. 11, Lesson 2)

Extra Practice See page 291, Set B.

Audio Tutor 1/36 Listen and Understand

# Model Division by Two-Digit Divisors

**Objective** Model division by two-digit divisors.

**STANDARDS** M4N7.d, M4P3, M4P5

**Materials**
base-ten blocks

## Work Together

You can use base-ten blocks to model division by a two-digit divisor.

Work with a partner. Use base-ten blocks to find 34 ÷ 11.

**STEP 1** Show 34 with the base-ten blocks.

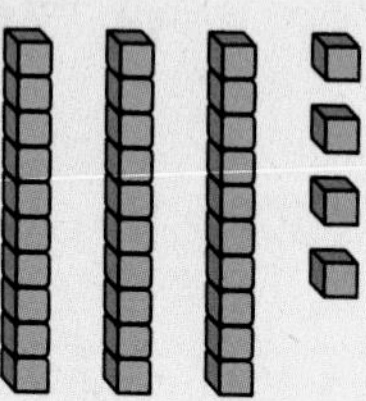

$11\overline{)34}$

- How many tens do you have?
- How many ones?

**STEP 2** Estimate to find about how many groups there will be.

- About how many groups will there be?

34 ÷ 11
↓ ↓
30 ÷ 10 = 3

**STEP 3** Use your estimate. Try to divide 3 tens 4 ones into 3 groups of 11.

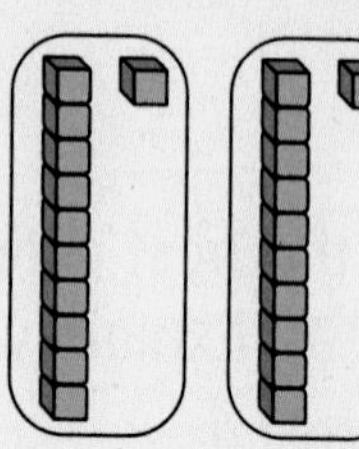

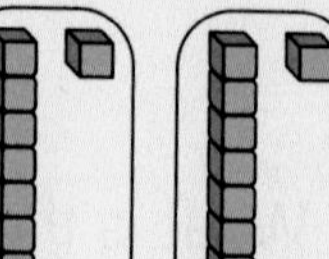

```
   3 R1
11)34   Multiply. 3 × 11
 − 33   Subtract. 34 − 33 = 1
    1   Compare. 1 < 11
```

- What is the quotient?

**Use base-ten blocks to find 158 ÷ 31.**

**STEP 1** Show 158 with base-ten blocks.

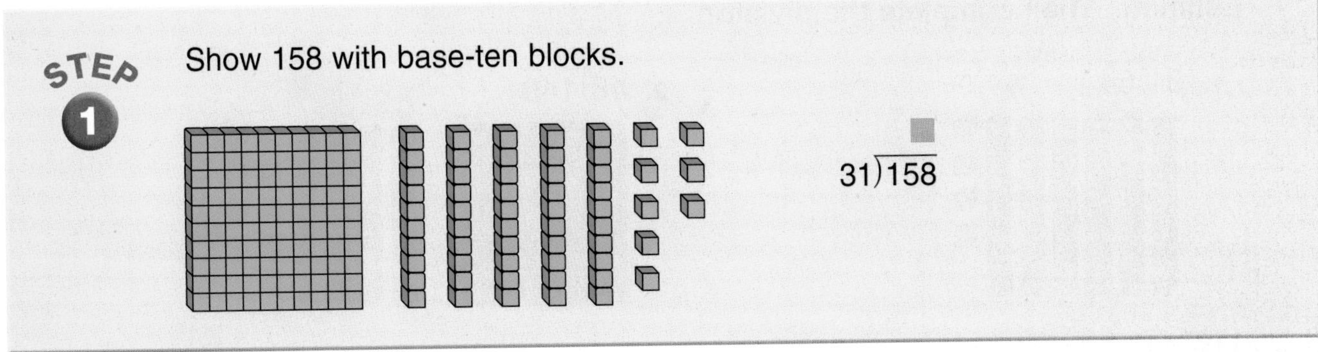


**STEP 2** Estimate to find about how many groups there will be.

158 ÷ 31

↓ ↓

150 ÷ 30 = 5

- About how many groups will there be?

**STEP 3** There is 1 hundred. You cannot divide it into five groups. So regroup 1 hundred as 10 tens.

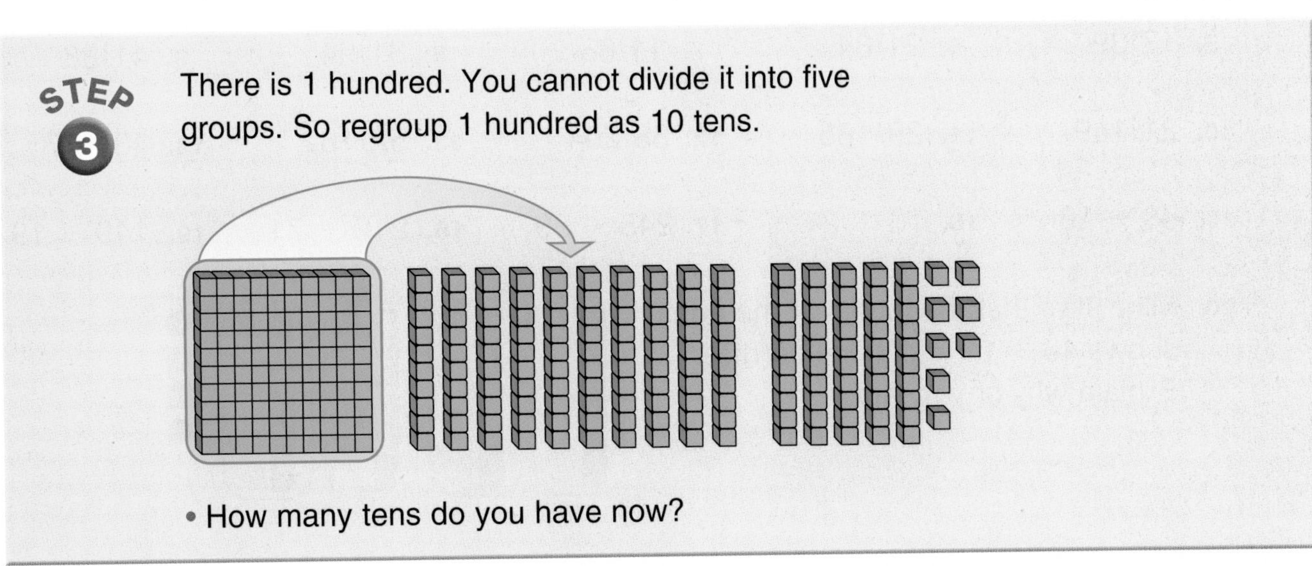

- How many tens do you have now?

**STEP 4** Try to divide the tens and ones into 5 groups of 31.

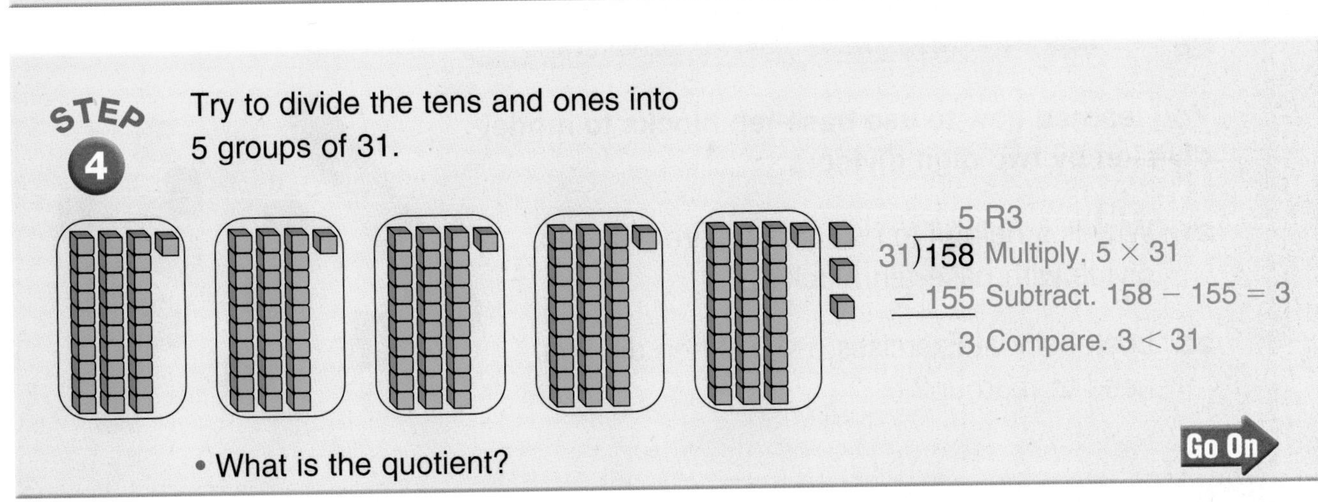


- What is the quotient?

Go On

## On Your Own

**Estimate. Then complete the division.**

1. $31\overline{)64}$

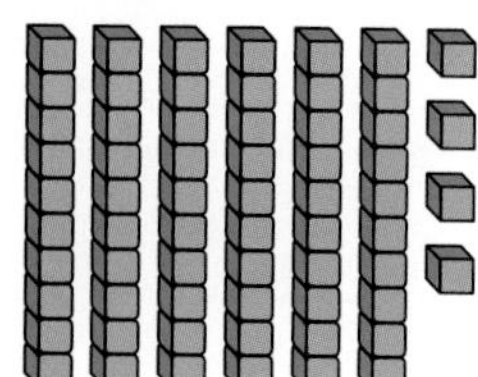

2. $48\overline{)149}$

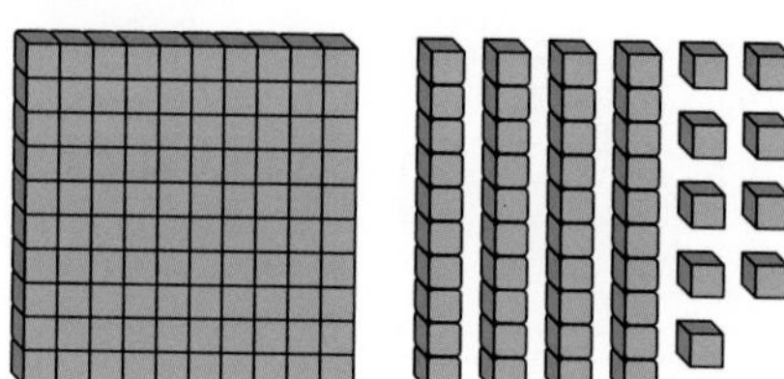

3. $22\overline{)45}$

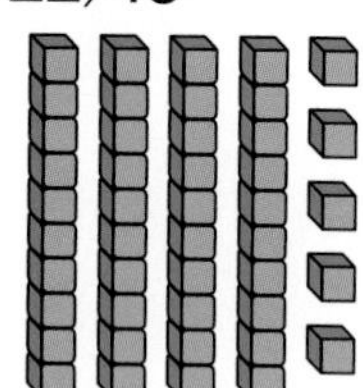

4. $27\overline{)168}$

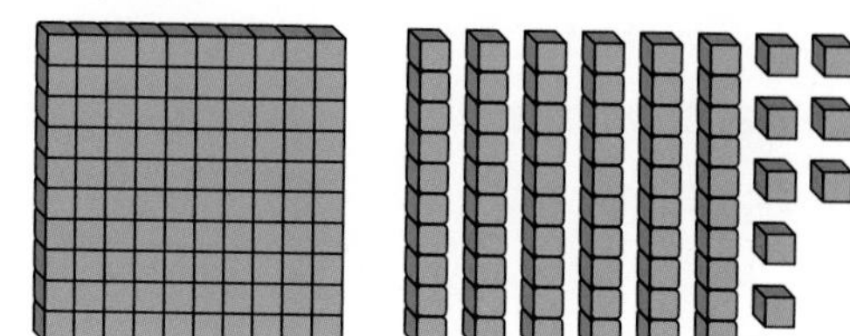

**Use models to divide.**

5. $17\overline{)39}$
6. $21\overline{)84}$
7. $11\overline{)68}$
8. $31\overline{)94}$
9. $41\overline{)88}$
10. $21\overline{)149}$
11. $29\overline{)185}$
12. $38\overline{)204}$
13. $52\overline{)162}$
14. $43\overline{)177}$
15. $88 \div 28$
16. $73 \div 24$
17. $245 \div 39$
18. $219 \div 71$
19. $149 \div 19$
20. Mike says that the model at the right shows $48 \div 11 = 4$. Is he correct? Explain why or why not.

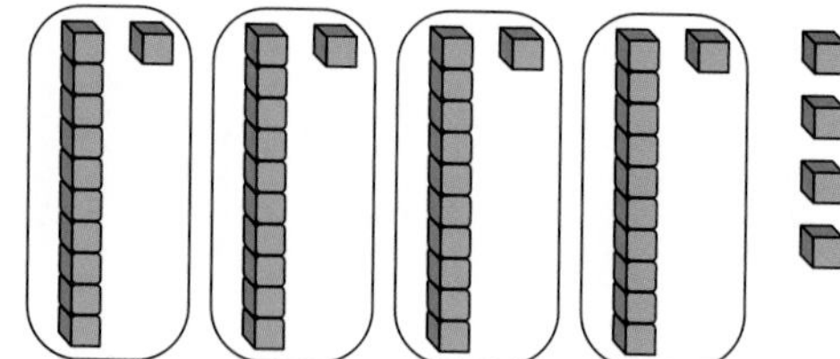

### Talk About It • Write About It

**You learned how to use base-ten blocks to model division by two-digit divisors.**

21. Why is it helpful to estimate before trying to divide with base-ten blocks?
22. Look back at Exercises 5–19. When did you need to regroup?

Problem Solving

GPS

## Social Studies Connection

### Old Faithful

STANDARDS M4N4, M4P4

Old Faithful is a geyser in Yellowstone National Park. A geyser is a natural hot spring that erupts, sending water and steam into the air. Old Faithful erupts about once every 76 minutes.

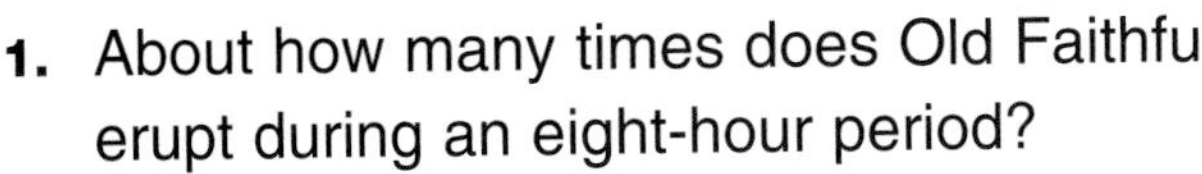

1. About how many times does Old Faithful erupt during an eight-hour period?

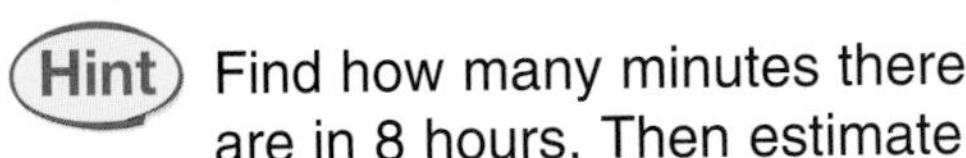

**Hint** Find how many minutes there are in 8 hours. Then estimate.

2. About how many times will Old Faithful erupt in a day? in a week? in a year?

*One eruption of Old Faithful sends out 3,700 to 8,400 gallons of boiling water.*

WEEKLY WR READER eduplace.com/map

## Quick Check

Check your understanding of Lessons 1–3.

**Use basic facts to help you divide.** (Lesson 1)

1. $15 \div 3 = ■$
   $150 \div 30 = ■$

2. $42 \div 7 = ■$
   $420 \div 70 = ■$

3. $64 \div 8 = ■$
   $6{,}400 \div 80 = ■$

4. $72 \div 9 = ■$
   $72{,}000 \div 90 = ■$

**Use a new dividend and a new divisor to estimate the quotient.** (Lesson 2)

5. $79 \div 38$ → $80 \div ■ = ■$

6. $542 \div 57$ → $■ \div 60 = ■$

7. $479 \div 82$ → $■ \div ■ = ■$

**Use models to divide.** (Lesson 3)

8. $12\overline{)62}$

9. $18\overline{)76}$

10. $29\overline{)146}$

Extra Practice at eduplace.com/map

Lesson 4

# One-Digit Quotients

**Objective** Divide when the quotient has one digit.

**Vocabulary**
dividend

## Learn About It

STANDARDS M4N4.b, M4N4.c, M4P1.b

Isabel's class is making tissue-paper art for the Elder Care Center. There are 235 sheets of tissue paper. If 28 students share the tissue paper equally, how many sheets can each student use? How many sheets will be left?

**Divide.** $235 \div 28$ **or** $28\overline{)235}$

**STEP 1** Estimate to decide where to place the first digit.

$28\overline{)235} \rightarrow 30\overline{)240}$ (8)

Write the first digit of the quotient in the ones place.

**STEP 2** Try the estimate. Divide.

$$\begin{array}{r} 8\text{ R}11 \\ 28\overline{)235} \\ -\,224 \\ \hline 11 \end{array}$$

Multiply. $8 \times 28$

Subtract. $235 - 224$

Compare. $11 < 28$

**Check your answer.**
Multiply. Then add.

$(28 \times 8) + 11 = 235$

The sum equals the **dividend**.

**Solution:** Each student can use 8 sheets of tissue paper. There will be 11 sheets left.

### Another Example

**Two-Digit Dividend**

Find $43 \div 19$.

Divide.

$$\begin{array}{r} 2\text{ R}5 \\ 19\overline{)43} \\ -\,38 \\ \hline 5 \end{array}$$

Check your answer.

$(19 \times 2) + 5 = 43$

## Guided Practice

**Estimate to decide where to place the first digit. Then divide.**

**1.** $17\overline{)62}$ **2.** $37\overline{)124}$ **3.** $92 \div 27$ **4.** $147 \div 28$

**Ask Yourself**

- How can I estimate the quotient?
- How do I check my answer?

**Explain Your Thinking** ▶ What does it mean if the remainder is greater than or equal to the divisor?

## Practice and Problem Solving

**Divide. Check your answer.**

5. $42\overline{)88}$
6. $32\overline{)99}$
7. $21\overline{)91}$
8. $46\overline{)55}$
9. $19\overline{)146}$
10. $27\overline{)177}$
11. $61\overline{)250}$
12. $89\overline{)725}$
13. $73 \div 22$
14. $81 \div 19$
15. $34 \div 11$
16. $74 \div 34$
17. $89 \div 36$
18. $197 \div 36$
19. $422 \div 83$
20. $413 \div 62$

**Algebra** • **Symbols** **Compare. Use >, <, or = for each ●.**

21. $305 \div 48$ ● $300 \div 48$
22. $795 \div 37$ ● $785 \div 37$
23. $400 \div 80$ ● $200 \div 40$
24. $800 \div 20$ ● $80 \div 2$
25. $362 \div 92$ ● $362 \div 90$
26. $735 \div 81$ ● $735 \div 79$

**Solve.**

27. **Reasoning** There are 85 paint brushes in a dozen jars. One of the jars contains 1 more brush than the others. How many brushes are in each jar?

28. **Multistep** There are 8 pictures with 6 flowers each and 11 pictures with 7 flowers each. Find the total number of flowers in all the pictures.

29. Elder Care residents made a quilt. There were 84 flowered fabric squares to put in 18 rows. If the residents put an equal number of flowered squares in each row, how many were in each row? How many squares were left?

## Sharpening Skills for CRCT

**Open Response**

**Decide whether each number is prime or composite.** (Ch. 10, Lesson 2)

30. 7
31. 39
32. 16
33. 28
34. 79
35. 59
36. 81
37. 43
38. 87

39. How do you know that 7 is not the correct quotient in the example below? (Ch. 11, Lesson 4)

$$\begin{array}{r} 7 \\ 28\overline{)176} \\ -\underline{196} \end{array}$$

Extra Practice See page 291, Set C.

Lesson 5

# Two-Digit Quotients

**Objective** Divide when the quotient has two digits.

## Learn About It

STANDARDS M4N4.b

Students at Riverside School collected 865 cans to recycle. They are packing the cans in 21 bags. Each bag holds the same number of cans. How many cans are in each bag? Are any cans left?

**Divide. 865 ÷ 21 or $21\overline{)865}$**

**STEP 1** Estimate to decide where to place the first digit in the quotient.

$21\overline{)865} \rightarrow \begin{array}{r} 40 \\ 20\overline{)800} \end{array}$

**STEP 2** Try the estimate. Divide.

$$\begin{array}{r} 4\phantom{5} \\ 21\overline{)865} \\ -\,84\phantom{5} \\ \hline 2\phantom{5} \end{array}$$

Multiply. 4 × 21 = 84
Subtract. 86 − 84 = 2
Compare. 2 < 21

Think
$\begin{array}{r} 4 \text{ tens} \\ 20\overline{)80} \text{ tens} \end{array}$

**STEP 3** Bring down the ones. Divide.

$$\begin{array}{r} 41 \text{ R4} \\ 21\overline{)865} \\ -84\downarrow \\ \hline 25 \\ -21 \\ \hline 4 \end{array}$$

Multiply. 1 × 21 = 21
Subtract. 25 − 21 = 4
Compare. 4 < 21

**STEP 4** Check your answer. Multiply. Then add.

$$\begin{array}{r} 21 \\ \times\ 41 \\ \hline 21 \\ +\,840 \\ \hline 861 \\ +\ \ 4 \\ \hline 865 \end{array}$$

← The sum equals the dividend, so the quotient is correct.

**Solution:** There are 41 cans in each bag. There are 4 cans left.

▶ You can use the same steps to divide a four-digit dividend.

**Divide. 1,278 ÷ 63 or 63)1,278**

**STEP 1** Estimate to decide where to place the first digit in the quotient.

$$63\overline{)1{,}278} \rightarrow \begin{array}{r} 20 \\ 60\overline{)1{,}200} \end{array}$$

**STEP 2** Try the estimate. Divide.

**Think:** $\begin{array}{r} 2 \text{ tens} \\ 60\overline{)120 \text{ tens}} \end{array}$

$$\begin{array}{r} 2 \\ 63\overline{)1{,}278} \\ -\,126 \\ \hline 1 \end{array}$$

Multiply. 2 × 63 = 126
Subtract. 127 − 126 = 1
Compare. 1 < 63

**STEP 3** Bring down the ones.

$$\begin{array}{r} 2 \\ 63\overline{)1{,}278} \\ -\,126\downarrow \\ \hline 18 \end{array}$$

← 18 < 63
There are not enough ones to divide.

**STEP 4** Write a zero in the ones place. Write the remainder.

$$\begin{array}{r} 20 \text{ R18} \\ 63\overline{)1{,}278} \\ -\,126 \\ \hline 18 \\ -\,0 \\ \hline \end{array}$$

**Check your answer.**
Multiply. Then add.

$$\begin{array}{r} 63 \\ \times\,20 \\ \hline 1{,}260 \\ +\,18 \\ \hline 1{,}278 \end{array}$$

The sum equals the dividend, so the quotient is correct.

**Solution:** 1,278 ÷ 63 → 20 R18

## Guided Practice

**Divide.**

1. 28)647
2. 42)886
3. 19)603
4. 44)2,222
5. 28)2,537
6. 81)6,643

**Ask Yourself**

- Where do I place the first digit in the quotient?
- Can I divide the tens?

**Explain Your Thinking** ▶ Why is it helpful to know the number of digits in a quotient before you divide?

Go On

## Practice and Problem Solving

**Divide. Check your answer.**

7. $18\overline{)582}$
8. $33\overline{)769}$
9. $24\overline{)258}$
10. $45\overline{)547}$
11. $51\overline{)4{,}598}$
12. $69\overline{)2{,}218}$
13. $77\overline{)6{,}319}$
14. $86\overline{)8{,}123}$
15. $657 \div 21$
16. $966 \div 31$
17. $577 \div 28$
18. $672 \div 48$
19. $3{,}526 \div 68$
20. $1{,}527 \div 28$
21. $4{,}769 \div 52$
22. $4{,}596 \div 89$

## Data Use the bar graph for Problems 23–25.

23. There are 6 classes in Grade 5. Each class recycled the same number of cans. How many cans did each class recycle?

24. The cans recycled by Grades 2, 3, and 4 were collected by 12 classes. Each class collected the same number of cans. How many cans did each class collect?

25. **Estimate** To the nearest hundred, about how many more cans were recycled by Grade 5 than by Grade 4?

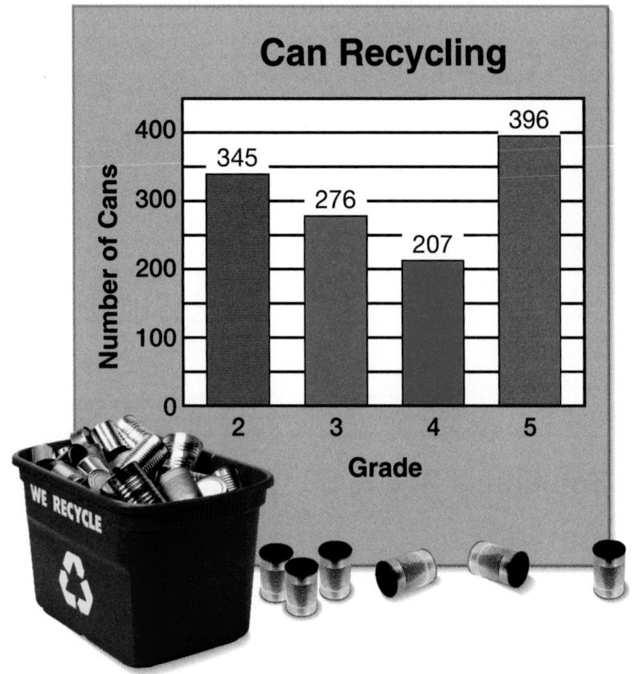

## Sharpening Skills for CRCT

GPS

**Open Response**

**Find the mean of the numbers.**
(Ch. 10, Lesson 5)

26. 2, 5, 8
27. 26, 51, 18, 25
28. $14, $67, $90
29. 3, 9, 20, 41, 82
30. 12, 19, 20, 17
31. 89, 102, 98, 91

**Multiple Choice**

32. What is the quotient? (Ch. 11, Lesson 5)

$346 \div 23$

A. 1 R11
B. 10 R23
C. 15
D. 15 R1



Extra Practice See page 291, Set D.

Problem Solving

GPS

# Math Reasoning

## Divide a Different Way

STANDARDS Maintains M3N4.a

You can use many different strategies to find the answer to a division problem. One strategy is to use repeated subtraction.

**Find 224 ÷ 56.**

- Start with 224. Subtract 56 repeatedly.
- Count how many times you subtracted 56.

$$\begin{array}{rl} 224 & \\ -\ 56 & ❶ \\ \hline 168 & \\ -\ 56 & ❷ \\ \hline 112 & \\ -\ 56 & ❸ \\ \hline 56 & \\ -\ 56 & ❹ \\ \hline 0 & \end{array}$$

You subtracted 56 four times, so there are 4 groups of 56 in 224. There is no remainder.

$56 + 56 + 56 + 56 = 224$

$4 \times 56 = 224$

and $224 \div 56 = 4$

**Find 296 ÷ 98.**

- Start with 296. Subtract 98 repeatedly.
- Count how many times you subtracted 98.

$$\begin{array}{rl} 296 & \\ -\ 98 & ❶ \\ \hline 198 & \\ -\ 98 & ❷ \\ \hline 100 & \\ -\ 98 & ❸ \\ \hline 2 & \end{array}$$

You subtracted 98 three times, so there are 3 groups of 98 in 296. The remainder is 2.

$98 + 98 + 98 + 2 = 296$

$(3 \times 98) + 2 = 296$

and $296 \div 98 \rightarrow 3\text{ R}2$

**Use repeated subtraction to find each quotient.**

1. $328 \div 82$
2. $350 \div 70$
3. $372 \div 93$
4. $125 \div 25$
5. $450 \div 50$
6. $193 \div 23$
7. $434 \div 62$
8. $729 \div 81$
9. $308 \div 51$
10. $525 \div 63$
11. $227 \div 72$
12. $170 \div 24$
13. **Analyze** What advantages are there in using repeated subtraction to find the quotient? What disadvantages are there?

Lesson 6

Audio Tutor 1/39 Listen and Understand

# Adjust the Quotient

**Objective** Adjust an estimate of the quotient to divide.

**STANDARDS** M4N4.b, M4N7.d, M4P2

## Learn About It

If your first estimate of a quotient is too large or too small, you need to adjust your estimate.

**Sometimes the estimate is too large.**

Find 368 ÷ 23.

Estimate first. $23\overline{)368} \rightarrow \overset{20}{20\overline{)400}}$

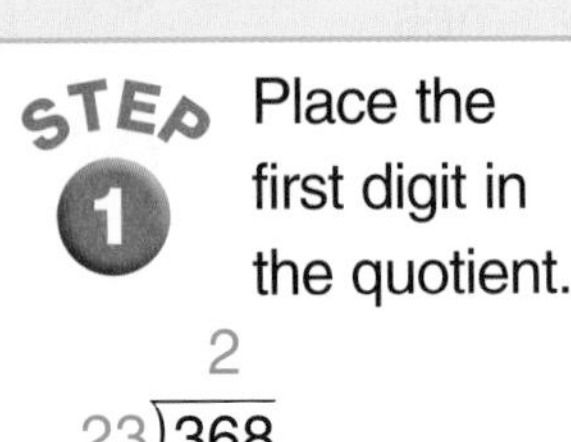

**STEP 1** Place the first digit in the quotient.

$\overset{2}{23\overline{)368}}$
$-46$

46 > 36
2 is too large.

**STEP 2** Adjust the estimate. Try 1.

$\overset{1}{23\overline{)368}}$
$-23$
13

13 < 23
1 is correct.

**STEP 3** Bring down the next digit. Try 7.

$\overset{17}{23\overline{)368}}$
$-23\downarrow$
138
$-161$

161 > 138
7 is too large.

**STEP 4** Try 6.

$\overset{16}{23\overline{)368}}$
$-23\downarrow$
138
$-138$
0

0 < 23
6 is correct.

**Solution:** 368 ÷ 23 = 16

**Remember**
To adjust something is to change it in order to make it fit.

**Sometimes the estimate is too small.**

Find 849 ÷ 16.

Estimate first. $16\overline{)849} \rightarrow \overset{40}{20\overline{)800}}$

**STEP 1** Place the first digit in the quotient.

$\overset{4}{16\overline{)849}}$
$-64$
20

20 > 16
4 is too small.

**STEP 2** Adjust the estimate. Try 5.

$\overset{5}{16\overline{)849}}$
$-80$
4

4 < 16
5 is correct.

**STEP 3** Bring down the next digit. Try 2.

$\overset{52}{16\overline{)849}}$
$-80\downarrow$
49
$-32$
17

17 > 16
2 is too small.

**STEP 4** Try 3.

$\overset{53\text{ R1}}{16\overline{)849}}$
$-80\downarrow$
49
$-48$
1

1 < 16
3 is correct.

**Solution:** $\overset{53\text{ R1}}{16\overline{)849}}$



Extra Help at **eduplace.com/map**

## Guided Practice

**Write *too large, too small,* or *correct* for each estimate of the quotient. Then find the correct answer.**

**Ask Yourself**

- How many digits will the quotient have?
- Do I need to adjust my estimate?

1. $12\overline{)654}$ estimate 60
2. $16\overline{)839}$ estimate 40
3. $26\overline{)583}$ estimate 20

**Explain Your Thinking** ▶ What should you do if your estimate is too large?

## Practice and Problem Solving

**Estimate. Then divide.**

4. $18\overline{)619}$
5. $54\overline{)983}$
6. $19\overline{)422}$
7. $31\overline{)342}$
8. $28\overline{)632}$
9. $42\overline{)794}$
10. $28\overline{)931}$
11. $26\overline{)626}$
12. $48\overline{)527}$
13. $19\overline{)564}$
14. 840 ÷ 24
15. 611 ÷ 33
16. 843 ÷ 16
17. 771 ÷ 44

**Data** **Use the list for Problems 18–20.**

18. For a community-service project, Mr. Li's class made a time capsule. A video was made of 12 classroom activities. How long is each activity if each one is the same length?

19. Fourteen students recorded messages on audiotapes. About how long is each message if each is the same length?

20. **Analyze** The essays fill a 42-page journal. All essays are the same number of pages except for one that is 3 pages longer than each of the others. How many pages long is each essay?

## Sharpening Skills for CRCT

**Open Response**

**Find the mean of the numbers.**
(Ch. 10, Lesson 5)

21. 6, 9, 12
22. 5, 12, 9, 26
23. \$12, \$15, \$45
24. 75, 23, 67, 38, 12

**Multiple Choice**

25. What is 418 ÷ 21? (Ch. 11, Lesson 6)

A. 18 R40
B. 19
C. 19 R19
D. 24 R14

Extra Practice See page 291, Set E.

Lesson 7

 **Audio Tutor 1**/40 Listen and Understand

# Problem-Solving Decision

## Multistep Problems

**Objective** Solve multistep problems.

**STANDARDS** Extends and enriches M4N7, M4P1.b

**Problem** Lucia and her dad will prepare corn on the cob for the volunteer firefighters' dinner. There are 3 bags of corn. Each bag holds 32 ears of corn. If 16 ears of corn fit in a pot, what is the least number of pots needed to cook all the corn at the same time?

It takes more than one step to solve this problem.

**You know these facts.**

- There are 3 bags of corn.
- Each bag holds 32 ears of corn.
- Each pot holds 16 ears of corn.

**STEP 1** Find the total number of ears of corn.

$3 \times 32 = 96$ ← total number of ears

(3: number of bags; 32: number in each bag)

There are 96 ears in all.

**STEP 2** Find the number of pots needed for all of the corn.

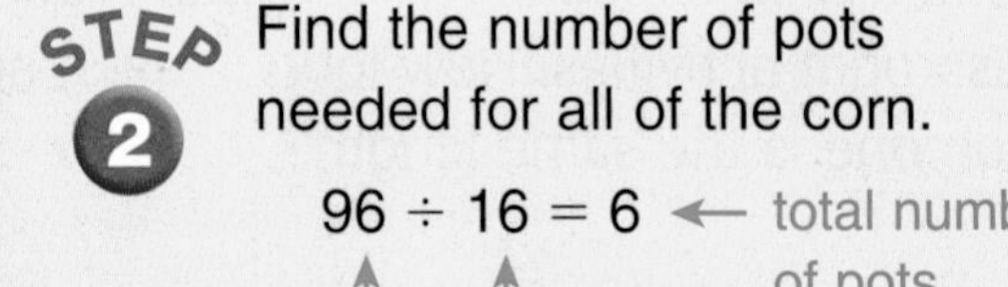

$96 \div 16 = 6$ ← total number of pots

(96: number of ears; 16: number of ears in each pot)

Six pots are needed.

**Solution:** Six pots are needed to cook all the corn.

## Try These

1. A firehouse pantry has 144 cans of vegetables and 220 cans of soup. Each shelf holds up to 52 cans. How many shelves are needed for all the cans?
2. An adult's dinner costs $8. A family of 2 adults and 2 children pay $26 for their dinners. How much does a child's dinner cost?
3. Layla's dad bought 10 dozen tomatoes for the dinner. The tomatoes were equally divided among 20 bags. How many tomatoes were in each bag?
4. After the dinner, Ben collected 92 cans and 48 bottles. If he received 5¢ for each can or bottle, about how much money did Ben receive?

# Math Challenge

## Hit the Target

STANDARDS M4N4.b

**Place the digits to find each Target Number.**
**Use a calculator to help you.**

**1.** Digits: 2, 2, 4, 7
Target Number: 3

■■ ÷ ■■ = ■

**2.** Digits: 0, 1, 5, 9
Target Number: 6

■■ ÷ ■■ = ■

**3.** Digits: 0, 1, 3, 4, 7
Target Number: 20

■■■ ÷ ■■ = ■■

**4.** Digits: 0, 1, 2, 3, 6
Target Number: 30

■■■ ÷ ■■ = ■■

**5.** Digits: 2, 2, 4, 6, 7
Target Number: 16

■■■ ÷ ■■ = ■■

**6.** Digits: 0, 1, 4, 5, 8
Target Number: 18

■■■ ÷ ■■ = ■■

**7.** Digits: 2, 8, 9, 9
Target Number: 124

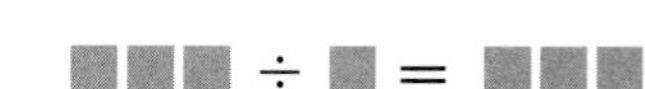

■■■ ÷ ■ = ■■■

**8.** Digits: 4, 4, 6, 7
Target Number: 124

■■■ ÷ ■ = ■■■

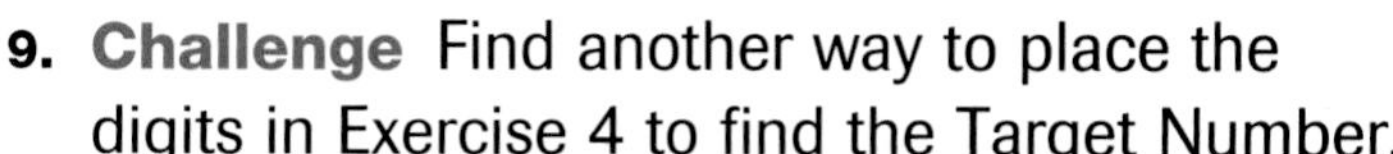

**9.** **Challenge** Find another way to place the digits in Exercise 4 to find the Target Number.

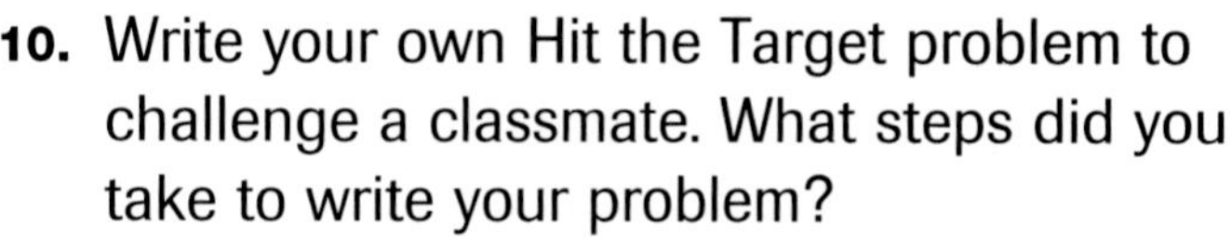

**10.** Write your own Hit the Target problem to challenge a classmate. What steps did you take to write your problem?

# Chapter Review/Test

Study Guide page SG13

## VOCABULARY

**Choose the best word to complete each sentence.**

**Vocabulary**
- divisor
- multiple
- quotient
- dividend

1. In the division sentence 480 ÷ 12 = 40, the number 40 is the _____.
2. In the division sentence 27 ÷ 3 = 9, the number 27 is the _____.
3. The number by which another number is divided is the _____.

## CONCEPTS AND SKILLS

**Estimate each quotient.** (Lesson 2, pp. 274–275)

4. 99 ÷ 54
5. 152 ÷ 33
6. 349 ÷ 68

**Divide.** (Lessons 1, 3–6, pp. 272–273, 276–287)

7. $40\overline{)360}$
8. $50\overline{)4,500}$
9. $80\overline{)72,000}$
10. $13\overline{)72}$
11. $24\overline{)92}$
12. $35\overline{)140}$
13. $27\overline{)540}$
14. $42\overline{)635}$
15. $15\overline{)645}$
16. $33\overline{)585}$
17. $28\overline{)2,397}$
18. $45\overline{)3,475}$

## PROBLEM SOLVING

**Solve.** (Lesson 7, p. 288)

19. Mr. Tucker pays a total of $24 for movie tickets. He buys two adult tickets for $6 each. He also buys four tickets for his children. What is the price of a child's ticket?
20. Bree is unpacking boxes of books. She has 6 boxes that each hold 36 books. If 18 books fit on each shelf, what is the least number of shelves needed for the books?

**Write About It**

**Show You Understand**

- Explain how you would estimate to find 3,599 ÷ 62.
- Predict whether the exact answer will be greater than or less than your estimate. Explain your prediction.
- Find the exact answer. Was your prediction correct?

# Extra Practice

## Set A (Lesson 1, pp. 272–273)

**Use basic facts to help you divide.**

1. $120 \div 30$
2. $240 \div 60$
3. $6{,}300 \div 70$
4. $8{,}100 \div 90$
5. $30\overline{)180}$
6. $40\overline{)3{,}600}$
7. $80\overline{)5{,}600}$
8. $50\overline{)25{,}000}$
9. $3{,}500 \div n = 50$
10. $n \div 8 = 600$
11. $4{,}800 \div 60 = n$

## Set B (Lesson 2, pp. 274–275)

**Estimate each quotient.**

1. $58 \div 31$
2. $79 \div 19$
3. $102 \div 49$
4. $542 \div 89$
5. $318 \div 82$
6. $325 \div 44$
7. $447 \div 53$
8. $719 \div 78$

## Set C (Lesson 4, pp. 280–281)

**Divide. Check your answer.**

1. $16\overline{)80}$
2. $28\overline{)34}$
3. $55\overline{)198}$
4. $72\overline{)398}$
5. $84 \div 42$
6. $96 \div 25$
7. $129 \div 14$
8. $230 \div 46$
9. $126 \div 18$
10. $248 \div 62$
11. $620 \div 77$
12. $766 \div 85$

## Set D (Lesson 5, pp. 282–284)

**Divide. Check your answer.**

1. $18\overline{)865}$
2. $28\overline{)569}$
3. $42\overline{)894}$
4. $31\overline{)716}$
5. $31\overline{)2{,}499}$
6. $47\overline{)3{,}620}$
7. $19\overline{)1{,}452}$
8. $29\overline{)1{,}894}$

## Set E (Lesson 6, pp. 286–287)

**Estimate. Then divide.**

1. $842 \div 23$
2. $943 \div 25$
3. $581 \div 32$
4. $849 \div 16$
5. $467 \div 38$
6. $685 \div 23$
7. $784 \div 44$
8. $587 \div 22$

Extra Practice at eduplace.com/map

# A Giant in DANGER

Every winter, female Northern Right Whales visit the warm waters near the shores of Georgia and northern Florida. There they give birth to baby whales, called calves. It is the only known place in the world where members of this whale species are born.

The Northern Right Whale is Georgia's official state marine mammal. It is also the most endangered large whale in the world. Northern Right Whales have been protected from hunting since 1935, but their population has not increased much since then. Fewer than 400 Northern Right Whales are alive today. Scientists worry that, even though people are trying to protect them, the Northern Right Whale could be extinct in 200 years.

## Problem Solving

**Suppose scientists are studying an adult female Northern Right Whale with the characteristics below. Use the information in the table to solve Problems 1–4.**

| Characteristics of an Adult Female Northern Right Whale | |
|---|---|
| Length | 15 meters |
| Weight | 60,000 kilograms |
| Amount of food eaten each day | 1,800 kilograms |

1. Suppose a Northern Right Whale calf is 4 meters long when it is born. How many 4-meter-long newborn calves would need to line up next to the adult female whale to at least equal the adult's length?

2. A football field is about 91 meters from end zone to end zone. Estimate how many times longer the football field is than the female adult whale.

3. African elephants are the largest living land animal. This female Northern Right Whale weighs as much as 12 male adult African elephants. About how much does one male adult African elephant weigh?

4. A bottlenose dolphin eats about 12 kilograms of food each day. About how many dolphins would it take to eat the same amount of food as this female Northern Right Whale in one day?

## Enrichment: Divisibility Rules

A number is **divisible** when it can be divided by another number and there is no remainder.

| Divisibility Rules | Examples |
|---|---|
| **Even numbers** are divisible by 2. Even numbers end with 0, 2, 4, 6, or 8 in the ones place. | These numbers are divisible by 2.<br>630 632 634 636 638 |
| Numbers divisible by 5 end with 0 or 5 in the ones place. | These numbers are divisible by 5.<br>630 635 640 645 650 |
| Numbers divisible by 10 end with 0 in the ones place. | These numbers are divisible by 10.<br>600 610 620 630 640 |
| If a number is divisible by 3, the sum of the digits is divisible by 3. | The number 630 is divisible by 3.<br>$630 \rightarrow 6 + 3 + 0 = 9$<br>$9 \div 3 = 3$ |
| If a number is divisible by 9, the sum of the digits is divisible by 9. | The number 630 is divisible by 9.<br>$630 \rightarrow 6 + 3 + 0 = 9$<br>$9 \div 9 = 1$ |

## Try These!

**Tell whether each number is divisible by 2, 3, 5, 9, or 10.**

1. 30
2. 45
3. 84
4. 95
5. 130
6. 180
7. 502
8. 2,000
9. **Challenge** If a number is divisible by both 2 and 3, is it divisible by 6? Try some examples. Explain your answer.
10. Can an **odd number** be divisible by 2? by 4? Try some examples.

# Divide and Conquer

**STANDARDS** Maintains M3N4.e

You can use the base-ten blocks found on Education Place at **eduplace.com/kids/map** to practice division.

**Follow these steps to find 163 ÷ 5.**

- At **Change Mat,** choose **Empty.**
- To show 163:
  Put your pointer over the **Stamp** tool.
  Click the hundreds block.
  Then click the tens block 6 times.
  Next, click the ones block 3 times.
- To regroup 1 hundred as 10 tens, click the right arrow in the hundreds column.
- Click the **Hand** tool. Put 15 of the tens into 5 equal groups.
- To regroup the remaining 1 ten as 10 ones, click the right arrow in the tens column 1 time.
- Click the **Hand** tool. Divide the 13 ones into the 5 groups.

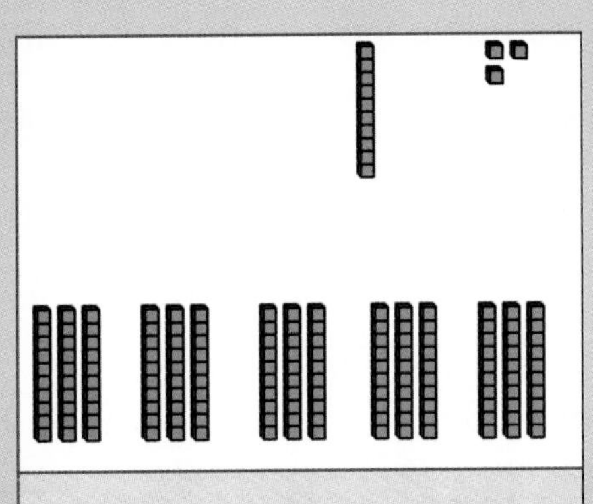

**Solution:** There are 3 tens blocks and 2 ones blocks in each group with 3 ones blocks left over. So 163 ÷ 5 → 32 R3.

**Use the base-ten blocks to find each quotient.**

**1.** 43 ÷ 3 **2.** 65 ÷ 2 **3.** 74 ÷ 3 **4.** 377 ÷ 6

**5.** 112 ÷ 5 **6.** 212 ÷ 4 **7.** 225 ÷ 3 **8.** 131 ÷ 4

**9.** **Create and Solve** Write a word problem that uses division. Use the base-ten blocks to solve.

# Unit 4 Test

Study Guide pages SG13–14, SG28–29, SG41

## VOCABULARY Open Response

**Choose the best word to complete each sentence.**

**Vocabulary**
- divisor
- quotient
- dividend
- remainder

1. The number that is left after one whole number is divided by another is the ____.
2. The number by which a number is being divided is the ____.
3. The number that is divided in a division problem is the ____.

## CONCEPTS AND SKILLS Open Response

**Use basic facts to help you divide.** (Chapters 8, 11)

4. $80 \div 4$
5. $1{,}200 \div 3$
6. $2{,}100 \div 7$
7. $5{,}600 \div 8$
8. $240 \div 60$
9. $1{,}800 \div 90$
10. $36{,}000 \div 40$
11. $56{,}000 \div 80$

**Estimate.** (Chapters 8, 11)

12. $6\overline{)34}$
13. $9\overline{)350}$
14. $7\overline{)567}$
15. $5\overline{)245}$
16. $48\overline{)97}$
17. $19\overline{)169}$
18. $31\overline{)222}$
19. $68\overline{)349}$

**Divide. Check your answers.** (Chapters 8, 9, 11)

20. $4\overline{)85}$
21. $3\overline{)67}$
22. $65 \div 5$
23. $76 \div 4$
24. $4\overline{)448}$
25. $7\overline{)938}$
26. $\$5.04 \div 9$
27. $\$6.15 \div 5$
28. $8\overline{)1{,}128}$
29. $15\overline{)53}$
30. $12\overline{)99}$
31. $5\overline{)32{,}566}$
32. $23\overline{)576}$
33. $52\overline{)607}$
34. $97\overline{)8{,}148}$
35. $58\overline{)3{,}596}$

**List two multiples for each number.** (Chapter 10)

36. 7
37. 3
38. 9
39. 6

**List the factors for each number. Tell if the number is prime or composite.** (Chapter 10)

40. 4
41. 5
42. 17
43. 12

**Find the mean of the numbers in each group.** (Chapter 10)

**44.** 93, 72, 78

**45.** \$57, \$24, \$99, \$108

**46.** 8, 378, 123, 49, 187

**PROBLEM SOLVING** Open Response

**47.** Jenny has 55 CDs in a display case. One shelf has 7 CDs. All the other shelves have 8 CDs each. How many shelves are in the display case?

**48.** Guitar strings cost 2 times as much as a set of picks. A tuner costs 8 times as much as the picks. The tuner costs \$24. How much do the strings cost?

**49.** A sign says: "Buy 4 post cards, get a 5th post card FREE!" If Hector wants 25 post cards, how many does he have to buy at the regular price?

**50.** Jo delivers 24 papers to each class on 2 floors. The first floor has 15 classes. She delivers 624 papers. How many classes are on the second floor?

## Performance Task

| Item | Number of Items per box |
|---|---|
| 20 dishes | 5 |
| 43 glasses | 9 |
| 28 bowls | 5 |
| 84 books | 7 |

**Task** Andrew donates various items to a local hospital. The table above shows the items he wants to donate and the number of each item he can pack in a box.

a. How many boxes will Andrew need? Show your work.

b. Andrew decides to get larger boxes. The larger boxes can fit double the number of items. Create a new table to show how many of each item will fit in the new boxes.

c. How many of the larger boxes will Andrew need? Explain your answer.

# Getting Ready for CRCT

**Solve Problems 1–10.**

*Look at the example below.*

Mr. Benz is slicing bagels into 4 equal pieces. There are 24 students in his class. If each student gets 2 pieces, how many bagels will Mr. Benz slice?

A. 6

B. 12

C. 24

D. 48

**THINK**

Multiply to find the total number of pieces needed.

24 students $\times$ 2 pieces = 48 pieces

Now find how many bagels are needed to make 48 pieces.

48 pieces $\div$ 4 pieces = 12 bagels

Therefore, you should choose **B**.

## Multiple Choice

1. Which shows 8,596,023 rounded to the nearest hundred thousand?

A. 9,000,000

B. 8,600,000

C. 8,500,000

D. 8,590,000

(Chapter 2, Lesson 5)

2. What is the value of *n*?

$$(2 + 9) - (6 + 3) = n$$

A. 0

B. 1

C. 2

D. 3

(Chapter 5, Lesson 1)

3. One pack of baseball cards contains 10 cards. There are 36 packs in a box and 20 boxes in a case. How many baseball cards are in a case?

A. 7,200

B. 3,600

C. 720

D. 360

(Chapter 11, Lesson 7)

4. When the heights of the mountains are rounded to the nearest hundred, about what is the difference in their heights?

| Mt. Everest | Mt. Kilimanjaro |
|---|---|
| 29,035 feet | 19,340 feet |

A. 9,000 feet

B. 9,500 feet

C. 9,700 feet

D. 10,000 feet

(Chapter 3, Lesson 3)



For Test-Taking Tips, See Page 658.

## Open Response

5. A farmer plants 26 rows of tomato plants, with 105 plants in each row. How many plants does the farmer plant? Write a number sentence to show how to find the answer.

(Chapter 7, Lesson 6)

6. Raul's class picks 1,200 apples. The class has 30 boxes and puts an equal number of apples into each box. How many apples are in each box?

(Chapter 11, Lesson 1)

7. One page in a photo album holds 8 photos. If Sue has 87 photos, how many pages in the photo album can she fill completely?

(Chapter 8, Lesson 3)

8. The table shows a pattern for the number of divisions and the number of teams in a soccer league. Based on the pattern, how many divisions will there be when there are 32 teams?

| Soccer League | |
|---|---|
| **Number of Divisions** | **Number of Teams** |
| 2 | 8 |
| 3 | 12 |
| 4 | 16 |
| 5 | 20 |

(Chapter 4, Lesson 3)

## Extended Response

9. On Day 1, James read 9 pages of a book. On Day 2, he read twice as many pages as on Day 1. At the start of Day 3, he had 35 pages left to read.

   a. How many pages are in the book?

   b. Explain what steps you used to find the answer.

   c. On what day did James finish reading the book if he read 7 pages each remaining day? Explain how you found your answer.

(Chapter 11, Lesson 7)

10. Anna buys 6 boxes of balloons. There are 76 balloons in each box.

   a. About how many balloons does Anna buy?

   b. Exactly how many balloons does Anna buy? Is your answer reasonable? Explain how you know.

(Chapter 6, Lesson 4)

**Education Place**

Look for Cumulative Test Prep at **eduplace.com/map** for more practice.

# Vocabulary Wrap-Up for Unit 4

**Look back at the big ideas and vocabulary in this unit.**

## Big Ideas

Sometimes you need to regroup when you divide.

A multiple of a number is a product of that number and any whole number.

You can use basic facts to help you place the first digit in a quotient.

### Key Vocabulary

**regroup**
**multiple**
**product**
**quotient**

## Math Conversations

**Use your new vocabulary to discuss these big ideas.**

1. Explain how to find the mean of four numbers.
2. Explain how to regroup to divide 98 by 8.
3. Explain how multiplication and division are related.
4. Explain the difference between a prime number and a composite number.
5. **Write About It** Look through catalogs and newspaper ads. Then explain how you can use division when you shop.

# UNIT 5

# Measurement and Graphing

# Reading Mathematics

## Reviewing Vocabulary

**Here are some math vocabulary words that you should know.**

| | |
|---|---|
| **capacity** | the amount that a container can hold |
| **centimeter (cm)** | a metric unit used to measure length |
| **mass** | the amount of matter in an object |
| **ounce (oz)** | a customary unit used to measure weight |

## Reading Words and Symbols

You can describe the capacity of an object by using customary units or metric units.

**Customary Units**

**Read:** The pitcher holds about one quart.

**Write, using symbols:** The pitcher holds about 1 qt.

**Metric Units**

**Read:** The pitcher holds about one liter.

**Write, using symbols:** The pitcher holds about 1 L.

**Use words and symbols to answer the questions.**

1. What is the length of the eraser?

0 1 2
inches

2. What is the mass of the apple?

# Reading Questions on CRCT

**Choose the correct answer for each.**

3. What is the approximate weight of the apples?

A. 1 pound

B. 2 pounds

C. 3 pounds

D. 4 pounds

**Approximate** means "close to" or "about."

4. What unit of measure would you use to determine the mass of a crayon?

A. degrees

B. grams

C. meters

D. seconds

**Determine** means "find out" or "decide."

5. Which word completes this sentence?

An elephant's weight can be measured in _____.

A. gallons

B. inches

C. miles

D. tons

**Completes** means "finishes" or "fills in."

# Learning Vocabulary

**Watch for these words in this unit. Write their definitions in your journal.**

**century**
**decade**
**kilogram (kg)**
**degrees Celsius (°C)**
**degrees Fahrenheit (°F)**
**interval**
**outlier**
**line graph**

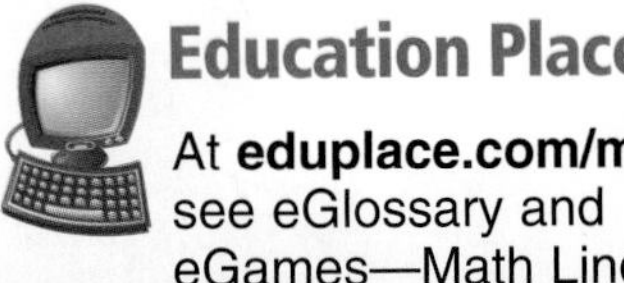

## Education Place

At **eduplace.com/map** see eGlossary and eGames—Math Lingo.

## Literature Connection

Read "Lengths of Time" on Page 650. Then work with a partner to answer the questions about the story.

# Customary and Metric Measurement

## PERFORMANCE PREVIEW

### Using Data

The Cherokee rose, the state flower of Georgia, can grow as high as 6 meters! The table shows how tall one rose grew in 4 years. How tall do you think the rose would be after 6 years? How can you use the information in the chart to make your estimate?

**Growth of a Cherokee Rose**

| Number of Years | Height in Centimeters |
|---|---|
| 1 | 60 |
| 2 | 120 |
| 3 | 180 |
| 4 | 240 |

# Use What You Know

**Use this page to review and remember what you need to know for this chapter.**

## VOCABULARY

**Choose the best word to complete each sentence.**

1. A pencil weighs about one _____.
2. A grocer sells potatoes by the _____.
3. The amount of water in a swimming pool would best be measured in _____.

**Vocabulary**

quart
ounce
pound
gallons

## CONCEPTS AND SKILLS

**Measure to the nearest inch.**

4. 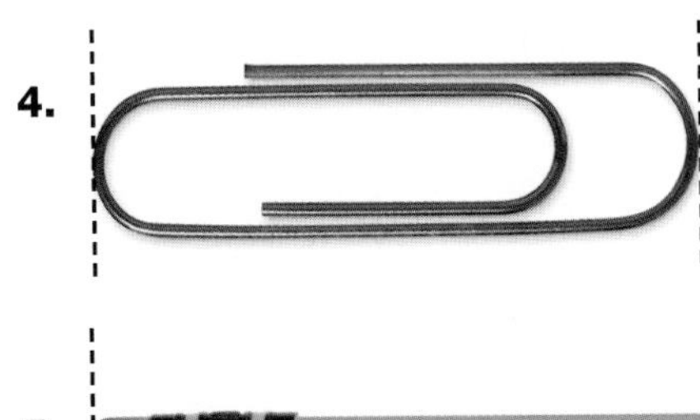

5.

**Choose the better unit of measure.**

6. the width of a book
   **a.** meters **b.** centimeters
7. the length of a car
   **a.** meters **b.** kilometers
8. the length of an eraser
   **a.** inches **b.** feet
9. the distance between towns
   **a.** yards **b.** miles

**Write About It**

10. Name 4 measuring tools that you have used. Describe how to use them and tell what you could measure with them.

Facts Practice, See page 670.

# Explore Customary Units of Length

**Objective** Estimate and measure lengths, using an inch ruler.

**STANDARDS** Maintains M3M2.b, M4P3

## Work Together

Work with a partner to estimate length and then measure, using an inch ruler.

**STEP 1** Estimate the length of the pea pod above. Record your estimate in a table like the one at the right.

| Estimate: |
| --- |
| Nearest inch: |
| Nearest half inch: |
| Nearest quarter inch: |

**STEP 2** Use an inch ruler to measure the pea pod to the nearest inch. Use a half-inch mark to decide which inch mark is closer to the end of the pea pod. Record the length.

*If the end is exactly at the half-inch mark, round to the next inch.*

**STEP 3** Now measure the pea pod to the nearest half inch. Use a quarter-inch mark to decide which half-inch mark is closer to the end. Record the length.

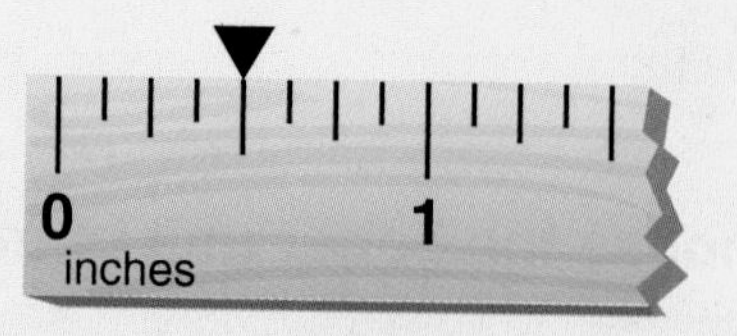


**STEP 4** Measure the pea pod to the nearest quarter inch. Use an eighth-inch mark to decide which quarter-inch mark is closer to the end.

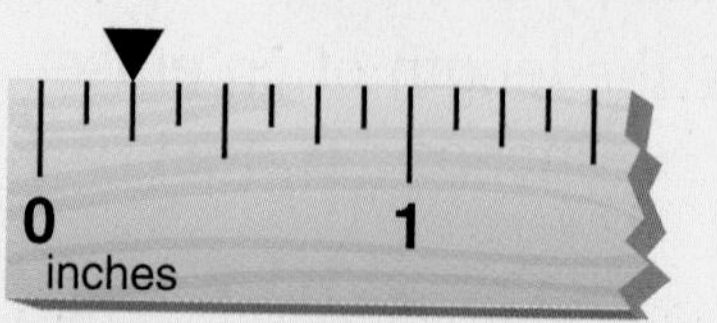


*The more marks your ruler has, the more accurately you will be able to measure.*

Compare your estimate and the three measurements of the pea pod. Which is closest to the actual length of the pea pod?

STEP 5

Find five objects to measure. Estimate the length of each object to the nearest inch. Then measure each object to the nearest inch, half inch, and quarter inch. Record your work.

## On Your Own

**Measure to the nearest inch, half inch, and quarter inch.**

1. 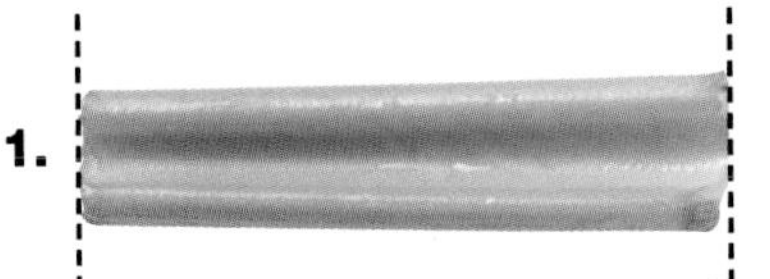

2. 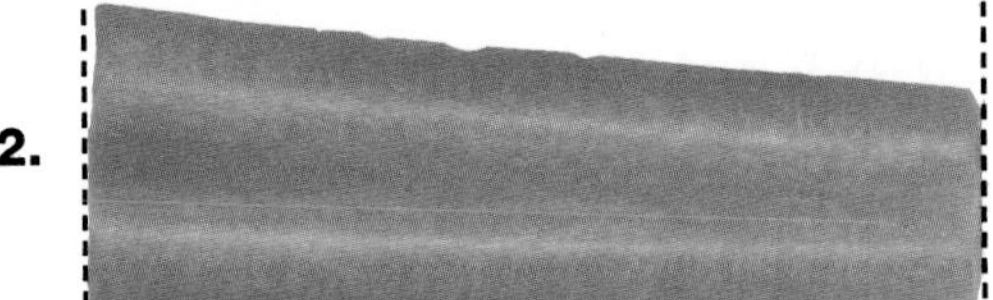

**Estimate the length of each object to the nearest inch. Then measure to the nearest inch, half inch, and quarter inch.**

3. 

4. 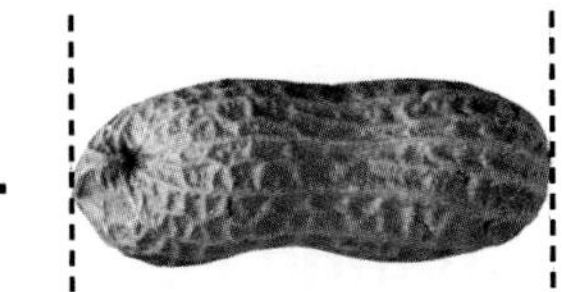

## Talk About It • Write About It

**You have learned to measure to the nearest inch, half inch, and quarter inch.**

5. One green bean is less than 5 inches long, and another is more than 5 inches long. When they are measured to the nearest inch, both are about 5 inches long. Explain how this is possible.

6. What is the length of this green bean to the nearest quarter inch?

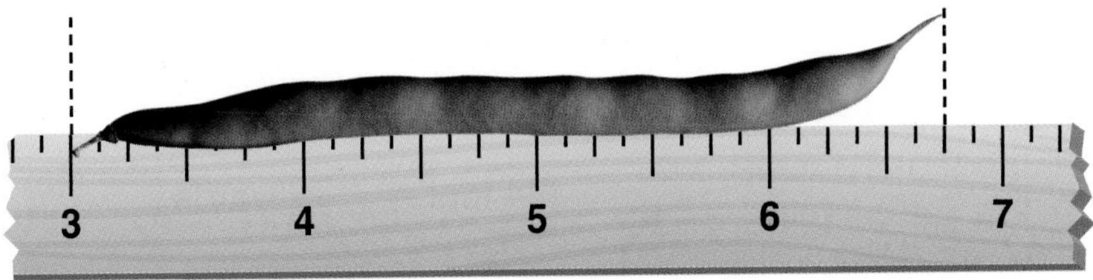

Lesson 2

Audio Tutor 2/1 Listen and Understand

# Inch, Foot, Yard, Mile

**Objective** Change units of length.

**STANDARDS** M4M1.c, Maintains M3M2, M4P1.b

## Learn About It

The fourth grade planted flowers in the school courtyard. The length of the flower bed is 9 feet. What is the length in inches? in yards?

Inch, foot, yard, and mile are customary units of measure.

### Change Feet to Inches

When you change from larger units to smaller units, the number of units increases. So multiply.

Multiply by the number of inches in 1 foot.

| 9 | × | 12 | = | 108 |
|---|---|---|---|---|
| ↑ | | ↑ | | ↑ |
| number of feet | | inches in foot | | inches in 9 feet |

**Customary Units of Length**

| | | |
|---|---|---|
| 1 foot (ft) | = | 12 inches (in.) |
| 1 yard (yd) | = | 3 feet |
| 1 yard (yd) | = | 36 inches |
| 1 mile (mi) | = | 1,760 yards |
| 1 mile (mi) | = | 5,280 feet |

### Change Feet to Yards

When you change from smaller units to larger units, the number of units decreases. So divide.

Divide by the number of feet in 1 yard.

| 9 | ÷ | 3 | = | 3 |
|---|---|---|---|---|
| ↑ | | ↑ | | ↑ |
| number of feet | | feet in 1 yard | | yards in 9 feet |

**Solution:** The length of the flower bed is 108 inches, or 3 yards.

## Other Examples

**A. Miles to Yards**

2 miles = ____ yards

$2 \times 1{,}760 = 3{,}520$

2 miles = 3,520 yards.

Think
Miles are larger than yards, so multiply.

**B. Feet to Yards**

144 feet = ____ yards

$144 \div 3 = 48$

144 feet = 48 yards.

Think
Feet are smaller than yards, so divide.

## Guided Practice

**Find each missing number.**

1. 72 ft = ____ yd
2. ____ in. = 6 ft
3. 2 mi = ____ ft
4. ____ yd = 144 in.

**Ask Yourself**

- Am I converting to a larger or smaller unit?
- Should I multiply or divide?

**Explain Your Thinking** ▶ What unit of measure would you use to measure the length of your classroom?

## Practice and Problem Solving

**Find each missing number.**

5. 72 yd = ____ ft
6. 5 ft = ____ in.
7. 10 yd = ____ ft
8. 4 mi = ____ ft
9. ____ yd = 3 mi
10. 21 ft = ____ yd

**Compare. Write >, <, or = for each ⬤.**

11. 3 ft ⬤ 36 in.
12. 2 yd ⬤ 60 in.
13. 5,280 yd ⬤ 2 mi
14. 4 yd ⬤ 108 in.
15. 5 ft ⬤ 60 in.
16. 7 yd ⬤ 28 ft

**Copy and complete the tables. Write the rule for each table.**

17.

| ft | 2 | 3 | 5 | 8 | 9 | 12 |
|---|---|---|---|---|---|---|
| in. | 24 | 36 | ■ | ■ | ■ | ■ |

18.

| ft | 3 | 6 | 9 | 12 | 15 | 30 |
|---|---|---|---|---|---|---|
| yd | 1 | ■ | 3 | ■ | ■ | ■ |

**Solve.**

19. Alicia has a board that is 2 yards long. She cuts a 4-foot length for a fence. How long is the remaining piece?

20. Seth estimates the length of his garden to be 20 feet. Sarah estimates it to be 7 yards. If the actual length is 19 feet, which is the better estimate?

## Sharpening Skills for CRCT

**Open Response**

**Solve.** (Ch. 4, Lesson 5)

21. $35 \div 7$
22. $8 \times 9$
23. $56 \div 8$
24. $90 \div 10$
25. $6 \times 7$
26. $9 \times 5$
27. $54 \div 9$
28. $8 \times 7$
29. $64 \div 8$

**Multiple Choice**

30. Which is the best unit for measuring the distance from New York to Chicago? (Ch. 12, Lesson 2)

A. inch
B. foot
C. yard
D. mile

Extra Practice See page 331, Set A.

Lesson 3

# Customary Units of Capacity

**Objective** Change units of capacity.

## Learn About It

**STANDARDS** M4M1.c, Maintains M3M5.b, M4P1.b

Angela's watering can holds 8 quarts of water. How many cups is that? how many gallons?

Gallons, quarts, pints, and cups all measure capacity, the amount a container can hold.

### Change Quarts to Cups

When you change from larger units to smaller units, the number of units increases. So multiply.

Multiply by the number of cups in 1 quart.

$8 \times 4 = 32$

8 ↑ number of quarts; 4 ↑ cups in 1 quart; 32 ↑ cups in 8 quarts

| Customary Units of Capacity | | |
|---|---|---|
| 1 pint (pt) | = | 2 cups (c) |
| 1 quart (qt) | = | 2 pints |
| 1 quart (qt) | = | 4 cups |
| 1 gallon (gal) | = | 4 quarts |
| 1 gallon (gal) | = | 8 pints |
| 1 gallon (gal) | = | 16 cups |

### Change Quarts to Gallons

When you change from smaller units to larger units, the number of units decreases. So divide.

Divide by the number of quarts in 1 gallon.

$8 \div 4 = 2$

8 ↑ number of quarts; 4 ↑ quarts in 1 gallon; 2 ↑ gallons in 8 quarts

**Solution:** The watering can holds 32 cups, or 2 gallons, of water.

## Other Examples

**A. Cups to Pints**

10 cups = ____ pints

$10 \div 2 = 5$

10 cups = 5 pints

Think
Cups are smaller than pints, so divide.

**B. Gallons to Pints**

3 gallons = ____ pints

$3 \times 8 = 24$

3 gallons = 24 pints

Think
Gallons are larger than pints, so multiply.

## Guided Practice

**Find each missing number.**

1. 8 c = ____ pt
2. ____ qt = 5 gal
3. 16 pt = ____ qt
4. 2 qt = ____ c

**Ask Yourself**

- Am I converting to a larger or smaller unit?
- Should I multiply or divide?

**Explain Your Thinking** ▶ Describe how you found the missing number in Exercise 2.

## Practice and Problem Solving

**Find each missing number.**

5. 14 c = ____ pt
6. 8 gal = ____ qt
7. 9 pt = ____ c
8. ____ qt = 10 pt
9. 4 pt = ____ qt
10. 16 c = ____ qt

**Choose the unit you would use to measure the capacity of each item. Write *cup, pint, quart,* or *gallon.***

11. 

12. 

13. 

14. 

**Compare. Write >, <, or = for each ⬬.**

15. 4 pt ⬬ 6 c
16. 8 gal ⬬ 30 qt
17. 13 pt ⬬ 8 qt
18. 16 c ⬬ 8 qt
19. 16 pt ⬬ 4 gal
20. 2 qt ⬬ 4 c

21. **Explain** Which is the better buy, 4 quarts of plant food for $5.00 or one half gallon for $3.00? Explain how you got your answer.

22. Jane has 5 cups of water. Al has 3 pints and Bert has 1 quart of water. List amounts in order from least to greatest.

## Sharpening Skills for CRCT

**Open Response**

**Round each number to the nearest hundred. Then estimate.** (Ch. 3, Lesson 3)

23. 5,321 − 2,192
24. 2,896 + 1,419
25. 7,099 − 3,299
26. 4,650 + 4,506

27. How many times must Taylor fill his 1-pint measuring cup to make a recipe calling for $\frac{1}{2}$ gallon of water? Explain how you got your answer. (Ch. 12, Lesson 3)

Extra Practice See page 331, Set B.

Hands On Lesson 4

# Customary Units of Weight

**Objective** Estimate and measure, using customary units of weight.

 **STANDARDS** M4M1, M4P1.b

**Vocabulary**

**tons**

**Materials**
balance scale
1-pound weight
1-ounce weight

## Learn About It

Ounces, pounds, and **tons** are units of weight. They are used to show how heavy an object is.

*A strawberry weighs about one ounce.*

*A bunch of grapes weighs about one pound.*

*A tractor weighs about one ton.*

**Try this activity to measure and compare weight.**

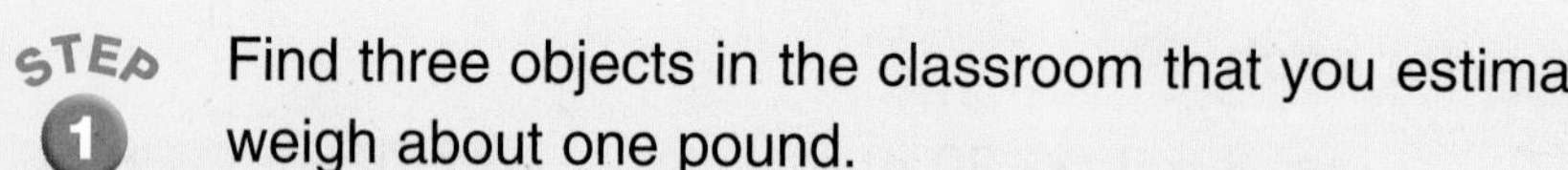

**STEP 1** Find three objects in the classroom that you estimate weigh about one pound.

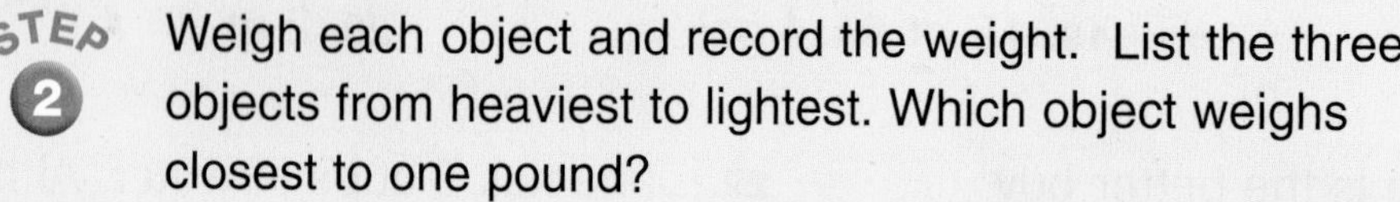

**STEP 2** Weigh each object and record the weight. List the three objects from heaviest to lightest. Which object weighs closest to one pound?

**STEP 3** Use the object closest to one pound to predict what other things in the classroom weigh. Make a list of four things that weigh more than, less than, and about one pound.

**STEP 4** Repeat Step 1 and Step 2, looking for four objects in the classroom that weigh about 1 ounce. Which object weighs closest to one ounce?

▶ Look at the truck. How many tons of watermelons are on it?

## Change Pounds to Tons

When you change from smaller units to larger units, the number of units decreases. So divide.

Divide by the number of pounds in 1 ton.

| 4,000 | ÷ | 2,000 | = | 2 |
|---|---|---|---|---|
| ↑ | | ↑ | | ↑ |
| number of pounds | | pounds in 1 ton | | tons in 4,000 pounds |

| Customary Units of Weight | | |
|---|---|---|
| 1 pound (lb) | = | 16 ounces (oz) |
| 1 ton (T) | = | 2,000 pounds |

**Solution:** The truck carries 2 tons of watermelons.

▶ If one watermelon weighs 10 pounds, how many ounces does it weigh?

## Change Pounds to Ounces

When you change from larger units to smaller units, the number of units increases. So multiply.

Multiply by the number of ounces in 1 pound.

| 10 | × | 16 | = | 160 |
|---|---|---|---|---|
| ↑ | | ↑ | | ↑ |
| number of pounds | | ounces in 1 pound | | ounces in 10 pounds |

**Solution:** The watermelon weighs 160 ounces.

## Guided Practice

**Find each missing number.**

1. 8,000 lb = ____ T
2. 5 lb = ____ oz
3. 112 oz = ____ lb
4. ____ lb = 3 T

**Ask Yourself**

- Am I converting to a larger or smaller unit?
- Should I multiply or divide?

**Explain Your Thinking** ▶ Do small objects always weigh less than large ones? Give examples to support your answer.

## Practice and Problem Solving

**Find each missing number.**

5. ____ lb = 16 T
6. 48 oz = ____ lb
7. ____ oz = 2 lb
8. 144 oz = ____ lb
9. 8,000 lb = ____ T
10. 10 lb = ____ oz

**What is the best unit to weigh these items? Write *ounce, pound,* or *ton.***

11. a bunch of bananas
12. a paper clip
13. a car
14. an elephant
15. a handful of blueberries
16. a table

**Compare. Write >, <, or = for each ●.**

17. 38 oz ● 2 lb
18. 3,000 lb ● 3T
19. 5 lb ● 80 oz
20. 2 lb ● 40 oz
21. 90 oz ● 6 lb
22. 2 T ● 3,000 lb

23. Shonte bought a 9-pound watermelon that cost $0.50 per pound. How much did she pay?

24. Darlene bought 3 pounds of peaches, 6 ounces of cherries and 14 ounces of plums. What was the total weight of her purchases?

25. Mario bought 3 pounds of fruit. He bought strawberries, cherries, grapes, and blueberries. How much did each type of fruit weigh if they weighed the same?

## Sharpening Skills for CRCT

### Open Response

**Round each number to the nearest hundred. Then estimate.** (Ch. 3, Lesson 3)

26. 7,091 + 2,802
27. 3,399 − 1,239
28. 4,511 + 5,499
29. 1,887 − 1,102
30. 3,271 + 4,010
31. 6,487 − 2,296

### Multiple Choice

32. How many ounces are in 5 pounds? (Ch. 12, Lesson 4)

A. 16 ounces
B. 20 ounces
C. 80 ounces
D. 2,000 ounces



Extra Practice See page 331, Set C.

## Visual Thinking
### Balancing Act

STANDARDS M4M1.b, M4M1.c, Prepares for M5M3.a

Which containers should you move so that each group has the same amount of juice?

Group A

Group B

## Science Connection
### A Lot of Elephant!

An African elephant can weigh 12 tons. How many pounds is that?

An elephant can drink as much as 40 gallons of water a day. How many quarts is that?

An elephant's tusk can be as long as 8 feet. How many inches is that?

## Brain Teaser

A snail is climbing a15-foot fence. Every day it climbs 3 feet, but slides back 1 foot every night. How long does it take the snail to climb to the top of the fence?

**Education Place**

Check out **eduplace.com/map** for more brain teasers.

Lesson 5

**Audio Tutor 2/12 Listen and Understand**

# Problem-Solving Decision

## Too Much or Too Little Information

**Objective** Find the information you need to solve a problem.

**STANDARDS** M4D1.d, M4P1.b

**Problem** Sam sold 38 seed packets. He collected $19.00. April sold four times as many seed packets as Sam. How many seed packets did April sell?

**Ask Yourself**

| What is the question? | What do I need to know? | What do I know? |
| --- | --- | --- |
| • How many seed packets did April sell? | • How many packets did Sam sell? | • Sam sold 38 packets.<br>• April sold 4 times as many packets as Sam. |

**Solve the problem.**

$$\begin{array}{r} 38 \\ \times\ 4 \\ \hline 152 \end{array}$$

38 ← number of packets Sam sold
× 4 ← 4 times as many as Sam
152 ← number of packets April sold

**Solution:** April sold 152 seed packets.

## Try These

**Solve. If not enough information is given, tell what information is needed to solve the problem.**

1. Rebecca's club sold 343 flower and vegetable seed packets altogether. They collected $171.50. Were more flower or vegetable seeds sold?
2. Nate bought 8 one-pound packages of crocus bulbs for $1.50 a pound and a box of fertilizer for $4.00. How much did he spend on bulbs?
3. Ann planted 16 tulips and 12 lilies. She planted twice as many daffodils as tulips. How many daffodils did she plant?
4. Lee planted marigold seeds in pots. Each pot held 20 ounces of soil. What was the weight of all the soil used?



Extra Help at eduplace.com/map

Problem Solving

GPS

## Art Connection

### Mobile Math

STANDARDS M4M1.b, M4P4

Hanging sculptures like the one in the photo are called mobiles. The artist needs to carefully balance the construction.

Calder might have used an equation like this to balance his mobile.

Use some of the shapes below to construct an imaginary mobile. Draw a picture equation to show how it will balance.

| 3 oz | 5 oz | 4 oz | 4 oz | 1 lb | 8 oz | 2 oz |
|---|---|---|---|---|---|---|

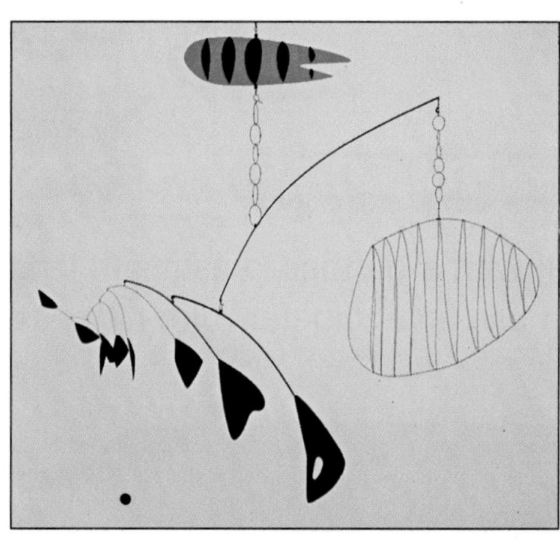

*"Lobster Trap and Fish Tail" by Alexander Calder (1939)*

WEEKLY WR READER eduplace.com/map

Quick Check

Check your understanding of Lessons 1–5.

**Measure to the nearest inch, half inch, and quarter inch.** (Lesson 1)

**1.** **2.** **3.**

**Compare. Write >, <, or = for each ⬮.** (Lessons 2–4)

**4.** 2 yd ⬮ 66 in. **5.** 72 in. ⬮ 6 ft **6.** 9 gal ⬮ 30 qt

**7.** 8,500 lb ⬮ 8 T **8.** 60 oz ⬮ 4 lb **9.** 7 lb ⬮ 112 oz

**Solve.** (Lesson 5)

**10.** Mrs. Juba used 20 oranges to make 8 cups of juice. How many quarts of juice did she make?

Hands On Lesson 6

# Explore Metric Units of Length

**Vocabulary**
millimeter (mm)

**Objective** Estimate and measure lengths using a centimeter ruler.

 **STANDARDS** M4M1.c, Maintains M3M2.b, M4P3

## Work Together

Work with a partner to estimate lengths.
Then use a centimeter ruler to measure lengths.

**STEP 1** Estimate the length of the cattail above. Record your estimate in a table like the one shown.

| Object | Estimate | Nearest Centimeter | Nearest Millimeter |
|---|---|---|---|
| cattail | | | |
| | | | |
| | | | |

**STEP 2** Use a centimeter ruler to measure the length of the cattail to the nearest centimeter. Use a half-centimeter mark to decide which centimeter mark is closer to the end of the cattail. Record the length in your table.

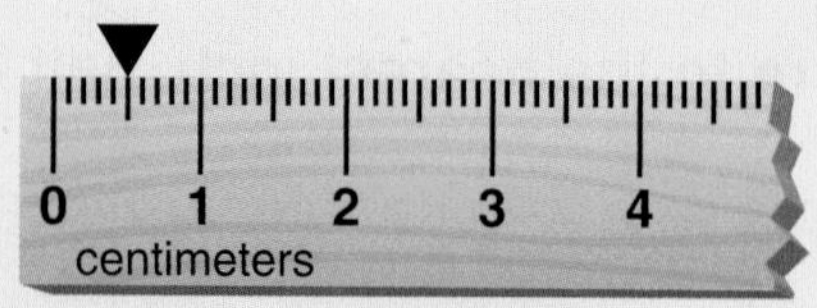


*If the end is exactly halfway between centimeters, round to the next centimeter.*

**STEP 3** Now measure the cattail to the nearest **millimeter**. Decide which millimeter mark is closer to the end of the cattail. Record the length in millimeters in your table.

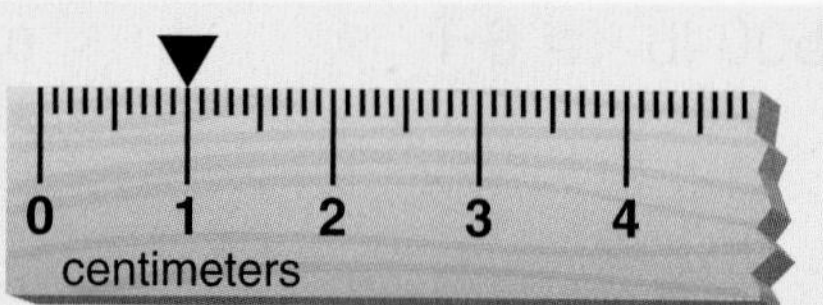


*There are 10 millimeters in 1 centimeter.*

Find 5 objects to measure. Estimate the length of each object to the nearest centimeter. Then measure each object to the nearest centimeter. Record your work in your table.

| Object | Estimate | Nearest Centimeter |
|---|---|---|
| cattail | | |

## On Your Own

**Measure the length to the nearest centimeter and millimeter.**

1. 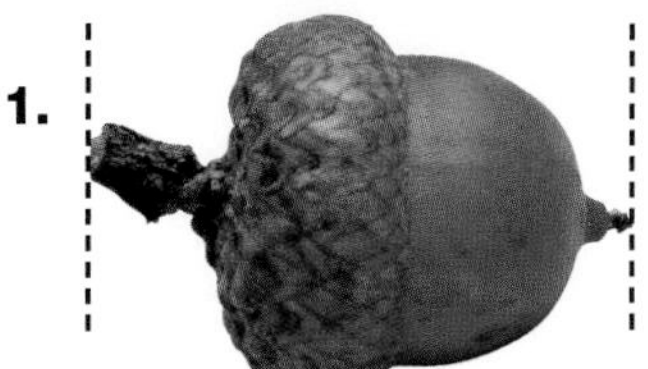

2. 

**Estimate the length. Then measure each object to the nearest centimeter and millimeter.**

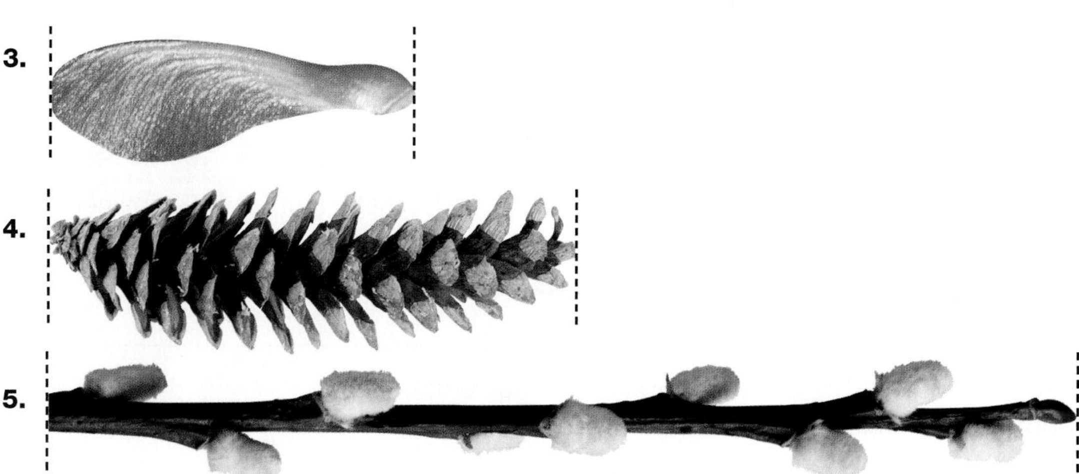


## Talk About It • Write About It

**You have learned to measure lengths in centimeters and millimeters.**

6. Suppose you know how tall a plant is in centimeters. Explain how you can tell how tall it is in millimeters.

7. Suppose you are measuring a piece of wood for a birdhouse. Would it be better to measure in centimeters or in millimeters? Explain your thinking.

Audio Tutor 2/3 Listen and Understand

Lesson 7

# Metric Units of Length

**Objective** Change metric units of length.

**STANDARDS** M4M1.c, M4P1.b, Maintains M3M2

**Vocabulary**

- millimeter (mm)
- centimeter (cm)
- decimeter (dm)
- meter (m)
- kilometer (km)

## Learn About It

**Millimeters**, **centimeters**, **decimeters**, **meters**, and **kilometers** are metric units used to measure length.

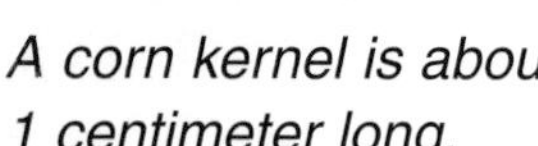

*A corn kernel is about 1 centimeter long.*

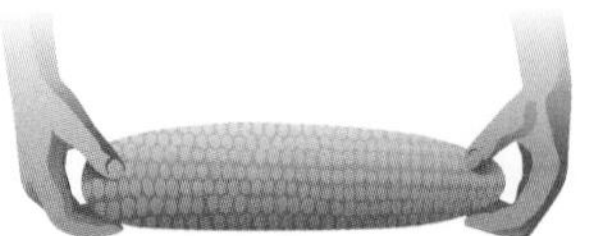

*An ear of corn is about 2 decimeters long.*

*A young corn plant is about 1 meter tall.*

*A road can be about 1 kilometer long.*

### Change Meters to Decimeters

When you change from larger units to smaller units, the number of units increases. So multiply.

Multiply by the number of decimeters in 1 meter.

$$4{,}000 \times 10 = 40{,}000$$

4,000 ↑ number of meters; 10 ↑ decimeters in 1 meter; 40,000 ↑ decimeters in 4,000 meters

4,000 meters = 40,000 decimeters

**Metric Units of Length**

| | | |
|---|---|---|
| 1 centimeter (cm) | = | 10 millimeters (mm) |
| 1 decimeter (dm) | = | 10 centimeters |
| 1 meter (m) | = | 10 decimeters |
| 1 kilometer (km) | = | 1,000 meters |

### Change Meters to Kilometers

When you change from smaller units to larger units, the number of units decreases. So divide.

Divide by the number of meters in 1 kilometer.

$$4{,}000 \div 1{,}000 = 4$$

4,000 ↑ number of meters; 1,000 ↑ meters in 1 kilometer; 4 ↑ kilometers in 4,000 meters

4,000 meters = 4 kilometers

## Other Examples

**A. Meters to Centimeters**

5 meters = ____ centimeters

$5 \times 100 = 500$

5 meters = 500 centimeters

**B. Millimeters to Centimeters**

80 millimeters = ____ centimeters

$80 \div 10 = 8$

80 millimeters = 8 centimeters

## Guided Practice

**Find each missing number.**

1. 40 cm = ____ mm
2. 200 cm = ____ m
3. 3 km = ____ m
4. 50 cm = ____ dm

**Ask Yourself**

- Am I converting to a larger or smaller unit?
- Should I multiply or divide?

**Explain Your Thinking** ▶ What is the best unit to use when measuring the distance between two cities?

## Practice and Problem Solving

**Find each missing number.**

5. 50 km = ____ m
6. 600 mm = ____ cm
7. ____ mm = 9 cm
8. 3 m = ____ cm
9. 5,000 m = ____ km
10. ____ dm = 40 cm

**Choose the better estimate of length.**

11. length of a garden row
    a. 10 m  b. 10 mm
12. width of your fingertip
    a. 1 dm  b. 1 cm
13. the length of a street
    a. 3 km  b. 3 dm
14. the height of a window
    a. 1 m  b. 10 mm

**Copy and complete the tables. Write the rule for each table.**

15.

| km | 1 | 3 | 5 | 7 | 8 |
|---|---|---|---|---|---|
| m | 1,000 | ■ | ■ | ■ | ■ |

16.

| mm | 10 | 20 | 30 | 60 | 80 |
|---|---|---|---|---|---|
| cm | 1 | ■ | ■ | ■ | ■ |

17. **Estimate** Sue estimates that there are 9 dm between plants. Lee estimates 1 m. The actual distance is 97 cm. Who made the closer estimate?

18. Maxine has a piece of string that is 2 m long. If she cuts off a piece that is 105 cm long, will she have at least 35 cm left?

## GPS Sharpening Skills for CRCT

### Open Response

**Solve.** (Ch. 4, Lesson 5)

19. 72 ÷ 9
20. 36 ÷ 6
21. 56 ÷ 7
22. 49 ÷ 7
23. 27 ÷ 9
24. 72 ÷ 8

### Multiple Choice

25. Which length is closest to 1 kilometer? (Ch. 12, Lesson 7)

A. 10 dm
C. 1,000 cm
B. 900 m
D. 999 m

Extra Practice See page 331, Set D.

Hands On Lesson 8

# Metric Units of Capacity

**Objective** Change metric units of capacity.

 **STANDARDS** M4M1.c, Prepares for M5M3, M4P1.b

**Vocabulary**
**liter (L)**
**milliliter (mL)**

## Learn About It

**Materials**
containers of various sizes
liter measure marked in mL
water

**Liter** and **milliliter** are units used to measure capacity in the metric system.

This bottle holds 1 liter.

This eyedropper holds 1 milliliter.

| Metric Units of Capacity |
|---|
| 1 liter (L) = 1,000 milliters (mL) |

**Try this activity to measure metric capacity.**

**STEP 1** Find three containers that you estimate will each hold about a liter of water.

**STEP 2** Fill the liter measure with water. Pour it into each of the containers you selected.

| Container Estimated | More or Less Than 1 Liter |
|---|---|
| Container 1 | |
| Container 2 | |
| Container 3 | |
| | |

**STEP 3** Decide if the capacity of each container is greater than, less than, or equal to a liter.

- Which container has a capacity closest to one liter? Explain how you know.

## Other Examples

**A. Liters to Milliliters**

4 liters = ____ milliliters

$4 \times 1{,}000 = 4{,}000$

4 liters = 4,000 milliliters

**B. Milliliters to Liters**

2,000 milliliters = ____ liters

$2{,}000 \div 1{,}000 = 2$

2,000 milliliters = 2 liters

## Guided Practice

**Ask Yourself**

- Am I converting to a larger or smaller unit?
- Should I multiply or divide?

**Find each missing number.**

**1.** 9 L = ____ mL

**2.** ____ L = 5,000 mL

**3.** 3,000 mL = ____ L

**4.** ____ mL = 4 L

**Explain Your Thinking** ▶ Why is it useful to measure capacity by using milliliters and liters instead of by using a small container and a large container?

## Practice and Problem Solving

**Find each missing number.**

**5.** ____ mL = 3 L

**6.** ____ L = 2,000 mL

**7.** 6,000 mL = ____ L

**8.** 10,000 mL = ____ L

**9.** 4,000 mL = ____ L

**10.** 25 L = ____ mL

**Choose the better estimate of capacity for each item.**

**11.**

**a.** 20 mL **b.** 20 L

**12.**

**a.** 400 mL **b.** 400 L

**13.**

**a.** 250 mL **b.** 25 L

**14.**

**a.** 8 mL **b.** 8 L

**15.**

**a.** 215 mL **b.** 215 L

**16.**

**a.** 280 mL **b.** 28 L

Go On

**Choose the better unit to measure each capacity.**
**Write *milliliters* or *liters.***

**17.** a glass of milk **18.** a kitchen sink **19.** the juice from one lemon

**20.** a bathtub **21.** a spoon **22.** a swimming pool

**Compare. Write >, <, or = for each ●.**

**23.** 6 mL ● 6,000 L **24.** 8 L ● 8,000 mL **25.** 30 L ● 300 mL

**26.** 4,500 mL ● 45 L **27.** 4 L ● 350 mL **28.** 2,000 mL ● 2 L

**29.** 7 L ● 7,000 mL **30.** 550 mL ● 5 L **31.** 60 L ● 60,000 mL

**Solve.**

**32.** Carla has 4 bottles of water. Each bottle has a capacity of 500 mL. How many liters of water can the bottles hold altogether?

**33.** It takes 12 average-size oranges to make 1 liter of orange juice. How many mL of juice can be expected from 18 oranges?

**34.** **Estimate** A recipe calls for 250 mL of apple juice. If the recipe is tripled, will a 1 L container of apple juice be enough?

**35.** A large cooler can hold 20 L and a small cooler can hold 5 L. How many more milliliters can a large cooler hold than a small cooler?

## Data Use the recipe for Problems 36–40.

**36.** How many liters will Sonya's punch recipe make?

**37.** How many 250 mL servings are in this recipe?

**38.** If each serving is 250 mL, how many liters of punch will be needed for 40 servings?

**39.** How many more milliliters of lemon-lime soda are in this recipe than orange juice?

**40.** **Money** How much will each 250 mL serving cost if the ingredients in the recipe cost a total of $5.60?

Extra Practice See page 331, Set E.

## Sharpening Skills for CRCT

**Open Response**

**Write the time in two ways.** (Grade 3)

**41.** 

**42.** 

**43.** Anna wants to write 7,000 milliliters, using the fewest digits. How else could she write this capacity? (Chapter 12, Lesson 8)

Explain how you got your answer.

# Math Reasoning

## Using Benchmarks

Activity

**STANDARDS** Reviews M3M2.c

Materials: centimeter or inch ruler
yardstick or meter stick

Here are some useful ways to estimate length.

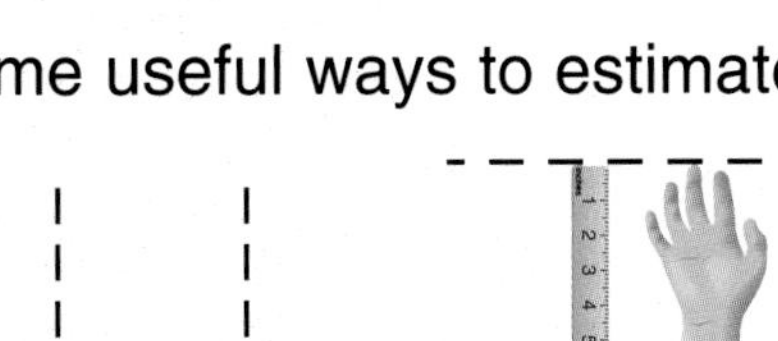

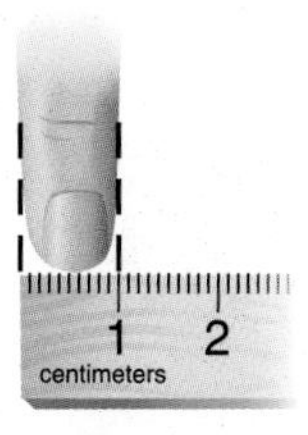


**1 centimeter**

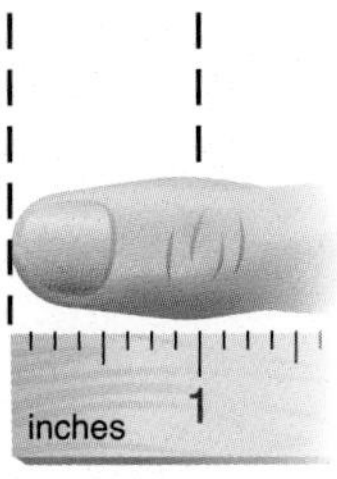


**1 inch**

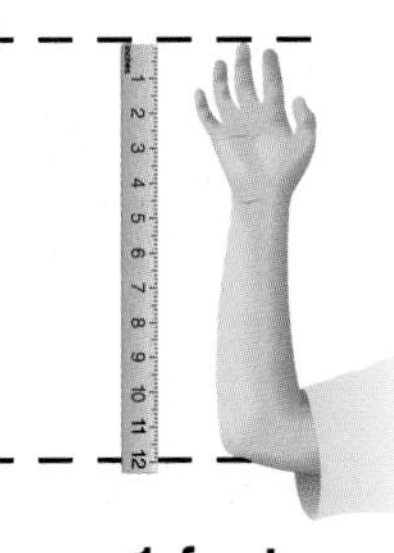

**1 foot**

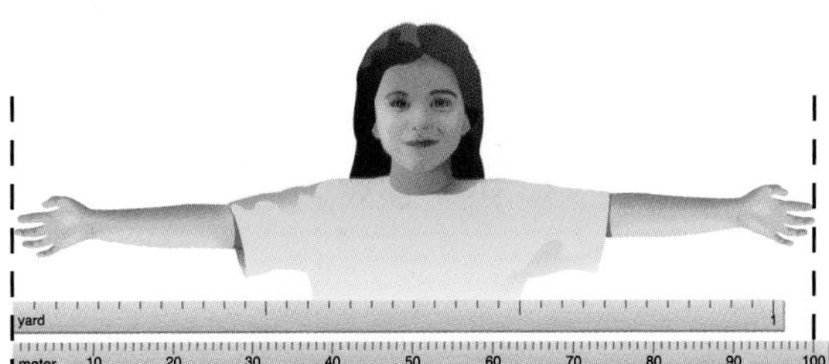


**1 yard or 1 meter**

**Work with a partner.**

STEP 1 Check the measurements shown above to find your personal benchmarks for length.

- Is your finger about 1 centimeter wide?
- Is the first joint in your thumb about 1 inch long?
- Does your arm from elbow to hand measure about 1 foot?
- Does your arm span measure about 1 yard? 1 meter?

STEP 2 Use your personal benchmarks to estimate the length of 5 objects in the classroom. Order and record your estimates. Then measure the objects using metric or customary units. Order and record your measurements.

How close were your estimates?

Hands On Lesson 9

# Metric Units of Mass

**Objective** Change metric units of mass.

**STANDARDS** M4M1, M4P1.b

**Vocabulary**
**gram (g)**
**kilogram (kg)**

**Materials**
balance
metric masses

## Learn About It

These four pumpkin seeds have a mass of 1 gram. The pumpkin has a mass of 45 kilograms.

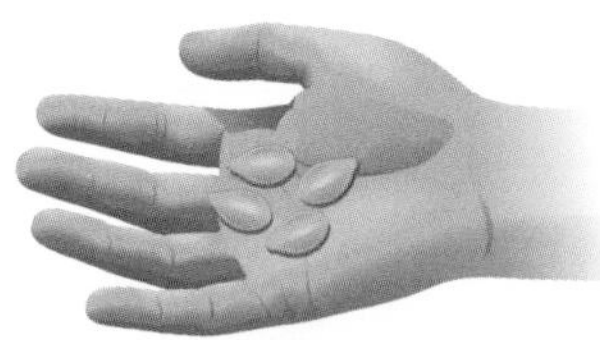

**Gram** and **kilogram** are metric units of mass.

**Try this activity to measure and compare mass.**

**STEP 1** Find three objects in the classroom that you estimate will have a mass of 500 grams, 1 gram, and 100 grams.

**STEP 2** Determine each object's mass and record it. List the three objects from heaviest to lightest.

**STEP 3** Use the objects you found to predict the mass of other things in the classroom. Make a list of things that have a mass of about 1 gram, about 100 grams, and about 500 grams.

| Metric Units of Mass |
|---|
| 1 kilogram (kg) = 1,000 grams (g) |

### Other Examples

**A. Kilograms to Grams**

3 kilograms = ____ grams

$3 \times 1,000 = 3,000$

3 kilograms = 3,000 grams

**B. Grams to Kilograms**

2,000 grams = ____ kilograms

$2,000 \div 1,000 = 2$

2,000 grams = 2 kilograms

## Guided Practice

**Find each missing number.**

1. 8 kg = _____ g
2. _____ kg = 9,000 g
3. _____ kg = 5,000 g
4. 7 kg = _____ g

**Ask Yourself**

- Am I converting to a larger or smaller unit?
- Should I multiply or divide?

**Explain Your Thinking** ▶ Why is mental math useful in converting kilograms to grams?

## Practice and Problem Solving

**Find each missing number.**

5. 5 kg = _____ g
6. _____ kg = 3,000 g
7. _____ g = 8 kg
8. 10 kg = _____ g
9. _____ g = 4 kg
10. 6 kg = _____ g

**Choose the better unit to measure each. Write *gram* or *kilogram*.**

11. a paper clip
12. a stapler
13. a desk
14. a dictionary
15. a pencil
16. a cherry

**Choose the better estimate of the weight of each.**

17. 

**a.** 40 g **b.** 4 kg

18. 

**a.** 450 g **b.** 45 kg

19. 

**a.** 60g **b.** 6 kg

20. 

**a.** 8 g **b.** 8 kg

21. 

**a.** 100 g **b.** 10 kg

22. 

**a.** 300 g **b.** 300 kg

Go On

**Compare. Write >, <, or = for each ●.**

23. 95 kg ● 950 g
24. 3 kg ● 3,000 g
25. 1,000 g ● 2 kg
26. 5 g ● 5,000 kg
27. 25 kg ● 2,500 g
28. 700 g ● 7 kg
29. 3 kg ● 6,000 g
30. 125 kg ● 4,000 g
31. 1,990 g ● 19 kg

**Solve.**

32. **Estimate** Workers put apples in baskets that hold about 12 kg each. The workers filled 17 baskets. About how many kg of apples did they put in baskets?

33. **Write About It** A 500-gram bag of peanuts costs $2, and 2-kg bag costs $6.50. What is the least expensive way to buy 5 kg of peanuts?

34. Paul sold 3-kg bags of apples for $3.90 each. He sold pears for $1.20 per kg. He found that he had sold 15 kg of apples and 7 kg of pears. How much money did he collect?

35. Delroy weighed the pumpkins shown below. What is the average mass of the pumpkins?

36. Delroy decided to sell the pumpkins for 1 cent per gram. How much money will he collect if he sells all the pumpkins?

Extra Practice See page 331, Set F.

## Sharpening Skills for CRCT

**Open Response**

**Estimate. Then Divide.** (Ch. 11, Lesson 6)

**37.** $16\overline{)339}$

**38.** $22\overline{)628}$

**39.** 893 ÷ 47

**40.** 990 ÷ 38

**41.** The local market sells cornmeal in 2,000-gram bags. Kristen needs 5 kilograms of cornmeal to make cornbread for the town fair. How many bags of cornmeal should she buy? Will she have any cornmeal left over? (Chapter 12, Lesson 9)

Problem Solving

GPS

## Calculator Connection
### Crafty Conversions

STANDARDS M4M1.b

**Use your calculator to estimate conversions between metric and customary units.**

**1.** 5 yd is about ____ m

**2.** 12 oz is about ____ g

**3.** 36 lb is about ____ kg

**4.** 5 mi is about ____ km

**5.** 10 cm is about ____ in.

**6.** 6 qt is about ____ L

**7.** 3 m is about ____ ft

**8.** 4 ft is about ____ cm

| Estimated Equivalents |
|---|
| **Length** |
| 1 in. is about 2.5 cm |
| 1 yd is about 0.9 m |
| 1 mi is about 1.6 km |
| **Weight/Mass** |
| 1 oz is about 28 g |
| 1lb is about 0.5 kg |
| **Capacity** |
| 1 qt is about 0.9 L |

# Chapter Review/Test

Study Guide pages SG30–32

## VOCABULARY

**Choose the best word to complete each sentence.**

1. A unit used to describe mass is a ____.
2. A unit used to describe length is a ____.
3. A unit used to describe liquid measure is a ____.

**Vocabulary**

- mile
- liter
- gram
- weight

## CONCEPTS AND SKILLS

**Measure this ribbon.** (Lessons 1 and 6, pp. 306–307, pp. 318–319)

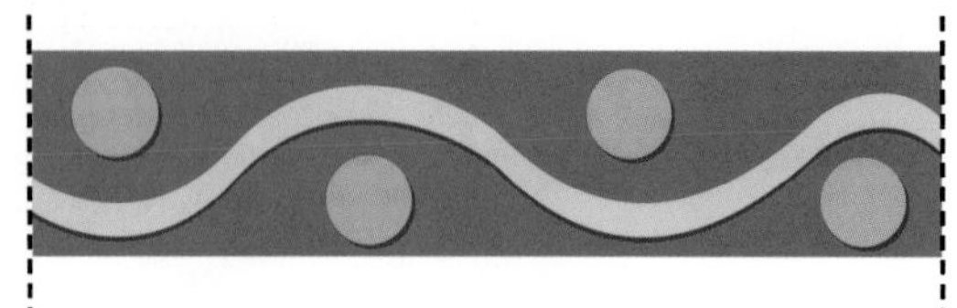

4. to the nearest inch
5. to the nearest quarter inch
6. to the nearest centimeter
7. to the nearest millimeter

**Find each missing number.** (Lessons 2–4, pp. 308–314)

8. 4 yd = ____ in.
9. 60 ft = ____ yd
10. 2 mi = ____ ft
11. 5 gal = ____ qt
12. 12 c = ____ pt
13. 2 gal = ____ c
14. 4 lb = ____ oz
15. 2 T = ____ lb
16. 32 oz = ____ lb

**Choose the metric unit you would use to describe each.** (Lessons 7–9, pp. 320–328)

17. the length of a flea
18. the capacity of a sink
19. the mass of a pencil

## PROBLEM SOLVING

**Solve.** (Lesson 5, p. 316)

20. Maria is 3 feet 9 inches tall. Naeem is 47 inches tall. Paula is 5 feet tall. What is the difference in inches between Paula's height and Naeem's height?

**Show You Understand**

Tony has a 22 gallon aquarium. Ian said that it holds 90 quarts of water. Is Ian correct?

Explain why or why not.

# Extra Practice

## Set A (Lesson 2, pp. 308–309)

**Find each missing number.**

1. 3 yd = ____ in.
2. 24 in. = ____ ft
3. ____ in. = 6 ft
4. ____ ft = 1 mi
5. 4 yd = ____ ft
6. 3 mi = ____ yd

## Set B (Lesson 3, pp. 310–311)

**Find each missing number.**

1. 16 c = ____ pt
2. 4 gal = ____ c
3. 8 pt = ____ gal
4. ____ gal = 12 qt
5. 11 pt = ____ c
6. ____ pt = 6 qt

## Set C (Lesson 4, pp. 312–314)

**Compare. Write >, <, or = for each ●.**

1. 3,000 lb ● 3 T
2. 6 lb ● 80 oz
3. 36 oz ● 2 lb

## Set D (Lesson 7, pp. 320–321)

**Find each missing number.**

1. 3 dm = ____ cm
2. 5 cm = ____ mm
3. 200 cm = ____ m
4. ____ km = 5,000 m
5. 30 cm = ____ dm
6. 700 mm = ____ cm

## Set E (Lesson 8, pp. 322–324)

**Find each missing number.**

1. 2 L = ____ mL
2. ____ L = 6,000 mL
3. ____ mL = 10 L
4. 4000 mL = ____ L
5. ____ mL = 8 L
6. 5 L = ____ mL

## Set F (Lesson 9, pp. 326–328)

**Compare. Write >, <, or = for each ●.**

1. 2 kg ● 2,500 g
2. 17 kg ● 17,000 g
3. 850 g ● 85 kg

# Time and Temperature

INVESTIGATION

## Using Data

Flamingos are beautiful pink birds that live in tropical climates. Look at the list of facts about flamingos. About how many weeks does it take a flamingo egg to hatch? What information do you need to write each of the Flamingos facts in terms of weeks?

### Flamingos

- It takes between 26 and 31 days for a flamingo egg to hatch.
- It takes between 1 and 3 years for the gray flamingo chick to turn pink.
- A flamingo can live up to 50 years.

# Use What You Know

**Use this page to review and remember what you need to know for this chapter.**

## VOCABULARY

**Choose the best term to complete each sentence.**

1. The tool for measuring temperature is a ____.
2. Temperature can be measured in ____.
3. A ____ shows the days, weeks, and months in a year.

**Vocabulary**

year
calendar
thermometer
degrees Fahrenheit

## CONCEPTS AND SKILLS

**Write each time in two different ways.**

4. 

5. 

6. 

**Use the calendar for Questions 7–9.**

7. The first Monday of September is Labor Day. What is the date?
8. What is the date of the third Wednesday?
9. How many Fridays are there in the month shown?

SCHOOL

**September**

| Sun. | Mon. | Tue. | Wed. | Thu. | Fri. | Sat. |
|---|---|---|---|---|---|---|
| | | | | 1 | 2 | 3 |
| 4 | 5 | 6 | 7 | 8 | 9 | 10 |
| 11 | 12 | 13 | 14 | 15 | 16 | 17 |
| 18 | 19 | 20 | 21 | 22 | 23 | 24 |
| 25 | 26 | 27 | 28 | 29 | 30 | |

**Write About It**

10. Why is 7:30 sometimes called half past seven? Use words or pictures to explain your thinking.

Facts Practice, See page 671.

Lesson 1

# Calendar

**Objective** Use a calendar to find elapsed time.

**Vocabulary**
**decade**
**century**

## Learn About It

 **STANDARDS** Maintains M3M1

A cardinal laid eggs on Monday, April 25. They hatched 13 days later. On what day and date did the eggs hatch?

You can use a calendar to find elapsed time by counting the number of days.

Find April 25. Start counting forward from the next day. Count 13 days.

**APRIL**

| S | M | T | W | T | F | S |
|---|---|---|---|---|---|---|
| | | | | | 1 | 2 |
| 3 | 4 | 5 | 6 | 7 | 8 | 9 |
| 10 | 11 | 12 | 13 | 14 | 15 | 16 |
| 17 | 18 | 19 | 20 | 21 | 22 | 23 |
| 24 | 25 | 26 | 27 | 28 | 29 | 30 |

**MAY**

| S | M | T | W | T | F | S |
|---|---|---|---|---|---|---|
| 1 | 2 | 3 | 4 | 5 | 6 | 7 |
| 8 | 9 | 10 | 11 | 12 | 13 | 14 |
| 15 | 16 | 17 | 18 | 19 | 20 | 21 |
| 22 | 23 | 24 | 25 | 26 | 27 | 28 |
| 29 | 30 | 31 | | | | |

**Units of Time**

1 week = 7 days
1 year = 12 months
1 year = 52 weeks
1 year = 365 days
1 leap year = 366 days

**Solution:** The eggs hatched on Sunday, May 8.

### Other Examples

**A.** A **decade** is equal to 10 years. How many years equal 5 decades?

Think
1 decade = 10 years
So 5 decades = 5 × 10, or 50 years

5 decades = 50 years

**B.** A **century** is equal to 100 years. How many years equal 5 centuries?

Think
1 century = 100 years
So 5 centuries = 5 × 100 or 500 years

5 centuries = 500 years

## Guided Practice

**Use the calendars above for Questions 1–4.**

1. Write the day and date 10 days after May 3.
2. Write the day and date 2 weeks before May 10.
3. Write the date and time $7\frac{1}{2}$ hours after May 26 at 9:00 P.M.
4. Write the date and time 11 hours before April 22 at 6:00 P.M.

**Ask Yourself**

- On what day do I begin counting?
- Should I count forward or backward?
- How many days do I count?

**Explain Your Thinking** ▶ What multiplication fact could you use to find how many years are in 8 decades? 4 centuries?

## Practice and Problem Solving

**Use the calendars on Page 334. Write the day and date.**

**5.** 2 days before May 4

**6.** 6 days after May 22

**7.** 2 weeks before May 9

**8.** The winner of the dance-a-thon began dancing April 12 at 7:00 P.M. He stopped dancing on April 14 at 5:15 A.M. How long did he dance? Write your answer in days, hours, and minutes.

**9.** Sarah's family drove cross-country. They left home at 6:00 A.M. on May 3. They arrived at their destination on May 6 at 11:30 P.M. How long did they travel? Write your answer in days and hours.

**Find each missing number.**

**10.** 2 years = ____ weeks

**11.** 2 years 3 months = ____ months

**12.** 1 year 2 weeks = ____ weeks

**13.** 6 centuries = ____ decades

**14.** 4 decades 3 years = ____ years

**15.** How many days is it from February 23 to March 15 in a leap year when February has 29 days?

**Use the calendars on Page 334 and the schedule on the right for Problems 16–18.**

**16.** How many meetings are planned for Bird Watching?

**17.** Jed plans to attend the series on *Habits of Chipmunks* and *Trees and Bushes.* How many meetings will that be?

**18.** Mark wants to attend the series Animals of the Night and one other series. What other series can he attend?

## Sharpening Skills for CRCT

### Open Response

**Write each number in word form.**

(Ch. 1, Lesson 2)

**19.** 406 **20.** 758 **21.** 10,002

**22.** 4,250 **23.** 9,345 **24.** 16,400

**25.** 20,250 **26.** 900,050 **27.** 607,844

### Multiple Choice

**28.** On April 7, Edmundo is looking forward to the school trip, which is in 5 days. What is the date of the school trip?

(Ch. 13, Lesson 1)

A. April 2 C. April 12

B. April 7 D. April 13

Extra Practice See page 353, Set A.

Lesson 2

Audio Tutor 2/4 Listen and Understand

# Elapsed Time

**Objective** Find elapsed times.

**STANDARDS** Maintains M3M

**Vocabulary**

**elapsed time**

**A.M.**

**P.M.**

## Learn About It

Mariah finds that a tour of the Raptor Center is full when she arrives at 11:00 A.M. How long will she have to wait for the next tour?

**Elapsed time** is the time that passes between one time and another.

**A.M.** is used for the hours between 12 midnight and 12 noon.

**P.M.** is used for the hours between 12 noon and 12 midnight.

▶ **You can use a clock to find how long it will be until the next tour.**

Start at 11:00.

Count the hours.
11:00 to 1:00 is 2 hours.

Then count the minutes.
1:00 to 1:45 is 45 minutes.

**Solution:** Mariah will have to wait 2 hours and 45 minutes.

▶ **If the tour starts at 1:45 P.M. and lasts 50 minutes, at what time does the tour end?**

If you know when the tour starts and how long it lasts, you can find when the tour ends.

Start at 1:45.

Count ahead 50 minutes to 2:35.

**Solution:** The tour ends at 2:35 P.M.



Extra Help at **eduplace.com/map**

You also can add or subtract to find elapsed time.

| Units of Time |
|---|
| 60 second(s) = 1 minute (min) |
| 60 minutes = 1 hour (h) |
| 24 hours = 1 day (d) |
| 7 days = 1 week (wk) |

▶ **If a tour begins at 1:45 P.M. and lasts 50 minutes, at what time does the tour end?**

$$\begin{array}{r} 1 \text{ h } 45 \text{ min} \\ + \quad 50 \text{ min} \\ \hline 1 \text{ h } 95 \text{ min or } 2 \text{ h } 35 \text{ min} \end{array}$$

Think
60 min = 1 h

**Solution:** The tour ends at 2:35 P.M.

▶ **Mariah plans to arrive at the Raptor Center at 11 A.M. It is a 1 hour 15 minute ride by car. At what time should she leave home?**

$$\begin{array}{r} \overset{10}{\cancel{11}} \text{h} \quad \overset{60}{\cancel{0}} \text{ min} \\ - \ 1\text{h } 15 \text{ min} \\ \hline 9\text{h } 45 \text{ min} \end{array}$$

Think
Rename 11 h 0 min as 10 h 60 min.

**Solution:** Mariah should leave home at 9:45 A.M.

## Another Example

**Reading Time to the Second**

**Read or Write** 6:23:15
six twenty-three and fifteen seconds, or
twenty-three minutes fifteen seconds after six.

## Guided Practice

**Tell what time it will be.**

**1.** in 3 hours

**2.** in 20 minutes

**3.** in 5 minutes

**Ask Yourself**

- At what time do I start counting?
- Do I need to count hours?
- Do I need to count minutes?

**Explain Your Thinking** ▶ How much time will elapse between 3:20 A.M. and 9:45 P.M.? How did you find the elapsed time?

## Practice and Problem Solving

**Tell what time it will be.**

**4.** in 4 hours

**5.** in 15 minutes

**6.** in 13 minutes

**7.** in 10 hours

**Look at each pair of times. Write how much time has passed.**

**8.** Start: 1:05 P.M.
End: 6:15 P.M.

**9.** Start: 6:50 A.M.
End: 9:57 A.M.

**10.** Start: 8:35 A.M.
End: 1:40 P.M.

**11.** Start: 11:45 A.M.
End: 3:20 P.M.

**12.** Start: 9:10 P.M.
End: 12:34 A.M.

**13.** Start: 7:40 A.M.
End: 11:47 P.M.

**Write the time shown on the clock before the hour and then after the hour.**

**14.**

**15.**

**16.**

**17.**

**Find each missing number.**

**18.** 2 hours = ____ minutes

**19.** 3 minutes = ____ seconds

**20.** 90 minutes = 1 hour ____ minutes

**21.** 1 hour 25 minutes = ____ minutes

**22.** 4 minutes = ____ seconds

**23.** 95 minutes = 1 hour ____ minutes

**24.** Greg spent 2 hours 45 minutes visiting the Raptor Center. He arrived at 11:40 in the morning. What time did he leave?

**25.** Rita went to the Raptor Center at half-past four in the afternoon. How long was she there if she left at 8:25 P.M.?

**26.** **What's Wrong?** Bird-watching videos are shown every 20 minutes. The last video was at 2:25 P.M. Ann says that the next videos will be at 2:45 P.M. and 2:65 P.M. What did Ann do wrong?

**27.** **Analyze** Mr. Motts started working at the Raptor Center at 2:40 P.M. He led a tour for 2 hours 10 minutes. Then he worked in the office for 90 minutes. Was he finished before 7 P.M.?



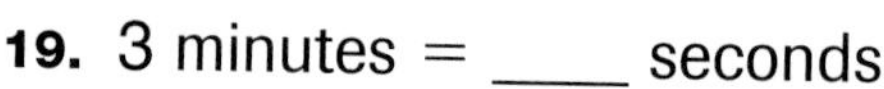
Extra Practice See page 353, Set B.

## Sharpening Skills for CRCT

**Open Response**

**Round each number to the nearest ten cents. Then estimate.** (Ch. 3, Lesson 3)

**28.** \$0.57 + \$0.81 **29.** \$0.49 − \$0.22

**30.** \$4.65 + \$8.32 **31.** \$9.44 − \$0.11

**Multiple Choice**

**32.** A yard sale starts at 8:30 A.M. and ends at 1:00 P.M. How long is the yard sale? (Ch. 13, Lesson 2 )

A. 3 h 30 min C. 4 h 30 min

B. 4 h D. 7 h 30 min

# Math Reasoning
## Estimating Time

STANDARDS Maintains M3M1

You don't always need to know the exact time. Sometimes you can use an estimate.

**Use the clocks for Problems 1–2.**

**You can estimate time to the nearest quarter hour.**

**1.** Suppose it takes 15 minutes to walk to the library. To the nearest quarter hour, at what time would you arrive?

**You can estimate time to the nearest 5 minutes.**

**2.** Suppose a friend stops to ask what time it is. If you round to the nearest 5 minutes, what time will you tell your friend?

**You can estimate elapsed time.**

**3.** The sign at the right lists the movies that are showing at the Raptor Center. How long will each movie last

**a.** to the nearest quarter hour?

**b.** to the nearest 5 minutes?

**MOVIE TIMES AT THE RAPTOR CENTER**

| | |
|---|---|
| The Eagle Soars | 11:00 A.M.–11:22 A.M. |
| Owls of the Night | 1:15 P.M.–2:43 P.M. |
| Hawks on High | 2:10 P.M.–3:24 P.M. |

Lesson 3

# Problem-Solving Strategy

## Guess and Check

**Objective** Use the Guess and Check strategy to solve a problem.

 **STANDARDS** M4N7.a, M4P1.b

**Sometimes a good way to solve a problem is to guess and check.**

**Problem** A nature photographer took some pictures of puffins and otters. She photographed 21 animals with 66 legs altogether. How many puffins and otters did she photograph?

**UNDERSTAND**

**This is what you know.**

- The 21 animals have 66 legs altogether.
- Puffins have 2 legs and otters have 4 legs.

**PLAN**

**Use the Guess and Check strategy.**

Guess two numbers. Then check to see if they are correct. If not, use your result to improve your next guess.

**SOLVE**

**Use your result to make your next guess.**

| 1st Guess | 2nd Guess | 3rd Guess |
|---|---|---|
| 14 otters → 56 legs<br>7 puffins → 14 legs<br>21 animals 70 legs<br>Check: Too many legs. Guess again. | 11 otters → 44 legs<br>10 puffins → 20 legs<br>21 animals 64 legs<br>Check: Too few legs. Guess again. | 12 otters → 48 legs<br>9 puffins → 18 legs<br>21 animals 66 legs<br>Check: This is the answer. |

**Solution:** She photographed 9 puffins and 12 otters.

**LOOK BACK**

**Reread the problem.**
Does the solution fit the facts of the problem?

## Guided Practice

**Use the Ask Yourself questions to help you solve each problem.**

1. Altogether, there are 10 birds and bees in Ali's garden. If the birds and bees have 48 legs in all, how many birds and bees are there?

   **Hint** A bee has 6 legs.

2. Tim and Jared collect trading cards of rare birds. Tim has 8 more cards than Jared. Together they have 104 cards. How many cards does each boy have?

### Ask Yourself

UNDERSTAND **What facts do I know?**

PLAN **What numbers would be a reasonable first guess?**

SOLVE **How can I use my result to improve my next guess?**

LOOK BACK **Did I go back to the problem to check my answer?**

## Independent Practice

**Use Guess and Check to solve each problem.**

3. A photographer said that the only animals he saw on an island were lizards and parrots. He saw 8 animals with 22 legs altogether on that island. How many lizards and parrots did he see?

4. **Money** On a nature tour the guide collects \$260 in fares. He collects only \$10 bills and \$20 bills. He collects 22 bills in all. How many of each kind of bill does the guide collect?

5. Carol has 8 booklets about birds. Some of the booklets have 26 pages and the others have 41 pages. How many of each size booklet does she have if the pages total 253?

6. The product of two numbers is 24. The difference between the numbers is 10. What are the numbers?

Go On

# Mixed Problem Solving

**Solve. Show your work. Tell what strategy you used.**

7. In a bike race, there are judges posted at the beginning and end of each mile. If the race is 10 miles long, how many judges are needed?

8. Ten bicycles and tricycles are lined up at the park. Jerry counts a total of 24 wheels. How many bicycles are there?

9. Tyrone invited 8 friends to his party. He asked each friend to bring two other friends. How many people will come to Tyrone's party?

10. Five friends stood in line. Jamie was fourth in line. Jose stood right behind Ned. Lee was not third or last. Alice was also in line. In what order did the friends stand?

**You Choose**

**Strategy**
- Act It Out
- Draw a Picture
- Guess and Check
- Use Logical Reasoning
- Write an Equation

**Computation Method**
- Mental Math
- Estimation
- Paper and Pencil
- Calculator

## Data Use the graph to solve Problems 11–13.

Students at Whitney School planted trees on Arbor Day. The graph at the right shows the number of trees planted by Grades 3–6.

11. How many trees were planted altogether?

12. Suppose it takes 15 minutes to plant each tree. How long will it take the fourth grade to plant all their trees?

13. Altogether, how many more trees did the fifth and sixth graders plant than the fourth graders?

14. **You Decide** Meg has $200 to buy trees. She can choose 2 kinds of trees. Pine trees cost $10, elm trees cost $8, and oak trees cost $12 each. How many of each type of tree can Meg buy?

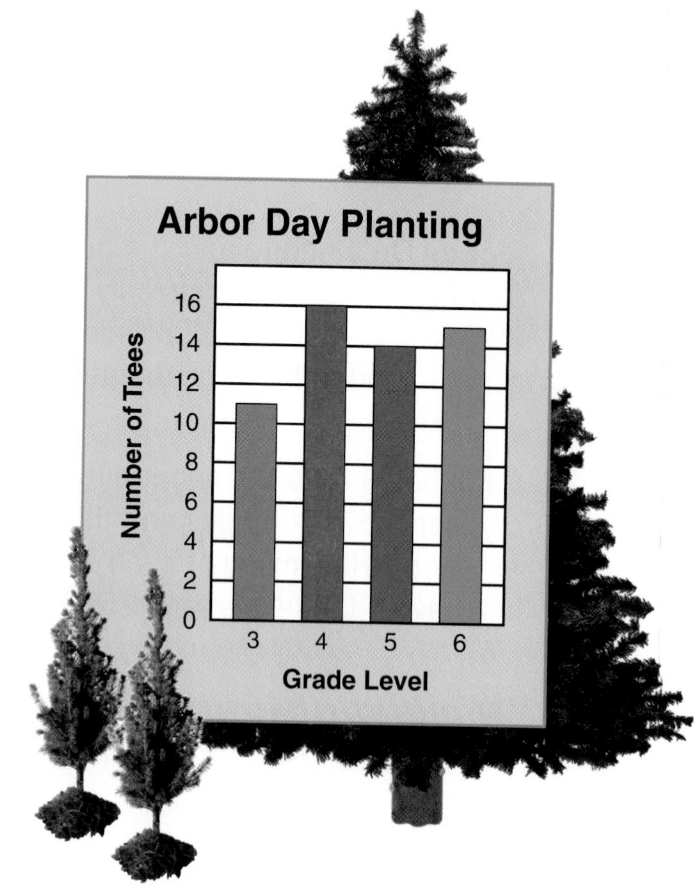

# Problem Solving on CRCT

**Multiple Choice**

**Choose the letter of the correct answer.**

1. The length of a pencil is 16 centimeters. How many millimeters are equal to 16 centimeters?

   A. 16,000

   B. 1,600

   C. 160

   D. 16

(Chapter 12, Lesson 7)

2. About how much water can this sink hold?

   A. 160 gallons

   B. 10 gallons

   C. 10 quarts

   D. 600 quarts

(Chapter 12, Lesson 3)

**Open Response**

**Solve each problem.**

3. Sixty-seven students are taking part in a game. Teams can have no fewer than 3 and no more than 8 members. What is the smallest number of teams possible? Draw a diagram or write an equation to explain your answer.

(Chapter 8, Lesson 3)

4. A soccer team begins practice at quarter after 3 and ends practice at quarter to 5. How many minutes does the team practice? Explain how you found your answer.

(Chapter 13, Lesson 2)

5. Students sold three types of stuffed animals at the school carnival. The table shows how much money they raised.

| Stuffed Animals Sold | |
|---|---|
| **Animal** | **Amount Raised** |
| Lion | $400 |
| Falcon | $124 |
| Otter | $342 |

   a. How much did each lion cost if 80 lions were sold? Use a basic division fact to help you divide.

   b. Each falcon sold for $4. Estimate how many falcons were sold. Write the basic fact you used.

   c. 57 otters were sold. Did the otters cost more or less than the lions? Could you round to the greatest place to solve this problem? Explain your thinking.

(Chapter 11)

**Education Place**

See **eduplace.com/map** for more Test-Taking Tips.

Lesson 4

Audio Tutor 2/5 Listen and Understand

# Temperature and Negative Numbers

**Objective** Use a thermometer to read temperatures above and below zero.

**STANDARDS** Prepares for a future grade, M4P2

**Vocabulary**

- positive numbers
- negative numbers
- degrees Fahrenheit (°F)
- degrees Celsius (°C)

## Learn About It

A thermometer can be used to measure temperature in degrees Fahrenheit or degrees Celsius.

**You can think of a thermometer as a vertical number line.**

- Temperatures above zero are **positive numbers**.
- Temperatures below zero are **negative numbers**.

Negative numbers are less than 0. | Positive numbers are greater than 0.

⁻15 ⁻10 ⁻5 0 5 10 15

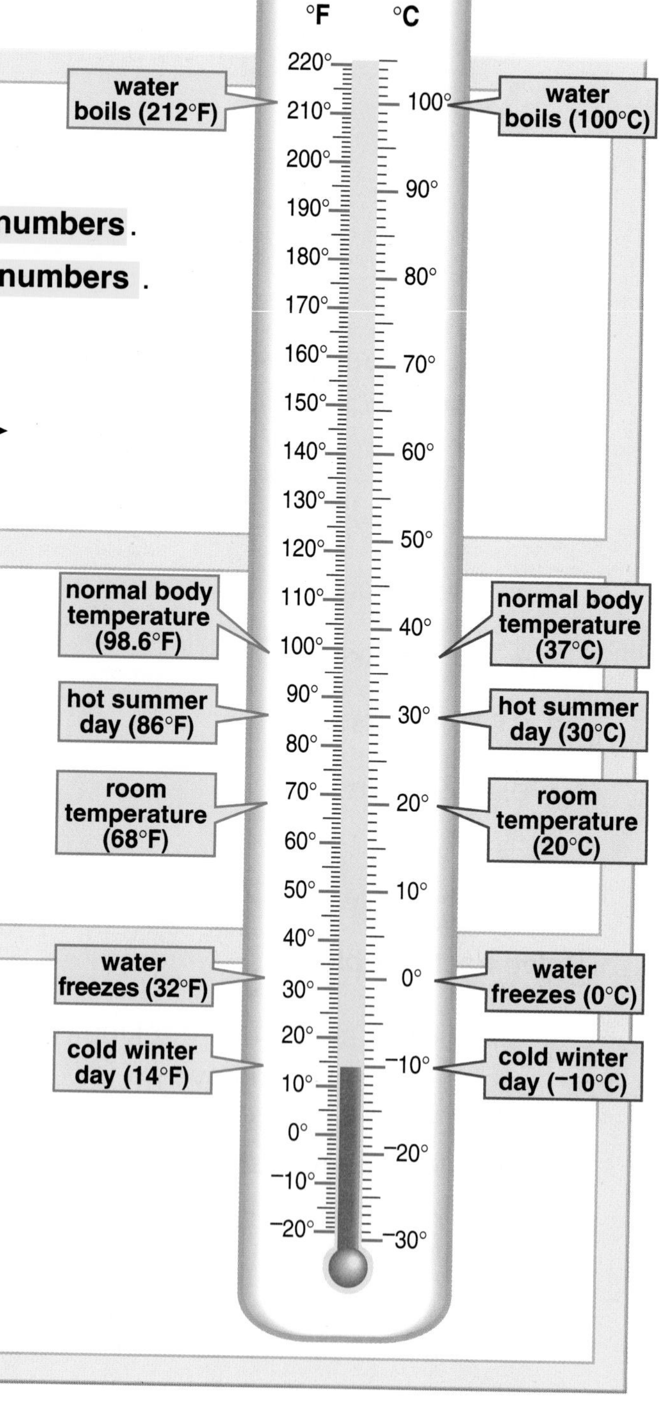


**Degrees Fahrenheit (°F)** are customary units of temperature.

The temperature shown on this thermometer is 14°F.

**Write:** 14°F

**Say:** fourteen degrees Fahrenheit

**Degrees Celsius (°C)** are metric units of temperature.

The temperature shown on this thermometer is ⁻10°C.

**Write:** ⁻10°C

**Say:** negative ten degrees Celsius or ten degrees below zero Celsius

**Use a thermometer to find the difference between two temperatures.**

**Count up or down on the thermometer to find the difference.**

**A.** 70°F and 42°F

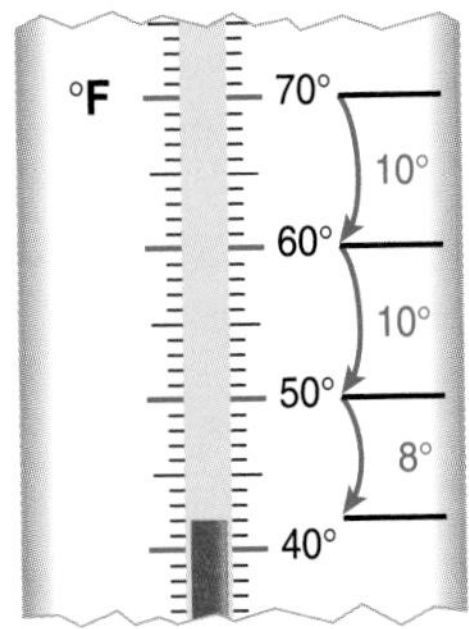


10 + 10 + 8 = 28
The difference is 28°.

**B.** -15°C and 8°C

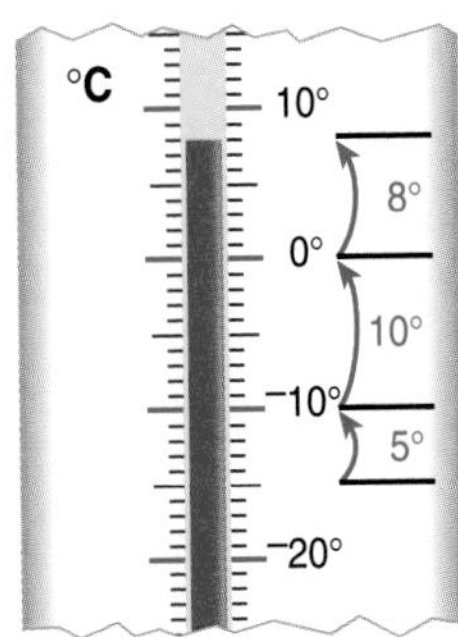


5 + 10 + 8 = 23
The difference is 23°.

## Guided Practice

**Ask Yourself**

- What numbers is the temperature between?
- Is the temperature positive or negative?
- Is the temperature in degrees Fahrenheit or degrees Celsius?

**Write each temperature.**

**1.** °F 50° 40°

**2.** °C 0° -10°

**3.** °F 90° 80°

**Find the difference between the temperatures.**

**4.** 2°C and 4°C
**5.** -3°F and 2°F
**6.** 27°F and 45°F
**7.** -8°F and 15°F
**8.** -12°C and -26°C
**9.** 13°C and -2°C

**Choose the better estimate of the temperature.**

**10.** a cold day
**a.** -10°C **b.** 30°C

**11.** a hot day
**a.** 90°F **b.** 37°F

**12.** room temperature
**a.** 20°F **b.** 70°F

**Explain Your Thinking** Which is lower, 5°C or -15°C? How do you know?

Go On

## Practice and Problem Solving

**Write each temperature.**

**13.** °F 20° 10°

**14.** °C 30° 20°

**15.** °F −10° −20°

**16.** °C −20° −30°

**Write the temperature shown on each thermometer. Then write the difference between the two temperatures.**

**17.** °C 30° 20°

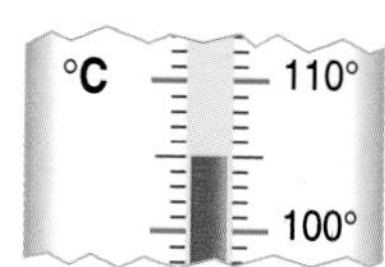


**18.** °F 50° 40°

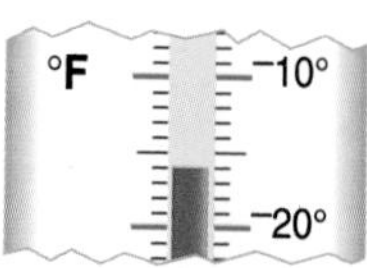


**Find the difference between the temperatures.**

**19.** 88°F and 110°F

**20.** −5°C and 10°C

**21.** −3°F and −10°F

**22.** 27°C and 13°C

**23.** 71°F and 39°F

**24.** −26°C and −8°C

**Choose the better estimate of the temperature.**

**25.** room temperature
**a.** 22°C **b.** 39°C

**26.** swim at the beach
**a.** 32°F **b.** 85°F

**27.** cup of hot soup
**a.** 73°C **b.** 14°C

**28.** build a snowman
**a.** 10°C **b.** −10°C

**29.** rake leaves
**a.** 20°F **b.** 60°F

**30.** play baseball
**a.** 75°F **b.** 17°F

### Data Use the table for Problems 31–32.

**31.** Was the difference in temperature greater between 6:00 A.M. and noon or between noon and 6:00 P.M.?

**32.** **Reasoning** Do you think the temperature at 7:00 A.M. was greater than or less than 70°F? Explain.

**33.** **Analyze** After the sun rose one morning, the temperature rose 5°. In the afternoon, the temperature fell 3°. If the temperature was 24°C then, what was the temperature when the sun rose?

**Temperatures on July 27**

| Time | Temperature |
|---|---|
| 6:00 A.M. | 64°F |
| 9:00 A.M. | 70°F |
| Noon | 87°F |
| 3:00 P.M. | 78°F |
| 6:00 P.M. | 71°F |



Extra Practice See page 353, Set C

# Real World Connection

## Why Do We Leap?

STANDARDS Extends M4N4, M4P4

Earth takes a little more than 365 days to orbit the sun, but our calendars usually have only 365 days. After several hundred years, the extra time would build up, and our seasons would be turned around.

Long ago, people came up with a solution—leap year. Every fourth year, an extra day is added to February.

- You can use division to find out which years are leap years. Pick any five years from 1904 to 2005. If you can divide the year evenly by 4, it is a leap year.
- How many leap years did you pick?

WEEKLY WR READER eduplace.com/map

## Quick Check

Check your understanding of Lessons 1–4.

**Find each missing number.** (Lesson 1)

**1.** 2 years = ____ weeks  **2.** 3 weeks = ____ days

**Look at each pair of times. Write how much time has passed.** (Lesson 2)

**3.** Start: 2:20 P.M.
End: 3:05 P.M.

**4.** Start: 10:35 A.M.
End: 12:15 P.M.

**5.** Start: 9:03 A.M.
End: 10:10 P.M.

**Find the difference between the temperatures.** (Lesson 4)

**6.** 15°C and 23°C  **7.** ⁻4°F and 12°F  **8.** 7°C and ⁻7°C

**Solve.** (Lessons 3 and 4)

**9.** There are 3 more dogs than cats in a pet store. There are 21 cats and dogs altogether. How many cats are there?

**10.** At 9 A.M. the temperature was ⁻3°F. At 3 P.M. the temperature was 15° warmer. What was the temperature at 3 P.M.?

Lesson 5

# Problem-Solving Application

## Use Temperature

**Objective** Solve problems about temperature.

 **STANDARDS** Prepares for a future grade, M4P1.a, M4P1.b, M4P1.d

**You can use what you know about finding temperature to solve problems.**

**Problem** Antarctica is the coldest continent on Earth. The temperature at noon one day is $^{-}6$°F. The temperature rises 4 degrees over the next two hours. Then by 8:00 P.M. the temperature falls 7 degrees. What is the temperature at 8:00 P.M.?

### UNDERSTAND

**This is what you know.**

- The temperature is $^{-}6$°F at noon.
- The temperature rises 4 degrees and then falls 7 degrees by 8:00 P.M.

### PLAN

**You can use a thermometer to count up and down.**

### SOLVE

**Count up or count down.**

- Start at $^{-}6$°F.
- Count up 4 degrees.
- Count down 7 degrees.

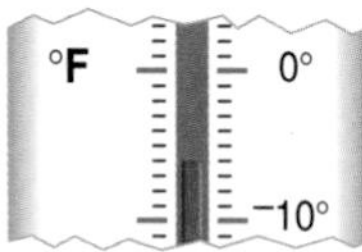


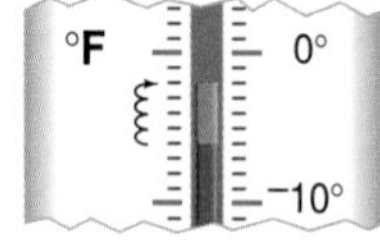


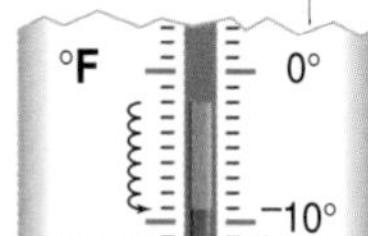


**Solution:** The temperature is $^{-}9$°F at 8:00 P.M.

### LOOK BACK

**Check your answer to see if it's reasonable. Since the temperature fell more than it rose, the answer should be less than $^{-}6$°F. $^{-}9$°F is less than $^{-}6$°F, so the answer is reasonable.**

## Guided Practice

**Use the Ask Yourself questions to help you solve each problem.**

**Ask Yourself**

**What do I know?**

**Can I use a thermometer?**

**Did I count up or count down the correct number of degrees?**

**Does my answer make sense?**

1. If it is 68°F inside and 24°F outside, how many degrees lower is the temperature outside than inside?

2. Mina recorded the temperature at noon. It then fell 6 degrees. Later it rose 4 degrees. If the last temperature was 17°C, what was it at noon?

Hint Should you count up or count down?

## Independent Practice

3. The temperature was 70°F in the morning. It rose 17 degrees during the day and then dropped 9 degrees by 6 P.M. What was the temperature at 6 P.M.?

4. At 10 A.M. the temperature was ⁻14°F at a bird research station in Antarctica. If the temperature rose 2 degrees every hour, what was the temperature at 3 P.M.?

5. Suppose the temperature falls 1 degree Celsius for every 100 meters you climb. If your thermometer shows 2°C now, what will it show after you climb 400 meters?

6. A thermometer shows 16°F. The wind makes the air feel 20 degrees colder. How cold does it feel?

7. On Monday the low temperature was ⁻37°C and the high temperature was ⁻12°C. On Tuesday the low temperature was ⁻23°C and the high was 4°C. Which day had the greatest difference in temperature?

Go On

# Mixed Problem Solving

**Solve. Show your work. Tell what strategy you used.**

**You Choose**

**Strategy**

- Find a Pattern
- Guess and Check
- Work Backward
- Write an Equation

**Computation Method**

- Mental Math
- Estimation
- Paper and Pencil
- Calculator

8. Mr. Ordono's class collected a total of 172 cans for a food drive. Jacob collected 16 cans and Lakia collected 9 cans. How many cans did the rest of the class collect?

9. **Money** Ben and Norman earned $63 together last weekend. Norman earned $9 more than Ben. How much did Ben earn?

10. Ashley swam 2 laps on Monday, 4 laps on Tuesday, 7 laps on Wednesday, and 11 laps on Thursday. If she continues at the same rate, how many laps is she likely to swim on Friday?

**Solve. Tell which method you used.**

11. Arctic terns migrate about 10,000 miles. This is about the same distance as two round trips from New York to Los Angeles. About how many miles apart are New York and Los Angeles?

12. Look at the caption at the right. About how long was it between the time Albert Crary arrived at the North Pole and at the South Pole?

13. **Explain** Marsha plans to cut a piece of string 97 inches long to show the wingspan of the American White Pelican. She has 7 feet of string. Is that enough? How do you know?

*Albert Paddock Crary was the first person to reach both the North Pole and the South Pole. He arrived at the North Pole in 1952, and the South Pole in 1961.*

GPS Activity

# Math Reasoning
## In Hot Water!

**Materials:**
1 glass of hot water from the tap
1 glass of cold water from the tap
2 Fahrenheit thermometers

Have you ever left a cold drink outside on a hot day? When you try to drink it later, it's as hot as the air around it.

**Try this activity to see how a liquid's temperature changes over time.**

1. Make a table like the one at the right.
2. Measure the room temperature and record it.
3. Measure the temperature of each glass of water and record it.
   - What is the difference between each water temperature and the room temperature at the beginning of the experiment?
   - Predict which glass will reach room temperature first.
4. Repeat the water measurements every half hour and record them.
   - At what time did both glasses of water reach the same temperature?

| | Water Temperature (°F) | |
|---|---|---|
| Time | Cold Water | Hot Water |
| 9:00 A.M. | | |
| 9:30 A.M. | | |
| 10:00 A.M. | | |
| 10:30 A.M. | | |
| 11:00 A.M. | | |
| 11:30 A.M. | | |

Room Temperature ____ °F

# Chapter Review/Test

## VOCABULARY

**Choose the best term to complete each sentence.**

**Vocabulary**
- decade
- century
- positive number
- negative number
- elapsed time

1. The time that passes between one time and another is ____.
2. A number that is less than 0 is a ____.
3. There are 10 years in a ____.
4. There are 100 years in a ____.

## CONCEPTS AND SKILLS

**Find each missing number.** (Lesson 1, pp. 334–335)

5. 4 weeks = ____ days
6. 1 year = ____ days
7. 5 years = ____ months
8. 21 days = ____ weeks
9. leap year = ____ days
10. ____ weeks = 1 year
11. 3 decades 2 years = ____ years
12. 2 centuries 3 decades = ____ years

**Look at each pair of times. Write how much time has passed.** (Lesson 2, pp. 336–338)

13. Start: 9:00 A.M.<br>End: 6:45 P.M.
14. Start: 4:10 P.M.<br>End: 5:53 P.M.
15. Start: 8:17 A.M.<br>End: 11:00 A.M.

**Find the difference between the temperatures.** (Lesson 4, pp. 344–347)

16. 25°F and 7°F
17. 12°C and $^{-}5$°C
18. $^{-}8$°F and $^{-}6$°F

## PROBLEM SOLVING

**Solve.** (Lessons 3, 5, pp. 340–342, 348–350)

19. There are 13 children and dogs in the park. Altogether there are 34 legs. How many children and how many dogs are there?
20. Kelly read the temperature at noon. It rose 10 degrees by 3 P.M. then fell 5 degrees by 6 P.M. If the temperature was 3°F at 6 P.M., what was it at noon?

**Show You Understand**

Frank says that when it's 30°C, it is time to wear a warm coat. Is he correct? Explain why or why not.

# Extra Practice

## Set A (Lesson 1, pp. 334–335)

**Use the calendar.**

1. Write the day and date 3 days before January 26.
2. Write the day and date 5 days after January 8.
3. Write the day and date 2 weeks after January 1.
4. Write the day and date 1 week before January 11.

| January | | | | | | |
|---|---|---|---|---|---|---|
| Sun. | Mon. | Tue. | Wed. | Thu. | Fri. | Sat. |
| | | | | | | 1 |
| 2 | 3 | 4 | 5 | 6 | 7 | 8 |
| 9 | 10 | 11 | 12 | 13 | 14 | 15 |
| 16 | 17 | 18 | 19 | 20 | 21 | 22 |
| 23 | 24 | 25 | 26 | 27 | 28 | 29 |
| 30 | 31 | | | | | |

**Find each missing number.**

5. 3 weeks = _____ days
6. 1 year = _____ days
7. 2 decades = _____ years
8. 52 weeks = _____ year
9. 1 year 6 months = _____ months
10. 3 centuries = _____ years

## Set B (Lesson 2, pp. 336–339)

**Tell what time it will be.**

1. in 3 hours

2. in 20 minutes

3. in 17 minutes

## Set C (Lesson 4, pp. 344–347)

**Write the temperature shown on each thermometer.**
**Then write the difference between the two temperatures.**

1.

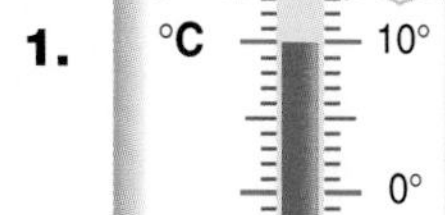


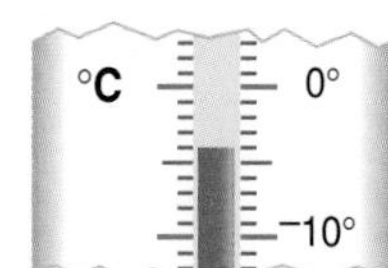


2.

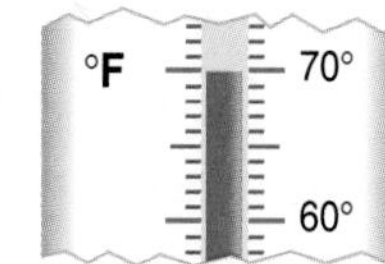


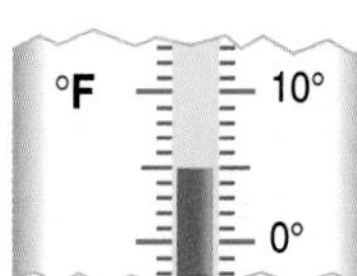


**Find the difference between the temperatures.**

3. 5°C and 12°C
4. $^-3$°F and 10°F
5. $^-9$°C and $^-4$°C

Extra Practice at **eduplace.com/map**

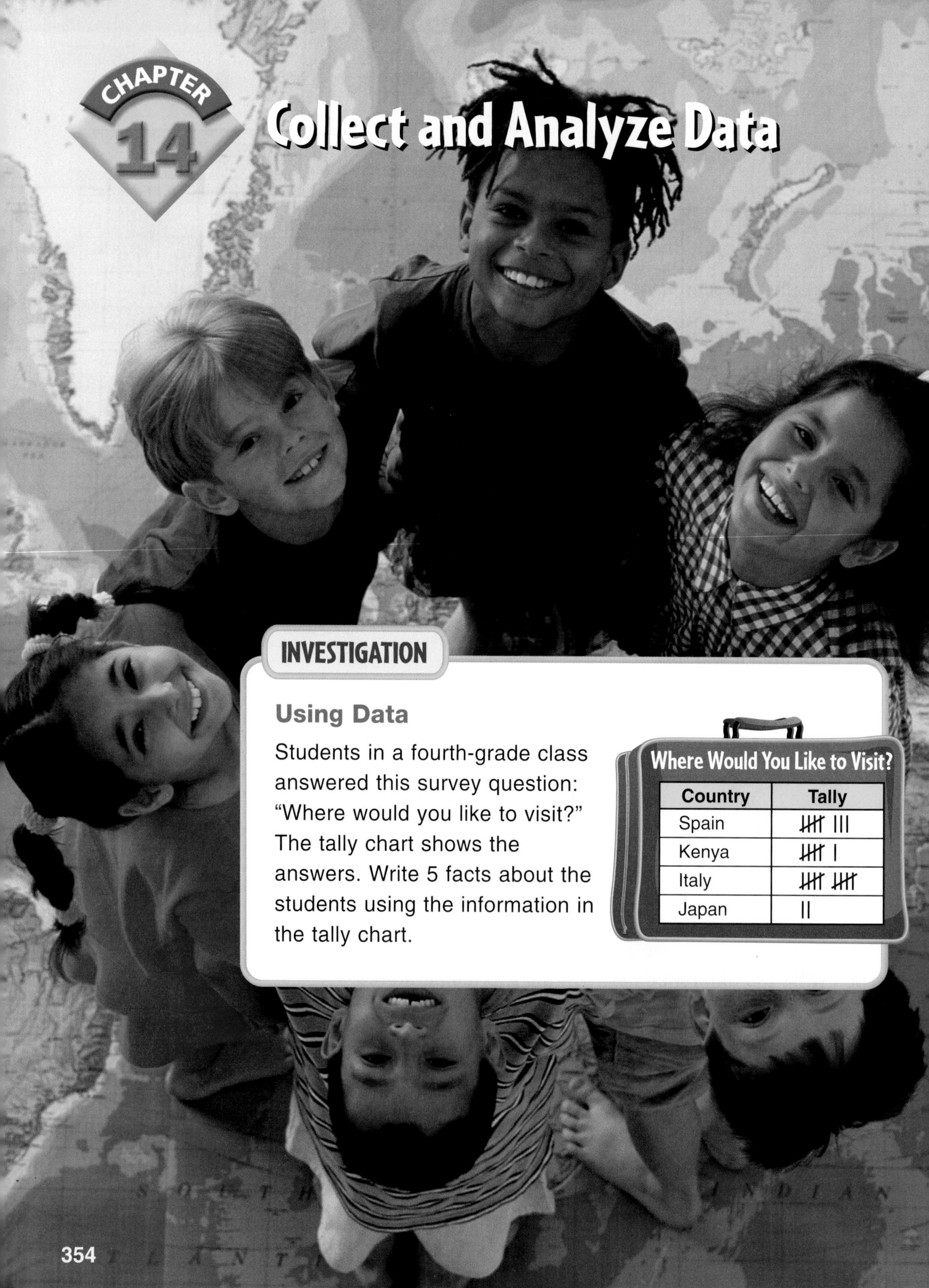

CHAPTER 14

# Collect and Analyze Data

## INVESTIGATION

### Using Data

Students in a fourth-grade class answered this survey question: "Where would you like to visit?" The tally chart shows the answers. Write 5 facts about the students using the information in the tally chart.

**Where Would You Like to Visit?**

| Country | Tally |
|---|---|
| Spain | 𝍸 III |
| Kenya | 𝍸 I |
| Italy | 𝍸 𝍸 |
| Japan | II |

**Use this page to review and remember what you need to know for this chapter.**

## VOCABULARY

**Choose the best term to complete each sentence.**

1. A graph that uses pictures to show data is a ____.
2. One way to collect information is to take a ____.
3. The symbols ~~||||~~ are called ____.

**Vocabulary**

- survey
- bar graph
- pictograph
- tally marks

## CONCEPTS AND SKILLS

**The tally chart at the right shows the number of hours Alicia trained for a marathon. Use the tally chart for Problems 4–6.**

4. In which week did Alicia train the most?
5. How many more hours did she train in Week 4 than in Week 1?
6. What is the total number of hours Alicia trained in 4 weeks?

**Alicia's Marathon Training**

| Week | Hours of Training |
|---|---|
| 1 | ~~||||~~ |
| 2 | ~~||||~~ ~~||||~~ ||| |
| 3 | ~~||||~~ || |
| 4 | ~~||||~~ ~~||||~~ ~~||||~~ | |

**Order the numbers from least to greatest.**

7. 89 72 86 64
8. 163 314 145 278
9. 948 762 1,045 926

**Write About It**

10. What would be a good interval on a bar graph for the following data? Explain your reasoning.

15 16 20 22 25 28

Facts Practice, See page 664.

Hands On Lesson 1

# Collect and Organize Data

**Vocabulary**
data
survey

**Objective** Conduct a survey and organize information.

STANDARDS M4D1, M4P2, M4P3

**Materials**
Tally Charts
(Learning Tool 17)

## Work Together

A survey is one way to collect information, or **data**. When you conduct a **survey**, you ask a question and record the answers.

The question for a class survey was, "What do you like to eat?"

- Thirty students answered the question.
- The answer choices were *chicken nuggets, corn, French fries, salad,* and *tuna sandwich.*
- The answer *chicken nuggets* was given most often. Thirteen students liked chicken nuggets best.

**What Do You Like to Eat?**

| Answer | Tally | Number |
|---|---|---|
| Chicken nuggets | 𝍸 𝍸 III | 13 |
| Corn | 𝍸 II | 7 |
| French fries | 𝍸 I | 6 |
| Salad | | 0 |
| Tuna sandwich | IIII | 4 |

Work with a partner. Conduct a survey and organize your data.

STEP 1 Write a question that has 3 or 4 possible answers. List the possible answers in a tally chart like the one shown.

**Question:**____________

| Answer | Tally | Number |
|---|---|---|
| | | |
| | | |
| | | |

STEP 2 Survey 20 people. Allow each person to give only one answer. Make a tally mark for each answer. Then add the tally marks for each answer.

STEP 3 Analyze your data.

- How would you describe the results of your survey?

## On Your Own

**Use the tally chart for Problems 1–6.**

1. What is the survey question?
2. Which answer was given most often? least often?
3. How many students answered the survey question?
4. How many students named the two most popular activities?
5. What is the order of activities from most to least popular?
6. **What's Wrong?** Dora says that more than half the class likes swimming or visiting grandparents best. Explain why that is not true.

| What Is Your Favorite Summer Activity? | | |
|---|---|---|
| **Activity** | **Tally** | **Number** |
| Bicycling | 𝍸 𝍸 \|\| | 12 |
| Going to camp | \|\|\| | 3 |
| Playing video games | 𝍸 \| | 6 |
| Swimming | 𝍸 𝍸 𝍸 \| | 16 |
| Visiting grandparents | \|\|\|\| | 4 |

**Use the list at the right to make a tally chart. Then solve Problems 7–10.**

7. What are the possible answers on your tally chart?
8. How many students never bring their lunch to school?
9. How many students sometimes bring their lunch to school?
10. How many students sometimes or always bring their lunch to school?

How Often Do You Bring Your Lunch to School?

| | |
|---|---|
| Sandy | always |
| Gina | sometimes |
| Wilson | never |
| Paco | sometimes |
| Joy | sometimes |
| Rosalie | always |
| Bob | sometimes |
| Joanna | sometimes |
| Will | always |

Go On

**Conduct your own survey. Use the survey question "What do you like to eat?" or "What is your favorite summer activity?" Use the survey for Problems 11–13.**

11. How many students did you survey?

12. Compare your survey results to the survey results on pages 356 or 357. Are the results similar or different? Explain.

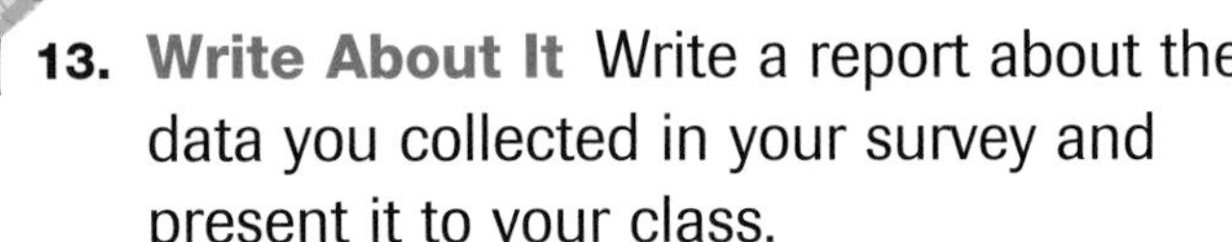

13. **Write About It** Write a report about the data you collected in your survey and present it to your class.

**Use the tally chart for Problems 14–19. Write *true* or *false* for each statement.**

14. The greatest number of people in the survey recycle newspapers.

15. More people recycle glass than cans.

16. There were a total of 28 answers to the survey question.

17. From least to greatest, the order of recycled items is cardboard, plastic, glass, cans, newspapers.

18. More people recycle newspapers than plastic and cans combined.

19. **Create and Solve** Use the tally chart to write a word problem. Then solve the problem.

**What Items Do You Recycle?**

| Answer | Tally | Number |
|---|---|---|
| Cans | 𝍸 III | 8 |
| Cardboard | I | 1 |
| Glass | 𝍸 I | 6 |
| Newspapers | 𝍸 𝍸 II | 12 |
| Plastic | II | 2 |

**Talk About It • Write About It**

**You learned to conduct a survey and collect data.**

20. Suppose a principal wants to know what color people prefer for the walls of a cafeteria. Does it make sense for the principal to survey only fourth-graders? Why or why not?

21. Can a survey tell you anything about the opinions of people who did not take part in the survey? Explain your answer.

Game

Activity

GPS

# Igba-ita

STANDARDS M4D1

In parts of Africa, people use small shells called cowries to play *Igba-ita*. You and a partner can play a similar game with pennies instead of cowries.

**2 Players**

**What You'll Need**
- 20 pennies for each player
- *Igba-Ita* Scoring sheets (Learning Tool 18)

## How to Play

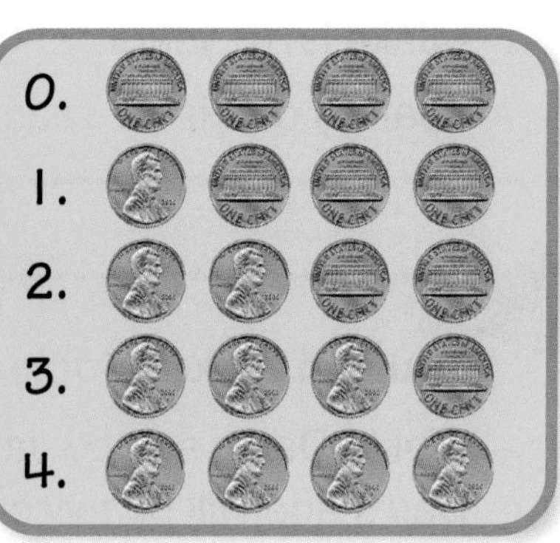


1. Look at the picture to see all the different ways four pennies tossed at the same time can land.

2. Make a scoring sheet. Write the numbers 0–4 in a column down the left side of your paper.

3. Take turns tossing four pennies. After each round, count the number of heads you and your partner tossed. The player with the greater number of heads tossed takes all eight pennies. Toss again if both players toss the same number of heads. Mark the scoring sheet with the number of heads each player tossed.

4. Keep playing until one player has all the pennies.

Lesson 2

# Problem-Solving Strategy

## Make a Table

**Objective** Organize data in a table to solve a problem.

 **STANDARDS** Maintains M3D1.a, M4P1.a, M4P1.b

**Problem** Jake is 18 years old. Jake's dad is 41 years old. How old will they both be when Jake's dad is twice as old as Jake?

UNDERSTAND

**This is what you know.**

- Jake is 18 years old now.
- Jake's dad is 41 years old now.

PLAN

**You can make a table to help you solve the problem.**

Divide Dad's age by Jake's age. When the quotient is 2, Dad's age will be twice Jake's age.

SOLVE

**Make a table.**

- Divide Dad's age by Jake's age. Write the quotient in the table.
- Keep adding one year to each person's age.
- Divide until you find an exact quotient of 2.

**Think:** $2 \times 23 = 46$

**Solution:** When Jake is 23, his dad will be 46.

| Jake's Age | Dad's Age | Dad's Age ÷ Jake's Age |
|---|---|---|
| 18 | 41 | 41 ÷ 18 → 2 R5 |
| 19 | 42 | 42 ÷ 19 → 2 R4 |
| 20 | 43 | 43 ÷ 20 → 2 R3 |
| 21 | 44 | 44 ÷ 21 → 2 R2 |
| 22 | 45 | 45 ÷ 22 → 2 R1 |
| 23 | 46 | 46 ÷ 23 = 2 |

LOOK BACK

**Look back at the problem.**

Does the solution answer the question?
Does the answer make sense?

## Guided Practice

**Use the Ask Yourself questions to help you solve each problem.**

1. Scott is 9 years old, and his sister is 2 years old. How old will each be when Scott is twice his sister's age?

2. Ellen's aunt is 34 years old. Ellen is 15 years old. At what age will Ellen be exactly half her aunt's age? How old will Ellen's aunt be then?

   **Hint** Ellen's aunt will be twice Ellen's age.

UNDERSTAND **What do I know?**

PLAN **Can I make a table?**

SOLVE
- **Did I start with the correct numbers?**
- **Did I choose the correct operation?**

**Does my solution answer the question?**

## Independent Practice

**Make a table to solve each problem.**

3. Six people are in Steve's family. Each person is 8 inches taller than the next person. The tallest person is 70 inches tall. How tall is the shortest person?

4. Steve has $12. His sister Emily has $7. Steve earns $3 a week, and Emily earns $2 a week doing chores. How much money will each have when Steve has exactly $10 more than Emily?

5. Steve has read 5 books. Each week he reads 3 more books. Emily has read 6 books. Each week she reads 2 more. How many books will each have read when they have read a total of 41 books?

6. A fast-growing weed doubles its height every week. It is now 3 centimeters tall. How tall will it be at the end of 5 weeks?

Go On

# Mixed Problem Solving

**Solve. Show your work. Tell what strategy you used.**

**You Choose**

**Strategy**
- Find a Pattern
- Make a Table
- Use Logical Reasoning
- Work Backward
- Write an Equation

**Computation Method**
- Mental Math
- Estimation
- Paper and Pencil
- Calculator

7. Dalia, Jen, and Brad are wearing jackets that are either red, blue, or gray. Each is wearing a different color. Brad's jacket is not red. Jen's jacket is not red or blue. What color is each person's jacket?

8. Susan is 9 years old. Her uncle is 24 years old. At what age will Susan be half her uncle's age? How old will her uncle be then?

9. **Measurement** What is Martha's height in feet and inches if she is 10 inches less than five feet?

10. Copy the table below. Fill in the missing numbers so that the sum of the numbers in each row and column is equal.

| 6 | | 3 |
|---|---|---|
| | | 2 |
| 4 | | 17 |

**Data** **Use the graph about class birthdays for Problems 11–14.**

11. Which season has the greatest number of birthdays?

12. How many birthdays are in autumn and winter?

13. How many fewer birthdays are in summer than in the rest of the year?

14. How many people were surveyed?

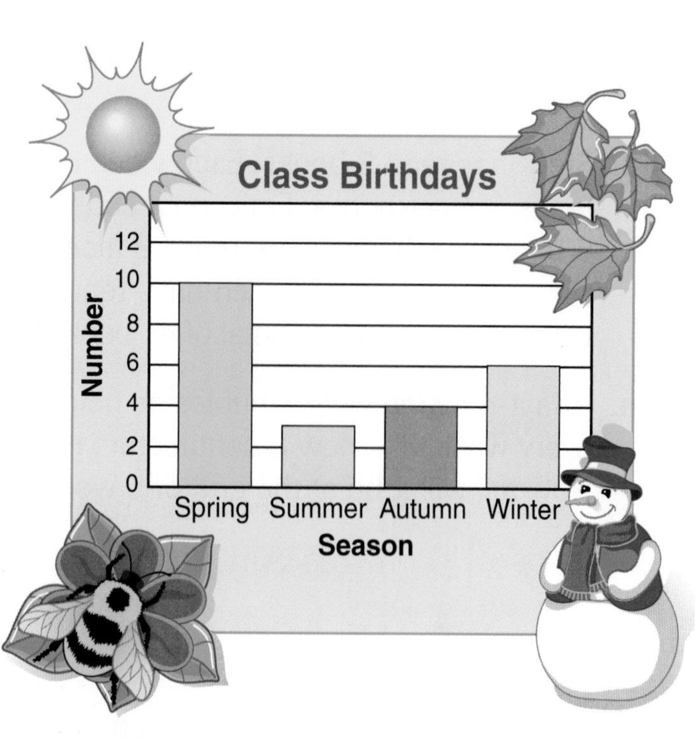

# Problem Solving on CRCT

**Choose the letter of the correct answer.**

**Multiple Choice**

1. The temperature at 3:00 P.M. was 2 degrees higher than the temperature at 2:00 P.M. If it was 6°C at 2:00 P.M., what was the temperature at 3:00 P.M.?

   A. ⁻2°C
   B. 2°C
   C. 4°C
   D. 8°C

   (Chapter 13, Lesson 4)

2. Marlena can pack 28 books into one box. How many boxes does she need in order to pack 224 books?

   A. 7
   B. 8
   C. 78
   D. 196

   (Chapter 11, Lesson 4)

**Open Response**

**Solve each problem.**

3. Students estimated a doorway's height.

| Name | Estimate |
|---|---|
| Andrew | 2 yd |
| Sarah | 75 in. |
| Christy | 6 ft 1 in. |
| Mike | 2 yd 1 ft |

   The actual height is 6 ft 8 in. Whose estimate is closest to the actual height?

   (Chapter 12, Lesson 2)

4. Al uses 8 pins to hang 3 drawings.

   If Al hangs a total of 6 drawings the same way, how many pins will he use?

   (Chapter 10, Lesson 3)

5. The table shows the weights of some squash Greg grew in his garden.

**Garden Squash**

| Squash | Weight |
|---|---|
| Zucchini | 16 oz |
| Acorn | 32 oz |
| Spaghetti | 5 lb |
| Pumpkin | 18 lb |

   a. The zucchini weighs one pound. Greg grew a patty pan squash that is smaller than the zucchini. What is the best unit to use to weigh the patty pan squash? Explain.

   b. How many pounds does the acorn squash weigh?

   c. How many ounces does the spaghetti squash weigh?

   d. Would 10 grams or 10 kilograms be a better estimate for the mass of the pumpkin? Explain your answer.

   (Chapter 12, Lessons 4, 9)

**Education Place**

See **eduplace.com/map** for more Test-Taking Tips.

# Mean, Median, Mode, and Range

**Objective** Find the mean, median, mode, and range of a set of data.

**Vocabulary**
mean
median
mode
range

## Work Together

 **STANDARDS** M4D1.b, M4P2, M4P3

The graph below shows the results of a survey of fourth-graders who have baseball cards. Work with a partner to describe the data in the graph in different ways.

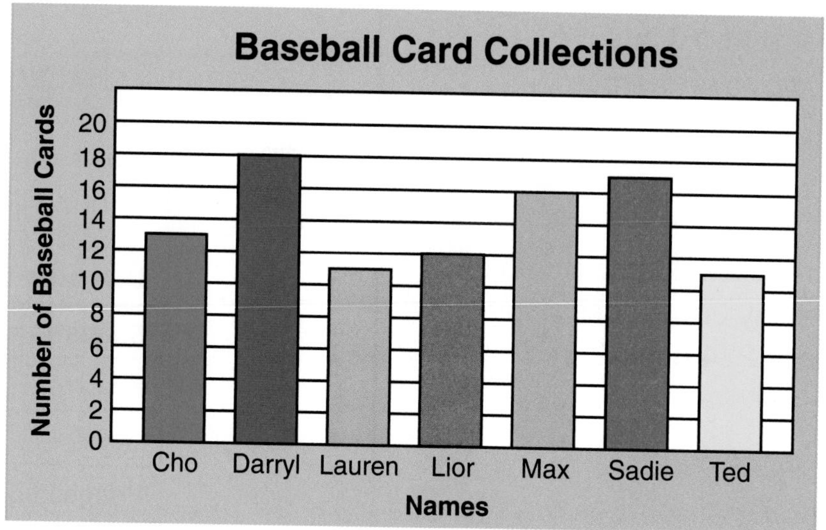


**STEP 1** Find the **mean** of the data. First, find the sum of the numbers: 13 + 18 + 11 + 12 + 16 + 17 + 11 = 98.

Divide the sum by the number of addends: 98 ÷ 7.

- What is the mean number of baseball cards?

**STEP 2** Find the **median** of the data.

When a set of numbers is ordered from least to greatest, the middle number is called the median.

- What is the median number of baseball cards?

When there are two middle numbers in a data set, the median is the mean of those two numbers. Look at the data.

12, 12, 13, 15, 15, 15

13 + 15 = 28

28 ÷ 2 = 14

The median is 14.

**STEP 3** Find the **mode** of the data.

The number that occurs most often in a data set is called the mode.

- What is the number of baseball cards that occurs most often?

Find the **range** of the data.

The difference between the greatest number and the least number is the range.

- What is the range of the number of baseball cards?

Use the results of your work to describe the number of baseball cards that the fourth graders surveyed have.

- Do you think your description would also describe your class? Explain.

## On Your Own

**Use the data in the graph to answer Problems 1–5.**

Sandra and her friends like to read. They keep track of how many books they each read. The graph shows the data for this year.

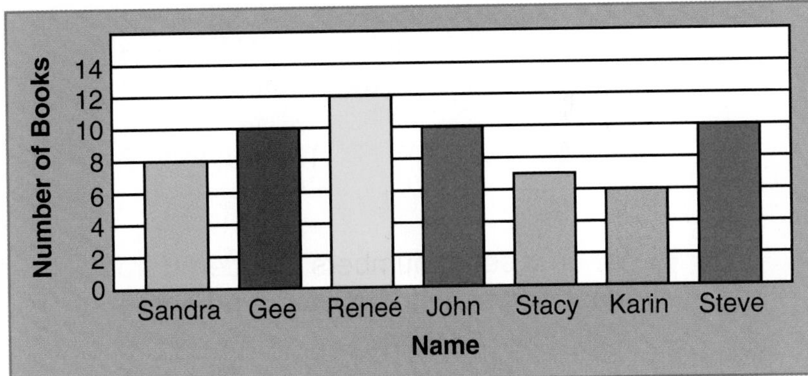

1. Use a calculator to find the mean number of books read.
2. Sandra says that most of her friends read more books than she did. Is she correct? Explain how you know.
3. What is the mode of the data?
4. What is the range of the data? How did you find it?

5. **Analyze** Josie, a new student, moved to town this year. She read 17 books over the summer. If this information is added to the data, how will it change the mean, median, mode, and range?

**You learned to find the mean, median, mode, and range of a set of data.**

6. Explain why it is helpful to put the data in order from least to greatest before you find the median, mode, and range.
7. Does the mode or the median give a better description of Sandra's friends? Explain your thinking.

Lesson 4

Audio Tutor 2/6 Listen and Understand

# Line Plots

**Objective** Make a line plot to represent data.

**Vocabulary**
line plot
range
median
mode

## Learn About It

STANDARDS M4D

Cindy and Pete surveyed their classmates about family pets and made a tally chart. Then they made a line plot like the one below to show the data they collected.

A **line plot** is a way to represent data using X's. You can use a line plot to find the median, mode, and range of a data set.

**How many pets do you have?**

| Number | Tally |
|---|---|
| 0 | \|\|\|\| |
| 1 | ~~\|\|\|\|~~ \| |
| 2 | \|\| |
| 3 | \|\| |
| 4 | |
| 5 | \| |

▶ To find the **range**, look at the number line on the line plot. Subtract the least value from the greatest value.

5 − 0 = 5 The range is 5.

▶ When a set of numbers is ordered from least to greatest, the middle number is called the **median**.

0 0 0 0 1 1 1 1 1 1 2 2 3 3 5

The median, or middle, of the data set is 1.

| | | | | | |
|---|---|---|---|---|---|
| | X | | | | |
| | X | | | | |
| X | X | | | | |
| X | X | | | | |
| X | X | X | X | | |
| X | X | X | X | | X |
| 0 | 1 | 2 | 3 | 4 | 5 |

**Number of Pets**

▶ To find the **mode**, look for the number that has the most X's. Some data sets do not have a mode. Others have one or more modes.

The mode is 1.

## Guided Practice

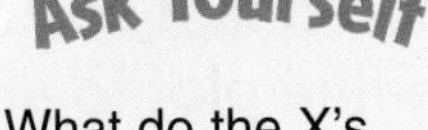


- What do the X's represent?
- What does the number line represent?

**Seven students weighed their dogs. The line plot shows the data. Use it for Problems 1–3.**

1. What is the range of the data?

2. What are the median and the mode of the data?

3. Suppose there was another dog weighing 15 kg. What would the median and mode be then?

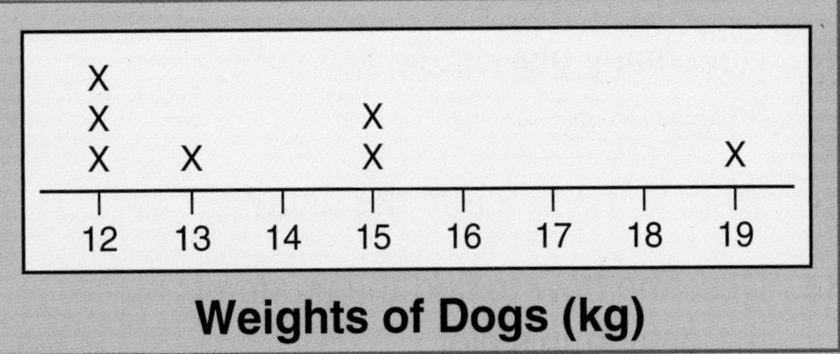

**Weights of Dogs (kg)**

**Explain Your Thinking** ▶ What is the mean of the data in the line plot above? How did you find it?

## Practice and Problem Solving

**Use the line plot at the right for Problems 4–6.**

4. How many hours of TV did most fourth-graders watch on Tuesday?

5. What is the range of the data?

6. What are the mean, median, and mode of the data?

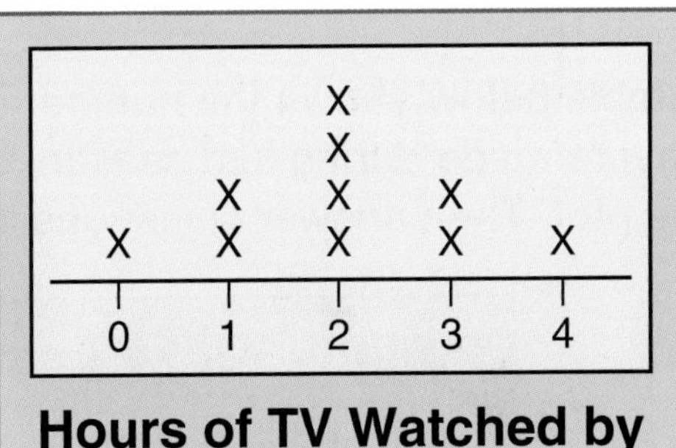

**Hours of TV Watched by Fourth-Graders on Tuesday**

**This line plot shows the hours students spent reading each week. Use the line plot to answer Problems 7–10.**

7. How many students read for 2 hours each week?

8. How many students answered the survey? Explain your answer.

9. Did more students read for 3 hours or for 5 hours?

10. Describe how to find the median number of hours spent reading for the data in this plot.

**Hours Spent Reading**

Go On

**Ari asked the players on his soccer team how many goals they scored last season. This line plot shows the results. Use the line plot to answer Problems 11–15.**

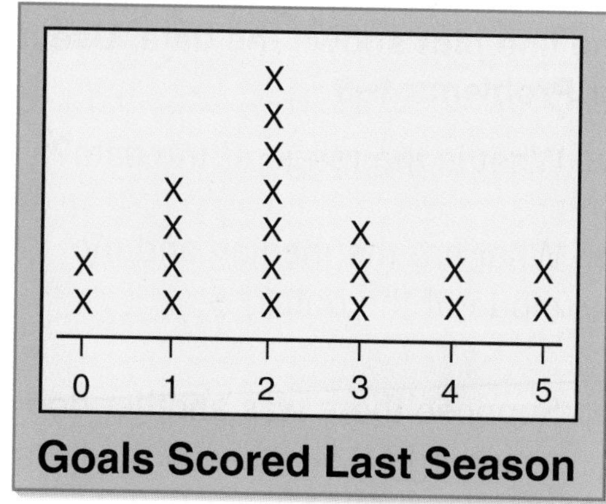


11. How many players scored exactly 4 goals?

12. How many players scored at least 2 goals?

13. How many players did Ari survey altogether?

14. What is the range of the data?

15. Describe how to find the mode of the data in this plot.

16. Decide on a survey question for which the answers are numbers. There should be three or four possible answers. Conduct the survey and record your answers on a line plot.

**The table below shows the number of penalty kicks that 5 players made during last season. Use the data to make a line plot. Then answer Questions 17–21.**

| Penalty Kicks Last Season | |
|---|---|
| **Name of Player** | **Number of Penalty Kicks** |
| Josh | 4 |
| Kristen | 5 |
| Louis | 8 |
| Terrell | 5 |
| Sean | 3 |

17. When you drew the line plot, what numbers did you use?

18. What do the X's on your plot stand for?

19. How many players got more than 1 kick?

20. What is the median of the data?

21. What is the mode of the data?



Extra Practice, See page 373, Set A.

Problem Solving

GPS

## Math Reasoning

### Mode of a Set

STANDARDS Prepares for a future grade.

Mode can describe data sets that are not numerical. These dog tags are grouped by size. The mode for size is medium.

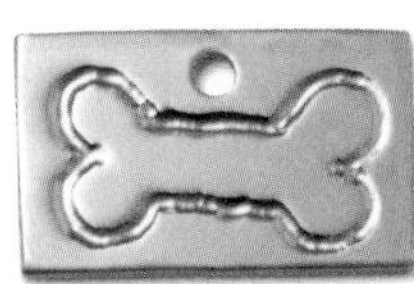

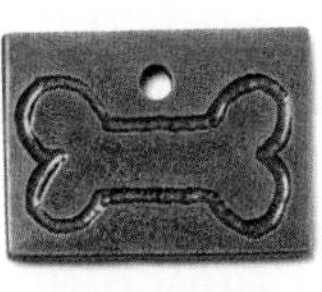
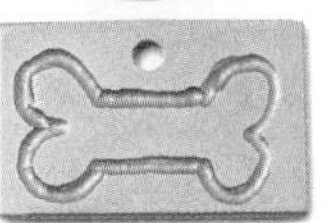
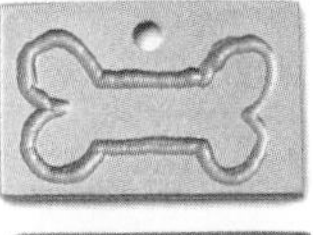
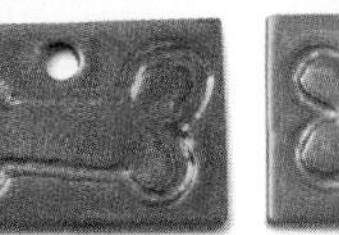
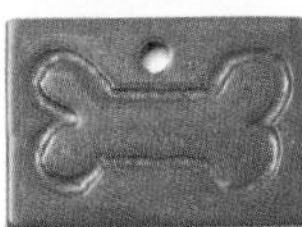

1. What is the mode for dog-tag shape: octagon, rectangle, or circle?
2. What is the mode for dog-tag color: red, blue, silver, gold, or green?

Quick Check

Check your understanding of Lessons 1–4.

**Use the tally chart.** (Lesson 1)

**What Is Your Favorite Color?**

| Color | Tally |
|---|---|
| Blue | 𝍸 ||| |
| Green | |||| |

1. How many people chose blue?
2. How many people were surveyed?

**Use the line plot.** (Lessons 3–4)

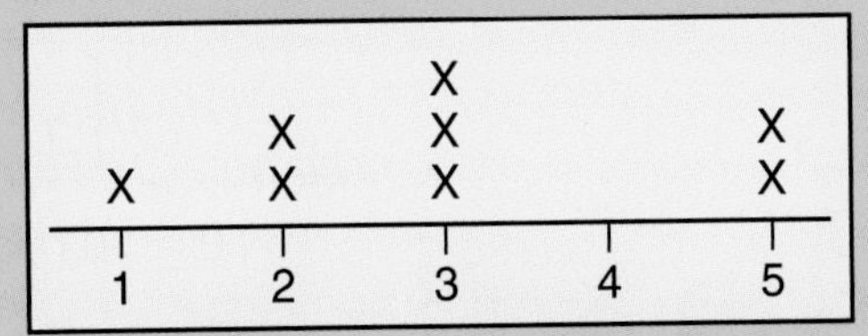

**Size of Litters for Eight Animals**

3. What is the range of the data set?
4. What is the mean?

**Solve.** (Lesson 2)

5. Lee saves $3 in Week 1. Each week, he doubles the amount he saves. What is the amount he saves in Week 5?

Lesson 5

 **Audio Tutor 2/7** Listen and Understand

# Stem-and-Leaf Plots

**Objective** Read and make stem-and-leaf plots.

**STANDARDS** Extends and enriches M5D2

**Vocabulary**
**stem-and-leaf plot**
**outlier**

## Learn About It

Another way to organize data is with a **stem-and-leaf plot**. A stem-and-leaf plot shows information arranged by place value.

The table at the right shows how many minutes nine students spent doing chores. You can make a stem-and-leaf plot of the data.

**Minutes Spent Doing Chores**

| Name | Minutes |
|---|---|
| Akio | 77 |
| Bonnie | 30 |
| Daniel | 38 |
| Ella | 45 |
| Julie | 40 |
| Miguel | 35 |
| Payat | 55 |
| Sarah | 50 |
| Tanya | 35 |

- First, order the data from least to greatest.

| 30 | 35 | 35 | 38 | 40 | 45 | 50 | 55 | 77 |
|---|---|---|---|---|---|---|---|---|

- Then make a stem-and-leaf plot with digits in order from least to greatest.

**Minutes Spent Doing Chores**

| Stem | Leaves |
|---|---|
| 3 | 0 5 5 8 |
| 4 | 0 5 |
| 5 | 0 5 |
| 6 | |
| 7 | 7 |

3 | 0 = 30 minutes

Each stem is the tens digit of each number.

Each leaf is the ones digit of each number.

The stem 7 and the leaf 7 tell you that one student spent 77 minutes doing chores. The number 77 is called an **outlier** because it is far from the other numbers.

You can use a stem-and-leaf plot to find the mean, median, mode, and range of the data set.

- What are these measures?



Extra Help at **eduplace.com/map**

## Guided Practice

**The stem-and-leaf plot shows the amount of money Mia earned baby-sitting. Use the plot for Problems 1–3.**

1. What is the median of the data?
2. What is the mode of the data?
3. Is there an outlier? What does that tell you about the data?

**Ask Yourself**

- What place do the stems represent?
- What place do the leaves represent?

**Mia's Earnings**

| Stem | Leaves |
|---|---|
| 1 | 0 2 3 7 8 8 |
| 2 | 0 0 2 5 |
| 3 | 4 |

1 | 0 = $10

**Explain Your Thinking** ▶ How are the stems and the leaves different in a stem-and-leaf plot?

## Practice and Problem Solving

**The list on the right shows how many minutes Lionel practiced the piano on eleven different days. Use the list for Problems 4–8.**

**Lionel's Piano Practice (minutes)**

| | |
|---|---|
| 60 | 55 |
| 50 | 30 |
| 65 | 46 |
| 48 | 63 |
| 60 | 57 |
| 60 | |

4. Use the data to make a stem-and-leaf plot. Then use your stem-and-leaf plot for Problems 5–8.
5. How many leaves are in your stem-and-leaf plot? What do they represent?
6. What was the least number of minutes Lionel practiced?
7. What is the median number of minutes Lionel spent practicing?
8. **Analyze** Is the range a good way to describe Lionel's practice time? Why?

## Sharpening Skills for CRCT

**Open Response**

**Find each missing number.** (Ch. 12, Lesson 3)

9. 3 pints = ____ cups
10. 1 gallon = ____ quarts
11. 8 cups = ____ quarts

12. Make a stem-and-leaf plot for the data. (Ch. 14, Lesson 5)

| My Miniature Golf Scores |
|---|
| 35, 40, 39, 45, 41, 32, 38, 44, 57 |

Extra Practice, See page 373, Set B.

# Chapter Review/Test

## VOCABULARY

**Choose the best term to complete each sentence.**

| Vocabulary |
|---|
| mean |
| range |
| median |
| stem-and-leaf plot |

1. The difference between the greatest number and the least number in a set of data is the ____.
2. A way of displaying data as tens and ones is a ____.
3. When a set of numbers is arranged in order, the middle number is the ____.

## CONCEPTS AND SKILLS

**Use the line plot for Problems 4–6.** (Lessons 3, 4, pp. 364–368)

| 0 | 1 | 2 | 3 | 4 | 5 |
|---|---|---|---|---|---|
| | | | X | | |
| | | X | X | | |
| | | X | X | | X |
| | X | X | X | X | X |

**Number of Runs in 11 Games**

4. What is the median of the data?
5. What is the range of the data?
6. What is the mode of the data?

**Use the stem-and-leaf plot for Problems 7 and 8.** (Lesson 5, pp. 370–371)

**Test Scores**

| Stem | Leaves |
|---|---|
| 5 | 0 |
| 6 | |
| 7 | 2 4 8 |
| 8 | 3 6 7 7 |

5 | 0 = 50

7. How many scores are there?
8. Is there an outlier? If so, which score is it?

## PROBLEM SOLVING

**Make tables to solve Problems 9 and 10.** (Lesson 2, pp. 360–362)

9. Jamal is 19 years old. Billy is 3 years old. How old will each one be when Jamal is three times as old as Billy?
10. A blue bus leaves every 3 minutes. A red bus leaves every 5 minutes. Both leave at 6:00 P.M. When is the next time a blue bus and a red bus will leave at the same time?

### Write About It

**Show You Understand**

Do you think that a survey of 100 people will give more reliable information than a survey of 10 people? Explain your thinking.

# Extra Practice

## Set A (Lesson 4, pp. 366–368)

**Use the line plot for Problems 1–6.**

1. How many campers are there?
2. Are any of the campers younger than 8 years old?
3. What is the age of the oldest camper?
4. What is the range of the data?
5. What is the mode?
6. What is the median?

**Ages of Campers**

| Age | 8 | 9 | 10 | 11 | 12 |
|---|---|---|---|---|---|
| Number of X's | X X X X | X X X X X X | X X X | X X | X |

## Set B (Lesson 5, pp. 370–371)

**Use the stem-and-leaf plot at the right for Problems 1–5.**

1. How many days are recorded?
2. Which temperature is an outlier?
3. What is the range?
4. What is the median?
5. What is the mode?

**Daily High Temperatures in September (°F)**

| Stem | Leaves |
|---|---|
| 4 | 9 |
| 5 | |
| 6 | 6 8 9 9 |
| 7 | 0 0 0 1 2 2 3 5 7 9 |

4 | 9 = 49

**Use the stem-and-leaf plot at the right for Problems 6–10.**

6. Which measure–the mean, median, mode, or range–helps you understand the difference between the team's best and worst games?
7. What was the highest score?
8. What is the mean of the scores between 80 and 89?
9. What is the median score?
10. Is there an outlier? Explain your reasoning.

**Basketball Scores**

| Stem | Leaves |
|---|---|
| 6 | 8 9 |
| 7 | 1 5 6 6 |
| 8 | 4 7 8 8 8 |
| 9 | 0 |

6 | 8 = 68

# Graph Data

## INVESTIGATION

### Using Data

To estimate the distance between you and a thunderstorm, count the number of seconds between a lightning flash and the sound of thunder. If you see a lightning flash, how could you use the graph to find out how far away the thunderstorm is?

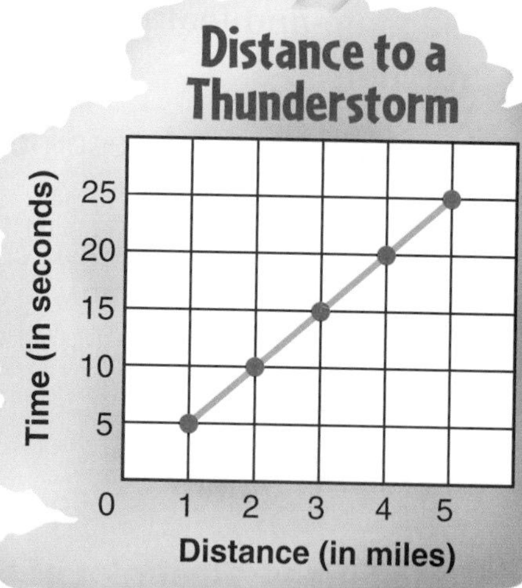

# Use What You Know

**Use this page to review and remember what you need to know for this chapter.**

## VOCABULARY

**Choose the best term to complete each sentence.**

1. When you ask people questions, one way to keep track of the answers is to use a ____.
2. The difference between the greatest number and the least number in a set of data is the ____.
3. A number that names a part of a whole is a ____.

**Vocabulary**
- mean
- range
- fraction
- tally chart

## CONCEPTS AND SKILLS

**Write a fraction for the shaded part.**

4. 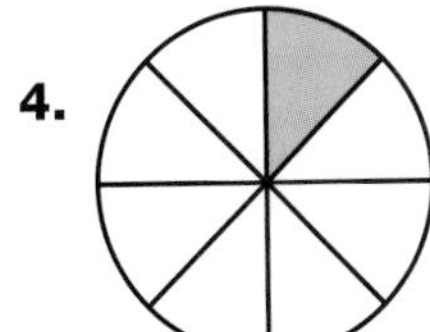

5. 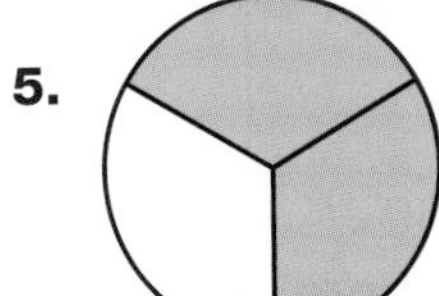

6. 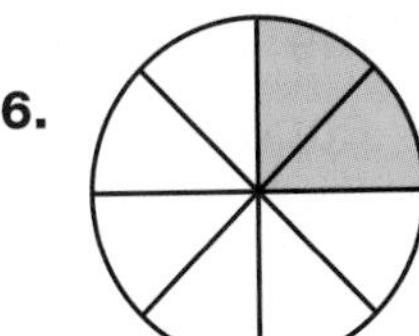

**Use the bar graph for Problems 7–9.**

7. How many more animal books than sports books does Robin have?
8. Robin has about the same number of sports books as what other type of book?
9. How many animal and mystery books does Robin have altogether?

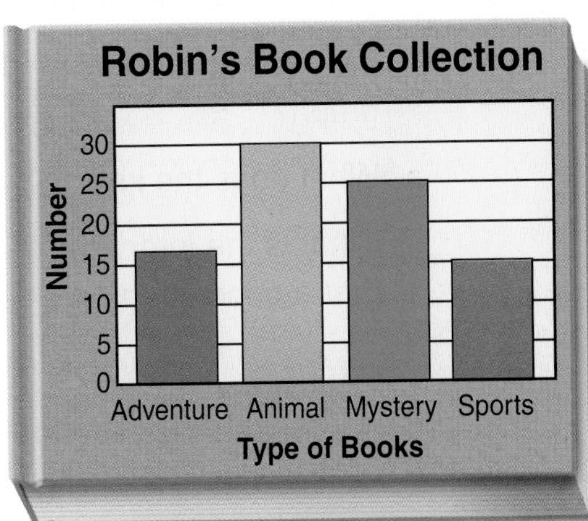


**Write About It**

10. Think about what you know about pictographs and bar graphs. Explain how a bar graph is different from a pictograph.

Facts Practice, See page 665.

# Double Bar Graphs

**Objective** Make a double bar graph to compare two sets of data.

**STANDARDS** M4D1.a, M4P3

## Vocabulary

**double bar graph**
**key**
**interval**

### Materials

Grid Paper (Learning Tool 19)
colored pencils

## Work Together

A **double bar graph** can be used to compare two sets of data.

The table on the right shows the number of rainy days during May, June, and July in Cleveland, Ohio, and Raleigh, North Carolina.

Work with a partner to make a double bar graph to compare the data.

**Number of Rainy Days**

| | May | June | July |
|---|---|---|---|
| Cleveland, OH | 13 | 11 | 10 |
| Raleigh, NC | 10 | 9 | 11 |

**STEP 1** Choose a title and labels for the graph. Then choose colors for the **key.** The key shows what each bar stands for.

Next, choose an interval. The difference between two numbers on the scale is the **interval.**

- What is the title of the graph?
- What are the labels on the graph?
- What does the key show?
- What is the interval? Why is that a good interval to use?

## Guided Practice

**Use the graph on Page 380 and the Ask Yourself questions to help you solve each problem.**

1. Explain what happened between Point *A* and Point *B*. Tell how you know.

   Hint How are temperature and time related?

2. Between which two points did the temperature drop the most? What explanation could there be?

**Ask Yourself**

- How can I tell when the temperature is going up?
- How can I tell when time is passing?

## Independent Practice

**Use the graph at the right for Problems 3–5.**

3. Was it colder at the start of the day or at the end of the day?
4. Between which two consecutive points did the greatest change occur? Can you tell how much the temperature changed during that time? Explain.
5. Did more time pass between Point *A* and Point *B* or between Point *C* and Point *E*?

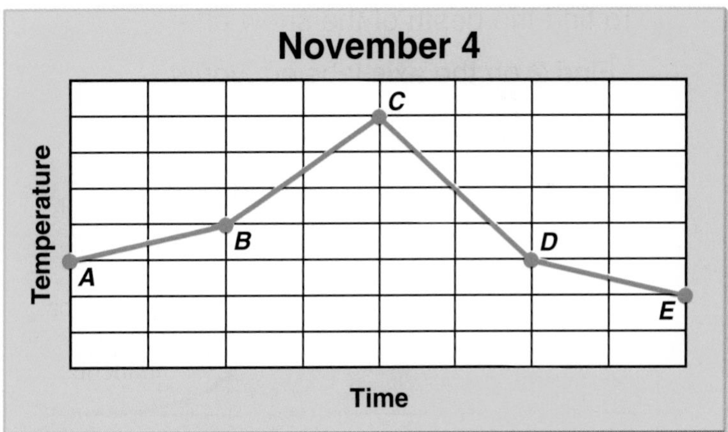


**Use the graph at the right for Problems 6 and 7.**

6. The graph shows the change in height during a climb and the time spent climbing. Which points show when the climbers probably stopped for lunch?
7. Explain what happened between Point *A* and Point *B*. Tell how you know.
8. **Represent** Make a line graph without numbers. Show that the distance around a tree increases as the tree grows taller.

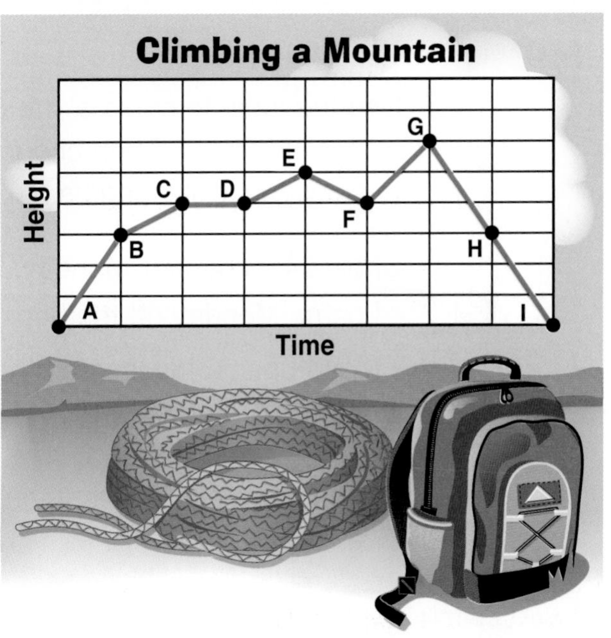

**Audio Tutor 2**/9 Listen and Understand

# Read and Make Line Graphs

**Objective** Read and make a line graph.

**STANDARDS** M4D1.a, M4D1.b, M4P3

**Vocabulary**
line graph

**Materials**
Grid Paper
(Learning Tool 21)

## Learn About It

You can use a **line graph** to show how data change over time. This line graph shows how much snow fell in 4 hours. How deep was the snow after 2 hours?

To find the depth of the snow after 2 hours,

- Find 2 on the axis labeled *Hours*.
- Move up to the line of the graph.
- Move left to the axis labeled *Depth*. Read the depth in inches.

**Depth of Snow**

Depth (inches): 0, 1, 2, 3, 4, 5, 6, 7, 8, 9, 10

Hours: 1, 2, 3, 4

The vertical axis represents depth in inches.

The horizontal axis represents time in hours.

**Solution:** After 2 hours, the snow was 4 inches deep.

**Try this activity to make a line graph.**

**STEP 1** Use the table to make a line graph. Write a title and labels. Then choose a scale to show the icicle lengths.

**STEP 2** Show 24 inches for Monday.
- Locate Monday on the horizontal axis.
- Move up to 24 inches on the vertical axis.
- Place a point where both lines meet.

**STEP 3** Continue placing points, then connect them.

**Icicle Lengths**

| Day | Length |
|---|---|
| Monday | 24 inches |
| Tuesday | 20 inches |
| Wednesday | 12 inches |
| Thursday | 16 inches |
| Friday | 20 inches |



Extra Practice, see page 389, Set B.

## Guided Practice

**Use the *Depth of Snow* graph on Page 382 for Problems 1–3.**

1. What was the depth of snow after 3 hours?
2. About what is the depth of snow after $2\frac{1}{2}$ hours?
3. The graph line goes up from left to right. Could the direction of the line ever change? Explain.

**Ask Yourself**

- What do the numbers on the side and bottom of the graph represent?

**Explain Your Thinking** ▶ What is the pattern on the Depth of Snow graph? If the pattern continues, what will the depth of the snow be after 5 hours?

## Practice and Problem Solving

4. Use the table at the right to make a line graph. Then use your line graph for Problems 5–7.
5. What happened to the temperatures from Thursday through Sunday?
6. **Predict** Would you expect the high temperature on the day after Sunday to be 20°F, 60°F, or 90°F? Explain your answer.
7. What is the range of the temperatures on your graph?

**Daily High Temperatures**

| Day | Temperature |
|---|---|
| Monday | 40°F |
| Tuesday | 45°F |
| Wednesday | 30°F |
| Thursday | 40°F |
| Friday | 35°F |
| Saturday | 30°F |
| Sunday | 25°F |

## Quick Check

**Check your understanding for Lessons 1–4.**

**Use the graphs for Problems 1 and 2.** (Lessons 1, 3, 4)

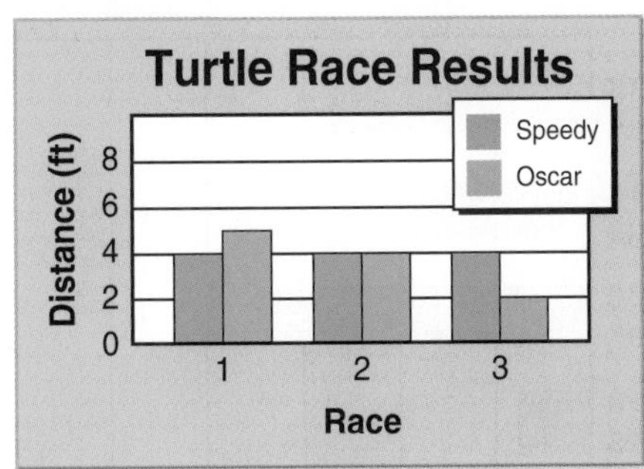


1. How far did Oscar travel in the race he won?

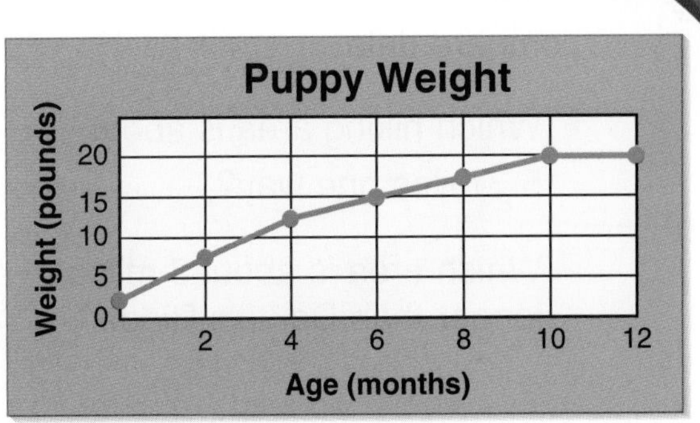


2. How much weight did the puppy gain between 6 months and 1 year?

Extra Practice at eduplace.com/map

# Analyze Graphs

**Objective** Use graphs to display different types of data.

**STANDARDS** M4D1.a, M4D1.b, M4D1.c

**Materials**
Grid Paper
(Learning Tools 19, 20, and 21)

## Learn About It

Brian is doing a report on Death Valley, one of the hottest places in the world. These graphs show data about Death Valley in different ways.

*On July 10, 1913, a high temperature of 134°F was recorded at Greenland Ranch in California's Death Valley.*

▶ A **line graph** is a good way to show change over time.

- About how hot is it at 9:00 A.M.? How do you know?
- Between which two times does the temperature increase about 20°?

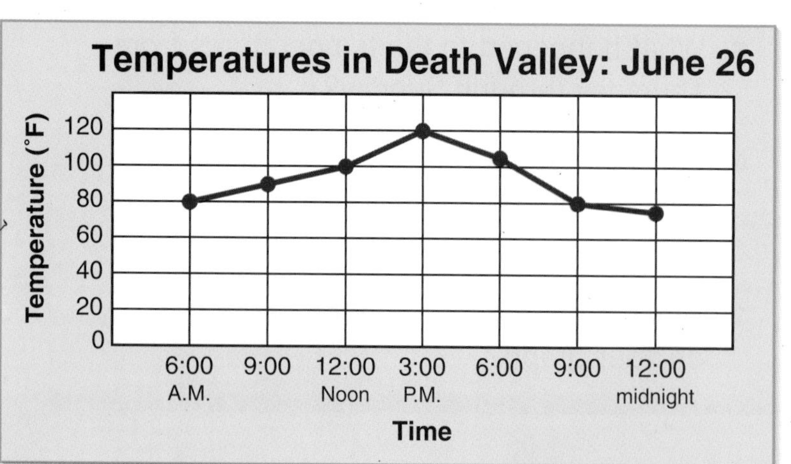


▶ A **bar graph** lets you compare data.

- Which hiking area is about $5\frac{1}{2}$ miles one way?
- Which area is about 3 miles longer than Dante's Ridge?

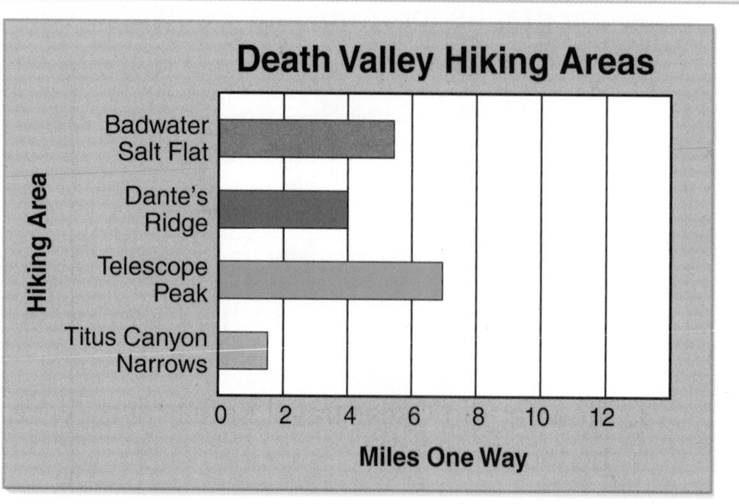

A **circle graph** shows the parts of a whole. It is a good choice for showing a budget.

- Which item will use about half the vacation budget?
- Which budget item will cost about the same amount as a car rental?

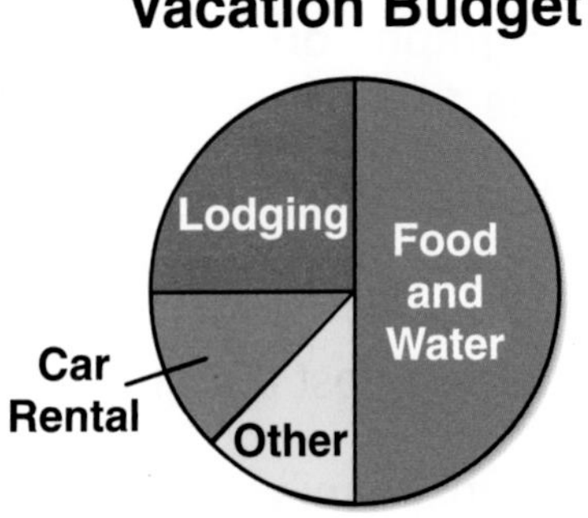


A **pictograph** uses a key instead of a scale. The pictograph shows the results of a survey that asked students to vote on the best month to visit Death Valley.

- Which month got the most votes?
- What does the symbol stand for?

**Best Month to Visit Death Valley**

| | |
|---|---|
| March | |
| April | |
| May | |
| June | |
| July | |

Each = 2 votes.

**Make a graph to analyze the results of a survey.**

STEP 1 Choose a survey question like the one shown on the right. Then conduct a survey and record the data.

- How many students did you survey?

STEP 2 Make a graph to display the data you collected.

- Why did you choose the type of graph you did?

STEP 3 Write two questions about the data that can be answered using your graph.

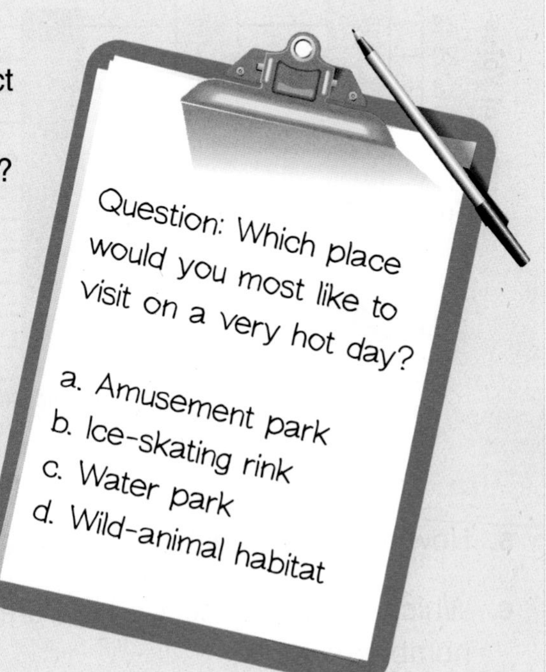


Go On

## Guided Practice

**Use the graphs on Pages 384 and 385 for Problems 1–4.**

1. Between which two times on June 26 does the temperature increase the most?
2. What will cost about twice as much as a car rental?
3. If Brian's family wants to hike a total of about 3 miles out and back, to which hiking area should they go?
4. How many votes were recorded on the pictograph?

**Ask Yourself**

- What is the purpose of the graph?
- Did I read the data on the graph correctly?

**Explain Your Thinking** ▶ Would a pictograph have been another good way to represent the data about Death Valley hiking areas? Why or why not?

## Practice and Problem Solving

**The graphs below show the results of a local election. Use the graphs to answer questions 5–7.**

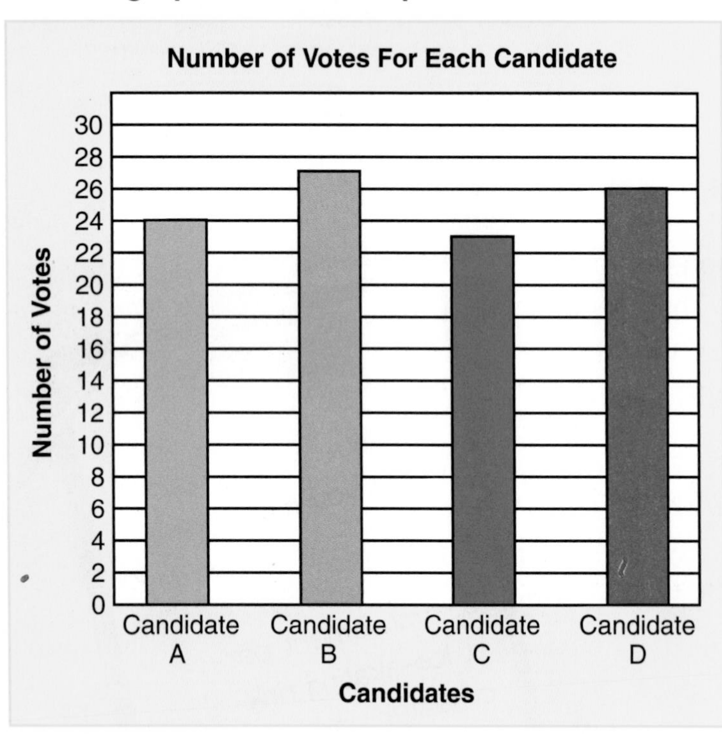


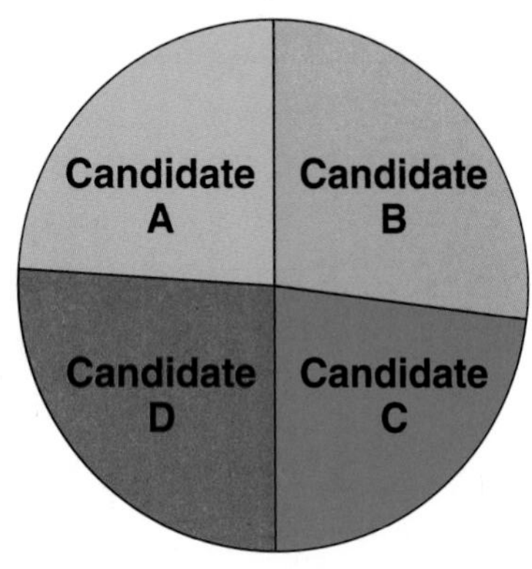


5. How many votes did candidate A get?
6. Which candidate received the greatest number of votes?
7. Did you use the same graph to answer both questions? Explain your answer.
8. **Create and Solve** What could the graph to the right be showing? Create a title, scale, and labels for the graph.

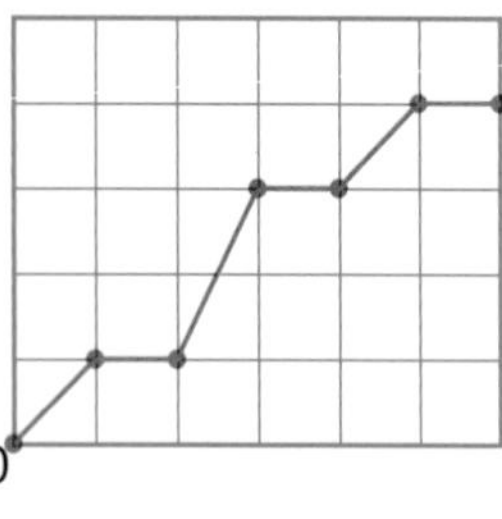




Extra Practice See page 389, Set C.

## Sharpening Skills for CRCT

**Open Response**

**Find the mean, median, mode, and range for each set of data.** (Ch. 14, Lesson 3)

**12.** 14, 3, 8, 1, 14

**13.** 5, 3, 11, 5

**14.** 13, 1, 13, 6, 2

**15.** 30, 40, 20, 30

**16.** 9, 6, 12, 9, 9

**17.** 15, 23, 17, 25

**18.** A line graph that shows the distance a bicyclist rode on a 1-hour trip levels off between two points in the middle of the graph. (Ch. 15, Lesson 5)

How could you explain this?

# Math Reasoning
## Comparing Graphs

**STANDARDS** M4D1.c

Every ten years, the United States takes a census. In the 2000 U.S. Census, 8,186,453 people were counted in Georgia. 2,414,770 of those counted were people age 19 and younger.

The graphs on this page show data about these young people in two different ways. Answer the following questions about the graphs.

1. Name the two types of graphs shown.
2. Which of the graphs most clearly illustrates how many people are in each group?
3. Which of the graphs is the least helpful when looking for differences between the two groups?

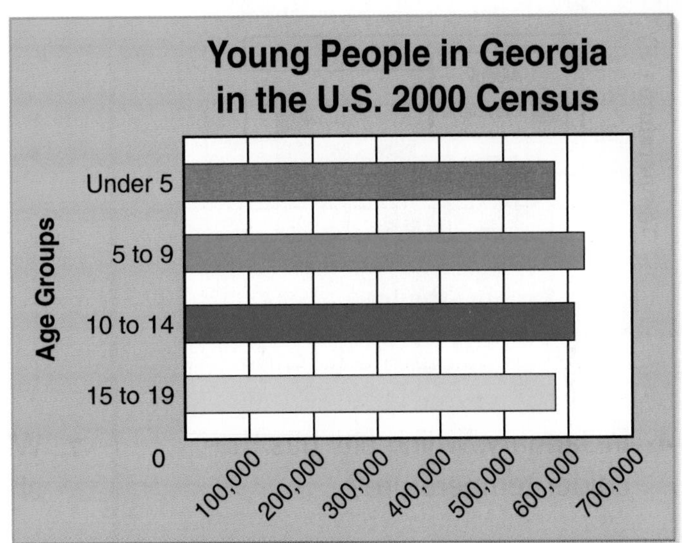


**Young People in Georgia in the U.S. 2000 Census**

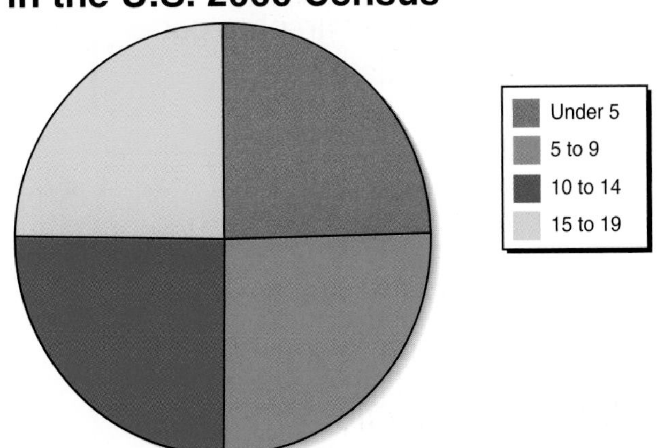

# Chapter Review/Test

Study Guide pages SG44–48

## VOCABULARY

**Choose the best term to complete each sentence.**

**Vocabulary**
- key
- interval
- line graph
- circle graph
- double bar graph

1. A ____ uses bars to compare two sets of data.
2. The difference between two numbers on a scale is the ____.
3. A ____ shows the parts that make up a whole.

## CONCEPTS AND SKILLS

**Use the graphs to answer Problems 4–9.** (Lessons 1, 2, 5, pp. 376–379, 384–386)

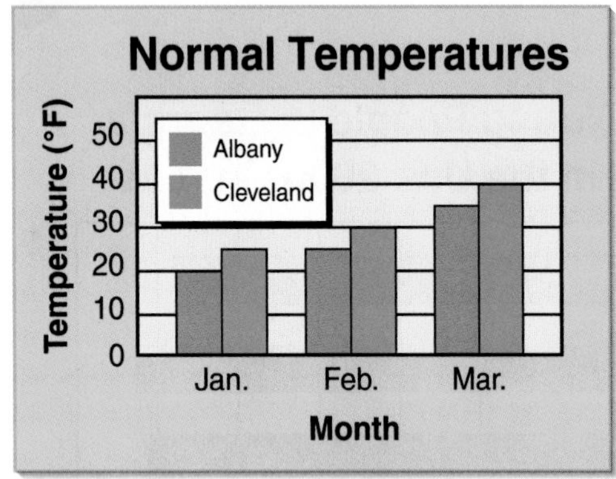


4. In January, which city has the colder temperature?
5. In March, is it warmer in Albany or in Cleveland?
6. Why is a double bar graph a good choice for these data?

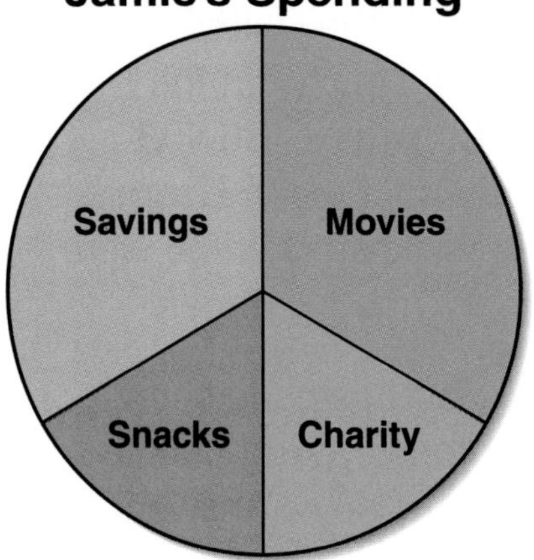


7. What fraction of Jamie's money does she save?
8. Does Jamie spend more on movies or on snacks?
9. Why is a circle graph a good choice for these data?

## PROBLEM SOLVING

**Solve.** (Lessons 3, 4, pp. 380–383)

10. Draw a line graph to show the total distance hikers walked in a day.

**Write About It**

**Show You Understand**

What kind of graph would best display changes in the high temperature outside a school during one week? Why?

# Extra Practice

## Set A (Lesson 2, pp. 378–379)

**Use the circle graph for Problems 1–3.**

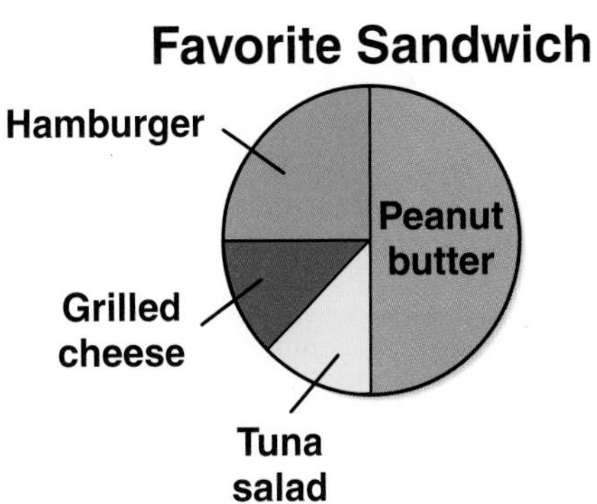


1. What fraction of people chose peanut butter?
2. Did more people choose hamburger or tuna salad as their favorite sandwich?
3. Which choice shows about twice as many votes as grilled cheese?

## Set B (Lesson 4, pp. 382–383)

**Use the line graph for Problems 1–3.**

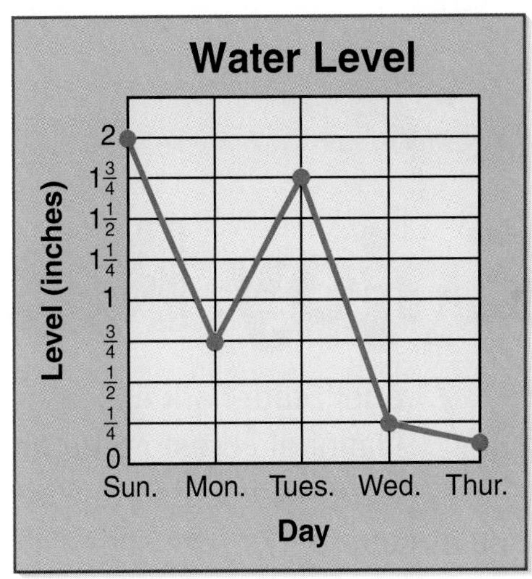


1. On which day was the water level the greatest?
2. On which days was the water level less than 1 inch?
3. Between which two days did the water level decrease the most?

## Set C (Lesson 5, pp. 384–386)

**Write the letter of the graph that shows the information given in each problem.**

A. 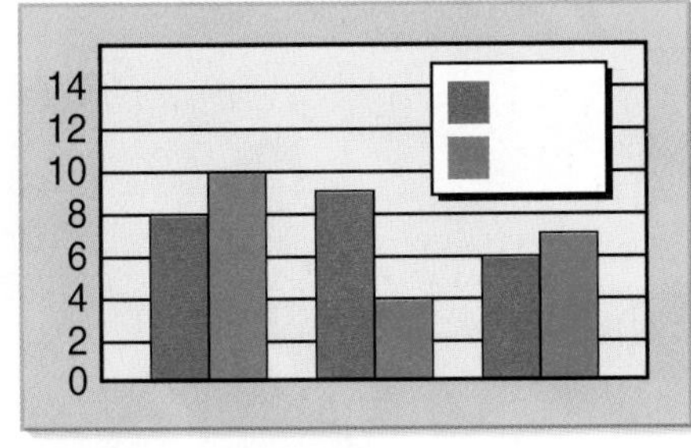

B. 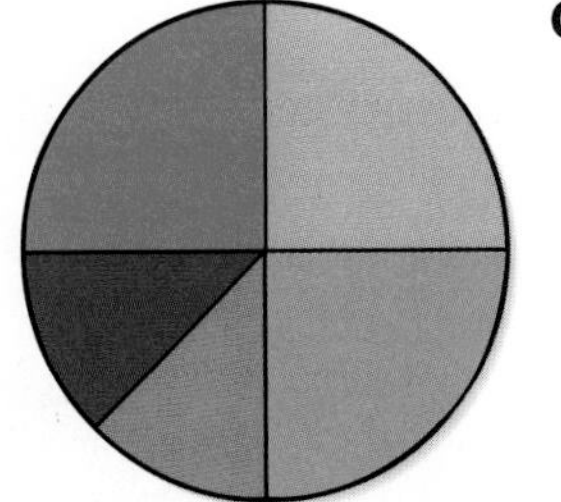

C. 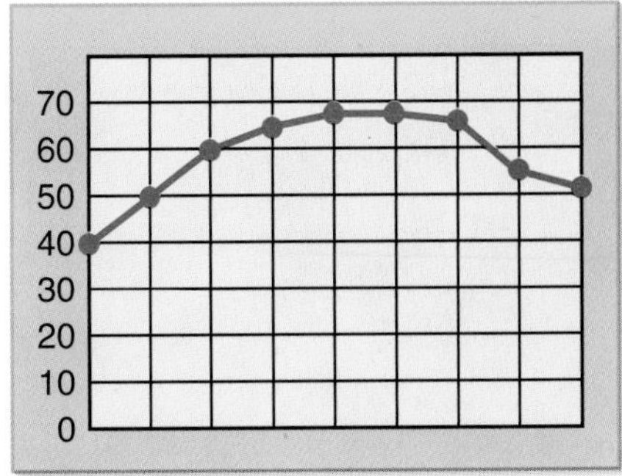

1. the amount spent on party supplies
2. changes in temperature during a day
3. a comparison of scores by two teams in three games

Extra Practice at **eduplace.com/map**

# Enjoy Nature

Vogel State Park lies in the Chattahoochee National Forest in the mountains of northern Georgia. It is one of Georgia's oldest and most popular state parks. The scenic park features Lake Trahlyta and provides a route to the Appalachian Trail.

While in the park, guests can enjoy many activities, including swimming, fishing, and hiking. Visitors can also spend the night in the park at one of the 103 campsites or 35 cottages.

## Problem Solving

**The tally chart and pictograph below show two different ways to display the same information. Use the tally chart and pictograph for Problems 1–4.**

| Cottages at Vogel State Park | |
|---|---|
| **Number of People Who Can Stay in a Cottage** | **Tally** |
| 2 | \|\|\|\| |
| 4 | 𝍸 𝍸 \| |
| 6 | 𝍸 𝍸 |
| 8 | 𝍸 \|\|\| |
| 10 | \|\| |

| Cottages at Vogel State Park | |
|---|---|
| 2 | ⌂ ⌂ |
| 4 | ⌂ ⌂ ⌂ ⌂ ⌂ ⌂(half) |
| 6 | ⌂ ⌂ ⌂ ⌂ ⌂ |
| 8 | ⌂ ⌂ ⌂ ⌂ |
| 10 | ⌂ |

1. What do the numbers on the side of the pictograph stand for?

2. What should the key be for each cottage symbol in the pictograph?

3. Do any cottages shelter 12 people?

4. Make a bar graph that shows the same information that appears in the tally chart and pictograph. How many cottages shelter 4 people? Is it easier to use the pictograph or the bar graph to answer this question?

STANDARDS M4D1.d, M4P5

# Careful Collecting

You can use different types of graphs to display certain kinds of information. Remember that with any graph you use to represent data, you need to be careful when you collect the information. If there are mistakes in the way you collect your data, your graph will reflect those errors.

Celia and Alexi work together on a project for science class. They recorded the temperature at 8 A.M. over the course of a week. The graph below displays the data they collected.

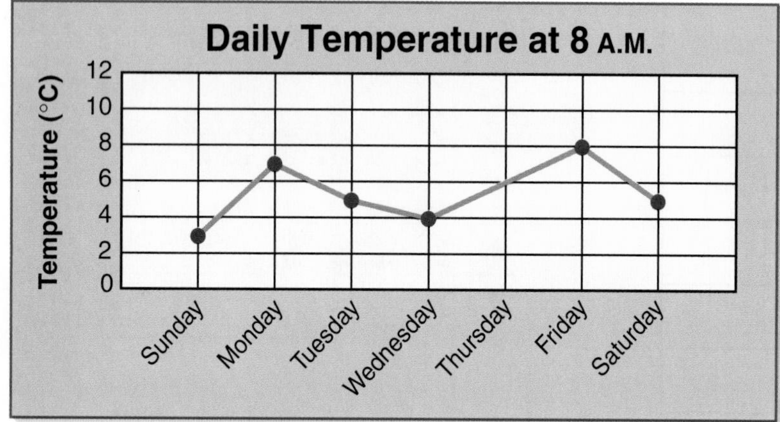


There is no data point for Thursday on the graph. The line moves from Wednesday in a straight line to Friday. What might have caused this missing data point?

- **Missing Information**

Celia and Alexi may have forgotten to collect data on Thursday. If they failed to collect data for one day, their graph will be missing some information. This could lead to a misleading or inaccurate graph.

## Try These!

**Use the line graph above to answer the questions.**

1. Based on the graph, can you make a reasonable estimate of what the temperature was on Thursday? Why or why not?

2. Suppose Celia and Alexi checked Thursday's newspaper and found out the temperature was 4°C. How would the graph change to reflect the new data?

# Watch 'em Grow!

**STANDARDS** M4D1.a

Mrs. Spinelli's class is growing vegetables in the school garden. The table on the right shows the growth of one of their tomato plants over 5 weeks.

| Tomato Plant Growth | |
|---|---|
| **Week** | **Height** |
| 1 | 2 inches |
| 2 | 3 inches |
| 3 | 6 inches |
| 4 | 6 inches |
| 5 | 8 inches |

**You can use Graphers to make a line graph of the data.**

- Click [Work Out] then [Go].
- Click [Create New Data] then [Go].
- Click [Time Data] then [Go].
- Click [icon], then [icon] then [Go].
- Click [Data Maker]. Click 1 two times to represent the height of the plant after 1 week. Click 2 three times to represent the height of the plant after 2 weeks. Repeat for rest of the data. Then click [Done].
- Click [Graphs], then [icon], then [Go].
- Click [Unit] below the graph and type "Week."
- Click [Units] above the graph and type "Tomato Plant Growth in Inches."
- Click [Tools] then [icon].

**Use the line graph you created for Problems 1–4.**

1. How tall was the tomato plant at the end of Week 4?
2. How many inches did the tomato plant grow between Week 1 and Week 3?
3. Between which two weeks did the growth of the tomato plant show the greatest increase?
4. What are the mean, median, mode, and range of the heights? How did you find the mean?

# Unit 5 Test

Study Guide pages SG30–32

**VOCABULARY** Open Response

**Choose the correct word to complete each sentence.**

| Vocabulary |
|---|
| mode |
| median |
| interval |
| capacity |

1. The amount that a container can hold is its ____.
2. The middle number in a set of numbers ordered from least to greatest is the ____.
3. The difference between two numbers on the scale of a bar graph is the ____.

**CONCEPTS AND SKILLS** Open Response

**Find each missing number.** (Chapter 12)

4. __ pt = 32 c
5. 6 L = __ mL
6. __ lb = 48 oz
7. 2 dm = __ cm
8. __ g = 7 kg
9. 60 yd = __ ft

**Look at each pair of times. Write how much time has elapsed.** (Chapter 13)

10. Start: 3:42 A.M.<br>End: 7:07 A.M.
11. Start: 8:15 A.M.<br>End: 1:05 P.M.
12. Start: 10:20 P.M.<br>End: 2:35 A.M.

**Write each temperature.** (Chapter 13)

13. °F 70° 60°

14. 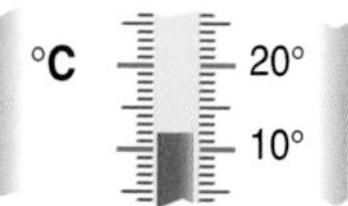


15. 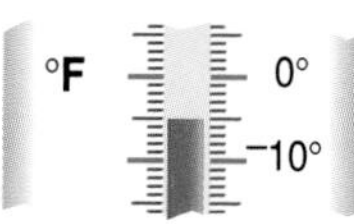


16. 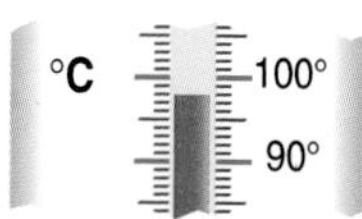


**Use the line graph for Problems 17–19.** (Chapter 15)

17. Which months had the same amount of rainfall?
18. How much rain fell in the wettest month? Which month was it?
19. About how much rain fell between the beginning of May and the end of July?

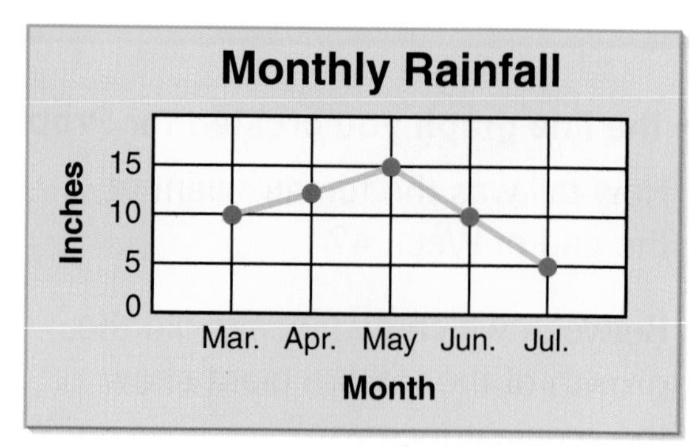

**Use the data in the table for Problems 20 and 21.** (Chapter 14)

| Minutes Jacob Played in His Soccer Games | | | | |
|---|---|---|---|---|
| 1 | 25 | 13 | 13 | 20 |
| 13 | 14 | 25 | 20 | |

**20.** Use the data to make a stem-and-leaf plot.

**21.** Find the mean, median, and mode of the data.

**PROBLEM SOLVING** Open Response

**22.** A comic book doubled in price every 10 years. It cost $20 in 1950. How much did it cost 5 decades later?

**23.** Jim bought 4 muffins for $2.50 each and 2 snack bars for $1.25 each. How much did he spend on muffins?

**24.** In a park, there are 25 people and dogs with a total of 70 legs. How many people are there?

**25.** It is 17°F at 8 P.M. If it gets 4° colder each hour for 3 hours, what will the temperature be then?

## Performance Task

| Tree A Growth | |
|---|---|
| Year 1 | 500 cm |
| Year 2 | 400 cm |
| Year 3 | 200 cm |
| Year 4 | 100 cm |

| Tree B Growth | |
|---|---|
| Year 1 | 400 cm |
| Year 2 | 300 cm |
| Year 3 | 300 cm |
| Year 4 | 200 cm |

**Task** A scientist has asked you to chart the growth of two trees. The tables above show the growth of two trees over four years.

a. Change the information in the tables from centimeters to meters. Make two new tables to display the heights in meters.

b. Make a double bar graph to compare the number of meters the trees grew each year. How did you label the graph? What scale did you use?

c. Which tree grew more during the first year? Did this tree also grow faster in the following years? Explain.

d. Make line graphs to show the number of meters the trees grow each year. Compare and contrast the two line graphs.

# Getting Ready for CRCT

**Solve Problems 1–10.**

*Look at the example below.*

The students in Britney's class voted on their favorite season. The results are shown in the pictograph below.

| Favorite Seasons | |
|---|---|
| Fall | ☆☆☆☆ |
| Winter | ☆☆☆½ |
| Spring | ☆☆☆☆☆☆ |
| Summer | ☆☆☆☆☆☆☆☆ |

Each ☆ = 2 votes.

Which statement is TRUE?

A. Winter is the most popular season.

B. Spring got more votes than summer.

C. Fall is the least favorite season.

D. Spring got more votes than winter.

**THINK**

**A** is **NOT TRUE** because winter does not have the greatest number of stars.

**B** is **NOT TRUE** because the number of stars for spring is less than the number of stars for summer.

**C** is **NOT TRUE** because fall does not have the fewest stars.

**D** is **TRUE** because there are more stars for spring than for winter.

So choose **D**.

## Multiple Choice

1. Find the product.

**731 × 8 = ■**

A. 5,600

B. 5,648

C. 5,848

D. 6,848

(Chapter 6, Lesson 6)

2. Katrina bought 3 pounds of apples. How much do the apples weigh in ounces?

A. 12

B. 16

C. 36

D. 48

(Chapter 12, Lesson 4)

3. An orbit is the time it takes for a planet to go around the Sun. Mercury's orbit lasts 88 Earth days. How many times does Mercury orbit the Sun in 440 Earth days?

A. 3

B. 4

C. 5

D. 6

(Chapter 11, Lesson 4)



For Test-Taking Tips, See page 658.

## Open Response

4. Khai wants to have $45 at the end of 5 weeks. If every week she saves the amount, how much does she need to save each week?

(Chapter 4, Lesson 4)

5. Copy and complete the function table.

| Rule: ________ | |
|---|---|
| *x* | *y* |
| 1 | 6 |
| ■ | 18 |
| 10 | 60 |
| 12 | ■ |

(Chapter 12, Lesson 9)

6. Which is heavier, 60 grams or 6 kilograms? Explain.

(Chapter 13, Lesson 2)

7. Sarah asked 20 classmates to name their favorite pet. The circle graph below represents her results.

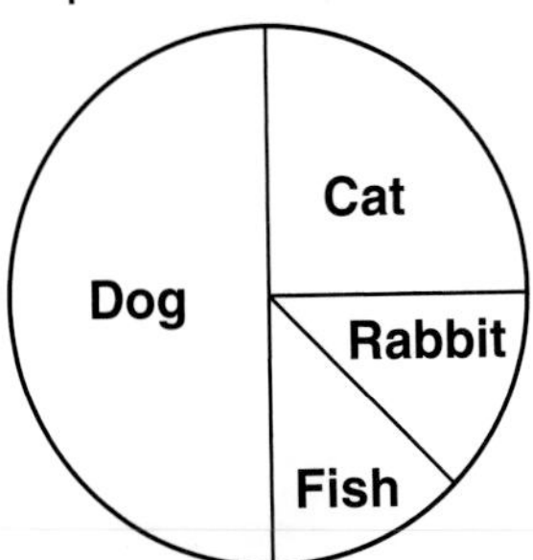


Which pet is the most popular? Explain how you know.

(Chapter 15, Lesson 1)

8. A carton holds 12 eggs. If Jon has 11 cartons of eggs, how many eggs does he have?

(Chapter 4, Lesson 6)

## Extended Response

9. The graph shows how many cans of food were collected by each grade during a food drive.

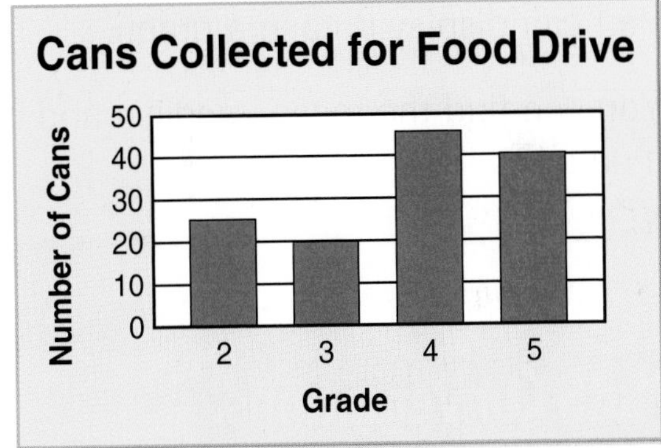


a. Which grade collected the MOST cans of food?

b. How many cans of food did the third grade collect?

c. Which grade collected twice as many cans as Grade 3?

d. If Grade 3 had collected twice as many cans of food, would it have collected more cans than Grade 4? Explain.

(Chapter 2, Lesson 6)

**Education Place**

Look for Cumulative Test Prep at **eduplace.com/map** for more practice.

# Vocabulary Wrap-Up for Unit 5

**Look back at the big ideas and vocabulary in this unit.**

## Big Ideas

You can use multiplication and division to convert from one unit of measure to another.

You can measure elapsed time on a calendar or a clock.

You can display data in a graph.

You can find the mean, median, and mode of a data set.

### Key Vocabulary

**data**
**elapsed time**
**mean**
**median**
**mode**

## Math Conversations

**Use your new vocabulary to discuss these big ideas.**

1. Explain how you can find the number of inches in 6 feet.

2. Explain the difference between the mean, median, and mode of a data set.

3. Explain how bar graphs and line graphs are alike and different.

4. **Write About It** Measure the height of different textbooks to the nearest half inch. Make a bar graph to display the data. Find the median, mode, and range of the data.

# UNIT 6

# Geometry and Measurement

# Reading Mathematics

## Reviewing Vocabulary

**Here are some math vocabulary words that you should know.**

| | | |
|---|---|---|
| **angle** | two rays with a common endpoint | |
| **line** | a straight path of points that goes on without end in both directions | |
| **line segment** | a part of a line with two endpoints | |
| **triangle** | a polygon with 3 sides | |

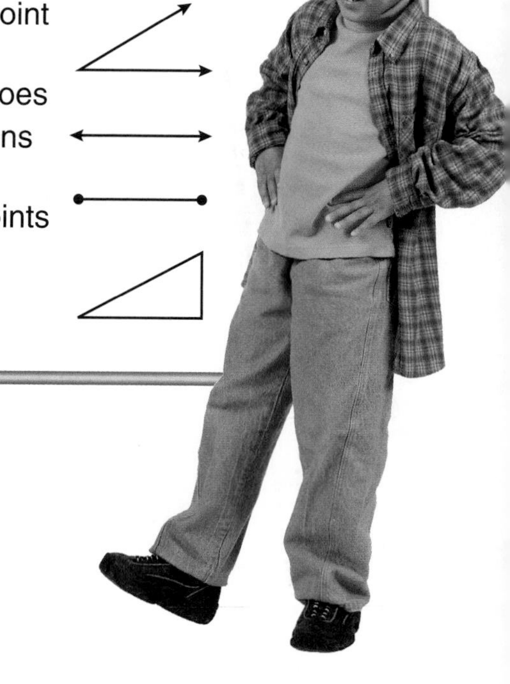

## Reading Words and Symbols

There are many different geometric figures.

Look at the names of these polygons.

| 3 sides, 3 angles | 4 sides, 4 angles | 4 equal sides, 4 equal angles |
|---|---|---|
| | 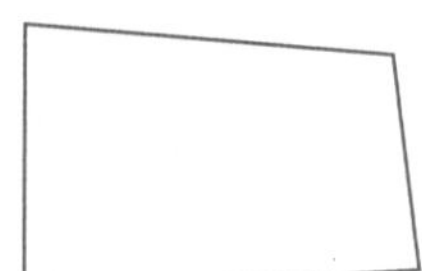 |  |
| **Write:** triangle | **Write:** quadrilateral | **Write:** square |

**Use the figure at the right for Problems 1–2.**

1. What figure is shown at the right?
2. Are there other names you could give the figure? Explain your thinking.

# Reading Questions on CRCT

**Choose the correct answer for each.**

**3.** Which figure is a square?

A. □

B. ▭

C. ▱

D. ⏢

**Figure** means "shape."

**4.** Which pair of figures shows two quadrilaterals?

A. ○ □

B. □ ◺

C. ⬠ ⬡

D. ▯ ⏢

**Pair** means "group of two."

**5.** How many quadrilaterals appear inside the circular figure at the right?

A. 3

B. 4

C. 5

D. 9

**Circular** means "shaped like a circle."

# Learning Vocabulary

**Watch for these words in this unit. Write their definitions in your journal.**

- **line segment**
- **ray**
- **acute angle**
- **protractor**
- **rhombus**
- **trapezoid**
- **congruent**

## Education Place

At **eduplace.com/map** see eGlossary and eGames—Math Lingo.

## Literature Connection

Read "Dividing the Cheese" on Page 651. Then work with a partner to answer the questions about the story.

# Plane Figures

## PERFORMANCE PREVIEW

### Using Data

Quilting is a popular activity in Georgia. In fact, a group of quilters formed the Georgia Quilt Council in 1983. Quilts are often made with the figures you study in math class, such as triangles and squares. The chart shows the number of sides different figures have. How many of each figure can you find in the photo of the quilt?

| Name of Figure | Number of Sides |
|---|---|
| Triangle | 3 |
| Quadrilateral | 4 |
| Pentagon | 5 |
| Hexagon | 6 |

# Use What You Know

**Use this page to review and remember what you need to know for this chapter.**

## VOCABULARY

**Vocabulary**
- line
- circle
- triangle
- rectangle

**Choose the best word to complete each sentence.**

1. A straight path of points that goes on without end in both directions is a ____.
2. A polygon with exactly three sides is a ____.
3. A ____ is a polygon with opposite sides parallel and four right angles.

## CONCEPTS AND SKILLS

**Tell whether each figure is a line, a line segment, or an angle.**

4. 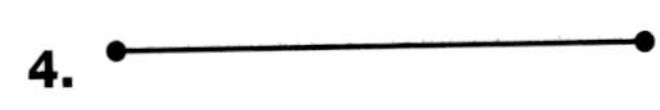
5. 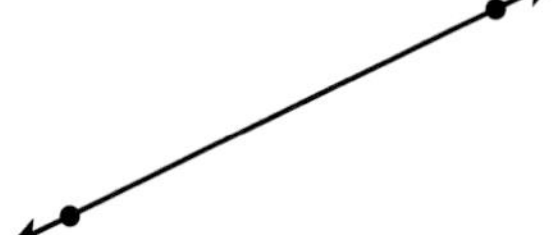
6. 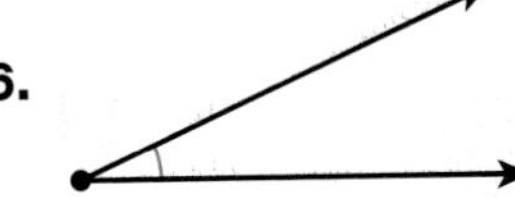

**Draw a polygon for each description. Name the polygon you drew.**

7. a figure with four equal sides
8. a figure with five sides
9. a figure with two pairs of parallel sides

**Write About It**

10. Use as many different words as you can to describe this figure. Tell why those words are good descriptions.

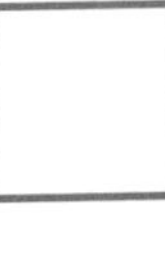

Facts Practice, See Page 667.

Lesson 1

# Points, Lines, and Line Segments

**Objective** Identify geometric figures.

 **STANDARDS** M4G1.b, M4P3

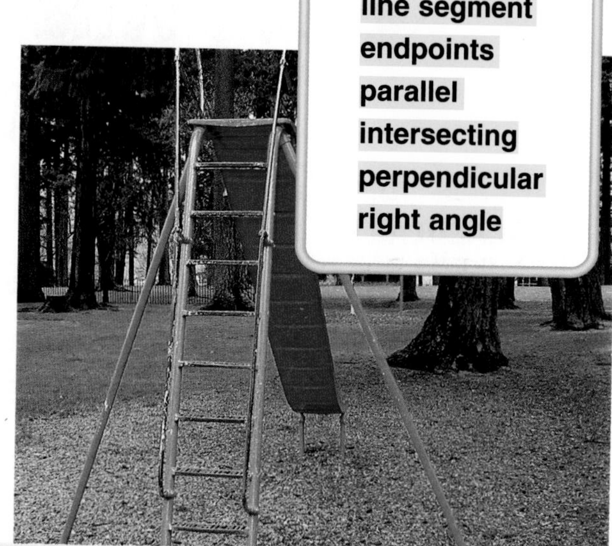

**Vocabulary**

line segment
endpoints
parallel
intersecting
perpendicular
right angle

## Learn About It

Many everyday things can model geometric figures. The period at the end of this sentence is a model of a point. A solid painted stripe in the middle of a straight road is a model of a line. The rungs on a metal ladder are models of parallel line segments.

### Geometric Figures

A point is a location in space.

• *B*

**Say:** point *B*
**Write:** *B*

You can draw a line through any two points. A line goes on without end in both directions.

**Say:** line *CD* or line *DC*
**Write:** $\overleftrightarrow{CD}$ or $\overleftrightarrow{DC}$

A **line segment** is part of a line. It has two **endpoints**.

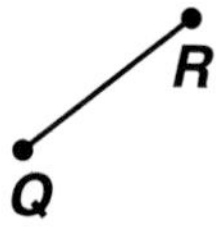


**Say:** line segment *QR* or line segment *RQ*
**Write:** $\overline{QR}$ or $\overline{RQ}$

Lines that are always the same distance apart are **parallel**.

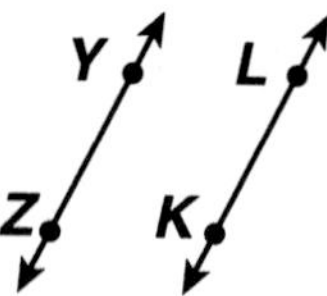


**Say:** Line *ZY* is parallel to line *KL*.
**Write:** $\overleftrightarrow{ZY} \parallel \overleftrightarrow{KL}$

The symbol $\parallel$ means "is parallel to."

Lines that cross each other are **intersecting**.

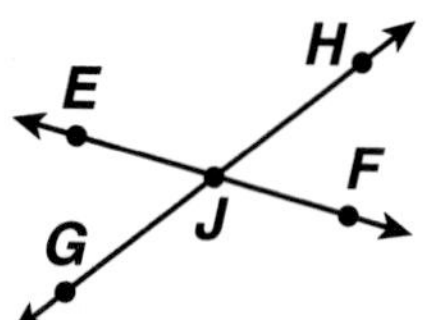


**Say:** Line *EF* and line *GH* intersect at point *J*.

Two lines that form right angles are **perpendicular**.

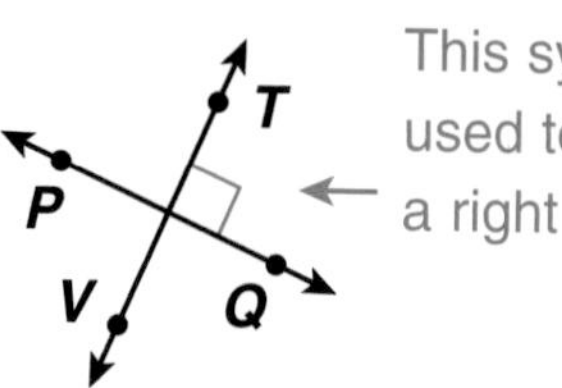


This symbol is used to show a right angle.

**Say:** Line *PQ* is perpendicular to line *TV*
**Write:** $\overleftrightarrow{PQ} \perp \overleftrightarrow{TV}$

The symbol $\perp$ means "is perpendicular to."

▶ In the picture at the right, the horizontal line is perpendicular to the vertical line. At their intersection, they form right angles.

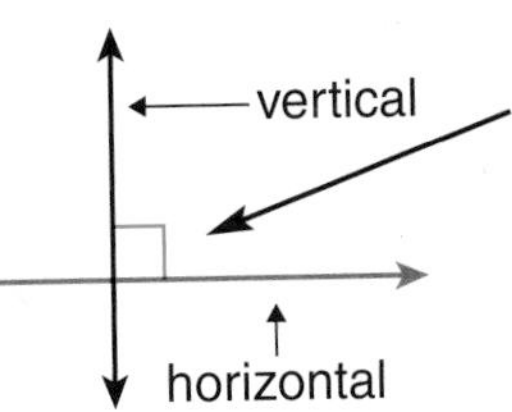


The angle makes a square corner, which is called a **right angle**.

## Guided Practice

**Ask Yourself**

- Which point will I write first to name the figure?
- What symbol stands for the figure?

**Use words and symbols to name each figure.**

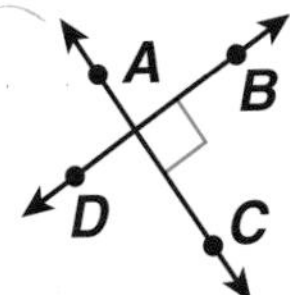


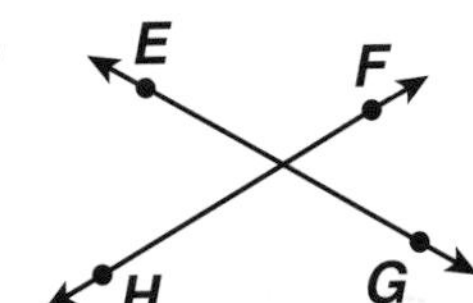


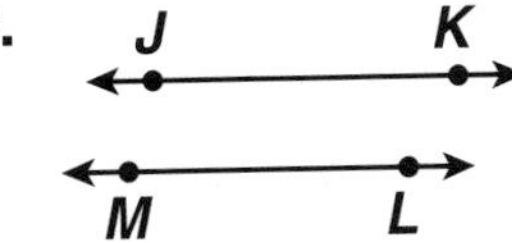

**Write *parallel, intersecting,* or *perpendicular* to describe the relationship between each pair of lines.**

4. A B C D

5. E F G H

6. J K M L

7. T S R U

**Explain Your Thinking** ▶ Can two lines be both intersecting and perpendicular? Can two lines be both intersecting and parallel? Explain your thinking.

## Practice and Problem Solving

**Use words and symbols to name each figure.**

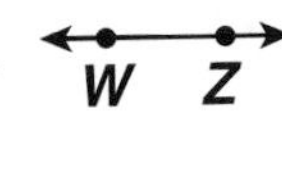


11. • Q

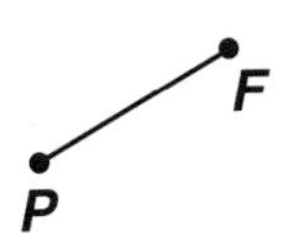


**Write *parallel, intersecting,* or *perpendicular* to describe the relationship between each pair of lines.**

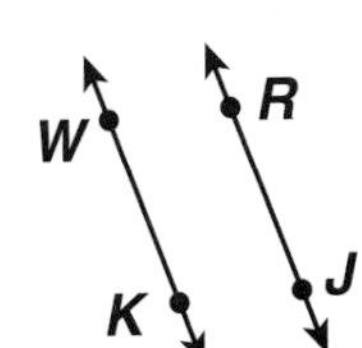


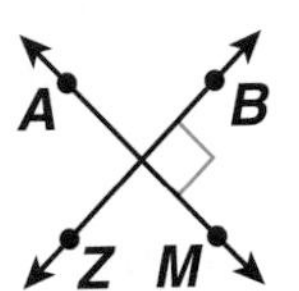


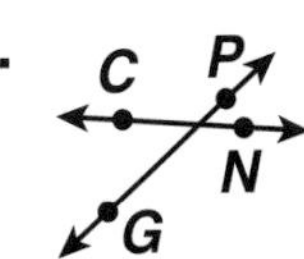


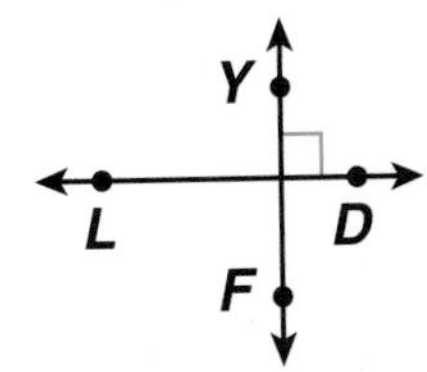


Go On

**Draw an example of each.**

**17.** line segment $JK$

**18.** line $MN$

**19.** horizontal line segment $WY$

**20.** $\overleftrightarrow{EF} \parallel \overleftrightarrow{GH}$

**21.** $\overleftrightarrow{AB} \perp \overleftrightarrow{CD}$

**22.** horizontal $\overline{PQ}$ and vertical $\overline{PR}$

**23.** $\overleftrightarrow{CD}$ intersecting $\overleftrightarrow{ST}$

**24.** $\overline{VW} \parallel \overline{XY}$

**25.** $\overline{AB} \perp \overline{QR}$

**Write *true* or *false* for each sentence. You can draw a picture to help find the answer.**

**26.** If two lines are parallel, they never meet.

**27.** If a line is horizontal, it is parallel to a vertical line.

**28.** If two lines intersect, they are always perpendicular.

**29.** If two lines are perpendicular, they are also parallel.

**Use the drawing at the right for Problems 30–33.**

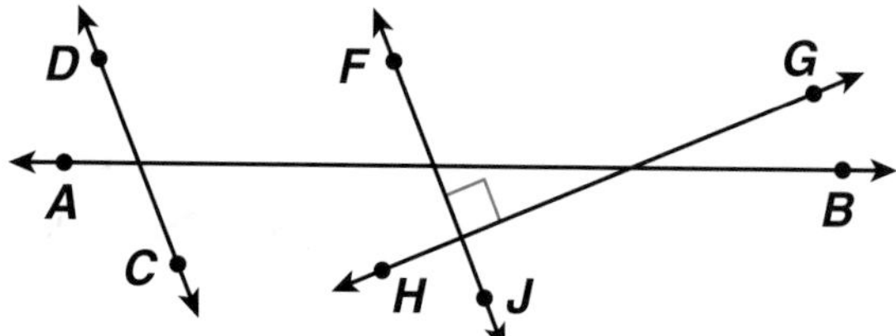


**30.** Name a line.

**31.** Name a pair of perpendicular lines.

**32.** Name a pair of parallel lines.

**33.** **Explain** Is $\overleftrightarrow{AB}$ is perpendicular to $\overleftrightarrow{FJ}$? Explain your answer.

**34.** **Write About It** Look around your classroom. Describe something that shows a pair of parallel lines. Then describe something that shows a pair of perpendicular lines.

## Sharpening Skills for CRCT

### Open Response

**What letter is likely to come next in each pattern?** (Grade 3)

**35.** t u u v v v w w w w x x x x ____

**36.** a b a b c a b c d a b c d ____

**37.** m n m n o m n o p m n o p ____

**38.** a c a c e a c e g a c e g ____

**39.** Which lines in the diagram below appear to be perpendicular? Explain your answer.

(Ch. 16, Lesson 1)

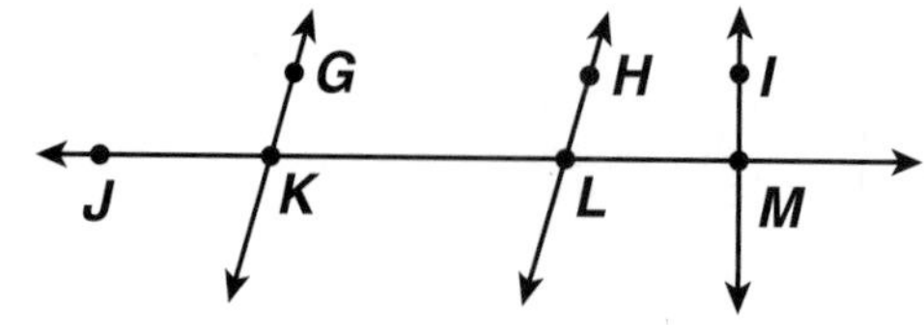




Extra Practice See page 427, Set A.

Game

GPS Activity

# Triple Concentration

**2 Players**

STANDARDS Maintains M3G1.b

**What You'll Need** • 18 Game Cards (Learning Tool 22)

## How to Play

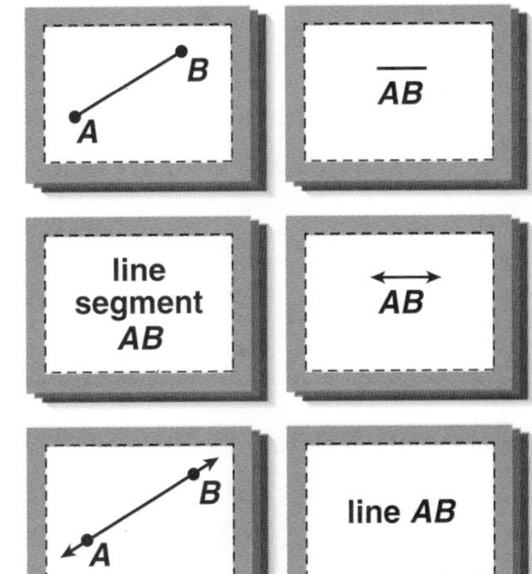


1. Make 3 copies of each card shown on the right.
2. Shuffle the cards. Place them face down in a 3 by 6 array.
3. 
   - The first player turns up three cards.
   - If all the cards match (picture, name, and symbol), the player collects those cards.
   - If the cards do not match, the player turns the cards face down. The next player takes a turn.
4. Players take turns until all matches have been made. The player with the most cards wins.

Lesson 2

# Rays and Angles

**Objective** Name and describe rays and angles.

## Vocabulary

- ray
- angle
- sides
- vertex
- obtuse angle
- acute angle
- straight angle

## Learn About It

You have learned about lines and line segments.

Rays and angles are also geometric figures.

▶ A **ray** is a part of a line. It has one endpoint and goes on without end in one direction.

**Say:** ray *BA*
**Write:** $\overrightarrow{BA}$

▶ An **angle** is formed by two rays with a common endpoint. The rays are the **sides** of the angle. The common endpoint is the **vertex** of the angle.

| Say | Write |
|---|---|
| angle *C* | ∠*C* |
| angle *BCD* | ∠*BCD* |
| angle *DCB* | ∠*DCB* |

← Each of the angle names in the chart can be used to name the angle on the right.

← When naming an angle, the vertex is the middle letter.

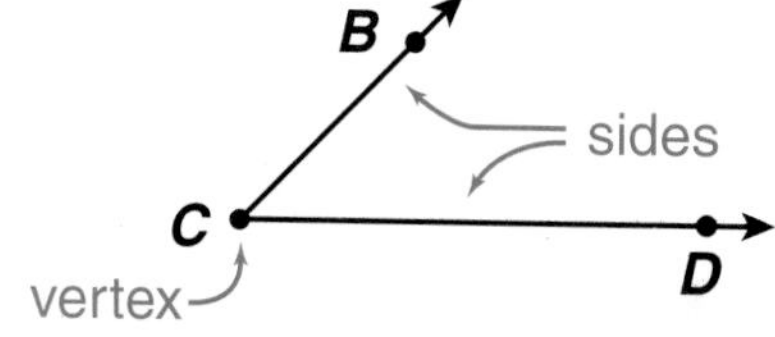


Angles are classified by the size of the opening between the sides.

This angle forms a square corner.

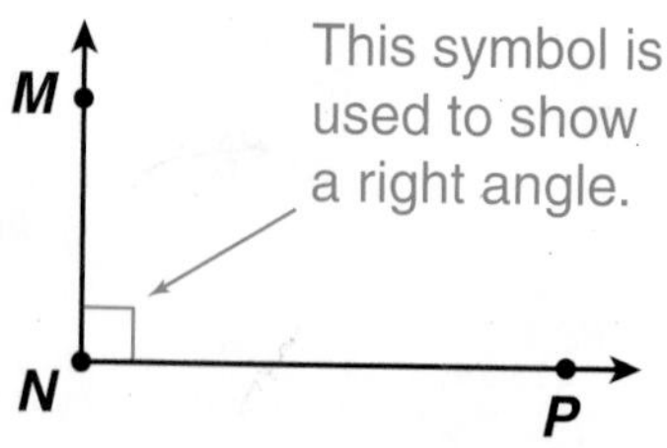


∠*MNP* is a right angle.

This angle is greater than a right angle.

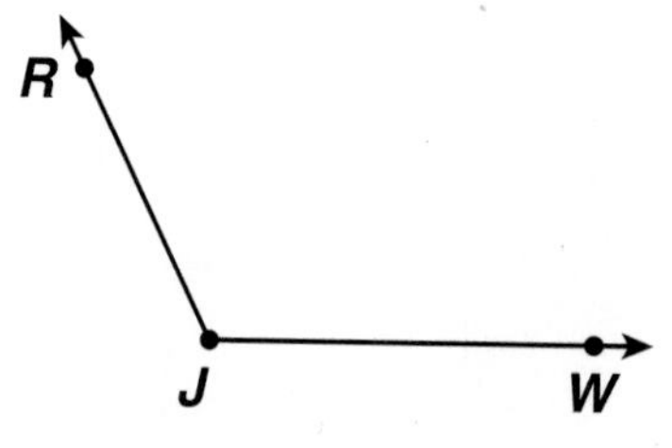


∠*RJW* is an **obtuse angle**.

This angle is less than a right angle.

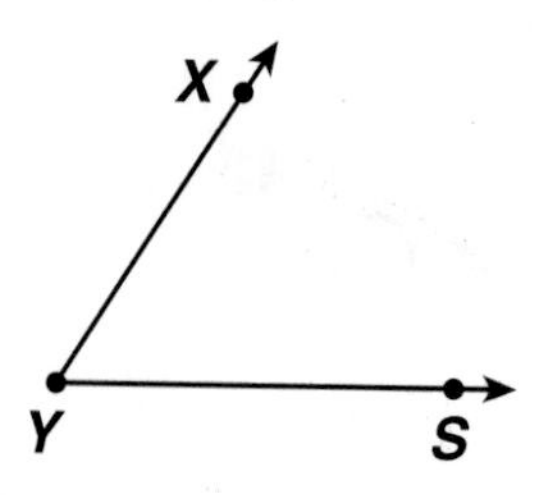


∠*XYS* is an **acute angle**.

This angle forms a straight line.

∠*FGH* is a **straight angle**.

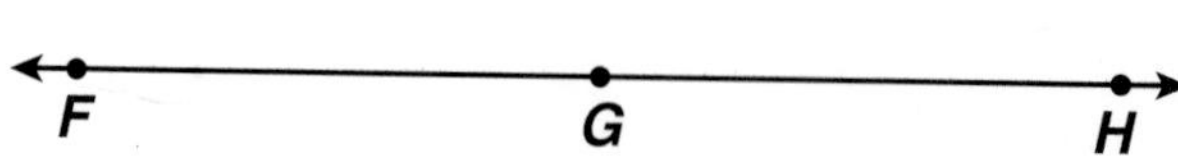

## Some polygons are regular. Some are irregular.

**Regular polygons**

All sides have equal lengths.
All angles have the same measure.

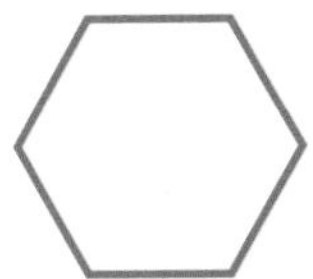

Regular Hexagon

**Irregular polygons**

Some sides have different lengths.
Some angles have different measures.

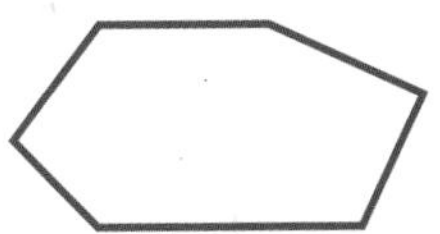

Irregular Hexagon

## Some quadrilaterals have special names.

A rectangle has opposite sides parallel and four right angles.

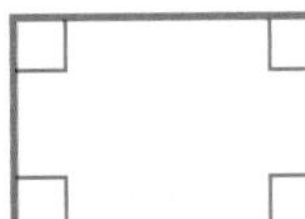

A square has four sides of the same length and four right angles.

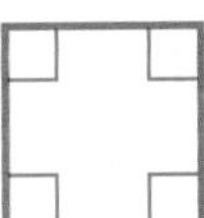

A **trapezoid** has only one pair of parallel sides.

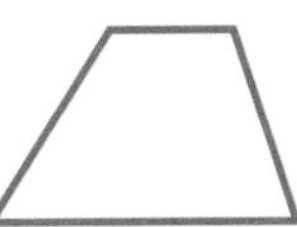

A parallelogram has opposite sides parallel and of the same length.

A **rhombus** has opposite sides parallel and four sides of the same length.

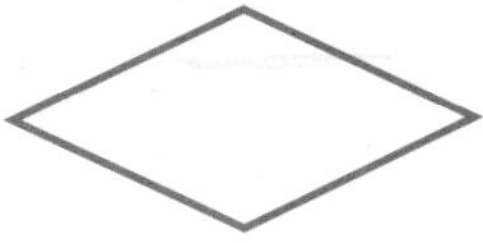

## Polygons with more than 3 sides have diagonals.

A **diagonal** of a polygon is a line segment that connects two vertices. A diagonal is never a side of a polygon.

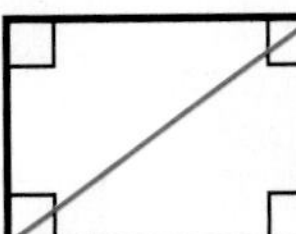

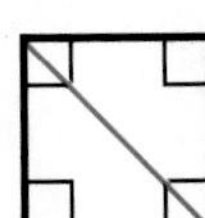

Go On

## Guided Practice

**Name each polygon. If the polygon is a quadrilateral, write all names that apply.**

1. 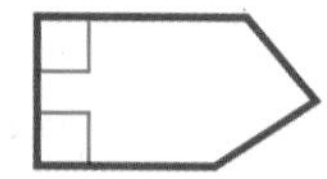

2. 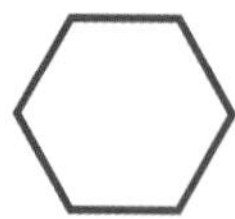

3. 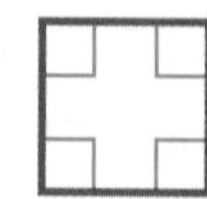

### Ask Yourself

- How many sides does the polygon have?
- If there are 4 sides, are there any parallel sides or right angles?

**Explain Your Thinking** ▶ Why is a circle not a polygon?

## Practice and Problem Solving

**Name each polygon. If the polygon is a quadrilateral, write all names that apply.**

4. 

5. 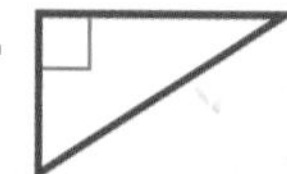

6. 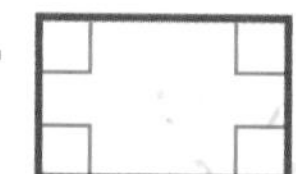

7. 

**Tell if each figure is a polygon or not. For a polygon, tell if it appears to be regular or irregular.**

8. 

9. 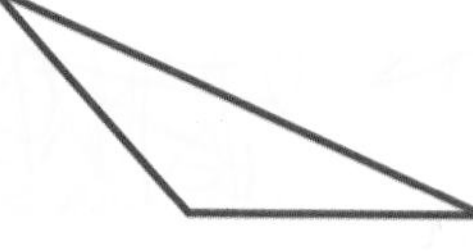

10. 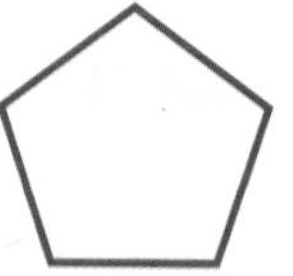

11. 

**Solve.**

12. **Write About It** Describe three different figures you see in the swing set on the right. Include the number of sides and angles.

13. **Analyze** I have an even number of sides. I have more sides than a pentagon, but fewer sides than an octagon. What kind of polygon am I?

Extra Practice See page 427, Set C.

Problem Solving

GPS

## Math Reasoning

### Measure Angles with Paper

STANDARD M4M2.a

**You can make a paper tool to measure different angles without a protractor.**

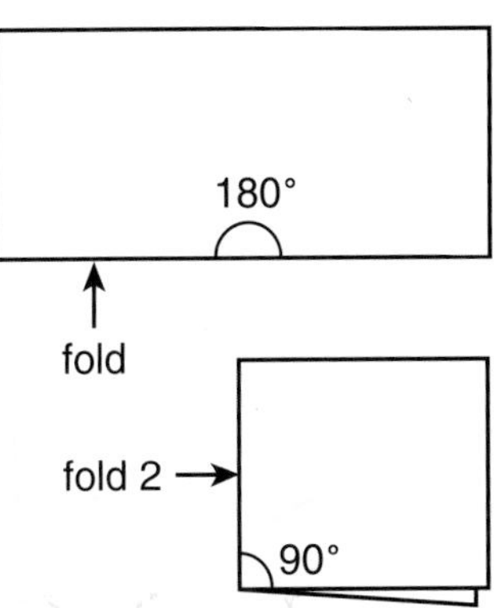


- Fold a piece of paper in half the long way. The fold is a 180° angle. Turn the paper so that the fold is facing you. Label the 180° angle.
- Fold the paper in half from left to right. The fold is a 90° angle. Label the 90° angle.
- Fold the two folded sides together. You have made a 45° angle. Label the 45° angle.

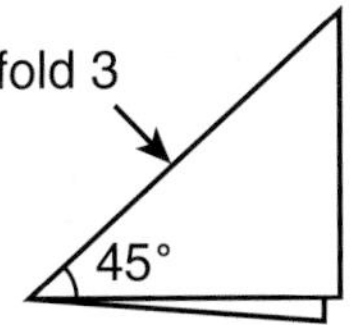


**You can use your paper tool to measure angles in your classroom. Find each of the 3 angles and write down where you found the angle.**

## Quick Check

Check your understanding of Lessons 1–4.

**Use the drawing on the right for Problems 1–2.** (Lesson 1)

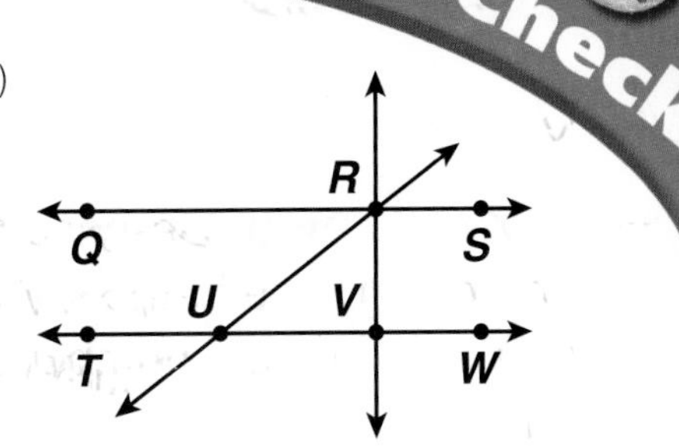


1. Name a pair of parallel lines.
2. Name a pair of intersecting lines that are not perpendicular.

**Classify each angle as *acute, obtuse, right,* or *straight.*** (Lessons 2, 3)

3.

4. 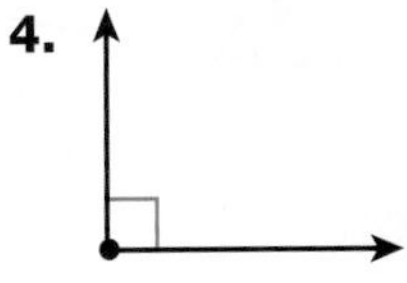

5. 

6. 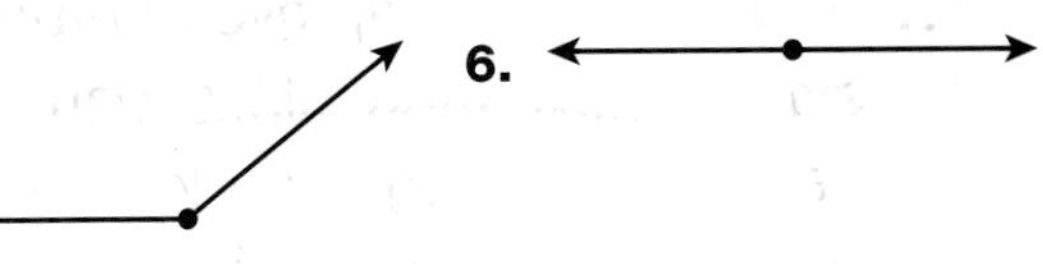

**Name each polygon.** (Lesson 4)

7. 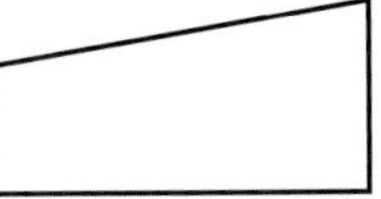

8. 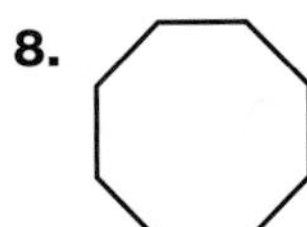

9. 

10. 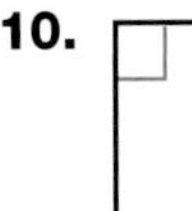 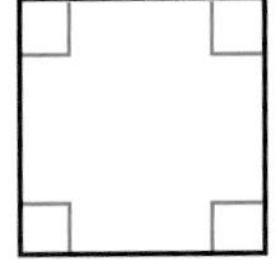

Lesson 5

# Classify Triangles

**Objective** Identify and classify triangles.

 **STANDARDS** M4G1.a, M4P2

**Vocabulary**

- equilateral triangle
- isosceles triangle
- scalene triangle
- right triangle
- obtuse triangle
- acute triangle

## Learn About It

Triangles are used to build many things, even jungle gyms! Triangles help make structures rigid and strong.

**You can classify triangles by the lengths of their sides.**

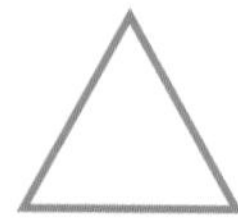

**Equilateral Triangle**
All sides are the same length.

**Isosceles Triangle**
At least two sides are the same length.

**Scalene Triangle**
No sides are the same length.

**You can classify triangles by the measures of their angles.**

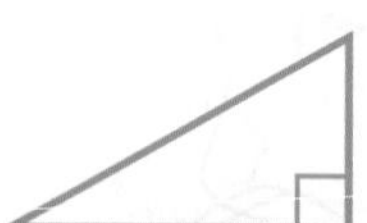

**Right Triangle**
One angle is a right angle.

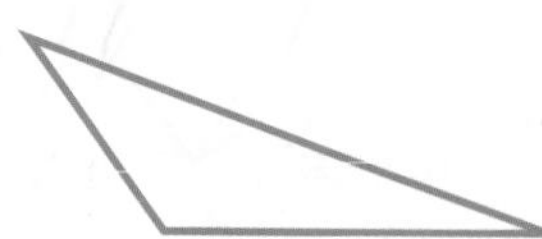

**Obtuse Triangle**
One angle is an obtuse angle.

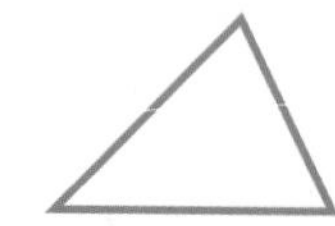

**Acute Triangle**
All angles are acute angles.

## Guided Practice

**Classify each triangle as *equilateral, isosceles,* or *scalene* and as *right, obtuse,* or *acute.***

**1.** 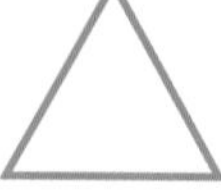

**2.** 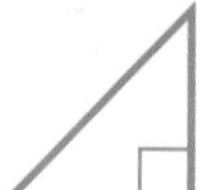

**3.** 

**Ask Yourself**

- Are any sides the same length?
- What kinds of angles does the triangle have?

**Explain Your Thinking** Can a triangle be both isosceles and obtuse? Explain why or why not.

## Practice and Problem Solving

**Classify each triangle as *equilateral, isosceles,* or *scalene* and as *right, obtuse,* or *acute.***

**4.** 

**5.** 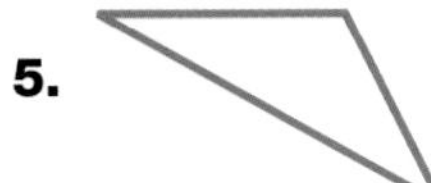

**6.** 

**7.** 

**8.** 

**9.** 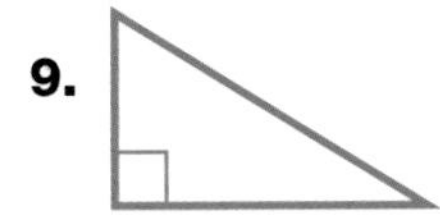

**10.** 

**11.** 

**Draw one example of each triangle described below.**

**12.** an equilateral triangle that is also an acute triangle

**13.** an isosceles triangle that is also a right triangle

**14.** a scalene triangle that is also an obtuse triangle

**Solve.**

**15.** **Analyze** A triangle measures 3 cm on one side. The other two sides are twice as long as the first side. Is the triangle equilateral, isosceles, or scalene? Explain your reasoning.

**16.** Look at the picture of the jungle gym at the right. Draw the triangles you see. Classify each triangle as *acute, obtuse,* or *right.*

## Sharpening Skills for CRCT

### Open Response

**Find the product.** (Ch. 6, Lesson 7)

**17.** 11,495 × 3

**18.** 24,459 × 3

**19.** 45,395 × 8

**20.** 78,231 × 6

### Multiple Choice

**21.** Which is NOT an acute triangle? (Ch. 16, Lesson 5)

A. 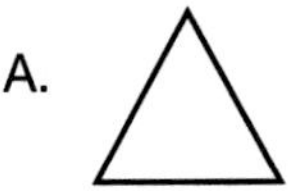

C. 

B. 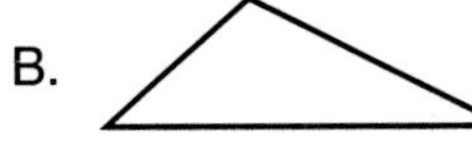

D. 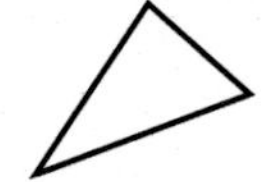

Extra Practice See page 427, Set D.

Lesson 6

**Audio Tutor 2/11** Listen and Understand

# Problem-Solving Strategy

## Find a Pattern

**Objective** Find patterns to solve problems.

**STANDARDS** M4A1.a, M4P1.b

**Problem** John is using tiles to design a mural for a playground. If he continues the pattern, which group of tiles should he use for the unfinished section?

**UNDERSTAND**

**This is what you know.**

- The tiles form a pattern.
- The colors are red, blue, green, and yellow.

**PLAN**

**You can find the pattern and continue it.**

**SOLVE**

**Find a pattern.**

- Look for a color pattern in the columns from top to bottom. You see a column of red, green, red beside a column of blue, yellow, blue, yellow. This pattern repeats.
- Then look at the diagonal rows. What pattern do you see?

Choose the group of tiles that completes the pattern of the columns and the pattern of the diagonals.

**a.** 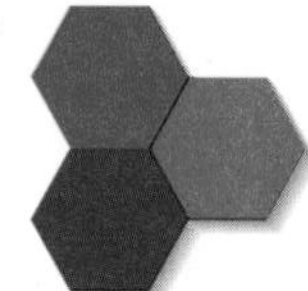 **b.**  **c.**  **d.** 

**Solution:** Choice **c** completes the pattern.

**LOOK BACK**

**Why would the other choices not complete the pattern?**

## Guided Practice

**Use the Ask Yourself questions to help you solve each problem.**

### Ask Yourself

UNDERSTAND **What facts do I know?**

PLAN **Can I find the pattern?**

SOLVE **Can I describe how the pattern repeats or changes?**

LOOK BACK **Did I check that my answer completes the pattern?**

1. Describe the pattern. What figures will complete the pattern?

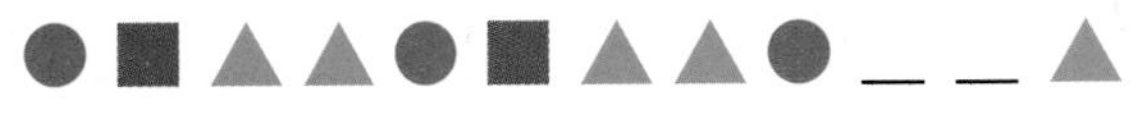

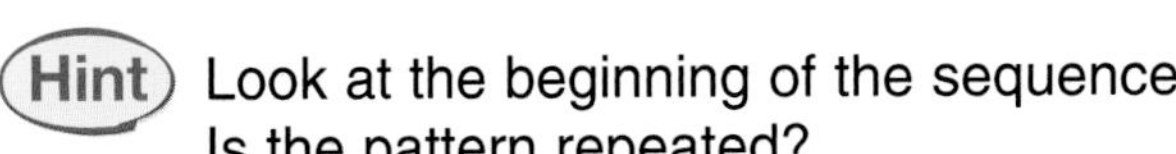

Hint Look at the beginning of the sequence. Is the pattern repeated?

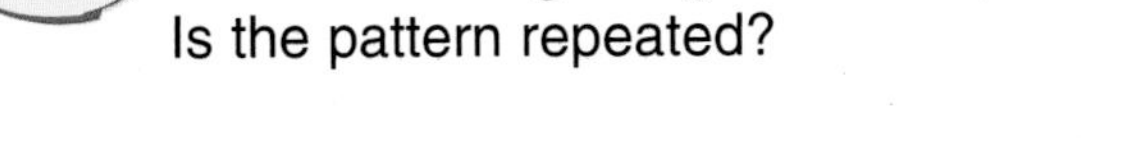

2. Which piece completes the pattern?

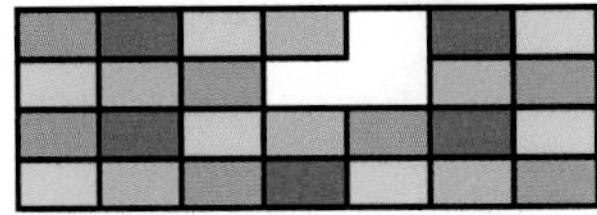

a.  b.  c.  d. 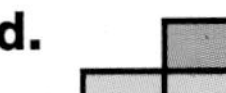

## Independent Practice

**Find the pattern to solve each problem.**

3. Nia makes the design on the right. Describe the pattern. What figures will complete the pattern?

4. **Represent** A border has a repeating design that shows a triangle, a circle, and a pentagon in a row. The triangle is just before the pentagon. The circle is first. Draw the first eight figures in the design.

5. The pattern on the right can also be shown as 1, 3, 6, 10. What would be the next two figures and numbers in the pattern?

6. **Analyze** Vincent made a design in which 3 out of every 7 quadrilaterals were green. Vincent colored 56 quadrilaterals. How many quadrilaterals did Vincent color green?

Go On

# Mixed Problem Solving

**Solve. Show your work. Tell what strategy you used.**

7. **Money** Ms. Flores counted 13 bills and found they totaled $110. She had only $5 and $10 bills. How many of each kind of bill did she have?

8. Antoine created a design on the computer. He printed the design, but two figures did not print. What are the missing figures?

9. A fruit stand sells different sizes of fruit baskets. Each piece of fruit costs $3, and the basket costs $11. What is the price of a fruit basket with 6 pieces of fruit?

**You Choose**

**Strategy**
- Find a Pattern
- Guess and Check
- Make an Organized List
- Write an Equation

**Computation Method**
- Mental Math
- Estimation
- Paper and Pencil
- Calculator

## Data **Evan and Ariana used shapes to make puppets. Use the double bar graph for Problems 10–14.**

10. How many shapes did Evan use?

11. Who used more shapes, Evan or Ariana?

12. How many more triangles would Evan have to use in order to use the same number as Ariana?

13. Ariana used equal numbers of which two shapes?

14. **Explain** Since all squares are rectangles, can you use the graph to find how many squares Evan used? Explain your thinking.

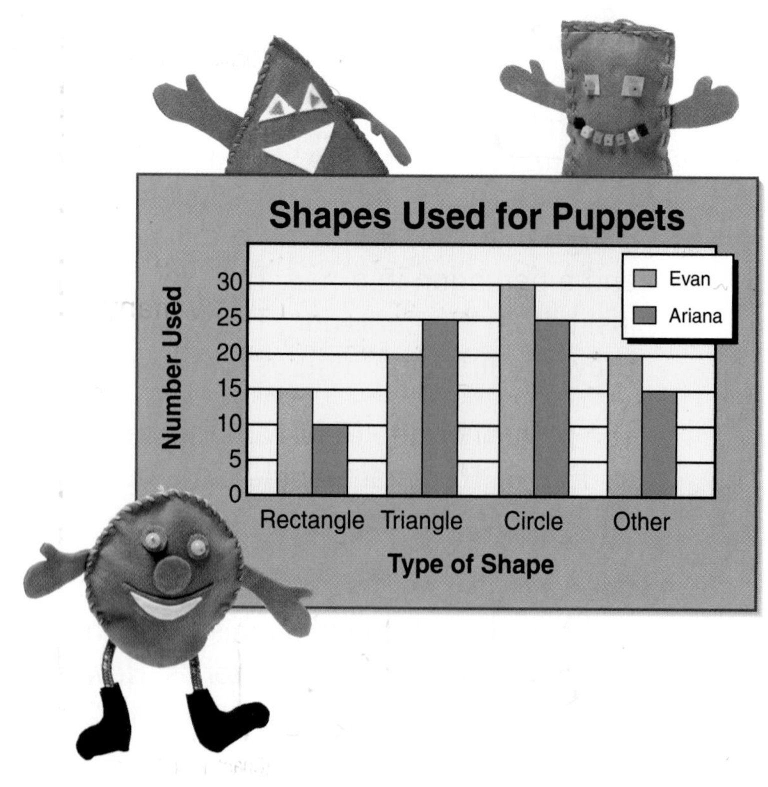

# Problem Solving on CRCT

**Choose the letter of the correct answer.**

1. A library has 42 shelves of books with about 25 books on each shelf. About how many books are there?

   A. about 100

   B. about 200

   C. about 1,000

   D. about 2,000

   (Chapter 7, Lesson 5)

2. The fourth-grade classes at Hilltop School have 23, 26, 29, and 22 students. What is the average number of students in a fourth-grade class?

   A. 20

   B. 24

   C. 25

   D. 29

   (Chapter 10, Lesson 5)

**Open Response**

**Solve each problem.**

3. This stem-and-leaf plot shows the ages of people at a picnic. How many people are at the picnic? Explain.

**Ages of People at a Picnic**

| Stem | Leaves |
|---|---|
| 3 | 0 1 4 5 |
| 4 | 2 4 6 7 9 |
| 5 | 0 2 |
| 6 | 0 1 |

(Chapter 14, Lesson 5)

4. Dale's family took a trip. They spent the following amounts on T-shirts.

   $10, $14, $10, $16, $50

   **Explain** Which best describes the cost of a T-shirt: the mean, the median, the mode, or the range? Why?

   (Chapter 14, Lesson 3)

5. The graph shows the distance the Dunn family drove on one day of their vacation.

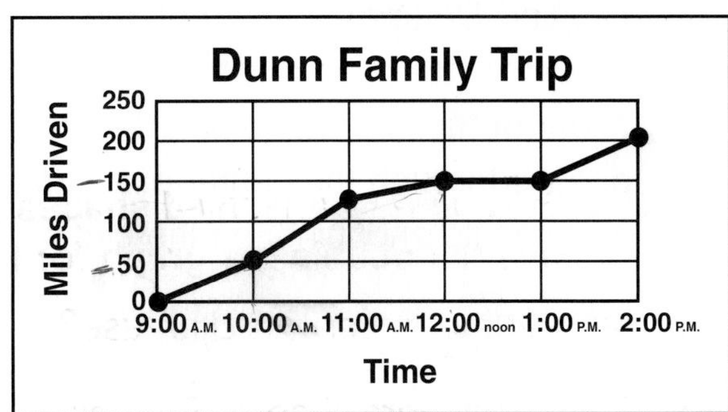


   a. What kind of graph is this? Why was it used to display this data?

   b. How many miles did the family drive between 10:00 A.M. and 12:00?

   c. During what hour did the family travel the greatest distance? About how far did they travel? Explain.

   d. What happened between 12:00 noon and 1:00 P.M.?

   (Chapter 15, Lesson 3)

**Education Place**

See **eduplace.com/map** for more Test-Taking Tips.

Lesson 7

Audio Tutor 2/12 Listen and Understand

# Circles

**Objective** Identify parts of a circle.

**STANDARDS** M4M2.b, Maintains M3G1.d, M4P2

## Vocabulary

- **circle**
- **center**
- **radius (radii)**
- **diameter**
- **chord**

## Learn About It

A **circle** is made up of all points in a plane that are the same distance from a given point in that plane, called the center. Point *D* is the **center** of the circle below.

### Circles

A **radius** is any line segment that joins a point on the circle to the center of the circle.

$\overline{DE}$ or $\overline{ED}$ is a radius of this circle.
$\overline{DG}$ and $\overline{DF}$ are also radii of this circle.

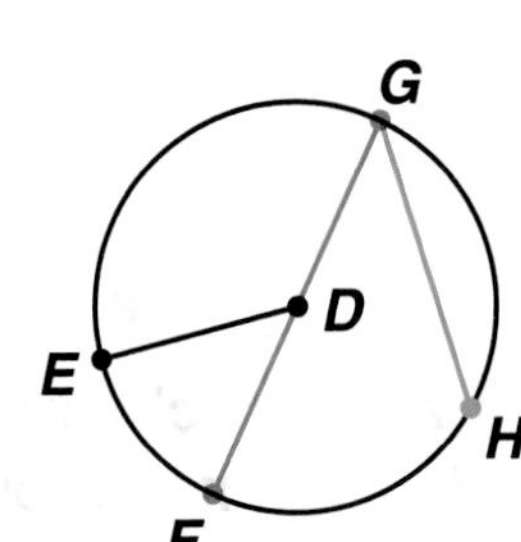


A **diameter** is any line segment that passes through the center of a circle and has its endpoints on the circle.

$\overline{GF}$ or $\overline{FG}$ is a diameter of this circle.

A **chord** is any line segment that has its endpoints on the circle. It does not need to pass through the center.

$\overline{GH}$ or $\overline{HG}$ is a chord of this circle.
The diameter, $\overline{GF}$, is also a chord.

▶ The number of degrees (°) in a full circle is 360. You can turn an object around the point that is the center of a circle.

Each turn is measured from the start position. The start position is at the mark for 0°.

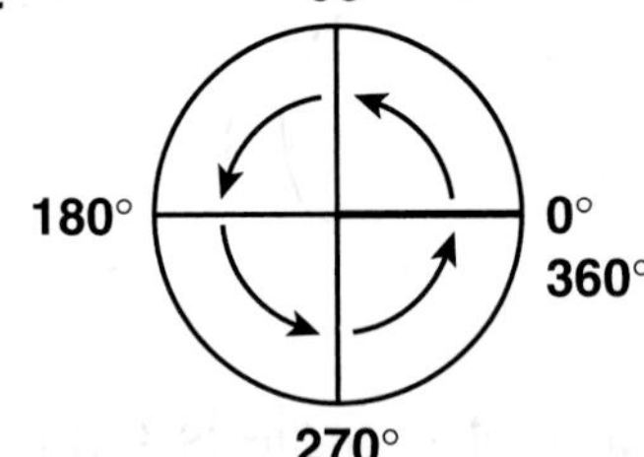


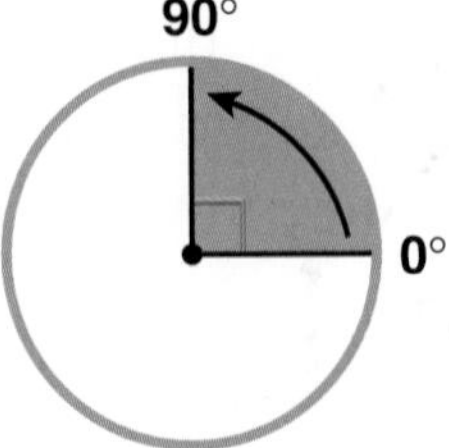


A quarter turn is 90°.

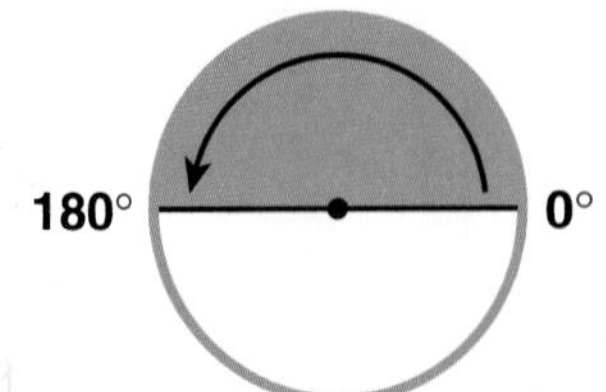


A half turn is 180°.

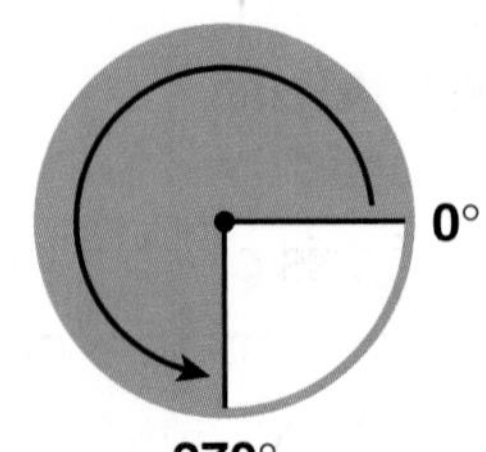


A three-quarter turn is 270°.

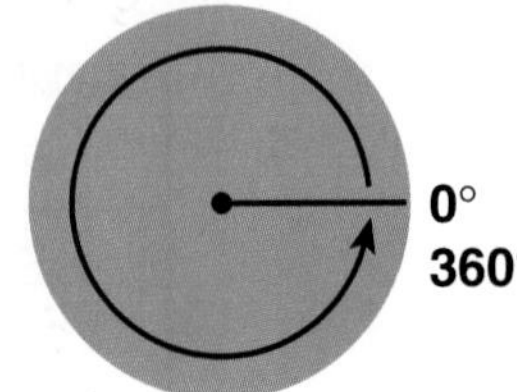


A full turn is 360°.

## Guided Practice

**Name the parts of the circle. Write *center, radius, diameter,* or *chord.***

1. $G$
2. $\overline{FH}$
3. $\overline{DE}$
4. $\overline{FG}$

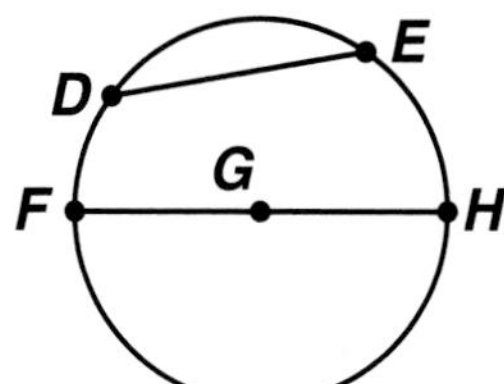


**Ask Yourself**

- Does the line segment connect a point on the circle to the center?
- Does the line segment pass through the center of the circle?

**Explain Your Thinking** ▶ How does the length of a diameter of a circle compare to the length of its radius?

## Practice and Problem Solving

**Name the part of each circle that is shown in red. Write *center, radius, diameter,* or *chord.***

5. 
6. 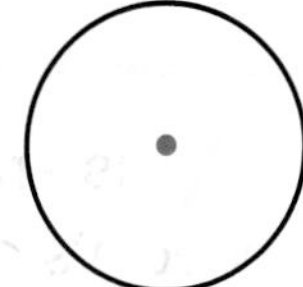
7. 
8. 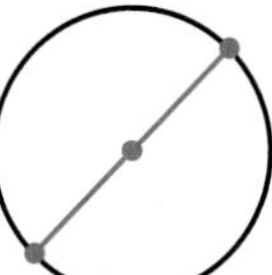

**Solve.**

9. Look at the circles below. Describe the pattern. Then draw the missing figures in the pattern.

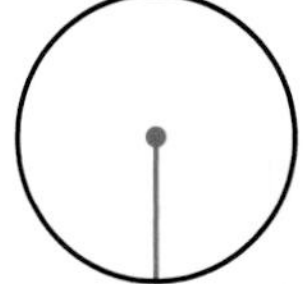 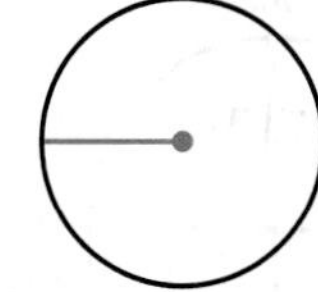 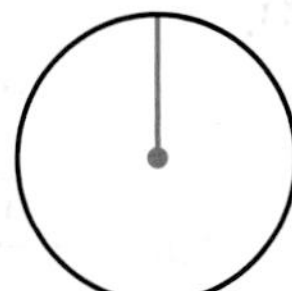 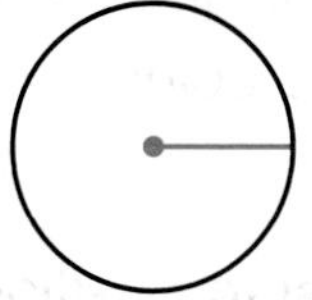 ________ ________  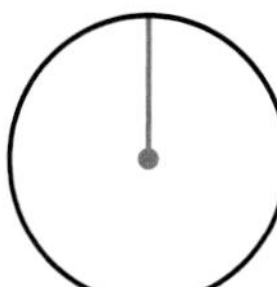

10. One radius of a circle is 4 meters long. How long would a different radius of the same circle be? Why?

11. If the minute hand of this clock moves from 12 to 6, will it have made a quarter turn, a half turn, or a three-quarter turn? What time will it be when the minute hand has made a full turn?

Go On

**Marvin and Lisa are riding the wheel on the right. Use the picture for Problems 12–14.**

12. The arrow shows the direction the wheel is turning. Which best describes the turn needed to move Marvin to Lisa's location—half turn, quarter turn, or full turn?

13. From the starting position, which best describes the turn needed to move Lisa to Marvin's position—quarter turn, half turn, or three-quarter turn?

14. How many degrees has the wheel turned each time Lisa arrives back in the same place she started?

**For Exercises 15–17, trace around a circular object. Draw the part or parts of the circle described.**

15. two radii that do not form a diameter

16. a chord that is not a diameter

17. a horizontal diameter and a vertical diameter

## Data Use the circle graph for Problems 18–22.

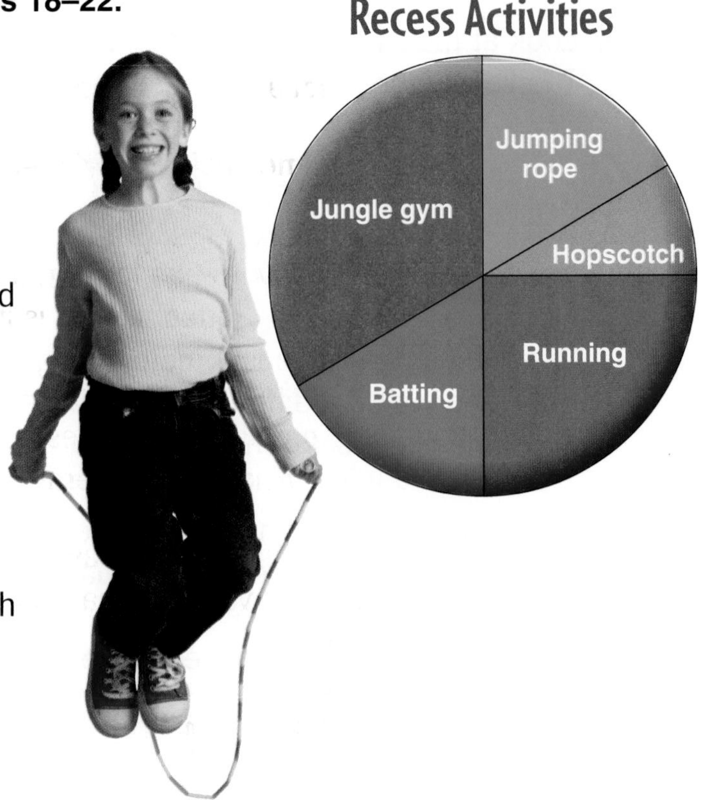


18. In which activity did the greatest number of students participate?

19. Which activity did about $\frac{1}{4}$ of the students do?

20. **Mental Math** If 50 fourth-graders had recess, about how many of them did either jungle gym or jumping rope?

21. **Analyze** Which two activities had about the same number of students participating?

22. **Create and Solve** Make a circle graph and write two questions about it. Give your questions to a classmate to solve.



Extra Practice See page 427, Set E.

## Sharpening Skills for CRCT

**Open Response**

**Choose a graph to display the data. Write *bar graph*, *circle graph*, *line graph*, or *pictograph*. Explain your choice.**
(Ch. 15, Lesson 5)

**23.** wind speeds during a storm

**24.** the number of goals scored by 4 hockey players during one month

**25.** the results of a survey that asked students to choose their favorite pet

**26.** A circle has a diameter labeled $\overline{FG}$. Could $F$ be the center of the circle? Explain your thinking.
(Ch. 16, Lesson 7)

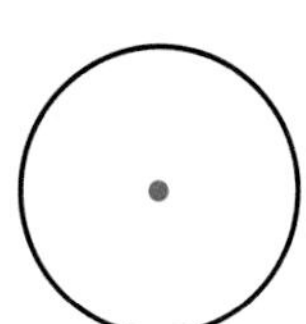

## Problem Solving

# Logical Reasoning
## Quadrilaterals

STANDARDS M4G1.d

rectangle square trapezoid parallelogram rhombus

**Use the models to name each quadrilateral described below.**

1. This quadrilateral always has four right angles and four equal sides. What quadrilateral is it?
2. This quadrilateral always has opposite sides that are parallel and four equal sides. It does not have to have right angles. What quadrilateral is it?
3. This quadrilateral has only one pair of parallel sides. It does not have to have any equal sides. Which quadrilateral is it?

WEEKLY WR READER eduplace.com/map

# Chapter Review/Test

Study Guide pages SG33–35, SG48

## VOCABULARY

**Choose the best word to complete each sentence.**

1. A line segment that joins a point on a circle to the center of the circle is a ____.
2. Two lines that intersect to form right angles are ____.
3. A quadrilateral that has only one pair of parallel sides is a ____.

**Vocabulary**
- radius
- triangle
- trapezoid
- perpendicular

## CONCEPTS AND SKILLS

**Use words and symbols to name each figure.** (Lessons 1–2, pp. 404–409)

4. 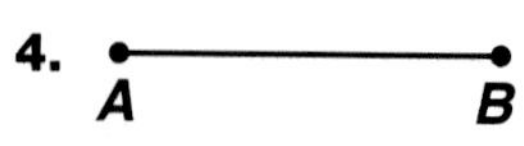


5. 

6. 

7. • G

**Classify each angle as *acute, straight, obtuse,* or *right.*** (Lessons 2–3, pp. 408–411)

8. 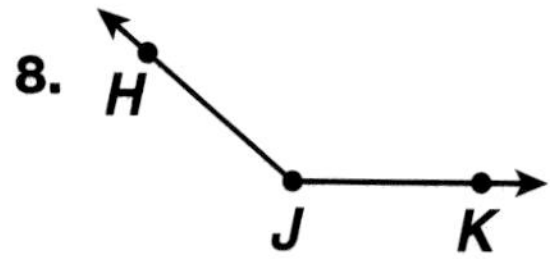


9. 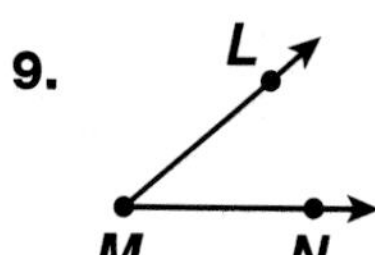


10. 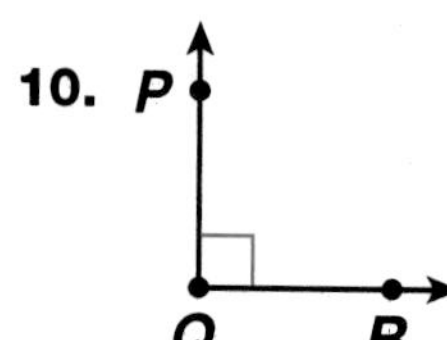


11. S T U

**Name each polygon. Write all the names that apply.** (Lessons 4–5, pp. 412–417)

12.
13.
14.
15.

**Name the part of each circle that is shown in red.** (Lesson 7, pp. 422–424)

16.
17. 
18. 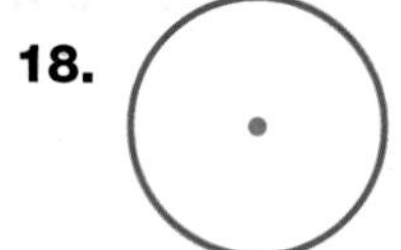
19. 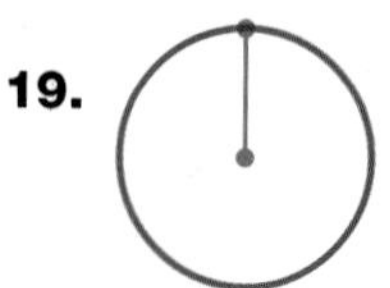

## PROBLEM SOLVING

**Solve.** (Lesson 6, pp. 418–420)

20. Look at the design. If the pattern continues, what kind of polygon should the fifteenth figure be?

**Write About It**

**Show You Understand**

How are an equilateral triangle and an isosceles triangle alike? How are they different?

# Extra Practice

## Set A (Lesson 1, pp. 404–406)

**Use words and symbols to name each figure.**

**1.** 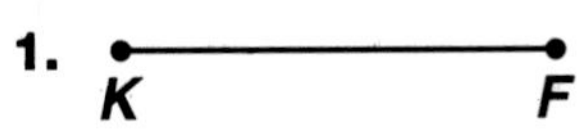


**2.** • *M*

**3.** 

**4.** • *X* • *Y*

**Write *parallel, intersecting,* or *perpendicular*.**

**5.** 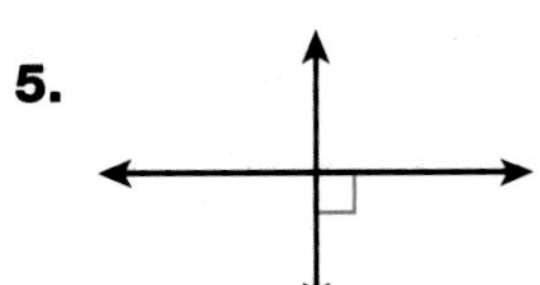

**6.** 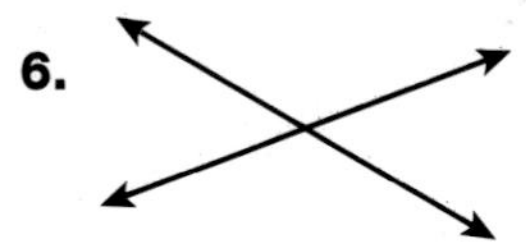

**7.** 

**8.** 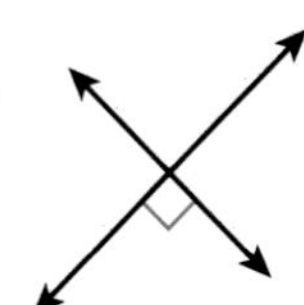

## Set B (Lesson 2, pp. 408–409)

**Classify each angle as *acute, obtuse, right,* or *straight*.**

**1.** 

**2.** 

**3.** 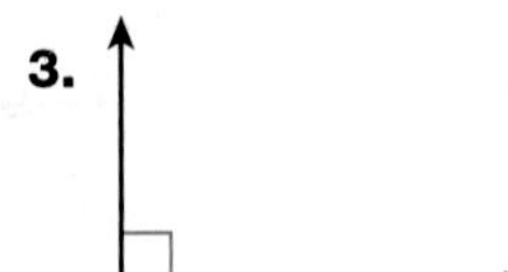

**4.** 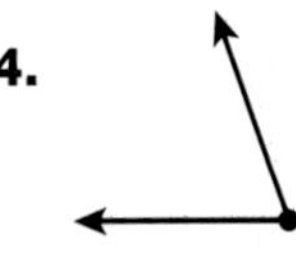

## Set C (Lesson 4, pp. 412–414)

**Name each polygon. Write all names that apply.**

**1.** 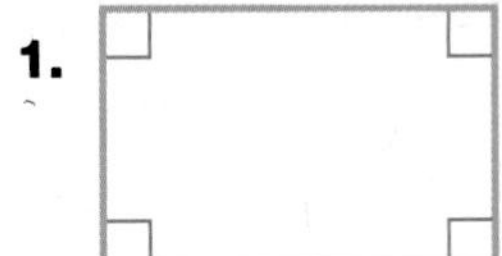

**2.** 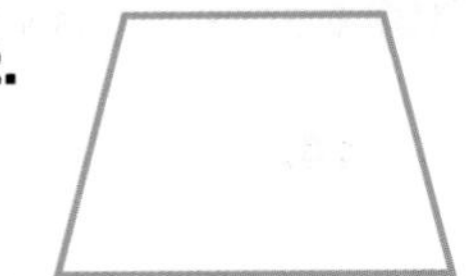

**3.** 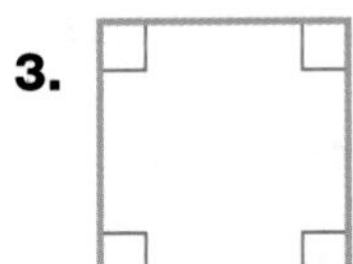

**4.** 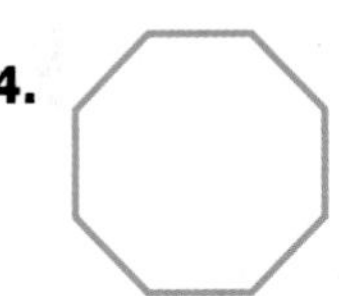

## Set D (Lesson 5, pp. 416–417)

**Classify each triangle as *equilateral, isosceles,* or *scalene*.**

**1.** 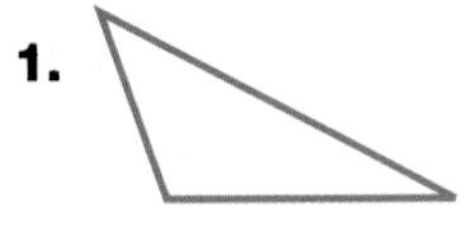

**2.** 

**3.** 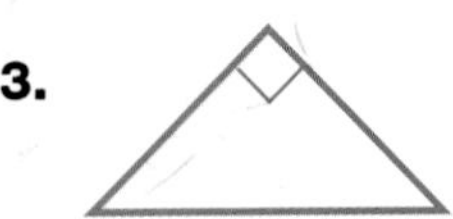

**4.** 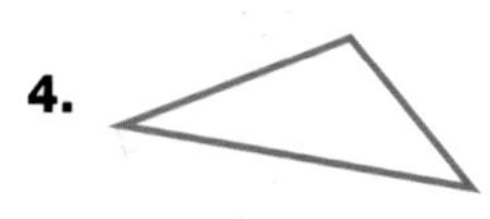

**5.** 

## Set E (Lesson 7, pp. 422–424)

**Name the part of each circle that is shown in red.**

**1.** 

**2.** 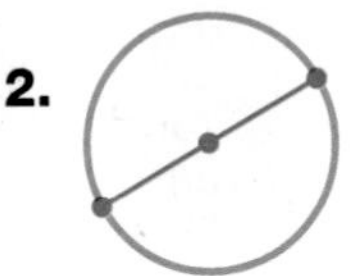

**3.** 

**4.** 

**5.** 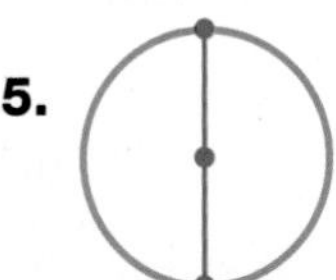

# CHAPTER 17 Congruence, Symmetry, and Transformations

## INVESTIGATION

### Using Data

A ladybug is a small oval-shaped bug with spots on its wings. You can identify the species of ladybug by its pattern of spots. Look at the 6 different species of ladybugs at the right. Describe the pattern of spots shown on each ladybug.

# Use What You Know

**Use this page to review and remember what you need to know for this chapter.**

## VOCABULARY

**Choose the best term to complete each sentence.**

1. A location in space is called a ____.
2. A ____ goes on without end in both directions.
3. A ____ always has four sides of the same length.
4. A quadrilateral that has exactly one pair of parallel sides is a ____.

**Vocabulary**
- ray
- line
- point
- rhombus
- trapezoid

## CONCEPTS AND SKILLS

**Choose the figure that appears to be the same size and shape as the first figure. Write *a*, *b*, or *c*.**

5. 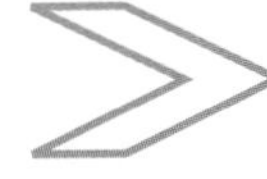

a. 
b. 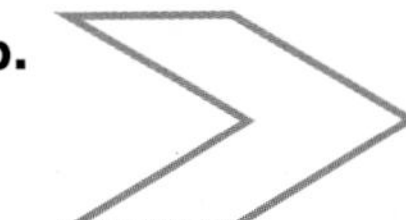
c. 

6. 

a. 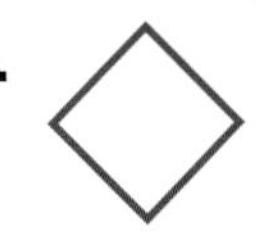
b. 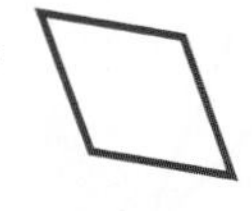
c. 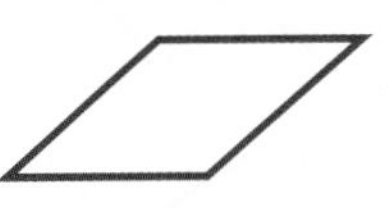

**Does the dashed line divide the figure into two parts that match exactly? Write *yes* or *no*.**

7. 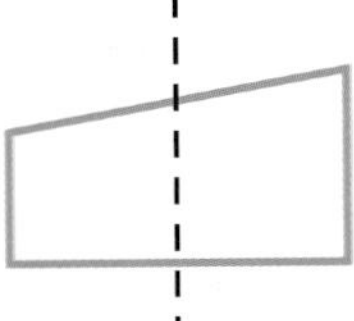
8. 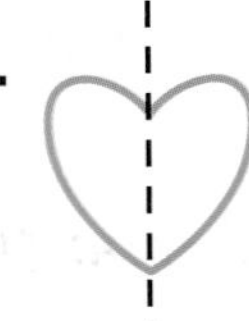
9. 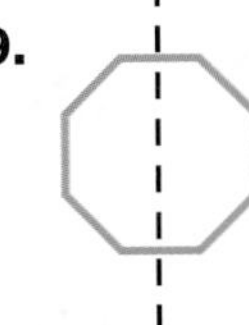

**Write About It**

10. How are a square, rhombus, trapezoid, and parallelogram the same? How are they different?

Facts Practice, See Page 666.

Audio Tutor 2/13 Listen and Understand

# Congruent Figures

**Objective** Learn about figures that have the same size and shape.

**STANDARDS** Prepares for M5G1, M4P2

**Vocabulary**
**congruent**

**Materials**
grid paper
scissors

## Learn About It

Sari is designing a puzzle on her computer. Look at the puzzle and the puzzle piece. You can tell that the piece belongs in the puzzle because it is the same size and shape as the empty space.

Plane figures that have the same size and shape are **congruent** figures.

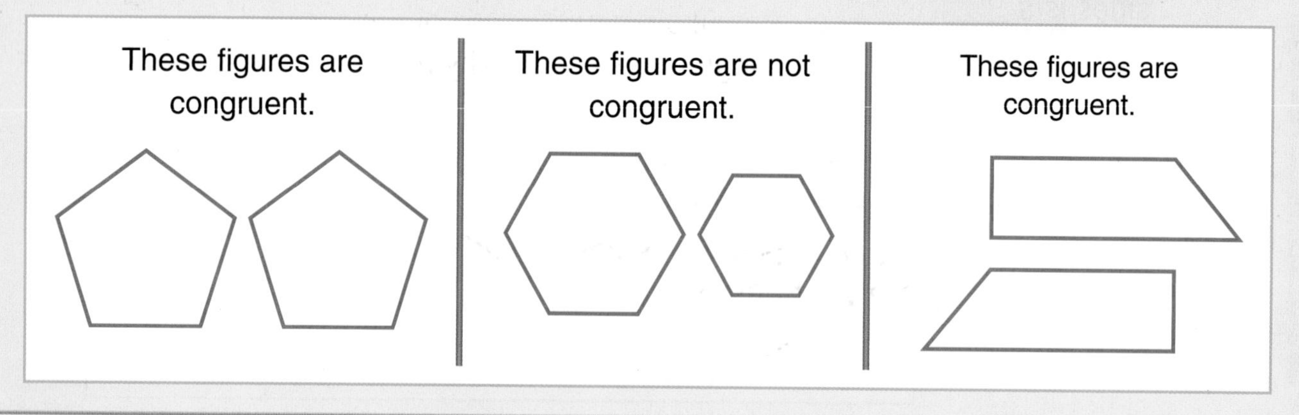


**Try this activity to explore congruence.**

**STEP 1** Copy Figures A, B, C, and D on grid paper. Cut out Figures B, C, and D. Look at the figures. Which figures appear to be congruent?

**STEP 2** Place each cut-out figure on top of Figure A, turning it to check for congruence. Which figure is congruent to A? How do you know?

**STEP 3** Draw another figure on grid paper. Cut it out. Trace it. Are these two new figures congruent? Explain.

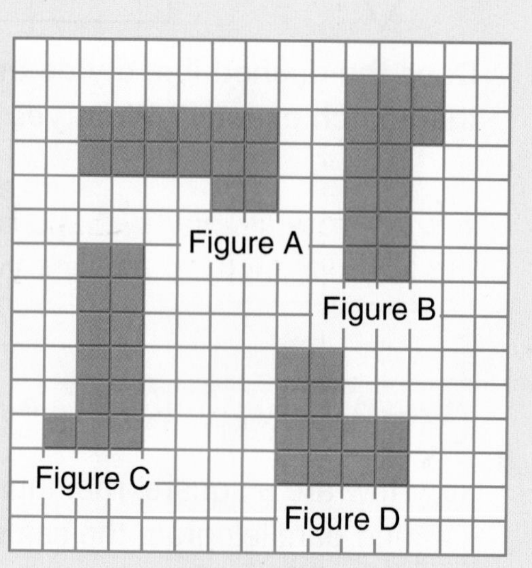

## Guided Practice

**Ask Yourself**

- Are the figures the same size?
- Are the figures the same shape?

**Do the figures in each pair appear to be congruent? Write *yes* or *no*.**

1. 

2. 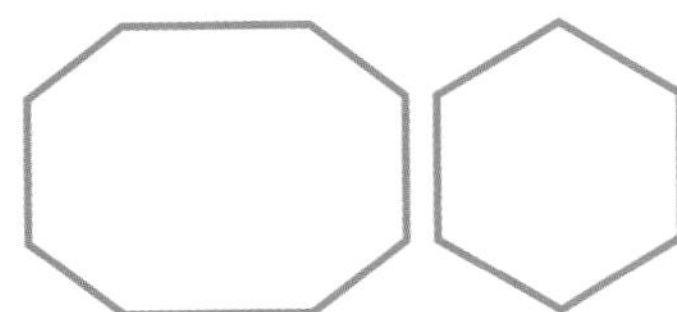

3. 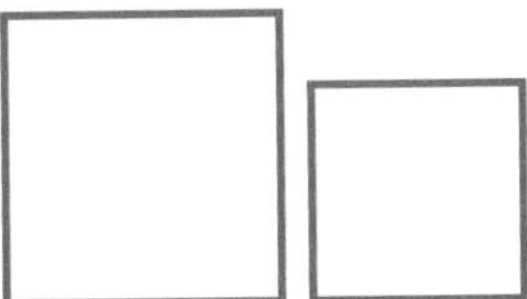

4. 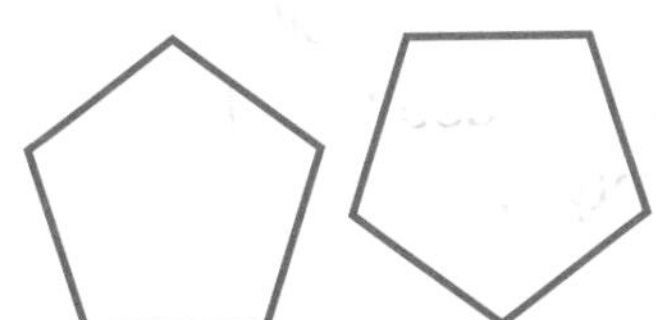

5. Draw a figure congruent to the figures in Exercise 4. Explain how you know it is congruent.

**Explain Your Thinking** ▶ Are all circles with radii of 4 inches congruent? Why or why not?

## Practice and Problem Solving

**Do the figures in each pair appear to be congruent? Write *yes* or *no*. Explain your answer.**

6. 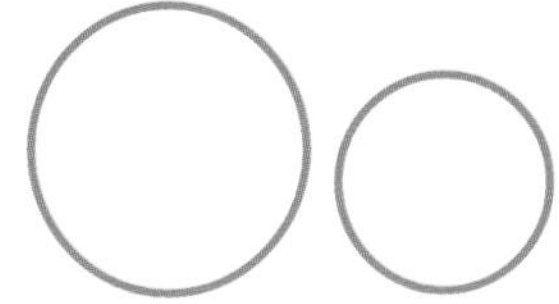

7. 

8. 

9. 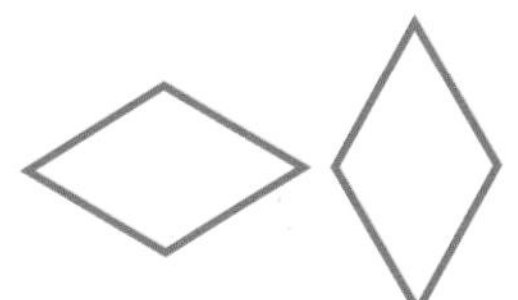

10. 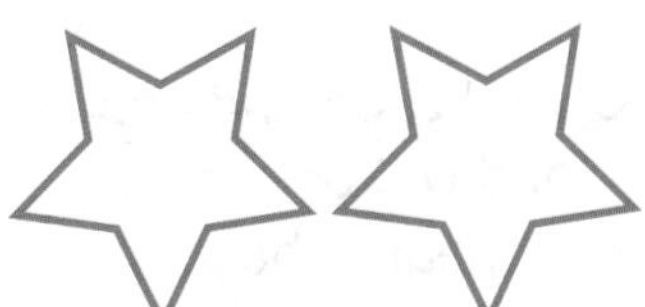

11. 

**Draw a figure like each shape below. Then draw a figure congruent to the one you drew.**

12. 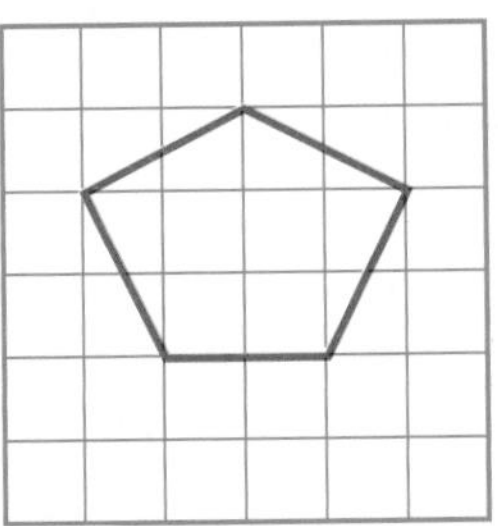

13. 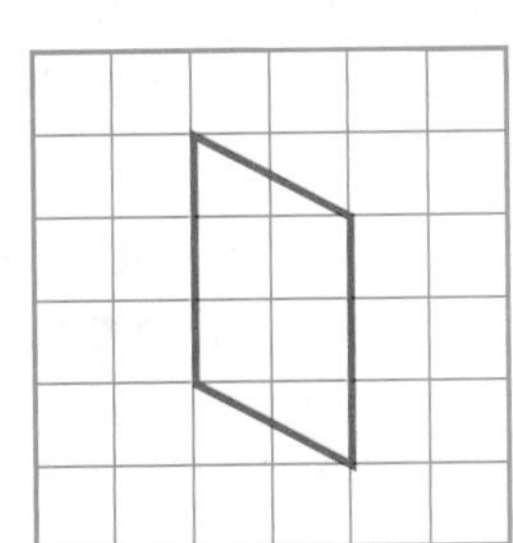

Go On

**Use the figures at the right for Problems 14–16.**

14. **Measurement** Parallelograms have 2 pairs of opposite sides that are congruent. Use a centimeter ruler. Which of the figures at the right are parallelograms?

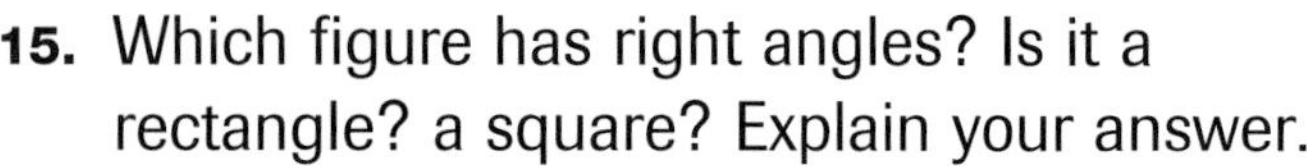

15. Which figure has right angles? Is it a rectangle? a square? Explain your answer.

16. **Analyze** Six congruent triangles form Figure D. What geometric figure is it? Draw a picture of another way to combine the triangles to make a different geometric figure.

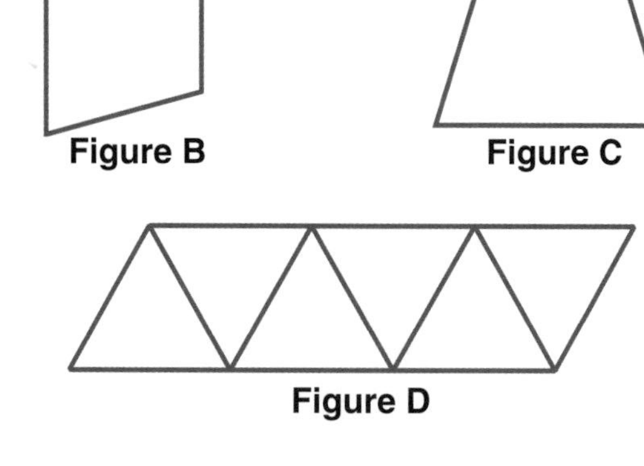


17. **Reasoning** Copy the Venn Diagram at the right. *Trapezoid* and *Square* are the terms that are missing from the diagram. Which term should go in the green section? Which should go in the pink section? Explain how you decided.

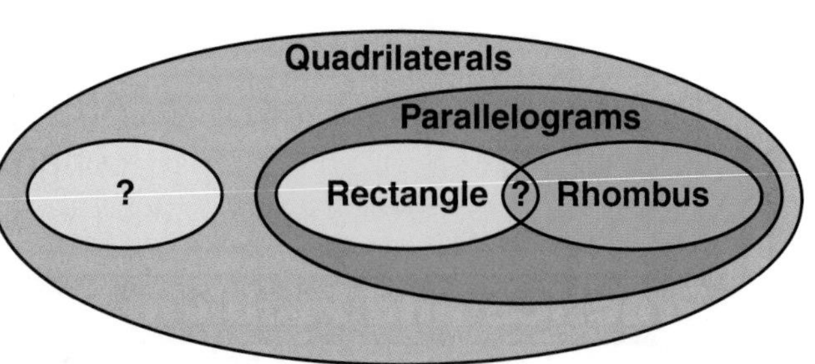


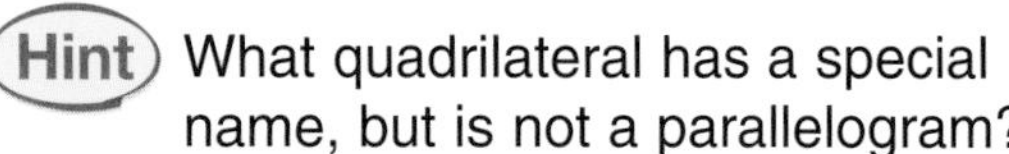

**Hint** What quadrilateral has a special name, but is not a parallelogram?

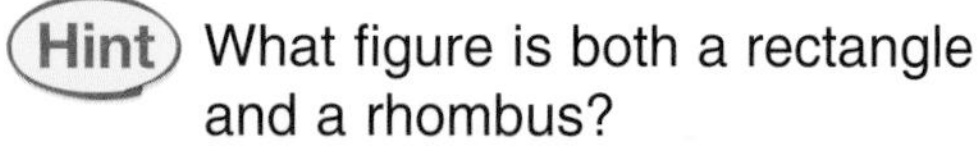

**Hint** What figure is both a rectangle and a rhombus?

## GPS Sharpening Skills for CRCT

### Open Response

**Identify each figure. Write all the names that apply.** (Ch. 16, Lessons 1, 4–5)

18. 

19. 

20. 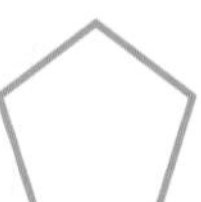

21. 

22. 

23. 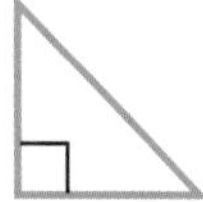

### Multiple Choice

24. Which figure appears to be congruent to this figure?
(Ch. 17, Lesson 1)

A.

C. 

B. 

D. 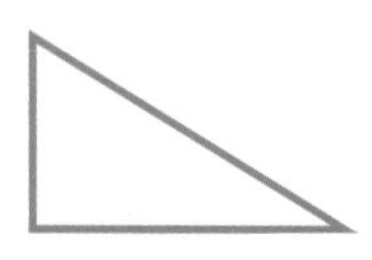



Extra Practice See page 449, Set A.

Problem Solving

GPS

# Math Reasoning

## Similar Figures

STANDARDS M4G1.d

You have learned that congruent figures are the same size and shape. **Similar** figures are the same shape, but not necessarily the same size.

**Vocabulary**

**similar**

**Look at the figures below.**

| Same shape<br>Not the same size | Not the same shape<br>Not the same size | Same shape<br>Same size |
|---|---|---|
|  | 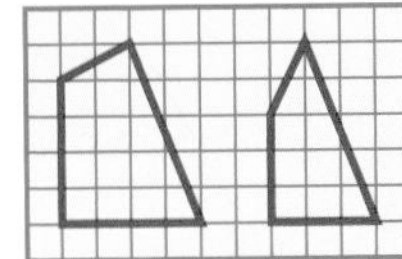 | 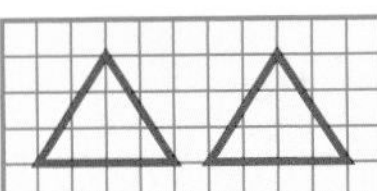 |
| Similar<br>Not Congruent | Not Similar<br>Not Congruent | Similar<br>Congruent |

**Tell if the figures in each pair are *congruent, similar,* or *neither.***

1. 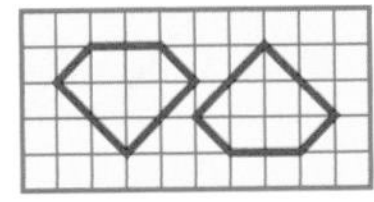

2. 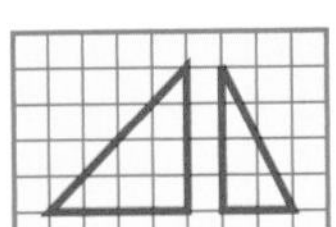

3. 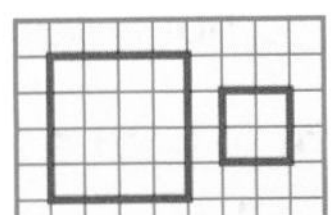

**Write *true* or *false* for each sentence. Then draw an example to support your answer.**

4. All squares are similar.
5. If shapes are similar, they must be congruent.
6. All hexagons are similar.
7. If shapes are congruent, they must be similar.
8. All circles are similar.
9. If shapes are *not* congruent, they cannot be similar.

 **Audio Tutor 2**/14 Listen and Understand

# Rotations, Reflections, and Translations

**Objective** Learn about rotations, reflections, and translations.

**STANDARDS** M4M2.b, M4P5

**Vocabulary**

- **rotation**
- **reflection**
- **translation**
- **transformations**

**Materials**
trapezoid pattern block or Learning Tool 25
grid paper

## Learn About It

Vincent is a graphic artist. He is designing a logo for his company's product. He moves the figure shown in different ways to create the logo.

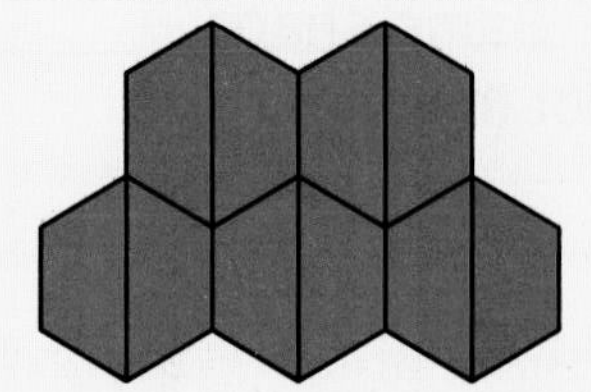

There are different ways to move a figure.

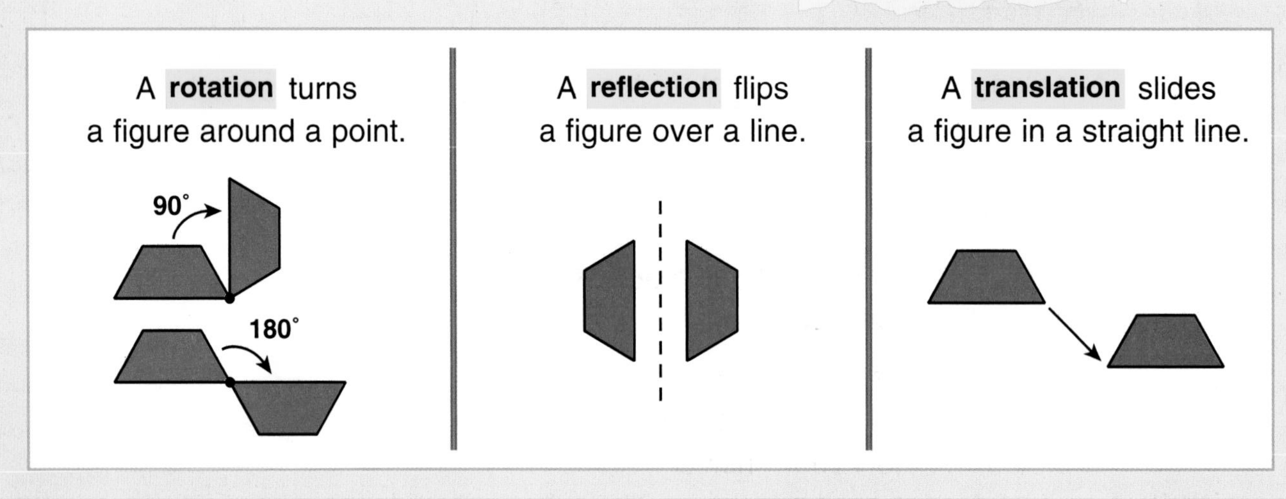


Rotations, reflections, and translations are called **transformations**.

**Try this activity to show rotations, reflections, and translations.**

**STEP 1** Trace the pattern block on grid paper. Rotate it around the point shown. Trace the resulting figure.

**STEP 2** Trace the block again. Flip it across the dotted line shown. Trace the resulting figure.

**STEP 3** Trace the block again. Slide it in a line as shown. Trace the resulting figure.

- Are the figures you drew congruent? Explain how you know.

## Guided Practice

**Tell how each figure was moved. Write *rotation, reflection,* or *translation*.**

**1.** 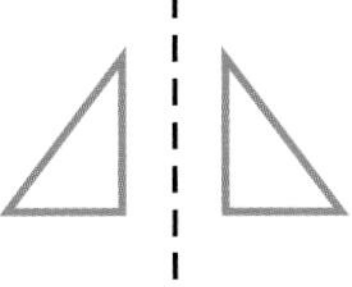

**2.** 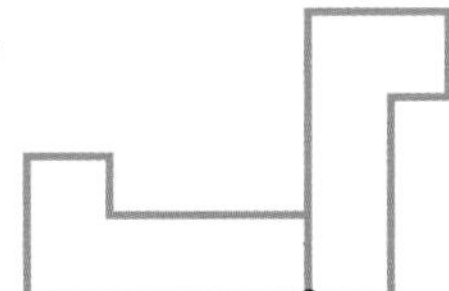

### Ask Yourself

- Was the figure turned around a point?
- Was the figure flipped over a line?
- Was the figure slid along a straight line?

**Explain Your Thinking** ▶ Look at the figures in Exercise 2. Are they congruent? How can you use transformations to find out?

## Practice and Problem Solving

**Tell how each figure was moved. Write *rotation*, *reflection*, or *translation*.**

**3.** 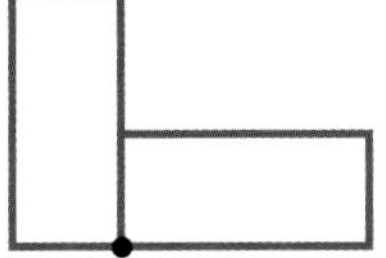

**4.** 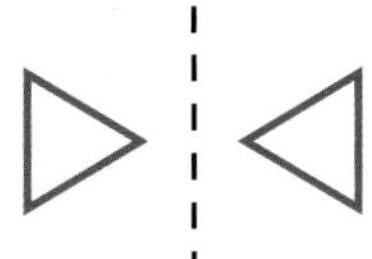

**5.** 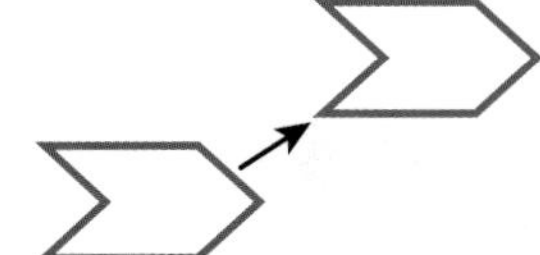

**Copy Figure A on grid paper and cut it out. Use the cut-out figure for Problems 6–7.**

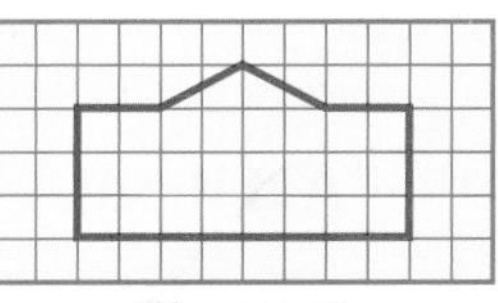

Figure A

**6.** **Represent** Vincent rotated Figure A 90° to the right. What does the figure look like now? Draw a picture to show your answer.

**7.** **Predict** If you flip Figure A, what will it look like? Draw the resulting figure. Is this the only answer? Explain.

**8.** Vincent is designing another logo. He started with Figure B. How did he move the figure to make Figure C? Explain your answer.

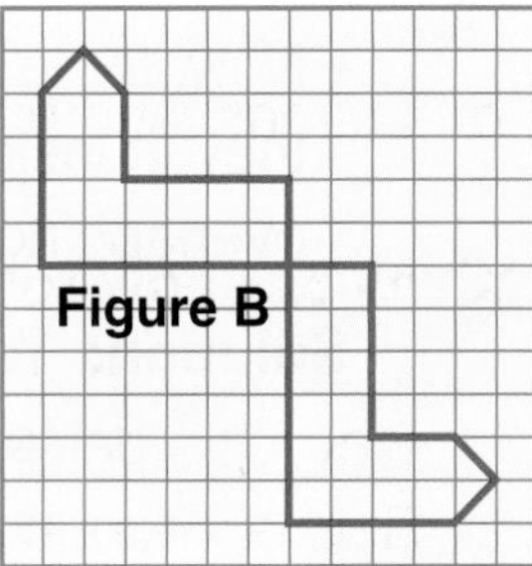


Figure C

## GPS Sharpening Skills for CRCT

**Open Response**

**Solve each equation.** (Ch. 5, Lesson 4)

**9.** $12 = n + 4$

**10.** $16 - n = 9$

**11.** $40n = 120$

**12.** $n \div 5 = 27$

**13.** Suppose the letter P was rotated 180° to the left. What would it look like? Draw a picture to show your answer. (Ch. 17, Lesson 2)

Extra Practice See page 449, Set B.

Lesson 3

# Problem-Solving Strategy

## Act It Out

**Objective** Learn how to solve a problem by using a model to act it out.

 **STANDARDS** M4G1, M4P1.b

**Problem** Can these five figures be arranged to form a figure that is congruent to the large square at the right?

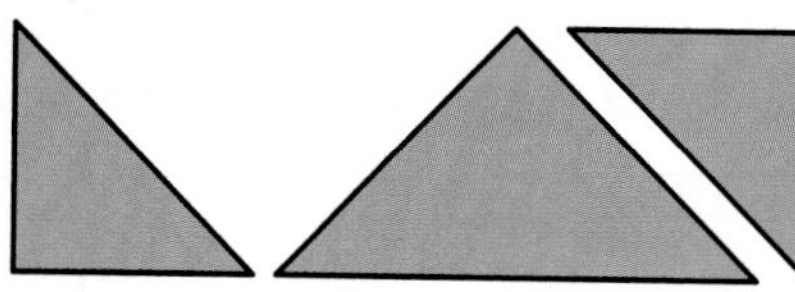

**UNDERSTAND**

**This is what you know.**

Congruent figures have the same size and shape.

**PLAN**

**You can make and use models to solve the problem.**

**SOLVE**

**Act it out.**

- To make models, trace the five figures and the large square on grid paper. Cut out the five figures.
- Now, try to arrange the five figures so that they fit inside the large square without overlapping.

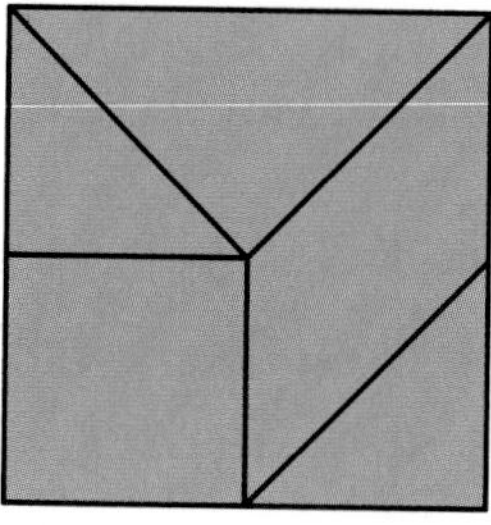

**Solution:** Yes, the five figures can be arranged to form a figure that is congruent to the large square.

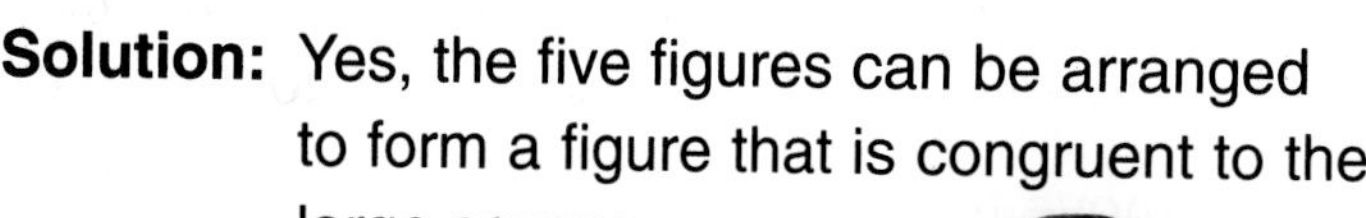

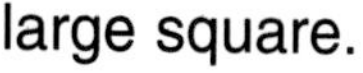

**LOOK BACK**

**Look back at the problem.**

How can you be sure your answer is correct?

## Guided Practice

**Use the figures on Page 436 to solve each problem. Make a drawing to show your answer.**

1. Arrange all the figures except the largest triangle to form a figure congruent to the parallelogram below.

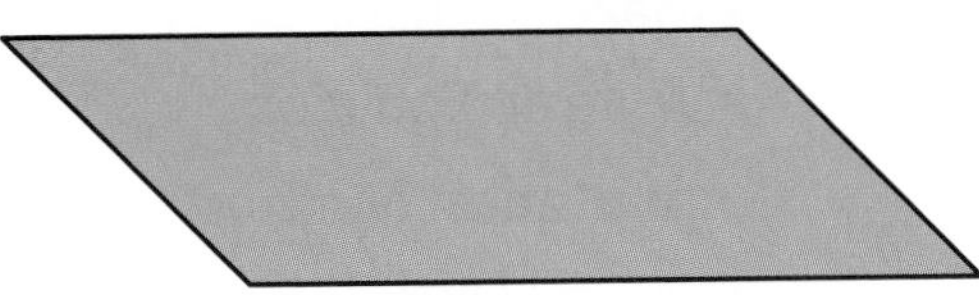

### Ask Yourself

**UNDERSTAND** **What facts do I know?**

**PLAN** **Can I make a model?**

**SOLVE**
- **Did I make and use the correct models?**
- **Does the figure I made match the figure in the problem exactly?**

**Did I check to see if my answer is correct?**

2. Arrange the largest triangle, the parallelogram, and one of the small triangles to form a figure congruent to the quadrilateral at the right.

Where must right angles be?

## Independent Practice

**Use the figures on Page 436 for Problems 3 and 4. Make a drawing to show your answer.**

3. Use four of the figures to form a figure congruent to the pentagon shown below.

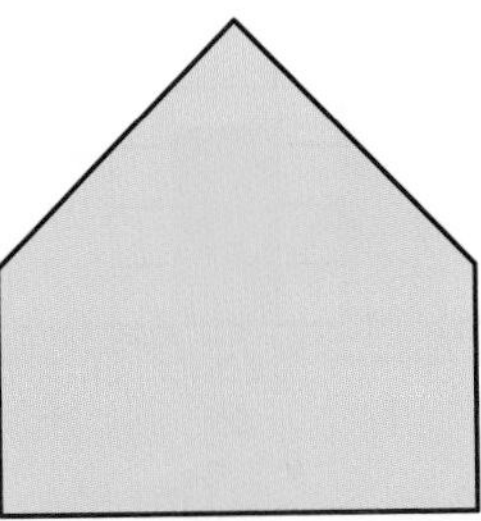

4. Use all five of the figures to form a figure congruent to the triangle shown below.

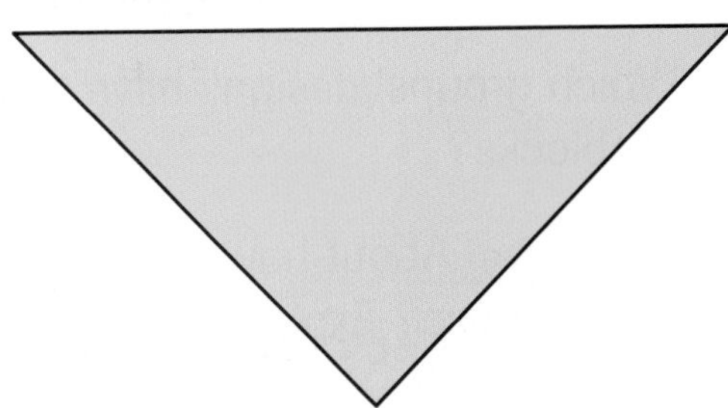

5. Can 12 toothpicks be used to form 4 congruent squares?

6. Can 9 toothpicks be used to form 4 congruent triangles?

# Mixed Problem Solving

**Solve. Show your work. Tell what strategy you used.**

7. A salad costs $1.50 more than a sandwich. Together the salad and sandwich cost $10.50. How much does each cost?

8. Guitar lessons start at 3:30 P.M. Each lesson is 45 minutes long. There are 6 lessons scheduled. At what time does the last lesson start?

9. Lorenzo draws 20 circles in a row. Each circle has a diameter of 25 mm. Each circle touches the next circle at only one point. What is the length of the row of circles?

10. Danny has two buckets. One holds 7 quarts and the other holds 4 quarts. How can Danny use the two buckets to measure 6 quarts?

**You Choose**

**Strategy**
- Act it Out
- Draw a picture
- Guess and Check
- Make a Table
- Write an Equation

**Computation Method**
- Mental Math
- Estimation
- Paper and Pencil
- Calculator

**Data** **Groups of students are using blocks to make designs in art class. The graph shows the number of blocks in four groups' designs. Use the bar graph for Problems 11–14.**

11. Which group used the greatest number of blocks? How many did they use?

12. **Explain** Did Group 3 or Group 4 use more blocks? Explain how you know.

13. Which groups' designs have more than 50 blocks?

14. **Estimate** About how many blocks did Group 4 use? Explain how you made your estimate.

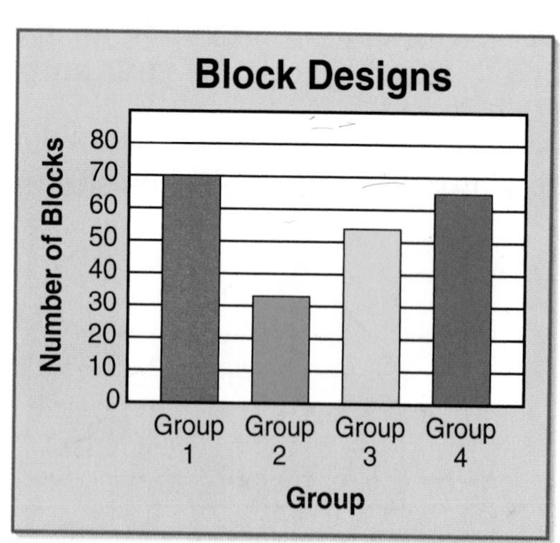


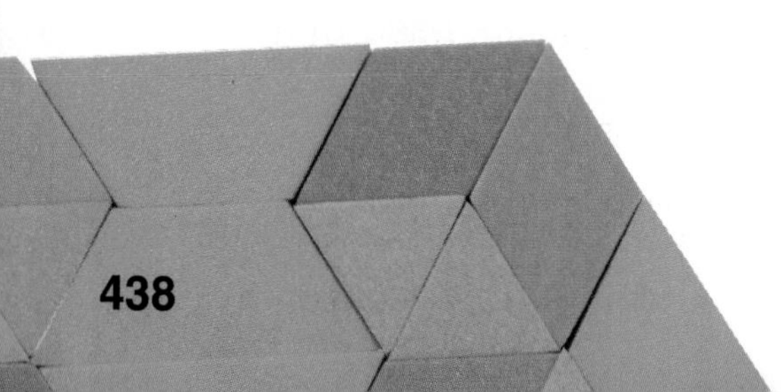

# Problem Solving on CRCT

Multiple Choice

**Choose the letter of the correct answer.**

1. Dan multiplied (5 × 2) × 3. Paul multiplied 5 × (2 × 3). What property says that they both got the same answer?

   A. Zero Property

   B. Commutative Property

   C. Property of One

   D. Associative Property

2. A glove costs $25.50. A bat costs $10.45. Jim buys 3 gloves and 4 bats for his club. What is the total cost?

   A. $35.95

   B. $118.30

   C. $133.35

   D. $147.45

Open Response

**Solve each problem.**

3. 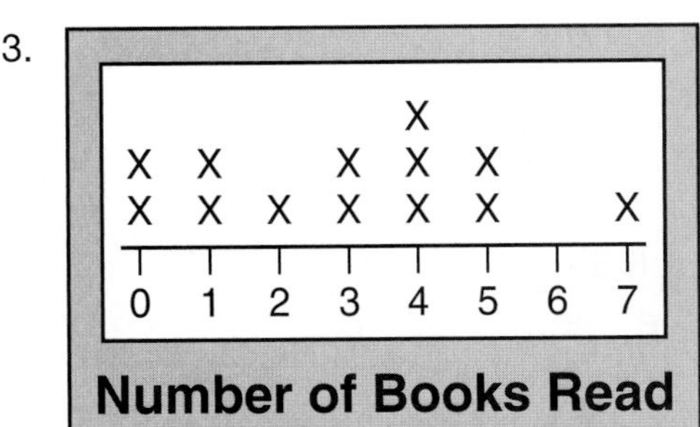


   **Explain** Which is greater, the median or the mean of the data? Explain.

4. At 10:00 A.M. the temperature was 3°C. By noon, it was 2 degrees higher. By 2:00 P.M., it was 3 degrees lower than it was at noon. What was the temperature at 2:00 P.M.?

   **Represent** Use a number line to solve the problem.

5. Toby and Anna work for a florist. Potted flowers are on sale for $4.89 each. A sign reads, "Buy 2 plants and get one free." The pictograph below shows the assortment of plants.

| Potted Summer Flowers | |
|---|---|
| Pansies | ❀❀❀❀❀❀ |
| Zinnias | ❀❀❀❀❀❀❀❀❀❀❀ |
| Daisies | ❀❀❀❀❀❀❀❀ |
| Petunias | ❀❀❀❀ |
| Snapdragons | ❀❀❀❀❀❀❀ |

❀ = 5 plants

   a. Toby and Anna displayed the plants in rows. Decide how many rows of plants they might set up.

   b. Mr. Perez wanted 5 potted daisies and 4 potted pansies. How many plants did he pay for? How much will he spend? Show your work.

   c. At the end of the sale, Toby and Anna collected almost $420. Make a diagram to show about how many plants were given away free.

**Education Place**

Check out **eduplace.com/map** for more Test-Taking Tips.

# Symmetry

**Objective** Learn how to identify figures that can be folded into matching parts.

**STANDARDS** M4M2.b, M4P2

**line symmetry**
**line of symmetry**
**rotational symmetry**

**Materials**
grid paper

## Learn About It

Amir's art class made photo albums. Amir is decorating the front of his album with geometric shapes. He folds the paper in half before he cuts to be sure the two parts of his shape match exactly.

A figure has **line symmetry** if it can be folded in half so the two parts match exactly. The fold line is a **line of symmetry**.

- Figures can have one or more than one line of symmetry.

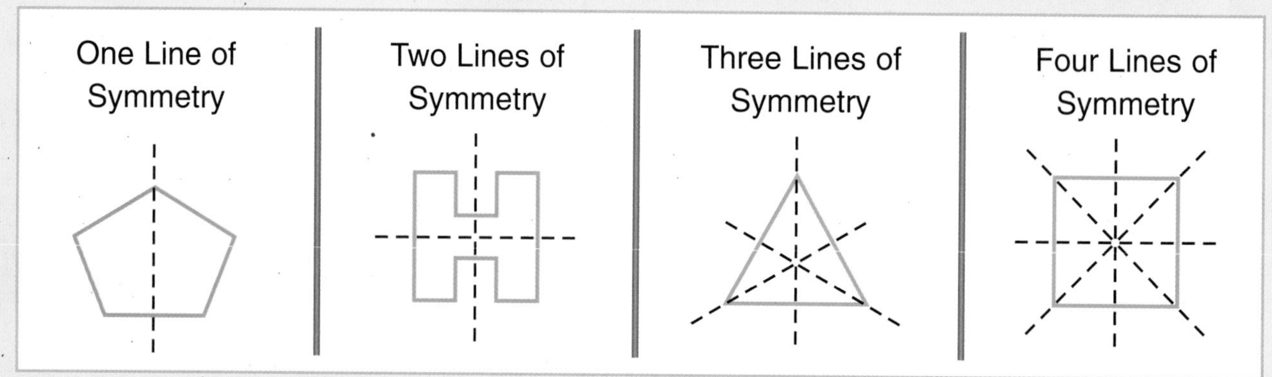


- Some figures have **rotational symmetry**.

A figure has rotational symmetry if you can rotate it less than a full turn (360°) around a point and it looks the same as it did before the turn.

**quarter turn 90°** | **half turn 180°** | **three-quarter turn 270°** | **full turn 360°**

**Try this activity to explore symmetry.**

Trace Figure A and cut it out. Try to fold it so the two parts match. If you can, draw a line of symmetry on the fold line. Repeat for Figure B.

- Which figure has a line of symmetry?
- Does it have more than one? How can you tell?

**Figure A**

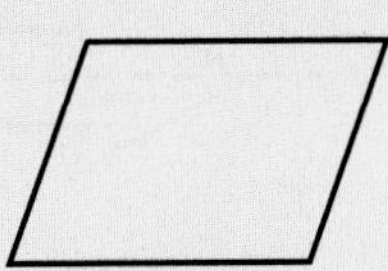

**Figure B**

On grid paper draw a dashed line of symmetry and the design shown at the right.

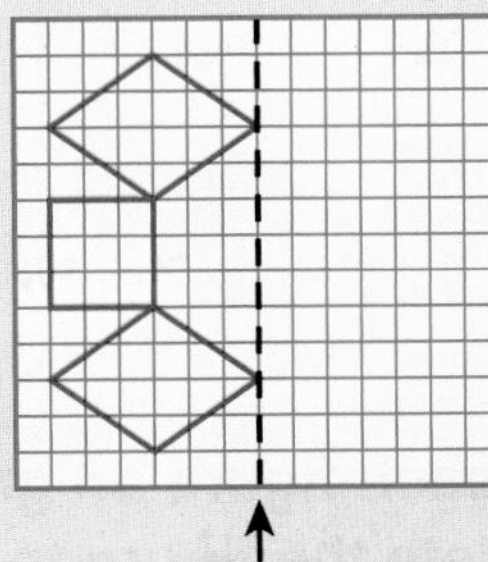

Draw a mirror image of the design on the right side of the line.

- How did you transform the figures on the left to get the figures on the right? Explain.
- How do you know the dashed line is a line of symmetry?

## Guided Practice

**Ask Yourself**

- Do the two parts match exactly?
- How does the figure look when I turn it less than 360°?

**Is the dashed line a line of symmetry? Write *yes* or *no*.**

1. 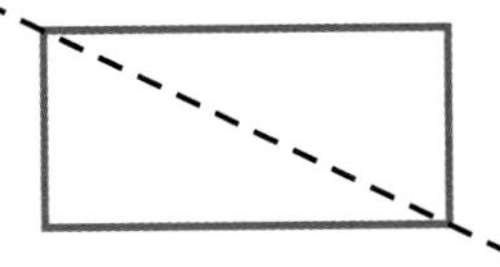

2. 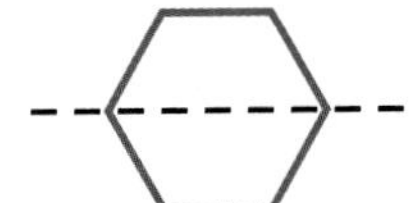

**Trace each figure. Does the figure have rotational symmetry? Write *yes* or *no*.**

3. 

4. 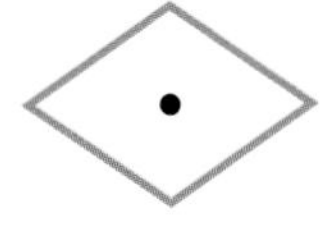

5. 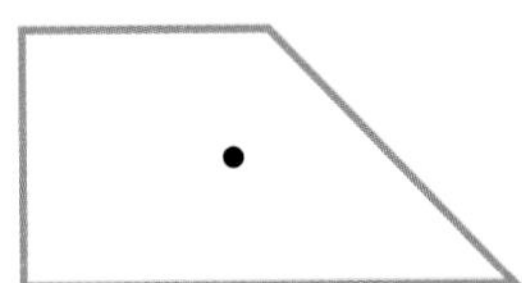

**Explain Your Thinking** ▶ How can you use a tracing of a figure to find out if it has rotational symmetry?

## Practice and Problem Solving

Is the dashed line a line of symmetry? Write *yes* or *no*.

6. 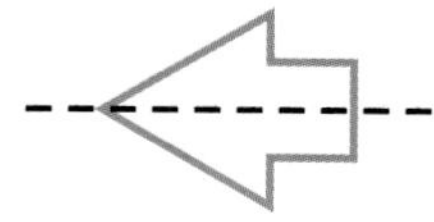

7. 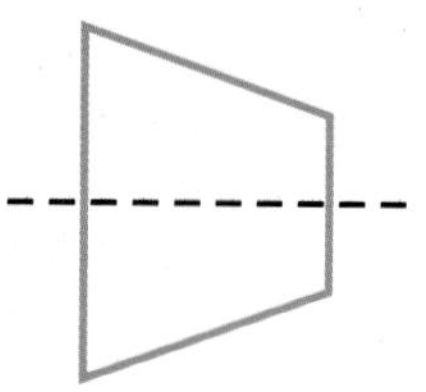

8. 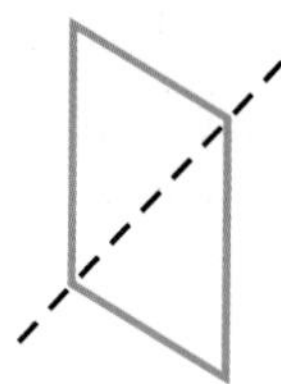

9. 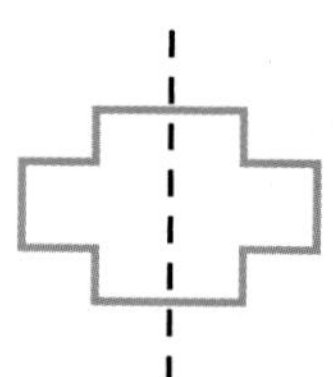

How many lines of symmetry does the figure have?

10. 

11. 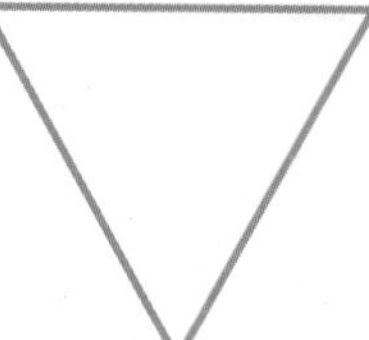

12. 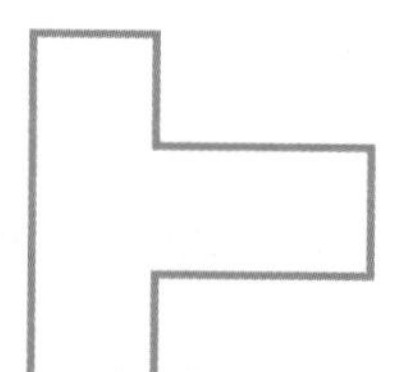

13. 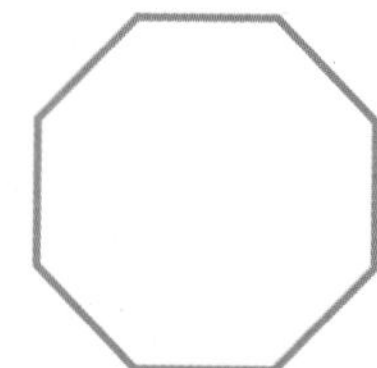

Draw each figure on grid paper. Draw the line of symmetry. Complete the figure to show line symmetry.

14. 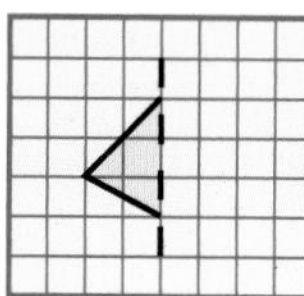

15. 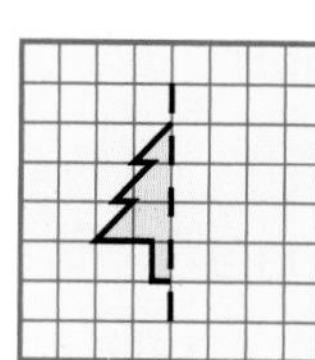

16. 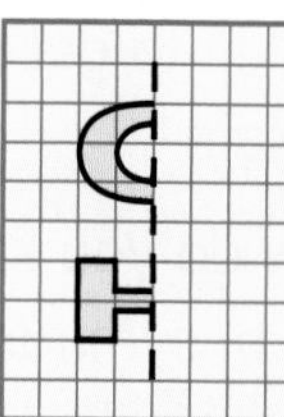

17. 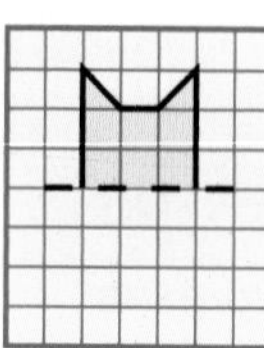

18. 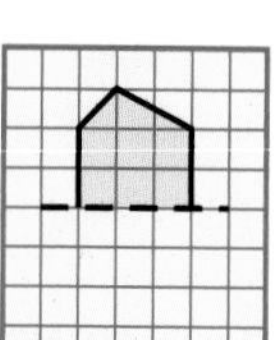

19. 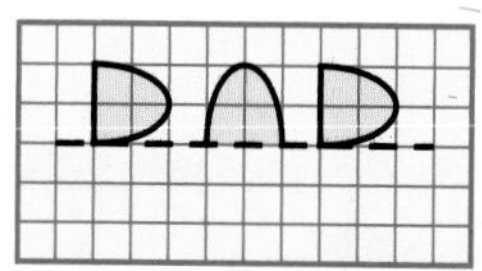

Trace each figure. Does the figure have rotational symmetry? Write *yes* or *no*.

20. 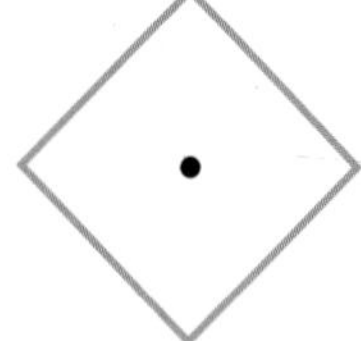

21. 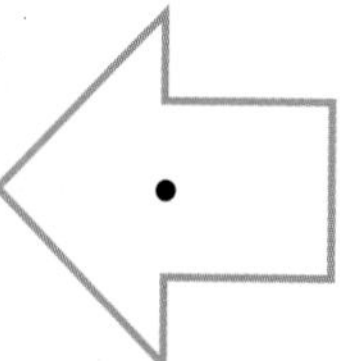

22. 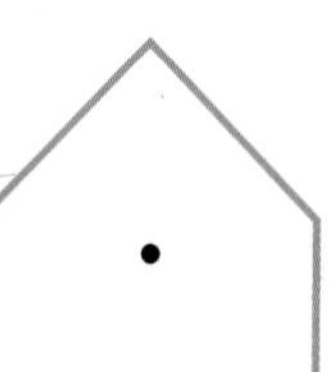

23. 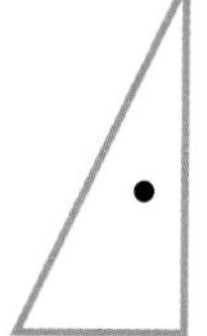

24. 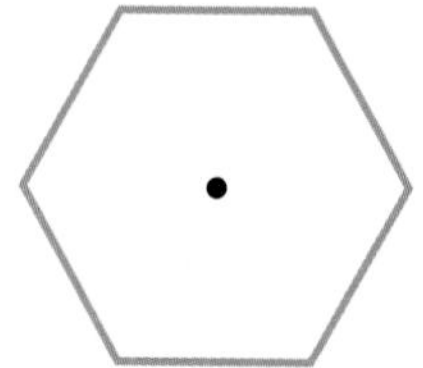

25. 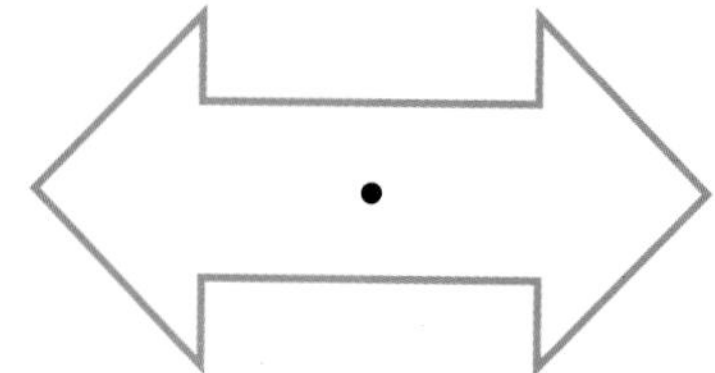



Extra Practice, See page 449, Set C.

**Solve.**

26. **Represent** Suppose each of the letters below is rotated a half turn around the point. Draw a picture to show what each letter would look like.

a. 

b.

c. 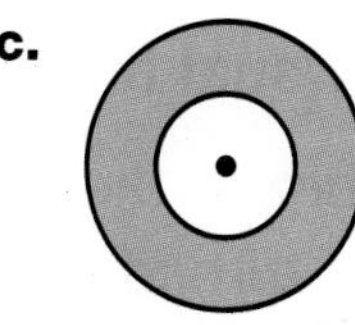

d. 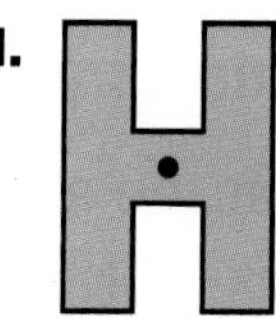

27. Which of the letters in Exercise 26 have rotational symmetry? How do you know?

28. Which of the letters in Exercise 26 have line symmetry? Use a drawing to help you explain.

29. **Explain** Amir made the figure below in art class. Trace the figure. Turn it. Does the figure have rotational symmetry around the point? Explain how you got your answer.

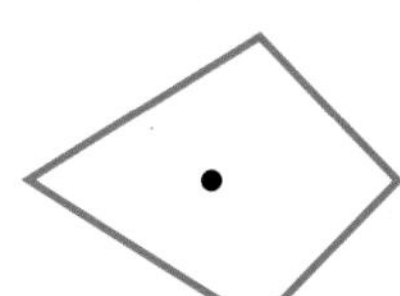

30. Trace the circle below. Cut it out. Fold it on line segment *NP*. What happens to points *M* and *O*? How many lines of symmetry does a circle have? Explain your thinking.

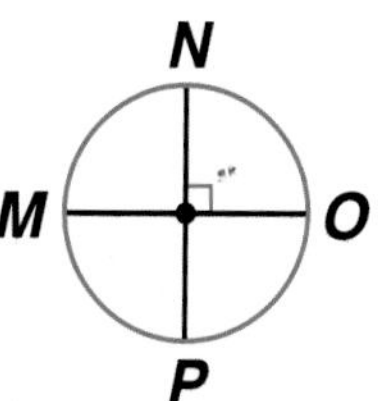


## Quick Check

Check your understanding for Lessons 1–4.

**Do the figures in each pair appear to be congruent? Write *yes* or *no*.** (Lesson 1)

1. 

2. 

**Tell how each figure was moved. Write *rotation*, *reflection*, or *translation*.** (Lesson 2)

3. 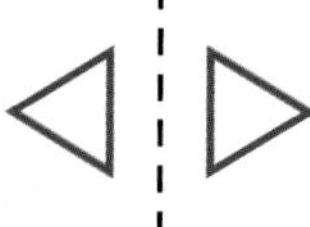

4. 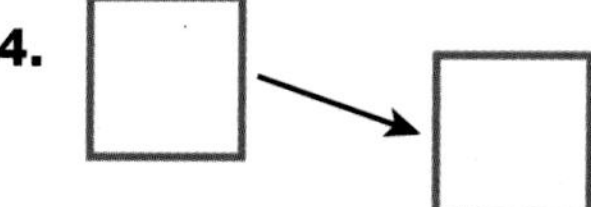

5. 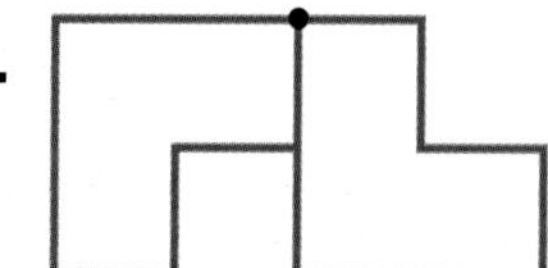

Lesson 5

# Problem-Solving Application

## Visual Thinking

**Objective** Solve problems using visual thinking.

 **STANDARDS** M4M2.b, M4P1.b, M4P1.d

**Sometimes you can use visual thinking to solve problems.**

Look at the arrow on the box at the right. What will the box look like when it is turned upside down?

### UNDERSTAND

**This is what you know.**

- The arrow is in the lower right-hand corner of the box.
- The arrow is pointing up.
- The box is going to be turned upside down.

### PLAN

**You can use visual thinking to solve the problem.**

### SOLVE

**Use visual thinking to move the box in your mind.**

- The arrow will be in the upper left-hand corner of the box.
- The arrow will point down.

Then decide which of the choices below shows the box after it is turned.

**a.** 

**b.** 

**c.** 

**Solution:** When the box is turned upside down, it will look like choice *b*.

### LOOK BACK

**Look back at the problem.**

How else could you have solved this problem?

## Guided Practice

**Use the Ask Yourself questions to help you solve each problem.**

### Ask Yourself

UNDERSTAND **What facts do I know?**

PLAN **Can I use visual thinking to solve the problem?**

SOLVE **Did I move the objects correctly in my mind?**

LOOK BACK **Did I check to be sure my answer is correct?**

1. What will be the next figure in this pattern? Choose *a, b,* or *c.*

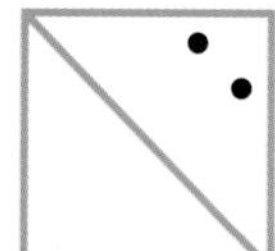
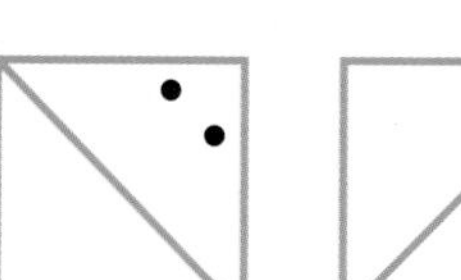
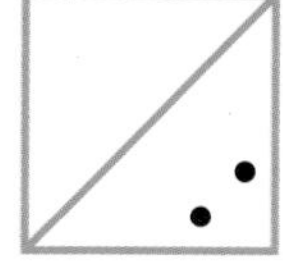
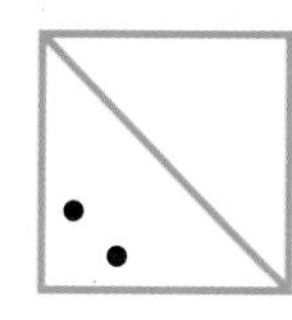

**a.** 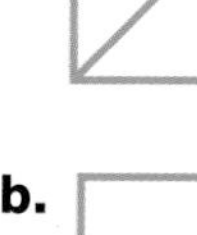 **b.** 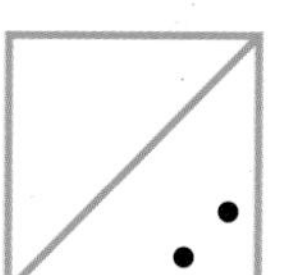 **c.** 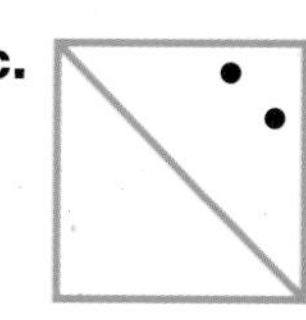

2. Willis drew the figure at the right. How many right triangles are in the figure? Explain your solution.

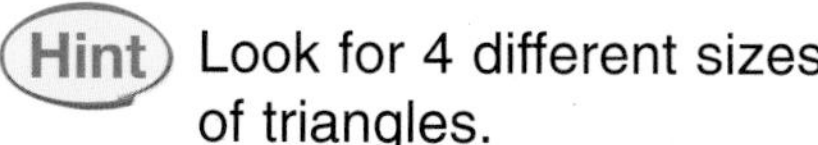

Look for 4 different sizes of triangles.

## Independent Practice

**Solve.**

3. Tammy punched holes in the folded piece of paper at the right. What will the paper look like when it is unfolded? Choose a, b, or c.

**a.** 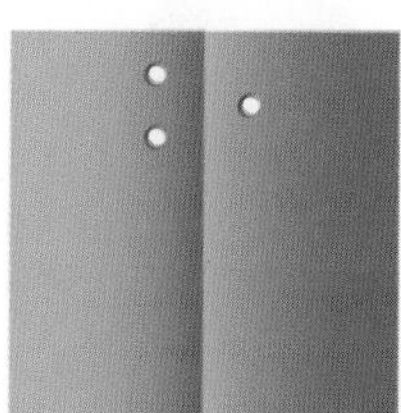 **b.** 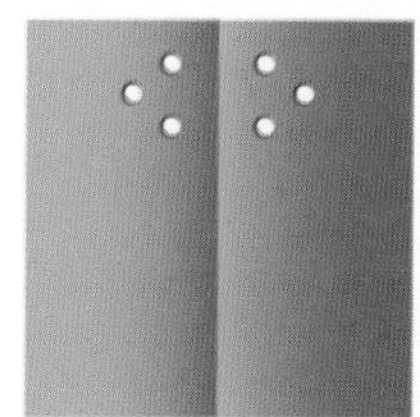 **c.** 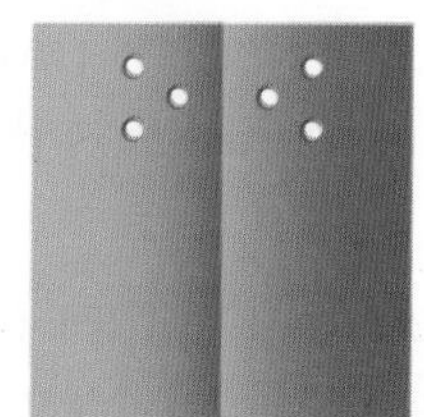

4. Sarah bought some tiles like the one below to fill in the pattern in the floor shown at the right. How many tiles did she buy? Explain your answer.

Go On

# Mixed Problem Solving

**Solve. Show your work. Tell what strategy you used.**

5. Sammy bought art supplies for \$4.95. His mom gave him \$5.00. Then he bought paper for \$12.50. He had \$6.50 left. How much money did Sammy have at the start?

6. At a craft store, 2 pieces of felt cost 75¢. Three pieces of felt cost 95¢, and four pieces of felt cost \$1.15. If the prices follow a pattern, how much are seven pieces of felt likely to cost?

7. Five teams are competing in a tournament. Each team must compete against each of the other teams once. How many rounds of competition are needed?

**You Choose**

**Strategy**
- Find a Pattern
- Guess and Check
- Solve a Simpler Problem
- Work Backward

**Computation Method**
- Mental Math
- Estimation
- Paper and Pencil
- Calculator

**Solve. Show your work. Tell which method you used.**

8. Matt is sponge-painting designs on shirts. He buys one shirt for \$7.25 and 2 packages of sponges for \$2.95 each. He pays with a \$20 bill. About how much change does he receive?

9. One shirt has 10 rows with 12 shapes in each row. A second shirt has 13 rows with 10 shapes in each row. Which shirt has the most shapes?

10. **Money** Supplies for another craft project cost \$29.99. Matt has \$15.50. How much more money does he need?

11. A craft store sold 135,375 sponge stamps in January, 104,476 in February, and 85,904 in March. How many sponge stamps were sold in those 3 months?

## Sharpening Skills for CRCT

**Open Response**

**Name each polygon.** (Ch. 16, Lesson 4)

**12.** 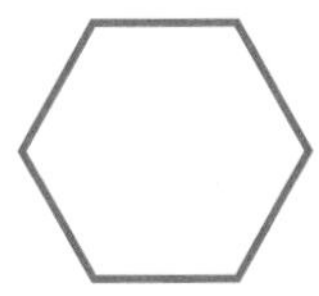

**13.** 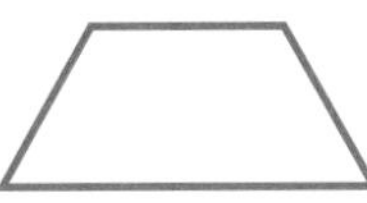

**14.** 

**15.** 

**16.** Twelve toothpicks are arranged as shown. Can you remove 2 of the toothpicks so that only 2 squares remain? Draw a picture to show your answer.

(Ch. 17, Lesson 5)

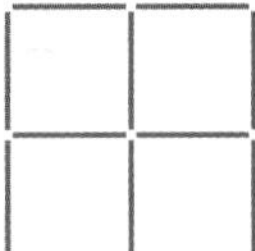

# Visual Thinking
## Kuba Cloth Patterns

STANDARDS Reviews M3A1.a.

Many of the patterns Kuba weavers use today are the same patterns that have been used for hundreds of years!

**You can make your own Kuba pattern.**

- Trace pattern blocks or other small objects.
- Cut out the figures you traced.
- Turn, flip, or slide your figures to create a pattern.

*The Kuba people of central Africa use geometry to weave patterns into cloth.*

# Chapter Review/Test

Study Guide
page SG33

**Vocabulary**

reflection
congruent
translation
line symmetry

## VOCABULARY

**Choose the best term to complete each sentence.**

1. If a figure can be folded along a line so that the two parts match exactly, it has ____.
2. Figures that have the same size and shape are ____ figures.
3. A change in position resulting from a slide is called a ____.

## CONCEPTS AND SKILLS

**Do the figures in each pair appear to be congruent? Write *yes* or *no*.** (Lesson 1, pp. 430–433)

4. 

5. 

**Tell how each figure was moved. Write *rotation*, *reflection*, or *translation*.** (Lesson 2, pp. 434–435)

6. 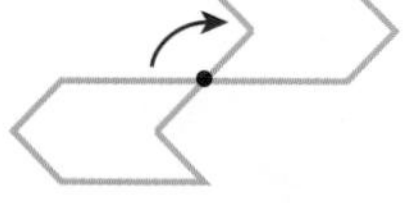

7. 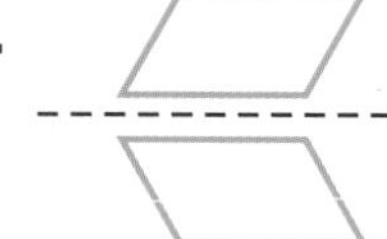

**Which figures have both line symmetry and rotational symmetry?** (Lesson 4, pp. 440–443)

8. a.  b.  c.  d. 

## PROBLEM SOLVING

**Solve. Draw a picture to show your answer.** (Lesson 3, 5, pp. 436–439, 444–447)

9. How can you cut the letter X in half so that the two parts match exactly?
10. What will the letter Y look like if it is turned 90° to the left?

**Show You Understand**

Consuela thinks that circles are always congruent. Is she correct? Explain why or why not.

# Extra Practice

## Set A (Lesson 1, pp. 430–433)

**Do the figures in each pair appear to be congruent? Write *yes* or *no*.**

1. 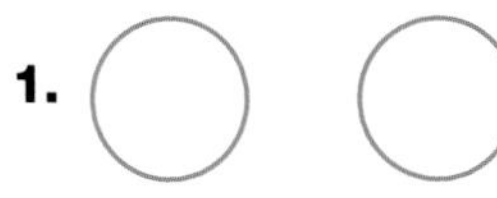

2. 

3. 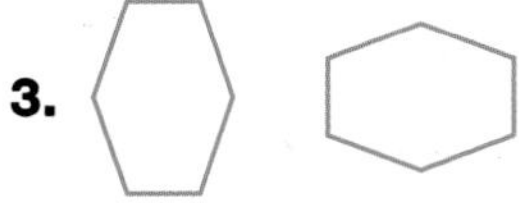

4. 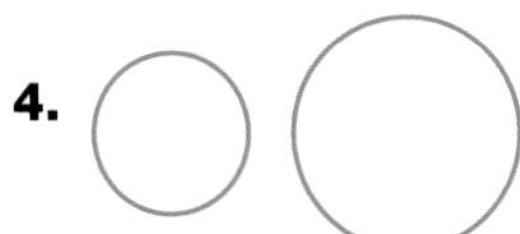

5. 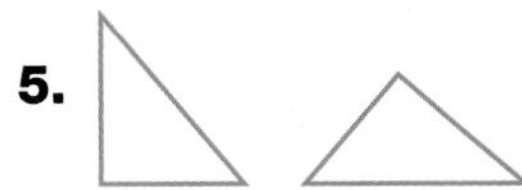

6. 

## Set B (Lesson 2, pp. 434–435)

**Tell how each figure was moved. Write *rotation*, *reflection*, or *translation*.**

1.

2. 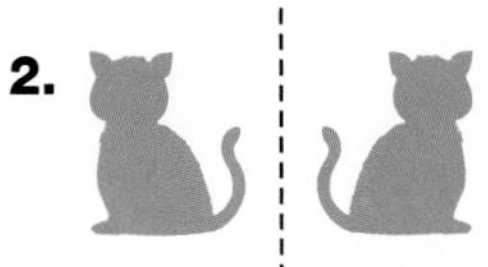

3. 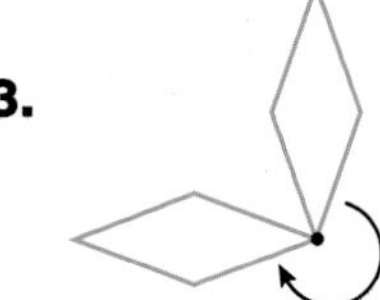

4. 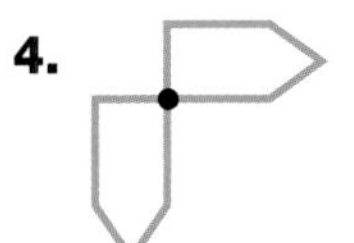

5. 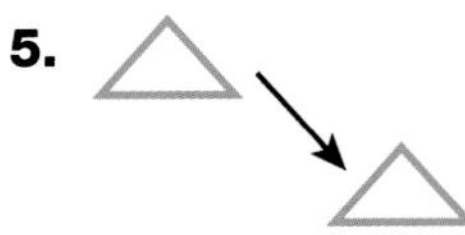

6. 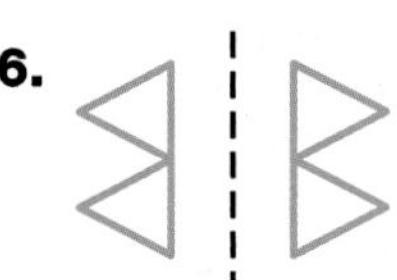

## Set C (Lesson 4, pp. 440–443)

**Is the dashed line a line of symmetry? Write *yes* or *no*.**

1.

2. 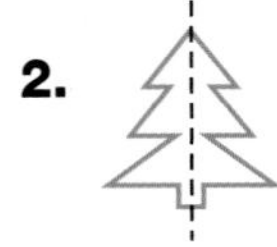

3. 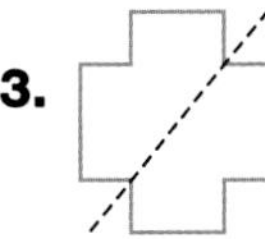

4. 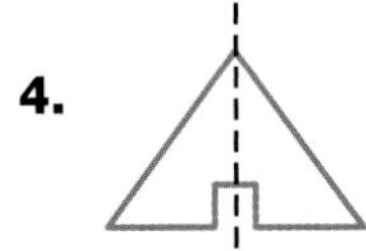

5. 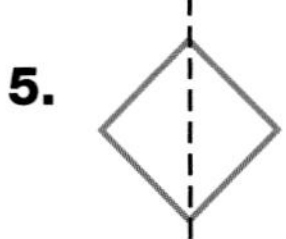

6. 

**Does the figure have rotational symmetry? Write *yes* or *no*.**

7.

8. 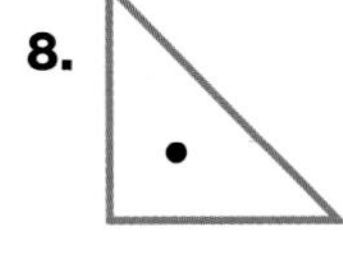

9. 

10. 

11. 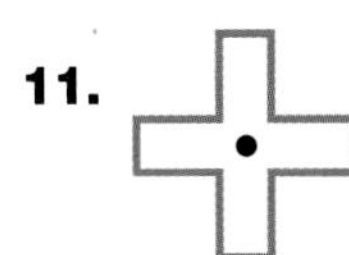

12. 

CHAPTER 18

# Perimeter, Area, and Volume

## INVESTIGATION

### Using Data

An architect draws a blueprint before a house is built. A carpenter then follows the blueprint when building the house. Imagine that you are an interior designer. You need to fit certain items of furniture into the bedrooms. How could you use the blueprint to determine whether you have enough room for the furniture? What other information would you need?

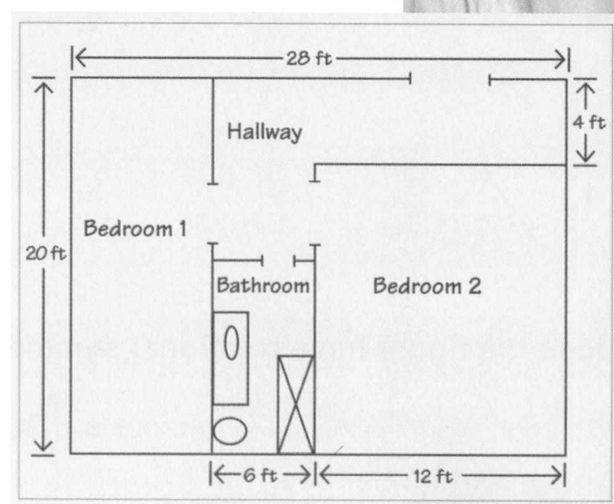

Use this page to review and remember what you need to know for this chapter.

## VOCABULARY

**Choose the best word to complete each statement.**

**Vocabulary**
- square
- hexagon
- octagon
- pentagon
- triangle

1. A polygon with five sides is a ____.
2. A polygon with eight sides is an ____.
3. A polygon with four equal sides is a ____.
4. A polygon with six sides is a ____.

## CONCEPTS AND SKILLS

**Solve.**

5. $83 \times 3$
6. $45 \times 7$
7. $68 \times 44$
8. $75 + 24 + 5$
9. $26 + 7 + 14 + 3$
10. $32 + 19 + 23$

**Write *regular* or *irregular* for each figure.**

11. 
12. 
13. 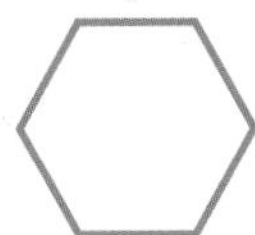

**Find each missing number.**

14. 12 in. = _____ ft
15. _____ yd = 3 ft
16. 36 in. = _____ yd
17. 7 km = _____ m
18. 3 m = _____ cm
19. 500 cm = _____ m

20. How are regular polygons and irregular polygons the same? How are they different? Explain your reasoning.

Facts Practice, See Page 668.

# Explore Perimeter and Area

**Objective** Use models to explore perimeter and area.

**Vocabulary**
**perimeter**
**area**

**Materials**
grid paper
(Learning Tool 27)

## Work Together

 **STANDARDS** Maintains M3M3 and M3M4, M4P2, M4P3

Does the **perimeter**, or distance around a figure, determine the number of square units needed to cover the figure?

Work with a partner to find out.

Look at the figures at the right. Find the perimeter of each figure by counting the number of units around the outside of the figure.

- Record your answers in a table like the one below.

| Figure | Perimeter | Area |
|---|---|---|
| Square A | 12 units | ■ square units |
| Rectangle B | ■ units | ■ square units |

**Square A**

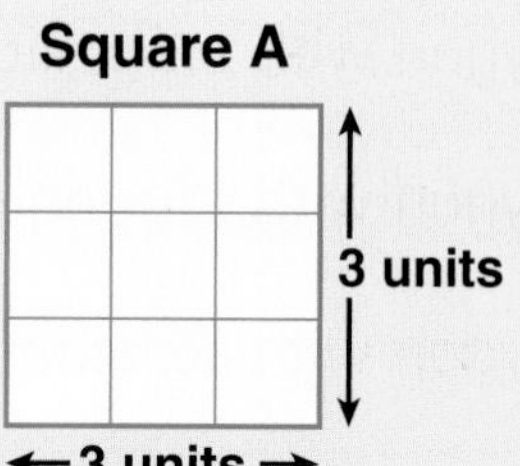


**Rectangle B**

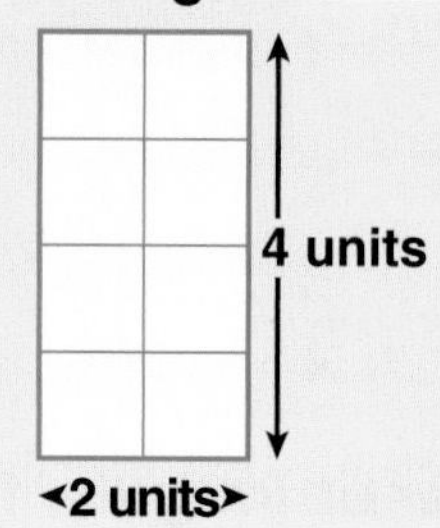

Now find the number of square units needed to cover each of the figures.

The number of square units needed to cover a figure is the **area** of the figure.

- Count to find the area of each figure.
- Record your answers in your table.

Look at your table.

- Can a square have the same perimeter as a rectangle?
- Can rectangles and squares with the same perimeter have different areas?

## On Your Own

**Find the perimeter and area of each figure. Record your answers in a table like this:**

| | Figure | Perimeter | Area |
|---|---|---|---|
| **1.** | Rectangle C | units | square units |
| **2.** | Square D | units | square units |
| **3.** | Rectangle E | units | square units |

**Rectangle C**

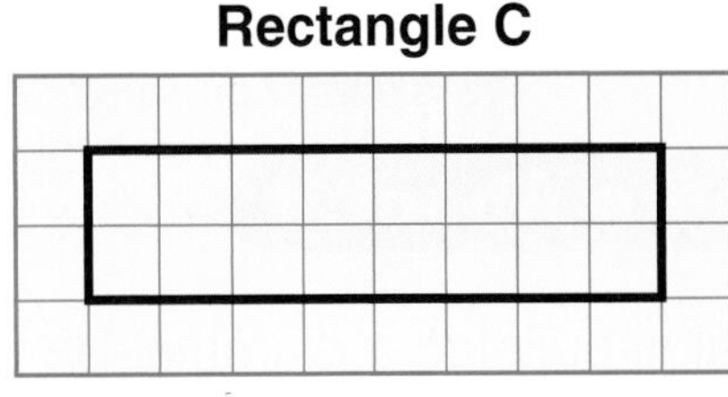

**Square D**

**Rectangle E**

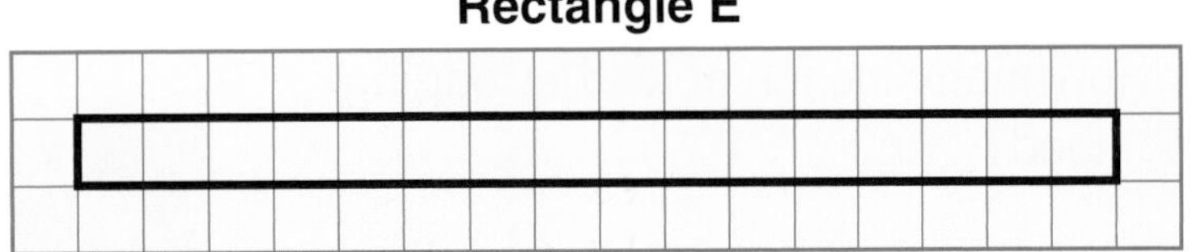

**Use your table to answer these questions.**

**4.** Can a square have the same area as a rectangle?

**5.** Can rectangles and squares with the same area have different perimeters?

**Use grid paper for Problems 6–8.**

**6.** Draw a rectangle with an area of 20 square units and a perimeter greater than 20 units.

**7.** Draw a rectangle with an area of 18 square units and a perimeter of 18 units.

**8.** **Analyze** If you double the length and width of a figure will its area double also? Double the length and width of figures C, D, and E above. What can you conclude?

### Talk About It • Write About It

**You learned how perimeter and area can be measured.**

**9.** How are perimeter and area different?

**10.** Suppose two figures have different shapes. If one figure has a greater perimeter than the other, does it also have a greater area? Explain your thinking.

**Audio Tutor 2/15** Listen and Understand

Algebra

# Perimeter

**Objective** Find perimeters of polygons.

**STANDARDS** Maintains M3M3.a, M3M3.b, M3M3.c, and M3M3.d

**perimeter**

**Materials**
ruler

## Learn About It

Paul is building a diorama. He plans to glue a strip of leather around the edge. The diorama is 12 inches long and 8 inches wide. How many inches of leather edging will he need?

To find the length of the edges, find the **perimeter** or distance around the diorama.

### Different Ways to Find Perimeter

**Way 1** **You can add the lengths of the sides.**

Perimeter $= l + w + l + w$

$P = 12 \text{ in.} + 8 \text{ in.} + 12 \text{ in.} + 8 \text{ in.}$

$P = 40 \text{ in.}$

**Way 2** **You can use the formula to find the perimeter of a rectangle.**

Perimeter $= (2 \times l) + (2 \times w)$

$P = (2 \times 12 \text{ in.}) + (2 \times 8 \text{ in.})$

$P = 24 \text{ in.} + 16 \text{ in.}$

$P = 40 \text{ in.}$

**Remember**
Do what is in parentheses first.

**Solution:** Paul needs 40 inches of leather edging.

**Estimate and then find the perimeter of objects.**

**STEP 1** Choose three objects in your classroom.

**STEP 2** Estimate what the perimeter of each might be. Record your estimate.

**STEP 3** Use your ruler to find the exact perimeter. Record the actual perimeter.

## Guided Practice

**Ask Yourself**

- Is the figure a regular or irregular polygon?
- Can I use a formula?

**Find the perimeter of each polygon.**

1. 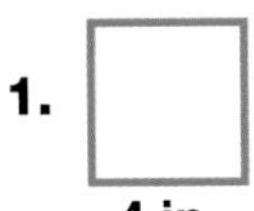 4 in.

2. 3 ft

3. 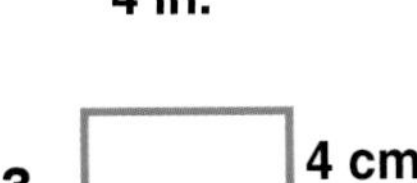 4 cm, 8 cm

4. 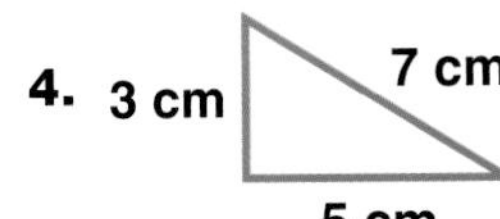 3 cm, 7 cm, 5 cm

**Explain Your Thinking** ▶ Write a formula for finding the perimeter of a square.

## Practice and Problem Solving

**Find the perimeter of each polygon.**

5.  20 cm, 60 cm

6. 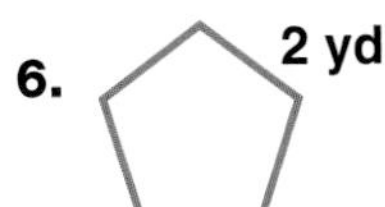 2 yd

7. 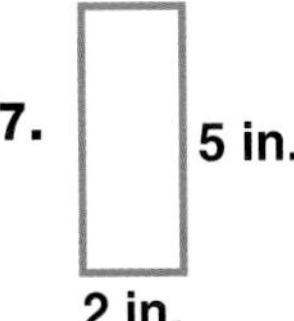 5 in., 2 in.

**Write a formula to find each perimeter. Then solve.**

8. a regular pentagon with sides 8 cm long

9. a regular hexagon with sides 8 cm long

10. a regular octagon with sides 8 cm long

**Solve.**

11. A rectangular room is 15 feet long and 7 yards wide. Find the perimeter in feet. Then find the perimeter in yards.

12. **Explain** Reggie is making sandals. He traced his foot on grid paper. How can he find its perimeter with a piece of string and a ruler?

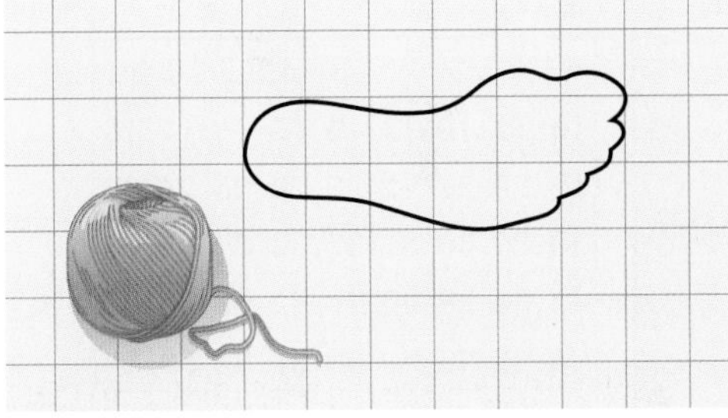

## Sharpening Skills for CRCT

GPS

### Open Response

**Write >, <, or = for each ⬬.** (Ch. 3, Lesson 1)

13. $9 + 4 - 3$ ⬬ $7 + 8$

14. $13 - 5$ ⬬ $2 + 6$

15. $5 + 9 - 1$ ⬬ $4 + 8$

16. $4 + 7 - 2$ ⬬ $5 + 8 - 3$

### Multiple Choice

17. The perimeter of a square is 36 cm. What is the length of one side of the square? (Ch. 18, Lesson 2)

A. 4 cm
B. 9 cm
C. 32 cm
D. 40 cm

Extra Practice See page 475, Set A.

Algebra

# Area

**Objective** Find the area of a rectangle.

STANDARDS Maintains M3M4, M4P2

**Vocabulary**
area

**Materials**
rulers

Jake's grandfather is building a patio. He wants to know how many square feet of slate he needs to order.

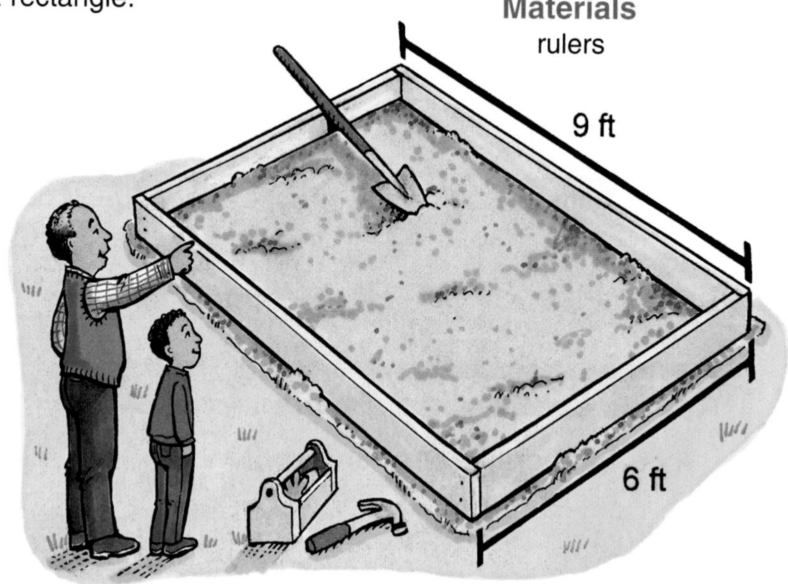


To find how much slate is needed, you need to find the **area** or square units within the patio. You can find area in two ways.

## Different Ways to Find Area

**Way 1 You can draw a model and count the squares.**

| 1 | 2 | 3 | 4 | 5 | 6 | 7 | 8 | 9 |
|---|---|---|---|---|---|---|---|---|
| 10 | 11 | 12 | 13 | 14 | 15 | 16 | 17 | 18 |
| 19 | 20 | 21 | 22 | 23 | 24 | 25 | 26 | 27 |
| 28 | 29 | 30 | 31 | 32 | 33 | 34 | 35 | 36 |
| 37 | 38 | 39 | 40 | 41 | 42 | 43 | 44 | 45 |
| 46 | 47 | 48 | 49 | 50 | 51 | 52 | 53 | 54 |

Each square is 1 square foot or 1 $ft^2$.

**Way 2 You can use the formula to find the area of a rectangle.**

Area = length × width

Area = $l \times w$

$A = 9 \text{ ft} \times 6 \text{ ft}$

$A = 54 \text{ ft}^2$ or 54 square feet

**Solution:** The patio will be 54 square feet in area. So, he will need 54 square feet of slate.

## Another Example

### Area of a Square

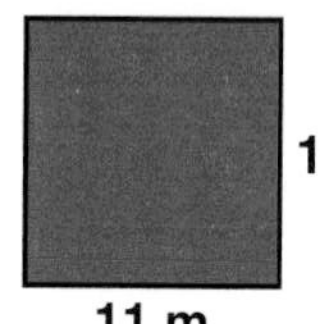


$A = s \times s$

$A = 11 \text{ m} \times 11 \text{ m}$

$A = 121 \text{ m}^2$

**Remember**
Each side of a square is the same length.

**Try this activity to estimate and find the area of objects.**

**STEP 1** Find three flat rectangular objects in your classroom.

**STEP 2** Estimate what the area of each might be. Record your estimate.

**STEP 3** Use your ruler and a formula to find the area of each object. Record the actual area. How did your estimate compare to the actual area?

## Guided Practice

**Ask Yourself**

- What formula can I use?
- What unit do I need?

**Use a formula to find the area of each figure.**

**1.** 2 mi, 3 mi

**2.** 16 ft, 16 ft

**3.** 12 in., 25 in.

**4.** 4 cm, 4 cm

**5.** 6 m, 24 m

**6.**

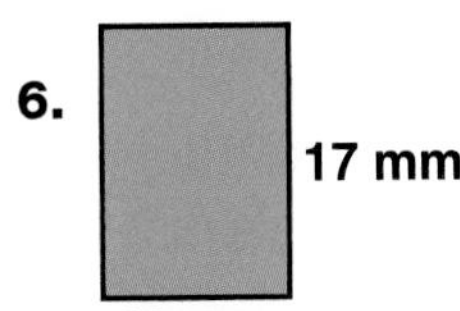


**Explain Your Thinking** ▶ How could you find the perimeter of a square that has an area of 25 square inches?

## Practice and Problem Solving

**Find the area of each figure.**

**7.** 14 in., 14 in.

**8.** 2 mi, 5 mi

**9.** 12 yd, 9 yd

**10.** 7 m, 12 m

**11.** 16 cm, 20 cm

**12.** 3 km, 21 km

Go On

**Find the perimeter and area for each rectangle.**

13. 14 m long, 6 m wide
14. 3 yd long, 7 yd wide
15. 15 cm long, 4 cm wide
16. 5 ft long, 13 ft wide
17. 2 in. long, 16 in. wide
18. 8 mm long, 26 mm wide

**Which of the figures below have the same perimeter but different areas?**

**19.**

**a.**

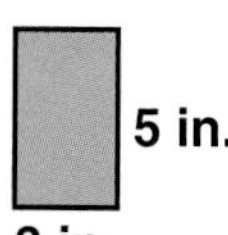


**b.**

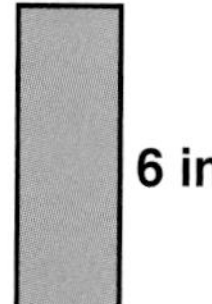


**c.**

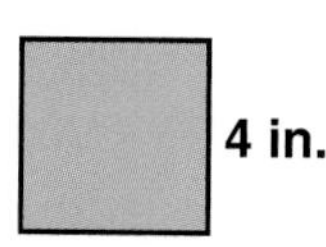


**d.**

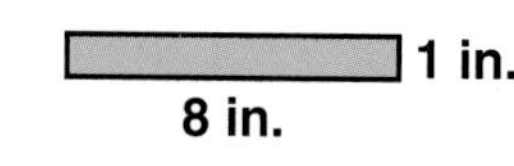


**Solve.**

20. The area of Kahli's closet is 15 square feet. One side is 3 feet long. How long is the other side? What did you do to get your answer?

21. **Analyze** Does the area of a rectangle double when the length and width are doubled? How do you know?

**Data** **Use the floor plan at the right for Problems 22–26.**

22. Is the floor space of the living room greater or less than 200 square feet? How much greater or less?

23. **Money** Anna wants to tile the kitchen floor. Each tile is 1 foot square and costs $1.75. How much will it cost for the tiles?

24. The rug in the living room is 10 feet by 8 feet. How much floor space is not covered by the rug?

25. **What's Wrong?** Ben finds the total perimeter of the three rooms by doubling the perimeter of the living room. Explain why that is not correct.

26. **You Decide** Suppose you added two rooms onto the floor plan shown. What size might each be? What would the total area of the five rooms become?

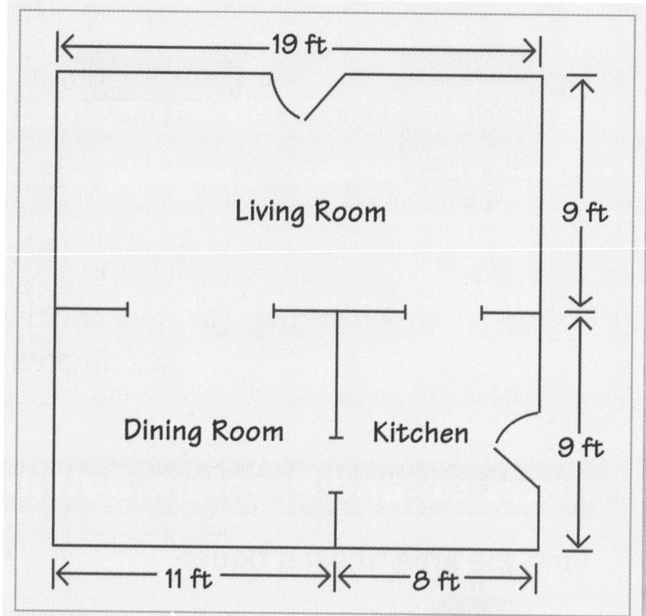

Extra Practice See page 475, Set B.

Problem Solving

GPS

# Measurement Sense

## Area of a Right Triangle

STANDARDS Prepares for M5M1.c, M5M1.d

You can use the area of a rectangle to find the area of this right triangle.

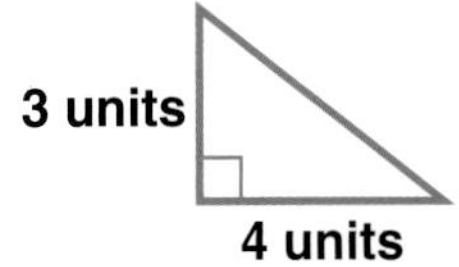


- Think of the right triangle as half of a rectangle.
- Find the area of the rectangle.
  4 units × 3 units = 12 square units
- Now divide the area of the rectangle by 2.
  12 square units ÷ 2 = 6 square units

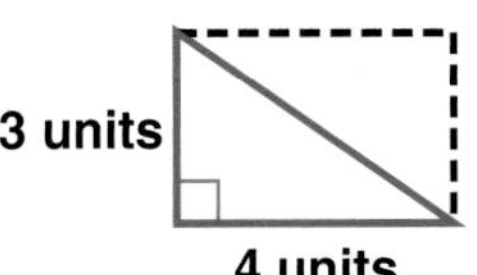


The area of the triangle is 6 square units.

**Find the area of each right triangle.**

**1.** 4 cm, 7 cm

**2.** 10 mm, 10 mm

**3.** 6 m, 3 m

Quick Check

**Check your understanding of Lessons 1–3.**

**Find the perimeter of each figure.** (Lessons 1–2)

**1.**

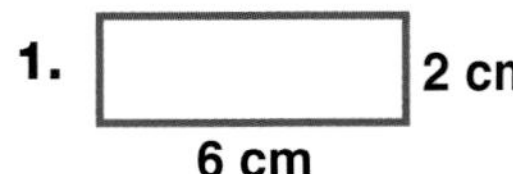


**2.** 5 in., 5 in.

**3.** 8 cm, 8 cm, 5 cm

**4.**

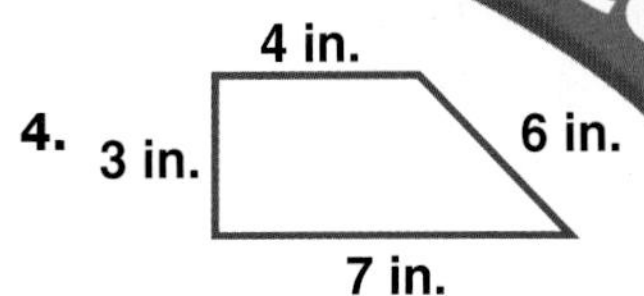


**Find the area of each figure.** (Lessons 1 and 3)

**5.**

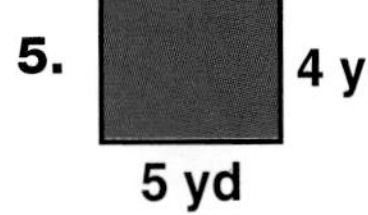


**6.** 7 in., 2 in.

**7.**

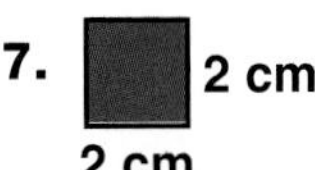


**8.**

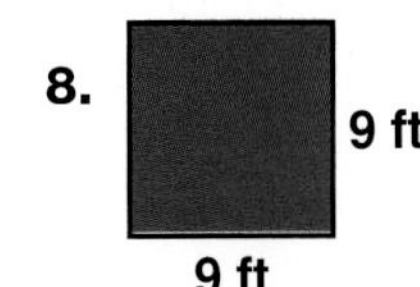


**Write a formula to find the perimeter. Then solve.** (Lesson 2)

**9.** a regular octagon; each side is 7 cm

**Write a formula to find the area. Then solve.** (Lesson 3)

**10.** a rectangle 9 in. long and 7 in. wide

Lesson 4

Algebra

# Perimeter and Area of Complex Figures

**Objective** Find the perimeter and area of figures that are not rectangles.

## Learn About It

STANDARDS Prepares for M5M1.f, Extends and enriches M3M3, M4P2

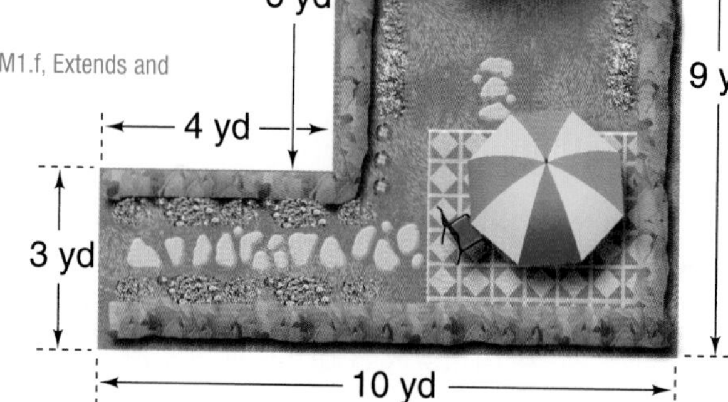


Andy wants to put a fence around his garden. The space he will use is shown at the right. How much fence should he buy? What is the area of his garden?

**Find the perimeter.**

Add the lengths of the sides.

Perimeter = 10 yd + 3 yd + 4 yd + 6 yd + 6 yd + 9 yd

$P$ = 38 yd

**Solution:** He should buy 38 yards of fence.

**Find the area.**

STEP 1 Separate the figure into a rectangle and a square.

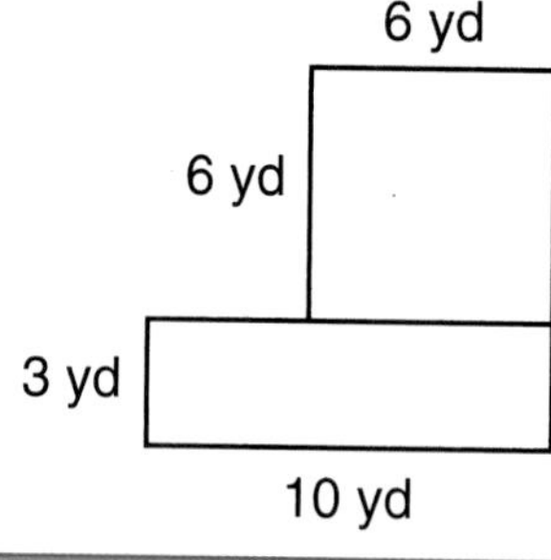


STEP 2 Use a formula to find the area of each figure.

**Area of the Rectangle**

Area = $l \times w$

$A$ = 10 yd × 3 yd

$A$ = 30 yd$^2$

**Area of the Square**

Area = $s \times s$

$A$ = 6 yd × 6 yd

$A$ = 36 yd$^2$

STEP 3 Add both areas to find the area of the whole figure.

30 yd$^2$ + 36 yd$^2$ = 66 yd$^2$

**Solution:** The area of the garden is 66 square yards.

## Guided Practice

**Find the perimeter and area of each figure.**

**1.**

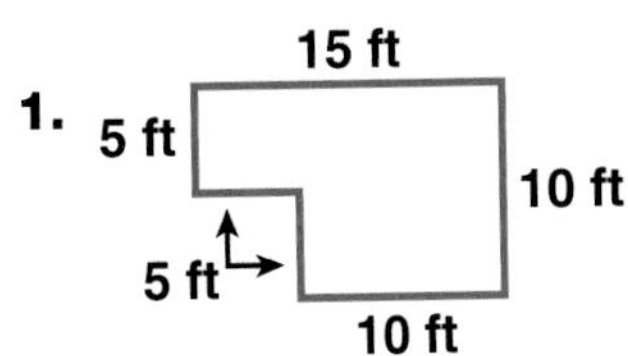


**2.**

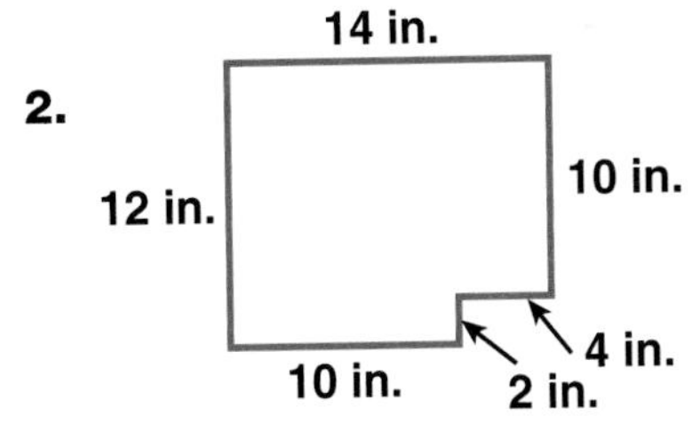


**Ask Yourself**

- How can I divide the figure into squares and rectangles?
- How should I label the answer?

**Explain Your Thinking** ▶ How could you find the area of your classroom? What tools would you need? What formula would you use?

## Practice and Problem Solving

**Find the perimeter and area of each figure.**

**3.**

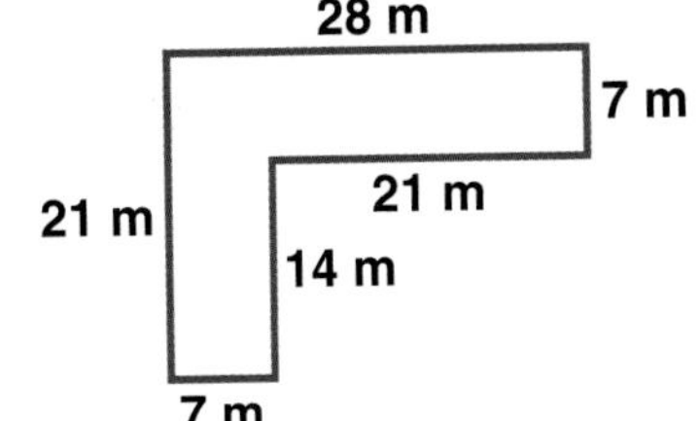


**4.**

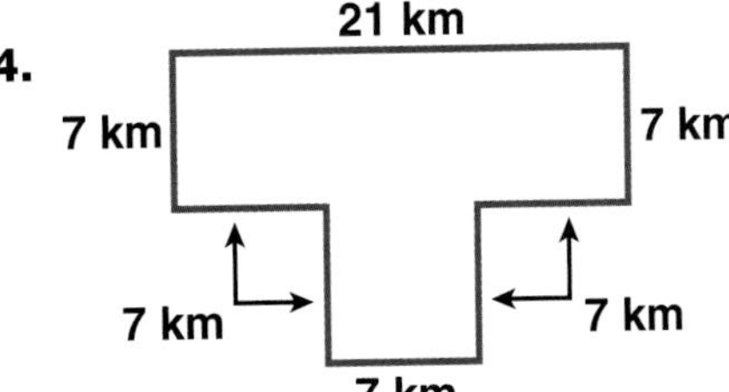


**5.**

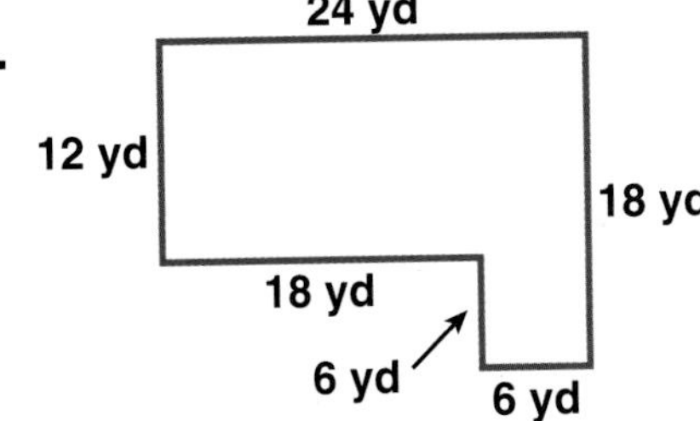


**6.**

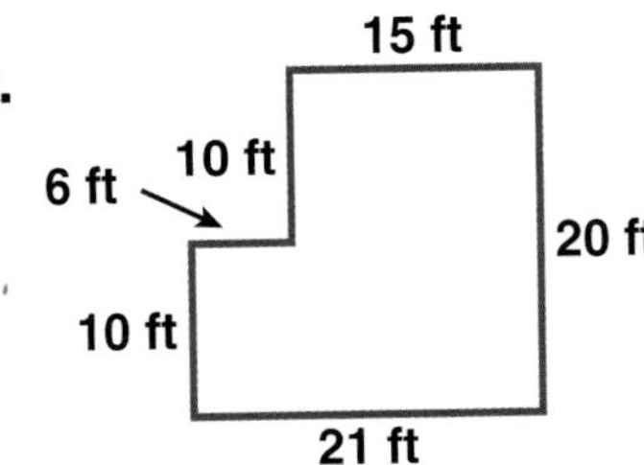


**7.**

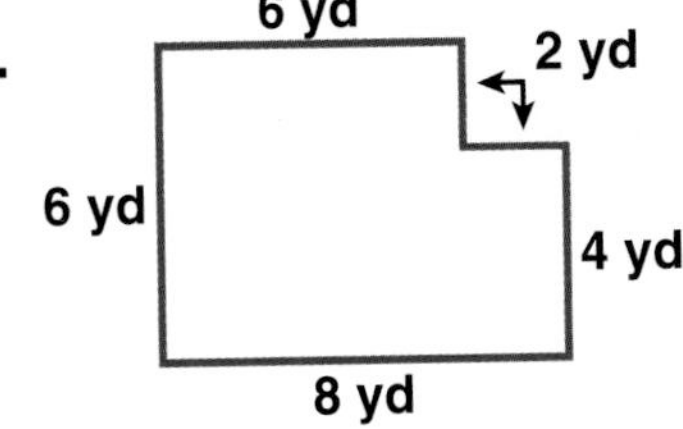


**8.**

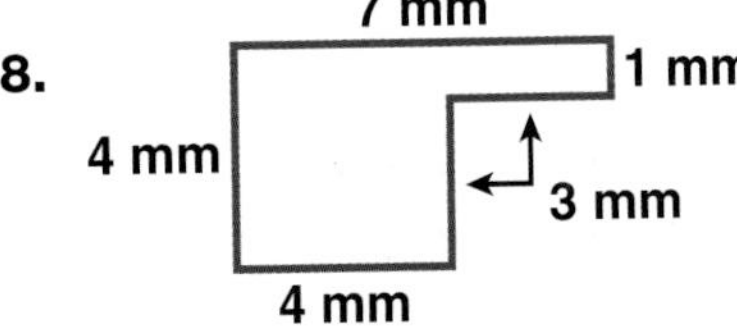


Go On

Find the length of each missing side.

9. 

x; 4 in.; 4 in.; 8 in.

Perimeter = 24 inches

10. 

12 m; 6 m; 8 m; 5 m; x; 7 m

Perimeter = 40 meters

11. 

7 yd; 2 yd; 5 yd; x; 5 yd; 2 yd

Perimeter = 24 yards

## Data Use the drawing of Dee's backyard below and the table at the right for Problems 12–15.

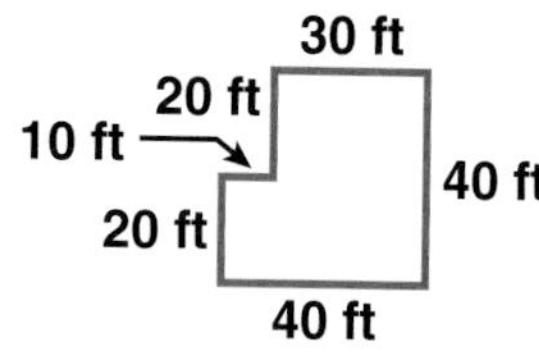

**How Much Grass Seed to Buy**

| Area (ft²) | Pounds of Seed |
|---|---|
| 1,000 | 1 |
| 1,500 | 2 |
| 2,000 | 3 |
| 2,500 | 4 |

12. **Money** Dee needs to put a fence around this yard. Fencing costs $3 per foot. How many feet of fencing are needed? How much will it cost?

13. **Analyze** Dee wants to put grass seed on the yard. How many pounds of grass seed will she need?

14. Joel purchased 3 pounds of grass seed. What might the length and width of his yard be?

15. **Write Your Own** Use the data in the table to write a problem. Give your problem to a classmate to solve.

## Sharpening Skills for CRCT

**Open Response**

**Is the dashed line a line of symmetry? Write *yes* or *no*.** (Ch. 17, Lesson 4)

16. 

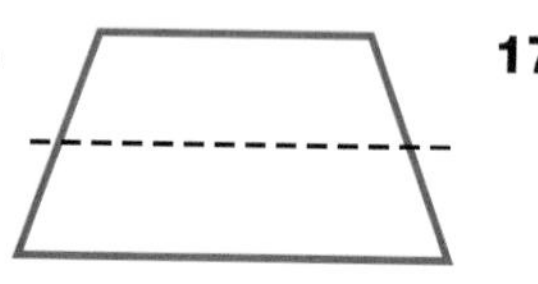

17. 

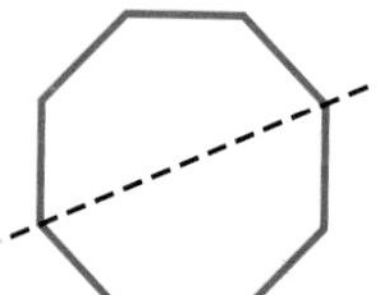

18. Aldo plans to put new tiles on the kitchen floor. How many square yards of tile does he need if the kitchen measures 9 feet by 12 feet? (Ch. 18, Lesson 4)

Explain your thinking.



Extra Practice See Page 475, Set C.

## Visual Thinking

### Estimating Area

**Look at the shape below.**

You can use grid paper to help you estimate the area of unusual shapes like this one by counting the square units within the shape.

- If the shape covers $\frac{1}{2}$ or more than $\frac{1}{2}$ of a square, count it as 1 square unit.
- If the shape covers less than $\frac{1}{2}$ of a square, don't count it.

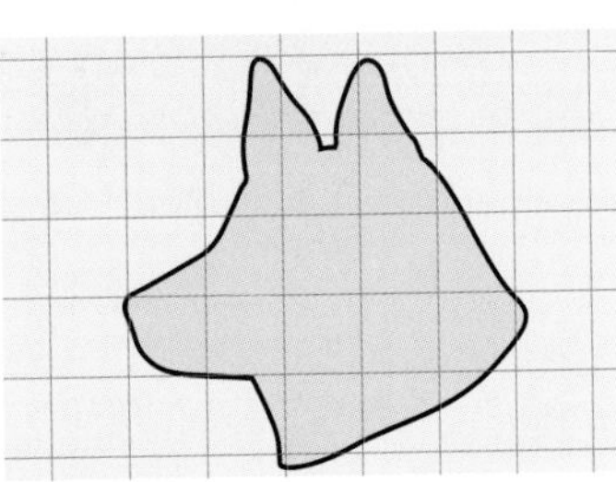

The area is about 15 square units.

**Estimate the area of these shapes.**

1. 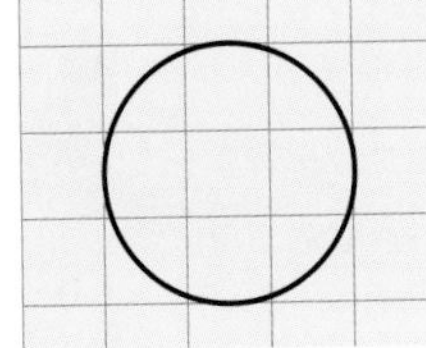

2. 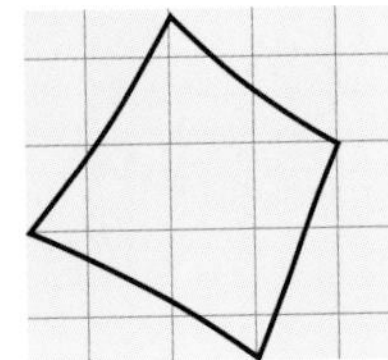

3. 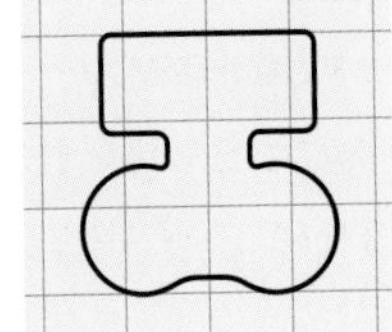

**STANDARDS** Maintains M3M4.a, M3M4.b, and M3M1.a

## Art Connection

### Stencil Patterns

Vivian is stenciling a border on her bedroom wall. Which of the pieces below will complete the unfinished section? Explain how you know.

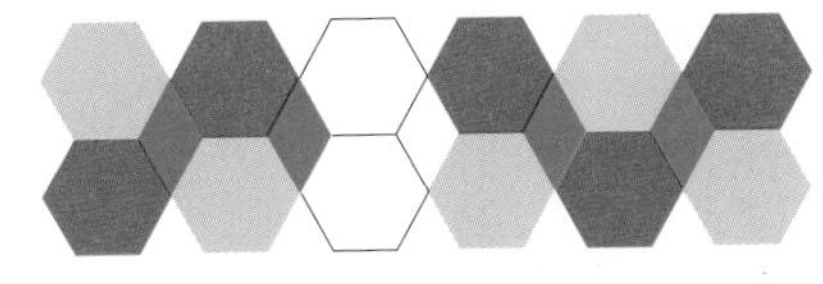

**a.** 

**b.** 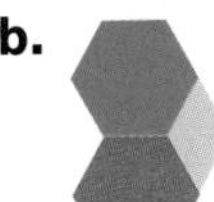

**c.**  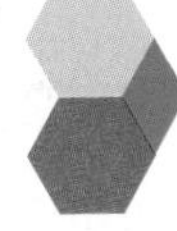

## Brain Teaser

**Mr. Tanz is building a 48-foot fence along one side of his yard. He plans to put a post on each end. He wants to place the remaining posts every 8 feet.**

**How many posts does he need?**

**Education Place**

Check out **eduplace.com/map** for more brain teasers.

# Solid Figures and Nets

**Objective** Identify and make solid shapes.

 **STANDARDS** M4G2.a, M4G2.b, M4G2.c

**Vocabulary**
- faces
- edge
- vertex (vertices)
- net

**Materials**
Learning Tools 28–33
scissors
tape

## Learn About It

Sand castles are fun to make. You create solid figures when you build sand castles. Solid figures are objects that take up space.

This solid figure is called a cube.

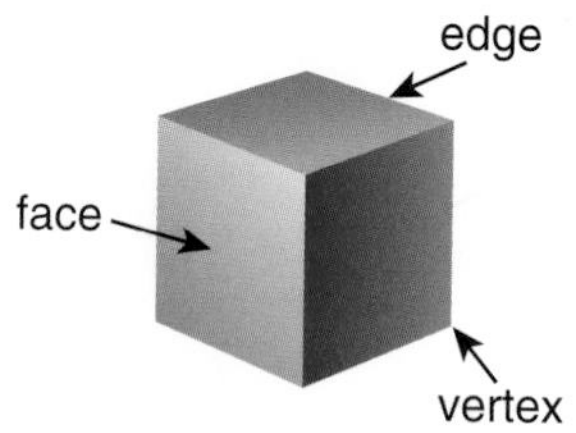


- A cube has 6 **faces**.
- Two faces meet to form an **edge**.
- The point where 3 edges meet is a **vertex**. A cube has 8 vertices.

**Here are more solid figures.**

### Solid Figures

**The faces of these solid figures are polygons.**

Cube

Rectangular Prism

Triangular Prism

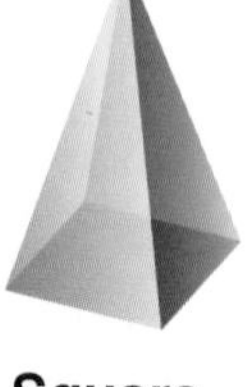

Square Pyramid

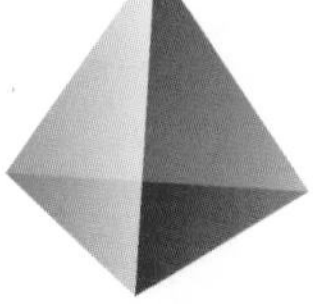

Triangular Pyramid

**These solid figures are not made up of polygons.**

Cylinder

Cone

Sphere

Look at the rectangular prisms below.

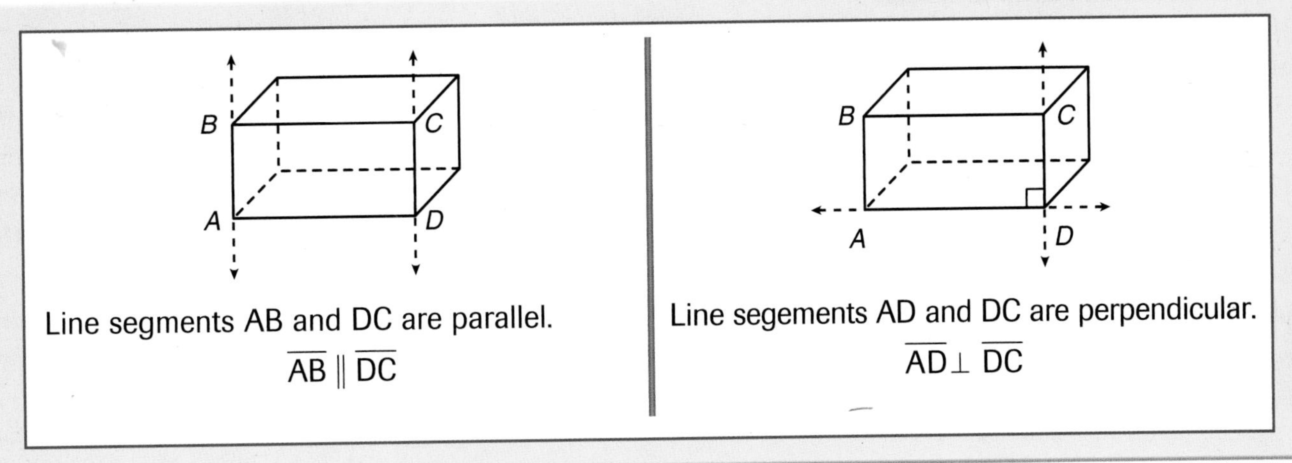


Line segments AB and DC are parallel.
$\overline{AB} \parallel \overline{DC}$

Line segements AD and DC are perpendicular.
$\overline{AD} \perp \overline{DC}$

Knowing about parallel and perpendicular lines in a solid figure will help you as you make solid shapes in the activity below.

These patterns are **nets**. If you cut out a net and fold it on the dotted lines, you can make a solid figure.

## Nets

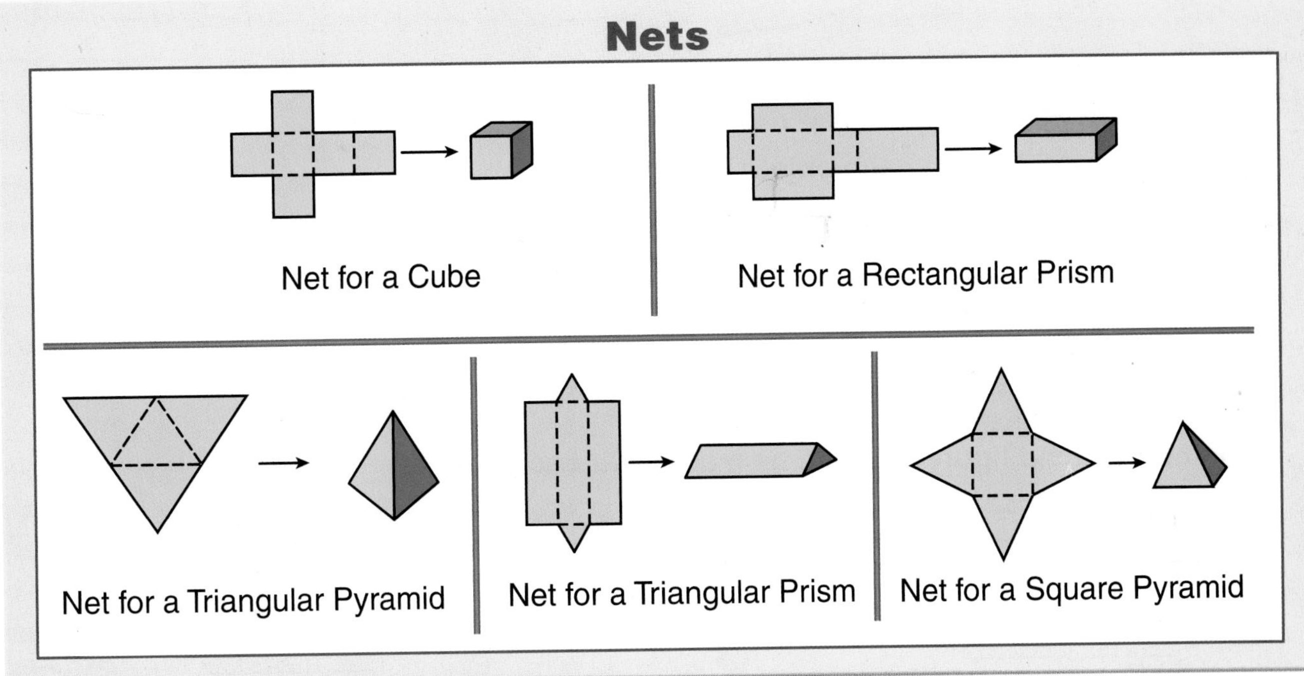

Net for a Cube

Net for a Rectangular Prism

Net for a Triangular Pyramid

Net for a Triangular Prism

Net for a Square Pyramid

**Try this activity to make solid figures.**

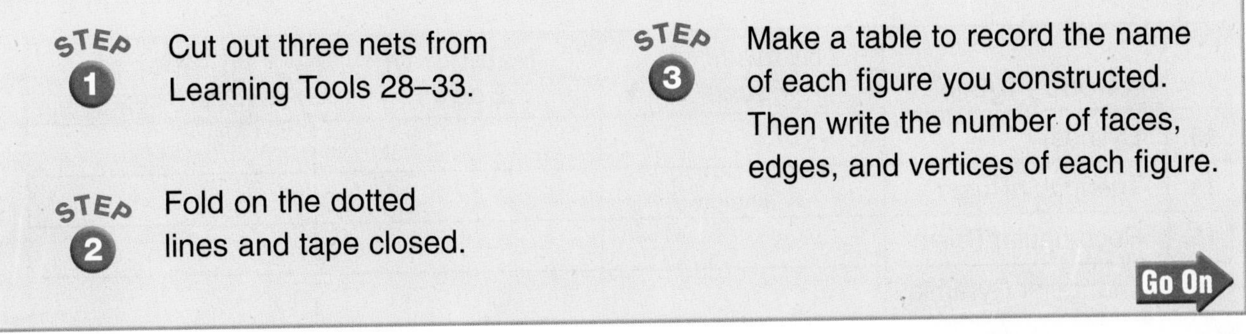

STEP 1 Cut out three nets from Learning Tools 28–33.

STEP 2 Fold on the dotted lines and tape closed.

STEP 3 Make a table to record the name of each figure you constructed. Then write the number of faces, edges, and vertices of each figure.

Go On

## Guided Practice

**Name each solid figure.**

1. 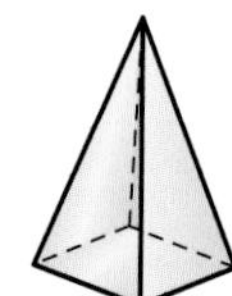

2. 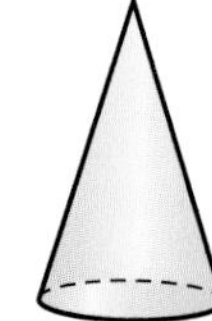

3. 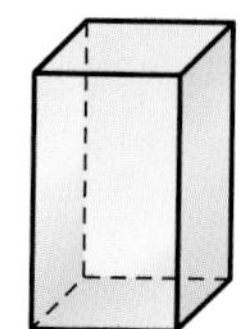

**Ask Yourself**

- Are the faces of the solid figure polygons or circles?
- How many faces will the solid figure have when the net is folded?

4. Look at one face of the figure in Exercise 3. How many pairs of parallel lines does it have?

5. Which net can be folded to make a cube?

a. 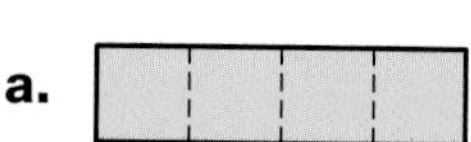

b. 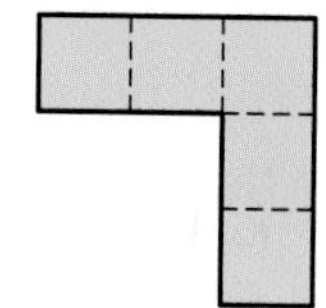

c. 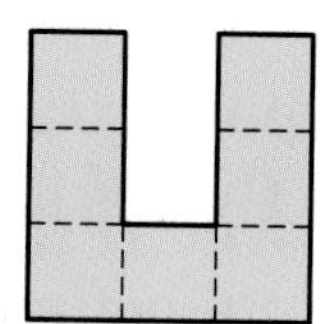

d. 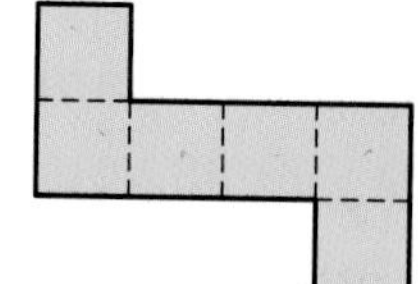

**Explain Your Thinking** ▶ Which solid figure has faces that are all triangles?

## Practice and Problem Solving

**Name the solid figure each object looks like.**

6. 

7. 

8. 

9. 

**Name the solid figure that can be made with each net.**

10. 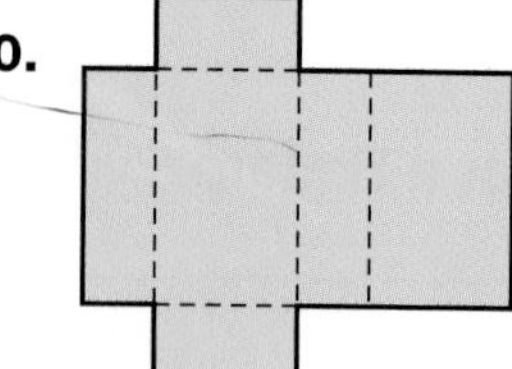

11. 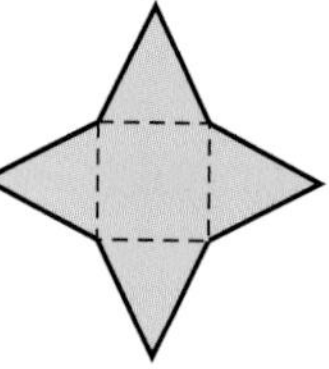

12. 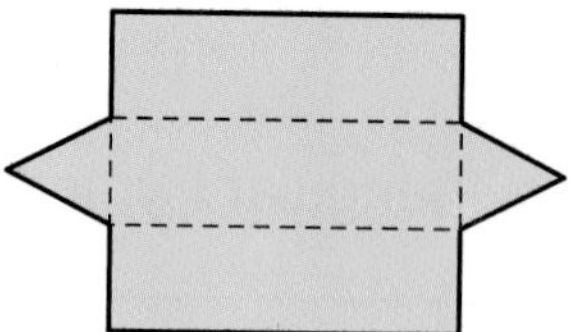

**Copy and complete the table.**

| | Solid Figure | Number of Faces | Number of Edges | Number of Vertices |
|---|---|---|---|---|
| 13. | Cylinder | | | |
| 14. | Triangular Prism | | | |
| 15. | Rectangular Prism | | | |
| 16. | Triangular Pyramid | | | |

## Guided Practice

**Use the Ask Yourself questions to help you solve each problem.**

1. Thomas's workbench measures 19 inches by 36 inches. What is the perimeter of his workbench?

2. Sarah will place the treasure box on her desk. The desk measures 24 inches by 30 inches. How much room will be left on the desk?

**Hint** Remember to subtract the area of the treasure box.

### Ask Yourself

**UNDERSTAND** **Does the question ask me to find perimeter, area, or volume?**

**PLAN** **What formula should I use?**

**SOLVE** **Did I answer with the correct unit?**

**LOOK BACK** **Did I need inches, square inches or cubic inches?**

## Independent Practice

**Use a formula to solve.**

3. Suppose a toolbox is 1 foot high, 20 inches long, and 9 inches wide. How much space is inside the toolbox?

4. A workshop is 10 feet on each side. What area will be left for working if 6 square feet are used for a workbench?

5. **Mental Math** A garage wall that measures 10 feet by 30 feet needs to be painted. How many square feet is that?

6. **Analyze** You have 72 cm of wood to make a picture frame. How can you cut the wood to make a frame with the greatest area for a picture? What shape will it be?

Go On

# Mixed Problem Solving

**Solve. Show your work. Tell what strategy you used.**

7. There are 8 teams competing in a soccer tournament. Each team plays every other team once. How many games are played?

8. Mary planted flowers every 6 inches along a garden path. She planted them at the beginning, end, and along both sides of the 14-foot path. How many flowers did she plant?

9. Steven is thinking of a number. If he multiplies the number by 6 and then adds 123, the result is 621. What number is he thinking of?

**You Choose**

**Strategy**
- Draw a Picture
- Solve a Simpler Problem
- Work Backward
- Write an Equation

**Computation Method**
- Mental Math
- Estimation
- Paper and Pencil
- Calculator

**Solve. Tell which method you chose.**

10. **Money** Mr. Brown's class put 8 small plants and 5 large plants in a terrarium. The small plants cost $2.19 each. The large plants cost $3.86 each. About how much was spent on plants?

11. Sheila is starting a train trip. Her watch indicates that it is now 12 noon. The trip will end 2 days later at 3 P.M. How many hours will she be traveling?

12. Mike is framing a square picture that measures 20 inches on each side. What is the length of wood he will need for the frame?

13. A factory produces birdbaths. Workers can make 50 birdbaths in 30 minutes. How many birdbaths can be made in an 8-hour day? in a 40-hour week?

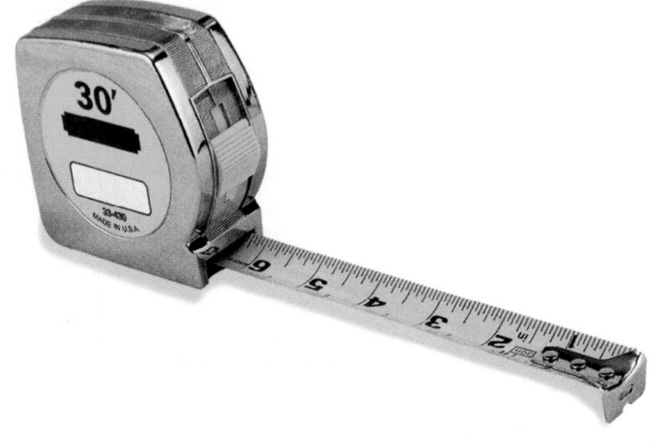

# Art Connection

## Be an Artist

Activity

GPS

STANDARDS M4G2.c

**Materials:** tape, safety scissors, Learning Tools 29, 30, 31, and 32

**Construct solid figures using nets.**

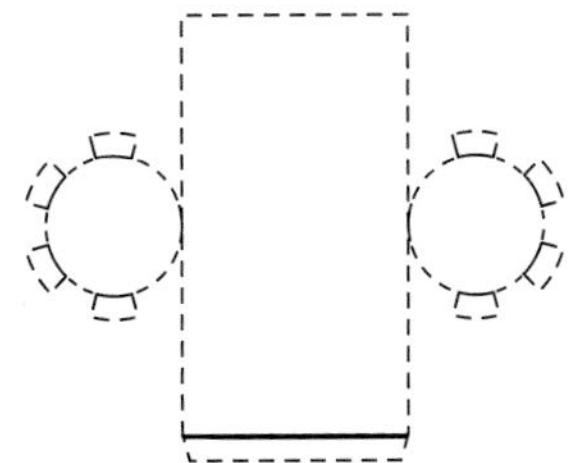

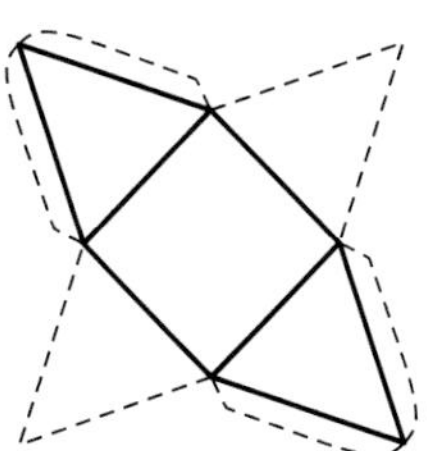

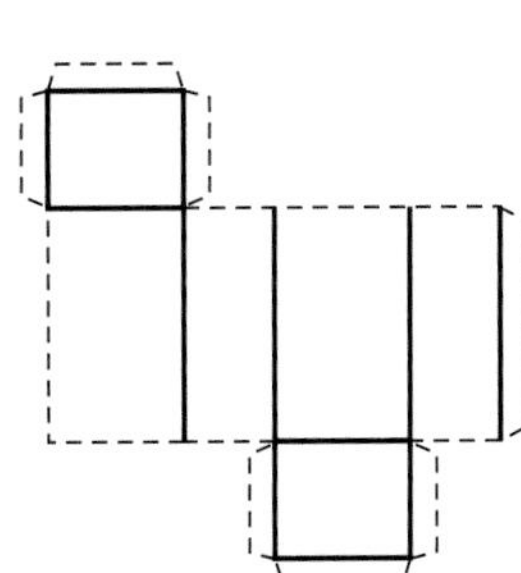

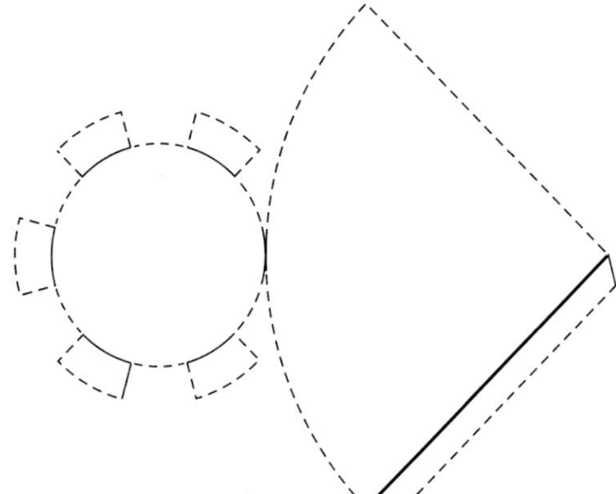

**Complete the following steps for all four nets.**

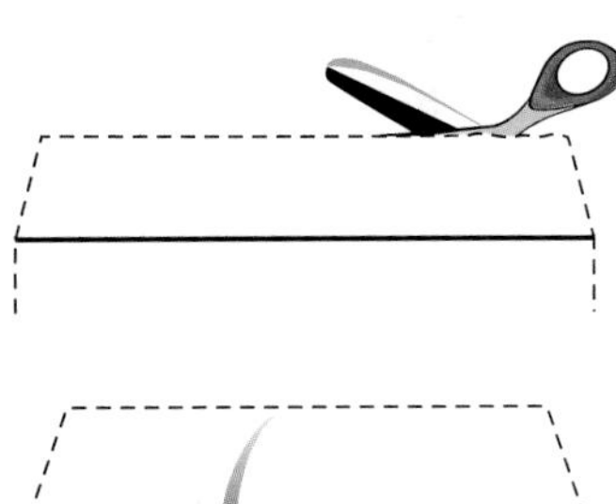

1. Cut along the dashed lines.
2. Fold along the solid lines.
3. Tape along the edges of the figure.
4. Name the solid figures you constructed.

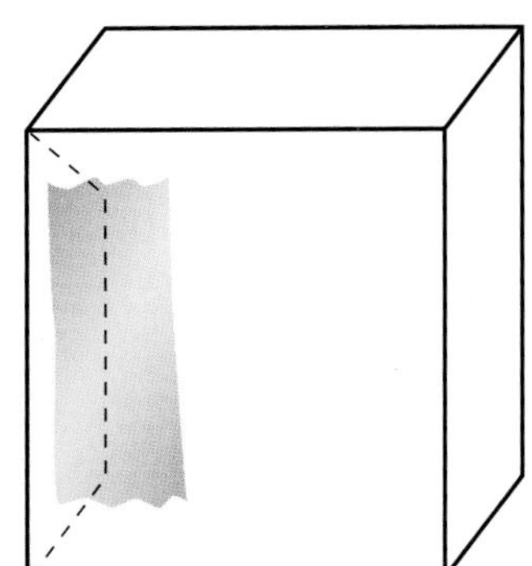

# Chapter Review/Test

Study Guide pages SG36–38

## VOCABULARY

**Choose the best word to complete each sentence.**

**Vocabulary**
- area
- vertex
- volume
- perimeter

1. The number of cubic units in a solid figure is the ____.
2. The point where 3 edges of a solid figure meet is a ____.
3. The number of square units in a region is the ____.

## CONCEPTS AND SKILLS

**Find the perimeter and area of each figure.** (Lessons 1–4, pp. 452–462)

4. 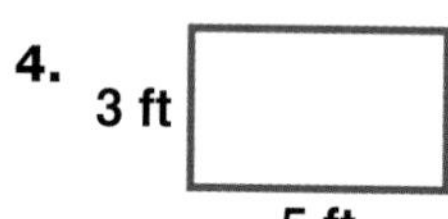


5. 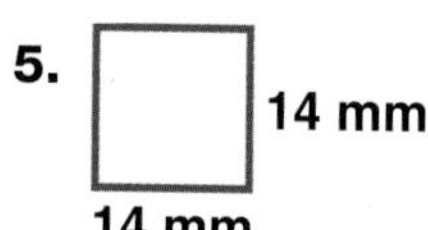


**Name the solid figure that can be made with the net.** (Lesson 5, pp. 464–467)

6. 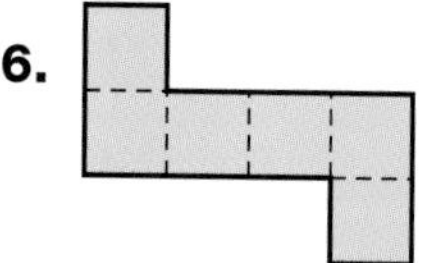

**Find the volume of each figure.** (Lesson 6, pp. 468–469)

7. 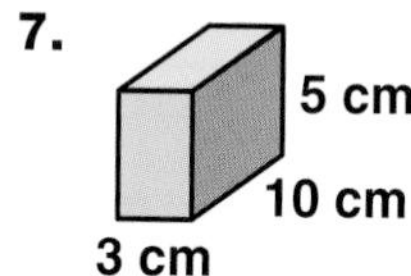


8. 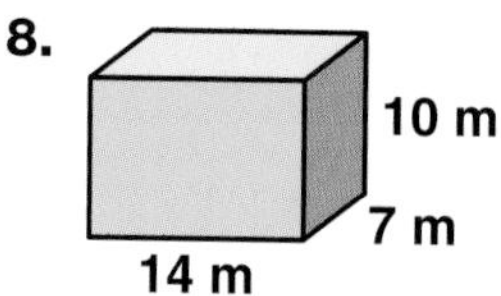


## PROBLEM SOLVING

**Use a formula to solve.** (Lesson 7, pp. 470–472)

9. Mrs. Cortez wants to buy wall-to-wall carpeting. The room is 10 feet wide and 12 feet long. How much carpeting does she need?
10. The volume of a box is 24 cubic inches. The height is 2 inches and the width is 3 inches. What is the length?

**Write About It**

**Show You Understand**

Kim has a rectangle with an area of 12 square inches. Mona says the length can only be 6 inches, and the width can only be 2 inches. Is she correct?

Explain your reasoning.

# Extra Practice

## Set A (Lesson 2, pp. 454–455)

**Write a formula to find each perimeter. Then solve.**

1. a square with sides 7 centimeters long
2. a regular pentagon with sides 3 meters long
3. a rectangle with sides 2 feet and 5 feet long

## Set B (Lesson 3 pp. 456–458)

**Find the area of each figure.**

1. a rectangle with sides 4 inches and 6 inches long
2. a square with sides 13 millimeters long
3. a rectangle with sides 5 feet and 9 feet long

## Set C (Lesson 4, pp. 460–462)

**Find the perimeter and area of each figure.**

1.

2 ft
5 ft
3 ft
6 ft
2 ft
8 ft

2. 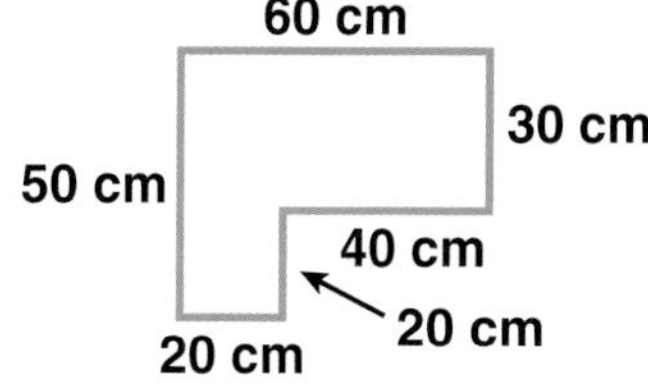


3. 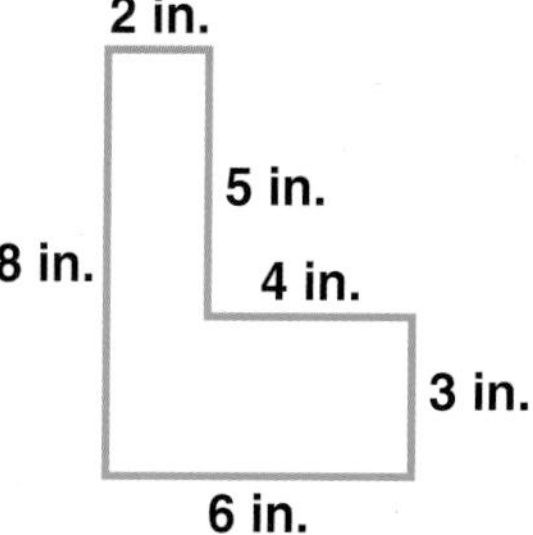


## Set D (Lesson 5, pp. 464–467)

**Name the solid figure that can be made with each net.**

1. 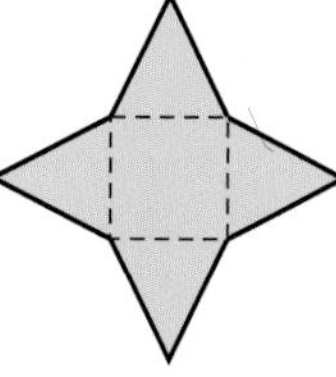

2. 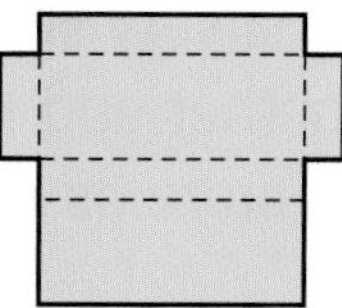

3. 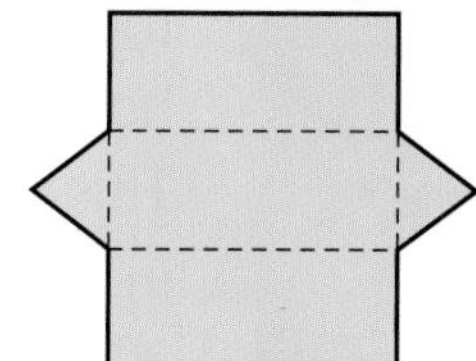

## Set E (Lesson 6, pp. 468–469)

**Find the volume of each figure.**

1. 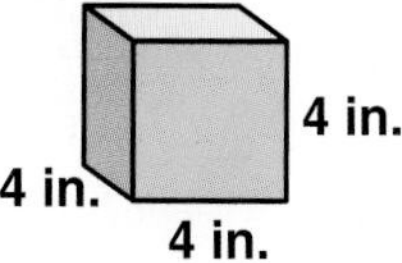


2. 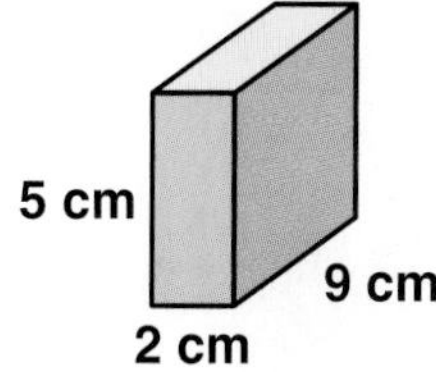


3. 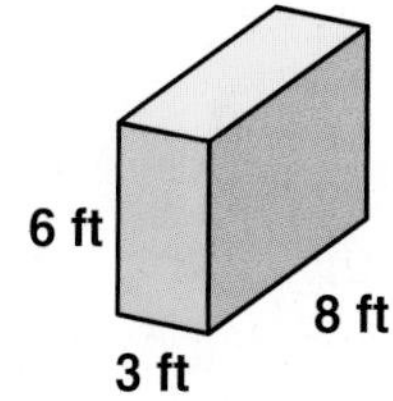

# A Home of Hexagons

Think about the rooms in the house where you live. If you draw them as two-dimensional shapes, they are probably shaped like squares or rectangles. However, the Georgia state insect prefers a different shape. Honeybees use hexagons to build the "rooms" of their homes.

The hexagons in a honeycomb are openings into room-like spaces called cells, where honeybees store honey for the winter. The queen bee of a colony also lays eggs in the honeycomb cells. After the baby bees hatch, they can eat the honey stored in the cells.

Honeycombs are made of wax. Their walls are very thin, but the honeycomb structure is very strong. The hexagons in a honeycomb fit tightly together and leave no wasted space. This allows honeybees to store as much honey as possible in a small space.

# UNIT 7

# Fractions and Decimals

# Reading Mathematics

## Reviewing Vocabulary

**Here are some math vocabulary words that you should know.**

| | |
|---|---|
| **fraction** | a number that names a part of a whole or part of a group |
| **denominator** | the number below the bar in a fraction that tells how many equal parts there are |
| **numerator** | the number above the bar in a fraction that tells how many equal parts have been counted |
| **decimal** | a number with one or more digits to the right of a decimal point |
| **decimal point** | a symbol (.) used to separate the ones and tenths places in a decimal |

## Reading Words and Symbols

Fractions and decimals both name parts of a whole. Look at the rectangle on the right.

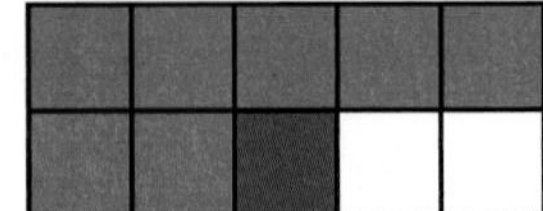

**Read:** Seven tenths of the rectangle is red.

**Write as a fraction:** $\frac{7}{10}$ of the rectangle is red.

**Write as a decimal:** 0.7 of the rectangle is red.

**Use words and symbols to answer the questions.**

1. In the fraction $\frac{7}{10}$, which number is the numerator? What does that number mean?
2. What decimal names the part of the rectangle that is blue? How would you write it as a fraction?

# Reading Questions on CRCT

**Choose the correct answer for each.**

**3.** Which statement is false?

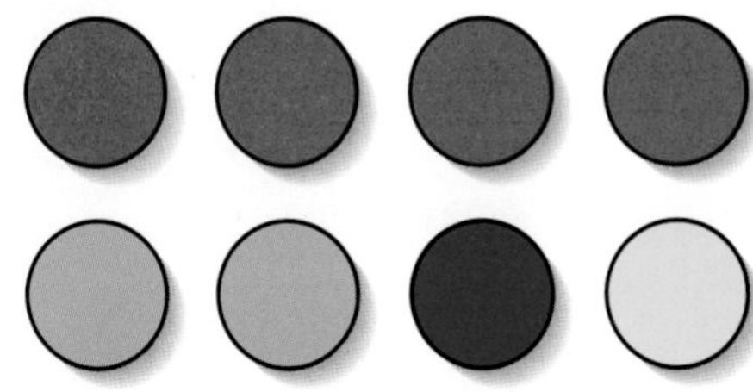

A. $\frac{1}{8}$ of the circles are blue.

B. $\frac{2}{8}$ of the circles are green.

C. $\frac{1}{2}$ of the circles are red.

D. $\frac{8}{8}$ of the circles are yellow.

**False** means "not true" or "wrong."

**4.** Which fraction represents the green part of the rectangle?

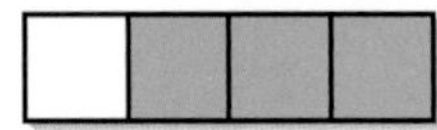

A. $\frac{1}{4}$

B. $\frac{1}{2}$

C. $\frac{2}{3}$

D. $\frac{3}{4}$

**Represents** means "stands for," or "shows," or "names."

**5.** Which decimal represents the shaded part of the rectangle?

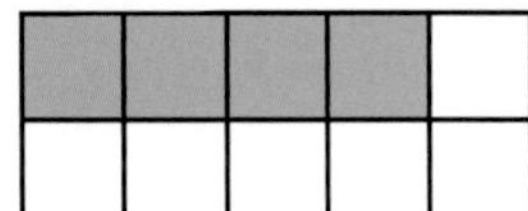

A. 0.3

B. 0.4

C. 0.5

D. 0.6

**Shaded** means "colored in."

# Learning Vocabulary

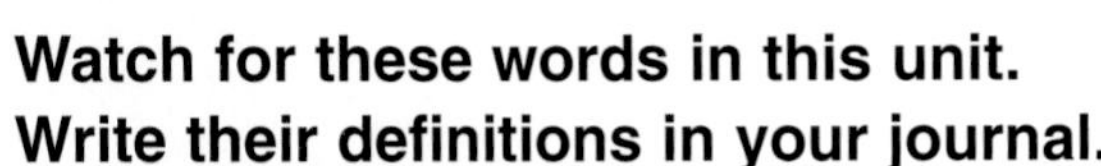

**Watch for these words in this unit. Write their definitions in your journal.**

**equivalent fractions**

**improper fraction**

**mixed fraction**

**tenth**

**hundredth**

## Education Place

At **eduplace.com/map** see eGlossary and eGames—Math Lingo.

## Literature Connection

Read "Hold the Meat!" on Pages 652–653. Then work with a partner to answer the questions about the story.

# Understand Fractions

## PERFORMANCE PREVIEW

### Using Data

The Venn diagram shows the flowers that 10 students like best. What fraction of the students like both azaleas and peach blossoms? How might the teacher use this information to decorate the classroom?

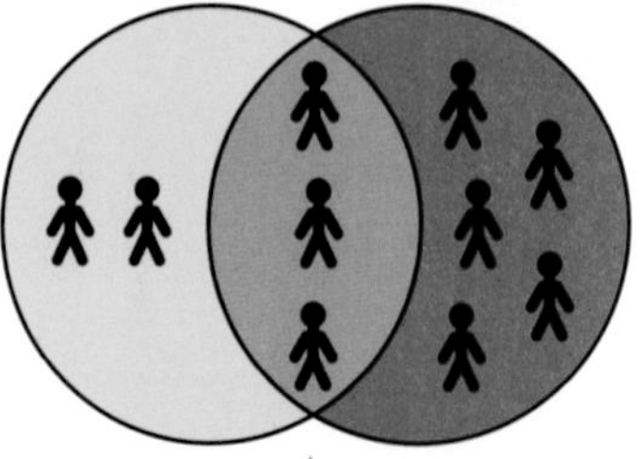

▶ A fraction is in **simplest form** when 1 is the only number that divides both the numerator and the denominator with no remainder.

| These fractions are in simplest form. | These fractions are not in simplest form. |
|---|---|
| $\frac{1}{2}$ $\frac{2}{3}$ $\frac{3}{8}$ $\frac{2}{7}$ $\frac{5}{9}$ | $\frac{2}{4}$ $\frac{4}{8}$ $\frac{3}{15}$ $\frac{6}{9}$ $\frac{8}{12}$ |

Juan and Brooke both used equivalent fractions to write $\frac{12}{18}$ in simplest form.

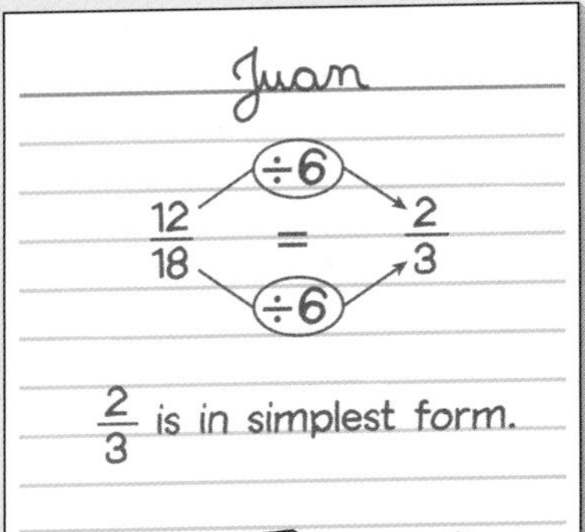


Brooke

$\frac{12}{18} = \frac{12 \div 2}{18 \div 2} = \frac{6}{9}$

$\frac{6}{9} = \frac{6 \div 3}{9 \div 3} = \frac{2}{3}$

$\frac{2}{3}$ is in simplest form.

Could Brooke have divided by 3 first?

$\frac{2}{3}$ is in simplest form because 1 is the only number that can divide both 2 and 3 with no remainder.

- How are Juan's work and Brooke's work alike?
- How are they different?

## Guided Practice

**Ask Yourself**

- Did I multiply or divide the numerator and the denominator by the same number?

**Write each fraction in simplest form. Then write another equivalent fraction.**

**1.** $\frac{2}{6}$ **2.** $\frac{4}{10}$ **3.** $\frac{6}{12}$ **4.** $\frac{10}{16}$

**Complete the equivalent fraction. What number did you multiply or divide the numerator or denominator by?**

**5.** $\frac{1}{2} = \frac{3}{■}$ **6.** $\frac{15}{20} = \frac{■}{4}$ **7.** $\frac{4}{10} = \frac{■}{5}$ **8.** $\frac{2}{3} = \frac{4}{■}$

**Explain Your Thinking** ▶ Can you always multiply or divide to find equivalent fractions?

Go On

## ...tice and Problem Solving

...e fractions in each pair equivalent? Explain how you know.

... $\frac{?}{8}$ $\frac{4}{16}$    10. $\frac{2}{4}$ $\frac{5}{10}$    11. $\frac{6}{9}$ $\frac{8}{12}$

12. $\frac{5}{5}$ $\frac{8}{8}$    13. $\frac{6}{15}$ $\frac{2}{5}$    14. $\frac{14}{16}$ $\frac{7}{9}$

**Write each fraction in simplest form. Then write another equivalent fraction.**

15. $\frac{3}{9}$    16. $\frac{6}{8}$    17. $\frac{9}{12}$    18. $\frac{6}{15}$    19. $\frac{15}{18}$

20. $\frac{4}{14}$    21. $\frac{2}{3}$    22. $\frac{20}{20}$    23. $\frac{9}{21}$    24. $\frac{18}{36}$

## $x$ Algebra • Variables Find the value of $x$.

25. $\frac{x}{4} = \frac{2}{8}$    26. $\frac{9}{12} = \frac{x}{4}$    27. $\frac{x}{5} = \frac{15}{15}$

28. $\frac{10}{x} = \frac{2}{3}$    29. $\frac{18}{27} = \frac{2}{x}$    30. $\frac{x}{42} = \frac{1}{7}$

**Use the recipe for Problems 31–33.**

31. Are the amounts of cranberry juice and pineapple juice equivalent? Explain.

32. Reni made 12 servings of her fruit shake for her friends. How many bananas did she use?

33. Lila will make one serving of Reni's recipe. How much cranberry juice does she need? Use fraction strips to solve the problem.

34. **Write About It** Justine says that $\frac{2}{3}$ and $\frac{16}{25}$ are equivalent fractions. Is she correct? Explain your thinking.

35. **Reasoning** Can you add the same number to the numerator and denominator to find equivalent fractions? Why or why not?

### Reni's Fruit Shake

1 large banana
1 cup strawberries
1 mango, cubed
$\frac{3}{4}$ cup cranberry juice
$\frac{1}{2}$ cup pineapple juice
1 cup ice cubes

Put all ingredients in blender.
Blend until thick and smooth.
**Makes 3 servings.**



Extra Practice See page 513, Set B.

## Sharpening Skills for CRCT

### Open Response

**Solve.** (Ch. 6, Lesson 4; Ch. 8, Lesson 2)

**36.** $4\overline{)78}$ **37.** $8\overline{)26}$ **38.** $18 \times 7$

**39.** $6\overline{)45}$ **40.** $86 \times 3$ **41.** $25 \times 9$

**42.** $31 \times 4$ **43.** $8\overline{)38}$ **44.** $4\overline{)89}$

**45.** Dora's team won 10 of 15 games. Pedro's team played 6 games and won the same fraction of their games as Dora's. How many games did Pedro's team win? Explain your thinking. (Ch. 19, Lesson 3)

Game

GPS Activity

# Fraction Match-up

**2 Players**

**STANDARDS** M4N6.a

**What You'll Need** • 16 index cards (Learning Tool 37)

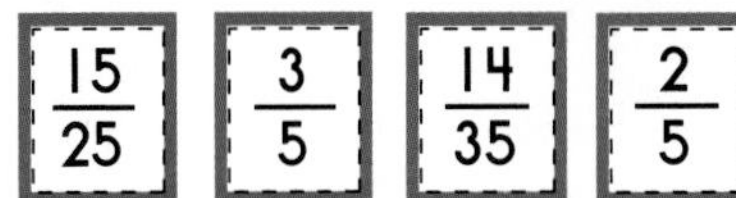


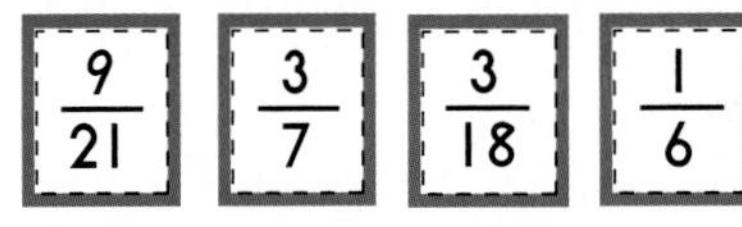


12/40 3/10 15/24 5/8

### How to Play

1. Use Learning Tool 37 or make 16 cards like the ones shown.
2. Shuffle the cards. Place them facedown in any order in a 4 × 4 array.
3. A player turns over any two cards. If the cards show two equivalent fractions, the player keeps both cards. If not, the player turns the cards over and places them in the same positions.
4. Players take turns repeating Step 3 until all 8 matches have been made. The player with the greater number of cards is the winner.

 **Audio Tutor 2/19 Listen and Understand**

# Compare and Order Fractions

**Objective** Compare and order fractions.

**STANDARDS** M4N6.a, Prepares for M5N4.f, M4P2

## Learn About It

Clay used $\frac{2}{6}$ of his garden for pumpkins, $\frac{1}{2}$ for lettuce, and $\frac{1}{6}$ for tomatoes. Was more of his garden used for pumpkins or for tomatoes?

To compare fractions that have the same denominators, just compare the numerators.

**Compare $\frac{2}{6}$ and $\frac{1}{6}$.**

pumpkins → $\frac{1}{6}$ $\frac{1}{6}$ $\frac{2}{6}$

tomatoes → $\frac{1}{6}$ $\frac{1}{6}$

$2 > 1$, so $\frac{2}{6} > \frac{1}{6}$

**Solution:** Clay used more of his garden for pumpkins than tomatoes.

▶ You can also compare fractions with different denominators.

**Compare $\frac{2}{6}$ and $\frac{1}{2}$.**

## Different Ways to Compare $\frac{2}{6}$ and $\frac{1}{2}$

### Way 1 Use a model.

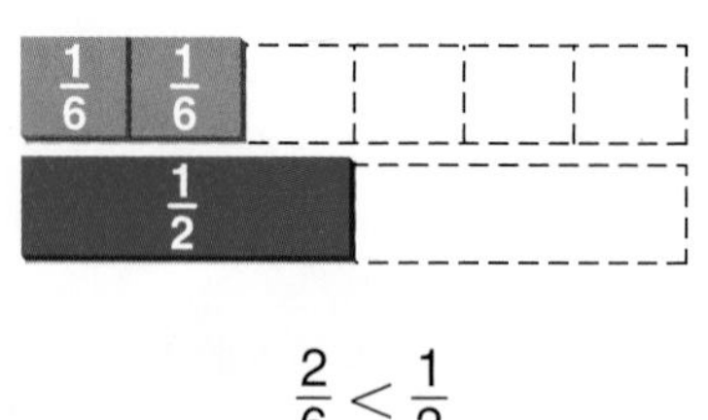


$\frac{2}{6} < \frac{1}{2}$

### Way 2 Find equivalent fractions. Then compare the numerators.

- Find a fraction equivalent to $\frac{1}{2}$ that has a denominator of 6.

$$\frac{1 \times 3}{2 \times 3} = \frac{3}{6} \quad \text{so} \quad \frac{1}{2} = \frac{3}{6}$$

- Then compare the numerators.

$\frac{2}{6} < \frac{3}{6}$, so $\frac{2}{6} < \frac{1}{2}$.

**Solution:** $\frac{2}{6}$ is less than $\frac{1}{2}$.



Extra Help at **eduplace.com/map**

▶ You can use what you know about comparing fractions to order fractions.

**Order $\frac{2}{6}$, $\frac{1}{2}$, and $\frac{1}{6}$ from least to greatest.**

## Different Ways to Order $\frac{2}{6}$, $\frac{1}{2}$, and $\frac{1}{6}$

### Way 1 Find equivalent fractions. Then compare the numerators.

- Find a fraction equivalent to $\frac{1}{2}$ that has a denominator of 6.

$$\frac{1}{2} \overset{\times 3}{=} \frac{3}{6}, \text{ so } \frac{1}{2} = \frac{3}{6}.$$

- Then compare the numerators and order the fractions.

$1 < 2 < 3$, so $\frac{1}{6} < \frac{2}{6} < \frac{1}{2}$

### Way 2 Use a number line.

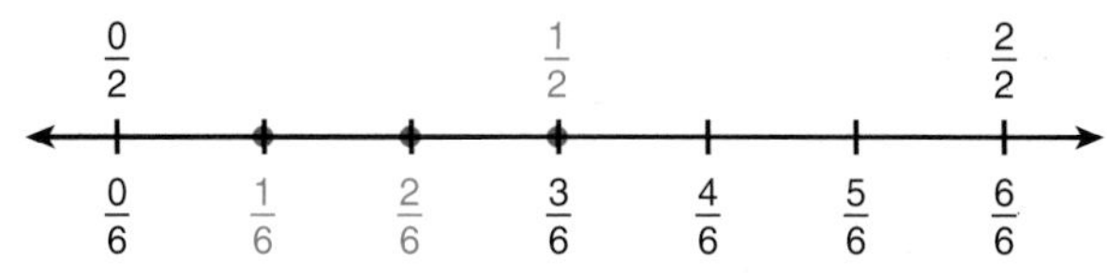


$\frac{1}{6}$ is farthest to the left.

$\frac{1}{2}$ is farthest to the right.

$\frac{2}{6}$ is in the middle.

So $\frac{1}{6} < \frac{2}{6} < \frac{1}{2}$

**Solution:** The order of the fractions from least to greatest is: $\frac{1}{6}$ $\frac{2}{6}$ $\frac{1}{2}$

## Guided Practice

**Ask Yourself**

- Do the fractions have like denominators?
- If not, how can I find equivalent fractions?

**Compare. Write >, <, or = for each ●.**

**1.** $\frac{3}{4}$ ● $\frac{5}{8}$

$\frac{1}{4}$ $\frac{1}{4}$ $\frac{1}{4}$

$\frac{1}{8}$ $\frac{1}{8}$ $\frac{1}{8}$ $\frac{1}{8}$ $\frac{1}{8}$

**2.** $\frac{2}{3}$ ● $\frac{5}{6}$

$\frac{1}{3}$ $\frac{1}{3}$

$\frac{1}{6}$ $\frac{1}{6}$ $\frac{1}{6}$ $\frac{1}{6}$ $\frac{1}{6}$

**3.** $\frac{4}{6}$ ● $\frac{2}{3}$

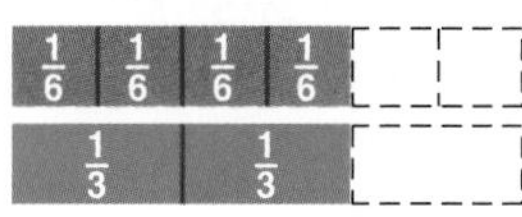


**Order the fractions from greatest to least. Draw number lines to help if you wish.**

**4.** $\frac{2}{7}$ $\frac{6}{7}$ $\frac{4}{7}$

**5.** $\frac{3}{4}$ $\frac{7}{8}$ $\frac{5}{8}$

**6.** $\frac{1}{5}$ $\frac{1}{10}$ $\frac{4}{5}$

**7.** $\frac{6}{12}$ $\frac{1}{3}$ $\frac{3}{3}$

**Explain Your Thinking** ▶ Suppose you have to order $\frac{2}{3}$, $\frac{1}{4}$, and $\frac{1}{2}$. What is the smallest denominator you can use to write equivalent fractions for $\frac{2}{3}$, $\frac{1}{4}$, and $\frac{1}{2}$?

## Practice and Problem Solving

**Compare. Write >, <, or = for each ⬬.**

**8.** $\frac{2}{6}$ ⬬ $\frac{4}{6}$

$\frac{1}{6}$ $\frac{1}{6}$

$\frac{1}{6}$ $\frac{1}{6}$ $\frac{1}{6}$ $\frac{1}{6}$

**9.** $\frac{1}{2}$ ⬬ $\frac{2}{4}$

$\frac{1}{2}$

$\frac{1}{4}$ $\frac{1}{4}$

**10.** $\frac{1}{4}$ ⬬ $\frac{3}{8}$

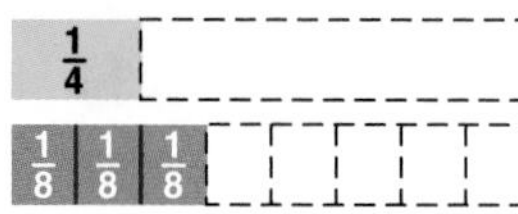


**11.** $\frac{6}{7}$ ⬬ $\frac{5}{7}$ **12.** $\frac{4}{9}$ ⬬ $\frac{1}{3}$ **13.** $\frac{3}{5}$ ⬬ $\frac{2}{10}$ **14.** $\frac{2}{3}$ ⬬ $\frac{1}{4}$

**Mental Math Write >, <, or = for each ⬬.**

**15.** 1 ⬬ $\frac{5}{6}$ **16.** $\frac{2}{4}$ ⬬ $\frac{2}{8}$ **17.** $\frac{3}{5}$ ⬬ $\frac{3}{8}$ **18.** 2 ⬬ $\frac{4}{8}$

**19.** $\frac{2}{5}$ ⬬ $\frac{4}{5}$ **20.** $\frac{6}{7}$ ⬬ 1 **21.** $\frac{2}{2}$ ⬬ 2 **22.** $\frac{3}{3}$ ⬬ $\frac{6}{6}$

**Order the fractions from least to greatest.**

**23.** $\frac{1}{5}$ $\frac{4}{5}$ $\frac{2}{5}$ **24.** $\frac{5}{7}$ $\frac{2}{7}$ $\frac{6}{7}$ **25.** $\frac{4}{8}$ $\frac{7}{8}$ $\frac{1}{8}$ **26.** $\frac{7}{12}$ $\frac{10}{12}$ $\frac{3}{4}$

**27.** $\frac{5}{8}$ $\frac{3}{4}$ $\frac{1}{4}$ **28.** $\frac{2}{3}$ $\frac{2}{6}$ $\frac{3}{6}$ **29.** $\frac{1}{2}$ $\frac{4}{6}$ $\frac{5}{12}$ **30.** $\frac{3}{4}$ $\frac{1}{2}$ $\frac{1}{3}$

**Solve.**

**31.** **Write About It** Why is it easier to compare fractions with the same rather than different denominators?

**32.** **Analyze** Explain why you can compare $\frac{2}{12}$ and $\frac{2}{16}$ without finding equivalent fractions.

**Data** **The table at the right shows results from the longest-green-bean contest at a fair. Use the table for Problems 33–35.**

**33.** Who entered a longer green bean, Sara or Brian?

**34.** List the lengths of the green beans in order from shortest to longest.

**35.** Which people entered green beans that were less than $\frac{2}{3}$ yd long?

**Longest Green Beans at County Fair**

| Name | Length |
|---|---|
| Sara | $\frac{5}{6}$ yd |
| Tom | $\frac{1}{2}$ yd |
| Brian | $\frac{7}{12}$ yd |



Extra Practice See page 513, Set C.

Problem Solving

GPS

## Social Studies Connection

### Flags of Africa

STANDARDS Extends M4N6, M4P4

Five students were studying African countries. They each drew and colored the flag of the country they were studying. From the clues, decide who colored each flag.

A

B

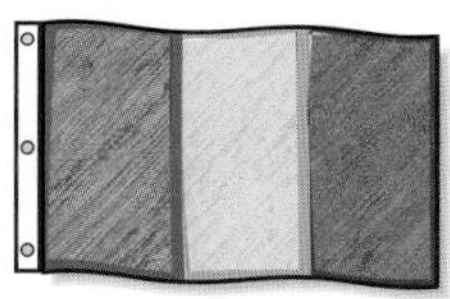
C

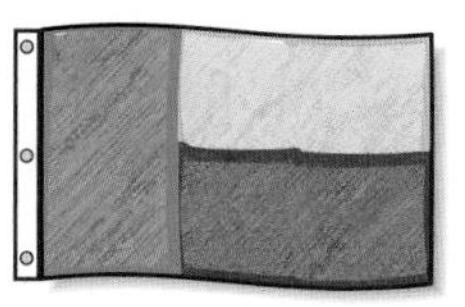
D

E

- José said, "Inga's flag and my flag are both $\frac{1}{3}$ red, with the red stripe on the right."
- Heather said, "My flag has the same colors as José's flag and Ken's flag."
- Ken said, "The thirds on my flag are not the same as the thirds on all the other flags."
- Maribeth said, "My flag is $\frac{2}{3}$ green."

**Challenge** Do research to find the name of each country being studied.

WEEKLY WR READER eduplace.com/map

Quick Check

Check your understanding of Lessons 1–4.

**Write a fraction for the part that is shaded. Then write a fraction for the part that is not shaded.** (Lesson 1)

1. 

2. 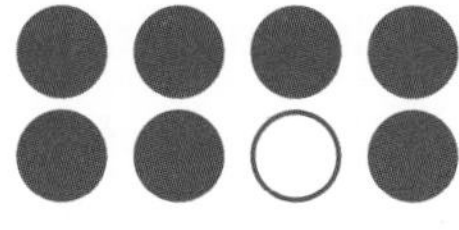

3. 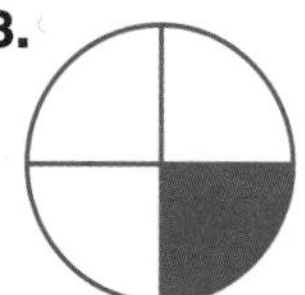

4. 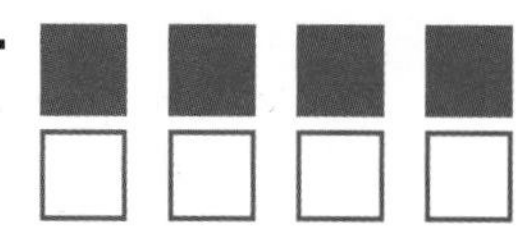

**Write each fraction in simplest form. Then write another equivalent fraction.** (Lessons 2–3)

5. $\frac{4}{6}$

6. $\frac{9}{12}$

7. $\frac{10}{20}$

8. $\frac{8}{18}$

**Order the fractions from greatest to least.** (Lesson 4)

9. $\frac{3}{4}$ $\frac{7}{8}$ $\frac{5}{8}$

10. $\frac{2}{5}$ $\frac{3}{10}$ $\frac{7}{10}$

Lesson 5

# Find Part of a Number

**Objective** Find a fractional part of a number.

 **STANDARDS** Maintains M3N5.d, M4P1.b

## Learn About It

Maria and her mother use 20 apples to make apple pies. One fourth of the apples are green and three fourths are red. How many apples are red?

**How can you find $\frac{3}{4}$ of 20?**

## Different Ways to Find $\frac{3}{4}$ of 20

### Way 1 You can use a model.

**STEP 1** The denominator, 4, tells you to separate the 20 counters into 4 equal groups.

**STEP 2** The numerator, 3, tells you to count the number in 3 groups.

4 equal groups

3 groups = 15

$\frac{3}{4}$ of 20 is 15.

### Way 2 You can use division and multiplication.

**STEP 1** Divide 20 by 4 to find the number in each group.

number of apples ↓ number of equal groups ↙

$20 \div 4 = 5$

↑ number in each group

**STEP 2** Multiply the number in each group by 3.

$5 \times 3 = 15$

$\frac{3}{4}$ of 20 is 15.

**Solution:** 15 apples are red.

## Guided Practice

**Find the fractional part of each number.**

**1.** 

$\frac{1}{4}$ of 8

**2.** 

$\frac{3}{5}$ of 10

**Ask Yourself**

- How many equal parts are there?
- How many equal parts do I need to count?

**3.** $\frac{2}{3}$ of 9 **4.** $\frac{1}{6}$ of 24 **5.** $\frac{2}{5}$ of 20 **6.** $\frac{3}{4}$ of 16 **7.** $\frac{4}{5}$ of 15

**Explain Your Thinking** ▶ How does knowing $\frac{1}{5}$ of 10 help you find $\frac{2}{5}$ of 10?

## Practice and Problem Solving

**Find the fractional part of each number.**

**8.** $\frac{1}{2}$ of 14 **9.** $\frac{2}{3}$ of 30 **10.** $\frac{1}{4}$ of 12 **11.** $\frac{3}{7}$ of 14 **12.** $\frac{2}{10}$ of 10

**13.** $\frac{3}{5}$ of 20 **14.** $\frac{7}{9}$ of 18 **15.** $\frac{3}{8}$ of 16 **16.** $\frac{5}{6}$ of 12 **17.** $\frac{3}{10}$ of 100

**Solve.**

**18.** Mina has 21 apples. Two thirds of the apples are green. How many of the apples are green?

**19.** Keisha's family eats $\frac{3}{4}$ of an 8-piece apple pie. How many pieces are not eaten?

**20.** **Analyze** Mike's dad has 100 quarters. He tells Mike that he can have either $\frac{3}{4}$ or $\frac{6}{10}$ of them. Which should Mike choose? Explain.

**21.** **Represent** Show why $\frac{2}{3}$ of 9 and $\frac{1}{3}$ of 18 name the same number. Use counters or draw a picture to explain your reasoning.

## GPS Sharpening Skills for CRCT

**Open Response**

**Solve.** (Ch. 6, Lessons 4, 6; Ch. 9, Lessons 2, 3)

**22.** $67 \times 8$ **23.** $105 \times 6$

**24.** $504 \div 7$ **25.** $\$5.60 \div 5$

**26.** $317 \div 9$ **27.** $\$7.24 \div 4$

**Multiple Choice**

**28.** Donya is $\frac{1}{4}$ as old as her sister, Amy. If Amy is 24, how old is Donya? (Ch. 19, Lesson 5)

A. 4 B. 6 C. 8 D. 14

Extra Practice See page 513, Set D.

# Lesson 6

Audio Tutor 2/20 Listen and Understand

# Problem-Solving Strategy Draw a Picture

**Objective** Draw a picture to solve a problem.

**STANDARDS** M4N6.a, M4P1.b

**Problem** Annie Aardvark's dinner was all ants. One half of the ants she ate were black, $\frac{1}{4}$ were red, and 6 were brown. How many ants did Annie eat?

**This is what you know.**

- $\frac{1}{2}$ were black ants.
- $\frac{1}{4}$ were red ants.
- 6 were brown ants.

PLAN

**You can draw a picture to help you solve the problem.**

**Draw a picture.**

- Draw a rectangle. Show the information given in the problem.
- Use what you know about fractions to solve the problem.

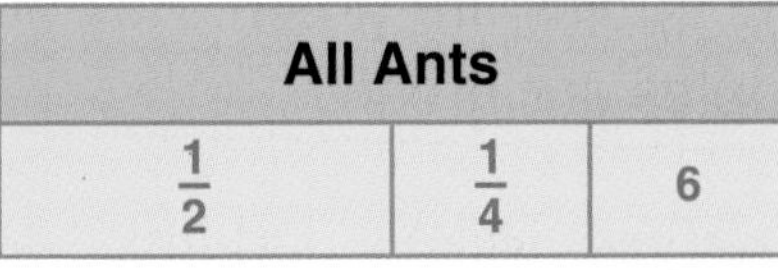

| All Ants | | |
|---|---|---|
| $\frac{1}{2}$ | $\frac{1}{4}$ | 6 |
| black ants | red ants | brown ants |

You know $\frac{1}{2} = \frac{2}{4}$ and $1 = \frac{4}{4}$.

So 6 brown ants are $\frac{1}{4}$ of all the ants.

Then $4 \times 6$, or 24, is the total number of ants.

Why do you multiply by 4?

| All Ants | | | |
|---|---|---|---|
| $\frac{1}{4}$ | $\frac{1}{4}$ | $\frac{1}{4}$ | $\frac{1}{4}$ |
| black ants | | red ants | 6 brown ants |

**Solution:** Annie ate 24 ants.

**Look back at the problem.**

Does the solution make sense?

## Guided Practice

**Use the Ask Yourself questions to help you solve each problem.**

1. Spencer Spider bought insects. Two sixths were centipedes, $\frac{1}{2}$ were millipedes, and 12 were flies. How many insects did he buy?

2. Betty Bat has a bug collection. Two eighths are flies, $\frac{3}{8}$ are locusts, and 9 are moths. How many flies are in her collection?

   Hint The answer is **not** 24.

### Ask Yourself

**What facts do I know?**

**Can I draw a picture?**

- **Did I separate the rectangle into equal parts?**
- **Did I label the parts?**
- **Did I find the number each part represents?**

LOOK BACK

**Did I solve the problem?**

## Independent Practice

**Draw a picture to solve each problem.**

3. Rodney spent half of his money on paint and $\frac{1}{6}$ on art paper. He had \$8 left. What was his starting amount?

4. All the students in Ann's art class must complete one final project. Three eighths painted, $\frac{1}{4}$ drew charcoal sketches, and 12 made pottery. How many students are there in Ann's class?

5. Tina collects colorful beads. Five twelfths are green, $\frac{1}{3}$ are red, and 9 are yellow. How many beads are red?

6. Carl made fruit punch. Half of it was orange juice, $\frac{2}{6}$ was cranberry juice, and 12 ounces was ginger ale. How many ounces of punch did he make?

Go On

# Mixed Problem Solving

**Solve. Show your work. Tell what strategy you used.**

7. **Money** Suppose you had only nickels and dimes in your pocket. Then you lost 10 coins that totaled 85 cents. How many of each coin did you lose?

8. Rico spent half of his money on admission to the museum and $\frac{1}{4}$ on lunch. He has \$5 left. What was his starting amount?

9. Colleen wants a computer game that costs \$64. She has \$30. If she saves \$5 a week, how many weeks will it take until she has enough money to buy the game?

**You Choose**

**Strategy**
- Draw a Picture
- Guess and Check
- Make a Table
- Write an Equation

**Computation Method**
- Mental Math
- Estimation
- Paper and Pencil
- Calculator

## Data Use the graph to solve Problems 10–13.

Each week Steve earns money by helping in art classes for younger students. The graph shows what he does with his money each week.

10. How much money does Steve earn each week?

11. How much more money does Steve spend on food than on art supplies?

12. Steve spends $\frac{1}{2}$ of his food money at school. How much does he spend on food at school?

13. After 9 weeks, how much money will Steve have earned? How much money will he have saved?

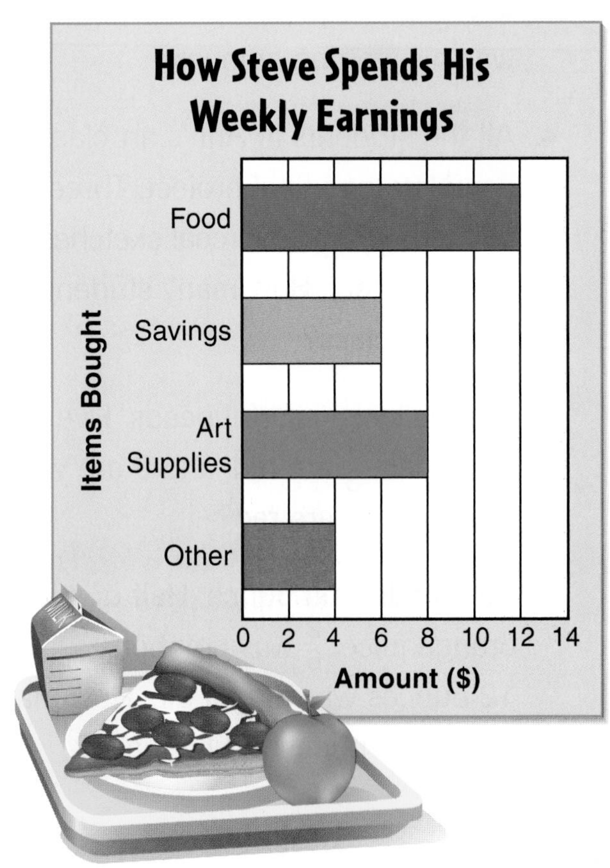

# Problem Solving on CRCT

Multiple Choice

**Choose the letter of the correct answer.**

1. Tina bought some bottled water for a bike trip. She drank 3 bottles. Then she bought 5 more. After drinking another 2 bottles, she had 4 bottles left. How many bottles of water did Tina start with?

   A. 14
   B. 12
   C. 10
   D. 4

   (Chapter 9, Lesson 5)

2. What is the next likely picture in this pattern?

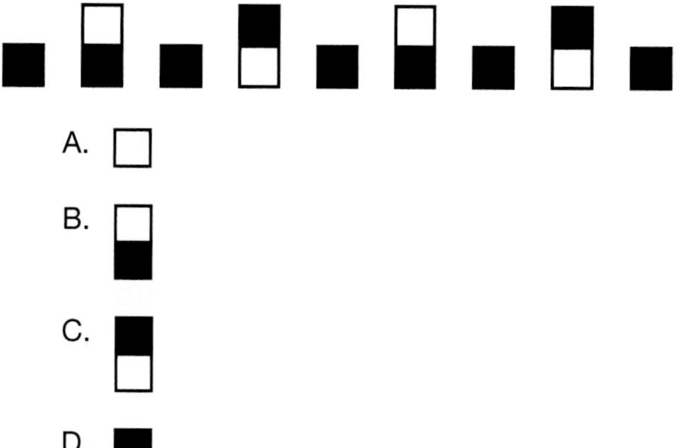


   (Chapter 16, Lesson 6)

Open Response

**Solve each problem.**

3. In a picture of turtles and parrots, there are 7 animals with 22 legs altogether. How many parrots are in the picture?

   **Represent** Support your solution with a picture or table.

   (Chapter 13, Lesson 3)

4. Tommy has 36 photos. He wants to put the photos in an album. He puts 4 photos on each page. How many pages will he use?

   **Represent** Write an equation that can be used to find the number of pages he will need.

   (Chapter 5, Lesson 5)

5. Nina is using the pattern of squares below to make a quilt.

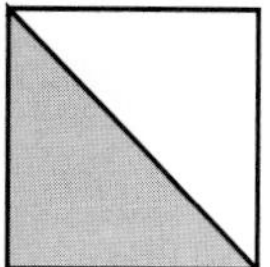 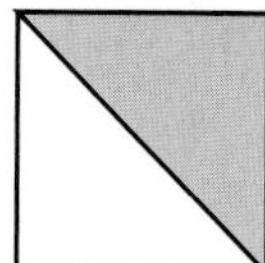 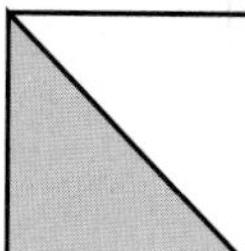 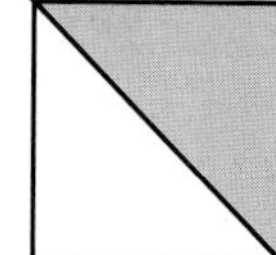

   a. Each square is made from two congruent parts. What shape is each part?

   b. What is the measure of each angle in one of the shaded sections of each square? Explain.

   c. To make the pattern for her quilt, Nina imagines rotating a square to determine how the next square will be attached. Use two different ways to describe the rotation from one square to the next.

   d. Use two different ways to describe how to rotate the first square in the pattern to get the third square in the pattern.

   (Chapter 17)

**Education Place**

See **eduplace.com/map** for more Test-Taking Tips.

Lesson 7

Audio Tutor 2/21 Listen and Understand

# Mixed Numbers and Improper Fractions

**Objective** Write mixed numbers and improper fractions.

**STANDARDS** M4N6.c, M4P1.b

**Vocabulary**
mixed number
improper fraction

## Learn About It

There are two whole waffles and one fourth of a waffle. There are nine fourths waffles.

**You can write the amount of waffles as a mixed number or as an improper fraction.**

▶ A **mixed number** is made up of a whole number and a fraction.

whole number → $2\frac{1}{4}$ ← fraction

To write a mixed number, count the wholes and parts.

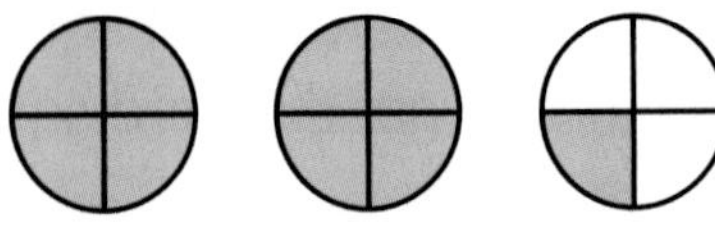

$\frac{4}{4} + \frac{4}{4} + \frac{1}{4} = 2\frac{1}{4}$

▶ An **improper fraction** has a numerator that is greater than or equal to its denominator.

$\frac{9}{4}$ ← improper fraction

To write an improper fraction, count the parts.

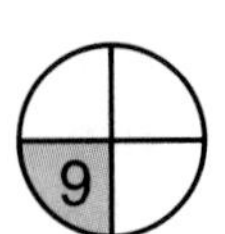



$\frac{9}{4}$

Here's how to change from one form to another.

**To change an improper fraction to a mixed number, you can divide.**

The fraction bar stands for "divided by." So $\frac{9}{4}$ means "9 divided by 4."

$$\begin{array}{r} 2 \\ 4\overline{)9} \\ -\ 8 \\ \hline 1 \end{array}$$

2 ← number of wholes

1 ← number of fourths

So $\frac{9}{4}$ is equal to $2\frac{1}{4}$.

**To change a mixed number to an improper fraction, you can multiply and add, as shown below.**

$$2\frac{1}{4} = \frac{9}{4}$$

9 ← (4 × 2) + 1

4 ← denominator stays the same

So $2\frac{1}{4} = \frac{9}{4}$.

## Other Examples

### Improper Fractions Equal to Whole Numbers

**A.**

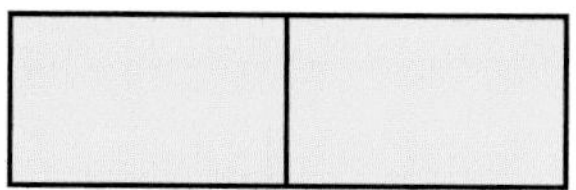

$\frac{2}{2} = 1$, because $2 \div 2 = 1$

**B.**

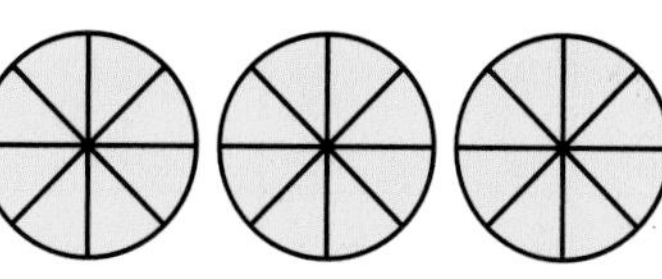

$\frac{24}{8} = 3$, because $24 \div 8 = 3$

## Guided Practice

**Write an improper fraction for the shaded parts. Then write each as a mixed number or as a whole number.**

**1.** 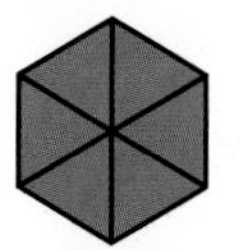 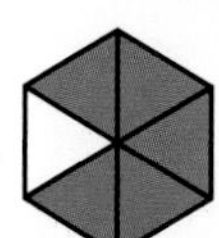

**2.** 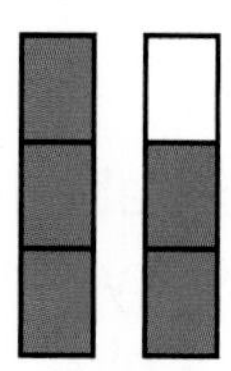

**3.** 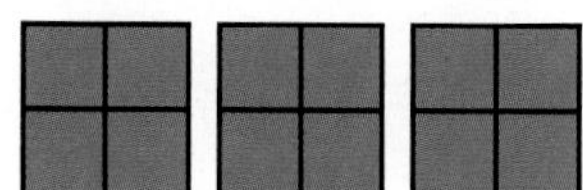

**4.** 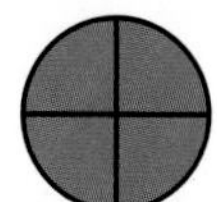

**Ask Yourself**

- Into how many equal parts is each figure divided?
- How many wholes are represented?

**Explain Your Thinking** ▶ How can you tell whether a fraction can be rewritten as a mixed number or as a whole number?

## Practice and Problem Solving

**Write an improper fraction and a mixed number or whole number to describe the shaded parts.**

**5.** 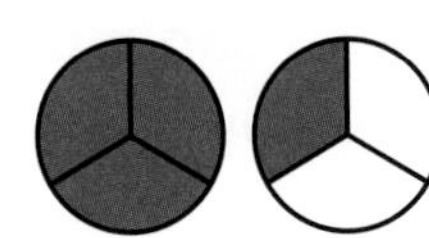

**6.** 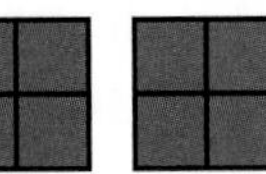

**7.** 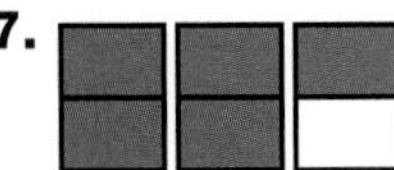

**Write a mixed number and an improper fraction for each letter.**

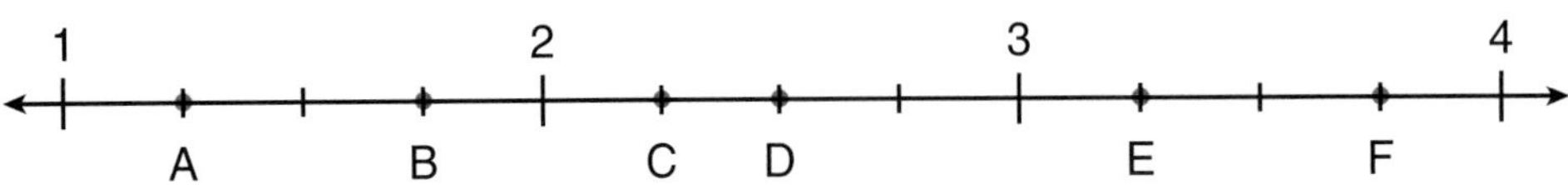


**8.** A **9.** C **10.** F **11.** D **12.** B **13.** E

**Copy and complete each table.**

| | Division | Improper Fraction | Mixed Numbers or Whole Numbers |
|---|---|---|---|
| **14.** | 16 ÷ 3 | $\frac{16}{3}$ | |
| **15.** | 19 ÷ 2 | | $9\frac{1}{2}$ |
| **16.** | | $\frac{11}{9}$ | |
| **17.** | | | $1\frac{7}{8}$ |

| | Division | Improper Fraction | Mixed Numbers or Whole Numbers |
|---|---|---|---|
| **18.** | | $\frac{28}{7}$ | |
| **19.** | | | $4\frac{4}{5}$ |
| **20.** | 10 ÷ 2 | | |
| **21.** | | $\frac{15}{6}$ | |

**Solve.**

**22.** Mr. Alvarez brought 5 oranges to a picnic. All the oranges were cut into halves. Each person ate one half of an orange, and there were no oranges left over. How many people ate oranges?

**23.** Michael is 5 years older than Elizabeth. Elizabeth is 8 years younger than José. Meredith is 2 years younger than José. If Meredith is 12 years old, how old is Michael?

**24.** **Reasoning** Ms. Carter made pies for the picnic. She brought enough so that each person could have $\frac{1}{8}$ of a pie. What is the least number of pies she could have made if 20 people were at the picnic?

Extra Practice See page 513, Set E.

## Sharpening Skills for CRCT

GPS

**Open Response**

**Find the fractional part of each number.**

**25.** $\frac{2}{3}$ of 15 ☆☆☆☆☆ ☆☆☆☆☆ ☆☆☆☆☆

**26.** $\frac{5}{6}$ of 18 □□□□□□ □□□□□□ □□□□□□

(Ch. 19, Lesson 5)

**Solve.**

**27.** Mr. Cronin's class made 4 pecan pies for the school bake sale. Each of the pies is cut into 8 equal pieces. Mr. Cronin bought 10 pieces of pie for a party. What fraction of 1 pie did he buy? Write your answer as an improper fraction in simplest form and as a mixed number.

(Ch. 19, Lesson 7)

# Math Reasoning

## Pie Pieces

Problem Solving GPS

**STANDARDS** Extends M4N6

**You can use these pies to help you round fractions.**

$\frac{1}{8}$ is close to 0.

Round $\frac{1}{8}$ to 0.

$\frac{3}{8}$ is close to $\frac{1}{2}$.

Round $\frac{3}{8}$ to $\frac{1}{2}$.

$\frac{7}{8}$ is close to 1.

Round $\frac{7}{8}$ to 1.

**Write whether the fraction rounds to 0, $\frac{1}{2}$, or 1.**

**1.** $\frac{1}{10}$ **2.** $\frac{5}{6}$ **3.** $\frac{4}{5}$ **4.** $\frac{2}{6}$

**5.** $\frac{3}{5}$ **6.** $\frac{9}{8}$ **7.** $\frac{4}{6}$ **8.** $\frac{4}{10}$

# Chapter Review/Test

Study Guide pages SG20–21

## VOCABULARY

**Choose the best term to complete each sentence.**

**Vocabulary**
- denominator
- simplest form
- mixed number
- improper fraction

**1.** The number 7 in $\frac{4}{7}$ is the ____ of the fraction.

**2.** If the only number that divides both the numerator and the denominator is 1, then the fraction is in ____.

**3.** If the denominator is less than the numerator, then the number is a(n) ____.

## CONCEPTS AND SKILLS

**Draw a picture to show each.** (Lesson 1, pp. 490–491; Lesson 7, pp. 508–510)

**4.** $\frac{6}{7}$ **5.** $\frac{8}{8}$ **6.** $1\frac{1}{3}$ **7.** $\frac{14}{5}$

**Write each fraction in simplest form. Then write another equivalent fraction.** (Lessons 2–3, pp. 492–497)

**8.** $\frac{6}{8}$ **9.** $\frac{3}{9}$ **10.** $\frac{4}{10}$ **11.** $\frac{12}{20}$

**Compare. Write >, <, or = for each ●.** (Lesson 4, pp. 498–500)

**12.** $\frac{3}{10}$ ● $\frac{7}{10}$ **13.** $\frac{5}{25}$ ● $\frac{1}{5}$ **14.** $\frac{5}{8}$ ● $\frac{6}{16}$ **15.** $\frac{2}{2}$ ● $\frac{5}{6}$

**Find the fractional part of each number.** (Lesson 5, pp. 502–503)

**16.** $\frac{3}{5}$ of 15 **17.** $\frac{1}{4}$ of 8 **18.** $\frac{1}{3}$ of 21

## PROBLEM SOLVING

**Solve.** (Lesson 6, pp. 504–507)

**19.** Mari collects books. One third of her books are fiction, $\frac{1}{6}$ are nature books, and 12 are mysteries. How many books are in Mari's collection?

**20.** Cody bought some sports cards. One half were baseball cards, 18 were soccer cards, and $\frac{1}{8}$ were football cards. How many sports cards did Cody buy?

**Write About It**

**Show You Understand**

**Bob wrote $\frac{13}{5}$ as a mixed number.**

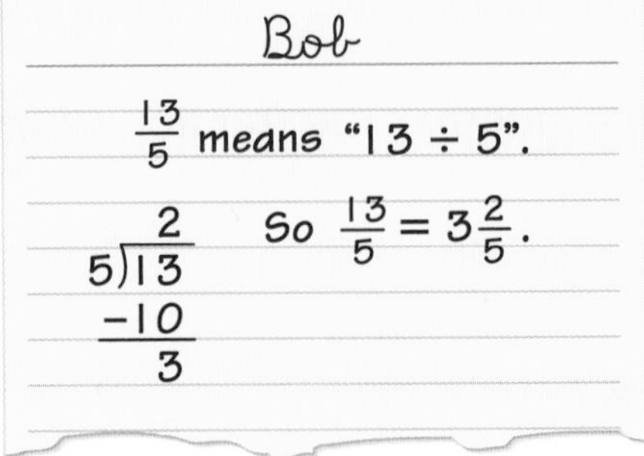


Explain what Bob did wrong. Then solve the problem correctly.

# Extra Practice

## Set A (Lesson 1, pp. 490–491)

**Write the fraction for the shaded part.**

1. 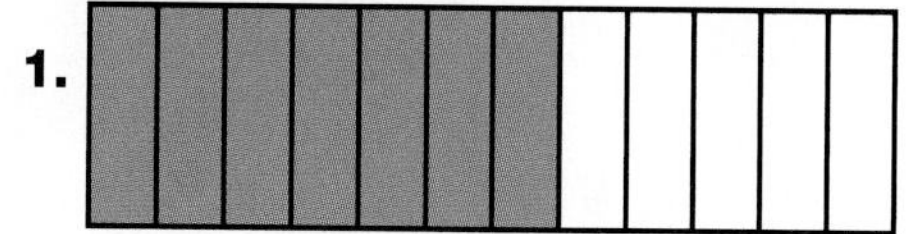

2. ★★★★ ★☆☆☆

3.

## Set B (Lesson 3, pp. 494–497)

**Write each fraction in simplest form. Then write another equivalent fraction.**

1. $\frac{2}{16}$ 2. $\frac{6}{12}$ 3. $\frac{4}{20}$ 4. $\frac{3}{9}$ 5. $\frac{10}{15}$ 6. $\frac{2}{14}$

## Set C (Lesson 4, pp. 498–500)

**Compare. Write >, <, or = for each ●.**

1. $\frac{2}{5}$ ● $\frac{3}{5}$ 2. $\frac{1}{2}$ ● $\frac{1}{6}$ 3. $\frac{5}{8}$ ● $\frac{3}{4}$ 4. $\frac{2}{3}$ ● $\frac{3}{9}$

**Order the fractions from least to greatest.**

5. $\frac{4}{10}$ $\frac{7}{10}$ $\frac{9}{10}$ 6. $\frac{3}{4}$ $\frac{2}{8}$ $\frac{2}{4}$ 7. $\frac{2}{5}$ $\frac{4}{15}$ $\frac{2}{3}$ 8. $\frac{1}{2}$ $\frac{3}{7}$ $\frac{5}{14}$

## Set D (Lesson 5, pp. 502–503)

**Find the fractional part of each number.**

1. $\frac{2}{4}$ of 16 2. $\frac{2}{3}$ of 21 3. $\frac{1}{2}$ of 18 4. $\frac{3}{5}$ of 15 5. $\frac{3}{4}$ of 12

## Set E (Lesson 7, pp. 508–510)

**Write each as an improper fraction.**

1. $3\frac{1}{5}$ 2. $4\frac{3}{4}$ 3. $2\frac{3}{7}$ 4. $5\frac{1}{2}$ 5. $1\frac{4}{9}$ 6. $3\frac{2}{3}$

**Write a mixed number or a whole number for each improper fraction.**

7. $\frac{11}{3}$ 8. $\frac{9}{2}$ 9. $\frac{21}{6}$ 10. $\frac{20}{3}$ 11. $\frac{8}{4}$ 12. $\frac{16}{5}$

# 20 Add and Subtract Fractions

INVESTIGATION

## Using Data

The chart on the right lists Family Fun Day activities. Plan a day for a family that likes outdoor activities. Plan for at least 5 hours. Tell the total time for activities and for eating.

**Family Fun Day**

| Activity | Time |
|---|---|
| Hike to River | $\frac{1}{2}$ hour |
| Rapids Ride | $2\frac{1}{2}$ hours |
| Lunch or Snack | $\frac{3}{4}$ hour |
| Canoe Ride | $1\frac{1}{4}$ hours |
| Hike to Camp | $\frac{3}{4}$ hour |

## Social Studies Connection

### Egyptian Fractions

**STANDARDS** Extends M4N6.b, M4P4

A **unit fraction** is a fraction that has 1 as its numerator. All ancient Egyptian fractions were written as unit fractions or as the sum of more than one unit fraction.

Look at the examples below.

- $\frac{1}{4}$ is a unit fraction, because its numerator is 1.

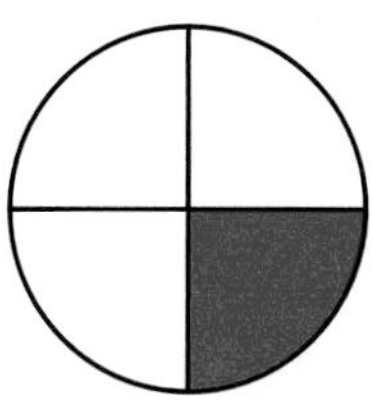

- $\frac{3}{4}$ is not a unit fraction, because its numerator is 3, not 1.

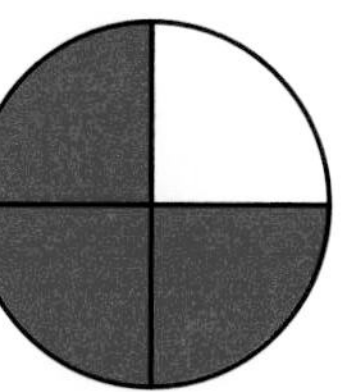

- In ancient Egypt, $\frac{3}{4}$ was written as the sum of unit fractions: $\frac{1}{2} + \frac{1}{4}$.

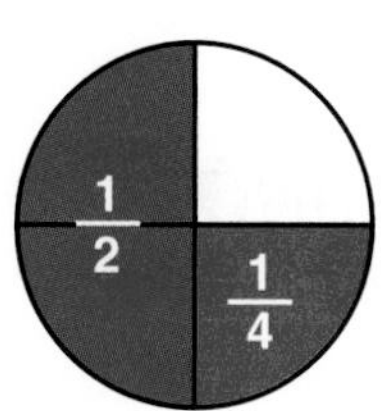


**Write each of these fractions as sums of unit fractions.**

**1.** $\frac{5}{8}$ **2.** $\frac{8}{15}$ **3.** $\frac{7}{12}$ **4.** $\frac{7}{8}$

**5.** $\frac{5}{6}$ **6.** $\frac{3}{8}$ **7.** $\frac{3}{5}$ **8.** $\frac{5}{12}$

WEEKLY WR READER eduplace.com/map

# Chapter Review/Test

Study Guide pages SG20–21

## VOCABULARY

**Choose the best term to complete each sentence.**

1. When you do not need an exact answer, you can ____.
2. The fractions $\frac{4}{6}$ and $\frac{3}{6}$ have ____.
3. The fractions $\frac{2}{7}$ and $\frac{1}{3}$ have ____.

**Vocabulary**

**estimate**

**like denominators**

**mixed number**

**unlike denominators**

## CONCEPTS AND SKILLS

**Add or subtract. Use fraction pieces if you wish. Write your answer in simplest form.** (Lessons 1, 2, 6, 7, pp. 516–521, 524–525)

4. $\frac{1}{3} + \frac{1}{3}$
5. $\frac{4}{6} + \frac{2}{6}$
6. $\frac{10}{12} - \frac{5}{12}$
7. $\frac{18}{24} - \frac{12}{24}$
8. $1\frac{1}{4} + 2\frac{1}{4}$
9. $5\frac{3}{5} + 4\frac{2}{5}$
10. $3\frac{2}{6} - 1\frac{1}{6}$
11. $7\frac{1}{9} - 4\frac{1}{9}$
12. $\frac{3}{5} + \frac{1}{10}$
13. $\frac{1}{4} + \frac{3}{8}$
14. $\frac{5}{6} - \frac{1}{2}$
15. $\frac{1}{3} - \frac{2}{12}$

**Estimate each sum. Write *greater than 1* or *less than 1*.** (Lesson 4, pp. 524–525)

16. $\frac{1}{4} + \frac{3}{8}$
17. $\frac{4}{5} + \frac{3}{4}$
18. $\frac{2}{9} + \frac{4}{12}$

## PROBLEM SOLVING

**Solve.** (Lessons 3, 8, pp. 522–523, 534–536)

19. At an arcade, four friends shared 25 tokens. If each person got the same number of tokens, how many tokens were left?
20. The circle graph shows the different coins Carl has. If Carl has 18 coins, how many of them are pennies?

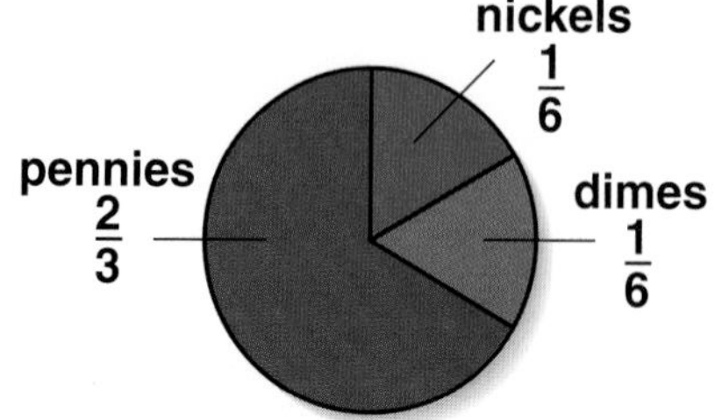


**Write About It**

**Show You Understand**

Jim used these fraction strips to solve a subtraction problem.

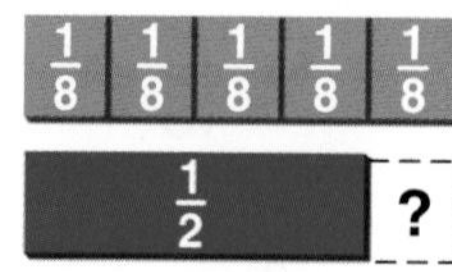


Jim's answer was $\frac{1}{8}$. What problem did he solve? Explain how you found your answer.

# Extra Practice

## Set A (Lesson 1, pp. 516–519)

**Add or subtract. Write your answer in simplest form.**

1. $\frac{3}{5} + \frac{2}{5}$
2. $\frac{2}{9} + \frac{4}{9}$
3. $\frac{3}{4} + \frac{1}{4}$
4. $\frac{6}{7} - \frac{5}{7}$
5. $\frac{2}{3} - \frac{2}{3}$
6. $\frac{4}{5} - \frac{1}{5}$
7. $\frac{4}{8} - \frac{2}{8}$
8. $\frac{4}{5} + \frac{4}{5}$
9. $\frac{5}{6} - \frac{2}{6}$
10. $\frac{7}{8} + \frac{5}{8}$
11. $\frac{3}{4} + \frac{3}{4}$
12. $\frac{7}{8} - \frac{1}{8}$
13. $\frac{2}{3} - \frac{1}{3}$
14. $\frac{5}{7} + \frac{4}{7}$

## Set B (Lesson 2, pp. 520–521)

**Add or subtract. Write your answer in simplest form.**

1. $2\frac{1}{9} + 3\frac{2}{9}$
2. $5\frac{4}{6} + 3\frac{2}{6}$
3. $4\frac{5}{12} - 3\frac{1}{12}$
4. $7\frac{8}{10} - 5\frac{3}{10}$
5. $2\frac{7}{8} + 4\frac{5}{8}$
6. $9\frac{5}{6} - 6\frac{4}{6}$
7. $6\frac{2}{4} - 4\frac{1}{4}$
8. $8\frac{3}{5} + 2\frac{4}{5}$
9. $5\frac{5}{7} - 2\frac{3}{7}$
10. $9\frac{3}{10} + 6\frac{7}{10}$
11. $2\frac{9}{10} - 2\frac{7}{10}$
12. $4\frac{1}{8} + 3\frac{5}{8}$
13. $1\frac{2}{3} + 2\frac{2}{3}$
14. $5\frac{5}{8} - 3\frac{3}{8}$

## Set C (Lesson 4, pp. 524–525)

**Estimate each sum. Write *greater than 1* or *less than 1*.**

1. $\frac{6}{8} + \frac{7}{8}$
2. $\frac{3}{8} + \frac{2}{5}$
3. $\frac{3}{10} + \frac{1}{3}$
4. $\frac{3}{4} + \frac{2}{3}$
5. $\frac{3}{5} + \frac{7}{10}$
6. $\frac{1}{5} + \frac{3}{12}$
7. $\frac{2}{3} + \frac{9}{10}$
8. $\frac{5}{8} + \frac{4}{7}$
9. $\frac{6}{10} + \frac{8}{15}$
10. $\frac{2}{3} + \frac{1}{2}$

**Estimate each sum. Write > or < for each ⬬.**

11. $\frac{1}{5} + \frac{3}{8}$ ⬬ $\frac{5}{8} + \frac{2}{3}$
12. $\frac{6}{8} + \frac{3}{5}$ ⬬ $\frac{7}{18} + \frac{4}{10}$
13. $\frac{1}{2} + \frac{3}{5}$ ⬬ $\frac{2}{5} + \frac{1}{8}$
14. $\frac{3}{4} + \frac{4}{5}$ ⬬ $\frac{1}{3} + \frac{3}{8}$
15. $\frac{1}{4} + \frac{2}{5}$ ⬬ $\frac{4}{5} + \frac{7}{10}$
16. $\frac{3}{9} + \frac{1}{3}$ ⬬ $\frac{2}{3} + \frac{7}{9}$

Extra Practice at eduplace.com/map

# Understand Decimals

## INVESTIGATION

### Using Data

A soccer game is broken up into either 2 or 4 equal sections of time. The table shows how long each section lasts for different age groups. How else could you write the numbers in the *Length of Section* column?

| Age Group | Length of Section |
|---|---|
| Under 12 | 0.25 hour |
| 12–17 | 0.50 hour |
| Over 17 | 0.75 hour |

# Use What You Know

**Use this page to review and remember what you need to know for this chapter.**

## VOCABULARY

**Choose the best word to complete each sentence.**

**Vocabulary**
- tenths
- improper
- equivalent
- hundredths

1. A whole can be divided into 100 equal parts called _____.
2. If two fractions name the same amount, they are called _____ fractions.
3. A whole can be divided into 10 equal parts called _____.

## CONCEPTS AND SKILLS

**Write a fraction to describe the shaded part.**

4. 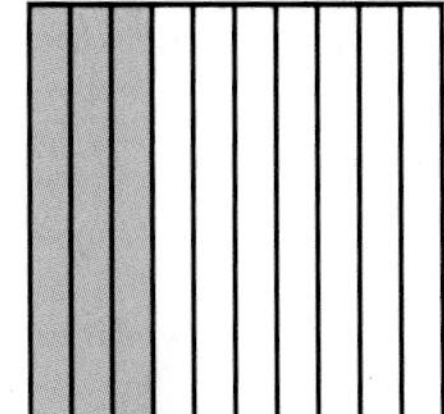
5. 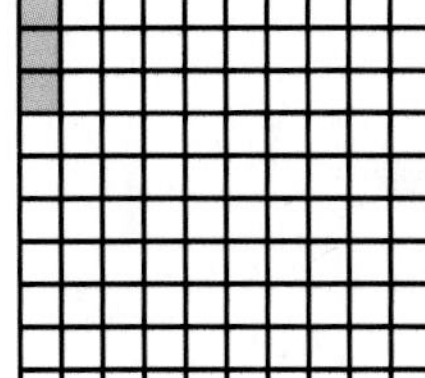
6. 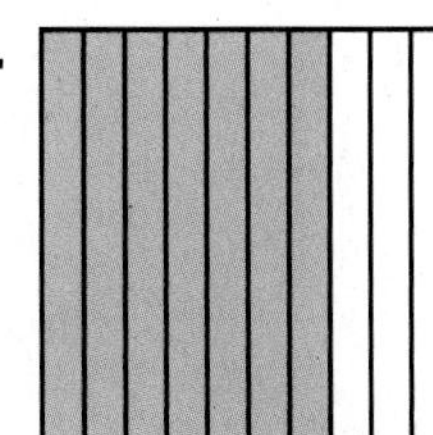
7. 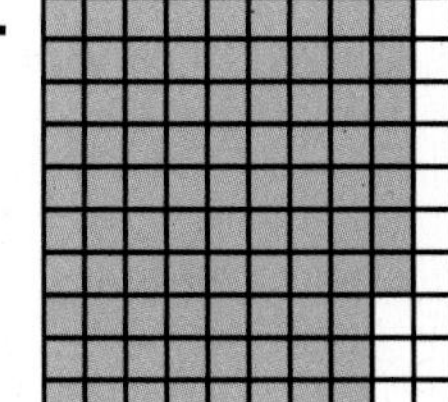

**Write each amount, using a dollar sign and a decimal point.**

8. 75¢
9. 2 dollars and 53 cents
10. 3 dollars and 4 cents
11. 10 dollars and 1 cent

**Find the value for each ■.**

12. $\frac{1}{2} = \frac{■}{10}$
13. $\frac{1}{5} = \frac{■}{10}$
14. $\frac{3}{5} = \frac{■}{10}$
15. $\frac{4}{5} = \frac{■}{10}$
16. $\frac{1}{4} = \frac{■}{100}$
17. $\frac{1}{2} = \frac{■}{100}$
18. $\frac{1}{25} = \frac{■}{100}$
19. $\frac{2}{5} = \frac{■}{100}$

**Write About It**

20. Draw pictures to show $\frac{5}{10}$ and $\frac{50}{100}$. How are these fractions alike? How are they different?

Facts Practice, See Page 669.

# Tenths and Hundredths

**Objective** Use models to show tenths and hundredths.

 **STANDARDS** M4N5, M4N1.a, M4P3

**Vocabulary**
- decimal
- decimal point
- tenth
- hundredth

**Materials**
Decimal Grids or Learning Tools 38 and 39

## Work Together

One way to show parts of a whole is to use fractions. Another way is to use decimals.

A **decimal** is a number with one or more digits to the right of the **decimal point**.

**Look at the models below.**

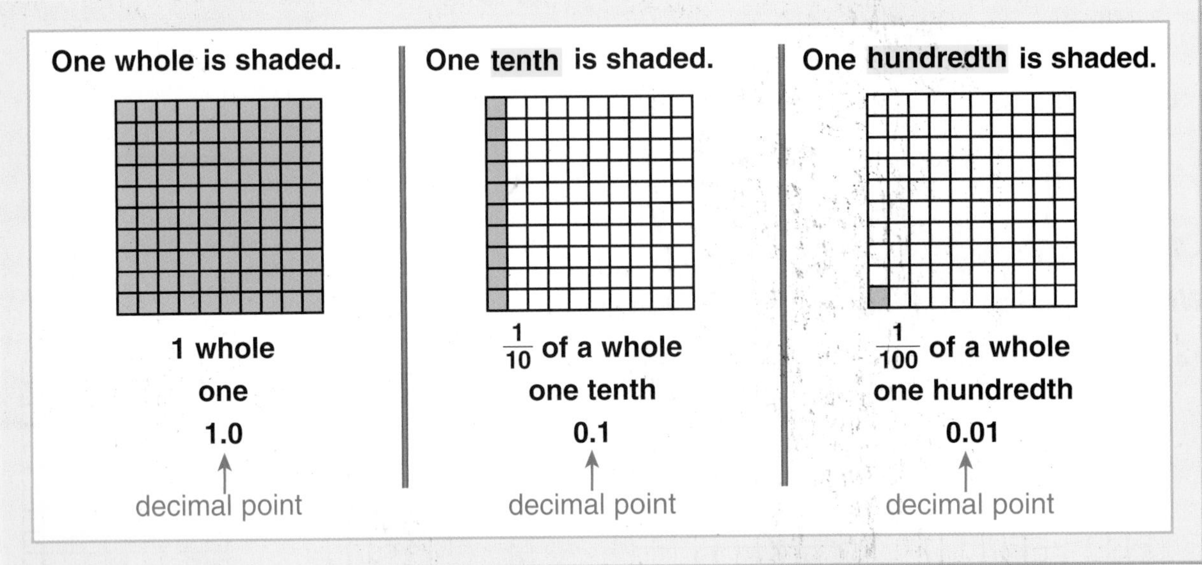


**Work with a partner to model decimals.**

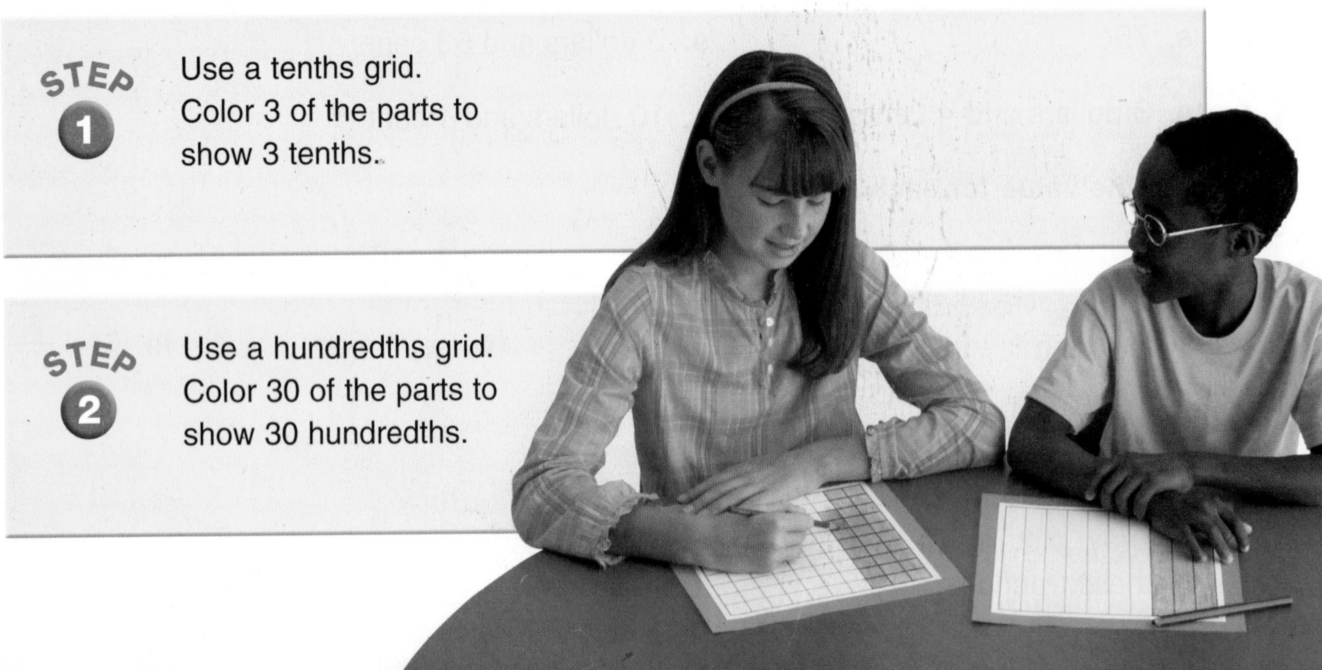

**STEP 1** Use a tenths grid. Color 3 of the parts to show 3 tenths.

**STEP 2** Use a hundredths grid. Color 30 of the parts to show 30 hundredths.

Compare your models.

- Is the same area colored in both models?
- How do you write 3 tenths as a decimal?
- How do you write 30 hundredths as a decimal?

Repeat Steps 1–3. This time show 0.6 and 0.60. Is the same area colored on both models?

## On Your Own

**Write a fraction and a decimal to describe each model.**

**1.** 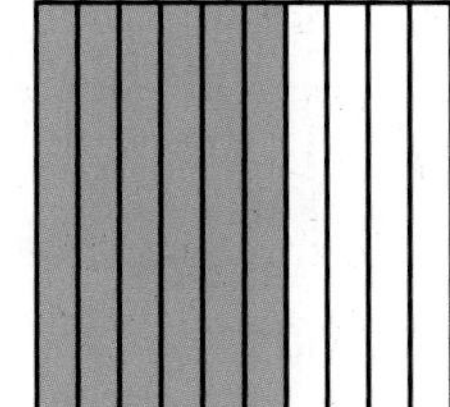

**2.** 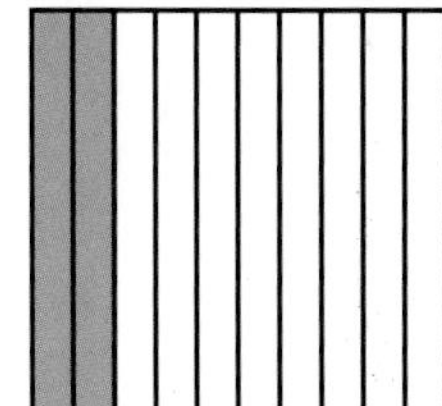

**3.** 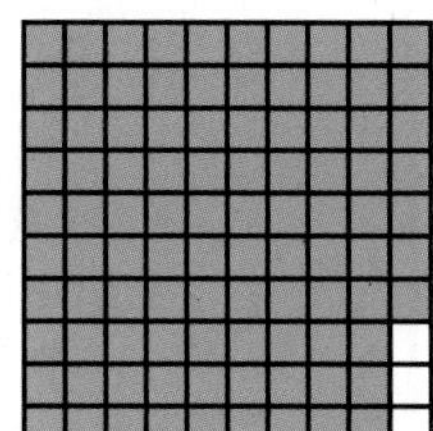

**4.** 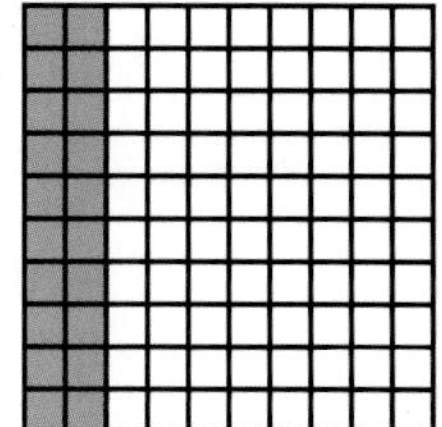

**Use grid paper. Draw a model to show each fraction. Then write each fraction as a decimal.**

**5.** $\frac{9}{10}$ **6.** $\frac{1}{10}$ **7.** $\frac{99}{100}$ **8.** $\frac{7}{100}$ **9.** $\frac{70}{100}$

**Use grid paper. Draw a model to show each decimal. Then write each decimal as a fraction.**

**10.** 0.3 **11.** 0.5 **12.** 0.01 **13.** 0.76 **14.** 0.54

### Talk About It • Write About It

**You learned how to represent fractions and decimals.**

**15.** How are 0.9 and 0.90 alike? How are they different?

**16.** Why is 0.1 greater than 0.01?

Audio Tutor 2/24 Listen and Understand

# Thousandths

**Objective** Write decimals for thousandths.

**STANDARDS** M4N5, M4N1.a, M4P2

**Vocabulary**
thousandths
equivalent decimals

**Materials**
Decimal Grids or Learning Tools 38, 39 and 40

## Learn About It

A whole can be divided into 1,000 equal parts called **thousandths**. Thousandths are even smaller than hundredths.

**Look at these models and place-value charts.**

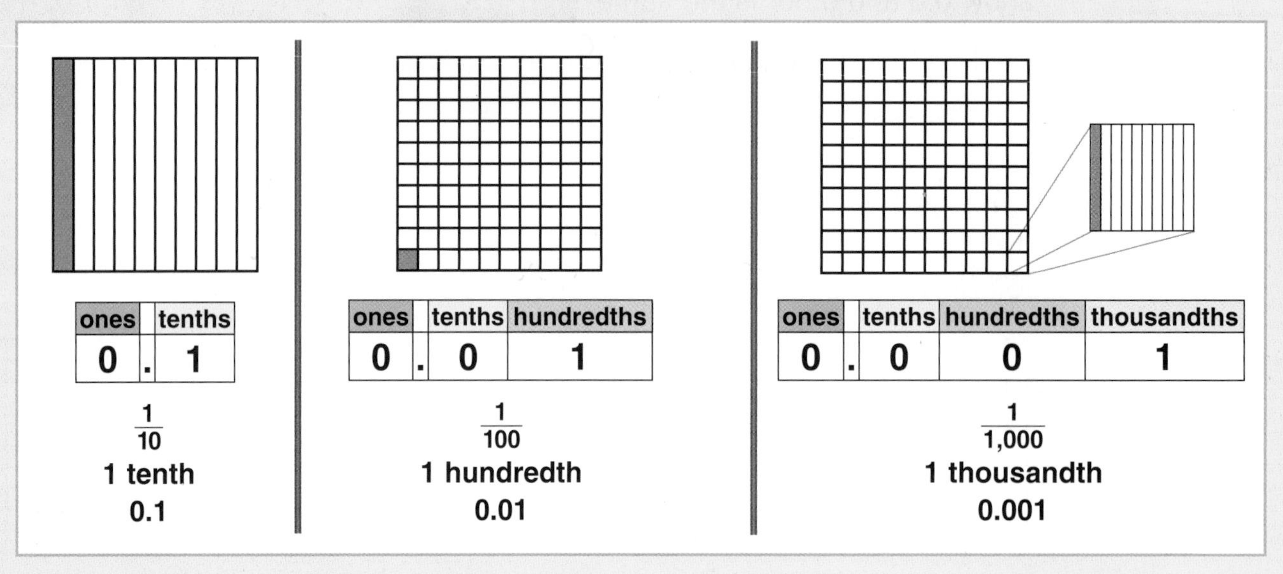


**Try this activity to explore thousandths.**

**STEP 1** Color 5 tenths on the tenths grid.

Color 50 hundredths on the hundredths grid.

Color 500 thousandths on the thousandths grid.

**STEP 2** Compare the 3 models that you colored.

- Do they all cover the same area?

▶ Decimals that name the same amount are called **equivalent decimals**.

0.5, 0.50, and 0.500 are equivalent decimals.

## Other Examples

**A. Zero in Tenths Place**

| Fraction | Decimal | Words |
|---|---|---|
| $\frac{21}{1,000}$ | 0.021 | twenty-one thousandths |

**B. Zero in Tenths and Hundredths Places**

| Fraction | Decimal | Words |
|---|---|---|
| $\frac{9}{1,000}$ | 0.009 | nine thousandths |

## Guided Practice

**Write each as a decimal.**

1. $\frac{782}{1,000}$ 2. $\frac{206}{1,000}$ 3. $\frac{45}{1,000}$ 4. $\frac{3}{1,000}$

5. 37 thousandths 6. 222 thousandths

**Ask Yourself**

- How many equal parts are there?
- How many digits do I put after the decimal point to show thousandths?

**Explain Your Thinking** ▶ Look at the place-value charts on Page 544. How does the value of the digit change as you move from left to right?

## Practice and Problem Solving

**Write each as a decimal.**

7. $\frac{356}{1,000}$ 8. $\frac{350}{1,000}$ 9. $\frac{49}{1,000}$ 10. $\frac{70}{1,000}$ 11. $\frac{3}{1,000}$

12. 450 thousandths 13. 6 thousandths 14. 15 thousandths

**Write each in word form.**

15. 0.005 16. 0.023 17. $\frac{455}{1,000}$ 18. 0.302 19. $\frac{300}{1,000}$

20. Mark walks $\frac{4}{10}$ mile to school. Carla walks 0.450 miles to school. Who walks farther? Explain how you know.

21. Cho Yia and her mother drive 0.7 kilometers to the store. Write an equivalent decimal for this distance.

22. **What's Wrong?** Look at Brian's work on the right. What's wrong with his reasoning?

Brian
300 > 30 so
0.300 > 0.30

## Sharpening Skills for CRCT

### Open Response

**Write all the factors of each number.**
(Ch. 10, Lesson 1)

23. 6 24. 24 25. 18
26. 25 27. 14 28. 27
29. 30 30. 20 31. 42

### Multiple Choice

32. Marcia's mother tells her that a liter is nine hundred forty-six thousandths of a quart. How do you write this number?
(Ch. 21, Lesson 2)

A. 0.946 C. 940.006
B. 900.046 D. 946,000

Extra Practice See page 565, Set A.

Lesson 3

# Mixed Numbers and Decimals

**Objective** Read, write, and model amounts greater than 1.

 **STANDARDS** M4N1.a, M4N1.b, M4N5.b, M4N5.a

## Learn About It

Melanie and Elena like to jog every day at their local park. There are two paths. Elena's favorite is the Blue Path. Melanie's favorite is the Red Path. The Red Path is two and eight tenths kilometers long.

**Here are different ways to show two and eight tenths.**

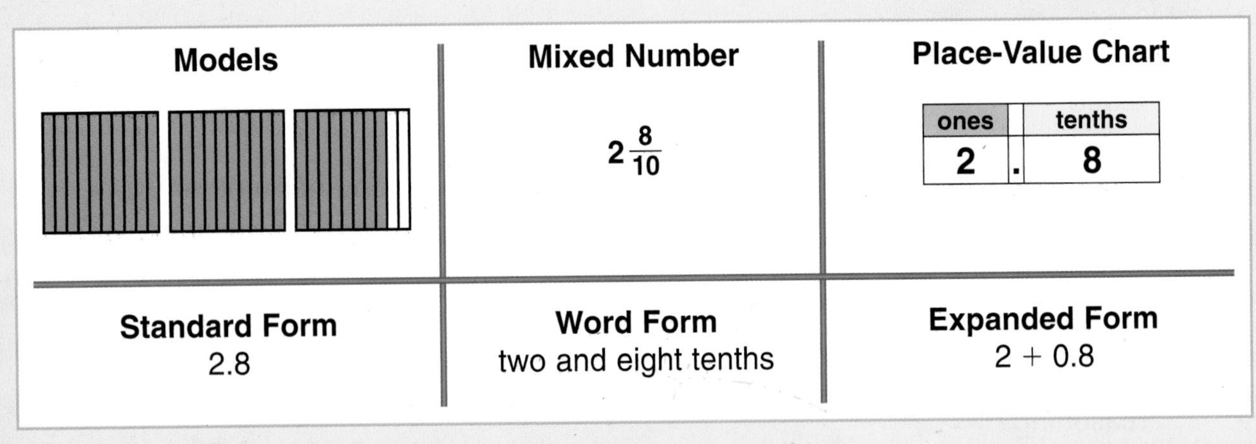

| Models | Mixed Number | Place-Value Chart |
|---|---|---|
| | $2\frac{8}{10}$ | ones: 2 . tenths: 8 |
| **Standard Form**<br>2.8 | **Word Form**<br>two and eight tenths | **Expanded Form**<br>2 + 0.8 |

**Here are different ways to show two and forty-five hundredths.**

| Models | Mixed Number | Place-Value Chart |
|---|---|---|
| | $2\frac{45}{100}$ | ones: 2 . tenths: 4 hundredths: 5 |
| **Standard Form**<br>2.45 | **Word Form**<br>two and forty-five hundredths | **Expanded Form**<br>2 + 0.4 + 0.05 |

▶ Thinking about money can help you understand decimals.

**Here are different ways to show $1.49.**

| Models | Mixed Number | Place Value Chart |
|---|---|---|
| | $1\frac{49}{100}$ | dollars (ones) \| . \| dimes (tenths) \| pennies (hundredths)<br>1 \| . \| 4 \| 9 |
| **Standard Form**<br>$1.49 | **Word Form**<br>one dollar and forty-nine cents | **Expanded Form**<br>$1 + $0.4 + $0.09 |

## Guided Practice

**Ask Yourself**

- What part is the whole number?
- What should the numerator be? What should the denominator be?

**Write a mixed number and a decimal to describe the shaded part in each model.**

1. 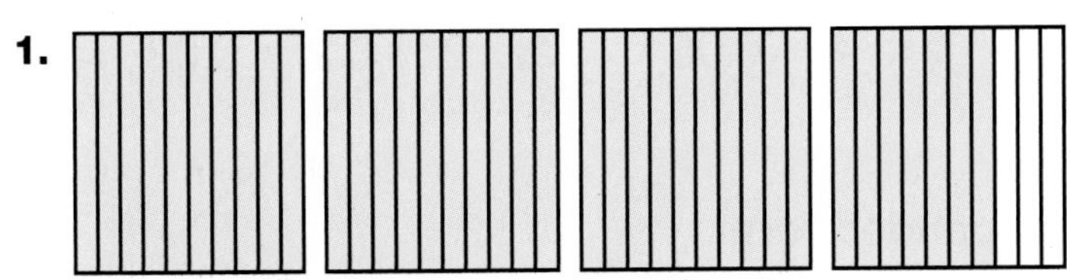

2.

3.

**Write each as a decimal.**

4. $5\frac{3}{10}$ 5. $9\frac{9}{10}$ 6. $26\frac{7}{10}$ 7. $15\frac{55}{100}$ 8. $12\frac{5}{100}$ 9. $2\frac{17}{1,000}$

10. seven tenths 11. twenty-two hundredths 12 one and 5 thousandths

**Explain Your Thinking** ▶ Look back at Exercise 7. Why is the value of each 5 different?

## Practice and Problem Solving

**Write a mixed number and a decimal to describe the shaded part.**

**13.**

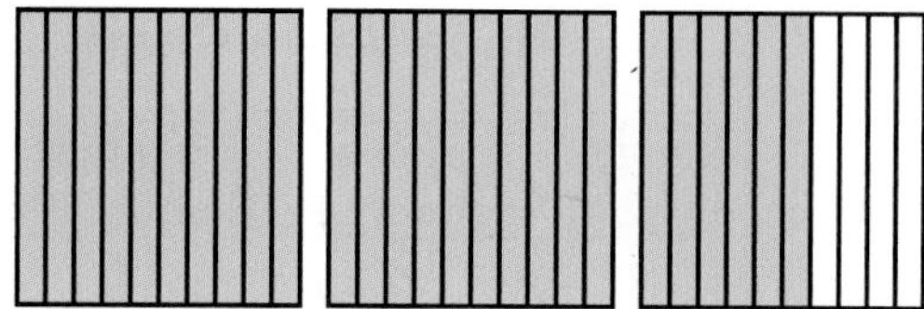

**14.**

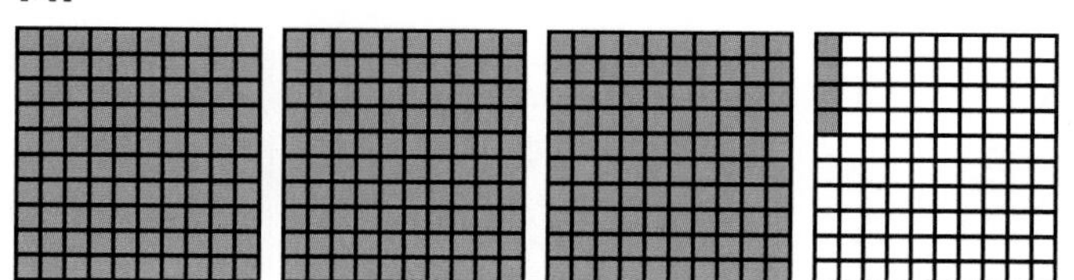

**Write each mixed number as a decimal.**

**15.** $1\frac{2}{10}$ **16.** $7\frac{7}{100}$ **17.** $4\frac{54}{100}$ **18.** $4\frac{7}{10}$ **19.** $34\frac{17}{100}$

**20.** $158\frac{85}{100}$ **21.** $175\frac{8}{100}$ **22.** $19\frac{38}{100}$ **23.** $45\frac{26}{1,000}$ **24.** $56\frac{3}{1,000}$

**Write each as a decimal in standard form.**

**25.** sixty-four hundredths

**26.** five and seven tenths

**27.** forty and four hundredths

**28.** three and sixteen thousandths

**29.** 7 + 0.5 **30.** 3 + 0.9 + 0.07 **31.** 4 + 0.06 **32.** 2 + 0.2 + 0.03 + 0.004

**Write each decimal in words and in expanded form.**

**33.** 0.4 **34.** 0.65 **35.** 5.03 **36.** 3.07 **37.** $3.98

**38.** 4.3 **39.** 5.67 **40.** 4.876 **41.** 0.005 **42.** 3.098

## Data Use the table for Problems 43–45.

**43. Measurement** On which day was there less than 1 inch of snow?

**44. Represent** Use a ruler to draw a line segment that shows the height of the snow that fell on Tuesday.

**45. Analyze** Melanie decided not to jog one day because eight and five tenths inches of snow fell on the day before. On which day of the week didn't she jog?

| Day | Inches of Snow |
|---|---|
| Monday | 3.0 inches |
| Tuesday | 3.5 inches |
| Wednesday | 0.5 inches |
| Thursday | 4.0 inches |
| Friday | 8.5 inches |



Extra Practice See page 565, Set B

# Use What You Know

**Use this page to review and remember what you need to know for this chapter.**

## VOCABULARY

**Choose the best term to complete each sentence.**

| Vocabulary |
|---|
| tenth |
| round |
| estimate |
| hundredth |
| decimal point |

1. When you find an approximate answer, you are making an ____.
2. One of ten equal parts of a whole is a ____.
3. The symbol that separates ones and tenths in a decimal is a ____.
4. You write \$3.59 as \$4.00 when you ____ to the nearest dollar.

## CONCEPTS AND SKILLS

**Write a decimal to describe the shaded part.**

5. 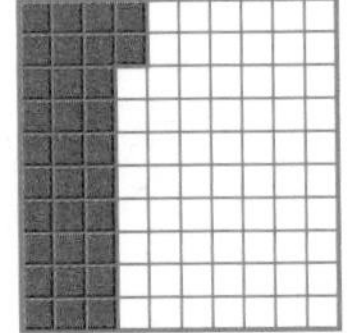

6. 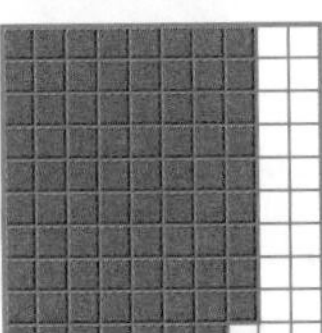

7. 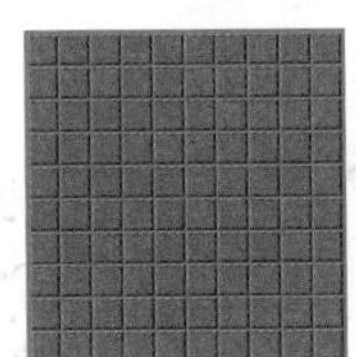 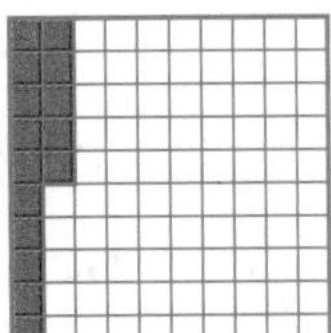

**Tell whether the underlined digit is in the *ones, tenths, hundredths,* or *thousandths* place.**

8. $0.\underline{4}21$
9. $5.61\underline{8}$
10. $1.2\underline{7}6$
11. $\underline{2}.015$

**Round each number to the place of the underlined digit.**

12. $\underline{4}3$
13. $2\underline{5}7$
14. $2\underline{9}8$
15. $3{,}\underline{1}39$
16. $\underline{4}{,}622$
17. $1\underline{4}{,}372$
18. $\underline{6}1{,}315$
19. $30\underline{9}{,}897$

**Write About It**

20. Why is 0.4 greater than 0.04? Use pictures, symbols, or words to explain your answer.

Facts Practice, See Page 669.

Lesson 1

 **Audio Tutor 2/27 Listen and Understand**

# Round Decimals

**Objective** Use rules or a number line to round decimals.

**STANDARDS** M4N2.c, M4N5.a, M4P2

## Learn About It

Ami sells nuts and vegetables at an outdoor market in Ghana. She has 1.35 kilograms of kola nuts to sell. What is the weight of the kola nuts to the nearest whole kilogram?

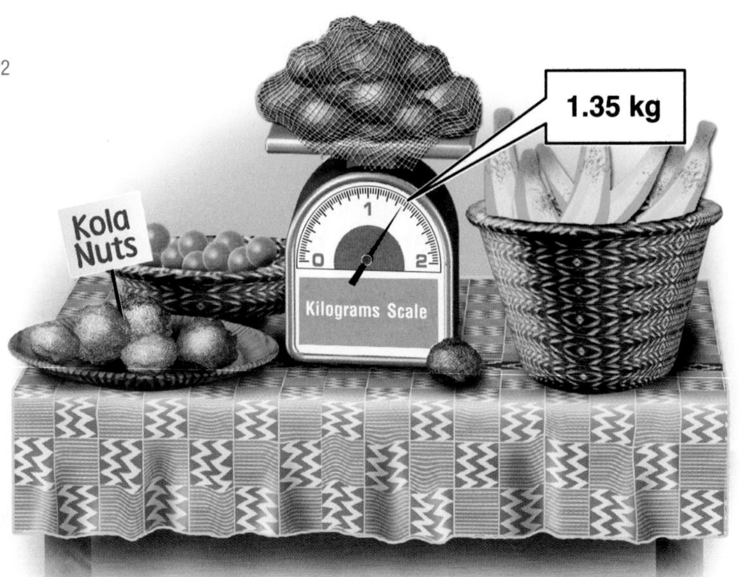


Here are some different ways to round decimals.

## Different Ways to Round 1.35

### Way 1 You can use a number line.

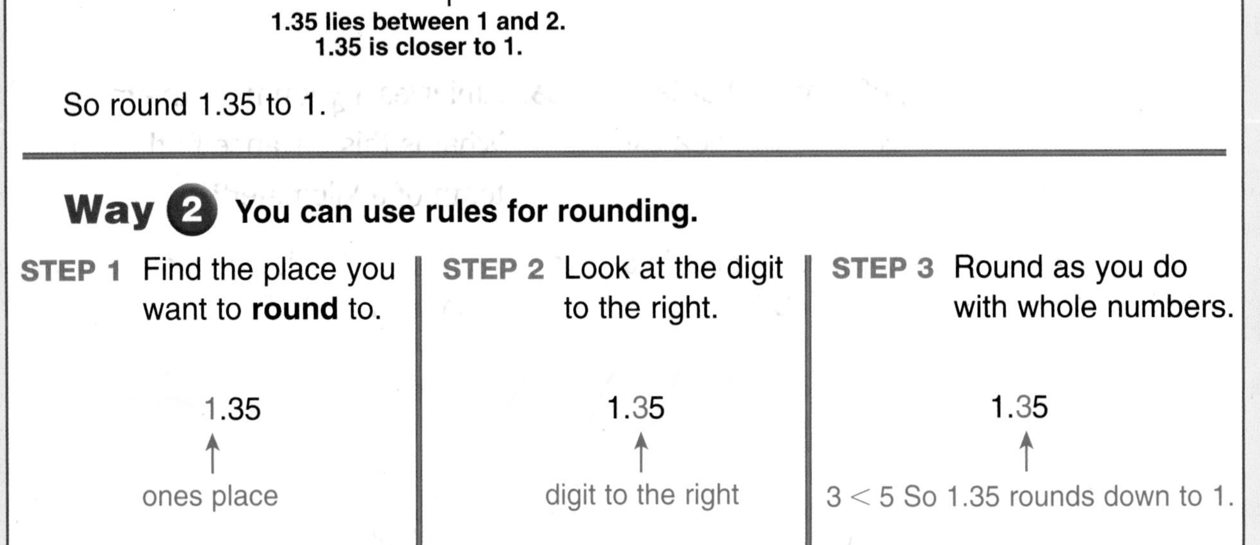

rounds to

1.00 1.10 1.20 1.30 1.40 1.50 1.60 1.70 1.80 1.90 2.00

**1.35 lies between 1 and 2.**
**1.35 is closer to 1.**

So round 1.35 to 1.

### Way 2 You can use rules for rounding.

**STEP 1** Find the place you want to **round** to.

1.35
↑
ones place

**STEP 2** Look at the digit to the right.

1.35
↑
digit to the right

**STEP 3** Round as you do with whole numbers.

1.35
↑
$3 < 5$ So 1.35 rounds down to 1.

**Solution:** The weight of the kola nuts to the nearest whole kilogram is 1 kilogram.

## Problem Solving

**Use the diagram at the right for Problems 1–3. Use the pictures at the bottom of the page for Problems 4 and 5.**

1. Suppose you see a barracuda swimming $\frac{1}{3}$ of the way down to the bottom. How many feet below the surface is that?

2. You see triggerfish $\frac{1}{2}$ of the way down to the bottom, a damselfish $\frac{3}{6}$ of the way down, and an angelfish $\frac{2}{3}$ of the way down. Which fish are swimming at the same depth?

3. An angelfish is swimming $\frac{2}{3}$ of the way to the bottom. A grouper is swimming $\frac{1}{6}$ of the water's depth deeper than the angelfish. How far down is the grouper swimming? Write the depth as a fraction and in feet.

4. Write the lengths of the fish below as improper fractions. Then list the fish in order from shortest to longest.

5. How much longer is the great barracuda than the gray triggerfish?

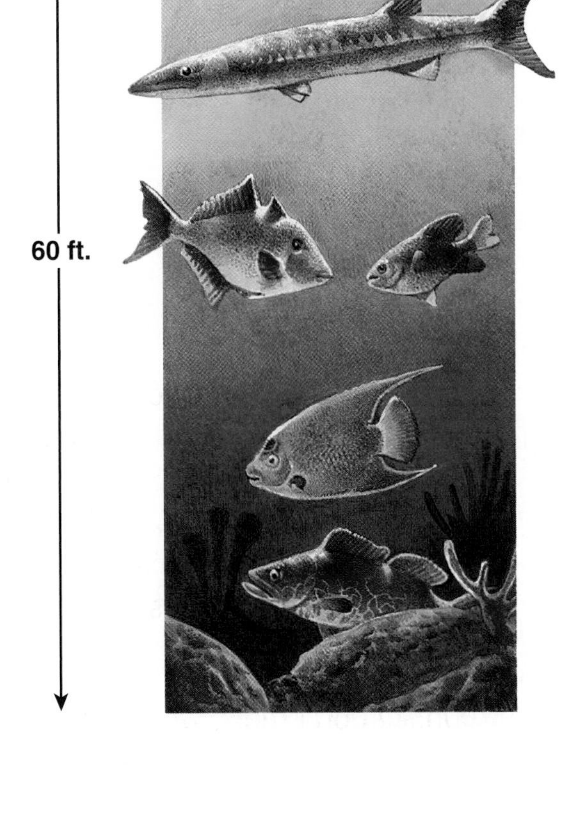


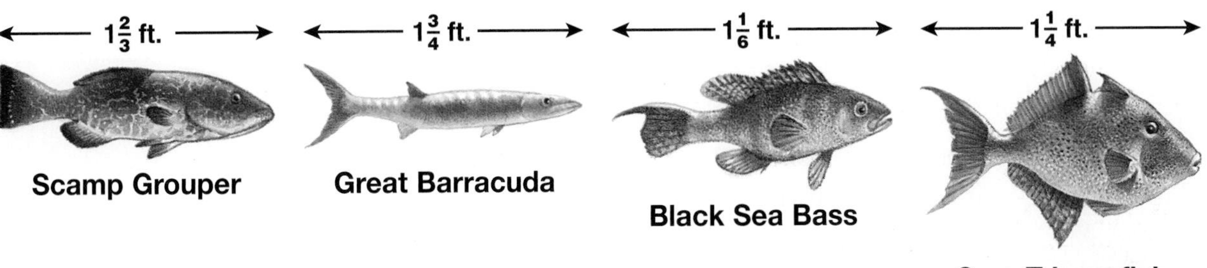

## Enrichment: Mixed Numbers and Improper Fractions

# It's a Hike!

There are two ways to write a fraction when the numerator is greater than the denominator. One way is to write a mixed number. A **mixed number** is made up of a whole number and a fraction. Another way is to write an **improper fraction,** a fraction that has a numerator greater than or equal to its denominator. A mixed number can be changed to an improper fraction, and an improper fraction can be changed to a mixed number.

The map at the right shows the istances of the trails between different scenic areas in a park. All of the distances, in miles, are improper fractions.

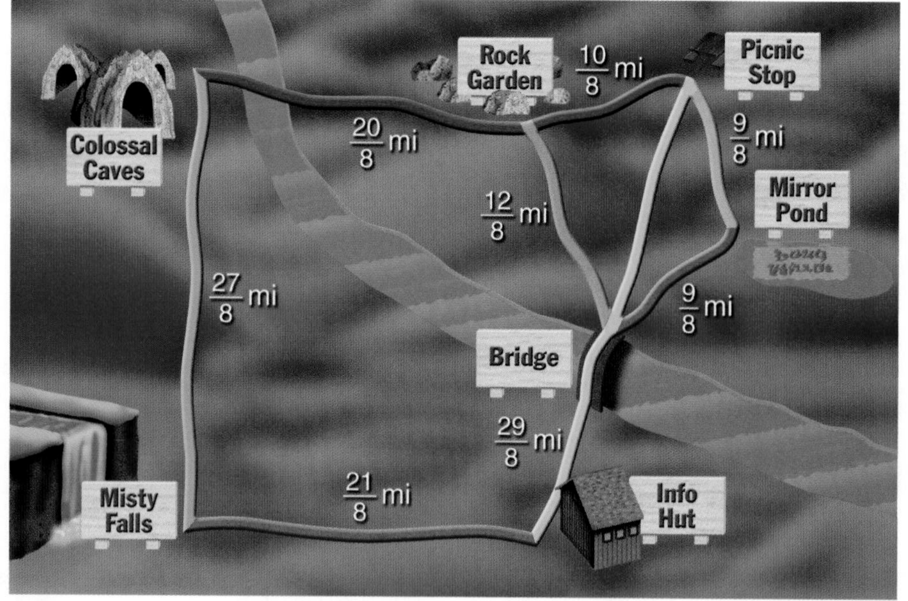


## Try These!

**Use the map to answer the questions.**

1. Change the distance of each trail to a mixed number. Write the distance in simplest form.

2. If you were at the Info Hut and wanted to arrive at the Colossal Caves but see Misty Falls along the way, how far would you have to hike? Write the total distance as a mixed number and in simplest form.

3. If the total distance of two trails from Mirror Pond to the Info Hut is $4\frac{2}{8}$ miles and you have hiked $1\frac{1}{8}$ miles already, how many more miles must you hike? Write the distance in simplest form.

# UNIT 8

# Multiply and Divide Decimals/ Graphing

# Reading Mathematics

## Reviewing Vocabulary

**Here are some math vocabulary words that you should know.**

| | |
|---|---|
| **dividend** | the number that is divided in a division problem |
| **factor** | a number that is multiplied in a multiplication problem |
| **ordered pair** | a pair of numbers in which one number is named as the first and the other number is named as the second |
| **product** | the result of a multiplication problem |
| **quotient** | the result of a division problem |

## Reading Words and Symbols

You can find the product of a decimal and a whole number by using the model. Look at the model.

Each grid has 4 tenths shaded.
There are 3 grids.
Together, there are 12 tenths shaded.

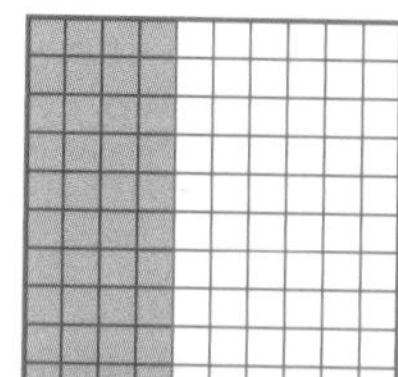

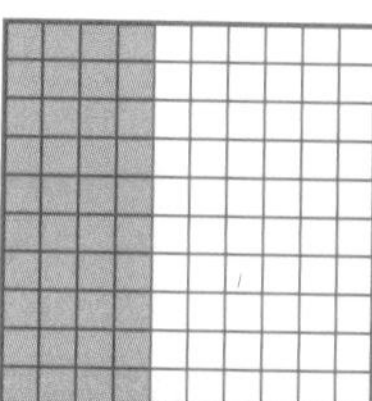

4 tenths $\times$ 3 = 12 tenths

- You can write this in words: twelve tenths
- You can write this as a decimal: 1.2

**Use the model to answer these questions.**

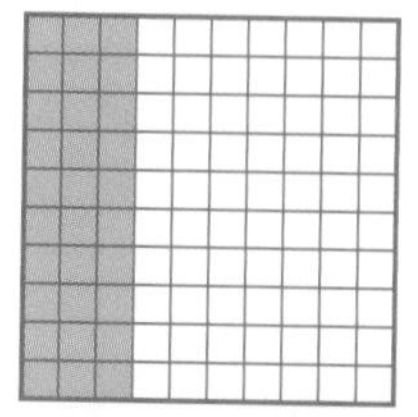

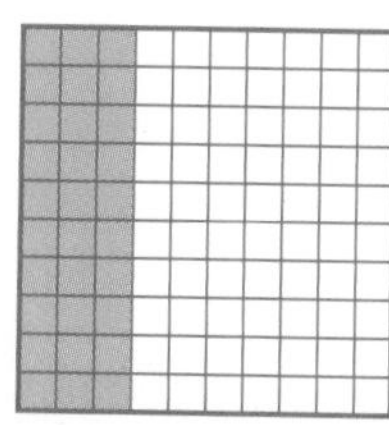

1. How many tenths are shaded altogether?
2. What multiplication expression does the model represent?

# Reading Questions on CRCT

**Choose the correct answer for each.**

**3.** Which statement describes the location of Point *A*?

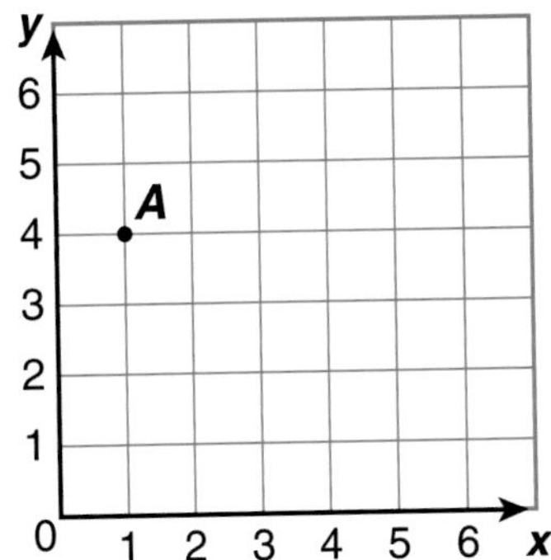


A. 2 units right and 3 units up

B. 3 units right and 2 units up

C. 1 unit right and 4 units up

D. 4 units right and 1 unit up

**Location** means "place" or "position."

**4.** Which decimal is shown by the model?

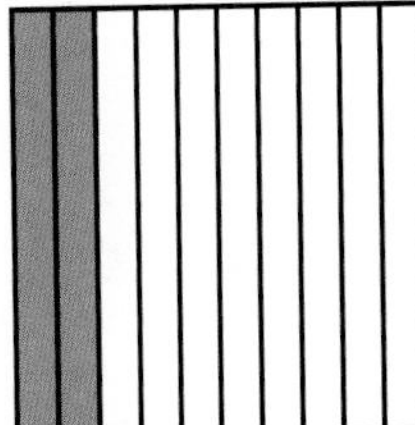

A. 0.1

B. 0.2

C. 0.3

D. 0.4

**Model** means "picture" or "example."

**5.** Which expression is the same as **3 tenths × 5?**

A. $0.1 \times 3$

B. $0.3 \times 5$

C. $0.3 \times 10$

D. $0.5 \times 3$

**Expression** means "group of numbers with operation symbols."

# Learning Vocabulary

**Watch for these words in this unit. Write their definitions in your journal.**

- **coordinates**
- **decimal**
- **integers**
- ***x*-axis**
- ***y*-axis**

## Education Place

At **eduplace.com/map** see eGlossary and eGames–Math Lingo.

## Literature Connection

Read "The Perfect Present" on Pages 654–655. Then work with a partner to answer the questions about the story.

# Multiplication and Division of Decimals

## PERFORMANCE PREVIEW

### Using Data

Built in 1838, the Little Cumberland Island Lighthouse is the southernmost lighthouse that still stands in Georgia. At the bottom, the lighthouse tower is 22 feet wide. The sides of the tower slope so that the top is 0.5 times as wide as the bottom. How could you use this data to find the width of the tower at the top?

# Extra Practice

## Set A (Lessons 1–2, pp. 616–619)

**Use the grid at the right for Exercises 1–8. Write the ordered pair for each point.**

**1.** *E* **2.** *F* **3.** *D* **4.** *A*

**Copy the grid. Plot and label each point.**

**5.** *G* (5, 0) **6.** *H* (3, 4) **7.** *I* (8, 3) **8.** *J* (5, 5)

## Set B (Lesson 3, pp. 620–623)

**Use the table to complete Exercises 1–3.**

**1.** Write the data in the table as ordered pairs. Use the number of packages as the first coordinate.

| Packages of Tomatoes | | | | | |
|---|---|---|---|---|---|
| Number of Packages | 1 | 2 | 3 | 4 | 5 |
| Number of Tomatoes | 3 | 6 | 9 | 12 | 15 |

**2.** Copy the grid. Plot the coordinates from Exercise 1. Then connect the points.

**3.** Extend your grid. Label the *x*-axis to 10 and the *y*-axis to 30. How many tomatoes would be in 7 packages? in 9 packages?

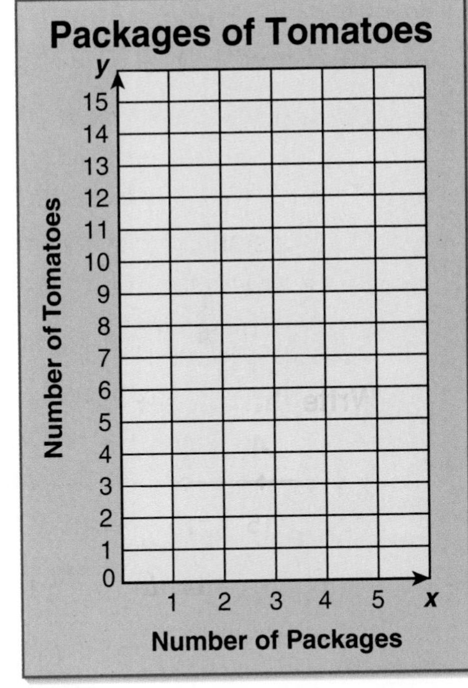


## Set C (Lesson 4, pp. 624–627)

**Write an integer for each situation.**

**1.** sea level

**2.** $15 owed

**3.** 14 floors above street level

**4.** 89 feet below sea level

**5.** $25 won

**6.** 75° above zero

Extra Practice at **eduplace.com/map**

# New Life For Worn Out Land

The Piedmont National Wildlife Refuge is located in central Georgia. It was created by order of President Franklin D. Roosevelt in 1939. It is made up of land that was once thought to be useless because it was "worn out" from farming and erosion. The refuge was created to bring wildlife back to an area that people, animals, and even most plants had abandoned.

Today, the refuge's forest, lake, ponds, and creeks are home to many kinds of animals, including the protected red-cockaded woodpecker, shortnose sturgeon, and bald eagle. Visitors can enjoy the scenery and wildlife any time during the year by walking along the nature trails, going on a wildlife drive, or by looking at exhibits in the visitor center.

## Problem Solving

**Use the table below to help solve Problems 1–4.**

| **Piedmont National Wildlife Trails** | |
|---|---|
| **Trail** | **Length (in miles)** |
| Red-cockaded Woodpecker Trail | 2.9 |
| Allison Lake Trail | 0.9 |
| Creek Trail | 0.8 |
| Pine Trail | 0.5 |

1. While visiting the Piedmont National Wildlife Refuge, Ms. Jones walked from the beginning to the end of Creek Trail and back again. What was the total distance that she walked?

2. Starting at different ends of the trail, Mr. Lin and Mrs. Lin walked toward each other on the Allison Lake Trail and met half-way. Find how far each of them walked before they met.

3. Ms. Gupta walks the Pine Trail every Saturday. How far has she walked on this trail after 4 weeks? After 7 weeks?

4. Mr. Morales walked the Red-cockaded Woodpecker Trail once, while Ms. Larsen walked the Allison Lake Trail three times. Who walked farther?

# Enrichment: Transformations

STANDARDS M4G3.a, M4G3.b

## Slips and Slides

A **slide** moves a figure up, down, or over along a line. When you slide a figure, its size and shape do not change.

See what happens when figure *ABC* slides 5 units right.

| | Ordered Pairs |
|---|---|
| Original Figure | *A* (2, 2) *B* (4, 4) *C* (5, 3) |
| Image | *A′* (7, 2) *B′* (9, 4) *C′* (10, 3) |

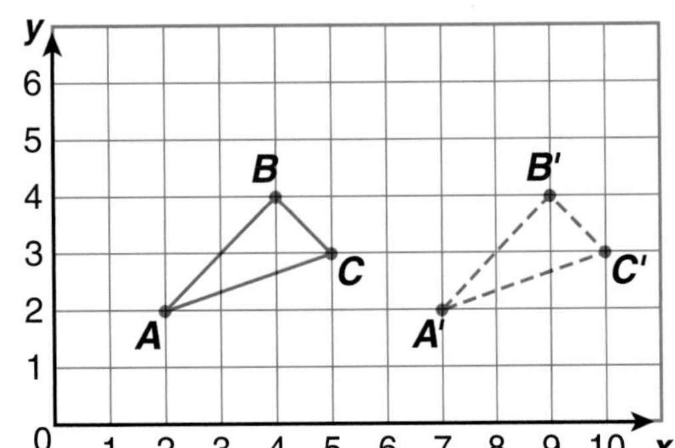

After you slide *ABC* to the right:

- *A* becomes *A′*, *B* becomes *B′*, and *C* becomes *C′*.
- The first coordinate of each point increases by 5.
- The second coordinate of each point does not change.

**The numbers in the coordinate change depending on how you slide.**

When you slide right or left,

- The first coordinate increases or decreases.
- The second coordinate stays the same.

When you slide up or down,

- The first coordinate stays the same.
- The second coordinate increases or decreases.

## Try These!

**Graph triangle *ABC* on grid paper. Slide triangle *ABC* the number of units given. Write the ordered pairs for the Points *A′*, *B′*, and *C′*.**

1. 1 unit left
2. 2 units down
3. 2 units up
4. 4 units right

# Get On Line!

 **STANDARDS** M4P5

Qwan was playing a game on the computer. In Round 1 he won 6 points. In Round 2 he lost 9 points. In Round 3 he won 4 points. How many points did Qwan have at the end of Round 3?

**You can use the number line found on Education Place at eduplace.com/kids/map to work with integers.**

- Click on 0 on the number line to start.
- To show Qwan's points at the end of Round 1, at **Choose Jump Size,** click on 6. Then click the **Jump Right** arrow.
- To show Qwan's points at the end of Round 2, change **Choose Jump Size.** Since Qwan lost 9 points, choose 9. Click the **Jump Left** arrow.
- To show Qwan's points at the end of Round 3, change **Choose Jump Size.** Since Qwan won 4 points, choose 4. Click the **Jump Right** arrow.

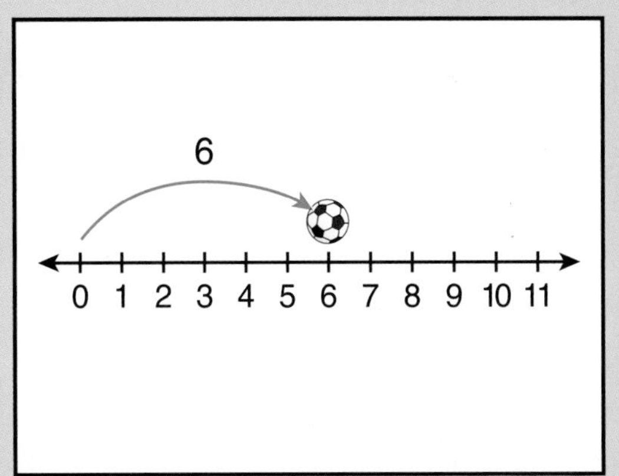


**Solution:** At the end of Round 3, Qwan had 1 point.

**Use the number line to help you solve each problem.**

1. Mia owes her brother \$3. She earns \$9. After paying her brother back, she spends \$5 on a book. How much money does Mia have left?
2. A scuba diver dove 9 feet below sea level. She swam up 6 feet. Next she dove down 2 feet. How many feet below sea level was the scuba diver?
3. One day, the temperature at 10 A.M. was 83°F. By 3 P.M. it had risen 9°. At 8 P.M. the temperature was 7° lower than it was at 3 P.M. What was the temperature at 8 P.M?
4. One day, the elevator in a building starts on the ground floor. It goes up 9 floors, down 3 and then up 2. How many floors above or below ground is the elevator?

# Unit 8 Test

Study Guide pages SG18, SG19, SG39, SG40

**VOCABULARY** Open Response

**Choose the best term to complete each sentence.**

1. The number of decimal places in the product equals the total number of ____ in the factors.

2. The point with the coordinates (0, 0) is called the ____.

3. The decimal point in the quotient is placed directly above the decimal point in the ____.

4. The horizontal number line on a coordinate grid is the ____.

**Vocabulary**

***x*-axis**
***y*-axis**
**origin**
**factor**
**dividend**
**decimal places**

**CONCEPTS AND SKILLS** Open Response

**Write the factor represented by the model. Then find the product.** (Chapter 23)

5. 3 × 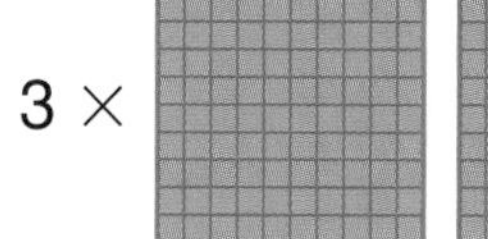 = ■

6. 9 × 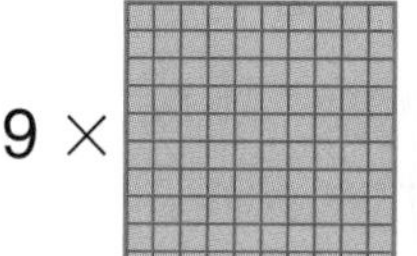 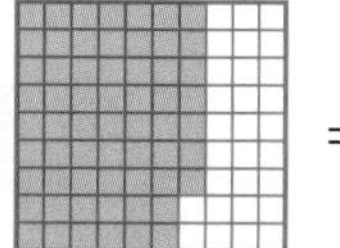 = ■

**Find the product or quotient.** (Chapter 23)

7. 0.2 × 6

8. 19.26 ÷ 9

9. 3.46 × 5

**Place the decimal point in each dividend to make each quotient correct.** (Chapter 23)

10. 2622 ÷ 6 = 4.37

11. 1267 ÷ 7 = 1.81

12. 273 ÷ 3 = 9.1

**Write the integer for each situation.** (Chapter 24)

13. 5 floors up

14. $10 spent

15. 6 degrees below zero

**Use the table and grid paper for Problems 16–18.**

**16.** Write pairs of data in the table as ordered pairs. Use the number of hours as the first coordinate.

**17.** Plot the ordered pairs on a coordinate graph.

**18.** How many hours does Carla have to work to earn $12?

**Carla's Baby-sitting Earnings**

| Hours Worked | Dollars Earned |
|---|---|
| 1 | 4 |
| 2 | 8 |
| 3 | 12 |

**PROBLEM SOLVING** Open Response

**19.** Use the digits 2, 4, and 8 to make as many three-digit numbers as you can. What are all the numbers?

**20.** Extend the graph you made for Problem 17. How much will Carla earn if she baby-sits for 4 hours?

## Performance Task

**Task** You are making a map of your hometown. The graph shows some of the locations.

a. Write the ordered pairs for the locations already labeled on the map.

b. Make a copy of the map. Draw and label the following locations on the map:

- park (8, 2)
- police department (8, 9)
- fire department (3, 8)
- museum (3, 5)

c. Write directions to get from the park to the school. How can you write the directions two different ways?

d. How are the points for the museum and fire department similar? How are they different?

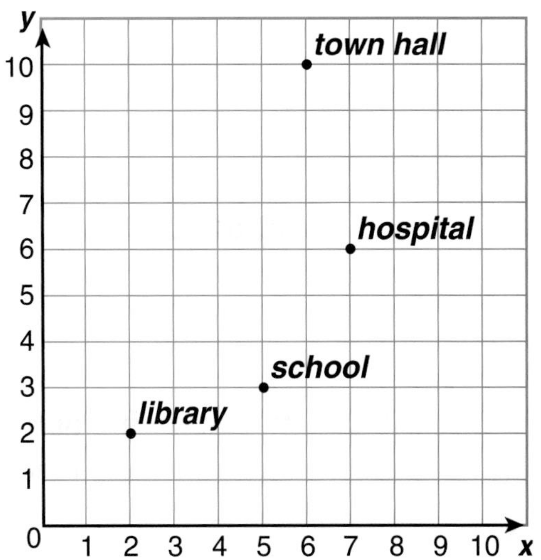

# Getting Ready for CRCT

**Solve Problems 1–10.**

*Look at the example below.*

Samantha drew a triangle with sides measuring 3 inches, 4 inches, and 3 inches. How should she classify the triangle? Explain your thinking.

**THINK**

You know that an isosceles triangle has two equal sides. You also know that all the angles in an acute triangle are less than 90°.

Draw a triangle with two sides that are 3 units long and one side that is 4 units long. You can see that all the angles are less than 90°.

So, you can classify the triangle as acute isosceles.

## Multiple Choice

1. What is the value of this expression?

$$4 + (14 - 6) \div 4$$

A. 3

B. 4

C. 6

D. 8

(Chapter 5, Lesson 1)

2. Which shows this trapezoid rotated 180°?

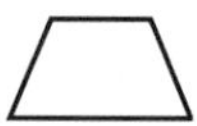

A.

B.

C.

D.

(Chapter 17, Lesson 2)

3. What shape will this net create?

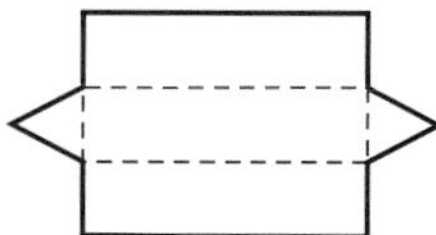

A. cone

B. cube

C. rectangular prism

D. triangular prism

(Chapter 18, Lesson 5)

4. Which set of numbers is listed from GREATEST to LEAST?

A. 0.75 1.25 2.80

B. 0.03 0.33 3.0

C. 1.50 0.45 0.05

D. 2.67 3.90 1.0

(Chapter 21, Lesson 6)



For Test-Taking Tips, See page 658.

## Open Response

5. Which unit of measure, grams or kilograms, would be better to measure the mass of a backpack full of books? Explain your thinking.

(Chapter 12, Lesson 9)

6. What fraction can be used to represent the shaded part of the figure below?

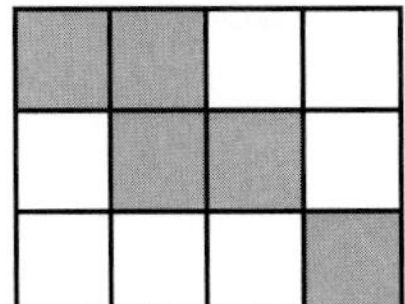

(Chapter 19, Lesson 1)

7. What are all the factors of 30?

(Chapter 10, Lesson 1)

8. Copy and complete the function table.

| **Rule:** ___________. | |
|---|---|
| **a** | **b** |
| 2 | 14 |
| ■ | 28 |
| 6 | ■ |
| 8 | 56 |

(Chapter 5, Lesson 6)

9. Write the coordinates for Point *A*.

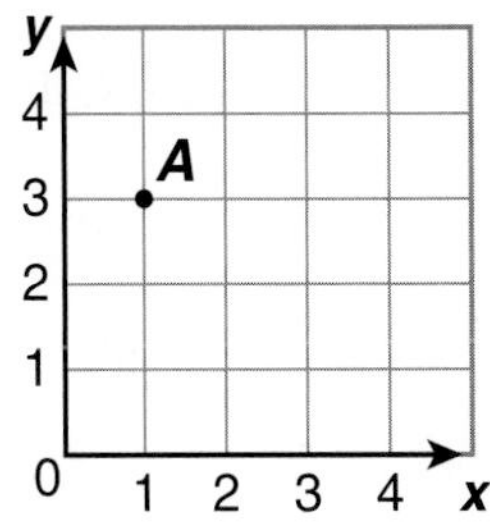


(Chapter 24, Lesson 2)

## Extended Response

10. Use the graph to answer the questions.

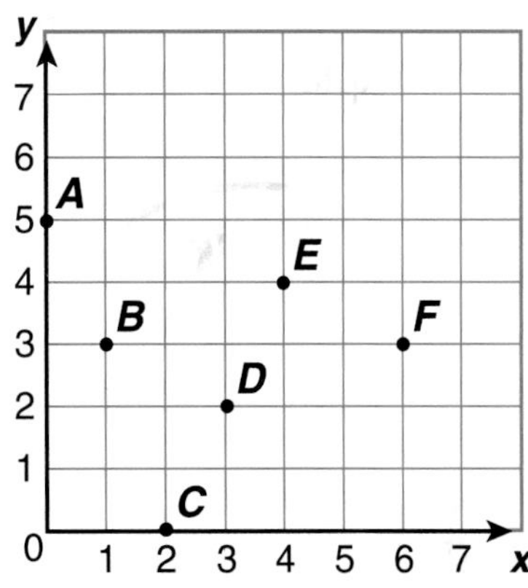


a. Name the ordered pairs for A and D.

b. B and F share a coordinate. What is it?

c. Write directions showing how to get to E if you start at (0, 0).

d. Write directions showing how to get from E to F.

(Chapter 24, Lesson 1)

**Education Place**

Look for Cumulative Test Prep at **eduplace.com/map** for more practice

# Vocabulary Wrap-Up for Unit 8

**Look back at the big ideas and vocabulary in this unit.**

## Big Ideas

You can find where to place the decimal point in a product by finding the total number of decimal places in the factors.

You can use coordinates to locate points on a grid.

### Key Vocabulary

**product**
**factor**
**coordinates**

## Math Conversations

**Use your new vocabulary to discuss these big ideas.**

1. Explain how you know where to place the decimal point when dividing with decimals.

2. Explain how to find the opposite of 7 on a number line.

3. Explain how to plot the ordered pairs in the table on the right to form a line.

| *x* | *y* |
|---|---|
| 1 | 1 |
| 2 | 3 |
| 3 | 5 |
| 4 | 7 |

4. **Write About It** Write a multiplication or division story problem that uses the numbers 2.5 and 3. Then solve your problem.

# Student Resources

Georgia Performance Standards

# Georgia Study Guide

**The Study Guide is organized by Georgia Performance Standard. You can use it as a resource to begin instruction in this standard or as an end-of-unit check of student understanding. The guide might also be helpful to students as a review before the CRCT.**

## Process Skills

**M4P1** Using the appropriate technology, students will solve problems that arise in mathematics and in other contexts.

- **a.** Solve non-routine word problems using the strategies of work backwards, use or make a table, and make an organized list, as well as all strategies learned in previous grades.
- **b.** Solve single and multi-step routine word problems related to all appropriate fourth grade math standards.
- **c.** Determine the operations(s) needed to solve a problem.
- **d.** Determine the most efficient way to solve a problem (mentally, paper/pencil, or calculator).

## Use Strategies

You have already learned a number of math strategies. This year, you will learn how to use other strategies, such as the *work backward* strategy.

In this strategy, you start with the information you know. Then you work backward, using **inverse operations** to solve. Addition and subtraction are inverse operations. Multiplication and division are inverse operations.

**Guided Practice**

**Use the Ask Yourself questions to help you solve each problem.**

1. Twice as many people went on the first aquarium tour as the second tour. Three times as many went on the third tour as the second tour. If 90 people went on the third tour, how many went on the first tour?

   Hint: What information should you start with?

2. At a zoo, there are 2 more penguins than walruses. There are half as many seals as penguins. There are 6 seals. How many walruses are at the zoo?

**Ask Yourself**

- UNDERSTAND: **What facts do I know?**
- PLAN: **What number do I know?**
- SOLVE: **Did I use inverse operations?**
- LOOK BACK: **Did I check by starting with my answer and working forward?**

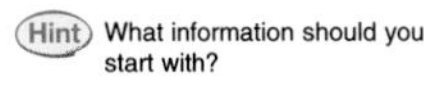

**Independent Practice**

**Solve.**

3. The Dunns bought aquarium supplies. One angelfish cost 2 times as much as the fish food. The filter cost 3 times as much as the angelfish. The filter cost $12. How much did the fish food cost?
4. At an aquarium there are twice as many sharks as turtles. There are 3 fewer seals than sharks. If there are 15 seals, how many turtles are there?
5. Kelley is thinking of a number. She adds 1, divides by 5, subtracts 2, and multiplies by 5. The result is 40. What is Kelley's number?
6. **Create and Solve** Make up a number puzzle like the one in Problem 5. Give your number puzzle to a classmate to solve.

Go On

**Chapter 9** Lesson 5 **241**

**In Your Text**

Understand the problem before you choose the operation or strategy to use to solve the problem.

**In Your Text**

Use the strategy *make a table* and *work backwards*.

**In Your Text**

*Pencil/paper* is the best way to solve problems 3 and 4.
*Mental math is the fastest way to solve problem 5.*

Georgia Study Guide

Georgia Performance Standards

# Process Skills

**M4P2** Students will investigate, develop, and evaluate mathematical arguments.

## Investigate Math Arguments

In math, an argument is not a disagreement.

A **math argument** is made up of the steps you use to solve a problem or the steps you use to prove you have done it correctly.

Since you first began your study of math, you have been developing skills for making and analyzing mathematical arguments.

You make math arguments when you state the steps in your solutions and defend them. You analyze math arguments when you evaluate the solutions of others.

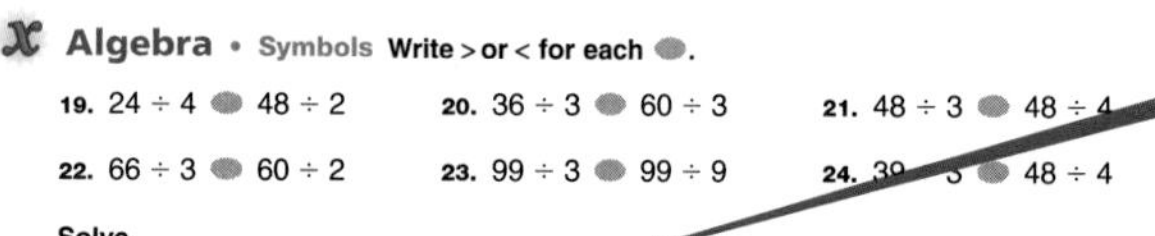

**Algebra** • Symbols Write > or < for each ●.

19. 24 ÷ 4 ● 48 ÷ 2
20. 36 ÷ 3 ● 60 ÷ 3
21. 48 ÷ 3 ● 48 ÷ 4
22. 66 ÷ 3 ● 60 ÷ 2
23. 99 ÷ 3 ● 99 ÷ 9
24. 39 ÷ 3 ● 48 ÷ 4

**Solve.**

25. José has 67 model cars in his collection. He wants to share them equally among 3 friends. How many cars will each friend get?
26. **Money** Jennifer has $29. She buys 2 model-car kits. Each kit costs the same amount. She has $1 left. How much does each kit cost?
27. How many different ways can 16 model cars be arranged in equal rows so there are at least 3 cars in each row and 1 car in a row by itself?
28. **Multistep** A shop sells 25 model cars for $9 each. It also sells 35 model trucks for $10 each. How much more does the shop receive for the model trucks than for the model cars?

**In Your Text**

Math Argument: I can prove my answer "22 cars" is correct by multiplying and adding: $22 \times 3 + 1 = 67$

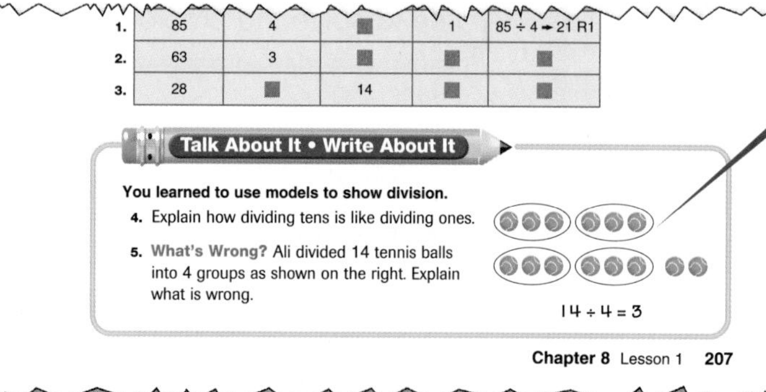

| | | | | | |
|---|---|---|---|---|---|
| 1. | 85 | 4 | ■ | 1 | 85 ÷ 4 → 21 R1 |
| 2. | 63 | 3 | ■ | ■ | ■ |
| 3. | 28 | ■ | 14 | ■ | ■ |

**Talk About It • Write About It**

**You learned to use models to show division.**

4. Explain how dividing tens is like dividing ones.
5. **What's Wrong?** Ali divided 14 tennis balls into 4 groups as shown on the right. Explain what is wrong.



Chapter 8 Lesson 1 207

**In Your Text**

Math Argument: There are 3 balls in each group with 2 left over. The sentence should include the 2 left over: $14 \div 4 = 3\text{ R}2$

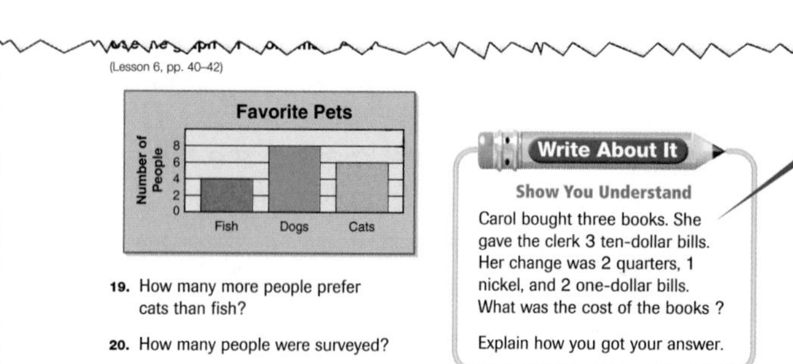

(Lesson 6, pp. 40–42)



19. How many more people prefer cats than fish?
20. How many people were surveyed?

**Write About It**

**Show You Understand**

Carol bought three books. She gave the clerk 3 ten-dollar bills. Her change was 2 quarters, 1 nickel, and 2 one-dollar bills. What was the cost of the books ?

Explain how you got your answer.

44 Chapter 2 Chapter Review/Test

**In Your Text**

Math Argument: Find the value of the change: $2.55. Subtract $2.55 from $30.00. The cost of the books is $27.45.

Georgia Study Guide

## Process Skills

**M4P3** Students will use the language of mathematics to express ideas precisely.

### Communicate Math Ideas

You know that you can communicate your ideas by writing and speaking. In math, you learn to use **math language** to express your ideas clearly.

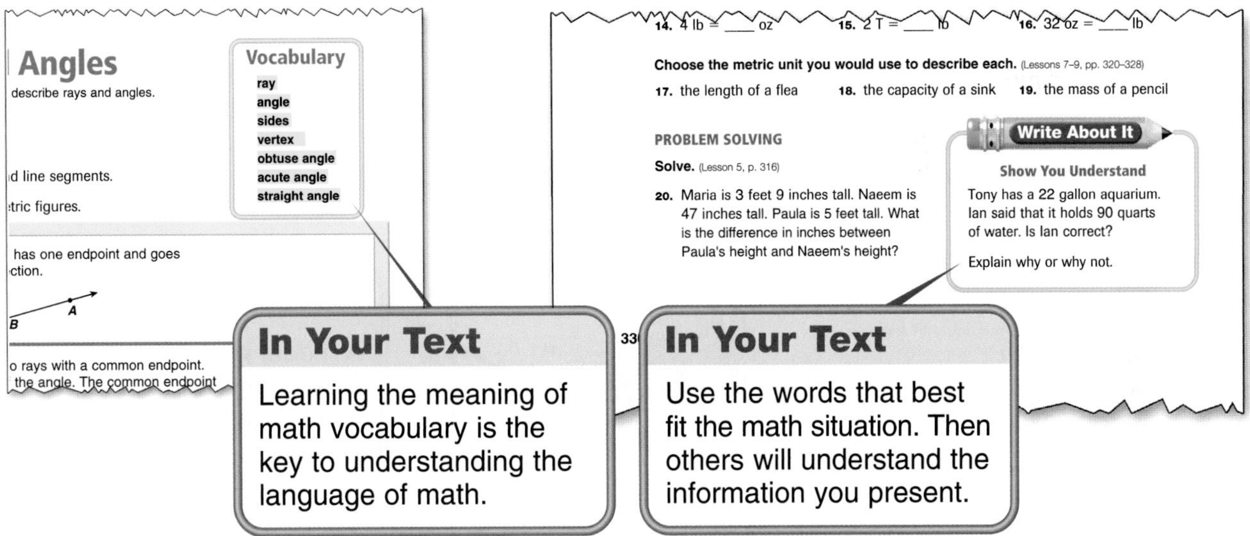


## Process Skills

**M4P4** Students will understand how mathematical ideas interconnect and build on one another and will apply math in other content areas.

### Make Math Connections

As you continue your study of math, you will see how ideas build, and how one idea **connects** to another.

You have also studied how math connects to other areas. For example, you have studied math-to-math connections. You know that addition and subtraction are related operations.

You have also studied how math connects to other areas. For example, when you use measurement skills in science, you make a math connection.

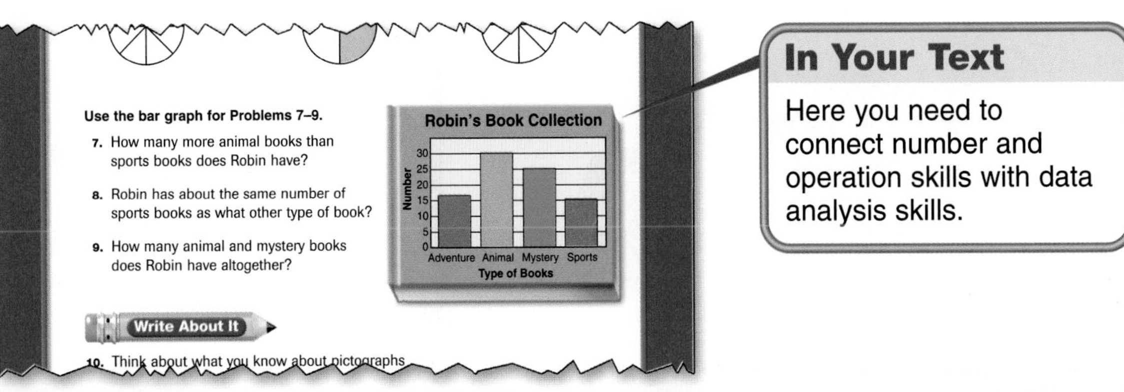


**In Your Text**

Here you need to connect number and operation skills with data analysis skills.

## Process Skills

**M4P5** Students will create and use pictures, manipulatives, models, and symbols to organize, record, and communicate mathematical ideas.

### Use Models

There are many tools you can use to show what you know about math. These tools include drawing pictures or diagrams, or using real objects to make a model.

In math, you can use many different models, These include base-ten blocks, sketches of geometric figures, and place-value models. When you represent an idea with a model, you demonstrate your understanding.

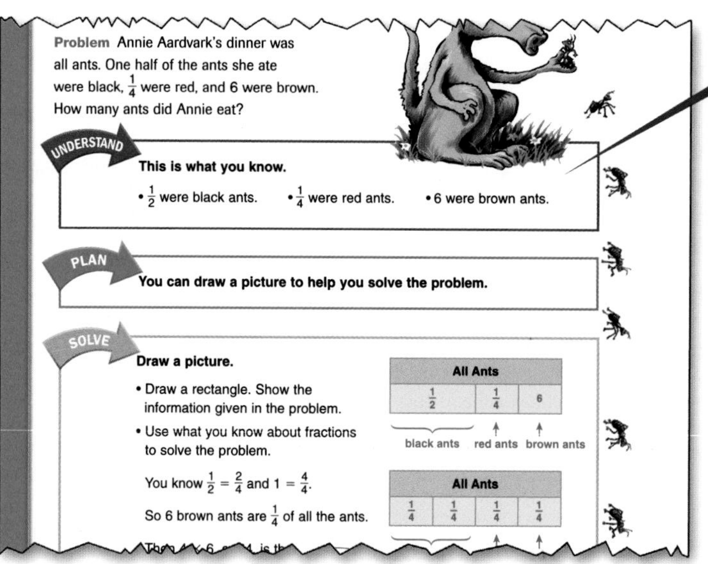


**In Your Text**

A model helps you understand and solve math problems.

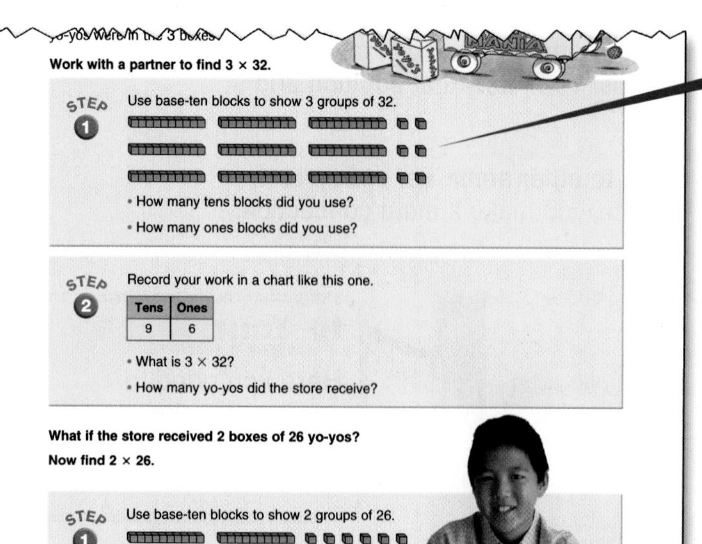


**In Your Text**

A model helps you visualize an idea and organize and explain your thinking.

Georgia Performance Standards

## Numbers and Operations

**M4N1.a** Identify place value names and places…through one million.

How can you find the place value of a digit in a number?

### Connect It

One way to find the place value of a digit is to use a place value chart. The chart below tells us the place of the digit 4 in the number 1,465,290.

| Millions | | | Thousands | | | Ones | | |
|---|---|---|---|---|---|---|---|---|
| hundreds | tens | ones | hundreds | tens | ones | hundreds | tens | ones |
| | | 1 | 4 | 6 | 5 | 2 | 9 | 0 |

The 4 is in the hundred thousands place. Remember, each place on the chart is ten times the place to its right.

**Read More**
See Unit 1 on pages 6–7, 14–15 to learn more about place value.

### Use Your Skills

Answer the following questions.

1. What is the place value of the underlined digit in 4,86<u>2</u>,399?
2. What digit is in ten thousands place in 1,423,976?
3. **Apply** How can place value be used to tell which number is greater–465 or 1,687?

## Numbers and Operations

**M4N1.b** Equate a number's word name, its standard form, and its expanded form.

What different ways you can write a whole number?

### Connect It

You can write a number such as 294,367 in three different ways.

**Standard form:** 294,367
**Expanded form:** 200,000 + 90,000 + 4,000 + 300 + 60 + 7
**Word form:** two hundred ninety-four thousand, three hundred sixty-seven

**Read More**
See Unit 1 on pages 6–7 to learn more about forms of whole numbers.

### Use Your Skills

Write each of the following numbers in two other forms.

1. ninety-four thousand, six hundred twenty
2. 700,000 + 5,000 + 800 + 10 + 6
3. 116,907
4. **Contrast** If two numbers are to be added, which form of the numbers would be easiest to use?

Georgia Performance Standards

## Numbers and Operations

**M4N1.b** Equate a number's word name, its standard form, and its expanded form.

What different ways can you write a decimal?

**Read More**
See Unit 7 on pages 546–548 to learn more about forms of numbers.

### Connect It

You can write a number such as 294.367 three different ways.

**Standard form:** 294.367

**Expanded form:** 200 + 90 + 4 + 0.3 + 0.06 + 0.007

**Word form:** two hundred ninety-four and three hundred sixty-seven thousandths.

When you read the number, remember the only time you say *and* is when you read the decimal point.

### Use Your Skills

Write each of the following numbers in two other ways.

1. 4.52
2. 78.012
3. three hundred eighty-nine
4. six hundred forty two and 7 thousandths
5. 5 + 0.7 + 0.04 + 0.002
6. 100 + 7 + 0.4 + 0.008
7. **Compare** Two of the following numbers are the same. Which number is different?

   4 + 500 + 0.80 + 0.006

   four and five hundred eighty-six thousandths

   4.586

## Numbers and Operations

**M4N2.a** Round numbers to the nearest ten, hundred, or thousand.

How do you round a number?

**Read More**
See Unit 1 on pages 38–39 to learn more about rounding.

### Connect It

Suppose you want to round the number 4,893 to the nearest ten.

You can draw a number line and find which ten the number is closest to.

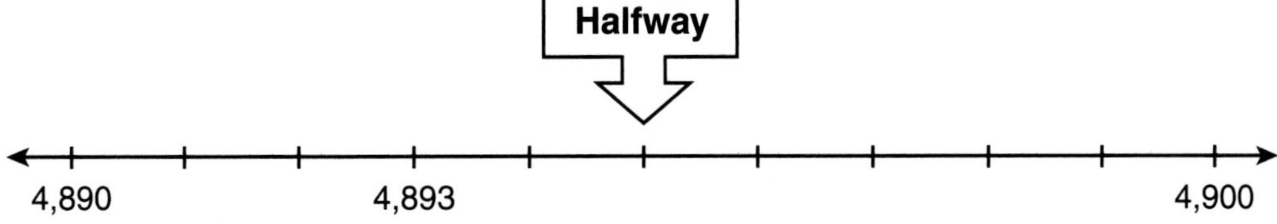


The number 4,893 is closer to 4,890 than it is to 4,900.

You can also use place value to round a number.

**Step 1:** Find the place you want to round to. Underline the digit in that place. 4,8<u>9</u>3

**Step 2:** Circle the digit to the right of the underlined digit. 4,8<u>9</u>(3)

**Step 3:** Look at the circled digit. This digit tells you whether the tens value in 4,8<u>9</u>3 is closer to 90 or 100. 4,8<u>9</u>(3)

3 is less than 5.
Round down to 90.
Change the 3 to a 0.

- If the circled digit is 5 or greater, round the underlined digit up to the next digit.
- If the circled digit is less than 5, do not change the underlined digit.
- Change any digit to the right of the underlined digit to a 0.

### Use Your Skills

Round the following numbers.

1. Round 473 to the nearest hundred.
2. Round 5,815 to the nearest ten.
3. Round 7,<u>4</u>93 to the place of the underlined digit.
4. Round 4,967 to the nearest thousand.
5. **Explain** Keesha sold 39 rolls of wrapping paper to raise money for her class. If she wanted to estimate the number of rolls she sold, would she round 39 to the nearest 10 or the nearest 100? Explain.

## Numbers and Operations

**M4N2.b** Describe situations in which rounding numbers would be appropriate and determine whether to round to the nearest ten, hundred, or thousand.

How do you decide when to round?

**Read More**
See Unit 2 on page 68 to learn more about when to round a number.

### Connect It

Estimation is a useful skill but it is not appropriate to use it for everything.

Sometimes the word *about* in a problem is a clue that you should estimate.
About how many pages are in a book that has 213 pages?
You could round the number of pages either to the nearest 10 or 100.
If you round to the nearest 100, there are about 200 pages.
If you round to the nearest 10, there are about 210 pages.

You might be asked how many pages you read last night. Then you could estimate and say that you read about 20 pages, or you could say that you read exactly 21 pages.

Often, the larger the number is, the more likely it is that an estimation will be used. For example, the population of Canton was 13,195 in 2003. If you are asked the population of Canton, you could say that the population of Canton was about 13,000 in 2003.

You should not always use estimation. You may have 24 students in your classroom. If someone asks how many students are in your class, they would probably want to know exactly how many students there are. So you should not say "about 20."

Estimation is also an excellent way to check your work to see if your answer is close to what it should be.

### Use Your Skills

Choose whether to estimate or give an exact answer.

1. A train leaves at 3:47 P.M. You need to arrive at the station at least 5 minutes before the train leaves. What time do you need to be at the station? Can you use an estimated time?
2. Three suitcases each weigh about 45 pounds. How much do they weigh altogether? Will your answer be exact or an estimate? Why?
3. Four friends will equally share the cost of lunch. The total cost for lunch is $19.40. How much will each friend pay? Do you need an exact answer or an estimate?
4. You want to buy 4 DVDs for $9.29 each. You have $37. Can you use an estimation to see if you have enough money, or do you need an exact answer?

## Numbers and Operations

**M4N2.c** Understand the meaning of rounding a decimal to the nearest whole number.

How do you round a decimal to a whole number?

**Read More**
See Unit 7 on pages 568–569 to learn more about rounding decimals.

### Connect It

If you round a decimal, such as 145.359, to a whole number, you are rounding it to the ones place.

- To round a decimal to a whole number, find the digit that is in the ones place. — 14<u>5</u>.359
- Then locate the digit in the tenths place. If the digit is 5 or greater, round up to the next greater whole number. If the digit is less than 5, the digit in the ones place stays the same. — 14<u>5</u>.(3)59; 3 is less than 5, round down; 14<u>5</u>.359 rounds to 145.

### Use Your Skills

Round each decimal to the nearest whole number.

**1.** 4.5 **2.** 5.46 **3.** 14.935 **4.** 59.37

**5. Apply** Fred lives 2.45 mi from the school. To the nearest mile, how far does he live from the school?

## Numbers and Operations

**M4N2.d** Estimate a sum or difference by rounding numbers and represent the results of computation as a rounded number.

How can rounding help you estimate when adding and subtracting?

**Read More**
See Unit 2 on pages 64–65 to learn more about rounding.

### Connect It

To estimate a sum or difference, round numbers before you compute.

Estimating a sum is simpler if we round both addends to the nearest 100.

| | | |
|---|---|---|
| 462 | rounds to → | 500 |
| + 289 | rounds to → | + 300 |
| | | 800 |

For a closer estimate, we can round to the nearest 10.

| | | |
|---|---|---|
| 738 | rounds to → | 740 |
| − 352 | rounds to → | − 350 |
| | | 390 |

### Use Your Skills

Round each number to the nearest hundred, then estimate.

**1.** 824 + 601 **2.** 5,986 + 345 **3.** 6,127 − 2,742

**4.** The population of a county was computed to be 25,891 people. What rounded number would you write to represent the population?

**5. Conclude** Maria needs to figure out how many tickets she can sell to a play. There are 340 seats, and 113 tickets have been sold. Should Maria estimate her answer? Why or why not?

## Numbers and Operations

**M4N2.d** Represent the results of computation as a rounded number when appropriate and estimate a sum or difference by rounding numbers.

How can you estimate a sum or difference of decimals?

**Read More**
See Unit 7 on page 570 to learn more about estimation.

### Connect It

To estimate the sum or difference of two decimal numbers, round the numbers to the nearest whole numbers. Then add or subtract the numbers.

$$\begin{array}{rcr} 5.6 & \text{rounds to} \rightarrow & 6 \\ \underline{+\ 4.3} & \text{rounds to} \rightarrow & \underline{+\ 4} \\ & & 10 \end{array}$$

The estimate of the sum is 10.

### Use Your Skills

Estimate each sum or difference.

**1.** 6.7 + 4.1

**2.** 5.2 − 3.9

**3.** 6.9 + 5.5

**4.** 14.2 − 4.7

**5.** The cost of fabric and other supplies was $34.33. What rounded number would you write to represent the cost of the fabric and other supplies?

**6.** **Analyze** Estimate the sum 4.8 + 3.6. Will the actual answer be more or less than your estimate? Why do you think so?

## Use Your Skills

Simplify each of the division exercises by dividing both the dividend and the divisor by the same number. Then write the quotient.

**1.** 6,000 ÷ 300 **2.** 99 ÷ 33 **3.** 540 ÷ 45 **4.** 512 ÷ 64

**5.** **Create** List two simpler divisions for 1,600 ÷ 64.

How do you know the value of a decimal?

# Numbers and Operations

**M4N5.a** Understand decimals are a part of the base-ten system.

**Read More**
See Unit 7 on pages 544–545 to learn more about decimal fractions.

## Connect It

Decimals appear to the right of the ones place in a place value chart. The place value chart below shows the number 1,465,290.379.

| Millions | Thousands | | | Ones | | | | | | |
|---|---|---|---|---|---|---|---|---|---|---|
| ones | hundreds | tens | ones | hundreds | tens | ones | | tenths | hundredths | thousandths |
| 1, | 4 | 6 | 5, | 2 | 9 | 0 | . | 3 | 7 | 9 |

The decimal point always comes between the ones and the tenths places. It separates the whole number and the decimal part of the number.

When you write a decimal in word form, you use the name of the place value farthest to the right.

0.074 = seventy-four *thousandths*
0.12 = twelve *hundredths*
0.6 = *six tenths*

## Use Your Skills

Write each decimal in word form.

**1.** 0.569 **2.** 0.482 **3.** 0.39 **4.** 0.006 **5.** 0.4

**6.** **Extend** You know that as you move from right to left on a place value chart, the value of each place increases 10 times from place to place. Express in your own words what happens to the value of each place as you move from left to right.

## Numbers and Operations

**M4N5.b** Understand the relative size of numbers and order 2-digit decimals.

How do you order decimals?

**Read More**
See Unit 7 on pages 542–543, and 558–559 to learn more about comparing decimal numbers.

### Connect It

You can use a place-value chart to compare and order decimals.

Order these decimal numbers from least to greatest.

2.4 2.45 2.34 2.1 1.96

Place the numbers in the chart, lining up the decimals points. Add zeros as place holders if you need to.

| ones | | tenths | hundredths |
|---|---|---|---|
| 2 | . | 4 | 0 |
| 2 | . | 4 | 5 |
| 2 | . | 3 | 4 |
| 2 | . | 1 | 0 |
| 1 | . | 9 | 6 |

**Step 1**

Start comparing digits in the ones place. Since 2 > 1, 1.96 is the least number.

**Step 2**

Compare the digits in the tenths place. 2.34 is greater than 2.10 because 3 > 1.

**Step 3**

There are 2 fours in the tenths place, compare the digits in the thousandths place. 5 > 0, so 2.45 > 2.40.

Ordered from least to greatest, the numbers are:

1.96 2.1 2.34 2.4 2.45

### Use Your Skills

Order the decimal numbers from least to greatest.

**1.** 4.3, 5.12, 4.75, 5.2

**2.** 6.79, 6.34, 6.3, 5.97

**3.** **Conclude** Three students measured different objects in their classroom. The measurements are 0.64 m, 0.72 m, and 0.46 m. Which is the shortest measurement? How do you know?

## Numbers and Operations

**M4N5.c** Add one and two-digit decimals.

How do you add decimals?

### Connect It

To add decimals, line up the decimal points and add the same as you add whole numbers. If the numbers do not have the same number of digits to the right of the decimal point, add zeros as place holders.

**Read More**
See Unit 7 on pages 572–574 to learn more about adding decimal numbers.

Add 4.56 and 5.7.

| ones | | tenths | hundredths |
|---|---|---|---|
| 4 | . | 5 | 6 |
| + 5 | . | 7 | 0 |
| 10 | . | 2 | 6 |

### Use Your Skills

Add.

**1.** 6.7 + 2.8 **2.** 4.78 + 1.55 **3.** 6.6 + 1.23 **4.** 1.95 + 4.77

**5.** **Apply** Martin earned $5.72 one day and $8.43 the next day. How much did he earn altogether?

## Numbers and Operations

**M4N5.c** Subtract one- and two-digit decimals.

How do you subtract decimals?

### Connect It

To subtract decimals, line up the decimal points, and subtract the same as you do whole numbers. If the numbers do not have the same number of digits to the right of the decimal point, add zeros as place holders.

**Read More**
See Unit 7 on pages 572–574 to learn more about subtracting decimal numbers.

Subtract 2.72 from 5.3.

| ones | | tenths | hundredths |
|---|---|---|---|
| 5 | . | 3 | 0 |
| − 2 | . | 7 | 2 |
| 2 | . | 5 | 8 |

### Use Your Skills

Subtract.

**1.** 3.4 − 1.7 **2.** 5.6 − 3.42 **3.** 9.24 − 7.36 **4.** 8.05 − 4.1

**5.** **Compare** Luis paid $8.43 for lunch and $15.76 for dinner. Which meal cost more? How much more did one meal cost than the other?

## Numbers and Operations

**M4N5.d** Model multiplication of decimal fractions by whole numbers.

How can you model multiplication of decimals by whole numbers?

### Connect It

You can use hundredths grids.

To model 0.2 × 4 draw four hundredths grids. Shade 0.2, or 0.20, of each grid. Then count how many tenths are shaded altogether.

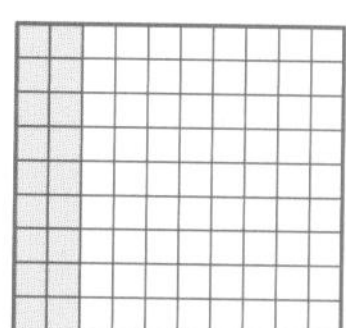
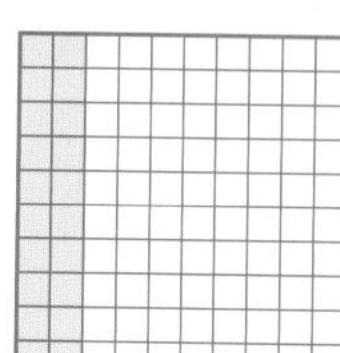
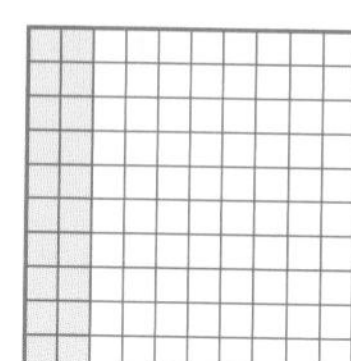
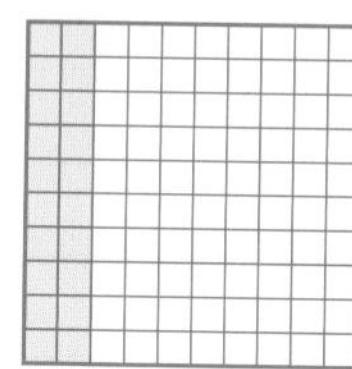

There are 8 tenths shaded. So 0.2 × 4 = 0.8

**Read More**
See Unit 8 on pages 596–597 to learn more about modeling multiplication of decimal numbers.

### Use Your Skills

Model each multiplication to find the answer.

**1.** 0.3 × 2

**2.** 0.5 × 3

**3.** **Illustrate** Eight friends plant 0.05 of a community garden. Make a model to show how much of the total garden they used.

## Numbers and Operations

**M4N5.d** Model division of decimals by whole numbers.

How can you model division of decimals by whole numbers?

### Connect It

You can use hundredths grids.

To model 0.8 ÷ 4 shade 0.8 of the grid. Divide the shaded area into equal groups of 4.

Each group has 0.2 of the entire grid.

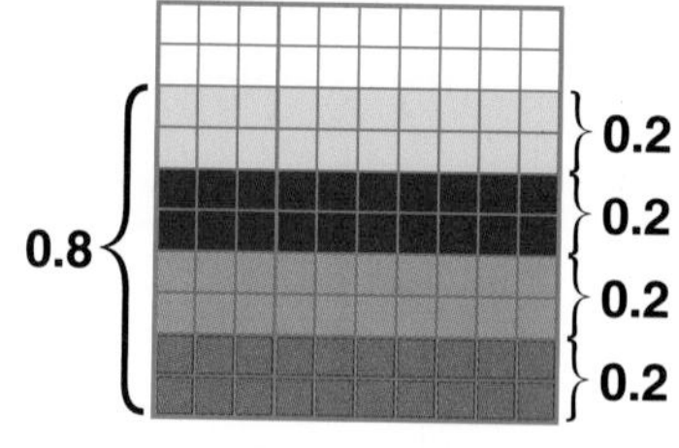

**0.8 ÷ 4 = 0.2**

**Read More**
See Unit 8 on pages 602–603 to learn more about modeling division of decimal numbers.

### Use Your Skills

Model each division problem to solve it. You may need to use more than one grid.

**1.** 0.9 ÷ 3

**2.** 1.8 ÷ 6

**3.** **Apply** Jorge baked 2 batches of cookies. He burned a few and ended up with 1.6 batches of cookies. If he gave the cookies to 8 of his friends, how much of the batches did each friend receive?

## Numbers and Operations

**M4N5.e** Multiply both one and two digit decimals by whole numbers.

How do you multiply decimals by whole numbers?

### Connect It

To multiply a decimal by a whole number, first multiply the two factors together as if you were multiplying whole numbers. Then count the number of places to the right of the decimal point in the decimal number. Your answer also needs to show the same number of places to the right of the decimal point.

$$\begin{array}{r} 4.52 \\ \times\ \ 3 \\ \hline 13.56 \end{array}$$

4.52 ← 2 places to the right

13.56 ← 2 places to the right

**Read More**
See Unit 8 on pages 598–600 to learn more about multiplying decimals by whole numbers.

### Use Your Skills

Multiply these factors.

**1.** 2.49 × 3

**2.** 8.2 × 9

**3.** **Connect** Susan earns $8.55 a day for a week raking leaves. What amount will she earn for the week?

## Numbers and Operations

**M4N5.e** Divide both one and two digit decimals by whole numbers.

How do you divide decimals by whole numbers?

### Connect It

When you divide a decimal by a whole number, set up the problem as if you were dividing whole numbers. Divide as if you were dividing whole numbers.

$$4\overline{)24.68}\quad 6\ 17$$

Then place the decimal point in the quotient directly above where it is in the dividend.

$$4\overline{)24.68}\quad 6.17$$

**Read More**
See Unit 8 on pages 608–610 to learn more about dividing decimals by whole numbers.

### Use Your Skills

Divide.

**1.** $7\overline{)2.8}$

**2.** $5\overline{)12.5}$

**3.** **Apply** Six students earned $48.42 for charity. If each student earned the same amount, how much did each student earn?

Georgia Performance Standards

## Numbers and Operations

**M4N6.a** Understand representations of simple equivalent fractions.

How do you know when fractions are equivalent?

### Connect It

Fractions are equivalent when they name the same amount. The strips show how fractions with denominators of 3, 6, and 12 relate to each other.

**Read More**
See Unit 7 on pages 492–496 to learn more about equivalent fractions.

How many sixths does it take to name the same amount as $\frac{1}{3}$? How many twelfths?

You can see from the table that $\frac{1}{3}$, $\frac{2}{6}$, and $\frac{4}{12}$ are equivalent fractions.

### Use Your Skills

For each fraction, name two equivalent fractions.

**1.** $\frac{1}{5}$

**2.** $\frac{1}{4}$

**3.** **Generalize** Explain how you know $\frac{4}{8}$ and $\frac{3}{6}$ are equivalent fractions. Use fraction strips or a number line to help.

## Numbers and Operations

**M4N6.b** Add and subtract fractions with like denominators.

How do you add and subtract fractions with the same denominator?

**Read More**
See Unit 7 on pages 516–517 to learn more about fractions with like denominators.

### Connect It

To add or subtract fractions with like denominators, add or subtract the numerators. The denominator stays the same. Simplify the fraction if possible.

Subtract $\frac{1}{6}$ from $\frac{5}{6}$.

$\frac{5}{6} - \frac{1}{6} = \frac{4}{6} = \frac{2}{3}$

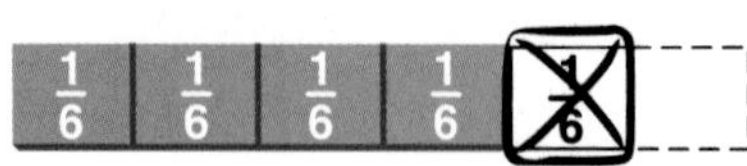


Add $\frac{4}{7}$ and $\frac{5}{7}$.

$\frac{4}{7} + \frac{5}{7} = \frac{9}{7} = 1\frac{2}{7}$

### Use Your Skills

Add or subtract these fractions.

**1.** $\frac{3}{4} + \frac{2}{4}$

**2.** $\frac{6}{11} - \frac{3}{11}$

**3.** **Discuss** Why don't you add or subtract the denominators when adding or subtracting fractions?

Georgia Study Guide

## Numbers and Operations

**M4N6.b** Add and subtract fractions and mixed numbers with common denominators.

How do you add and subtract mixed numbers with like denominators?

### Connect It

When you add mixed numbers with like denominators, add the fractions, then add the whole numbers. When you subtract, subtract the fractions, then subtract the whole numbers. Write the answers in simplest form.

Add $1\frac{3}{5} + 2\frac{4}{5} = 3\frac{7}{5} = 4\frac{2}{5}$ Subtract $4\frac{3}{8} - 2\frac{1}{8} = 2\frac{2}{8} = 2\frac{1}{4}$

**Read More**
See Unit 7 on page 520 to learn more about mixed numbers with like denominators.

### Use Your Skills

Add or subtract the following mixed numbers.

**1.** $5\frac{3}{5} + 2\frac{2}{5}$ **2.** $4\frac{7}{12} - 1\frac{5}{12}$

**3. Apply** There are 3 medium pizzas on the table. Cheryl eats $\frac{3}{8}$ of a pizza, Ali eats $\frac{1}{2}$ of a pizza, and John eats $\frac{3}{4}$ of a pizza. How can you decide how much pizza they ate altogether?

## Numbers and Operations

**M4N6.c** Convert and use mixed numbers and improper fractions interchangeably.

How do you write equivalent mixed numbers and improper fractions?

### Connect It

To change from a mixed number to an improper fraction, multiply the denominator by the whole number. Then add the numerator to this product to get the new numerator. The denominator stays the same.

$$3\frac{1}{5} = \frac{(5 \times 3 + 1)}{5} = \frac{16}{5}$$

To change from an improper fraction to a mixed number, divide the numerator by the denominator to get the whole number. The new fraction is the remainder over the denominator.

$$\frac{16}{5} = 16 \div 5 = 3 \text{ R1} = 3\frac{1}{5}$$

**Read More**
See Unit 7 on pages 508–510 to learn more about mixed numbers and improper fractions.

### Use Your Skills

Change to the equivalent mixed number or improper fraction.

**1.** $\frac{14}{3}$ **2.** $7\frac{2}{9}$

**3. Analyze** Why can't the improper fraction $\frac{15}{3}$ be written as a mixed number?

Georgia Performance Standards

# Numbers and Operations

**M4N7.a** Describe situations in which the four operations may be used and the relationships among them.

How do you know what operation to use to solve a problem?

**Read More**
See Unit 2 on pages 72–73, 88–89, and 104–105 to learn more about using operations.

## Connect It

Sometimes key words can help. The word *altogether* often tells you to add. The word *difference* may tell you to subtract. The phrase *how many equal groups* may mean you need to divide. The phrase *times as many* may mean to multiply.

You may need to use more than one operation to solve a problem. If you have used the correct operation to solve a problem, you can check your work by using the inverse operation. Multiplication and division are inverse operations, and addition and subtraction are inverse operations. Fact families of one operation are related to the fact families of the inverse operation.

For example, since $2 + 4 = 6$, then $6 - 4 = 2$.
Also, since $3 \times 4 = 12$, then $12 \div 4 = 3$.

## Use Your Skills

Decide whether you want more or fewer. You may be looking for equal groups. Then determine which operation to use to solve these problems. Solve and use the inverse operation to check your work. Show the related facts used in each problem.

1. Tonya needs 3 apples for one bowl of fruit salad. How many apples does she need for 5 bowls?
2. In a third grade class, 15 students wear tennis shoes, and 12 students wear other types of shoes. How many more students wear tennis shoes?
3. In a school, 27 students were absent on Monday, and 24 students were absent on Tuesday. How many students were absent on these days?
4. Peter earned $45 by mowing 9 lawns. He earned the same amount for each lawn he mowed. How much did he earn for each lawn?
5. **Relate** A student has 4 times as many CDs as her sister. Her sister has 5 CDs. Show how this problem can be solved either by addition or by multiplication.

## Numbers and Operations

**M4N7.d** Use mental math strategies to compute.

What other estimation strategies besides rounding can be used to estimate sums and differences?

**Read More**
See Unit 2 on page 67 to learn more about estimating.

### Connect It

**Front-end estimation.**

In front-end estimation, the first digits are added or subtracted.

$$\begin{array}{r} 586 \\ -\ 312 \\ \hline 200 \end{array} \rightarrow 500 - 300 = 200$$

Then adjust the estimate by looking at the other digits.

86 − 12 is more than 50, so we round to 100. Add 100 to 200: 100 + 200 = 300.

The estimate is about 300.

**Clustering**

If addends have similar values, you can estimate their sum by clustering.

Estimate 120 + 93 + 104.
The addends 120, 93, and 104 are all close to 100, so the sum is close to 300.

### Use Your Skills

Use front-end estimation or clustering to estimate each sum or difference.

**1.** 597 − 288

**2.** 415 + 393

**3.** **Choose** Would you use front-end estimation or clustering to estimate the sum of 499, 312, and 142? Why?

## Numbers and Operations

**M4N7.d** Use mental math strategies to compute.

How can you use mental math to multiply?

**Read More**
See Unit 3 on pages 146–147 to learn more about mental math and multiplication.

### Connect It

To multiply using mental math, you can use the basic multiplication facts you already know. You can also use patterns, such as patterns of zeros.

To multiply 4 × 60 using mental math, start with the basic multiplication fact, 4 × 6 = 24. — 4 × 6 = 24

Sixty has one 0, so we add one 0 to the product. — 4 × 60 = 240

### Use Your Skills

Use basic multiplication facts and patterns to find the products.

**1.** 4 × 800 **2.** 7 × 80 **3.** 6 × 9,000

**3.** **Discuss** A student multiplied 5 × 600 and said that the product was 3,000. Why does the product have 3 zeros and 600 has only 2 zeros?

## Numbers and Operations

**M4N7.d** Use mental math and estimation strategies to compute.

What strategies can you use to estimate a product?

### Connect It

You can estimate products by rounding factors to their greatest place.

$3 \times 47 = \blacksquare$
Round 47 to 50, and multiply: $3 \times 50 = 150$.
You rounded 47 up, so the actual answer is less than 150.

### Use Your Skills

Estimate each product.

**1.** $63 \times 4$

**2.** $75 \times 7$

**3.** **Analyze** To estimate the product of $75 \times 9$, which factor would you round? Why?

**Read More**
See Unit 3 on pages 148–149 to learn more about estimating products.

## Numbers and Operations

**M4N7.d** Use mental math and estimation strategies to compute.

How can you use mental math to divide?

### Connect It

You can use the basic division facts you already know and number patterns to divide using mental math.

Divide 1,800 by 3 using mental math,

Use the basic fact $18 \div 3 = 6$.

$$1{,}800 \div 3 = 600$$

Notice that the dividend has 2 more zeros than the basic fact, so the quotient must also have 2 more zeros.

### Use Your Skills

Use division facts and number patterns to divide these problems.

**1.** $500 \div 5$

**2.** $5{,}400 \div 6$

**3.** **Compare** How are the problems $4{,}000 \div 8$ and $400 \div 8$ alike?

**Read More**
See Unit 4 on pages 218–219 to learn more about mental math and division.

# Numbers and Operations

**M4N7.d** Use mental math and estimation strategies to compute.

What strategies can you use to estimate a quotient?

**Read More**
See Unit 4 on pages 220–222 to learn more about estimating quotients.

## Connect It

One way to estimate a quotient is to round the dividend.

Tyler collected 143 cans of food for the food pantry. He needs to prepare the cans in bags of 7 cans each. About how many bags of food can Tyler prepare?

To estimate the number of bags, round the dividend to a number that is close to 143 and is evenly divisible by 7. We can use a basic multiplication fact and multiples of 10 to decide what dividend to use.

Think: $2 \times 7 = 14$

Think: $20 \times 7 = 140$

$7\overline{)143}$ → $\begin{array}{r} 20 \\ 7\overline{)140} \end{array}$

Estimate: 20 bags

## Use Your Skills

Write the basic fact you would use to estimate. Then estimate the quotient.

**1.** $9\overline{)84}$

**2.** $5\overline{)223}$

**3.** $5\overline{)4{,}578}$

**4.** $8\overline{)62{,}388}$

**5.** **Discuss** Two students estimate $7\overline{)658}$. One estimates 100, the other estimates 90. Which estimate is closer? How do you know?

Georgia Performance Standards

## Measurement

**M4M1.a** Use standard and metric units to measure the weight of objects.

How can you find the weight of an object?

**Read More**
See Unit 5 on pages 312–314 to learn more about measuring weight.

### Connect It

The weight of an object tells how heavy the object is. A scale is used to measure weight. You can place an object on a scale and read the weight.

Sometimes a scale measures weight in both pounds (lb) and ounces (oz). Other scales, such as the ones used to weigh letters and small packages for mailing, measure weight only in ounces. A scale used to measure very heavy items, such as trucks, might measure weight in tons.

### Use Your Skills

Use a scale to weigh the following items.

**1.** your science book

**2.** your shoe

**3.** **Analyze** You want to weigh your cat using your bathroom scales. The cat will not stand still on the scales. How might you weigh your cat?

## Measurement

**M4M1.a** Use standard and metric units to measure the weight of objects.

How can you use a balance scale to measure mass?

**Read More**
See Unit 5 on pages 326–328 to learn more about metric measurements.

### Connect It

A balance scale can be used to measure the mass of an object. When you use a balance scale, you place the object you want to measure on one side. On the other side, you place known masses until the two sides balance. A balance scale used in the classroom usually measures mass in grams (g). Larger masses are measured in kilograms (kg).

### Use Your Skills

Use a balance scale to find the mass of these objects.

**1.** a marker

**2.** a paperback book

**3.** **Predict** Which do you think has greater mass, a new pencil or a quarter? Use a balance to check your prediction.

## Measurement

**M4M1.b** Know units used to measure weight (gram, kilogram, ounce, pound, and ton).

What units can you use to measure weight?

### Connect It

Customary units of weight include ounces (oz), pounds (lb), and tons (T).

16 oz = 1 lb          2,000 lb = 1 T

**Read More**
See Unit 5 on pages 312–314 to learn more about units of weight.

**Change Pounds to Ounces**

To change lb to oz you multiply.

How many ounces are in 24 pounds?

| 24 | × | 16 | = | 384 |
|---|---|---|---|---|
| ↑ | | ↑ | | ↑ |
| number of pounds | | ounces in a pound | | ounces in 24 pounds |

**Change Pounds to Tons**

To change lb to T you divide.

How many tons are in 6,000 pounds?

| 6,000 | ÷ | 2,000 | = | 3 |
|---|---|---|---|---|
| ↑ | | ↑ | | ↑ |
| number of pounds | | pounds in a ton | | tons in 6,000 pounds |

### Use Your Skills

Complete.

**1.** 12 lb = ■ oz          **2.** 8,000 lb = ■ T

**3.** **Extend** A car weighs 2 tons. How many ounces does it weigh?

## Measurement

**M4M1.b** Know units used to measure weight (gram, kilogram, ounce, pound, and ton).

What units can you use to measure mass?

### Connect It

Two metric units used to measure mass are kilograms (kg) and grams (g).

1,000 g = 1 kg

**Read More**
See Unit 5 on pages 326–328 to learn more about metric units of mass.

**Change Grams to Kilograms**

To change from g to kg, divide by 1,000.

2,000 g ÷ 1,000 g in a kg = 2 kg

**Change Kilograms to Grams**

To change from kg to g, multiply by 1,000.

4 kg × 1,000 g in a kg = 4,000 g

### Use Your Skills

Solve the following problems.

**1.** 5,000 g = ■ kg          **2.** 8 kg = ■ g

**3.** **Justify** A student wants to find the mass of a motorcycle. Would she measure this mass using grams or kilograms? Explain.

## Measurement

**M4M1.c** Compare one unit to another within a single system of measurement.

How can you compare customary units of measure?

### Connect It

If you know a customary measurement that uses one unit, you can use larger or smaller units to name an equivalent measurement.

How many inches are in 2 yards?

| 2 | × | 36 | = | 72 inches |
|---|---|---|---|---|
| ↑ | | ↑ | | ↑ |
| number of yards | | number of inches in a yard | | inches in 2 yards |

**Read More**
See Unit 5 on pages 308–314 to learn more about comparing customary units.

### Use Your Skills

Complete.

**1.** 20 quarts = ■ pints

**2.** 9 feet = ■ yards

**3.** **Compare** Which is greater 5 pounds or 85 ounces?

## Measurement

**M4M1.c** Compare one unit to another within a single system of measurement.

How can you compare metric units of measure?

### Connect It

If you know a metric measurement that uses one unit, you can use larger or smaller units to name an equipment measurement.

How many meters (m) are in 200 centimeters (cm)?

| 200 cm | ÷ | 100 | = | 2 m |
|---|---|---|---|---|
| ↑ | | ↑ | | ↑ |
| number of centimeters | | number of centimeters in a meter | | number of meters in 200 centimeters |

**Read More**
See Unit 5 on pages 318–328 to learn more about comparing metric units.

### Use Your Skills

Complete.

**1.** 3 kg = ■ g

**2.** 4,000 mL = ■ L

**3.** 3m = ■ cm

**4.** **Analyze** What metric units would be best to use to measure the mass and the length of a bicycle?

## Measurement

**M4M2.a** Use tools, such as a protractor or angle ruler, and other methods, such as paper folding or drawing a diagonal in a square, to measure angles.

How can you measure an angle?

**Read More**
See Unit 6 on pages 408, 410–411, and 415 to learn more about measuring angles.

### Connect It

One way to measure an angle is to use a protractor. Another way is to use what you know about right angles.

The vertices of a square are right angles (90°). If you draw a diagonal in a square, you divide both right angles in half with your line. Measure them with a protractor to see that the smaller angles all measure 45°.

A good way to develop a sense of angle size is to make a model using a piece of paper. Take a piece of notebook paper and fold it in half once. The angle measure at the fold is 180°, or a straight angle. If you fold the paper again along the first fold, your new fold is 90°. Fold once more at the vertex and you have a 45° angle. Measure it with a protractor. Fold it again to make a $22\frac{1}{2}°$ angle.

How many $22\frac{1}{2}°$ angles does it take to make a complete circle?

### Use Your Skills

Use a folded piece of paper or a protractor to measure each angle.

**1.**

**2.** 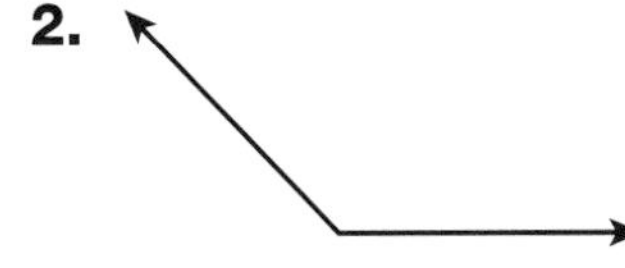

**3.** 

**4.** **Apply** Suppose you want to draw a 60° angle. Describe how you would draw a good estimate of the angle. Use your method to draw the angle and then measure it with a protractor. How close was your drawing to 60°?

## Measurement

**M4M2.b** Understand the meaning and measure of a half rotation (180°) and a full rotation (360°).

How can you tell how far a figure has been rotated?

### Read More

See Unit 6 on pages 422–424, 434–435, and 440–441 to learn more about rotations.

### Connect It

To know how far a figure has been rotated, you first need to identify the point around which it has been turned. It is helpful to think of the point at the center of a circle.

A full rotation means that a figure rotates 360° around a point until it returns to its starting point. You do this every time you spin around in a circle. That's why a full turn is called "a 360."

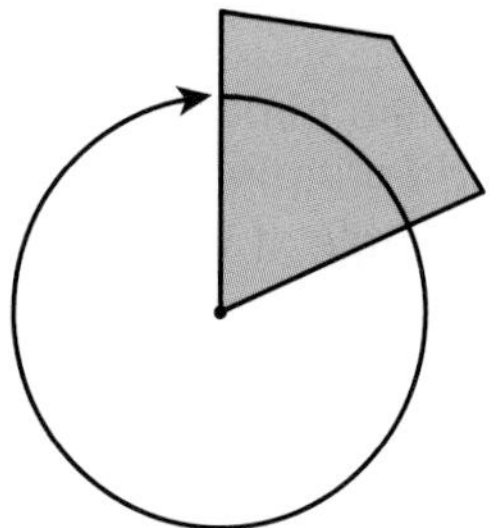

A half turn, or "a 180," happens when you turn halfway around and look in the opposite direction. To imagine a 90° turn, think of turning a quarter of a circle. You do this every time you turn directly left or right while walking.

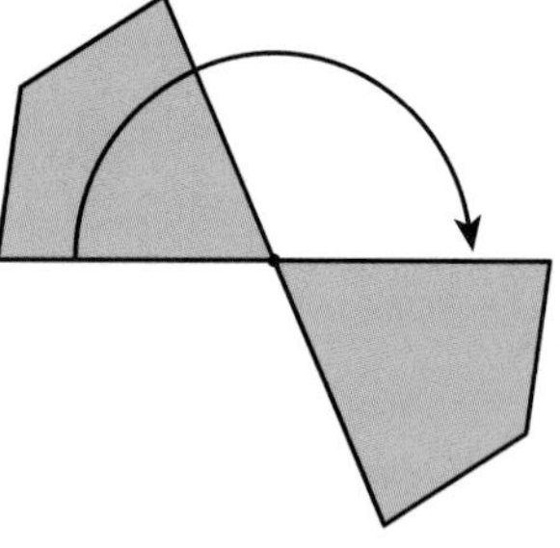

### Use Your Skills

Draw each rotation.

1. Draw a triangle. Draw a point at one of its vertices. Then draw what the same triangle will look like when it has been rotated a half turn.

2. Draw a rectangle with a point at one of its vertices. Then draw what the rectangle looks like when it has made a full rotation around that point.

3. **Extend** A clock shows 3:00. Two and a half hours pass. How many degrees has the minute hand turned? What number on the clock is the minute hand pointing to now?

## Geometry

**M4G1.a** Examine and compare angles in order to classify and identify triangles by their angles.

How can you classify a triangle by its angles?

**Read More**
See Unit 6 on pages 416–417 to learn more about classifying triangles.

### Connect It

No matter what triangle you examine, at least two of its angles must be acute, or less than 90°. You can classify the triangle by the size of its largest angle.

- If the largest angle is less than 90°, the triangle is an **acute triangle**.
- If the largest angle is exactly 90°, the triangle is a **right triangle**.
- If the largest angle is more than 90°, the triangle is an **obtuse triangle**.

### Use Your Skills

Classify each triangle.

**1.** 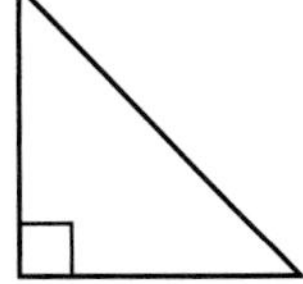

**2.** 

**3.** 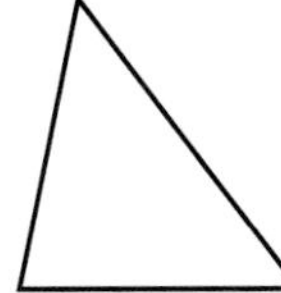

**4. Classify** A triangle has three equal sides. Is the triangle acute, right, or obtuse? Draw a picture to help you.

## Geometry

**M4G1.b** Describe parallel and perpendicular lines in plane geometric figures.

How do you identify parallel and perpendicular lines in plane figures?

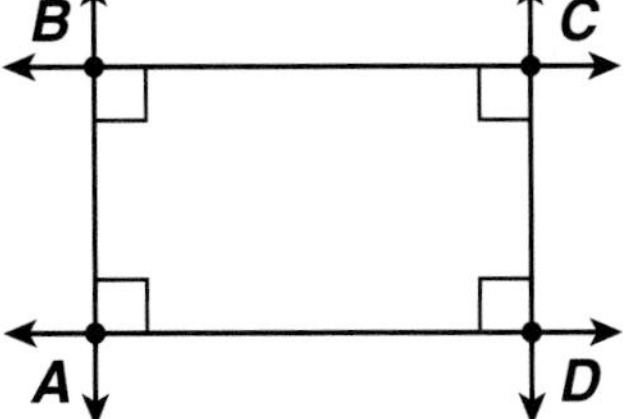


**Read More**
See Unit 6 on pages 404–406 to learn more about parallel and perpendicular lines.

### Connect It

Look at the figure at the right. Lines *AB* and *CD* are parallel to each other. So are lines *BC* and *AD*.

Line *AB* intersects line *AD* at a right angle. So line segment *AB* is perpendicular to line segment *AD* and angle *A* is a right angle.

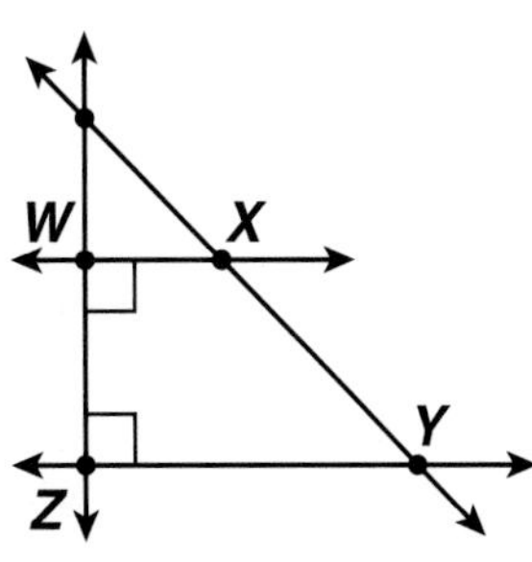


### Use Your Skills

Use the figure at the right to answer questions 1–3.

1. Name a  pair of line segments that are perpendicular.
2. Name a pair of lines that are parallel.
3. Name two lines that intersect but do not form a right angle.
4. **Connect** Why is the figure at the right known as a parallelogram?

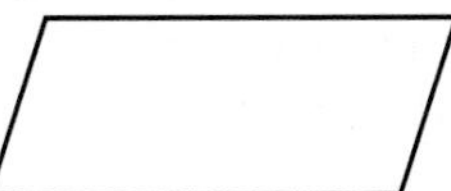

## Geometry

**M4G1.c** Examine and classify quadrilaterals (including parallelograms, squares, rectangles, trapezoids, and rhombi).

How are quadrilaterals similar and different?

**Read More**
See Unit 6 on page 413 to learn more about quadrilaterals.

### Connect It

The chart below shows some relationships among quadrilaterals.

| Features and Uses of Graphs | | | | |
|---|---|---|---|---|
| **Rectangle** | **Square** | **Trapezoid** | **Parallelogram** | **Rhombus** |
| Opposite sides equal in length and parallel; 4 right angles | Opposite sides parallel; 4 sides equal in length; 4 right angles | Only one pair of parallel sides | Opposite sides equal in length and parallel | Opposite sides parallel; 4 sides equal in length |

### Use Your Skills

Use the chart to help you answer each question.

1. How is a parallelogram like a rectangle?
2. How is a square like a rhombus?
3. How is a rectangle different from a square?

Name the figure described.

4. A four-sided polygon with opposite sides parallel.
5. A four-sided polygon with opposite sides parallel and all sides the same length.
6. A four-sided polygon with opposite sides parallel and four right angles.
7. A four-sided polygon with all sides the same length and four right angles.
8. **Analyze** Can a trapezoid have a right angle? Why or why not?

## Geometry

**M4G1.d** Compare and contrast the relationships among quadrilaterals.

How are quadrilaterals related to each other?

**Read More**
See Unit 6 on page 413 to learn more about relationships among quadrilaterals.

### Connect It

Some types of quadrilaterals share certain characteristics.

- Squares and rectangles have 4 right angles and parallel opposite sides of equal length. Squares have 4 sides of equal length. So squares are a special type of rectangle.
- Squares and rhombuses have 4 sides of equal length. Squares have 4 right angles. So squares are a special type of rhombus.
- Rectangles, squares, and rhombi are parallelograms because they have opposite sides that are parallel and equal in length.

### Use Your Skills

Name each quadrilateral. Write all names that apply.

**1.**

**2.** 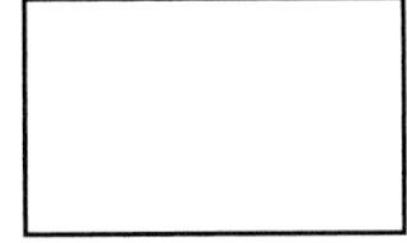

**3.** 

**4.** 

**5.** 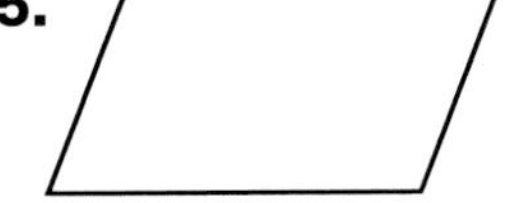

**6.** 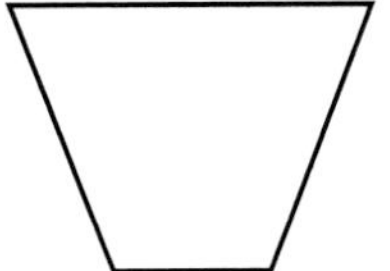

**7.** **Classify** It is correct to say that all squares are rectangles? Why is it not correct to say that all rectangles are squares?

## Geometry

**M4G2.a** Compare and contrast a cube and a rectangular prism in terms of the number and shape of their faces, edges, and vertices.

How are cubes and rectangular prisms alike and different?

**Read More**
See Unit 6 on pages 464–467 to learn more about solid figures.

### Connect It

What characteristics do a cube and rectangular prism share?

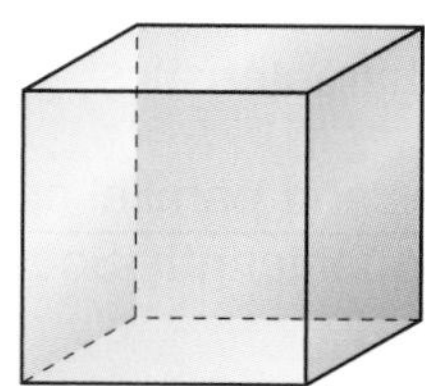

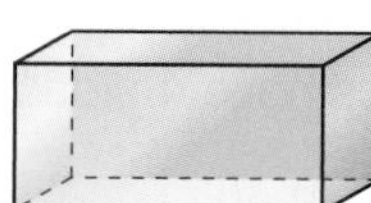

### Use Your Skills

Answer each question.

1. How many faces does a rectangular prism have? A cube?
2. How many vertices does a cube have? A rectangular prism?
3. How many edges does a rectangular prism have? A cube?
4. What shapes are the faces of a cube? Of a rectangular prism?
5. **Connect** Remember that a square is a special type of rectangle. How can you use that relationship to describe a cube in terms of a rectangular prism?

## Geometry

**M4G2.b** Describe parallel and perpendicular lines and planes in connection with rectangular prisms.

How do parallel and perpendicular lines relate to rectangular prisms?

**Read More**
See Unit 6 on pages 464–467 to learn more about rectangular prisms.

### Connect It

Look at the net for a rectangular prism. It is made up of line segments.

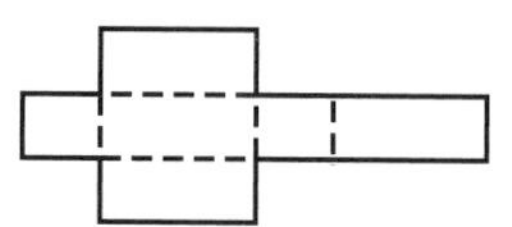

Suppose you redrew the net using the lines that contain the line segments.

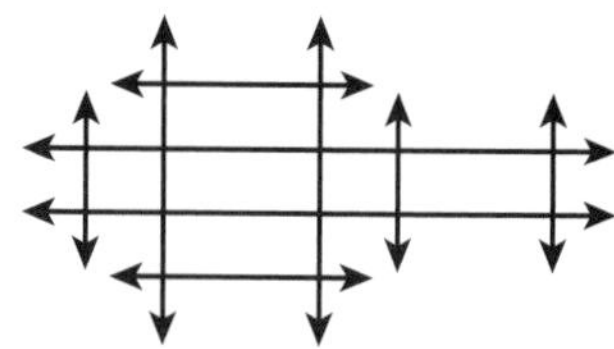

Since the faces of a rectangular prism are all rectangles, you know that the lines are either parallel or perpendicular to each other. So, you can conclude that all the edges of a rectangular prism are either parallel or perpendicular to each other.

### Use Your Skills

Answer these questions about the cube.

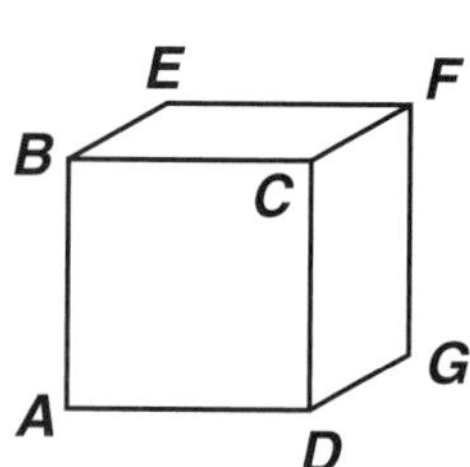


1. Using letters, list two pairs of edges that are parallel to each other.
2. Using letters, list two pairs of edges that are perpendicular to each other.
3. **Extend** How many pairs of parallel edges does a cube have? Hint: Determine how many pairs of parallel edges one face has. Then multiply.

Quaoar is the biggest object scientists have found in the Kuiper Belt so far. It is more than half the size of Pluto.

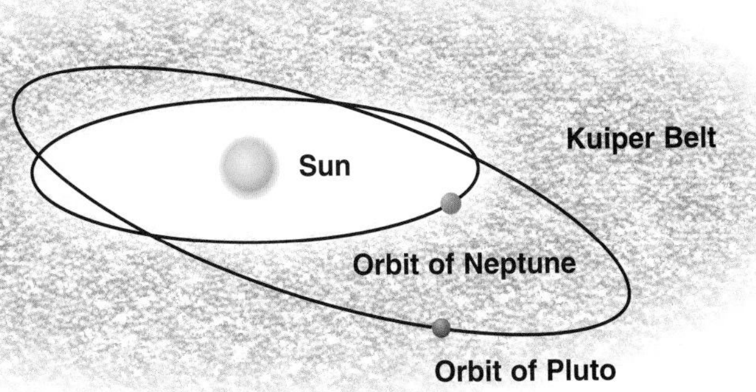


1. About how long should it take *New Horizons* to reach Pluto?
2. Is 248 an exact number as it is used in this article? Explain.

# Kid Camp

*from American Girl*

Last summer, Sarah Hennigsen of California knew she wanted to spend time with little kids. But at age ten, she felt she was too young to baby-sit by herself. So Sarah, her sister Molly, and their friend Aimee opened Sunshine Summer Camp. Each day for a week, 11 neighborhood kids came for an afternoon of crafts, snacks, and games.

"Mom was close by in case anything went wrong," Sarah says. "But everything went great!" By the end of the week, the girls had made more than $100 — plus tips!

Thinking about hosting a day camp? "Don't try games where very young kids have to take turns and only one person wins," warns Sarah. "Group games work better!"

1. Suppose Sarah and her camp partners charged $50 per camper for four weeks of camp. They wanted to earn $500 for that period of time. About how many campers would they need?

2. If the girls earned $20 in tips, about how much would each girl get if they split the tips evenly?

# GONE PRAWNING

*from Weekly Reader*

Many farms in the Midwest have cornfields that cover the landscape for miles. However, for the past few years, lack of rain has caused great concern. As corn crops dry up, so do the farmers' wallets.

In an attempt to save their farms, farmers who have ponds on their farms are trying alternate ways to bring in money. These farmers have begun stocking their ponds with prawns, which are shrimp-like animals. They can raise about 400 prawns in a pond that covers about a $\frac{1}{2}$ acre. The prawns sell for about \$8 a pound. Farmers can earn about ten times more money raising a $\frac{1}{2}$ acre of prawns than they can growing a $\frac{1}{2}$ acre of corn.

Many farmers across the drought-stricken Corn Belt plan to raise prawns to keep their farms afloat. Experts say that the United States imports about \$2 billion worth of shrimp per year, which is a good enough reason for the farmers to be hopeful.

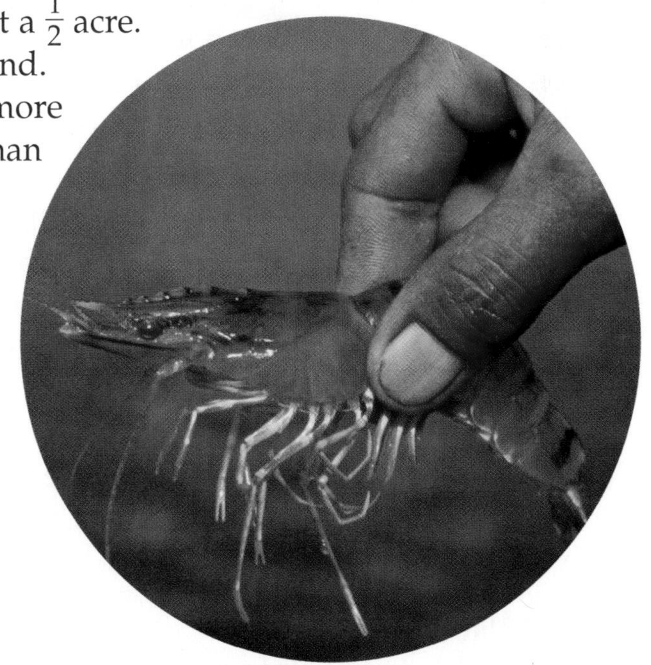

A farmer holding a prawn

1. Suppose there are 15 prawns in a pound and a customer wants to buy 6 pounds. How many prawns would that be? How much would they cost?

2. Write a short letter from a farmer who has switched from corn to prawns. Have him or her explain the reasons for switching.

# But I'm Not Tired

"Just five more minutes!" "I'm tired!" "I can't get up." If you have ever had trouble getting up in the morning, you are not alone. A new report says many U.S. kids do not get enough sleep.

Your body needs sleep and lots of it! "Evidence shows that elementary-age children need at least nine hours of sleep per night," says sleep expert Dr. Carl Hunt.

### Sleep Matters

Kids who do not sleep enough cannot do their best, experts say. A tired kid may

- be moody,
- forget things,
- act badly,
- have trouble learning,
- have trouble playing a sport.

Not sleeping enough can also affect kids' safety. Experts say children who are tired are more likely to suffer injuries.

Lots of kids lose sleep because they are busy. Many take part in after-school activities. Then they go home, eat dinner, and do homework. Afterward, many kids watch TV, play video games, and surf the Internet. That leaves less time for sleep.

Sometimes you may not be able to go to bed early. But, if you get a choice whether to stay up late, think twice. A good night's sleep can help you feel your best!

### Get a Good Night's Sleep!

Here are some tips for getting a good night's sleep.

- Relax with quiet time before bed.
- Go to bed at the same time each night.
- Don't eat a big meal right before going to sleep.

1. If Lauren gets 50 hours of sleep in a week, about how much sleep does she get each night?
2. To get the amount of sleep you need, how many hours must you sleep in a week?
3. Do you get enough sleep?

READING MATH

# Lengths of Time

BY PHYLLIS McGINLEY *from Wonderful Time*

Time is peculiar
And hardly exact.
Though minutes are minutes,
You'll find for a fact
(As the older you get
And the bigger you grow)
That time can
Hurrylikethis
Or plod, plod, slow.

Waiting for your dinner when you're hungry?
Down with the sniffles in your bed?
Notice how an hour crawls along and crawls along
Like a snail with his house on his head.

But when you are starting
A game in the park.
It's morning,
It's noon,
And suddenly it's dark.
And hours like seconds
Rush blurringly by.
Whoosh!
Like a plane in the sky.

1. What periods of time are mentioned in the poem?
2. Suppose the poet had placed numbers in the last stanza instead of using the words *morning, noon,* and *dark.* Would you have the same impression of time rushing by? Explain.

# DIVIDING THE CHEESE

Retold by Jackson Smith

Two foolish cats stole a piece of cheese. Neither cat trusted the other, so they agreed to ask the monkey to divide the cheese for them.

The monkey was glad to help. He fetched a scale. Then he started to divide the cheese. But instead of cutting the cheese in equal pieces, he made one portion larger than the other. He put both pieces on the scale. "Oh dear," said the monkey. "I'll just make it even."

The monkey began to eat the cheese from the heavier side. As he ate, the heavier piece became lighter than the other piece. Then the monkey ate from the other side. The cats became alarmed as they watched their snack disappear. "We've changed our minds," they said to the monkey. "We will divide the rest of the cheese ourselves."

"No, I must finish the job I started," said the monkey. And he continued to eat, first on one side, and then on the other, until the cheese was gone.

1. If the piece of cheese is square, how many ways could this be divided evenly between the two cats? How could it be divided evenly if the cats and the monkey were to share the piece? Draw a picture to show your solution.
2. What lesson does this folktale teach?

# HOLD THE MEAT!

*from American Girl*

"I became a vegetarian about six years ago. It isn't too hard for me. My mom doesn't eat much meat, so she and I fix veggies or tofu. And my dad and brother cook their own meat. If I'm going to someone's house, I tell him or her ahead of time that I don't eat meat so it won't be awkward. At restaurants, I can usually order a veggie plate.

"A few of my friends think it's strange that I'm a vegetarian, but most of them are supportive. I really don't remember how most meat tastes, except for seafood — I'm still looking for a good substitute for that! I'm happy with my choice, though, and I don't think I'll ever go back to eating meat." — Celeste, age 13, Ohio.

*continued on the next page*

# Great Shake

Whether or not you eat meat, you'll love this chocolatey treat. It's made with soy milk — and it packs as much protein as a hot dog!

**You will need:**

- An adult to help you
- A blender
- 2 peeled, frozen bananas, cut into chunks (peel and cut the bananas before freezing)
- $\frac{1}{2}$ cup chocolate soy milk
- 2 tablespoons chocolate syrup
- 2 tablespoons peanut butter

Ask an adult to blend ingredients until smooth.

Enjoy your soy!

1. Suppose you want to make this shake twice. How many cups of chocolate soy milk would you use? How many bananas?
2. If you decided to put in $1\frac{1}{2}$ tablespoons less peanut butter, how many tablespoons would you use?
3. How much chocolate syrup would be in the shake if you added $1\frac{1}{2}$ more tablespoons of chocolate syrup instead of the peanut butter?

# The Perfect Present

**BY E. RENEE HEISS**

*from Highlights*

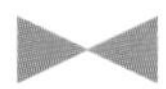

"A cow? You got me a cow for my birthday?" Grandma threw her arms up in the air when she saw what I had brought from the farm.

"But you said you wanted something to keep you company, Grandma. And I know you love milk."

"I don't have enough room for a cow," Grandma said.

I looked around the yard and had to agree with Grandma. So I took the cow away, and a few days later, I returned with a different birthday present.

"A pig? Now you're bringing me a pig?" Grandma threw her arms up in the air again. "I don't know how to care for a pig!"

"But the pig is smaller than the cow," I argued.

"I can't keep your pig, but I appreciate the thought," Grandma said.

A few days after that, I brought another gift from the farm for Grandma. But once again she threw her arms up in the air.

"A duck? I would need a pond in my backyard for a duck," Grandma explained.

"I'm sorry, Grandma," I said. "Next time I'm sure I'll have the perfect present for you."

The next time I rang the doorbell, Grandma didn't throw her arms in the air. She squealed with delight when she saw the present I had brought. It had a big red ribbon wrapped around it.

"This present will keep me company," she said. "It's not too big for my yard. It's not too difficult to care for. And it doesn't even need a pond in the backyard. It's perfect!"

Grandma smiled and put her arms around her perfect present — me!

1. What was the "perfect present"? Why is it perfect?

2. If the narrator brought his Grandma a horse, would she have been more likely, less likely, or equally likely to like the present as the "perfect present"? Explain your reasoning.

**Being a good math student includes reading carefully and doing your best on tests. On the next few pages, you'll find reading strategies, study hints, and test-taking tips to help you learn.**

# Use Reading Strategies to Think About Math

**What you learn during reading class can help you understand how to solve word problems.**

### Understand What the Question Is

Read the problem once to be sure it makes sense to you. Ask yourself the question in your own words. Picture the situation and make a drawing if it helps.

### Think About the Words

As you read, pay attention to the mathematical terms. If you don't understand a word, try to decide what it means by looking at the words around it.

### Be Sure You Have Enough Information

Identify the information you need. Look at tables or graphs as well as the words. Think about what you already know that may help.

### Plan What You Will Do

Think about the problem-solving plan and strategies. Decide what computation method is needed. Then make a plan and follow it.

### Evaluate Your Work

Look back at what the question asked, and check that your answer really answers that question. Be sure you have labeled your answer.

# Strategies for Taking Tests

**You need to think differently about how to answer various kinds of questions.**

### All Questions

If you can't answer a question, go on to the next question. You can return to it if there is time.

Always check your computation.

### Multiple-Choice Questions

Estimate the answer. This can help eliminate any unreasonable choices.

On bubble sheets, be sure you mark the bubble for the right question and for the right letter.

### Short-Answer Questions

Follow the directions carefully. You may need to show your work, write an explanation, or make a drawing.

If you can't give a complete answer, show what you do know. You may get credit for part of an answer.

### Long-Answer Questions

Take time to think about these questions because you often need to explain your answer.

When you finish, reread the question and answer to be sure you have answered the question correctly.

### Student Scoring Rubric

Your teacher may use a scoring rubric to evaluate your work. An example is on the next page. Not all rubrics are the same, so your teacher may use a different one.

## Scoring Rubric

| Rating | My work on this problem |
|---|---|
| **Exemplary** **(full credit)** | • has no errors, has the correct answer, and shows that I checked my answer. • is explained carefully and completely. • shows all needed diagrams, tables, or graphs. |
| **Proficient** **(some credit)** | • has small errors, has a close answer, and shows that I checked only the math. • is explained but may have missing parts. • shows most needed diagrams, tables, or graphs. |
| **Acceptable** **(little credit)** | • has some errors, has an answer, and shows that I did not check my answer. • is not explained carefully and completely. • shows few needed diagrams, tables, or graphs. |
| **Limited** **(very little credit)** | • has many errors and may not have an answer. • is not explained at all. • shows no needed diagrams, tables, or graphs. |

## Two Important Things You Can Do Before a Test

- Get plenty of sleep the night before.
- Eat a good breakfast in the morning.

# Your Plan for Problem Solving!

**Follow this four-part plan, and you'll become a problem-solving superstar!**

## Remember!

Always START at the "Understand" step and move on. But if you can't get an answer, don't give up. Just go back and start again.

UNDERSTAND

**Always be sure you know what the question means. Here are some hints to help you:**

- Read the problem and imagine the situation. Draw a picture if it helps.
- Replace any hard names you can't read with easier ones.
- Identify what the question is asking and say it in your own words.
- Look for words that help you decide whether to add, subtract, multiply, or divide.

**Start by making a plan.**
**Ask yourself:**

- What strategy should I use?
- Do I have too much or too little information?
- Should I do more than one step?
- Which operation should I use?
- Should I use estimation, paper and pencil, mental math, or a calculator?

**Strategy**
- Act It Out
- Draw a Picture
- Find a Pattern
- Guess and Check
- Make an Organized List
- Make a Table
- Solve a Simpler Problem
- Use Logical Reasoning
- Work Backward
- Write an Equation

**Finally! Now you're ready to solve the problem.**

- Carry out your plan.
- Adjust your plan if needed.
- Check your calculations.

**Congratulations! You've solved the problem.**
**But is it correct? Once you have an answer, ask:**

- Is my answer reasonable?
- Is my answer labeled correctly?
- Did I answer the question that was asked?
- Do I need to explain how I found the answer?

# Study Skills

**Knowing how to study math will help you do well in math class.**

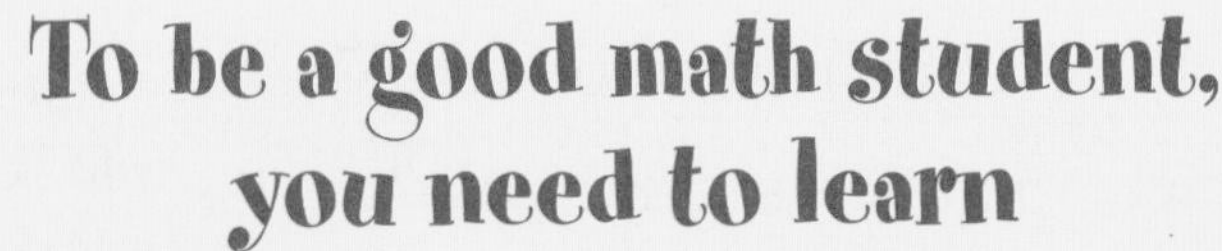

**To be a good math student, you need to learn**

- ★ **how to listen when your teacher is teaching.**
- ★ **how to work alone and with others.**
- ★ **how to plan your time.**

## Listening Skills

Listen carefully when your teacher is showing the class how to do something new. Try to understand what is being taught, as well as how to do each step.

If you don't understand what your teacher is showing the class, ask a question. Try to let your teacher know what you don't understand.

Listening carefully will also help you be ready to answer any questions your teacher may ask. You may be able to help another student by explaining how you understand what your teacher is saying.

**data** A set of information.

**decimal** A number with one or more digits to the right of a decimal point.

**decimal equivalent** A decimal that is equal to a whole number, a fraction, or another decimal.

**decimal point (.)** A symbol used to separate dollars and cents in money amounts or to separate ones and tenths in decimals.

*Example:* \$1.55
↑
decimal point

**degree (°)** A unit for measuring angles or temperature.

**degrees Celsius (°C)** The metric temperature scale.

**degrees Fahrenheit (°F)** The customary temperature scale.

**denominator** The number below the bar in a fraction.

*Example:* $\frac{1}{3}$ ← denominator

**diameter of a circle** A line segment that connects two points on a circle and passes through the center.

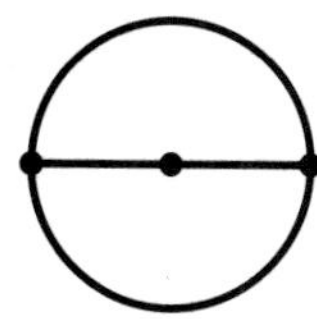

**difference** The answer in a subtraction problem.

*Example:* 12 − 5 = 7
↑
difference

**digit** Any one of the ten number symbols 0, 1, 2, 3, 4, 5, 6, 7, 8, and 9

**Distributive Property of Multiplication** The property which states that when two addends are multiplied by a factor, the product is the same as when each addend is multiplied by the factor and those products are added.

*Example:* $(2 + 3) \times 4 = (2 \times 4) + (3 \times 4)$

**dividend** The number that is divided in a division problem.

*Example:* 35 ÷ 7 = 5
↑
dividend

**divisible** Describes a number that can be divided into equal parts and has no remainder.

**divisor** The number by which the dividend is divided in a division problem.

*Example:* 35 ÷ 7 = 5
↑
divisor

**double bar graph** A graph in which data is compared by means of pairs of rectangular bars drawn next to each other.

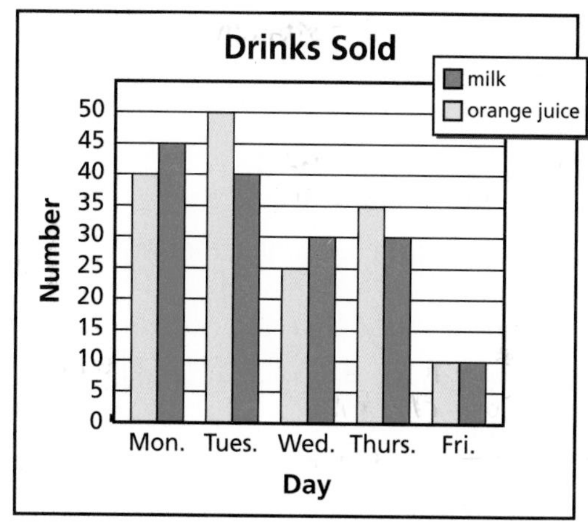


**doubles** A strategy for finding products.

*Example:* Since $2 \times 3 = 6$
Then $4 \times 3 = 6 + 6$
So $4 \times 3 = 12$

**edge** The line segment where two faces of a solid figure meet.

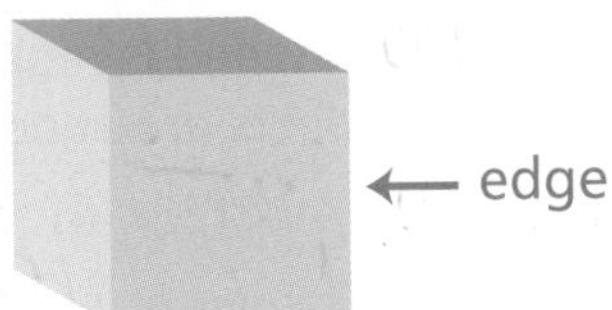


**elapsed time** The time that passes between the beginning and the end of an activity.

**endpoint** The point at either end of a line segment or the beginning point of a ray.

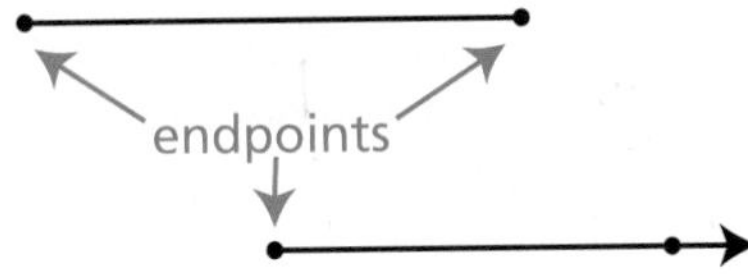


**equal** Having the same value.

**equation** A mathematical sentence with an equal sign.

*Examples:* $3 + 1 = 4$ and $2x + 5 = 9$

**equilateral triangle** A triangle that has three congruent sides.

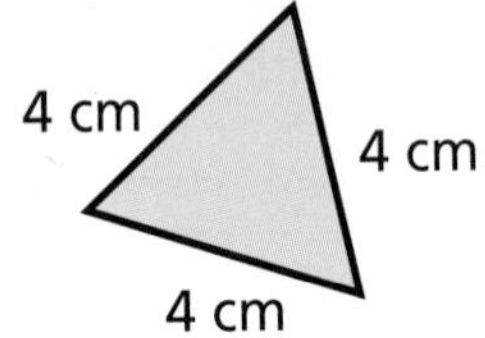


**equivalent decimals** Decimals that name the same amount.

**equivalent fractions** Fractions that name the same amount.

*Example:* $\frac{1}{2}$ and $\frac{3}{6}$

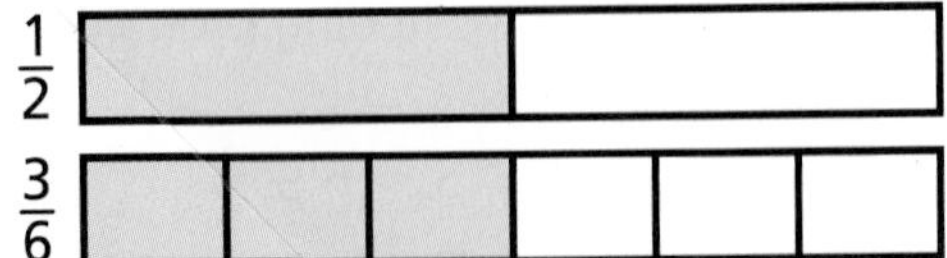


**estimate** A number close to an exact amount; to find about how many.

**evaluate** To find the value of an expression.

**even number** A whole number that is a multiple of 2. The ones digit in an even number is always 0, 2, 4, 6, or 8.

**expanded form** A number written to show the value of each digit.

*Example:* The expanded form of 2,345 is $2{,}000 + 300 + 40 + 5$.

**expression** A number or group of numbers with operation symbols. An expression may have a variable.

*Example:* $3 + n$

**face** A flat surface of a solid figure.

**fact family** Facts that are related, using the same numbers.

*Examples:* $1 + 4 = 5$; $4 + 1 = 5$
$5 - 4 = 1$; $5 - 1 = 4$

$3 \times 5 = 15$; $5 \times 3 = 15$
$15 \div 3 = 5$; $15 \div 5 = 3$

**factor** The numbers used in a multiplication problem.

*Example:* $7 \times 5 = 35$

↑ ↑
factors

**factor tree** A visual representation of the prime factors of a number.

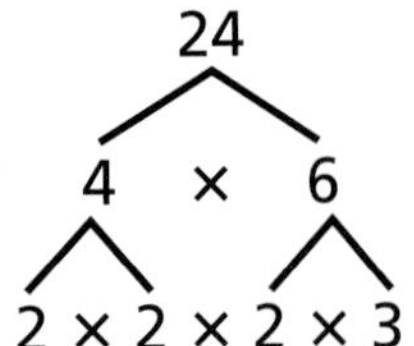

**formula** An expression that shows a mathematical rule.

**fraction** A number that names a part of a whole, a part of a collection, or a part of a region.

*Examples:* $\frac{1}{2}$, $\frac{3}{4}$, and $\frac{2}{3}$

**front-end estimation** A method of estimating sums, differences, products, and quotients using front digits.

**function table** A table of ordered pairs that follows a rule.

| Rule: $t = p \times 2$ | |
|---|---|
| Input ($p$) | Output ($t$) |
| 4 | 8 |
| 6 | 12 |
| 10 | 20 |

**Grouping Property of Addition** *See Associative Property of Addition*

**Grouping Property of Multiplication** *See Associative Property of Multiplication*

**hexagon** A polygon with six sides.

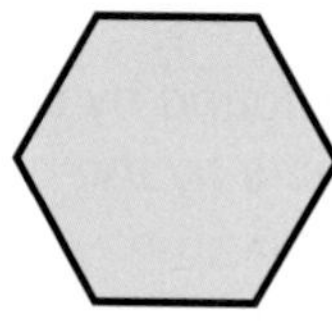

**horizontal axis** *See x-axis.*

**horizontal line** A line that lies straight across.

*Example:*

**hundredth** One of the equal parts when a whole is divided into 100 equal parts.

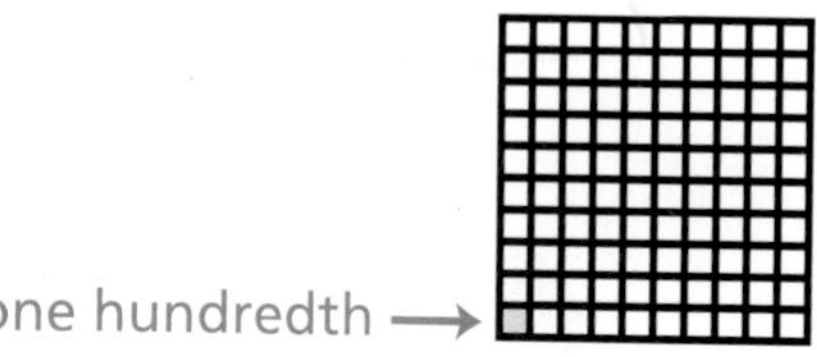

**improper fraction** A fraction that is greater than or equal to 1. The numerator in an improper fraction is greater than or equal to the denominator.

**inequality** Two expressions that are not equal. The symbols $>$, $<$, and $\neq$ show an inequality.

**integers** The set of positive whole numbers, their opposites (negative numbers), and 0.

**intersecting lines** Lines that meet or cross at a common point.

**interval** The difference between two numbers on a scale.

**inverse operations** Opposite operations.

*Examples:* Addition and subtraction are inverse operations. Multiplication and division are inverse operations.

**isosceles triangle** A triangle that has two congruent sides and two congruent angles.

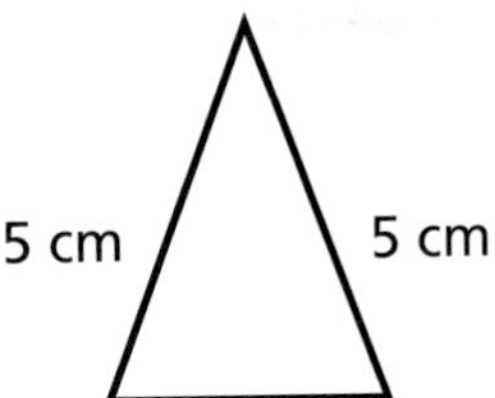

**key** A part of a map, graph, or chart that explains what symbols mean.

**like denominators** Denominators in two or more fractions that are the same.

**line** A straight path that extends in opposite directions with no endpoints.

**line graph** A graph that uses a line to show changes in data over time.

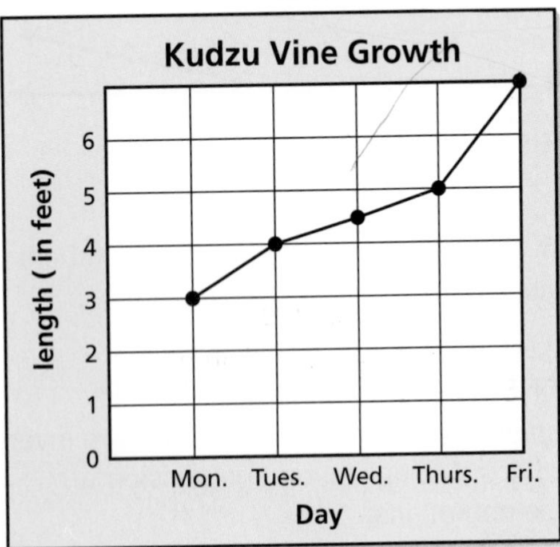


**line plot** A diagram that organizes data using a number line.

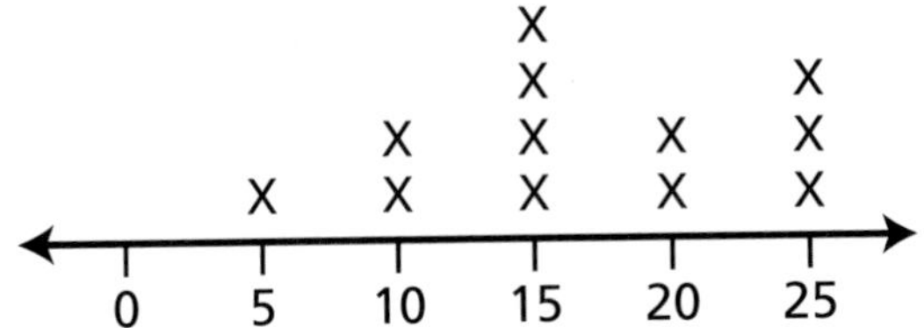


**line segment** A part of a line that has two endpoints.

**line symmetry** Describes whether a figure can be folded in half and its two parts match exactly.

**line of symmetry** The line along which a figure can be folded so that the two halves match exactly.

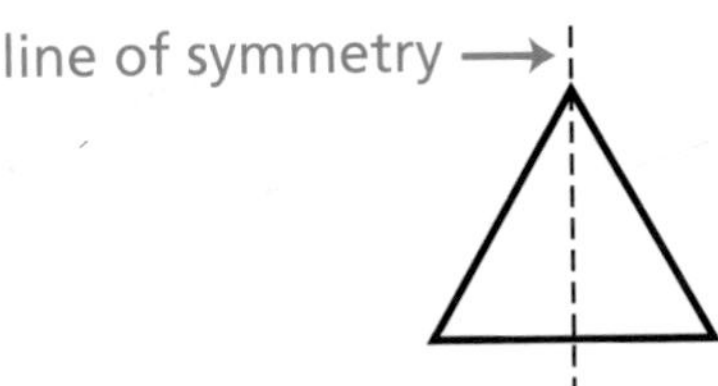

**mass** A measure of the amount of matter in an object.

**mean** The number found by dividing the sum of a group of numbers by the number of addends. Also called *average*.

*Example:*
$6 + 2 + 1 = 9$ $\quad$ $9 \div 3$ addends $= 3$
The average of 6, 2, and 1 is 3.

**median** The middle number when a set of numbers is arranged in order from least to greatest. For an even number of numbers, the median is the mean of the two middle numbers.

*Examples:* The median of 2, 5, 7, 9, and 10 is 7. The median of 2, 5, 7, and 12 is $(5 + 7) \div 2$, or 6.

**mixed number** A number containing a whole number part and a fraction part.

*Example:* $3\frac{1}{2}$

**mode** The number or numbers that occur most often in a set of data.

*Example:* The mode of 2, 3, 4, 4, and 6 is 4.

**multiple** A number that is the product of the given number and another number.

**negative numbers** Numbers that are less than 0.

*Examples:* $^-2$, $^-5$, and $^-26$

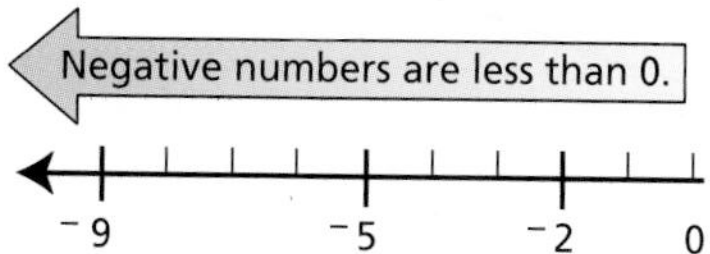


**net** A flat pattern that can be folded to make a solid.

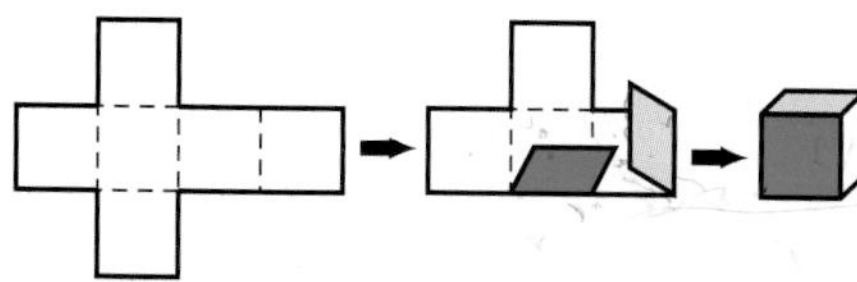

**number sentence** A mathematical sentence written in numerals and mathematical symbols. A number sentence always includes a greater than, less than, or equal sign.

*Examples:* $5 \times 5 = 19 + 6$
$2n \div 4 = 16$

**numerator** The number above the bar in a fraction.

*Example:* $\frac{1}{3}$ ← numerator

**obtuse angle** An angle that measures more than 90° and less than 180°.

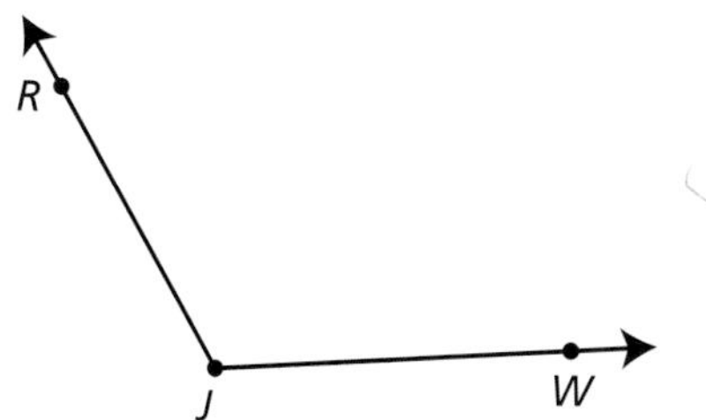


**obtuse triangle** A triangle that has one obtuse angle.

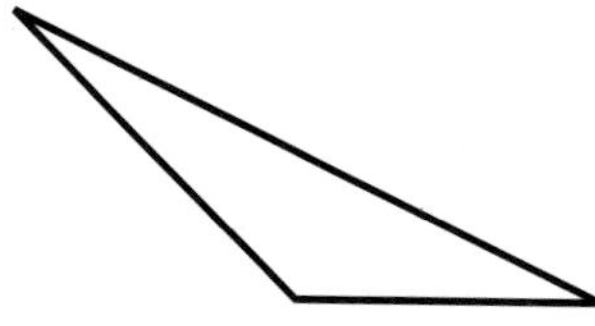

**octagon** A polygon with eight sides.

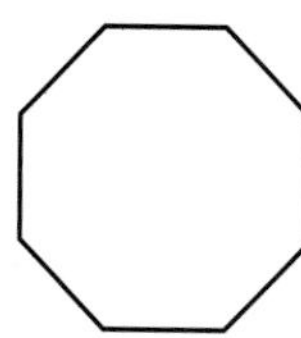

**odd number** A whole number that is not a multiple of 2. The ones digit in an odd number is 1, 3, 5, 7, or 9.

**order** To list numbers or items according to their value.

**order of operations** The order in which operations must be performed in order to arrive at a correct answer.

- First, do operations in parentheses.
- Then, do multiplication and division in order from left to right.
- Finally, do addition and subtraction in order from left to right.

**Order Property of Addition** *See Commutative Property of Addition.*

**Order Property of Multiplication** *See Commutative Property of Multiplication.*

**ordered pair** A pair of numbers used to locate a point on a grid such as (4, 5).

**ordinal number** A number used to show position.

**origin** A point assigned to zero on the number line or the point where the *x*- and *y*-axes intersect in a coordinate system.

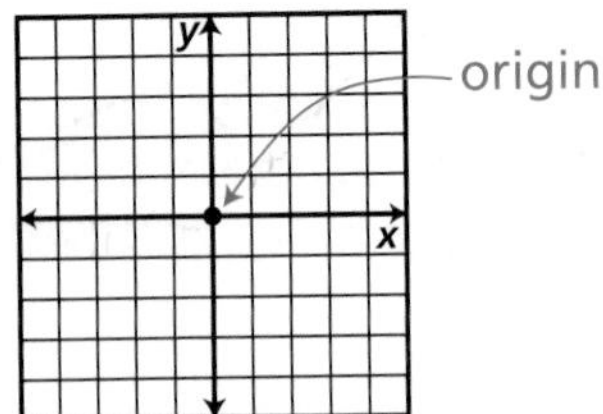


**outlier** A number or numbers that are at one or the other end of a set of data, arranged in order, where there is a gap between the end numbers and the rest of the data.

**P.M.** The time between 12:00 noon and 12:00 midnight.

**parallel lines** Lines that lie in the same plane and do not intersect. They are always the same distance apart.

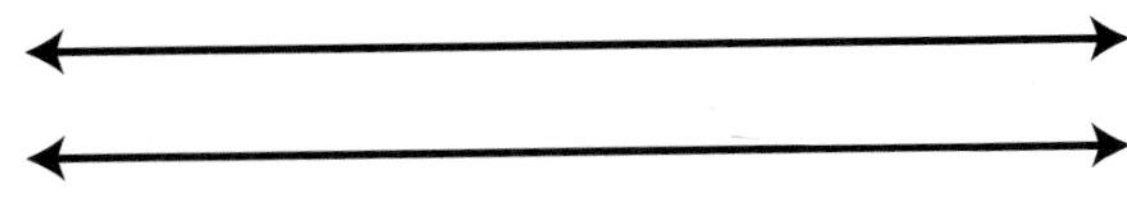

**parallelogram** A quadrilateral in which both pairs of opposite sides are parallel.

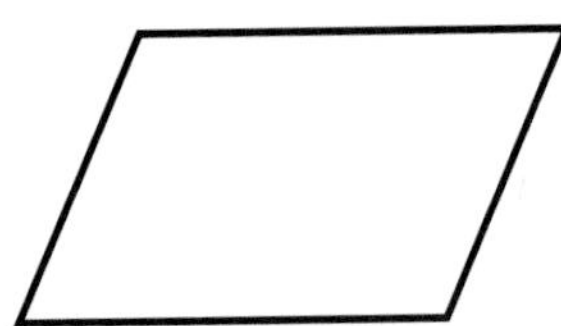

**parentheses** Used to show which operations should be done first.

**pentagon** A five-sided polygon.

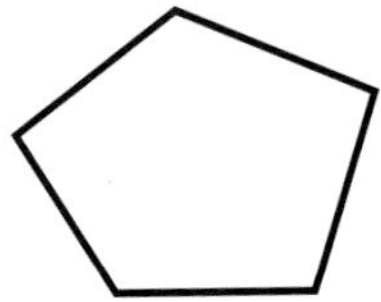

**percent (%)** Per hundred. The ratio of a number to 100.

*Example:* 9% means 9 out of 100 or $\frac{9}{100}$

**perimeter** The distance around the outside of a figure.

**period** Each group of 3 digits separated by a comma in a number.

**perpendicular lines** Two lines or line segments that cross or meet to form right angles.

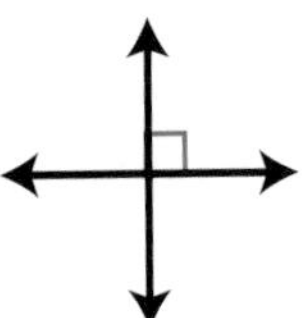

**pictograph** A graph in which information is shown by means of pictures or symbols.

| Book Sale | |
|---|---|
| Year 1 | |
| Year 2 | |
| Year 3 | |
| Year 4 | |

Each stands for 5 books sold.

**place value** The value of a digit in a number.

*Example:* The place value of 2 in 421,000 is 20,000.

**plane** A flat surface that extends in all directions without end.

**plane figure** A shape that is on a plane, such as an octagon or a triangle.

**plot** To place points in the coordinate plane.

**point** An exact location in space, represented by a dot.

**polygon** A simple closed plane figure made up of three or more line segments.

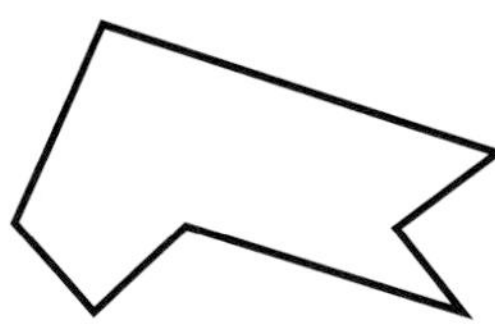

**positive numbers** Numbers that are greater than zero.

*Examples:* $^{+}2$, $^{+}5$, and $^{+}9$

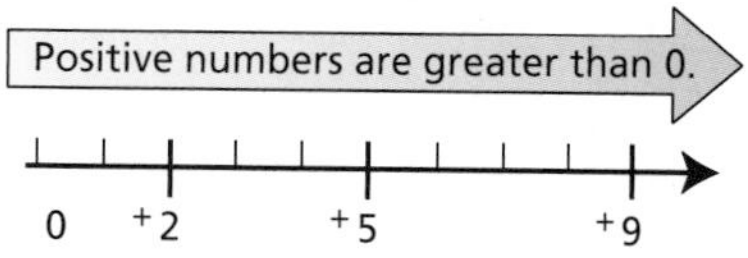


**prime factor** A factor that happens to also be a prime number.

**prime number** A whole number that has only itself and 1 as factors, such as 7 or 13.

**product** The answer in a multiplication problem.

*Example:* $7 \times 5 = 35$

↑ product

**proper fraction** *See fraction.*

**Property of One for Multiplication** The property which states that the product of 1 and any number is that number.

*Example:* $4 \times 1 = 4$

**protractor** A device used to measure and draw angles.

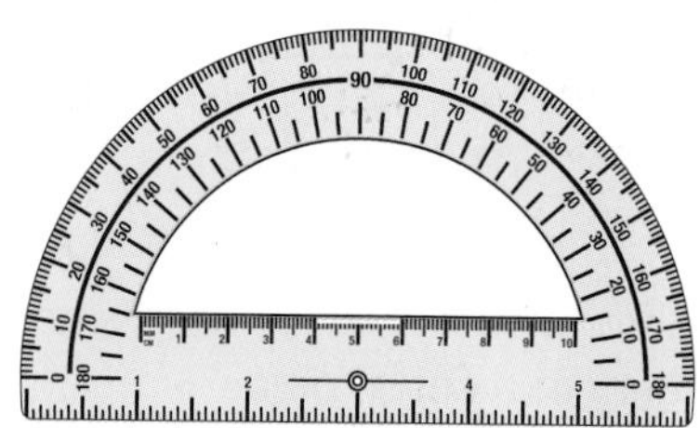

**pyramid** A solid figure whose base can be any polygon and whose faces are triangles.

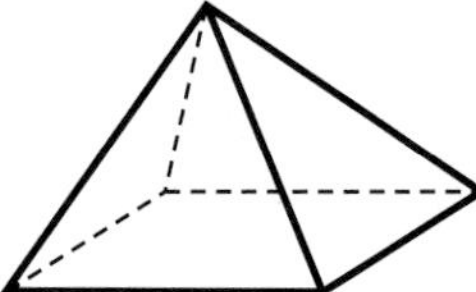

**quadrilateral** A polygon with four sides.

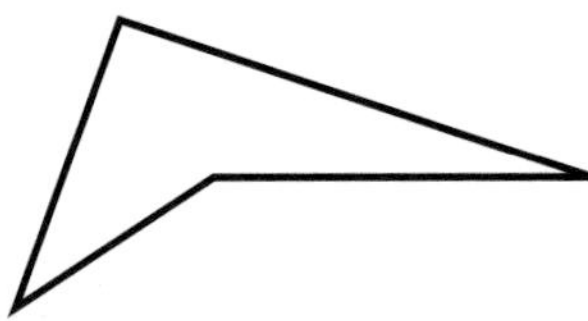

**quotient** The answer in a division problem.

*Example:* 35 ÷ 7= 5

↑

quotient

**radius (radii)** A segment that connects the center of a circle to any point on the circle.

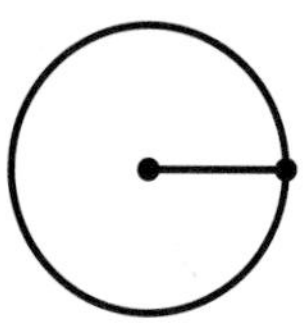

**range** The difference between the greatest and least numbers in a set of data.

*Example:* The range of 2, 3, 6, 8, and 9 is 7 Because 9 − 2 = 7

**ray** Part of a line that starts at an endpoint and goes on forever in one direction.

**rectangle** A parallelogram with four right angles.

**rectangular prism** A solid figure with six faces that are rectangles.

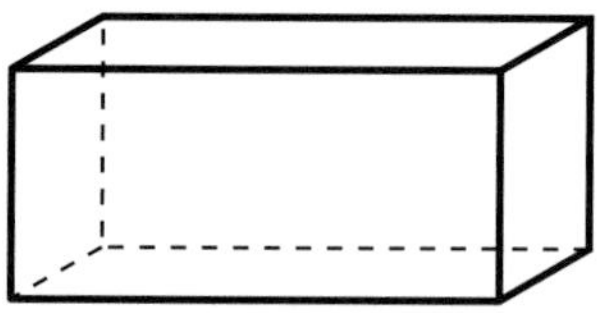

**rectangular pyramid** A solid figure whose base is a rectangle and whose faces are triangles.

**reflection** A move that makes a figure face in the opposite direction. It is also called a *flip*.

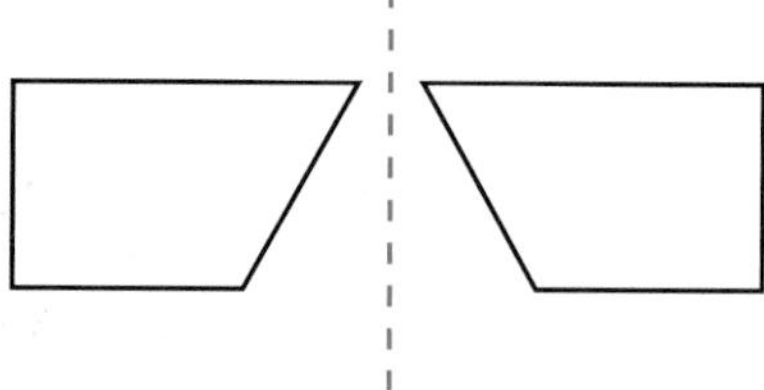

**regroup** To use place value to exchange equal amounts when renaming a number.

**regular polygons** Polygons whose sides are all the same length, and whose angles are the same measure.

**remainder** The number that is left after one whole number is divided by another.

**rhombus** A parallelogram with all four sides the same length.

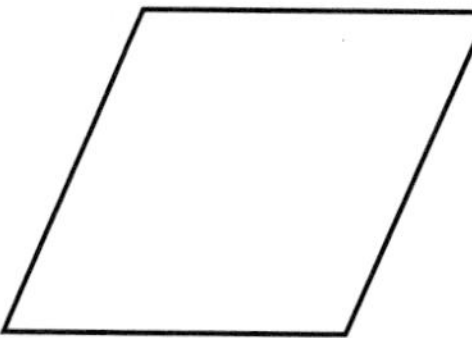

**right angle** An angle made when two line segments meet to form a square corner. It measures 90°.

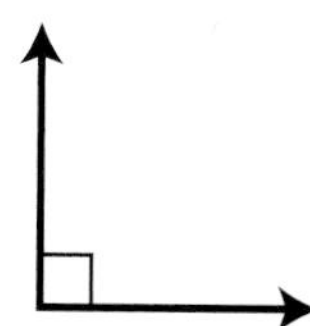

**right triangle** A triangle that has one right angle.

**rotation** A move that turns a figure around a point.

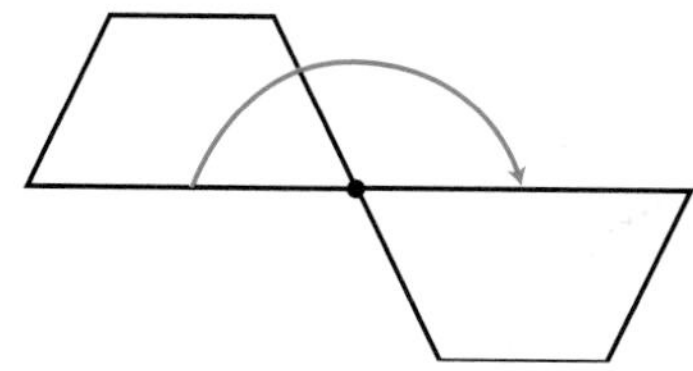

**rotational symmetry** A figure has rotational symmetry if, after the figure is rotated about a point, the figure is the same as when in its original position.

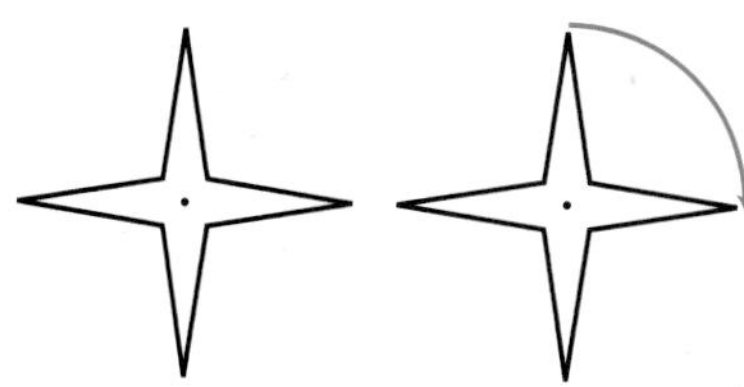

**round** To find about how many or how much by expressing a number to the nearest ten, hundred, thousand, and so on.

**scale** An arrangement of numbers in order with equal intervals.

**scalene triangle** A triangle with all sides of different length.

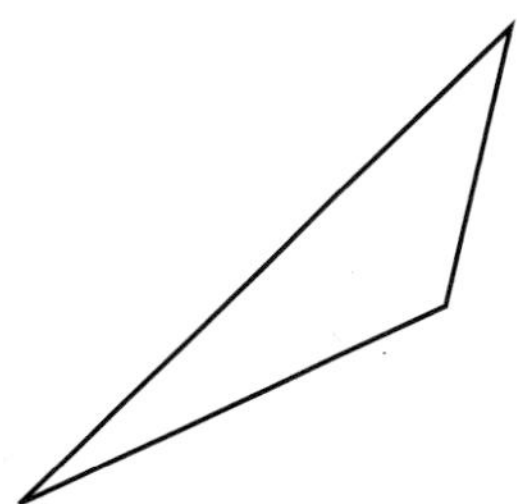

**short word form** A way to write a number by using digits and words to describe the periods of the number.

*Example:* The short word form of 2,345 is 2 thousand, 345.

**side (of a polygon)** One of the line segments that make up a polygon.

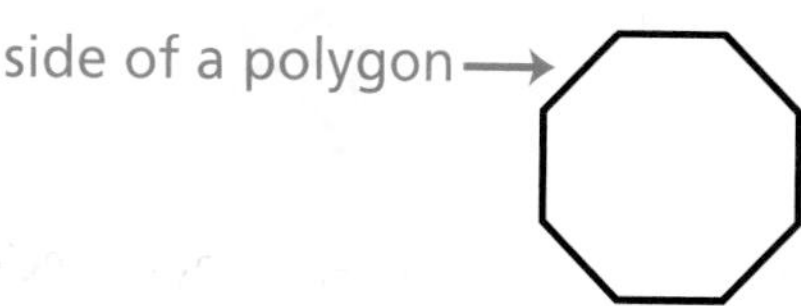


**side (of an angle)** One of the rays that make up an angle.

**similar figures** Figures that have the same shape but not necessarily the same size.

**simplest form of a fraction** A fraction whose numerator and denominator have the number 1 as the only common factor.

**sphere** A solid figure that is shaped like a round ball.

**square** A polygon with four right angles and four congruent sides.

**square number** The product of a number and itself.

**square pyramid** A pyramid that has a square base.

**standard form** The usual or common way of writing a number using digits.

*Example:* The standard form of two hundred twenty-seven is 227.

**stem-and-leaf plot** A table that organizes information by place value.

**sum** The answer in an addition problem.

*Example:* 5 + 8 = 13 ← sum

**survey** One method of collecting information.

**symmetric figure** A figure that has symmetry. *(See line symmetry, rotational symmetry.)*

**tenth** One of the equal parts when a whole is divided into 10 equal parts.

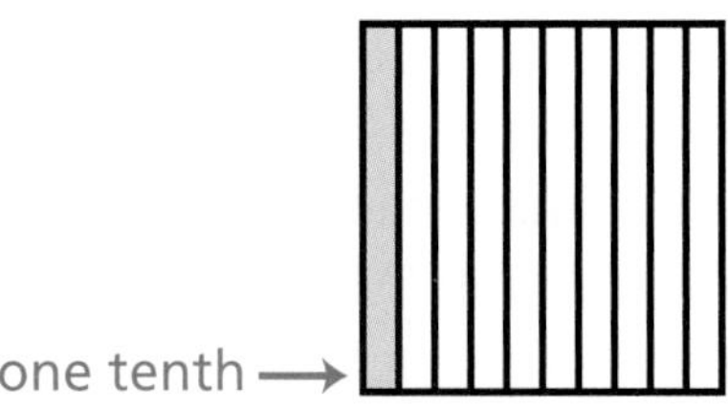


**thermometer** An instrument that measures temperature.

**thousandth** One of the equal parts when a whole is divided into 1,000 equal parts.

**transformation** The collective name that describes rotations, reflections, and translations.

**translation** An action that slides a figure in a straight line.

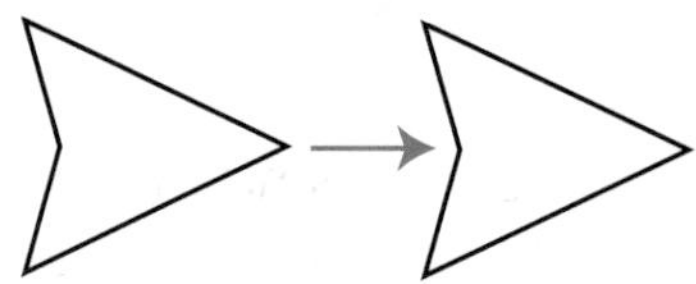

**trapezoid** A quadrilateral with two parallel sides.

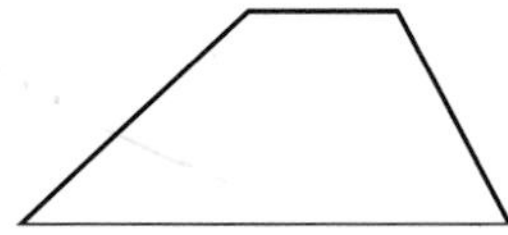

**triangle** A polygon with three sides and three vertices.

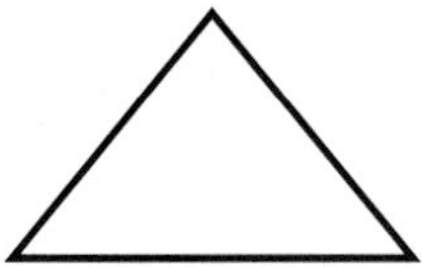

**triangular prism** A prism that has 2 triangular and 3 rectangular faces.

**triangular pyramid** A pyramid whose base is a triangle.

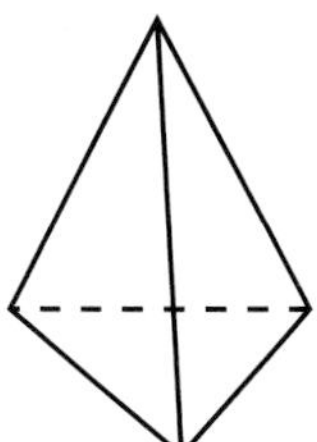

**unit fraction** A fraction whose numerator is 1.

*Examples:* $\frac{1}{3}, \frac{1}{5}, \frac{1}{8}$

**unlike denominators** Denominators that are not equal.

**variable** A letter or a symbol that represents a number in an algebraic expression.

**vertex of an angle (vertices)** A point common to the two sides of an angle.

**vertex of a polygon (vertices)** A point common to two sides of a polygon.

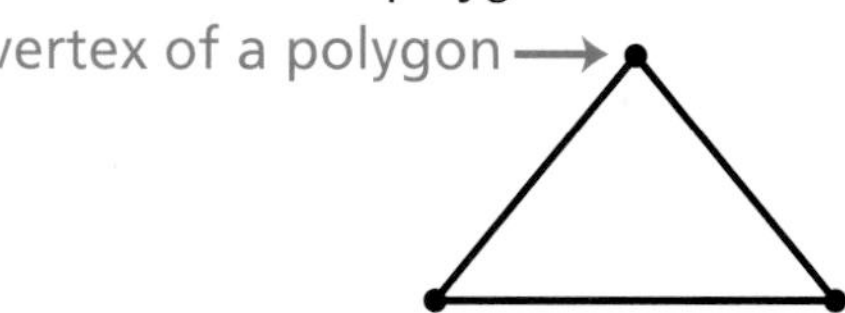


**vertex of a solid figure** A point where three or more edges meet.

**vertical line** A line that lies straight up and down.

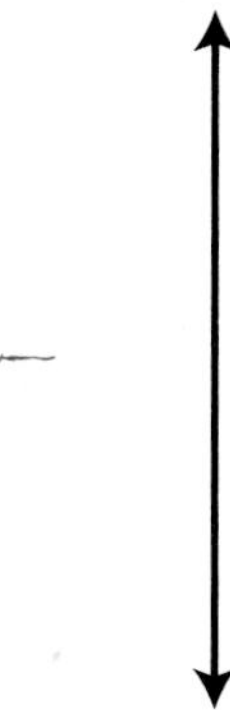

**volume** The number of cubic units that can fit inside a container or a solid figure.

**weight** The measure of how heavy something is.

**whole number** Any of the numbers 0, 1, 2, 3, 4, 5, and so on.

**word form** A way of using words to write a number.

*Example:* The number 12,345 in word form is twelve thousand, three hundred forty-five.

***x*-axis** The horizontal number line in a coordinate system. *Also called horizontal axis.*

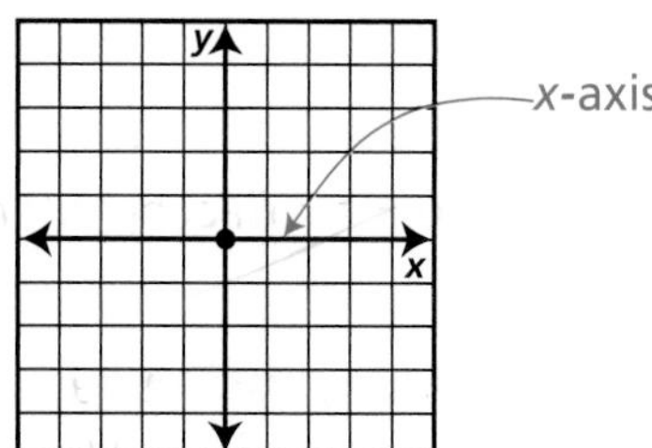

**x-coordinate** The first number of an ordered pair of numbers that names a point in a coordinate system.

**y-axis** The vertical number line in a coordinate system. Also called *vertical axis.*

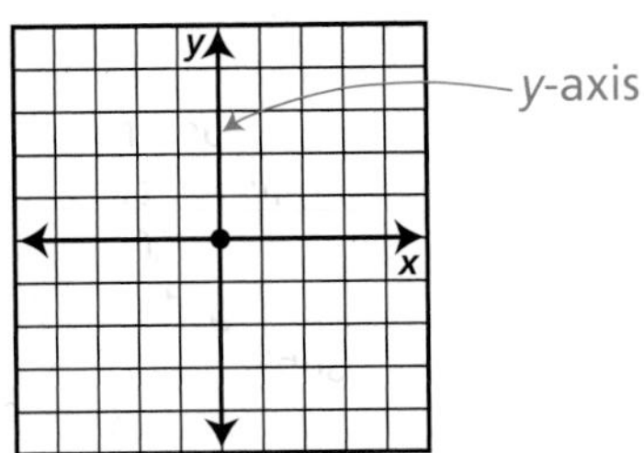


**y-coordinate** The second number of an ordered pair of numbers that names a point in a coordinate system.

**Zero Property of Addition** The property which states that the sum of any number and 0 is that number.

*Examples:* $9 + 0 = 9$ and $0 + 5 = 5$

**Zero Property of Multiplication** The property which states that the product of any number and 0 is 0.

*Examples:* $9 \times 0 = 0$ and $0 \times 5 = 0$

# Index

# redits continued

©The Museum of Modern Art/Licensed by SCALA/Art Resource, NY. **318** Dianne Huntress/Index Stock. **319** (tmr) (tml) (b) PhotoDisc/Getty Images. (m) Fred Whitehead/Earth Scenes. **323** (tl) (bl) Comstock. (tm) Artville. (bm) PhotoDisc/Getty Images. **326** Schmeul Thaler/Index Stock. **327** (bl) Artville. (br) DK Images. (tl) PhotoDisc/Getty Images. **332** (t) © Greg Stott/Masterfile. (b) Royalty Free/CORBIS. **336** Jim Brandenburg/Minden. **340** Frans Lanting/Minden. **341** (b) PhotoDisc/Getty Images. (t) Bob Elsdale/agefotostock. **342** (r) PhotoDisc/Getty Images. **348** Johnny Johnson/Index Stock. **349** © 2003 Johnny Johnson/AlaskaStock.com. **350** National Academies Archives. **354** Daniel Pangbourne Media/Getty Images. **356** Mary Kate Denny/Getty Images. **357** (b) PhotoDisc/Getty Images. **359** (t) © Chris Hellier/CORBIS. **360** © Peter Barrett/Masterfile. **370** (l) Comstock KLIPS. (r) PhotoDisc/Getty Images. **370** PhotoDisc/Getty Images. **374** Gandee Vasan/Getty Images. **382** Wayne B. Bilenduke/Getty Images. **386** (l) Robert Harding Picture Library Ltd/Alamy. **387** (l) © Tom Bean/CORBIS. (m) AP Photo/Brian Branch-Price. (r) © Andre Jenny/Focus Group/PictureQuest. **390** (c) Raymond Gehman/CORBIS. **391** (b) Peter Lavery/Masterfile. (br) © Graeme Teague Photography. **399** (tc) Georgia Department of Economic Development. **402** © Mark E. Gibson. (c) Georgia Department of Economic Development. **404** BongoPhoto. **412** HMCo. Film Archive. **414** James M. Mejuto. **417** Image 100/Alamy. **424** Rubberball Productions. **425** Hermitage, St. Petersburg, Russia/Bridgeman Art Library. **428** ©1996 Lynda Richardson/www.lyndarichardson.com. **450** © Bryan F. Peterson/CORBIS. **466** (ml)(mr) PhotoDisc/Getty Images. (l) HMCo. Film Archive. **471** © Coco McCoy/Rainbow/PictureQuest. **472** Comstock KLIPS. **473** PhotoDisc. **476-7** © Ralph A. Clevenger/CORBIS. **476** (m) "Symmetry Drawing E78 by M.C. Escher. © 2003 Cordon Art-Baarn-Holland. All rights reserved." **477** (b) © Scott T. Smith/CORBIS. **485** (tc) © Graeme Teague Photography. **488** (c) © Graeme Teague Photography. **490** Artville. **496** PhotoDisc/Getty Images. **502** Patricia Barry Levy/Index Stock. **510** (t) Comstock. **514** Karl Weatherly/Getty Images. **516** © Ariel Skelley/CORBIS. **519** © David Madison/Getty Images. **523** © Robert Franz/Index Stock/PictureQuest. **526** Mike Brinson/Getty Images. **529** PhotoDisc/Getty Images. **533** Artville. **534** (bl) PhotoDisc/Getty Images. (tr) Artville. **537** (b) Artville. **537** (t) © Sandro Vannini/CORBIS. **540** © Lynne Siler/Focus Group/PictureQuest. **546** Myrleen Cate/Index Stock. **549** (ml)(mr)(m) The Topps Company, Inc. (b) PhotoDisc/Getty Images. (t) © Bettman/CORBIS. **554** Copyright Kathy Goedeken. **555** (t) Copyright Kathy Goedeken. (b) Comstock. **559** © Rick Rickman/NewSport. **560** David Madison Sports Images, Inc. **566** (tl) Kevin Schafer/agefotostock. (tr) Peter Bowater/agefotostock. (ml) Kord.com/agefotostock. (mr) (bl) Jose Futse Raga/agefotostock. (br) David Allan Brandt/Getty Images. **574** (t) © Macduff Everton/CORBIS. (b) © Danny Lehman/CORBIS. **576** (t) Sea/Index Stock. (b) Pictures Colour Library. **577** Kendra Haste, Platform for Art-Gloucester Road Tube Station, galvanized wire mesh sculptures. **582-3** © Graeme Teague Photography. **582** (icon) © PhotoDisc/Getty Images. **584** (tr) Jane Faircloth/Transparencies, Inc. **591** (tc) © Graeme Teague Photography. **594** (c) © Graeme Teague Photography. **596** Pronk & Associates. **598** (tr) © foodfolio/Alamy. **600** Pronk & Associates. **601** (cr) Ray Boudreau Photography. **605** Barros & Barros/Getty Images. **606** (t) © Reuters NewMedia Inc./CORBIS (b) © AFP/CORBIS. **614** Roger Tully/Getty Images. **622** (r) Stockbyte. **626** © NRSC Ltd./Photo Researchers Inc. **628** © Cleo Photography/PhotoEdit. **634-5** Hollingsworth John and Karen/USFWS. **634** (b) Adam Jones/Getty Images. (br) Lee Canfield/TRANSPARENCIES Inc. **635** (b) Color Day Production/Getty Images. **647** NASA. **648** © Kevin R. Morris/CORBIS. **653** © PhotoDisc/Getty Images. **654** © Burke/Triolo Productions/FoodPix.

## ASSIGNMENT PHOTOGRAPHY

**643** © HMCo./Jade Albert.

**xxi** (b), **90, 146, 148, 157, 162, 252, 262** (b), **307** (t), **322, 324, 329, 376** (b), **436, 440** (r), **446, 465, 553, 604, 610** (b), **629** © HMCo./Greg Anthony.

**659-663** © HMCo./Joel Benjamin.

**297** (tr), **481** (tr) © HMCo./Ray Boudreau.

**xxx** (tr), **56, 142, 202, 302** (tr), **400, 486, 592** © HMCo./Dave Bradley.

**122, 186, 228, 454, 468, 594, 609, 624** © HMCo./Angela Coppola.

**492, 530** © HMCo./Peter Fox.

**xi** (br), **xii** (b), **2, 11, 37, 42, 54, 85, 98, 115, 124, 129, 140, 149-151, 160, 164, 181, 200, 206, 208, 209, 212, 217, 218, 233, 262** (t), **274** (b), **276, 280, 286, 287, 301, 312** (b), **316, 351, 359** (b), **398, 407, 433, 452, 467, 485, 494, 505, 542, 543, 556, 570, 572, 590, 599, 618, 642** © HMCo./Carol Kaplan.

**656** © HMCo./Ken Karp.

**vi** (bl), **xx** (r), **14, 16, 87, 88, 152, 170, 211, 602, 610** (t) © HMCo./Michael Indresano.

**xxiv, xxv, 497** © HMCo./Allan Landau.

**488** © HMCo./Tony Scarpetta.

**295** (c), **296** (tr), **300** (tr) (cr), **303** (tr), **480** (bl), **484** (tr), **636** (tr), **637** (tr), **639** (bl) © HMCo./Dave Starrett.

**195** (c), **395** (br) © HMCo./Ron Tanaka.

**522** © HMCo./Tracey Wheeler.

## ILLUSTRATION

**22, 35** (t), **101, 158, 188, 189, 334, 335, 339, 362, 381, 382, 383, 455, 456, 463, 506, 540, 578, 579** Argosy. **137, 195, 395** (c) Steve Attoe. **5, 311, 320, 325, 424, 464, 468** Ken Batelman. **656** (banner) Russell Benfanti. **533** William Brinkley. **194** Scott Cameron. **251** Estelle Carol. **395** (cr) Michael Cho. **155** Chris Costello. **134** Claudia Davila. **xviii, 655-56** Eldon Doty. **562** Julie Durrell. **314, 318** Neverne Covington. **92, 93** John Edwards Inc. **504, 655-56** Eldon Doty. **375, 460, 462, 464, 498, 500, 568** Joel Dubin. **xiii, xv, xvii, 282, 285, 288, 361, 456, 548** Ruth Flanigan. **236** Patrick Gnan. **616, 631** Jim Gordon. **182** Mike Gordon. **2, 37, 144, 147, 163, 183, 204, 217, 222, 237** (t), **242, 250, 279, 289, 425, 490, 496, 497, 533** (tr), **563** Ken Hansen. **652** Eileen Hine. **35** (b) Rob Hynes. **25, 347, 649-50** Nathan Jarvis. **50, 51** (tr)(c), **135, 590** Kelly Kennedy. **vii, 41, 70, 174, 175, 233, 265, 313, 366, 377, 379, 651** Dave Klug. **49** (b), **398** Bernadette Lau. **315** Brian Lies. **13, 125, 159, 261, 343, 363, 421, 557** Ruth Linstromberg. **645** Ethan Long. **50** (cr)(br) Tadeusz Majewski. **584** (cr) Jack McMaster. **50** (tr) Dirk Michiels. **614, 627** Karen Minot. **244** Ortelius Design. **48** (tr), **142, 143, 296** (bl), **302** (br), **394** (tr) June Park. **165, 166, 329** Precision Graphics. **43, 178** Chris Reed. **479** (c) Francois Robert. **xvi, 430,** Brucie Rosch. **623** Patrice Rossi. **121, 150** Alfred Schrier. **28, 365, 524, 525, 546, 552, 560** Rob Schuster. **295** (c) Ted Sivell. **237** Steve Snider. **104, 259, 263** George Ulrich. **328** David Wenzel.

All tech art by Pronk & Associates